THE AUDACIOUS ASCETIC

FLAGG MILLER

The Audacious Ascetic

*What the Bin Laden Tapes Reveal
about al-Qaʿida*

OXFORD
UNIVERSITY PRESS

Oxford University Press is a department of the
University of Oxford. It furthers the University's objective
of excellence in research, scholarship, and education
by publishing worldwide.

Oxford   New York
Auckland   Cape Town   Dar es Salaam   Hong Kong   Karachi
Kuala Lumpur   Madrid   Melbourne   Mexico City   Nairobi
New Delhi   Shanghai   Taipei   Toronto

With offices in
Argentina   Austria   Brazil   Chile   Czech Republic   France   Greece
Guatemala   Hungary   Italy   Japan   Poland   Portugal   Singapore
South Korea   Switzerland   Thailand   Turkey   Ukraine   Vietnam

Oxford is a registered trade mark of Oxford University Press
in the UK and certain other countries.

Published in the United States of America by
Oxford University Press
198 Madison Avenue, New York, NY 10016

Library of Congress Cataloging-in-Publication Data is available
Miller, Flagg.
The Audacious Ascetic: What the Bin Laden Tapes Reveal
about al-Qaʿida.
ISBN 978-0-19-026436-9

Printed in India on acid-free paper

CONTENTS

ACKNOWLEDGEMENTS

There are many to whom I owe thanks for the development of this book. Their patience and generosity kept me aloft when lonelier paths of research seemed interminable. For their support throughout, my wife and seven-year-old son deserve special mention. They have been steady companions in exploring the complexities of human experience everywhere.

My access to bin Laden's former audiotape collection beginning in 2003 was made possible through collaboration with anthropologist David Edwards, director of the Williams College Afghan Media Project. I am forever indebted to his confidence in me and to Williams College for facilitating my early archival and research efforts. I conducted my first stint of fieldwork and research for the book through a grant from the American Institute of Yemeni Studies in 2005. The following year, gratefully employed at the University of Wisconsin, Madison, I spent a semester developing chapters one, nine and twelve as a fellow at the university's Institute for Research in the Humanities. In 2007, I had moved to the University of California, Davis where I continued work with a new assembly of colleagues. I am especially grateful to former dean, Jessie Ann Owens, and my department chairs for allotting me the time and resources necessary to complete my work. A grant from the Hellman Foundation supplied rare funding for an Arabic research and translation assistant, Nour-Eddine Mouktabis, without whose labors my archival efforts would have been far less thorough. UCD staff members proved as adept in addressing my professional anxieties as they were convivial. They include members of the university's news and media relations team, Karen Nikos and Claudia Morain.

ACKNOWLEDGEMENTS

The book's organization, thesis and relevance would have been more modest were it not for invaluable support from beyond UC Davis. In 2009–10 I joined fellows at the Woodrow Wilson International Center in Washington, D.C. for a year of earnest discussion about pressing issues at home and abroad. Chapters eight and thirteen are indebted to my interactions while at the center. Two subsequent years of fellowship allowed me to refine the book's contributions. They were secured through support from the American Council of Learned Societies' Charles A. Ryskamp Fellowship in 2010–11, and through a University of California President's Faculty Research in the Humanities Fellowship in 2013–14. During this period, I had the privilege of submitting my research for consideration to a range of audiences both within academia and beyond. Host institutions included, roughly in order, the Modern Orient Center (ZMO) in Berlin, the University of Michigan's Near Eastern Studies department as well as its Linguistic Anthropology Group and Islamic Studies Program, Oxford University, Emory University's departments of anthropology and religion, George Washington University's Institute for Middle Eastern Studies, Georgetown University's School of Foreign Service, Qatar University, New York University, the Foreign Service Institute (Arlington, VA), Cornell University's Judith Reppy Institute for Peace and Conflict Studies, the University of California, Davis's anthropology department and militarization research cluster, Wesleyan College's Middle East Studies department, Dartmouth College, the University of Chicago's Middle East History and Theory Graduate Workshop, the National Defense University, Stanford University, Florida State University's department of religion, Harvard University, and most recently Yale University's anthropology department and Council on Middle East Studies.

Special thanks are due to a range of interviewees, readers, co-translators and facilitators. Paramount among them are Hurst's two anonymous readers as well as Michael Dwyer, without whose perspective and assiduous labor none of this would have been possible. To others' enormous generosity I can only gesture: 'Umar bin Laden, Abdullah Anis, Alexander Knysh, Zaina Bin Laden, Valerie Billing, Jean Sasson, Deputy Commissioner John Miller, Massa, Joe Brinley, Deborah Grosvenor, Katherine Zimmerman, Friedhelm Hoffman, Neil MacFarquhar, Henry Schuster, Esther Whitfield, Alex Strick van Linschoten, the Institute of Education (London), faculty colleagues in UC Davis's religious studies

ACKNOWLEDGEMENTS

department and Middle East/South Asia program, and research assistants Ahmed Mahmoud, Rabeah Hammood, Mohamed Amin, and Fatna Ballouchi.

Audio-recordings used for all translated excerpts featured at the start of each chapter can be heard on the website www.audaciousascetic.com. I am grateful to Charlie Turner and his colleagues at UC Davis's Academic Technology Services for their assistance with website development and the time-coded synchronization of audio material with translations.

INTRODUCTION

15 April 1998. Lahej governorate of southern Yemen. Village feast celebrating the Festival of the Sacrifice that concludes the holy month of Ramadan. Meal conversation with ʿAbdalla, leader of an al-Qaʿida front called the World Islamic Organization.[1]

―――――――

ʿAbdalla: Hey dog.

Me: Who's the dog?

ʿAbdalla: You. You're the dog.

Me: I am not a dog.

ʿAbdalla: My name is ʿAbdalla. In Islam, the name ʿAbdalla is the most revered of names. God created mankind to obey and serve him under the banner: 'There is no God but God alone and Muhammad is His Messenger.' The British, on the other hand: We used to call them Red Dogs since their faces were red.

Me: Well I'm not British and my face is not red.

ʿAbdalla: You are not welcome here. America hatches the greatest plots in the world. No power is more corrupt and sinister. No one wants you in our Muslim lands, so you would best head back to where you came from.

Me: That's not true. Many people have welcomed me here. They know perfectly well that I'm conducting research that will benefit the region.

By most measures, the outdoor feast for hundreds of villagers was an occasion for celebration. An hour later, tribal dancing broke out in a nearby market square. Delegations of dancers entered the square brandishing curved daggers and twirling in unison as they chanted poems. ʿAbdalla's darker mood was not his alone. One disgruntled elder, fresh back from Afghanistan, broke out a Klashnikov and swung it wildly at the first row of dancers. Before south Yemen's independence from the

1

British in 1967, his own clan had customary rights to lead the parade. They were religious *sayyids*, men who could trace genealogical descent to the Prophet Muhammad's own Quraish tribe. Three decades later, a Soviet-backed communist regime having killed or exiled religious elites and banned status hierarchies, everything had changed. To the relief of terrified parade goers, the assailant was coaxed away from pulling the trigger. He was tackled by whomever could lend a hand.

Such unnerving encounters were fortunately rare for me during my graduate fieldwork in Yemen. Pursuing a degree in linguistic anthropology, I had chosen to focus my research on changing traditions of tribal poetry. The topic was welcomed by Yemenis across the board. That afternoon, while sitting with an assortment of tribal shaikhs and guests, I had discovered that ʿAbdalla had more to say. Although the Cold War had ended, he predicted that Moscow was on the verge of a comeback. Within one year Russian forces would re-invade Yemen, beginning in Aden and continuing their advance across the Arab world. While America and "the Arabs" were enemies today, he insisted, they would join forces against this global front, struggling side by side in a third world war that would end in God's final Day of Judgment. ʿAbdalla smirked at me as my Yemeni colleagues in the room gave him a cold shoulder. "Perhaps we'll win you over one of these days."

The events of 11 September 2001 seemed adequate proof of ʿAbdalla's hair-brained predictions. Far from uniting Americans and Arabs, the attacks and their aftermath created even greater distrust. In the United States, Arabs, Muslims, and many people held to resemble them, experienced an increase in hate crimes that, in some cases, exceeded 1700 per cent.[2] Ten years later, a Pew research poll reported that more Americans held an unfavorable opinion of Islam (35 per cent) than those who held a favorable view (30 per cent), in contrast with findings just five years earlier.[3] In the Arab world, meanwhile, the ensuing militarization of America's foreign policy yielded even more dramatic trends in hostility. Already suffering from public anger over the crippling effects of U.S.-led sanctions in Iraq, and the unprecedented scale of Israeli settlement expansion, America's reputation garnered some of the strongest criticism from our long-term allies. A poll in 2004 showed a dramatic decline in favorable opinions of the United States among Egyptians (95% unfavorable versus 75% in 2002), Jordanians (78% versus 61%), Moroccans (88% versus 61%), and Saudi Arabians (94% versus 87%.)[4]

Still, if public opinion defied 'Abdalla's predictions, the decades of the 1990s and 2000s opened an epoch of bolstered military and economic ties between the United States and the Arab world that brought them even closer together. Beginning with the Gulf War of 1990–91, American-led coalition troops fought with Saudis, Egyptians, Syrians, Moroccans, Kuwaitis, Omanis, as well as some twenty-five other nations to drive Saddam Hussein's army out of Kuwait. In the years that followed, Qatar hosted the growth of America's two largest military bases in the region. Its Al-Udeid air base would become headquarters for the United States Central Command, the chief hub for managing American military operations in the Middle East, North Africa, and Central Asia. In the two years after 11 September, America's military budget increased by 73 per cent, totaling some $417.4 billion, half of the total U.S. discretionary budget.[5] Wars launched in Afghanistan and Iraq during this period would not only add further billions to the ledger. They would also ensure the centrality of these regions to Americans' sense of place and identity in a twenty-first-century world marked by heightened security concerns. Record-breaking arms sales to Arab allies, some of which topped $919 million by 2013, deepened and complicated a long-term American-Arab relationship.

Amidst the many currents of political and economic change that defined America's role in the post-Cold War period, Osama bin Laden came to acquire extraordinary power. Born in Saudi Arabia to a family made fabulously rich by construction and commercial ventures, he had already risen to celebrity by the time the first Gulf War occurred, as a result of his avid support for Arab freedom fighters struggling to liberate Soviet-occupied Afghanistan. To be sure, by most accounts, he faced decided setbacks through the 1990s. Opposing King 'Abdulla's decision to rely on American coalition forces to help drive Saddam's forces from Kuwait, he fell out of favor with the Saudis and their allies. So persistent were his demands on the Saudi monarchy that by 1994, he was stripped of his citizenship and family inheritance. A growing pariah across the Arab world for inciting Islamic resistance to authoritarian Sunni regimes elsewhere, he appears to have lost the vast remainder of his fortune through poor investments. In 1996, he became stateless after being kicked out of the Sudan. Curiously, however, his political and financial leverage not only survived these misfortunes but actually grew stronger. Described by the American Central Intelligence Agency in 1995 as the

"Ford Foundation of Sunni Islamic terrorism," his power seemed to transcend the surveillance and security mechanisms of the world's wealthiest states.[6] His capacity to threaten Western interests, especially American, tapped shadowy financial networks whose resilience puzzled the most acute observers. Even while being forced to retreat into Afghanistan's most rugged highlands, he was reported to have maintained steady access to tremendous wealth supplied to him by Arab political elites, private donors, charity organizations, foreign banks, shell companies, and a decentralized network of money brokers. With the attacks of 9/11, the full scope of bin Laden's exceptional capabilities were apparent to world audiences like never before. In the words of *New York Times* journalist Thomas Friedman, he was a "super-empowered angry man," one of a new class of individuals who took advantage of globalization's market, transportation, and communication networks and used them to challenge traditional state arrangements.[7] So extensive was his influence that top American officials viewed Iraq, a country without a notable al-Qaʿida presence prior to 2003, as dangerously subject to his sway. While Americans prepared for war, links between al-Qaʿida and Iraq became "accurate and not debatable."[8]

This book explores bin Laden's rise as both an ascetic adversary of Western globalization and an important rationale for expanding America's transnational security commitments within Arab and Islamic worlds especially. I focus, in particular, on the history of the concept of al-Qaʿida. Contrary to predictions of its elimination after bin Laden's death or the routing of what was called "al-Qaʿida Central" from Afghanistan in the decade following 9/11, al-Qaʿida remains very much in the news. Given conflicts during 2014 in Syria, Iraq, Egypt, and Yemen, we might speak of the organization's "rejuvenation." To do so, however, requires assuming that al-Qaʿida's apex was under bin Laden and that splinter groups and affiliates arising after 9/11 were successfully forced into retreat by virtue of being prevented from attacking the United States on its own soil, with the exception of a few isolated cases. I argue that the concept of al-Qaʿida has a longer and messier history. My encounter with Yemeni operative ʿAbdalla in 1998 provides a snapshot of how this history would unfold. Not only were Arabs and Muslims fast in becoming al-Qaʿida's primary victims, but bin Laden and his focus on the American "far enemy" would be comparatively marginal.

Al-Qaʿida's organization and ideology have been vigorous subjects of debate. According to political scientist Richard Jackson, scholars in the

West have typically held four perspectives.[9] First, there was the idea that al-Qaʿida is a hierarchical organization defined by a core group of top leaders, a secondary cadre of loyal operatives, and a wider coalition of supporters and ties with other groups.[10] Second, came the argument that al-Qaʿidaʾs hierarchy changes according to circumstances and reflects the priorities of a diffuse and adaptive web of both state and non-state actors.[11] From this perspective, al-Qaʿida was a "network of networks" and often worked through self-radicalized "lone wolves." A third approach, especially for those with an eye for political history, was that al-Qaʿida was one fairly short-lived branch of a much broader international jihadist movement.[12] Finally, came the argument that al-Qaʿida was more an ideological framework or source of inspiration that drew upon pan-Islamist vocabularies while trying to steer recruits toward specific conflict settings.[13]

I venture in new directions by exploring the ways in which al-Qaʿida works as discourse. Rather than unpacking al-Qaʿidaʾs organizational structure, network capacity, or ideology, I focus instead on how its leaders, supporters, and even detractors have talked about *al-qaʿida* in its Arabic sense as a "base" or "rule." In the Muslim world, such foundations (*qawaʿid* in the plural) are invoked by speakers in different contexts of reasoning and argumentation. In discussions of Islamic law, for example, jurists invoke these rules through catchy legal aphorisms: "Acts are judged by their intention" (*al-umuru bi-maqasidha*); "No harm shall be inflected or reciprocated in Islam" (*la darar wa la dirar*); "The law should work to alleviate people's hardships" (*al-mashaqqa tajlibu al-taysir*); and so forth. In discussions of theology, a basic *qaʿida* states that "Whatever exists can be seen" (*kullu mawjudin yura*), a rule that emphasizes empirical observation before metaphysics. In discussions of Arabic grammar, subjects come before predicates except in certain cases (*taqaddum al-mubtadaʾ ʿala al-khabar*). Since the eighth century Muslims had compiled vast compendia of such rule books (*qawaʿid*) that guided the faithful in aligning themselves with divine will. To a great extent, these tomes helped to bolster the authority of state establishments. *Al-qaʿida* discourse could focus very much on proper orders of power and knowledge: know the rule and its norms and all will be well. I'll suggest, in fact, that this rendition of *al-qaʿida* has made the concept far more conducive to furthering state interests than is typically thought plausible. I will also focus on how Muslim militants and reformers have disagreed with one another over what *qawaʿid* are and how they are to be applied.

I draw my insights primarily from a never before-studied collection of over one thousand five-hundred audio tapes that were formerly deposited in bin Laden's own residence in Kandahar, Afghanistan. The collection served as an audio library for those who gathered under bin Laden's roof between 1997 and 2001, during the years of al-Qaʿida's most coherent organizational momentum. Some of the speakers are al-Qaʿida's best-known militants, including twenty-four tapes of bin Laden himself, as well as tapes by ʿAbdalla ʿAzzam, Abu Musʿab Al-Suri, and Abu al-Walid Al-Misri, among others. Most of the tapes, however, contain speeches by figures known more for sticking to their books than their guns (see appendix A). These individuals were never members of al-Qaʿida, although as specialists in Islamic law, theology, ritual practice, and history they were held in great esteem by militants. Saudis rank foremost among them, followed by Egyptians, Peninsular Arabs (especially from Yemen, Kuwait, and Bahrain), Afghanis, Palestinians, Syrians, and Sudanese. Almost all speakers are Sunni Muslims, a branch representing the vast majority of Muslims in the world, although their traditions of legal interpretation are many. Some are established state clerics such as the former Chief Jurist (*mufti*) of Saudi Arabia, ʿAbd al-ʿAziz Ibn Baz, the leader of Yemen's largest Islamist party, ʿAbd al-Majid Al-Zindani, and Kuwait's unabashedly pro-West entrepreneur and intellectual Tariq Al-Suwaidan. The latter figure represents a breadth of thought contained on the tapes, and the ways militants found certain figures compelling—in Al-Suwaidan's case, his lectures on such leadership skills as "honor," painted in monumental golden letters forming an ocean ship on one cassette jacket—despite overt differences in political affiliation.

The tapes were originally acquired by the Cable News Network (hereafter CNN) in early 2002, a few months after al-Qaʿida and the Taliban had been routed from the city by American Special Forces, alongside Afghan troops and tribal leaders. CNN informed U.S. intelligence officials of the existence of this material. While they appear to have reviewed the tapes, they declined stewardship of the collection. Inundated after the fall of the Taliban with printed documents, computer hard drives, video cassettes, and other materials of more immediate intelligence value, officials advised CNN to pass the collection on to an academic community. A year later CNN arranged for the cassettes to be shipped to Williams College with the understanding that they would be made available for researchers.[14] In 2006, the tapes were moved to Yale

University where they have been converted into digital format and can now be heard.

Thanks to an anthropologist colleague at Williams, I first got involved in conducting research on the tapes when they arrived from CNN's Islamabad office. Since no inventory or description of the archive existed at the time, my main task over the next several years was to develop a report that could explain the significance of the collection for further studies of al-Qaʿida and bin Laden's role in particular. My first publication on the collection, released in 2008 in the *Journal of Language and Communication*, was accompanied by an article in the *New York Times*, and thereafter by media attention worldwide. At the outset of my article, I expressed surprise that after reviewing a great many of the tapes, some of which date to as late as November 2001, I had yet to find a single instance in which al-Qaʿida was spoken about as bin Laden's worldwide militant organization. Years later, after studying the collection exhaustively, I can update my findings: one tape, a recording produced in late October 2000 featuring a wedding celebration in honor of one of bin Laden's bodyguards, begins with an advertisement by "al-Qaʿida's publicity committee" (*al-lajnat al-iʿlaniyya li-l-qaʿida*). Chapter fourteen is devoted to my analysis of this tape. It is preceded by a chapter about another recording that, while not mentioning bin Laden or any organization associated with him, features a cartridge label whose title, "Listen—Plan—Carry Out ʿal-Qaʿida,'" (*Ismaʿ—Dabbir—Iʿmal ʿal-Qaʿida'*) suggests provenance from around 1999–2001.

I consider the audiotape collection's near complete silence on al-Qaʿida's association with bin Laden's global terrorist network in the years before 9/11 to be an opportunity rather than a loss. When I first began reviewing the tapes, I listened carefully for bin Laden's voice and any mention of al-Qaʿida's objectives by those most closely associated with the organization. What I heard instead a was range of lectures and discussions by over two hundred different speakers, most of whom were known to be established legal scholars with scant regard for bin Laden's style of reasoning. I also heard a vast range of amateur and extemporaneous recordings that were not designed for broad circulation: taxi cab conversations, chats over breakfast in make-shift kitchens, sounds of live battles as militants communicated on two-way radio transceivers, wedding ceremonies, celebrations before and after combat missions, poetry competitions, trivia games, lectures in training camp classrooms, interviews with leaders, telephone calls, studio-produced dramas of mock battles and their aftermath, and Islamic anthems sung late into the night. Much of this material was quite familiar to me and brought back memories of conversations and songs that I had come across while working with close friends in Yemen, the Arab Gulf, and the United States. I also heard ordinary views co-opted by heinous extremism. To help make sense of such shifts, I listened to the tapes with dozens of native Arabic speakers in the Middle East and United States, some of whom were ex-fighters themselves who had known bin Laden intimately. In time, I discovered not just how different bin Laden's world had been from that familiar to most of us. I learned much about what drew these worlds together.

A conventional view of al-Qaʿida maintains that the organization's ultimate goals are to drive America out of the Muslim world, to destroy Israel, and to create a jihadist caliphate larger than the Ottoman empire at its height.[15] Many statements by top al-Qaʿida leaders support just this formula. Questions arise, however, about how well these long-term objectives translate into the real concerns of people who might be inclined to take these leaders seriously. While militant ambitions to establish a caliphate are readily trotted out for non-Muslim audiences, speakers exercise far more restraint when lobbying for the notion among Muslim activists, as I discuss with respect to Palestinian militant ʿAbdalla ʿAzzam later in the book.[16] For ʿAzzam, struggling toward a pan-Islamic caliphate should take a back seat to more immediate and everyday objectives, among them seeking justice in one's own homeland. Muslims must cultivate a far broader repertoire of strategies, tactics, and methods for ensuring that the good fight isn't lost or perverted before it even begins. In this respect, al-Qaʿida theoreticians must position themselves within in-house debates about founding principles and practices. What makes a good Muslim? What is the nature of sin? How can the righteous remain vigilant against injustice? How much effort should one devote to seeking knowledge of other faiths and cultures? Which research topics are worth pursuing? What was the path of the pious forebears? What are the qualities of a good leader? How can a believer survive in the modern world while abiding by the Prophet Muhammad's example to his community? Such questions yield no easy answers. Different points of view and public disputation constitute the very terrain on which speakers engage with each other in attempts to find common cause. By linking these debates to changing discourse about al-Qaʻida's past, present, and future, I move beyond the tendency to lump Arab-Afghan radicals together under a single overarching narrative.

My greatest challenge in writing this book has been to find ways to accommodate the very thing that has come to define al-Qaʻida after roughly two decades of its making, namely, its leaders' adherence to a distinctly anti-American platform. Bin Laden was, of course, one of the most vocal and assiduous proponents of this message. Especially from 1996 onward, he branded himself as an ascetic warrior dedicated to a global Islamic struggle against the United States. He was not alone, however. Much of his discourse echoed sentiments among Saudi reformers mobilized during the 1980s and 1990s by a religious movement called "the Islamic Awakening" (al-sahwa al-islamiyya). Although the Saudi state had jailed, exiled, or co-opted the movement's most critical members by 1994, bin Laden's notoriety in the West continued to provide leverage to Saudi activists as they continued to jockey on various fronts. His calling card proved felicitous for similar reasons in other, largely Muslim-majority, countries whose state leaders worked to maintain legitimacy even as they defied popular resentment against deepened economic, political, and military collaboration with the United States. These countries included Afghanistan under a nascent Taliban leadership as well as Pakistan, India, Uzbekistan, Yemen, Qatar, Egypt, Jordan, Palestine, Eritrea, Ethiopia, Nigeria, Bosnia and Herzegovina, Malaysia, and others. Bin Laden's message played best among global television and print audiences. Given the United States' increasing pressure on an international community to stiffen sanctions against Iraq, his outbursts provided good copy as American, British, and Arab journalists sought to communicate the concerns of an increasingly angry Arab public. Beyond mass media scheduling, however, Western officials found purchase in a consistent message about bin Laden's global anti-American terrorist organization. As I show in later chapters, foremost among them were American federal prosecutors, intelligence analysts, law enforcement agents, foreign policy makers, and scholars who faced a new era of security challenges.

Bin Laden's exceptional role in global affairs was not immediately apparent to Muslim audiences familiar with his career. According to Egyptian American sociologist Saad Eddin Ibrahim, when interviewed for Al-Jazeera's first documentary on bin Laden in 1999:

With regards to bin Ladin, he is the exception that proves the rule (*al-istithnāʾ alladhi yuʾakkid al-qāʿida*). He was the youngest child, and since his family, despite its considerable wealth, is from the Hadramawt [in Yemen] and thus still considered marginal in Saudi Arabia, he was not fully accepted in Saudi society. Such marginalization sometimes explains a desire to rebel against the system. If one is unable to do this on the inside, one does it from the outside.[17]

Bin Laden's appeal to Arab audiences lay in what he shared with many a rebel. His rage against "the system" stemmed from a generational conflict between the young and the old, discrimination against ethnic minorities, entrenched status hierarchies, inequalities in citizenship, and a yearning for justice that one's own community could not deliver. Bin Laden's life story reminded audiences that money alone could never solve these problems. A well-stocked treasury could in fact make things worse. This was a universal message that invited rebellion on many fronts, beginning with those at one's doorstep. This book attends both to the religious mooring of such struggles and to how this foundation was overturned.

CHAPTER OVERVIEW

The idea of a "base" (*qāʿida*) set against outside forces of perceived economic and material corruption proves central to my argument. Accordingly, I devote the first three chapters to the ways Muslim discourses of self-abnegation or asceticism (*zuhd*) informed bin Laden's early life and views of his leadership. As throughout the book, each chapter begins with a translated excerpt from a selected audio recording in bin Laden's former collection. The opening excerpt in chapter one is taken from a speech bin Laden delivered in Tora Bora, Afghanistan in the summer of 1996. Since the speech was his first to be translated into English for Western audiences, it represents a key moment in perceptions of his vitriol. Dramatized with images of ruthless desert warriors, the oration came to be known as a "Declaration of War against Americans Occupying the Land of the Two Holy Sanctuaries." Much of the chapter provides an introduction to bin Laden's relevance among political reformers and opposition leaders in Saudi Arabia, whose "two holy mosques" of Mecca and Madina provided an anchor for his speech. I attend closely to audio recorded themes of *zuhd* left out of English translations as well as to complementary lectures on the topic elsewhere in the tape collection. While *zuhd* places value on leaving one's wealth and belongings aside in preparation for the afterlife, more important is self-discipline in this life, especially when in the presence of wealth close to home. Chapter two probes further into the productive relationship between wealth and self-abnegation through details of bin Laden's childhood, adolescence, and early years in the Islamic jihad against Soviet occupiers in Afghanistan. Entitled "Heart Pains," the chapter begins with an audio recording from 2000 in which, after a host of statistics detailing the proliferation of American military bases and personnel across the Middle East and North Africa, bin Laden levies a charge of fraud against the Saudi monarchy. Bin Laden's animosity toward an amalgamated "Crusader-Jewish occupation" needs contextualization. In 1979, the first year of bin Laden's involvement with the Arab-Afghan struggle, the Saudi state found ample reason to support a firebrand whose ascetic battle against an ostensible hoard of non-Muslim others also contained seeds for his own later isolation. Bin Laden's emphasis on the works of eighteenth-century Saudi reformer Muhammad Ibn ʿAbd al-Wahhab, draftsman for the state's own ideological charter, for example, as well as on Arabian tribal virtues played to the state's hand. All the more so when leveraged by security officials against political reform and opposition efforts from both Sunnis and Shiʿas.

Chapter three begins with the earliest of bin Laden's speeches in the collection and sets the tone for the book's subsequent chronological progression. Recorded in 1988, the featured speech addresses Saudi audiences' interests in the Arab-Afghan war effort. I focus on the first of bin Laden's training camps in Afghanistan and consider how his leadership and public perceptions of his work were tailored to narratives about this site. As a prelude to later chapters, I discuss relations between Arab and Afghan leaders who worked with bin Laden at the time and consider their various intellectual and political orientations. Before further unpacking the significance of bin Laden's original bases and their misconstrual by Western interpreters, I devote chapter four to the medium of the audio cassette. No study of al-Qaʿida is sufficient, I argue, without a serious consideration of media technologies and their political deployment. In contrast with clean genealogies of al-Qaʿida's founding theorists and their profiles, formative events and chronologies, the work of mediating Islamic jihad for specific audiences and occasions makes "bases," "rules," and their sponsors answerable to social projects whose histories and entailments are far more polyglot than is typically assumed. The chapter begins with an excerpted recording by a Muslim genie (*jinni*) who employs an audio recorder to win support for controversial views among Arab-Afghans. Using the genie's reflections on asceticism to inquire about the nature of the archival project underway in bin Laden's Kandahar residence between 1997 and 2001, I lay the groundwork for subsequent critical assessments of al-Qaʿida studies that have relied primarily on written, printed, and electronic records.

The next three chapters feature excerpts from public speeches made by bin Laden in Saudi Arabia and Yemen between 1989 and 1993. I focus on the ways audio recorded copies of bin Laden's speeches help situate his discourse amidst Islamic reform movements, whose relation to state authorities could not always be openly confrontational. Chapter five expands on earlier discussions of al-Qaʿida's origins by considering a lecture that identifies Islam's principal enemies as Shiʿa and Arab communists stretching from Afghanistan to the Arabian Peninsula. By comparing key themes in the speech with evidence from American federal prosecutors, journalists, and early al-Qaʿida analysts, I contest the common view that al-Qaʿida was founded by bin Laden in 1988 with the aim of preparing recruits for post-Soviet combat against non-Muslim enemies and, within a few years, the United States especially. I suggest, instead, that the organization emerged from plans to establish the Al-Faruq training camp in Afghanistan under Ayman Al-Zawahiri and Egyptian commanders who were dedicated primarily to supporting insurgencies against authoritarian regimes within the Muslim world itself. Chapter six, featuring a speech most likely delivered in Yemen, explores how bin Laden harnessed this focus on the near enemy by using doctrinal vocabularies familiar to his chief audiences in the region. While criticism of the Saudi regime remains acute, bin Laden's location outside the kingdom licenses a more radical denunciation of Muslim "hypocrites" across the world along with a call to take up arms against their leaders. Chapter seven explores the ways in which bin Laden was forced to mollify his critique of the Saudis in light of internal divisions within the Saudi Awakening movement. The price for such collaboration, I suggest, is a far more strident stance against the United States and its policies toward Israel and the Palestinians. Even this salvo requires muffling, however, given Saudi and Gulf Arab state sensitivities.

INTRODUCTION

I explore the implications of bin Laden's recourse to the example of Mohatma Gandhi as he tried to navigate these currents.

Chapter eight fleshes out tensions introduced in previous chapters between bin Laden's gestures toward more ecumenical forms of modern Islamic activism and his growing Arab-centric focus on the American enemy. Featuring a jocular, and at times irreverent, conversation between anonymous Arab militants as they prepare breakfast in an Afghan kitchen, the chapter draws attention to the ways bin Laden's own militant version of asceticism contrasts with its more pliant and accommodating counterpart among kitchen participants. With notes on the tape drawn from my interviews with bin Laden's son, 'Umar, I explore the tape's significance in mediating ideological differences that emerged in the early 1990s between a first generation of Arab-Afghans whose primary goal had been to defeat the Soviets and a second generation of younger, less experienced militants of uprooted transnational backgrounds who looked to broader horizons of militant engagement.

Chapters nine, ten, and eleven explore the ways in which bin Laden's rising notoriety among global television networks informed his speeches and shaped his role among militants from 1996–8. The first of these chapters begins with a longer excerpt from bin Laden's 1996 "Declaration of War" introduced in chapter one. Revisiting common assumptions, I show how bin Laden's unambiguous designation of the United States as Islam's prime enemy is couched in a tradition of in-house dissent against corrupt Muslim rulership. The last third of the speech, a section whose fourteen poems are delivered with stirring oratory on audio tape, though they are expurgated from most English translations, lays out the uncompromising tenor of such dissent. The chapter focuses on how bin Laden's message was downplayed or altered by Western political activists, intelligence analysts, and journalists in ways that found broader uptake by militants themselves. Chapter ten examines the first of bin Laden's recorded speeches from Kandahar, Afghanistan where he moved in March 1998 under the watchful eye of the Taliban. Evoking the theme of an "ancient house" in Mecca besieged by sixth-century Abyssinian Christians, bin Laden conjures up an image of pan-Islamic unity. The image, I argue, reflects modeling by CNN following its interview with him several weeks earlier. Most of the chapter explores the implications of bin Laden's much advertised anti-American ideology for Arab-Afghans and Taliban leaders. Chapter eleven delves further into

13

the ways bin Laden's growing status as a media sensation was contextualized by ordinary Arab-Afghan volunteers. It draws upon a recording featuring what is likely former Yemeni Guantánamo detainee, Salim Hamdan, as he cross-examines ABC Nightline news correspondents John Miller and Tarik Hamdi during their trip to one of bin Laden's camps in May 1998. The conversation provides insight into the mechanisms by which early depictions of bin Laden and his worldwide terrorist organization, drafted largely by American federal prosecutors, found their way back to bin Laden and his associates as they crafted talking points for their cause.

The final three chapters explore the ways al-Qaʿida's top commanders, advisors, and media consultants situated bin Laden's "far enemy" discourse, now amplified by global news coverage especially in the United States, in relation to the constraints of regionalized struggles and Islamic law in particular. Chapter twelve examines a lecture by Egyptian militant Mustafa Hamid (aka Abu al-Walid Al-Masri) on the tactics and virtues of establishing a militant "base" (qaʿida). Recorded in October 1998 at a Kandahar training camp, the tape reveals Hamid expressing doubts about the future of the Arab-Afghan struggle and urging recruits to return home and canvass the merits of applying Islamic law among broader audiences. I explore Hamid's discourse on al-qaʿida in relation to those of two other prominent Muslim jurists in the tape collection in order to show how he deploys the concept toward militancy. Chapter thirteen considers a more theological rendering of the qaʿida by the collection's top featured speaker, Syrian jurist ʿAbd al-Rahim Al-Tahhan. Focusing on a tape labeled "Listen, Plan, and Carry Out ʿal-Qaʿida'," I attend to the ways Al-Tahhan's discourse on Islamic law and creed lends itself to an existential reading that militants found useful, among them Saudi audiotape producers who re-branded his lectures in support of bin Laden's extremism during the late 1990s. Chapter fourteen examines the only other tape in the collection that is explicitly marketed under the "al-Qaʿida" label. The recording features a wedding celebration for one of bin Laden's bodyguards in October 2000. As I show, bin Laden and al-Qaʿida's increasingly controversial status among would-be followers after the 1998 United States Embassy bombings in East Africa, the victims of which were mostly Muslim, compelled them to try to reach broader audiences through innovative and more cosmopolitan renditions of an ascetic Arab ideal.

INTRODUCTION

In an epilogue, I review the lessons of the book for understanding and studying al-Qaʿida. Greater attention to the diversity of al-Qaʿida's primary enemies and targets is crucial to developing effective trans-national collaboration in fighting terrorism, especially given al-Qaʿida's horrific legacy among Muslims themselves.

1

THE MESSAGE (*AL-RISALA*)[1]

(August 1996 speech by Osama bin Laden. The Hindu Kush mountains, Afghanistan. Opening remarks, cassette no. 506.)

———

Praise be to God. We show Him gratitude, seek His help and ask for His pardon. We take refuge in God from the evils within us and our wrongful deeds. Who ever is guided by God will not be misled, and who ever is misled will never be guided. I bear witness that there is no god except God (*Allah*), Who has no associates, and I bear witness that Muhammad is His Slave and Messenger.

"O, you who believe! Be careful of your duty to God with the proper care which is due to Him, and do not die until you have rendered due submission."[2] "O mankind! Be careful of your duty to your Lord, who created you from a single being and created its mate of the same kind and spread from these two a multitude of men and women. Be careful of your duty to God, by whom you demand your rights of one another and attend to the ties of kinship; surely God ever watches over you."[3] "O you who believe! Be careful of your duty to God and speak the right word; He will make your conduct virtuous and will forgive you your faults; and whoever obeys God and His Messenger, he indeed achieves a mighty success."[4]

Praise be to God, it has been reported "I desire nothing but reform so far as I am able. My success in this task depends entirely on the help of God; in Him do I trust and to Him do I turn for everything."[5] Praise be to God, it has been reported "You are the best of the nations brought forth for mankind; you command what is right, forbid what is wrong and believe in God."[6]

17

God's blessing and salutations on His Slave and Messenger who said "If people see the oppressor and fail to restrain him with their hand, they draw close to an all encompassing punishment from God," as has been reported by Abu Da'ud Al-Tirmidhi.

Now then:

It should not be hidden from you that the people of Islam have suffered from injustice, oppression, and aggression by the Judeo-Christian alliance and their collaborators, to the extent that Muslims' blood became the cheapest and their wealth and natural resources loot in the hands of their enemies. Their blood was spilled in Palestine and Iraq. The horrifying pictures of the massacre of Qana, in Lebanon are still fresh in our minds. The same is true for the massacres in Tajikistan, Burma, Kashmir, Assam, the Philippines, Fatani, Ogadin, Somalia, Eritrea, Chechnya, and Bosnia and Herzegovina, where the massacres against Muslims that took place send shivers through the body.

Not only was all of this in full view and earshot of the entire world, but a clear conspiracy has developed between America and its allies to prevent the dispossessed from obtaining arms under the cover of the iniquitous United Nations.

The people of Islam realized that they are the main targets for the aggression of the Judeo-Crusader alliance. All false propaganda about "human rights" vanished under the blows and massacres that took place against Muslims everywhere. The latest of these aggressions on Muslims, a calamity that matches the greatest confronted since the death of the Prophet, God's blessings and salutations upon him, is the occupation of the Land of the Two Holy Sanctuaries—the foundation of the house of Islam, the place of the Revelation, the source of the message and the place of the noble Ka'ba, the direction of prayer for all Muslims—by the Christian armies of the Americans and their allies. "There is no power and might except through God."

In the shadows of this reality in which we live, in the shade of this blessed and sublime awakening that has extended over patches of this world and the Islamic world in particular, I meet with you today, after a long absence has been imposed on the scholars and preachers of Islam by the iniquitous Crusader campaign under the leadership of America. The latter fears that the Islamic community will be incited to rise against its enemies by the scholars and preachers of Islam who follow in the path of their pious forebears, may God be pleased with them, among them [the thirteenth-century scholar Taqi al-Din] Ibn Taymiyya and [the seventh-century judge] Al-'Izz Ibn 'Abd Al-Salam. Therefore the Crusader-Jewish alliance resorted to killing and arresting the most emblematic of sincere scholars and hard-working preachers. We need not commend any specific one of them to God.

They resorted to killing the struggler Shaikh 'Abdalla 'Azzam, God have mercy upon him. They arrested the struggler Shaikh Ahmad Yasin at the site of the ascension of our Prophet, God's blessings and salutations upon him, as well as the struggler Shaikh 'Umar 'Abd al-Rahman. In the same way, through America's determination, a very large number of scholars, preachers, and young people in the Land of the Two Holy Sanctuaries were imprisoned, among them the prominent Shaikh Salman Al-'Awda, Shaikh Safar Al-Hawali, Shaikh Ibrahim Al-Dubayan, Shaikh Yahya Al-Yahya and their brothers. "There is no power and might except through God."

In the wake of this injustice, we have suffered by being prevented from addressing the Muslims. We have been exiled from Pakistan, the Sudan and Afghanistan, hence this lengthy absence. But by the Grace of God, a safe base has become available in Khurasan on the summit of the Hindu Kush, this summit where by the Grace of God, the largest infidel military force of the world was destroyed, and the myth of the superpower withered before the strugglers' cries "God Is Greater."

Today, from atop the same summit of Afghanistan, we work to lift the injustice that had been imposed on the Islamic community by the Judeo-Crusader alliance, particularly after they have captured the Land of the Two Holy Sanctuaries. We ask God to bestow us with victory, for He is victory's patron and is most capable of it.

In the summer of 1996, Osama bin Laden was not a figure much known in the West. Few newspapers had published much about the man, despite his status as one of the most successful and well-financed recruiters of Arab fighters during Afghanistan's struggle against Soviet occupation during the 1980s.[7] Two years earlier, he had acquired notoriety for being expelled from Saudi Arabia. He had not only violated his promise to Saudi security officials not to continue supporting armed insurgents in Yemen. More urgent to Western officials, he had expressed opposition to the royal family's decision to host American and Western military forces in its defence against Saddam Hussein's forces during the Gulf War in 1990. Much of what Americans knew about bin Laden at the time was restricted to a handful of Central Intelligence Agency analysts who began focusing on bin Laden's activities in 1991.[8] Still, the Federal Bureau of Investigation, including the program responsible for tracking security threats abroad, had yet to open a file. This speech provided the FBI with the rationale to do so.[9]

A wind-blasted mountain eyrie, well removed from centers of power, was an unlikely place to launch a war on the eve of the twenty-first century. The technology on hand for public documentation, a simple tape recorder loaded with a Sony ninety-minute cassette, was hardly more auspicious. In fact, bin Laden was confronting the bleakest prospects of his career. During the late 1980s, as the Soviets prepared to withdraw from Afghanistan after nearly a decade of occupation, he had become Saudi Arabia's *cause célèbre*. His leadership of Arab volunteer fighters who had traveled to Afghanistan, "Arab-Afghans" as they were called, was considered to be a tribute to the extension of Islam's banner over infidel lands. By 1990, however, the Soviet Union had not only withdrawn from Afghanistan, but had ceased to exist. The war was over, the struggle, or *jihad*, victorious, and bin Laden's relevance in the post-Soviet world increasingly uncertain. Throughout his life, bin Laden's primary leverage had been financial, whether through membership in his father's multi-million dollar engineering and trading company or through his talents as a fund raiser. Once the first Gulf War began, however, his financial backers showed increasing restraint. Bin Laden's primary state sponsor, the Saudi royalty, redirected its wealth to shoring up regional security in collaboration with the United States. His opposition to foreign troop presence in the Saudi kingdom hardly helped, and, after King Fahd stripped him of his citizenship in 1994 for his maverick political views and financial support of militants, his own family disinherited him and he subtracted another $20 million of inheritance from his net worth. His biggest blow came in 1996, when after four years living and working in the Sudan, he was forced to leave the country, made stateless for the first time in his life. What hope he had in recovering $165 million in debts was soon dashed by the Sudanese, who informed him of their inability to pay back their loans. Six weeks before his mountain declaration, an unexpected cache of $5,000 had been met with unimaginable joy because he, his family, and his followers were ravenous and could not afford basic amenities.[10]

If bin Laden's material woes were acute, the challenges he faced in leading a militant struggle anywhere in the Islamic world were unprecedented. By mid-1996, favored battlefields in the Middle East and North Africa had dried up, God's warriors having been either co-opted by states with promises of Islamic reform or shamed into withdrawal by communities sick of bloodshed and puritanical zeal. Egypt's Muslim Brotherhood, long the state's principal opposition movement, had renewed its commitment to non-violent reform in efforts to distance itself from a four-year streak of militant attacks on Egyptians and foreigners alike; Algeria's horrific civil war in the early 1990s had led to a popular referendum in favor of the state and a military crackdown on

Islamic extremism; in the Palestinian territories, widespread protesting under the first Intifada, or "uprising," had subsided as the Palestinian Liberation Organization began a new round of peace negotiations with the Israeli government; in Yemen, a war with southern separatists in 1994 had given way to a period of state consolidation and the quelling of militant attacks against the socialist opposition; and in Saudi Arabia, the Islamic "Awakening" (*al-sahwa*) movement, so outspoken a critic of state abuses and capitulation to foreign interests during the 1980s and early 1990s, had dissipated under equally aggressive state consolidation and co-optation. Beyond the Middle East, frontiers of armed jihad were not much better. In the Balkans, war-torn communities that formerly had been privileged destinations for Arab militants deprived of their Soviet enemy in Afghanistan after 1990 were being patrolled by North Atlantic Treaty Organization peacekeeping forces. Southeast Asia's economic boom was being accompanied by public support for a Muslim corporate ethics that eschewed militant jihad. In Afghanistan itself, the Taliban, a popular armed resistance movement launched just two years earlier by ethnic Pashtun "students" (*taliban* in Pashto) of God's law, were open allies of the United States, despite their opposition to Afghanistan's standing government.[11] Among the American administration's top reasons for such support was to establish a regional front against Iran and China, whichever Afghan administration should come to power. More particular was the matter of securing a natural-gas pipeline through the Taliban heartlands that could deliver Central Asia's vast natural gas reserves to Western-bound ships in the Indian Ocean without Russian or Iranian interference. The United States hoped that the project would be awarded to the Union Oil Company of California (UNOCAL), an optimism that was backed by the support of Mulla 'Umar, paramount leader of the Taliban, who appreciated the revenues that UNOCAL could bring to southern Afghanistan's beleaguered people. Seven months later, bin Laden would present himself at Mulla 'Umar's doorstep in Kandahar in hopes of a favorable hearing.

These obstacles to leading a war against the United States were further complicated by a growing array of reports that bin Laden was not, in fact, a very good fighter. Throughout his life, many who encountered him found him to be shy, hesitant to talk, and persistently adolescent. His advocacy for armed jihad in Afghanistan, including his own brief experience combating the Soviets in 1987, certainly toughened his image.

By 1990, his reputation as Lion of Jihad had been secured through tireless efforts by Arab-Afghan propagandists supported by the powerful Saudi media industry. Such efforts included the use of audiocassettes; in 1990, a single speech by bin Laden sold 250,000 copies in Saudi Arabia alone. As he grew more controversial, however, copies of heroic speeches and narratives about him gradually disappeared. Compromising accounts of his leadership and military achievements began circulating among a growing number of Arab-Afghans who had fought alongside him or heard stories about him. The 1989 siege of Jalalabad against the communist Afghan government, newly liberated from the Soviets, had gone badly. Spearheaded by Pakistan's security apparatus, the Inter-Services Intelligence, with support from America's own Central Intelligence Agency, long the ISI's benefactor, the siege proved to be a virtual bloodbath for bin Laden's men.[12] Recruits at bin Laden's training camps complained about his poor organizational oversight and were put off by his tendency to refer even basic questions to Egyptian lieutenants.[13] Others were frustrated by his tendency to shirk deeper questions about the religious merit and ethics of jihad.[14] The seriousness of such reports was underscored by a more crippling trend: fewer and fewer recruits were coming to bin Laden's camps. Who exactly was the enemy now that the Soviets had left? The prospect of fighting other Muslims was deeply concerning to many, quite apart from the dwindling of financial support for the Afghan cause by Saudi and other Arab states. Bin Laden himself acknowledged as much when, in 1992, he and his supporters in Peshawar, Pakistan, packed up and headed to the Sudan, announcing to anyone who would listen that "al-Qaʿida is finished."[15]

Four years later, bin Laden sought a makeover. He hoped to be seen as someone who, despite his statelessness, personal shortcomings, and lack of funds, could command a war against the United States. What resources did he have to be taken seriously? What leadership style would he cultivate in trying to overcome the obstacles that confronted him? What was the nature of al-Qaʿida for militants and potential supporters during its most coherent years leading to the 11 September attacks in the United States, and what could bin Laden do to mobilize these views in his favor?

In exploring these questions, I rely in this book on a collection of audiotapes that were deposited in his residential compound in Kandahar, Afghanistan. Containing over 1,500 volumes, the collection functioned as an audio library for Arab-Afghans in bin Laden's coterie between 1997 and 2001. Featuring roughly 2,000 hours of lectures, speeches, and conversations, the tapes provide a record of the issues and debates that informed the worldviews of those who gathered in bin Laden's own home. Many of the collection's most represented speakers are among the Arab world's most esteemed Muslim jurists and preachers. The top seven include Saudi shaikhs 'A'id Al-Qarni, Salman Al-'Awda, Muhammad Ibn Salih Al-'Uthaimin (second, fourth, and sixth most featured speakers respectively), Kuwaiti scholar Ahmad Al-Qattan, Palestinian jurist and militant 'Abdalla 'Azzam, Yemeni shaikh 'Abd al-Majid Al-Zindani, and Syrian scholar 'Abd al-Rahim Al-Tahhan, the most well represented speaker in the collection. Given these individuals' accolades, the collection offers a unique resource for considering the ways Islam has been co-opted by what many have come to think of as history's most sophisticated terrorist organization. The cassettes provide an archive, however, not primarily of bin Laden's own distorted views and efforts to craft leadership, although I focus much on these in this book. The archive preserves a much more eclectic range of voices. Some are well known while others will never be identified. Some venture unequivocal support for bin Laden's goals while others express criticism. Some speak from generations past, including a preacher who died in the 1960s, while others recorded themselves as late as 18 November 2001. While roughly 98 per cent of the tapes are in Arabic, evidence on cassette cartridges and accompanying jackets contain printed and handwritten words betraying diverse origins and stages of transmission. Some of the tapes contain handwritten messages. "A gift to Shaikh Osama bin Laden," wrote one anonymous admirer in Arabic on a tape composed of anthems in a foreign tongue in tribute to his host. Other tapes contain notes for other recipients. Given the social and decentralized nature of audiocassette production and consumption in the Islamic world, and the ways tapes are regularly swapped among friends and would-be associates, the value of the collection is perhaps best understood as a collaborative audio recording archive that was given shape through bin Laden's stewardship by virtue of its location in his Kandahari residence. These and other observations on the culture and use of audiocassettes, and this archive in particular, are the topic of chapter four. In assessing the significance of the tapes for shaping al-Qa'ida's worldview, we should remember that while we cannot know exactly which tapes bin Laden himself listened to, we can safely say that these tapes were a communal resource, an audio "library" with borrowing privileges for residents, guests, and visitors in bin Laden's residence who wondered what to make of Arab-Afghan initiatives being mobilized under his roof. The vision of al-Qaʿida under bin Laden's leadership that emerges from these tapes, and that is the subject of this book, is more than one of his own making. It is a composite, tentative, and at times deeply conflicted vision, the inconsistencies of which reflect the circumstances of its place and time. If these inconsistencies are no less endemic to al-Qaʿida today than they were during its halcyon years, the archive provides a definitive record of how people closely involved with the world's most notorious militant movement sought to manage dissension through recourse to venerable traditions of Islamic theology, law, and cultural interpretation broadly writ.

Observers of al-Qaʿida's history and development have pointed out that its essential anti-Americanism was not, in fact, intrinsic to the organization itself but rather developed between the years 1996 and 2001.[16] Given the tape collection's assemblage during this important period, the tapes offer special lessons on why and how the United States became enemy number one. As noted by others, al-Qaʿida's militant founders and original charter, drafted in 1988, make no mention of America.[17] Neither, for that matter, was Russia or any of the Soviet republics mentioned as a target for the organization. Rather, al-Qaʿida's goals were broad to the point of inspired diplomacy: "To lift the word of God; to make His religion victorious." Under such a banner might sparring Islamic factions be reminded of common ground. As bin Laden himself looked into a future beyond Soviet control of Afghanistan, toppling the socialist government of South Yemen remained his primary militant objective, even as late as 1994.[18] America's threat to the Islamic world concerned him, of course, and was spoken about in no uncertain terms as early as the late 1980s, as evidenced on cassettes that I examine in later chapters. It was only after his expulsion from the Sudan, however, and most starkly in his summer speech from the peaks of the Hindu Kush, that the United States would become the principal subject of bin Laden's fiery discourse.

The tapes document the steady rise of anti-Americanism among Muslim militants through the 1990s. To some extent, militants draw from broader critiques of Western secularism and cultural depravity that had been a recurrent theme in the writings and sermons of conservative

Muslim reformers since the nineteenth century. As Muslim scholars under European colonial rule in countries like India, Egypt, and Algeria, such reformers invoked clean ideological boundaries between the political aspirations of an Islamic civilization, a superior form of modernity, and its predecessors. Central to these aims was the establishment of a moral community based on Islamic law, one that could, as bin Laden puts it in his opening supplications, "command what is right and forbid the wrong." Justice in such a community would ideally be secured by an Islamic state. For Sunni militants, however, the likelihood of securing an Islamic state had become increasingly remote over the course of the twentieth century, the 1924 abolition of the caliphate by Turkish nationalists having been a decisive blow. Iran's revolution against the United States-supported regime of Shah Reza Pahlavi in 1979 offered a shining example of statehood from the Shi'a world, and many Sunni militants would take inspiration from the Shah's successor, the Ayatolla Ruholla Khomeini. More auspicious were recent events in the Sunni pale. In the Sudan, a Revolutionary Command Council had seized power in 1989 with heavy support from political parties committed to Islamic law. In Afghanistan, Mulla 'Umar's Taliban leadership had been secured in 1994 with his appointment as the Commander of the Faithful (*amir al-mu'minin*), a title long reserved for Muslim caliphs. Still, state powers and their clerical representatives had, throughout the 1990s, secured an extraordinary compliance among Muslim revolutionaries across the Islamic world, as evidenced by bin Laden's own forced exile from the Sudan earlier that summer. Islamic states, however ideal, were still part of an international system of state regulation and surveillance. For these reasons, as we will learn throughout this book, militants' speeches frequently drift toward more emancipatory horizons of territorial reclamation by righteous minorities.

In the tape collection, militants cite the presence of American-led troops on the Arabian Peninsula as a principal reason for waging armed war against the West, though close behind this event lies their own leaders' servitude to American and "Jewish" interests in the region. For those sympathetic with bin Laden, few events confirmed the seriousness of his pitch about America's threat to Muslim lands, and the need to take up arms, more than the expanding scope of United States military operations in the Islamic world's historic heartlands. More broadly, of course, the United States was seen as the world's sole superpower after the fall of the Soviet Union in 1989, an opinion bolstered by the steady growth of America's arms industry and United States-led military operations across the globe. Muslim populations increasingly experienced these operations directly, most notably in the Persian Gulf war of 1990 when Iraqi forces were driven out of Kuwait by American-led coalition forces based mostly in Saudi Arabia. In the shadow and aftermath of the war, American troops along with a growing arsenal of private military subcontractors expanded operations in Iraq, Saudi Arabia, Kuwait, Turkey, the United Arab Emirates, Bahrain, Egypt, Oman, Yemen, and Somalia. Each initiative gave rise to debates and controversies that informed the consciousness of an expanding transnational Muslim community. For many Muslims, the United States' positive role in the Islamic world was deeply compromised by a lack of progress in Israeli-Palestinian peace negotiations. Especially vexing was its $3 billion annual aid package to Israel, a sum which, for many Muslims, seemed all the more egregious given nightly televised broadcasts showing Palestinian suffering and the rapid expansion of illegal Jewish settlements in the West Bank and Gaza.

In his summer of 1996 speech, bin Laden tapped these sentiments in presenting his case, the effect of which I'll consider further in chapter nine. Humble supplication sets the tone of the speech as bin Laden cites Qur'anic verses along with revered narratives of the Prophet Muhammad's words and deeds (*ahadith*, singular *hadith*). Islam requires Muslims to "speak the right word," but also to use physical force when necessary: "If people see the oppressor and fail to restrain him with their hand, they draw close to an all encompassing punishment from God." Immediately, bin Laden clarifies the enemy at large:

> It should not be hidden from you that the people of Islam have suffered from injustice, oppression, and aggression by the Judeo-Christian alliance and their collaborators, to the extent that the Muslim's blood became the cheapest and their wealth and natural resources as loot in the hands of the enemies.

Military and economic attacks rank paramount, whether in Palestine, under Israeli suzerainty; in Iraq, whose population was suffering under United Nations' economic sanctions and American bombing sorties designed to unseat Saddam Hussein; or in a host of other settings in the Middle East and beyond. The theft of vital elements—blood and natural resources—is made more unconscionable by the United Nations' "clear conspiracy" to deprive Muslims of weapons. Omitting the fact that, by 1990, the Saudis had become the United States' principle arms market, surpassing even the Israelis, bin Laden ventures further to locate the final culmination of Judeo-Christian aggression in the "Land of the Two Holy Sanctuaries," an epithet for Saudi Arabia employed by those who contest the house of Saud's claims to leadership and that refers instead to founding mosques in the cities of Mecca, the birthplace of the Prophet Muhammad, and Madina, site of the first Islamic community and Muhammad's tomb. Especially grievous for bin Laden is the "long absence" imposed on the "scholars and preachers of Islam by the iniquitous Crusader campaign under the leadership of America." Included among its ranks are clerics jailed by Saudi authorities such as Salman Al-ʿAwda and Safar Al-Hawali, as well as those from other countries who received training in Saudi Arabia but who were later jailed or killed on foreign shores. These include the alleged Palestinian militant cofounder of al-Qaʿida, ʿAbdalla ʿAzzam, and the Egyptian shaikh ʿUmar ʿAbd al-Rahman, imprisoned in the United States for his role in the 1993 World Trade Center bombings. "In the wake of this injustice," announces bin Laden, inserting himself into the ranks of these widely recognized scholars, "we have suffered by being prevented from addressing the Muslims. We have been exiled from Pakistan, the Sudan, and Afghanistan, hence this lengthy absence. But by the Grace of God, a safe base has become available in Khurasan on the summit of the Hindu Kush." Bin Laden's "safe base" (*qaʿida amina*), hovering over battlefields where Arab-Afghan fighters had wrested victory from godless Soviet infidels, would become the symbolic touchstone of his revolution.

Al-Qaʿida's spectacular base aside, bin Laden had a recruitment problem. In trying to build what would necessarily be a transnational corps of Muslim militants, he needed to convince audiences that efforts were best directed to attacking the United States rather than the more familiar arsenal of enemies at home, foremost among them their own authoritarian leaders. While many militants sympathized with those who worried about an expanding American empire and dreamed of its collapse, few could envision diverting resources from struggles in their homelands, or—imprisonment and exile having delayed the likelihood of near-term victory—in other Islamic countries perceived to be suffering under the occupation of infidels. Bin Laden himself had been among these skeptics just two years earlier. For every speech identifying America as a prime target are dozens of other speeches identifying other more classic enemies of Islam. These include idolators (*mushrikun*), ingrates who have rejected God's mission (*kufar*), communists, secularists, people electing submission to economic and material orders (*jahiliyya*), and "freemasons". All of these are more likely to characterize individuals or communities who would self-identify as Muslim than to characterize Jews, Christians, agnostics, or members of some other confessional group. The clerics and intellectuals who had appealed to militants throughout most of the twentieth century had developed their most critical vocabularies in opposition to those within the house of Islam, not beyond. Bin Laden's task would become no easier given the growing supply of volunteers from Saudi Arabia after 1997. As others have shown, few Saudis felt that attacking the United States was part of Islam's master plan.[19] While militants from countries lacking Muslim majorities also increasingly enlisted in camps by the late 1990s, they typically sought to drive infidel occupiers from Islamic lands rather than to take the fight back to their own countries. Especially after 1998, when al-Qaʿida's bombings of United States embassies in East Africa greatly amplified bin Laden's reputation across the world, militants who had been born in the West, or who had lived, worked, and received education in Western countries, were prone to make distinctions between one Western "enemy" and another. Abu Musʿab Al-Suri, for example, whose lectures to recruits are featured on nine cassettes in the collection, lived in Syria, Pakistan, Spain, and London before moving to Afghanistan to fight alongside bin Laden. He decried bin Laden's attacks against the East African embassies, feeling that bin Laden's blanket anti-Western tirades had distracted militants from more important strategic victories that would unite the Islamic community worldwide.[20] Even when prioritizing strikes against Western interests, for example, Al-Suri took pains to rank targets according to their likely success in uniting the Islamic community, beginning with "Centers of missionary activity and Christianization, the cultural envoys, and the institutions in charge of the American-Western civilizational and ideological invasion," followed by their regional economic assets (oil reserves, mines, then ocean facilities), diplomatic institutions, military entities, intelligence and security entities, and so forth.[21] Among cosmopolitan militants looking for tactical guidance in diverse locales, bin Laden's Declaration risked conflating American territory with America's perceived geopolitical war on Islam, the latter of which represented a more diffuse and urgent set of "missionary," "cultural," "civilizational," and "ideological" threats to Muslims. Bin Laden's inspired pledge to defend his sacred homeland from American occupiers was appreciated. Perhaps attacks within the United States would be a necessary corollary. But to what extent could he lead the larger war for oppressed Muslims everywhere? Could he set aside his own priorities in the Arab world, such as his own thirst for cleansing Saudi Arabia of foreign influences, in the interests of a more transnational Muslim community? Given that his ascendancy as a leader had been inextricably linked to his financial connections in the Kingdom, whether as the son of a multi-millionaire or as a gifted fundraiser, could he truly represent "the dispossessed," as he claimed to do in his late summer speech in 1996?

In 2002, the Qatar-based Al-Jazeera television channel broadcast an interview with Saudi scholar Muhsin Al-ʿAwaji, in which he was asked about the reasons for bin Laden's popularity among supporters.

> Bin Laden is perceived to be a man of honor, a man who abstains from the pleasures of this world, a brave man, and a man who believes in his principles and makes sacrifices for them…what the Saudis like best about bin Laden is his asceticism (*zuhd*). When the Saudi compares bin Laden to any child of wealthy parents, he sees that bin Laden left behind the pleasures of the hotels for the foxholes of jihad, while others compete among themselves for the wealth and palaces of this world.[22]

Throughout the book, I explore the ways in which bin Laden's reputation for asceticism helped define his leadership. Through the latter years of his life, bin Laden's worldly seclusion was animated for global audiences by his reluctance to release videos of himself and by a widely circulated photograph of him sporting a white turban and a controlled smirk. When pressed for his whereabouts, most experts pointed to his likely refuge in the Afghan-Pakistan borderlands. Others insisted that he had withdrawn to the deserts of Yemen or was dead. Traces of his continued existence reached audiences only through sound, in a voice that, deprived of its bodily host, seemed very eerie. When I mentioned my work to people during the years before bin Laden's death, I often get the reply "Are you listening to his actual voice?" followed by "What's that like?… Creepy?" The attacks of 11 September lent bin Laden a haunting shade.

And yet, how exactly was bin Laden's withdrawal construed by his different audiences? By his ability to elude capture by the world's most sophisticated and coordinated security networks? By his desertion of family and friends in pursuit of an enemy in far away lands? By his quest for an ideal Islamic order beyond the "wealth and palaces of this world"? Veils of withdrawal come in many folds, each with its cultural history. In Islam, asceticism has a venerable legacy in the examples of holy men and women, reformers as well as warriors, who found the attachments of this world too heavy. In the final section of his Declaration speech, bin Laden invokes this tradition, exhorting women, in particular, to lend support to male military and security personnel by "practicing asceticism from the world, and by boycotting American goods." He ventures further: "If economical boycotting is combined with the strugglers' military operations, then the defeat of the enemy would be even nearer, by God's permission." In bin Laden's speech, women's ascetic discipline, practiced through warfare against a Western economic order led by the United States, is not peripheral. As I discuss in chapter nine, their example inaugurates his call to every Muslim, and especially the youth, to launch armed jihad against the West. English-speaking audiences have been prevented from understanding the significance of asceticism in his Declaration given the poor quality of its original hasty translation. His statement "We expect the women of the Land of the Two Holy Sanctuaries and elsewhere to carry out their role *by practicing asceticism from the world, and* by boycotting American goods" has reached English readers without the reference to asceticism (italicized here). The function of asceticism is unambiguous in the audio recorded version of the speech in the collection. Shortly later, bin Laden underscores the urgency of asceticism, and its gendered undertones, when commending the leadership of Islam's second caliph 'Umar Ibn al-Khattab. One of Islam's earliest fighters, 'Umar was renowned for his spartan table of bread, olive oil, barley and coarse salt. Zealous to defend his new faith, most prominently in battles on Islam's expanding frontiers, 'Umar was also famous for his generosity, commending this virtue to his warriors on the eve of en epic battle with the Persians: "*Zuhd* is taking what is due from everyone who owes it and giving what is due to anyone who has a right to it." Bin Laden would regularly speak of 'Umar's leadership. When rallying Muslim listeners to martyrdom in the final section of his 1996 challenge to the Americans, bin Laden found natural recourse to 'Umar's example, noting that 'Umar's own sister Fatima had converted to Islam even slightly before him.

'Umar, however, like his sister, was also a renowned conciliator. In fact, most Muslims have long spurned ascetic inclinations toward the spartan rigors of war or monastic life. Narratives of asceticism typically focus on the ordeals of men and women who remain engaged with their communities whatever their faults. While pitched against the material excesses of this world, their struggles are inward rather than outward against the material orders of their age. In Arabic, *zuhd* is better rendered as "pious renunciation" than asceticism in the strict sense. Its essence has long been expressed in the lives of mystic saints, known as Friends of God (*waliyyulla*) or as Sufis who dissolve the ego while merging with the Divine self. As spiritual masters practiced in the esoteric aspects of Islam's holy writ, these mystics had long served as peacemakers among warring factions throughout the Islamic world. Their compounds were sacrosanct, their leadership exercised through words rather than weapons.

If bin Laden sought to lead through the example of asceticism, then he would again face serious obstacles. His commitment to militancy, violence and terror would need reconciling with asceticism's established call to God's House of Peace. As a former jihadi financier who had abandoned "the wealth and palaces of this world," he obviously struck a chord with a generation of Saudis and other Arabs who were fed up with unprecedented levels of state affluence and corruption, and who heard in bin Laden's speeches the heroic strains of a modern-day Robin Hood. As an Islamic voice, however, his pitch for all-out economic war against Americans and their allies, including Muslim leaders such as the Saudis themselves who courted them, would need considerable justification. This was especially the case given that Islamic asceticism had long made accommodations to the privileges of worldly belongings. Although the earliest Muslim ascetics had drawn much inspiration from Christian counterparts known for worldly withdrawal and starvations of the flesh, Islam's community of the righteous had become established enough by the tenth century to assert a code of ascetic virtues that could inspire the faithful within its own expanding empire. Property, goods, and a healthy economic livelihood were integral to religious life, as long as they did not distract one from God's higher purposes. Pleasure and moderate worldly indulgences were a natural part of human existence, as long as they didn't lead to capricious paths of desire.

One of the tapes in the collection, entitled "Poems about Asceticism," outlines the dangers of withdrawal and isolation.[23] Recorded in Burayda, a city in Saudi Arabia known for the ascetic zeal of an ultra-orthodox community, the cassette bears the imprint of Uhud Islamic Recordings, a recording studio named for a battle in CE 625 that is Islam's equivalent of the Alamo. After many moving poems about Muslims' courage in prevailing over defeat and death, a short essay on asceticism concludes the tape. It admonishes listeners against "renouncing wealth and showing off your ruggedness":

> Zuhd in Islam does not mean to isolate oneself from this worldly life as is practiced by the monks. Rather, it is a balanced asceticism, an asceticism of strength, calling towards God, working, and earning. [As the Qur'an states]: "And forget not thy share in this world."[24] This exemplifies God's upright approach, [as well as] the heartfelt approach of one who longs for the Afterlife even as he possesses wealth. It is an approach that does not prevent one from claiming one's share in this world, but rather, it encourages one to [build wealth (*recording briefly interrupted*)], as a task and duty. Asceticism should not be observed in the wrong way, leading one to neglect and weaken one's worldly life. God created good and lawful things in this world so that they may be enjoyed, so that people may work on earth to acquire and earn them. Thus, life grows and is renewed, and the role of the human race, as God's representative on earth, is fulfilled.

> [Humans'] ultimate goal and intention must be the Afterlife. It is important that they not deviate from this direction or become preoccupied with the goods of this world, failing in their duties. In this case, [however], using the goods of the world becomes a way of showing gratitude to Him who bestowed these blessings on us. Indeed, it is an act of worship that is rewarded by God. Some think that the ascetic is simply someone who renounces everything. Such is not the case, however. Setting aside your wealth and making a show of ruggedness is too much the stuff of those who seek adulation for what they do. Ascetic practice must be focused, above all, on human whims and desires. [As the Qur'an states] "and had restrained the soul from base animalistic desires (*hawa*)"[25]... Thus, asceticism ought to be observed and realized in the most ideal way. [It must be practiced] in accordance with God's balanced and upright approach, with no duplicity or excess therein, just as is mentioned in the holy Qur'an: "Thus have We made of you a nation justly balanced."

With winds buffeting the fourteen-thousand foot peaks around him, the windows of his family's rock hut covered with animal skins, and an audio-tape machine recording his declaration of war against the United States, bin Laden would not likely, in the summer of 1996, have won the appellation "balanced."

Nevertheless, in the months and years that followed, bin Laden and his followers would wrest virtue from a strain of asceticism that offered to redeem their actions and justify their rage at what they viewed as the towering arrogance of the West's most powerful economic nation. Audiocassettes such as "Poems about Asceticism" would provide Arab-Afghans who arrived at bin Laden's doorstep with a virtual sounding board that, while not entirely in line with what they knew of bin Laden or where he was going, gave shape to a political movement that was increasingly licensed in his name. In its broadest form, a militant rendition of asceticism, I will suggest, expresses certain solutions to political and moral conflict in the Arab world, especially in the Arab Gulf States including Saudi Arabia and the Yemen, and comes to distinguish al-Qa'ida's vision from that of other Muslim militant groups. Even as al-Qa'ida's chief message became open and unconditional enmity to the West, as terrorist strikes covered by global news networks would attest, bin Laden's leadership hinged on his ability to broker political and ideological alliances between Islamic militant groups whose different visions of political community obstruct cooperation. Striking at the interests of common Judeo-Christian enemies could underscore unity against outsiders, but diplomacy inside one's own community also proved key. If militants were specialists in the art of survival, not simply masters of self-annihilation, they needed ethical values that could attract recruits and enhance solidarity within existing state structures, however corrupt and impious they might be. Of special merit were virtues that functioned in more than one sense, tropes that supplied standards for public consensus even as they signaled the inverse worldviews of a minority committed to radical and sometimes violent change. Bin Laden's supporters would come to admire him greatly for knowing the rules for such sport. When speaking to audiences, bin Laden would employ dramatic historical narratives, irony, modes of comportment, and dress to tap into feelings of Muslim Arab persecution that had been transmitted over generations. Thin boundaries between open defiance and self-control would provide a whetting stone for building trust among companions. Asceticism proved instrumental in this regard. For bin Laden, asceticism was not simply a virtue of pious predecessors, a path blazed by heroic sage-warriors long ago that might lend dignity to the hard and compromised lives of God's modern strugglers. The ascetic's journey was a practice of realizing new social objectives, a set of body techniques through which society could be stripped of its frivolous baggage and rebuilt on purer foundations. In this sense, asceticism inaugurated radical departure as much as return. Daily combat against the "whims" and "desires" of this world required engagement with modernity's excesses, not retreat from them.

Bin Laden's own modern succubi, as recounted by family members, friends, and visitors, were more often technological appliances of diverse manufacture than they were age-old religious alliances bent on Muslim destruction. They included refrigerators, air conditioners, electric stoves, television sets, ice cubes, and modern medicine of any description, all of which he regularly banned from his homes. Desert suffering provided Osama with an anvil for smelting his twenty-first-century warrior code. At least the semblance of it did, for bin Laden also had a passion for expensive cars that was indulged well into his latter years, and he retained, from his days as an executive officer in his father's company, a comfortable relationship with telecommunications devices, computers, and media technologies that provided access to the latest information, even when he was forced into dank Afghani caves. Over time, bin Laden learned to reconcile such apparent contradictions by fashioning a specifically Western menagerie of demons, all of which threatened Muslims through particular patterns of consumption. By the late 1980s, his speeches made special mention of the dangers of importing American apples, Pepsi products, and Tobasco sauce, each of which contributed to Muslim subordination in degrees not only economic and cultural but also physical. In bin Laden's daily interactions with followers, the sacred integrity of the body became a worksite, its protection and defense against Western incursions key for realizing grander political ambitions. Rituals of body purification became especially important, however, because they brought grander and more distant battles to more familiar settings. As I show later when examining bin Laden's speeches as well as conversations and observations among associates, the very concept of "the rule" or "base" (al-qaʿida) acquired most significance for al-Qaʿida's teachers and recruits in local and embodied ways. Asceticism helped define the nature of such proximate struggles, their relation to wider political and religious boundaries, and the kind of knowledge required to triumph in both this world and the next.

In foregrounding the ways bin Laden's reputation as a leader was bolstered by an especially militant rendering of Muslim asceticism, I take a position that runs contrary to the usual assertions, made by Western analysts and their terrorists adversaries alike, that al-Qaʿida's primary enemy has always been the West, especially the United States. The latter perspective certainly accords with intelligence and security studies, the bulk of which are devoted to identifying the organization's threat to Western societies and, through predictive models, preventing future terrorist attacks. To be sure, anti-Americanism certainly becomes a rallying battle cry for bin Laden and other al-Qaʿida leaders, no more so than in the years following the 1996 Declaration of War. The determination and resourcefulness of al-Qaʿida's militants in attacking Western interests, including their capacity to launch terrorist attacks inside the United States and Europe, is enough to deserve serious attention. An honest survey of the cassette collection in bin Laden's house, however, requires acknowledging that for all the anti-West venom unleashed therein, even more animosity is directed toward what speakers believe to be the Islamic community's own weakest links, foremost among them, Muslims themselves. The havoc wrought by al-Qaʿida's ideology on Muslims across the world is evident enough to those who have lived and studied in Muslim societies, but is all too often forgotten or marginalized in studies of al-Qaʿida's public political discourse, much of which focuses on pan-Islamic unity in the face of external threats from the "far enemy." Efforts to redress this imbalance, and to recognize our commonalty with victims of al-Qaʿida's violence, both Muslim and non-Muslim alike, are instrumental to building allies in the struggle against religious radicalization and, in that sense, are a necessary part of any counter-terrorism initiative. My own efforts in this book begin with language. Like a traveler who discovers his inherited vocabulary is too thick to describe the color of a foreign encounter, I offer translations that might bridge some part of the gap between what we expect to find and the reality. The Arabic word *al-zuhd*, falling somewhere between asceticism, pious renunciation, and self-abnegation, provides a launching point.

In the following chapter, I explore the ways in which bin Laden's childhood and adolescence in Saudi Arabia have given shape to stories of his asceticism. His family's extraordinary wealth, built from scratch by his Yemeni father through favorable contracts both with the Saudi royal family and with American oil producers, lends a cosmopolitan tenor to his life that informs and also troubles popular views of his relation to worldly accumulation. Sensitive to the ways that new wealth opens one up to suspicion and distrust in the Kingdom, bin Laden strove through his early school years to uphold a higher standard than many of his contemporaries, even the most religious among them. Since he lacked the social status and authority of native Saudis, however, he also resorted to more ecumenical and at times adventurous strains of Muslim identity and political association than tended to be espoused in mainstream Islamic movements at the time. Before venturing back to bin Laden's formative years, it is worth highlighting where his estimation of an ascetic ideal ultimately leads.

In late December 2001, bin Laden found himself stateless once again. His chief state sponsors, the Afghan Taliban, had been driven from their headquarters in Kandahar by United States Special Operation Forces. The reason for his newly fugitive status was, of course, the 11 September attacks and evidence suggesting bin Laden's involvement in the financing and training of the perpetrators. Escaping to the peaks of Tora Bora in the Hindu Kush, where he had delivered his message to Americans nearly five years earlier, bin Laden once again delivered a speech praising the heroic youths of Islam. As martyrs for God's cause, he exclaims, they deserve eulogy from their countrymen. As activists worthy of emulation in this life, they win special praise for recognizing the values of monasticism even as they draw weapons to slaughter their foe:

> From the Land of the Two Holy Sanctuaries fifteen young men set forth—we pray to God to accept them as martyrs. They set forth from the land of faith, where lies the Muslims' greatest treasure, where faith takes root—as our Prophet rightly said, prayers be upon Him—in the Illuminated City [Madina], just as the snake finds sanctuary in its hole. Another two set forth from east of the Arabian Peninsula, from the Emirates, and another from the Levant, Ziyad Al-Jarrah—may God accept him as a martyr. Another set forth from Al-Kinana in Egypt, Mohammad 'Atta. May God accept all of them as martyrs. With their actions they provided a very great sign, a very great sign indeed, showing that it was this faith in their hearts that urged them to these many requirements, to give their soul to "There is no god but God alone"...
>
> Victory is not material gain; it is about sticking to your principles.
>
> And in the words of our Prophet, prayers be upon Him, there is the report about the young lad who took a stone when he was still uneducated and wavering between following a magician or a monk, and a wild beast blocked a road frequently used by people. He said "Today, I'll find out who is better, the monk or the magician." Because he was lacking in knowledge, he did not as yet understand which one was better, entrusting himself to his soul. So, he asked God to show him which one was better. If the monk was more

beloved to God Almighty, then he would be able to kill the animal. So the boy picked up the rock and threw it at the beast, and it dropped dead. The monk came to him and said: "My son, today you are better than me," despite his own learnedness and the ignorance of the boy. But God Almighty illumined this boy's heart with the light of faith, and he began to make sacrifices for the sake of "There is no god but God alone."

This is a unique and valuable narrative which the youths of Islam are waiting for their scholars to tell them, to hear them say to those [9/11 hijackers] who put their heads on the scales for "There is no god but God alone" what that learned monk had once said to the boy: "Today, you are better than us."

This is the truth. As relayed in the report of our Prophet, prayers be upon Him, the measure of virtue in this religion is the measure of faith. Virtue consists not only in collecting knowledge but in using it as well.

Earlier in the speech, bin Laden had focused on America's worldwide "Crusader campaign against Islam," a charge patched together with such a slough of conspiracies that, at one point, he even suggested that evidence for the 11 September attacks would more likely be found among the Irish Republican Army than among Muslims. Although American policies in Palestine and Iraq receives initial attention, bin Laden shifts mid-way through his speech toward a theme that unifies the bulk of what follows: "this haughty, domineering power, America, the Hubal of the age, is based on great economic power, but it is soft." Invoking memory of a pre-Islamic idol whose followers were defeated by the Prophet Muhammad's early companions, bin Laden slips into the role of an ostensible Muslim teacher. He can lecture about the evanescence of worldly gain and its relation to fundamentals of "truth" and "virtue" within the house of Islam.

The story of the boy, magician and monk gives insight into the ways bin Laden puts religion to his service. The story is drawn not from the Qur'an but rather from a sound report (*hadith*) about the Prophet Muhammad's own words that was committed to memory by early reliable transmitters and passed along to future generations through compilations featuring thousands of such reports. For Muslims, such reports are second in importance only to God's own revelation, and are especially valued for providing guidance in daily life when Qur'anic verses are ambiguous. This particular narrative recounts Muhammad's inspiration by a young boy who was invited by a pagan king to become apprentice to his court magician.[26] Choosing the counsel of a monk instead, the boy discovered faith in God to be a more powerful nostrum than any of the magicians' charms. One day, when accosted by a wild animal that was threatening travelers along a road, the boy was rewarded for his trust in the monk through God's intervention in helping him to kill the animal. The king's discovery of the boy's betrayal led to his torture and death by arrows, though not before the boy demonstrated God's awesome power once again. When the boy was ordered to submit to the king's pagan rites on pain of death, the henchmen ordered to push the youth off a cliff were instead launched into the abyss by a divine tremor from the highest peak.

Death-defying miracles on remote mountain peaks provide a regular theme in al-Qaʿida's literature.[27] They are no clearer than in bin Laden's descriptions of God's power in shaking the thrones of polytheist tyrants. Bin Laden's own recounting of the report focuses less on gory trials experienced by both the boy and the monk, and that feature in the original report as a common bond between them, than on the differences of knowledge that separate them. The monk, for all his erudition, proves too hesitant in taking up the fight against a bestial enemy. The boy, "uneducated" and "ignorant" though he is, proves to be the monk's superior because he weds faith and action. Drawing a lesson for his modern listeners, bin Laden states that scholars of the monk's quiet disposition have failed Islam's younger generations by not adequately testifying to the superior "knowledge" of the 9/11 hijackers. The victim in bin Laden's version of righteous youthful slaying is not only the beast but also older forms of knowledge preserved by Islam's most esteemed scholars. Monastic asceticism is certainly a cornerstone of faith, especially when used to refine one's erudition in the arts of overthrowing tyrant rulers. As bin Laden states, however, "Virtue consists not only in collecting knowledge but in using it as well." The word for "monk" (*rahib*), literally one afraid of God, proves most apt for militant reworking where it shares the same verbal root as the word "terrorist" (*irhabi*), one who, in militant discourse, turns fear into a weapon of divine justice. Students must learn from their teachers, but also finally break from them, using fear and terror to direct action against enemies in this world. The "principles" of this warrior code begin with shunning material gain. They also require new social investments. Earlier in the speech, bin Laden commends the 9/11 hijackers as "emigrants" (*muhajirun*), believers who have chosen "departure" (*hijra*) from their own established communities to embrace the faith of a more zealous collective. In CE 622,

the Prophet Muhammad launched the first such departure when rejecting the faith of his Meccan forebears, an event commemorated ever since
as the first year of the Islamic calendar. Joined by several hundred pious
emigrants, his destination was Yathrib, over two-hundred miles from
Mecca, and the collective they established there came to be known as
"the Enlightened City" (*al-madina al-munawwara*), or Madina. As bin
Laden prepares to extol the hijackers' particular brand of militant asceticism, he evokes this same memory of divine illumination, though with
a dizzying twist. The faith to which the young men return is like the hole
of a snake.

2

HEART PAINS

(Early-mid 2000 speech by Osama bin Laden entitled "The Presence of the Crusader-Jewish Occupation in the Heart of the Islamic world." Location unknown. Opening remarks, cassette no. 500.)

In the name of God, the Compassionate and Caring.

"Never will the Jews or the Christians be satisfied with you until you follow their way. Say: 'God's guidance is the only guidance.' Were you to follow their desires after the knowledge that has reached you, there would be none to protect or help you from the wrath of God."[1]

[*Introduction by an anonymous conference moderator:*]

My Muslim brother: Is there is a Crusader-Jewish occupation under way in the heart of the Islamic world? Has the Land of the Two Holy Sanctuaries, home to the honorable Kaʿba and sublime Prophet's Mosque, fallen to Crusader occupation? If such occupation exists, what are its goals? What are its particular shapes, varieties, and modes of dissemination? Is this the sole crime perpetrated by Crusaders and Jews against the Islamic community or is such occupation, in fact, only one episode in a series of ensuing crimes? What is the role of the American presence in enforcing a so-called 'operation of resignation and propagation,' and what is the role of the Islamic community in confronting this Crusader-Jewish attack?

My brother: to prepare yourself for responding to these and other questions, follow this conference with us.

[*Title of cassette announced:*] "The Crusader-Jewish Presence in the Heart of the Islamic World."

41

The Crusader-Jewish military presence in the Land of the Two Holy Sanctuaries. The American presence: 45,000 soldiers and experts, 130 fighter planes, military bases and cities in Hafr al-Batin, Dammam, Jeddah, Al-Kharja, Tabuk, Khamis Mushait, and Ta'if, and operational maneuvers conducted with international cooperation.

In occupied Palestine, the Zionist presence: 650,000 soldiers, 4,100 tanks, 9,480 armored cruisers and transportation vehicles, 1,790 artillery guns and missile launchers, 750 fighter planes, 3 submarines and 200 nuclear warheads.

In Egypt, the American presence: 20,000 soldiers, military bases west of Cairo, at the Suez Canal airport, and Ras Banyas. Military supply bases and operational maneuvers conducted with international cooperation.

In Kuwait, the American presence: 5,000 soldiers…

[*After statistics from a dozen other locations in the Middle East and North Africa are offered, Osama bin Laden begins speaking. The following excerpt is from the middle of his lecture.*]

Our respectable religious scholars have said, in the same fashion as their own scholarly predecessors, may God show mercy upon them, that there are ten clear ways that Islam can be legally nullified. Among them is supporting polytheists against believers. Assisting Jews against oppressed Muslims in Palestine is an example of such nullification. Whoever does this has certainly abandoned the community of Muhammad, God's blessings and salutations upon him.

What fraud is perpetrated against the pious community when those who have betrayed God and his Messenger are described as Guardians of the Believers! If you wish, consult the priceless words of the book *An Introduction to the Exalted*, a commentary on its predecessor *The Book of Monotheism* [written by eighteenth-century Saudi scholar Muhammad Ibn 'Abd al-Wahhab]. In one section of this [latter] book, Shaikh Muhammad, God's mercy upon him, said: whoever gives license to religious scholars and commanders to make licit what God has forbidden or make illicit what God has permitted has taken other gods than God alone as their Lord. In his *Introduction*, Shaikh 'Abd al-Rahman bin Hasan Al Al-Shaikh, God's mercy upon him, says: This is truly among the nullifications in Islam, and whoever does this has cast Islam's binding tie from his very core.

Not only are such people loyal to Jews and Christians. They also rule by [laws] other than those revealed by God. Even if they rule according to God's revelation in some matters, their judgement strays in other matters. It is well known to learned scholars that such practice is an example of the ways Islam is nullified. They have legislated and issued legal judgment on matters concerning the blood, belongings, and lands of Muslims in ways that fall outside God's revelation.

In so doing, they merely seek to comply with American pressure, with the United States of America, which appointed itself a rival and associate of God and legislated for people by laws other than God's own. Waging jihad against Americans and fighting them is thus the core of faith and monotheism. God, may He be exalted and glorified, ordered us to proclaim and abide by the testimony of monotheism: there is no god but God alone, and Muhammad is His Messenger. They [the Americans] likened themselves to a god who must be worshipped. Now the rulers of the region no longer worship the Lord of the Ancient House [the black cube in Mecca's Sacred Mosque that is reported to mark the site of Adam and later Abraham's first dwellings] and instead worship the lord of the White House. May whatever they deserve from God fall upon them.

To attribute faith to these [traitorous] people is to dilute the meaning of "There is no god but God alone, and Muhammad is His Messenger." Read, if you wish, the [early twentieth-century] treatise of [Saudi] Shaikh Muhammad bin Ibrahim Al Al-Shaikh—upon him be God's mercy—about man-made laws [in the Kingdom] and about his letters explaining how the country is being ruled by such laws. There is no might or power except through God. It is imperative to wake up the pious community…

Thus, the truthful scholars are all we have left.

These scholars must do their utmost to save the pious community. They must select a delegation from amongst themselves who might work together to appoint an Imam [a leader] for this community so that it can confront a worldwide rejection of God's guidance.

This will help us follow the path that has been prescribed for us. When a true leader is absent, it is incumbent upon people, as scholars have said—among them the [eleventh-century] Imam of the Two Holy Mosques [in Mecca and Madina Abu al-Maʿali] Ibn al-Juwayni, may God's mercy be upon him, in his book *Blessed Rain for the Nations in their Dark Confusion*. Al-Juwayni stated that if the sultan is absent in a given period, people of understanding and learning must appoint one of their own to rule amongst them according to God's revelation. He mentioned something to this effect.

I'm saying, then, that it is incumbent upon Muslims in the Islamic world to gather their dignitaries and form committees that would be in charge of appointing judges who would rule amongst them according to God's revelation. They must form committees to motivate and mobilize the pious community to show enmity to Jews and Christians, to boycott Jewish and American goods and products, and to do anything that may cause harm to the enemy. This is a duty of every Muslim man or woman. This pious community bears collective responsibility… [As is reported in a *hadith*] attributed to His Messenger, God's blessings and salutations upon him: "He who struggles against them with his hands is considered to be [a true] believer, as is he who

43

struggles against them with his tongue, as is he who struggles against them with his heart. Beyond this can be found not even a mustard seed of faith." Hence, all of us are responsible and all of us are strugglers (*mujahidun*). A man is a struggler, a young man is a struggler, a woman is a struggler; each person must do what they can—with the hands, and if this is impossible, then with the tongue, and if this is impossible, then with the heart.

It is therefore incumbent that women suckle our children on the enmity of Jews and Christians. This is necessary in order to disassociate ourselves from these polytheists, the enemies of Muhammad, God's blessings and salutations upon him. They must become ascetics in this world for the wellbeing of this pious community, for the wellbeing of its earlier generations. This is mentioned in [Muhammad Al-Bukhari's ninth-century compilation of sound *hadith* reports] *Sahih Al-Jami*: the wellbeing of this pious community lies in asceticism and conviction. Thus, we must all be ascetics in this world, and we must have strong conviction that God, Glorious and Exalted is He, will grant victory to His religion. He will continue doing so until we meet Him on the occasion that He is fully satisfied with us.

Responsibility lies on everyone's shoulders. Men must send their children to the fields of battle so that they can acquire military training to defend and support the religion of Muhammad, God's blessings and salutations upon him. As for picking and choosing from whatever suits us and is most pleasurable in religion: we would be deviating from the path of the Prophet, God's blessings and salutations upon him. It is authentically reported in *The Chronicles* [by eighth-century legal scholar Muhammad Al-Shaybani] that the Prophet set forth toward Tabuk during a period of extremely high temperatures to defend "There is no god but God alone, and Muhammad is His Messenger" [against assault by the Byzantines]. The Prophet, God's prayers be upon him, set out on the anniversary of the Battle of Uhud, when he had defended the banner of monotheism, injuring his noble face and breaking his front teeth.

What's the matter with us, then, when we sit back and don't set forth to defend our religion?

Over the course of the year 2000, bin Laden's reputation as a terrorist with global ambitions matured. His statements, audio recordings, and videos threatening unmitigated war against the United States and Western allies were readily transmitted to worldwide media networks. Solidifying his image as a militant who could orchestrate spectacular attacks worldwide was the August 1998 bombings of the American embassies in Nairobi, Kenya and Dar al-Salam, Tanzania. In the wake of these attacks, the sum of which left over two hundred dead and roughly five-thousand injured, the United States launched retaliatory missile strikes at al-Qaʿida's training camps in Afghanistan as well as at the Sudan's largest pharmaceutical plant, which intelligence reports identified as a chemical weapons procurer for bin Laden's men. Bin Laden escaped from these attacks not only unharmed but in some respects stronger. Afghan officials and Taliban leaders, his hosts at the time, rose to defend their homeland following tremendous public outcry against United States military involvement in the region. Three months later, when American officials posted a $5 million reward for information leading to the capture of bin Laden, the Taliban refused to hand him over, instead trying bin Laden in their own courts. Their verdict of "innocent" of wrongdoing by the end of the month echoed a sentiment growing among supporters of his anti-West platform worldwide, especially when charges of chemical weapons manufacturing at Sudan's Al-Shifaʾ factory proved unsustainable. In June of 1999, a documentary on bin Laden aired by Qatar's Al-Jazeera news network began with the following conundrum: "When bin Laden's name is mentioned, a number of conflicting ideas cross one's mind: Wealth, asceticism, terrorist, heroism, and jihad. What links all these words together is this man. Some people consider him to be a devil, while others believe him to be a fighter with a cause."

In some respects, the years since bin Laden's 1996 arrival in Afghanistan had gone well for him. By March of the following year, he had put down new roots with his family in Kandahar. In the years leading up to the 11 September attacks, al-Qaʿida would secure an estimated twenty training camps in the country, providing an educational infrastructure for some 10–20,000 militants.[2] Bin Laden had acquired just the "safe base" that he had envisioned in his Declaration of War. In other respects, however, bin Laden remained a pariah facing constant threats to his life and mission, even among his strongest supporters. At the time of his speech at the outset of this chapter, he had narrowly escaped six assassination attempts, at least half of them sponsored by the Saudis.[3] Many of bin Laden's troubles in Afghanistan stemmed from the fact that, despite his promises to his Taliban hosts, he could not stop fulminating against the West in much-publicized interviews with global media networks. By late 1998, an estimated 80 per cent of the Taliban leadership had come to oppose his presence in the country.[4] In their view, the several hundred Arab fighters that al-Qaʿida supplied in their campaigns in the north and eastern parts of the country did not offset the danger of bin Laden's obsession with publicity. In February 1999, Afghan officials, under pressure from the Taliban, seized his satellite phone and fax machine. Shortly after, the Taliban are reported to have closed down several al-Qaʿida training camps. Mulla ʿUmar, the Kandahar-based founder of the Taliban in 1994, remained bin Laden's sponsor, but relations with him were tense. Bin Laden repeatedly reneged on promises to give his host an oath of allegiance, instead claiming that only Afghans need submit to such procedures. In early 2000, ʿUmar declared bin Laden's fatwas void, a somewhat bizarre gesture for most Muslim authorities who knew of bin Laden's lack of authority to issue legal opinions. On top of these matters, top al-Qaʿida leaders themselves seem to have started back-pedaling from their colleague's privileging of the American enemy over corrupt Arab rulers at home. As reported by Mustafa Hamid, bin Laden's chief lieutenant at the time, al-Qaʿida's 1998 East Africa bombings and ensuing retaliatory American air strikes, when combined with international pressure on the Taliban to hand bin Laden over, were jeopardizing what many felt to be the long-term viability of the Islamic jihad worldwide.[5]

In many ways, bin Laden's speech in early–mid-2000 amplifies the anti-Americanism that defined his 1996 Declaration. Entitled *The Presence of the Crusader-Jewish Occupation in the Heart of the Islamic World*, the tape focuses on the "occupation" of the Middle East and North Africa by the latest wave of Christian Crusaders, especially Americans abetted by Jews. Statistics offered by an announcer at the tape's outset provide rhetorical leverage: "The American presence: 45,000 soldiers and experts, 130 fighter planes, military bases and cities…In occupied Palestine, the Zionist presence: 650,000 soldiers, 4,100 tanks…In Egypt, the American presence…In Kuwait, the American presence…"

If United States military operations remain the primary threat to Muslims, however, this latter speech situates the enemy's threat, both territorially and ideologically, in rather different ways. Whereas the earlier Declaration had focused on the entire Islamic world, identifying the "Land of the Two Holy Sanctuaries" (in Mecca and Madina) as the most egregious victim of "Judeo-Christian" enmity perpetrated by the United States, this speech focuses more resolutely on the Saudi context. If unity among Muslims of all stripes, including those not practicing their faith, had been a refrain in bin Laden's earlier tirade, cold and deliberate treachery by Saudi rulers themselves fuels rancor on this tape. Opening Qur'anic verses anticipate the treachery within, exhorting true believers to reject fellowship or guidance from Jews or Christians at the cost of being abandoned by God and his community. If armed jihad to defend Muslim territories worldwide had been the principle means for uprooting the enemy in 1996, here the arsenal of bin Laden's attack is whetted with a more developed militant theology. In contrast with their "desires" (*ahwa*), Muslims must anchor their actions in "learning" (*'ilm*). Those best equipped to exhibit such leadership are not the military personnel, security forces, or Muslim youth of all stripes highlighted earlier. Rather, they are religious leaders, "people of understanding and learning," as bin Laden calls them. His own selective vision of Islam and its champions is subsequently made apparent.

Foremost among religious leaders are established Saudi scholars. Bin Laden recommends the work of eighteenth-century Saudi reformer Muhammad Ibn 'Abd al-Wahhab, whose most famous treatise, *The Book of Monotheism*, provided audiences with a theological and legal tool-kit for building an Islamic state. Confronting Ottoman Turkish authorities in Saudi Arabia at the time, whose high taxes and cosmopolitan sophistication clashed with indigenous claims to leadership, 'Abd al-Wahhab argued that renewed campaigns to purge the peninsula of polytheism could serve the political goals of a more equitable pious community on one condition: absolute obedience had to be given to whoever had the power to lead. In 1744, his pledge to support a relatively marginal tribal leader, Muhammad Ibn Sa'ud, ensured the rising fortunes of the Saudi clan. By the mid-twentieth century, the Saudi state had secured an adequately compliant Wahhabi establishment, its freedom to enforce puritanical moral codes in the Kingdom contingent on submission to state-regulated "consultation" (*shura*) and "consensus" (*ijma'*). Still, dissent could be floated, and it was no more powerful than when voiced by descendents of Ibn 'Abd al-Wahhab himself, otherwise known as the "family of the Shaikh" (Al Al-Shaikh). Bin Laden singles out one of them for distinction: Muhammad bin Ibrahim, the juridical grandmaster of the conservative legal establishment until his death in 1969. One of the first in the Kingdom to invite dialogue with non-Wahhabis at a conference in 1954, bin Ibrahim's lesser-known theological writings on heresy would be resuscitated in the 1990s by virulent critics of the Saudi regime.[6] His adamancy against laws not fully consonant with Islam's revelation provides a foothold for bin Laden's charge, bolstered by an unusually peripatetic legal treatise, even for the eleventh century, that "people of understanding and learning must appoint one of their own to rule amongst them according to God's revelation."

Struggling to substantiate his call for regime change, bin Laden also urges mobilization by a broader field of religious activists. The "duty of every Muslim man or woman," he insists, is to seize the initiative in Islamic governance. They must form committees to choose rulers and to "motivate and mobilize the pious community." Support is found in a *hadith* that records one of the Prophet Muhammad's most influential statements on the obligation of Muslim believers to help correct wrongs and manage the public good: struggle (*jihad*) against traitors to the faith is obligatory, but can be waged with the hands, tongue, or heart. In the original report, such treachery is perpetrated by Muslims themselves who fail to honor the teachings of Islam's prophets. Bin Laden's enmity switches to an exclusive focus on "Jews and Christians," however, as he ventures a further tenuous qualification: struggle with "the hand" is preferable. At this point, seeking to expound upon the virtues of armed struggle against a polytheist enemy, bin Laden describes asceticism as key to inculcating the virtues of physical force. As in the 1996 Declaration, women are urged to take the lead in ascetic example, this time as child-rearers responsible for Islam's future generations. Through ascetic example, they must show children how to disassociate from Jews and Christians, enemies whose "polytheist" inclinations toward worldly belongings threaten to weaken the Muslim community and deprive it of "victory." Fathers who are responsible for their sons' welfare must follow suit, not hesitating to choose the more arduous path of religious duty and send their sons to battle. The hotter the weather the better.

We will continue to explore the ways anti-Americanism came to define bin Laden's goals and his antipathy for Jews and Christians in particular. I want to begin with more immediate questions that get us closer to understanding the nature of his leadership. Why asceticism? And why his focus on female asceticism, in particular? His repeated insistence that women lead by ascetic example seems ludicrous given how few female fighters have been involved in al-Qaʿida's militant operations. To begin answering these questions, I suggest starting with bin Laden's own family background and his upbringing in Saudi Arabia.

Details from his personal life provided his associates and sympathetic audiences with elemental materials for assembling their image of him as a leader.

Born on 10 March 1957, Osama identifies his place of birth as Riyadh, Saudi Arabia's historic capital and bastion of religious conservatism. As a child and adolescent, he was socialized in a more cosmopolitan environment. For over 100 years, Jeddah had been the Peninsula's busiest western port of call for travelers, merchants, and pilgrims across the Muslim world. Inter-marriage with Yemenis, Egyptians, Indians, and Javanese had long contributed to the city's diverse cultural heritage, and by the 1960s a growing health-care industry in town was bringing modern technological sophistication, education, and jobs, including for Saudi Arabia's first female doctors. The bin Laden family home was located in the city's first suburb, a middle-class neighborhood just outside the old city walls. Family members would regularly take cross-town trips to a cluster of private bungalows along the Red Sea. Those who knew Osama as an young child recall his love of nature and animals, especially dogs. They also knew of his father Muhammad's extraordinary wealth as an ingenious construction magnate who was overseeing the Kingdom's most important building projects. As the family wealth accumulated, so too did Muhammad's wives. Although never married to more than four at a time, in keeping with Islam's polygamy laws, Osama's affinal mothers would eventually number at least twenty one, the lot of which nurtured fifty three of his brothers and sisters. Osama was the eighteenth son, his mother, 'Aliyya, a Syrian by birth and married to his father for only a few years before their divorce. Rumors had it that 'Aliyya may have in fact been a concubine. In the city, she was called "the slave wife," as the saying goes, and Osama was "the son of a slave."

As Osama grew older, his bond with his mother, soon re-married to an employee of his father's, became second to none. During hard times in Afghanistan many years later, family members recount Osama's profound comfort in recalling stories about his mother and their earlier life together.[7] Summer trips to her family home in Latakia, Syria were filled with nostalgia, for it was there that Osama found endless pleasure roaming through a lush countryside, playing in streams and concocting adventures in the shadows of some of Saladin's most romantic castles. As a resort town along the coast, Latakia harbored a leisurely clientele, and Syria's version of Arab socialism ensured far more liberal attitudes toward cross-sex mixing, public entertainment, cultural interchange, and inter-faith encounters than did Saudi Arabia, even in its most cosmopolitan neighborhoods. ʿAliyyaʾs own family were ʿAlawites, adherents of a form of Shiʿism whose beliefs and rituals were considered anathema by many Sunni conservatives. Osamaʾs father had met fair-skinned ʿAliyya when on a business trip to the area and was not one to let religious orthodoxy stand in the way of practical necessity. Osama himself seems to have been equally circumspect about such sectarian strife. When at home, he passed the time reading and also watching television with his mother. One of his favorite shows was the American Western series *Fury*, about a boy from the Broken Wheel Ranch who is raised by a single father, his wife and first son having been lost in an automobile accident.

Relations with his father, Muhammad, were more complicated. Born in the rugged canyonlands of the Hadhramawt in eastern Yemen in 1908, Muhammad had used street-smarts, business savvy, and charisma to build a construction company whose net worth would eventually be valued at $5 billion. While such an achievement was a hard act to follow, details of his rise to power and his personal habits as family patriarch defied any attempt at emulation. Arriving penniless in Jeddah in the early 1930s, he found work as a brick-layer and mason for Aramco, an American company which was established to manage oil rights secured from KingʿAbd al-ʿAziz Ibn Saʿud by Standard Oil of California. Within a few years he had struck a deal with Aramco to start his own construction business. Offering the lowest contract bids in town, he also promised structural elegance and stability, touting connections with skilled craftsmen from regions known for their architectural splendor, such as the Hadhramawt and the Hijaz. By the 1950s, King ʿAbd al-ʿAziz Ibn Saʿud hired Muhammad to build his palaces in both Riyadh and Jeddah, oversee construction of the kingdomʾs most important highways and supervise a grand restoration project in Madina, hallowed site of Islamʾs first community and of the Prophet Muhammadʾs tomb. Such enterprises brought further rewards. Beginning in 1958, the Muhammad bin Laden Organization won a nearly decade-long commission to rebuild Jerusalemʾs Al-Aqsa Mosque, Islamʾs third holiest compound after those in Mecca and Madina. Gliding by helicopter from one worksite to the next, Muhammad garnered the unique privilege of being able to pray at all three destinations in a single day.

Like his other siblings, Osama enjoyed few opportunities to spend time with his father. One of his earliest memories seems to have been reciting a poem for Muhammad when he was four or five years old. In exchange for his performance, he recalls being given a hundred riyals, "a huge amount of money in those days."[8] The experience led to further impressive feats of memorization, including extended portions of the Qur'an.[9] Still, his father's schedule was not conducive to parent-child bonding. "In my whole life," explained Osama to his own son many years later, "I only saw your grandfather five times. Five times! Those very brief meetings, all but one with my large clan of brothers, were the only times my eyes saw your grandfather."[10] Osama's avoidance of any reference to "my father" when talking of the past was noted by his children, even as he extolled Muhammad's business ethics and loyalty to the king.[11] The one chance Osama had for a one-on-one encounter with his father was at his office in Jeddah at the age of nine. Plucking up extraordinary courage, he ventured to ask for a car.[12] He was given a red bicycle instead. Several weeks later, having passed the gift on to a brother, Osama discovered a brand new American Chrysler at his doorstep, this one painted in a shade of desert sand.[13]

The extravagance of Osama's story as a car owner aside, life under the mantle of his father appears to have been disciplined. In the very same year, he was put to work on his father's construction sites in town recording the names of workers and how much they were paid.[14] When Muhammad had something important to tell his children, he lined all twenty-plus of them up by height and presented the facts. Dissent or argument at any time met a severe response, often corporeal punishment by hand in full view of everyone assembled.[15] In comparison with his siblings, Osama seems to have reacted to such events by growing increasingly withdrawn. Remarks on Osama's shy, quiet, and guarded personality would become common in narratives by those who encountered him even through his adulthood. To some extent, his reticence to draw attention to himself would become a liability. His high school English teacher, a Briton who was hired by Jeddah's prestigious Al-Thaghr School to help implement an advanced Western educational curriculum, remarked: "In an intermediate-English class, I was trying to push the spoken aspects of the language. To succeed, the student needs to be prepared to make mistakes. They need to make a bit of an exhibition of themselves, and Osama was rather shy and reserved and perhaps a little afraid of making mistakes."[16] Osama's reluctance to acknowledge failure proved to be a handicap noted by family members, friends, and militant associates in years to come. At times, he seemed paralyzed by the demands of leadership, unwilling to acknowledge anything but total control and quick to blame others where fault might be shared.[17] Conversely, high expectations for himself, in the tradition of his father, struck others who knew him as the qualities of an ambitious and gifted young man. Many found him highly intelligent, observant, and brutally honest.[18] Thoughout his youth, he was known to be a better listener than speaker, a virtue much appreciated amongst the scholastic.[19] An intrinsic shyness was later held to have helped him survive in conflict zones when other more obvious leaders were marked for assassination.

And then, on 3 September 1967, his father died unexpectedly when his private Beechcraft airplane crashed in turbulent winds in a southern Saudi province. The fact that the pilot was American was itself hardly significant. At the time, private jets from the United States were in high demand among the Middle East's ultra elite, as were their pilots. His father's company, moreover, had established many strong ties with American corporations, among them Caterpillar, Morrison-Knudsen, and Trans-World Airlines. In fact, the bin Laden family would over time develop a comfortable relationship with American and Western values. A host of Osama's siblings spent extended periods of study abroad. Osama himself was known to have an easy, and at times jocular, relationship with American and European co-workers at the company's building sites.[20] Larger regional events unfolded, however, in ways that would substantially condition public attitudes toward American political power in the Middle East, particularly its relation to Arab and Muslim suffering. In June of the same year, a war pitting Israel against Egypt, Syria and Jordan had resulted in devastating territorial losses for the Arab nations. These included the Gaza Strip and the Sinai Peninsula, formerly under Egyptian control, the West Bank and East Jerusalem under Jordanian authority, and Syria's lush Golan Heights. Although Western nations withheld immediate military and tactical support, Arab press reports, bolstered by speeches from Egyptian president Gamal ʿAbd al-Naser, led most Arabs in the region to conclude that the war had been waged by Israeli, American, and British troops combined. The war was a "relapse" (naksa) that would plague the dreams of pan-Arabists for generations to come. In Tora Bora many years later, Osama would deride the alliance of America with Israel as a single bicycle with two wheels, the former made of wood and the latter made of steel.[21] If Israel was the harder enemy, it could be smashed by taking out its structural partner, beginning with its economy.[22]

Informing this event and its memories was an even more seismic ideological transformation: the growth of the Middle East's most powerful modern Islamist movement, the Muslim Brotherhood of Egypt, and its expansion into neighboring countries like Saudi Arabia. Founded in the fertile agricultural delta of Lower Egypt in 1928, the Brotherhood focused its activities on promoting a more Islamic educational environment in what had been, just six years earlier, a heavily regulated British protectorate. The Qur'an and Islam's established pathway (*Sunna*), as transmitted from the Prophet Muhammad and his Companions, were to provide the moral foundation for Muslim communities. Especially grievous was the abolition of the Ottoman Muslim caliphate by secular Turkish reformers in 1924, and along with it any hopes that a centralized governing institution might promote and regulate Islamic laws worldwide. For Brotherhood founder Hasan Al-Banna, however, religion was only part of Islam, understood to be a practice of everyday human conduct and not only a faith. Inspired by the writings of European Enlightenment thinkers that had percolated through the ranks of elite literati and scholars across the Middle East, Brotherhood members urged their audiences to think of education in its broadest senses. Students should not only read works on modern psychology, philosophy, economics, and the natural sciences. They should also venture beyond traditional academic disciplines through participation in community clubs, charitable associations, summer camps, and boy scout troops devoted to helping participants inculcate the proper Islamic virtues.

If the entire human race's conversion to Islam was part of the Brotherhood's long-term ambition, more immediate challenges to the faithful were presented at home among Muslims themselves. In Egypt, nationalists who deposed the pro-British king in 1953 declared an independent republic founded on strong principles of Arab socialism. Upon wresting control of the Suez Canal from the British in the following year, state leaders found the luxury of dissent too great, and after a Brotherhood member tried to assassinate 'Abd al-Naser during a speech commemorating the victory in Alexandria, over 20,000 citizens were arrested and jailed, most of them members of the Brotherhood. Over the next decade, as Egypt drew closer to the Soviet Union and Eastern Bloc countries, the Muslim Brotherhood was forced into withdrawal, its political offices closed and many of its members routinely imprisoned and tortured. Syria proved to be another fertile workshop for Muslim Brother ideals. With French anti-colonial origins in the 1930s, Muslim Brotherhood membership in the cities of Damascus, Hama, and Aleppo grew to represent a formidable political alliance. By the 1960s, members followed step in branding the state's platform of Arab socialism too hostile to Islam's rightful claims. After Syria's parliament ratified a constitution in 1973 that made no reference to Islam as the state religion, strikes turned violent. With an assassination attempt in 1976 followed by several years of murderous retribution, the organization was banned. The "Syrian Experience," as it came to be known, underscored the urgency of transnational militant collaboration, especially with branches in neighboring countries where worldwide objectives could be reinforced and then put to the service of internal divisions at home. The common enemy for Syrian militants was more Abrahamic than it was in Egypt. Embodied in the leadership of Hafez Al-Asad, president since 1970 and member of the same Shi'a sect of 'Alawis as Osama's mother and first wife, the enemy expressed more sinister designs as a "Nusayri," a derogatory term referring to the tenth-century Shi'a cleric Abu Shu'ayb Ibn Nusayr whose theological perfidy is held to have been inspired by Christians and Jews.[23] As the Muslim Brotherhood expanded its membership across the Middle East and North Africa, its original Egyptian imprint was modified to suit diverse political communities. While most branches remained committed to civil reform and accommodated multi-party elections, hard-liners argued that authoritarianism had become the only recourse for state elites whose Western and secular infatuations prohibited the advancement of Islam's national interests, primarily to the boon of Israel. Militants ventured further, penning treatises that justified struggle "by hand" against state rulers and their security forces.

Later in Kandahar, Osama would find ample material in his audiocassette collection for narrating the militant turn of Muslim Brothers in Egypt, Syria, Palestine, Kuwait, and other countries, as I discuss in later chapters. Shortly after his father's death, he acquired his first experiences with Brotherhood ideology while in Jeddah's Al-Thaghr school for middle and high school students, where he matriculated in 1968. Established by King Faisal to emulate equal opportunity between Saudis irrespective of birth, the free public school represented a break from the tribal and status-based hierarchies of private schools. In Osama's class of sixty-eight students were many poor and middle-class children, some of them the smartest in the class, and Saudis of international backgrounds were also well represented, especially Hadhramis from the bin Laden family's homeland.[24] The school uniform, modeled on English and American preparatory schools, was a button-down shirt with tie, gray slacks, black shoes and socks, and, in the winter, charcoal blazers.[25] Hardly the pressed white robe and cloth headdress that were customary for Saudi males, the uniform brandished a commitment to Western educational standards and the latest science curricula. Still, given the Kingdom's extreme shortage of citizens trained in modern educational methods, many teachers in the school were drawn from Egypt and Syria, a considerable proportion of them Muslim Brothers who had fled or been exiled from their home countries. By the time Osama was coming of age, Muslim Brothers had secured most of the faculty positions in Jeddah's King 'Abd al-'Aziz University, and their influence in Mecca, Madina, and Riyadh signaled the Saudi royalty's full commitment to integrating their lessons of "Islamic solidarity" (*tadamun islami*) with the more accommodating political doctrines of Wahhabism. At the Al-Thaghr School, Brotherhood teachings were conveyed through simple lessons in Islamic history and culture, lifestyle, health, and community activism. Extracurricular activities were especially popular since they took place after school and led to group bonding beyond school precincts.

The details of Osama's experience with his first Islamic study group in the eighth and ninth grade provide a sense of how currents in Brotherhood ideology influenced his worldview and what would ultimately become his own militant asceticism. At the time, Osama had a passion for soccer. The school's gym teacher, a charismatic Syrian who enjoyed considerable popularity among students, approached him and a few of his friends with a proposal. In exchange for a few hours of group study focused on memorizing the Qur'an, he would help them form a sports club, beginning with soccer drills immediately following their religious studies. Osama and his friends were seized with enthusiasm and were soon spending from two o'clock until five receiving private instructions from the coach. Gradually, the post-study soccer drills grew lackluster, however, and their Islamic lessons became lengthier and more involved. Much attention was given to *hadith* analysis, and when student attention began to drift, the Syrian seemed to have an endless supply of stories about Islamic luminaries, many of whom seemed to live in a realm transcending specific historical periods and places. A Saudi schoolmate of Osama's recalled one particular story in an interview with Steve Coll in 2005. It was: 'about a boy who found God— exactly like us, our age. He wanted to please God and he found that his father was standing in his way. The father was pulling the rug out from under him when he went to pray.' The Syrian 'told the story slowly, but he was referring to 'this brave boy' or 'this righteous boy' as he moved toward the story's climax. He explained that the father had a gun. He went through twenty minutes of the boy's preparation, step by step— the bullets, loading the gun, making a plan. Finally, the boy shot the father.' As he recounted this climax, the Syrian declared, 'Lord be praised—Islam was released in that home.' As the schoolmate recounted it, 'I watched the other boys, fourteen-year-old boys, their mouths open. By the grace of God, I said 'No' to myself…I had a feeling of anxiety. I began immediately to think of excuses and how I could avoid coming back.'[26]

While his schoolmate extracted himself from the group, Osama is reported to have intensified his commitment to the teacher's lessons. Letting his beard grow longer, he began lecturing other Al-Thaghr students about Islamic law and propriety, often with an unironed shirt meant to evoke dress customs in the Prophet's era.[27] By the age of sixteen, he would fast two days every week, an unusual discipline even among religious youths at the school.[28] Jamal Khashoggi, a Saudi journalist who knew Osama when he was living in Jeddah, recalled that:

Osama was just like many of us who had become part of the [Muslim] Brotherhood movement in Saudi Arabia. The only difference which set him apart from me and others, he was more religious. More religious, more literal, more fundamentalist. For example, he would not listen to music. He would not shake hands with a woman. He would not smoke. He would not watch television, unless it is news. He wouldn't play cards. He would not put a picture on his wall. But more than that, there was also a harsh or radical side in his life. I'm sure you have some people like that in your culture. For example, even though he comes from a rich family, he lives in a very simple house. He had no appreciation of art. He sees art as contrary to a Muslim. [He lived a] very simple, basic life. [He] doesn't attach himself to extravagant [or] to good living.[29]

If the Syrian coach's lesson on patricide led students to reflect on the deeper significance of killing a father, they were likely to have taken lesson on the necessity of radical measures against systems of authority that prevented Muslims from worshipping God. For bin Laden, the fight for justice involved rituals of physical and cultural asceticism that mainstream religious activists found hard to digest.

Osama's ascetic bent would be shaped and accentuated at the King 'Abd al-'Aziz University in Jeddah, where he matriculated in 1976. While he began pursuing a major in either business or civil administration, honoring family expectations that he help manage his father's company, he also joined private reading groups where he encountered more extremist writings. Among these were works by the thinker and essayist Sayyid Qutb, a member of Egypt's Muslim Brotherhood who was tortured by the Nasserist state in the mid-1950s and, after roughly a decade in prison, executed in 1966. Widely considered the intellectual heavyweight for modern militant Sunni Muslims, including al-Qaʿida itself, Qutb's book *Milestones* and also *In The Shade of the Qurʾan* found their way into Osama's hands during his first or second year in college.[30] Qutb's *Milestones* described Islam as a complete and organic "system" (*nizam*), a way of life (*manhaj*) that provides believers with guidance in how to eat, talk, marry, or conduct themselves piously in any other aspect of life. Vying against Islam's moral order is *jahiliyya*, wrote Qutb, a state of ignorance and barbarism marked by "rebellion against God's sovereignty on earth." Founded in the privileging of material interests over faith, *jahiliyya* leads to "one man's lordship over another," a relation of servitude that had reached its most developed form in the West and especially the United States, where Qutb spent several years pursuing graduate studies in education. Americans' passion for automobiles, well-manicured lawns, styled hair, and jazz struck Qutb as omens of a perverse ego-centrism. Still, the radicalism of Qutb's message was directed primarily toward forces within the house of Islam. While materialism and secular values were best illustrated in Western societies, Muslims would best be served through action against national leaders who failed to insist upon Islamic law. Such dignitaries committed polytheism (*shirk*) of the sort bin Laden decries in 2000 when chastising those who have "taken other gods than God alone as their Lord."

Even though Qutb depicts the West as civilization gone bad, his education in post-colonial Egypt and later in the United States exposed him to criticism from conservatives back at home. His call in *Milestones* to "preserve and develop the material fruits of the creative genius of Europe," though appealing in many ways to many Muslims, struck others as indicative of his wavering stance on Western secularism.[31] In Saudi Arabia, Qutb's literary background and metaphorical readings of the Qur'an put him at odds with Wahhabi literalists; the Lord's "ascension upon a throne" was nothing more, nothing less, and Qutb's inclination to view God's relevance as strictly political set a dangerous precedent for interpreting revealed law. More influential among Osama and his conservative activist friends, then, were the works of Sayyid Qutb's brother, Muhammad, who arrived in the Kingdom in the early 1970s after six years' imprisonment in Egypt. Once a week, Muhammad would lecture at the university in Jeddah, on leave from the prestigious "Mother of Villages" (*Umm Al-Qura*) University in Mecca where, with the commendations of a conservative Wahhabi faculty, he secured one of the first posts ever awarded to a Muslim Brother.[32] With a cracked and plaintive voice, Muhammad side-stepped his brother's fiery oratory about Muslim vanguards who must throw off yokes of oppression and band together to form a just Islamic state. He exhorted audiences instead to begin "the Islamic awakening" (*al-sahwa al-islamiyya*), as it came to be known, through internal reform. Questions of doctrine or "creed" (*'aqida*) lay at the heart of any political endeavor, as Ibn 'Abd al-Wahhab had argued some 250 years earlier. If Islamic governance was the ideal, Muslims must begin by making God's law paramount in their hearts. God was singular, of course, his will for mankind expressed clearly in revelations by the Prophet Muhammad, the last of the great Abrahamic messengers. Even more important than belief in divine omnipotence (*tawhid rububiyya*), however, was unity of moral conscience (*tawhid uluhiyya*), to be cultivated in daily practice. Many of Qutb's lectures admonished listeners to remember God in every waking moment, whether alone or in groups, speaking or listening, working or relaxing. Still, if his brother had found recourse to themes of organic growth, vitality, progress, and social justice when defending his radical views, Muhammad held a bleaker view of the Muslim condition, reminding his audiences of their essential shame and weakness. Amidst unprecedented economic prosperity in Saudi Arabia, as skyrocketing oil prices during the mid 1970s flooded the Kingdom with lavish public spending initiatives and foreign investment, especially from the United

States, Qutb railed against the assault of "modernism" (*hadatha*) and the treacherous loyalties of those who championed its cause. Life was but toil, struggle and strife. Qutb's fundamentalist tirades featured centrally in a required course on Islamic culture that Osama took while at the university, and would later feature on at least twelve cassettes in his Kandahar compound (his brother's lectures were notably absent).

The concept of *jahiliyya* proves central once again to Muhammad Qutb's vision of Islam's darkest foes. Four of Qutb's cassettes in bin Laden's collection are entitled *"Jahiliyya* Old and New," and together they expound upon ideas presented earlier in the *summa theologica* of his brother's works, a volume entitled *Twentieth-century Jahiliyya*, published in 1980. *Jahiliyya* is not simply a modern phenomenon, as his brother insisted, but is rooted in the ancient past, in a pre-Islamic age when Arab tribes served idols and lusted for booty in camel raids. Still, in no age has *jahili* zeal been more severe, its instruments more devastating, than in the present. Repeatedly evoking Manichaean contrasts between God and Satan, sincerity and treachery, the moral and perverse, Qutb blames Muslims above all for straying from the prescribed path. More passionately than his brother, Qutb focuses on Qur'anic injunctions to work for justice in this world by "commanding right and forbidding wrong" (*al-amr bi-l-ma'ruf wa-l-nahy 'an al-munkar*). Such discourse taps into a historic summons in many Muslim reform movements to take responsibility for the moral standing of one's community; its more radical strains would be signaled in bin Laden's recorded speech in 2000, when, drawing upon *hadith* traditions, Osama spoke of Muslims' "duty" to adopt vigilantism "by the hand." Qutb himself avoids the revolutionary populism of such "commanding," instead developing an argument for the importance of ascetic discipline that would find broader uptake among those struggling to liberate Muslim lands from occupation by infidels.

In the audio recordings *"Jahiliyya* Old and New" and also "The Islamic Awakening," both of which would be deposited in the Kandahar archive, Qutb argues that attending to divine commandments is the surest path to economic vitality, though not of a Western materialist bent. Where an Islamic economic system is regulated by justice, which is the distribution of wealth expressing God's moral order, the West's source of economic power comes from "liberty," in Qutb's vision a euphemism for exploitation in the name of amoral individualism. The bad seed corrupting

Islam's more responsible economic platform was originally Europe's industrial revolution, he explains, an event that introduced a division of labor whereby workers were alienated from the products of their labor, forced into exploitative production cartels using centralized mechanisms of espionage and compliance, and driven to competitive accumulation through manufactured fears of scarcity. Echoes of a Marxist critique ring out. These were the legacy of many a fiery treatise by Arab and Islamic theoreticians over the course of the twentieth century. Qutb distorts them with a more personified deus ex machina: the Jew. "By financing the industrial revolution through usury," Qutb states, "the pockets of the Jews filled with gold. Thus, they bought off governments, they bought off the media, and they bought off people's consciences." Qutb's narratives of a world-wide Jewish conspiracy rooted in global capitalism provide an extended coda for his lectures, and tap into currents of anti-Semitism that had long colored Muslim Brotherhood ideology. Still, Jews themselves, if the principal beneficiaries of industrial and financial systems run amock, are not the only targets selected for blame. Those who lend support to their materialist advantage, including Muslims themselves, commit the kind of polytheism that Osama would later describe as "nullifying" Islam. In his lecture "The Islamic Awakening," distributed by a Riyadh-based studio, Qutb sets the tone for ascetic disengagement from Jewish-dominated global capitalism through his selective reading of several Qur'anic verses about the "People of the Book," a standard phrase acknowledging the shared Abrahamic traditions of both Jews and Christians.[33] Qutb focuses on the following verse, implying that it refers exclusively to Jews alone:

[God] said about them: "Shame is pitched over them [like a tent] wherever they are found" (Al 'Imran 112). But there is an exception (istithna') in the verse: "Shame is pitched over them wherever they are found, except with a rope from God or a rope from people." The meaning of this is the following: the general rule (al-qa'ida al-da'ima) applying to them is [that they will be subject to] shame, and the exception to this rule is that [sometimes] they will enjoy fortification. And today, they are at the peak of this exception with a rope from God, because there isn't a thing that takes place in the universe without God's wish and desire. This is [the meaning of] the rope of God. With regards to "a rope from the people," what is meant by "people"? Who are the people who support the Jews? First among them, we would say "America." And those who delve deeper would say "And Russia too," because Russia used to support the Jews as well. And yet, "the people" is more comprehensive than just America and Russia. It means all people on earth today. All of them constitute a rope in support of the Jews, except those on whom your Lord had mercy, except those who proclaim "There is no god but God alone" with full knowledge of its meaning and implications, and who put into practice its requirements in the real world. All people, except the latter category, are supporting the Jews.

Jewish exceptionalism, Qutb insists, is secured not only by divine fiat, for God in his omnipotence commands all things, but by the support of America, Russia, and even Muslims themselves. In a legal and ideological idiom that I explore later in the book, Islamic reform begins by recognizing the ways in which general rules in Muslim ethics, such as the precept that, in Qutb's extremist view, all Jews are shameful, are routinely qualified through one's own actions and interpretations. As political doctrinology, Qutb's arguments launched a firestorm that would stoke the passions of students and activists for generations to come. At the King 'Abd al-'Aziz University, the message was clear: Muslims who lend support to Jews, and who cater more generally to the ideology of a New World Order underwritten by Western economic power, risk betraying Islam's basic tenet of monotheism. The stakes of such a position for Saudi Arabia's own leadership, including the Muhammad bin Laden Organization, could not have been more serious. By the time Osama was in his second year, the Kingdom was the United States' seventh largest export market, quite apart from arms sales and paramilitary assistance that totaled over half a billion dollars.

Osama's urge to "boycott Jewish and American goods and products," if prominent in his broad summons to Muslim militants in 2000, appears to have surfaced openly by 1982, three years after he left his university studies prematurely to help run the family business.[34] By the late 1980s, the theme had become a predictable element in his public speeches.[35] Still, for some who knew him well, such opinions seem to betray his comfortable relationship with cosmopolitan luxury and those who enjoyed it. Aside from his family's obvious connections with multimillion dollar corporations in both the United States and Europe, Osama seems to have been quite open to personal indulgences. In the mid 1980s, hospital patients in Peshawar, Pakistan recall him as a bit of a dandy when visiting with the war wounded: his *shalwar kameez*, a loose tunic over pants, was stitched from the best imported English cloth and he wore tailor-made safari boots from London. He even made a splash with excellent English chocolates.[36] In his earlier years, reports of a family trip to Sweden have him shopping in designer clothes stores and indulging in the haut cuisine of fine hotels.[37] At the age of fourteen, he and two of his half-brothers seem to have enrolled in an English language immersion course in Oxford, England, an experience that included punting on Oxford's meandering canals and being photographed with attractive female Spanish students their own age.[38] Although a *New York Times* obituary would report bin Laden never having traveled outside the Middle East, his son ʿUmar and wife describe a trip he took to Indianapolis, IN and Los Angeles, CA in 1979 in order to get the very latest medical treatment for his ailing son.[39]

If Osama's upbringing in a privileged and Westernized Saudi family indelibly marked his personality, his journey toward becoming a true enfant terrible who could capture world headlines with threats against the evil and hypocrisy of Western values would require resourcefulness. Osama needed an alibi, someone or something he could fall back on when his credentials for militant anti-Western leadership were called into question. It was in this state of moral compromise, of conflicted identities at the heart of his struggle for credibility, that he would discover the value of asceticism, or at least a mythical Arabian image of it, for reinforcing boundaries. Years later, his bodyguard would speak of bin Laden's "historical legitimacy" when comparing his leadership claims to those of al-Qaʿida's second-in-command Ayman Al-Zawahiri.[40] Such an assertion is odd given the bin Laden family's weak genealogical pedigree. Al-Zawahiri, after all, was born to venerable family of Arab notables that had included a rector of the one-thousand year old Al-Azhar University in Cairo, a founder and first general secretary of the Arab League, a president of Cairo University, and a founder of Riyadh's King Saʿud University. The bin Laden family's only claim to fame was tribal, their ancestors having once roamed the plains as Bedouin of the Al-Kinda tribe in Saudi Arabia's Najd province. Although the Najd had certainly been the homeland of the Saʿud family and its chief religious ally Muhammad Ibn ʿAbd al-Wahhab, blood connections to either of them could never be demonstrated. Osama's father was in fact routinely excluded from social networking among tribal families in the Kingdom. In defiance as well as unabashed tribute to his own ingenuity, he regularly reminded his family of their provincial Yemeni origins.[41] They were originally Qatanis, from an obscure tributary to the Hadhramawt valley whose only claim to fame was a tomb for an early Arabian prophet whose prayers led to the miraculous transformation of a rock into a pregnant, red she-camel. Al-Bahri's view of his boss's legitimacy conveys something of the mythic authenticity that would come to surround Osama's leadership, begging further questions about just how such authority could have been attributed to him.

Portents of Osama's formula for claiming historical legitimacy emerge in memoirs of family members who recall an increasing zeal for spartan domestic discipline during and after his university studies. His first wife, a Syrian cousin through his mother, 'Aliyya, recounts that after their marriage in 1974, "Osama was quite generous, but as time went on, he grew austere, believing that to be a good Muslim one must embrace simplicity."[42] One of his sons would recall that the couple's move to their first new home in 1983 signaled rigorous trials ahead for the entire family: "Regarding all things except modern transportation, our father decreed that we must live just as the Prophet had lived whenever possible."[43] In future years, the Prophet Muhammad's example would frequently be cited by Osama, in keeping with standard practice for would-be Muslim reformers. The challenges of re-creating a seventh-century environment in the modern world, much less one of Muhammad's description, naturally required invention. For Osama, they began with home-making and parenting. His houses, some of them with over twelve bedrooms, were shorn of decoration and all but the most essential furniture.[44] No television was permitted, and his children were instructed to lower their voices and speak with careful, measured words. Emotional displays among family members seemed to be a favorite subject for discipline. While his children were expected to be serious and avoid joking, an occasional smile was fine, as long as it didn't involve laughter exposing the teeth.[45] Corporeal punishment was frequent, much as his father had taught him, although Osama preferred the use of a cane.[46] "Life has to be a burden," he explained to his children when they complained to him about their hardships. "You will be made stronger if you are treated toughly."[47] Important lessons in self-discipline were conveyed especially when opportunities to eat or drink arose. His wives and children were expected to consume as little water as possible.[48] Snacks, coffee, ice, and American products of any description were banned, though his children snuck Pepsi products into the house when they could.[49] Breakfasts consisted of bread, eggs, cheese and yoghurt, and dinners were not elaborate, usually featuring rice, vegetables, and fruit.[50] Meat was served only if necessary, bread with oil and thyme being substituted instead. "You need to suffer. Hunger pangs will not hurt you," Osama would instruct his family when requests to supplement the diet were made. Food requiring chilling was impossible given Osama's adamancy against the use of refrigerators, and electric stoves were replaced with kerosene burners.[51] He also forbade the use of air conditioners even during the long Saudi summers, when temperatures climb to over 110 degrees fahrenheit. "Islamic beliefs are corrupted by modernization," he told his family.[52] Jeddah's rapid development during the mid 1970s and 1980s proved to be a suitable workshop for cultivating a mastery over bodily temptations, whether his or others'.

Lectures on asceticism or self-abnegation (al-zuhd) in his Kandahar audiotape library provide clues to how Osama's own interpretation deviated from mainstream views. Although Osama's discipline struck some observers as extreme, he was in some ways simply mirroring ordinary activities among Saudi Brothers who were urging their compatriots to seek physical and spiritual remove from the corruptions of modern society at the time. By the mid 1970s, massive urban development projects had been launched throughout the Kingdom as a result of skyrocketing oil prices during the Arab-Israeli war. Seeking to claim the moral high ground, the Brotherhood began to organize "desert camps" (mukhayyamat) for religious edification in the stark expanses (al-barr) outside major cities. Participants convened on weekends or in the summer to explore religious activism and identity in "free spaces" beyond traditional urban centers of learning.[53] "Families" were established, each named for a famous Islamic hero, and camp recruits ran obstacle courses, played soccer, and attended lectures on the cultivation of a modern Islamic lifestyle that could deepen rather then compromise one's faith. Much in keeping with Muslim Brother ideals in Egypt and Syria, Islam was viewed as a total way of life; extracurricular activities were instrumental to broader initiatives of moral education that included social development, group bonding and outreach. Still, a central component of the Saudi camps was building an identity set apart from the rest. Influenced in part by the Brotherhood's political notoriety abroad, participants called their movement an "Awakening" (sahwa), in step with the teachings of Muhammad Qutb and others, and devoted much of their attention to bringing personal daily practice in line with Islam's original monotheist creed. Physical and ethical departure from a morally compromised world was integral to this view.[54]

Osama's indebtedness to such Awakening camps was visible early on. Around the age of sixteen, seeking to put his high school gym teacher's lessons to use, he began leading his own religious studies courses in the northern outskirts of Jeddah where the only barrier to the desert beyond was a giant Pepsi-Cola factory. Every Monday and Thursday, the same days as his voluntary fast, he would gather together neighbors and residents from poorer quarters of the city for afternoon Islamic trivia contests, singing and conversation.[55] His first audiotape of jihadi anthems, highlighting the suffering of Muslims worldwide and Palestinians in particular, was cut around this time.[56] Still, his camps did not include Qur'anic study or *hadith* analysis, for Osama lacked the years of training required to speak confidently on these matters, and his initiatives were not sponsored by Islamist groups or scholars. Transportation and expenses were covered by himself. Over time, moreover, his lessons began to include military training exercises that were outlawed in Awakening camps.[57] Manly tests of stamina proved a sort of gauntlet for recruits. On one occasion, he praised those who had been pressed to follow him bare-footed across a searing patch of sand by saying "Your path was just as challenging whether you walked or ran. When you reach your highest limit it is like arriving in divine paradise!"[58] Religious justification for such views was often shallow. If pressed, Osama would defer to more credible authorities, a custom he continued, to some frustration by recruits, well into his Afghan years.[59] His leadership seems to have operated primarily through personal example, a virtue that he increasingly foisted upon members of his own family. By the mid 1980s, recruits began hearing about desert expeditions with his sons that involved long hikes without water. Asthmatic attacks experienced by several of them were routinely waved away. They must be prepared, he told them, for desert warfare when the West attacked the Muslim world.[60]

Osama's militant asceticism, cultivated acutely in the camps he ran, foreshadowed his growing divergence from the Saudi Awakening movement, despite his assertions a decade later that he represented their ideals on the world stage. Leaders of the Awakening movement were graduates of the Kingdom's top universities, established scholars even if their training and backgrounds represented important shifts from the state's traditional reliance on conservative Wahhabi clerics from the Najd. Osama had none of these accolades. His potential contributions as a religious opposition leader were impaired, in fact, by his father's close connections with American and European corporations, key elements of the royal family's sovereignty. Such familiarity with Western interests in the region could well have compromised his influence among militants, despite their exhortations to "know thy enemy."[61] In 1979, however, four cataclysmic events in the region helped to strengthen bin Laden's credibility among supporters as the Saudi state reacted to shore up its legitimacy.

Sixteen days into the new year, dramatic events in Iran opened a new chapter in perceptions of Islam's global contestation with the West. The country's premier Muhammad Reza Shah, whose Pahlavi family had ruled since 1925, fled Tehran under pressure from a coordinated mass revolt. Notorious for using a brutal security and intelligence apparatus called SAVAK to arrest, torture, and execute thousands of dissidents, the Shah had been installed in 1953 through assistance from the United States' Central Intelligence Agency after it helped overthrow the democratically elected government of Muhammad Mossadegh. During the course of the next decade, American economic and military aid rose to approximately $2 billion while American oil companies secured a contract for control over 40 per cent of Iranian oil (the rest being contracted out to the British, Dutch, and French.) Spearheading opposition to the Shah was the formidable Shi'i jurist and grand ayatollah Ruhallah Khomeini. While relations between Shi'a Iran and the avowedly Sunni polity of the Saudi state had been mixed, the ascendency of a politically active Muslim leader with a strong anti-West message, a sizeable oil reserve, and the mandate of a revolution sent tremors throughout the Saudi kingdom. The Persians would need a reply.

If the fall of a pro-Western neighbor was not concerning enough, the steady encroachment of Soviet troops into Afghanistan and, by the end of the year, Kabul's full-scale occupation by a foreign Communist army darkened Saudi Arabia's view of events over the horizon. Arabs had long ties with Afghanistan. In the first few decades of the twentieth century, Wahhabi proselytizers established centers of learning in neighboring Uzbekistan and, with a surge in the Kingdom's oil wealth during the 1960s, in the Islamic polity of Pakistan. With the latest Soviet deployment, however, Afghanistan's status as an anchor for communism in the region caught the attention of Muslims around the world, never more so than when tens of thousands of refugees began streaming toward Peshawar and a genuinely Islamic opposition began taking shape. For the Saudi monarchy, the timing of these events was auspicious. Having experienced unprecedented affluence over the previous two decades due to spectacular oil revenues and a commitment to the continued purchase of American goods, weapons and services that amounted to hundreds of millions of dollars, the state found ample reason to brandish its credentials as the traditional defender of Islam's holy mission worldwide. In the ensuing years, King Fahd's support for the Afghan cause would garner praise especially from Sunnis who felt threatened by the rising influence of Iran's Shi'a state. The Saudi clerical establishment, foremost among them 'Abd al-'Aziz Ibn Baz (with roughly ten cassettes in bin Ladin's collection), was quick to support the state's Afghan campaign by urging Muslims to contribute financially to the cause. Many Saudi reformers followed suit, though with more explicit anti-Shi'a rhetoric; these included Salman Al-'Awda (sixth most frequently-represented speaker) as well as Nasir Al-'Umar (eleventh most frequently-represented speaker). Not all Sunnis were convinced that the Afghan cause was good for Islam, however. Wahhabi doctrinalists angling for a political voice criticized the state's newfound commitments to Hanafism, Afghanistan's main legal school and one not well represented on the Arabian Peninsula. One of the most vocal exponents of this diatribe was Safar Al-Hawali, a man whose criticism of "Sufi" tendencies toward excessive veneration of shrines and Hanafi associationalism led him to spirited attacks against Arab-Afghan leader 'Abdalla 'Azzam;[62] over twenty five cassettes would make him the tenth most frequently featured speaker in bin Laden's collection. In light of such tensions, bin Laden would prove useful for the Saudis. Militantly pro-jihad, anti-communist, peripheral to the Saudi *sahwa* reform movement and, at the same time, an avowed champion of Arabian authenticity, he had the potential to service the King's public relations campaign remarkably well.

Two other events in 1979, both occurring within Saudi Arabia itself, presented further challenges to the monarchy's legitimacy. On 20 November 1979, the first day of the Islamic year 1400, the Sacred Mosque in Mecca was seized by several hundred Saudi rebels along with a smattering of foreign nationals. Not since the tenth century had such a maverick crew occupied Islam's holiest sanctuary, and for nearly two weeks Saudi Special Forces assisted by Pakistani and French commandos fought pitched battles to reclaim the compound. Through seven open letters circulated in advance, the leader of the rebels, a Saudi tribesman and former religious studies student of the Islamic University of Madina named Juhaiman Al-'Utaibi, staked out a clear position against the Saudi monarchy: he rejected its claims to moral governance, demanded the state's dissolution, and proposed the leadership of an obscure scholar named Muhammad bin 'Abdalla Al-Qahtani. The state media focused much on the colorful content of the first of the seven letters, much of which dwelled on the concept of the occulted *mahdi* (or *muhtadi* in Al-'Utaibi's parlance), a role which some of the rebels had attributed to Al-Qahtani. Most Saudis who knew of Al-'Utaibi's longer engagement with political activism understood his grievances to be more pragmatic.[63] Early opinion pieces published by leftist Kuwaiti newspapers charged the Saudi monarchy with Najdi exclusivism, nepotism, and egregious displays of material extravagance. Railing against Western cultural accommodations, Al-'Utaibi's writings appealed equally to religious reformers who begrudged the Saudi state for its capitulations to "Christian" powers obsessed with worldly accumulation, and called instead for a truer and more ascetic Islam. In light of King Fahd's extraordinary relationship with the United States, the specter of American influence was implicit although not directly addressed. Public anxieties were stoked during the course of Mecca's occupation by another very different form of protest, however, this time from the kingdom's Shi'a population. Inspired by events in Iran, Shi'a mourners representing some 10–15 per cent of the country's citizens gathered for the annual *'ashura* commemoration recalling the martyrdom of Hasan and Husain, sons of the seventh-century imam 'Ali Ibn Abi Talib. In doing so, they defied the monarchy's 1913 ban against public enactments of the rites. With the panic of Al-'Utaibi's sedition in the air, the Saudi government unleashed approximately 20,000 National Guard soldiers to disperse the mourners. In ensuing months, Shi'a activists mobilized to protest their status as second-class citizens. Clashes ensued, several demonstrators were killed, and very quickly debates about Shi'a social and economic deprivation engaged fundamental questions of national security. Whatever Saudis felt about the Meccan drama and ensuing Shi'a demonstrations, the state's extraordinary use of force against its own citizens during the long first month of Islam's fourteenth millennium steeled them toward the prospects of Islam's internal purging both at home and abroad.

In efforts to quash internal dissent, the Saudi monarchy would draw the clerical establishment (*'ulama'*) more firmly under its control during the years ahead, consolidating its authority by directing oil-boom revenues to those who would lend their voices to the "public good" (*maslaha*.)[64] Much favored among the state's luminaries was an ascetic discipline close to home, one embodied in exhortations toward Sunni ritual observance and national conferences on "culture" designed to bolster the state's tribal Arab authenticity. For those discomfited by the king's heavy hand in such initiatives, a more transnational and pan-Islamic temperament proved appealing, especially if linked, as the Muslim Brotherhood did, to national and cultural imperatives that could be contrasted with the West and secularism worldwide. Bin Laden's focus on combatting the Soviets in Afghanistan provided Saudis with the semblance of a clear front line, especially since the state and its citizens could be represented as ostensibly fighting the same good fight. His service to the cause was all the more effective given that his own brand of martial asceticism could be deployed, according to circumstances, both by the state and by its most ardent critics. For the state, images of steely Arab warriors fighting classical jihad against foreigners occupying Muslim lands played well among Saudis, especially given their experience with decades of Westernized development over which they had little control. For the Saudi opposition, the fight abroad was only the first step in a longer and more entrenched battle against Arab Muslims at home who turned from God's guidance in service of distorted principles. In the 1979 'Utaibi affair, accusations erupted over who was most culpable for hijacking Islam's sacred charter. On the heels of the crisis, bin Laden quickly rose to prominence. Opposing parties valued him for different reasons. For the monarchy, any chance that bin Laden's ascetic fervor would come back to haunt them was diminished by the fact that his family lacked tribal status and so presented no real threat to social hierarchies in the kingdom. Even more promising was the bin Laden Group's help in providing security personnel during the Al-'Utaibi affair with an invaluable weapon: blueprints of the Sacred Mosque that had been drafted during the company's earlier renovation of the site.[65]

Anticipating the double-edged asceticism that would give bin Laden much renown in future years, cassette no. 1255 in the collection dramatizes an attack two years later that would rock the Middle East. On

THE AUDACIOUS ASCETIC

6 October 1981, Egyptian president Anwar Sadat was assassinated at a military parade returning from a tribute to the tomb of famed nationalist and pan-Arab hero Gamal ʿAbd al-Nasir. Sadat had been the United States strongest Arab ally in the region; he had also helped engineer the Arabs' most comprehensive peace treaty with Israel in March of 1979 after bilateral talks at Camp David in Maryland. His assassins, led by twenty-four year old Lieutenant Khalid Al-Islambouli, would become the stuff of legend among Muslims opposed to Israeli policies as well as American involvement in the Muslim world. Recorded on audiocassette for a more discreet band of militants is a different member of the Islambouli family: Khalid's mother. Umm Khalid's voice, recorded in a twenty-minute interview by anonymous supporters, features the only woman speaker in bin Laden's tape collection. After recounting how she arrived at the site of her son's incarceration at a Cairene jail holding a bag of dates, sweets, and beverages, she tells listeners that she discovered her son and his comrades to have been executed. She coaches her audience on the ways God's justice is best served with ascetic resolve:

> I left the prison saying: "Praise be to God for honoring me with the martyrdom of my son." I left as everyone waiting outside stared at me. "What is this?" they said. "What kind of mother is she? *This* is a mother? What is she?" I swear. One of them even said to me: "You are a mother? You?" I replied: "Yes, I am his mother. But I want only one thing: while our men are in prison and I am with God, I hope that my Lord will grant me enough strength to claim my son's body, God willing, so that I may bury him in my hometown."

> This occurred at the military prosecutor's office. I went there myself to request retrieval of my son's body. The prosecutor said to me: "You shall not see it. Were it behind the sun you shall not see it." I told him: "Why? Do you think he will come out again to kill you all?" He smiled. I said: "Public opinion doesn't frighten you. The people do. You are afraid of human beings. Here is Islam. This is religion and no power on earth can wipe it out. God is enough for us and He is the best helper." He shot back: "Take it! It's just a body." As he returned to his desk, I discovered that I was holding a few sweets that I had brought and just picked up from the table, much like these [*perhaps gesturing to refreshments supplied by her interviewers*]. I said: "My son is now being hurried to the virgins of paradise. You all, however, remain to enjoy the glitter of this life. Eat, then. Drink and enjoy yourselves. These refreshments are to celebrate Khalid's martyrdom in our world."

> I then left repeating "There is no god but God alone!" and "God is Greater! God is Greater!" Some of them were even, I mean, crying. Some of them

were wondering who I was. They asked me: "Are you his mother?" As I was leaving, they asked me: "Are you his mother? Are you his mother?" "Yes," I told them, "I am his mother. I am the mother of the martyr." They asked me: "Are you the mother of the hero?" I said: "No, I am the mother of the martyr. In fact, the hero…the martyr…the hero who revived religion after you all disgraced it. You have trampled God's religion underfoot. You have entered mosques and stabbed muslims. You have thrown them in jails and killed those who remained in mosques. Your accountability is with God." And I left, praise be to God.

Khalid's battle cry resounded in defiance of Muslim rulers who might capitulate to Israeli-American interests. Umm Khalid's voice strikes closer to home. She addresses Khalid's lawyer as well as ordinary Egyptians, including those who, even if prone to label Khalid a "hero," might nevertheless be complicit in Egyptian state atrocities against true believers. While commending Khalid's martyrdom and journey "to the virgins of paradise," Umm Khalid pitches her message to those who would remain in this world to seek justice against the treachery of one's own co-religionists. Cuing listeners to the privileged role that women, in particular, might play in the Struggle, she reproaches her son's military prosecutor even while proffering a handful of sweets: "Eat, then. Drink and enjoy yourselves. These refreshments are to celebrate Khalid's martyrdom in our world." Embodying Abraham's will to sacrifice his own son, Ishmail, for God's benefit, Umm Khalid nevertheless breaks from the classic martyr narrative. Vacillating between "the hero…the martyr…the hero," she commemorates Khalid for his example to those who would remain alive to instigate Muslims toward excising hypocrisy within. Listeners might recall, after all, that Khalid had planned his assassination of Sadat with Muhammad 'Abd al-Salam Faraj, an electrical engineer whose jihadi treatise *The Neglected Duty* (*Al-Farida Al-Gha'iba*) waxed extensively on the duty of all Muslims to assail what he termed "the near enemy." So too did Khalid retain a copy of Al-'Utaibi's seven letters in his possession on the eve of his glorious struggle.[66] As ascetic witnesses to mens' martyrdom and imprisonment "behind the sun," women could honor the dead as well as shame the living, proving heroes to Islam's forsaken majority.

3

REMEMBERING THE LION'S DEN

(1988 speech by Osama bin Laden. Probably in Saudi Arabia. Cassette no. 508.[1] Concluding remarks, after a long lecture on the necessity of armed jihad and the lessons of combat against the Soviets in Afghanistan acquired during the previous year.)

So I say: whoever is presently thinking about infidels, Jews, advanced weapons, or some such, they all vanish before our struggle (*jihad*) in response to God and the Prophet, God's prayers be upon him. With regards to brothers there [in Afghanistan], they are determined to continue fighting until their ranks grow, praise be to God, Glorious and Exalted is He. I am not betraying any secret here; if some consider this to be a secret, then that is their prerogative. The Jews are now taking advantage of the concentration of Arabs who have gathered there, but it is inconceivable that Arabs should go and struggle for the liberation of a land of Muslim freedom fighters without first achieving liberation in Jerusalem. There is no doubt that they are planning against us.

I say: you have an opportunity to "go forth, whether light or heavy" in response to God, Glorious and Exalted is He.[2] You have the means to do so. Praise be to God, there is a training camp, for without it how long would we continue to remain silent, as the Shaikh mentioned [referring to Yemeni cleric 'Abd al-Majid Al-Zindani, who introduces bin Laden at the start of the tape]? Jerusalem has been taken from us during our lifetime. We were born to an age of humiliation imposed on Muslims. One of the ways that we have benefited from this struggle is to realize that one should never ever demean anyone, especially oneself.

73

THE AUDACIOUS ASCETIC

May God have mercy on Yahya [Shanyur of Jeddah]. He was a bit overweight, about one hundred kilograms [220 pounds]. I was urging him on at the time, according to God's command, for I urge on believers. Still, I lacked conviction inside myself that my instigation would come to any benefit. However God produced such tremendous benefit from it; by God, it was beyond your wildest imagination! How many caravan loads and weapons were moved! By himself, along with Amin [a fighter from Madina], who was injured that night, with seven more like them. When they had first arrived [in Pakistan], some of the brothers expressed the same feelings that I had: "These sons were brought here to struggle, but tomorrow they will just begin crying to you like some young men do in Madina and Jeddah." Days passed and these guys remained firm. They conducted 3,000 portages—3,000 portages!—each about seven kilometers as they carried weapons into Afghanistan. Aid organizations used their personnel, apparently calculating these portages exactly—this much was shipped to this mountain, that much elsewhere. When the Afghans had confirmed that the weapons arrived, the Saudi Relief Committee would compensate them for the expenses, may God reward them. Such matters are lengthy and our time is limited, so I urge you consider the lessons here and think about them so that you may respond to God's command.

Know that the lecturers, scholars, and merchants among you have a proper model in the Prophet, God's blessings and salutations upon him. I will give an example here: if one left his surplus wealth here, for example, and thinks that this will benefit Islam and Muslims, why would the Prophet, God's blessings and salutations upon him, have set forth from Madina to spread this religion? As is relayed in a sound *hadith* about the Prophet, God's blessings and salutations upon him: "I yearned to be killed in the path of God and then resurrected again." Moreover, the death of the Prophet, God's blessings and salutations upon him, brought to an end the blessing of revelation that descended from the heavens to the earth. So what of the person who has a bit of learning but grows afraid due to the devil's deceptions as he is told: "If you leave, who will raise people properly and teach them?" This is the way of Satan, my brothers.

I give another example about those who are not scholars—and everyone is endowed with goodness, God willing. This example concerns our brothers who are doctors, engineers, or other professionals, and it involves a tent. Imagine a tent. Naturally, the tent has ropes that strengthen it. Each person thinks that he holds one of these ropes and declares: "This is Islam's tent, how can we leave it? We are at the pivotal opening breach (*thaghr*)!" You, then, my brother, why don't you come forth? Each replies in turn "I am at the breach," "I am at the breach." The entire pious community tries to strengthen the ropes at the breaches while the main pole, without which a tent would not deserve the name, has yet to be erected! You see, if you try to construct a tent but leave the cloth on the ground, it is called "a cloth on the ground"! The main pole of Islam's tent is carrying weapons. This is related in a *hadith* of the Prophet, God's blessings and salutations upon him, a sound *hadith* in the compendium of [the ninth-century scholar] Muslim [Ibn al-Hajjaj]: "A sect within my pious community is in truth…[*pausing to rephrase*] manifestly continues to be in the truth. Those who abandon them can do them no harm, and they fight in the path of God." Among the characteristics of the victorious and proclaiming sect (*al-ta'ifa al-mansura al-nadiyya*) is fighting for the sake of God. Otherwise, if we make way for reasoning (*'aql*), allegorical interpretation (*ta'wil*), and voting, we will not be saved and we will be plunged into quarrelling. Nothing comes to a quarreling nation but tribulation.

The sum of all this is: after looping around them a second time, the infidels were struck with terror. They realized that the strugglers (*mujahidin*) had a way to maneuver around them. By God, the morale of the strugglers shot high. When you go there, you can ask them yourselves, by God's will; ask about the results of their brothers' deeds. By God, I even began to feel ashamed when in the presence of leaders who had witnessed the battle. Although we had been with them in the days before battle, and had interacted in the usual way, I grew ashamed when visiting them after they had advanced, stood firm and been martyred. I grew ashamed by their enormous generosity to us, to me and the other brothers who would visit them. When recounting events in their own words, their beauty increased, may God bring them prosperity. One time, Shaikh ['Abd al-Rasul] Sayyaf asked one of the [Afghani] leaders who was with us in the frontline camp: "How are the Arabs up front doing with you?" He answered: "Shaikh, they put our noses in the dirt for their courage, enthusiasm, and vehemence against the enemy."

So none of you should belittle himself. Praise be to God, Glorious and Exalted is He, [our enemies'] terror (*ru'b*) spread elsewhere. If before the struggle we had thought of Jerusalem, now the first things to cross our minds were America and Russia with the Jews. By God in whom there is no god but God alone! At one point several captives passed by from the ranks of infidel prisoners. They were told by our young lads who had formerly been considered incapable of confronting their attacks: "We are from a camp that is called 'the lion's den of supporters,' referring to the original supporters of God and the Prophet. Those humans who lent assistance to God were called 'The supporters of God' by witnesses who came to them. Thus we called it 'the lion's den of supporters.' The derivation of the title 'lion's den' comes from several verses [of the seventh-century poet Ka'b Ibn Malik], God's favor upon him. He used to praise God's Messenger, God's prayers and peace be upon him and his Companions. We cite some of them:

> Whoever roams forth smashing, confounding one another
> Like the wild burning of a reed torch: let them approach the lion's den
> Her swords sharpened between the feeding trough and the newly dug trench.[3]

It was the Raid of The Trench (*ghazwat al-khandaq*), and the name came from this."

It is said now that the camp became famous only ten days after the battles; it was perhaps the fifteenth day of the month. Among infidels, the place was known as Jayshair, though it was the place of the lions. The infidels had become terrified (*yirhabun*). They said, from what we heard, that anyone sent to this place called Jayshair would confront a massive and primeval emancipation (*al-fath al-buda'i al-kabir jiddan*) and would not return from it. And these youth—or rather God, Glorious and Exalted is He, and not us—sent down fear, as I mentioned earlier, Glorious and Exalted is He. It is not our place to use reason in thinking through the texts, something called independent legal interpretation (*ijtihad*) of the texts' meaning. "Go forth" (*infiru*), and we went forth!

Our brother 'Abd al-Hadi is here [in the audience] today. He was present at the camp when it was first established. It was set up by two youths who were born in Madina as well as myself, though I am not soliciting God's favor for anyone. Just three, by God the Great. They said: "You are crazy! Why are you going there? There is no problem between you and the enemy." I said: "By God, this is God's command: 'Go forth, whether light or heavy.'" By God's will, He sent us two men, then five more. Brother 'Abd al-Hadi came when there were five of us. God be my witness, when one of us would go into the wilderness [to urinate], he feared being abducted. The region was monstrous, with thick forests, the enemy within our sight and their vehicles within earshot.

I say through the grace of God, Glorious and Exalted is He: the experiment was successful, and we have not become harmed by what happens. I hope to God that we have paid some of our debts. In any case, it is necessary for the pious community, preachers, and people to publicize these events. The pious community must wake up. The community is waking up, by God's will. I relate these words and ask the forgiveness of God the Great.

Whatever Western analysts may say of bin Laden's post 9/11 interest in Palestine, his earliest recorded speeches leave little doubt that his road led through Jerusalem.[4] If Afghanistan promised heroic battles to test the souls of men, Jerusalem called the martyrs home. The potential for establishing a holy land in Palestine struck deep chords with Osama, even if they were mostly a wash of nostalgia. For the first ten years of his life, his father oversaw the re-construction of Jerusalem's Dome of the Rock, Islam's third holiest site after those in Mecca and Madina. The fate of the shrine became especially important for bin Laden and many other Muslims after the 1967 war, when Israel wrested control of the Temple Mount from Jordan along with East Jerusalem and the West

Bank. The 1973 Arab-Israeli war proved grievous for many Arabs who had championed the reconstruction as part of a larger project to restore the Palestinian homeland in preparation for their return from exile. Bin Laden would later date his religious awakening to the same year.[5]

And yet, if Palestinians loomed large in bin Laden's view, they were also largely figures on a larger tableau of civilizational struggles old and new. Rarely did the details of current political affairs from the region, so readily available in newspapers and media across the Arab world, enter into his vocabulary. He left such matters to those more experienced in the Palestinian-Israeli conflict than he, such as an unidentified preacher on cassette no. 491 whose speech on the recent outbreak of the Palestinian intifida in 1988 precedes his own. Bin Laden's discourse served different ends. Muslim Palestine and its Jewish Israeli counterpart were elements of a conspiracy that shifted back through time and forward into the future with the same underlying message: Arabs had been shamed and disgraced. In latter years, as we will learn, bin Laden would expand upon this theme with much historical verve, lingering frequently on twelfth-century combat with Byzantine Christians in the Holy Land and its peripheries. In the late 1980s, such dissertation was kept short. Bin Laden reminds his listeners at the outset of the speech cited above that "Jerusalem has been taken from us during our lifetime. We were born to an age of humiliation (*dhilla*) imposed on Muslims. One of the ways that we have benefited from this Struggle is to realize that one should never ever demean anyone, especially oneself." Renewed self-esteem could rally listeners toward victory. Redemption would come, however, only by taking up arms. No theme would feature as centrally in bin Laden's early speeches as the urgency of preparing oneself for combat. Under this banner, flown through the ages in as many shades of Muslim victimhood as could be mustered, bin Laden would evoke a wide swath of Islamic lands, each distinct for its own embattled heroes, legacies, and lessons for modern listeners. So too, under the appeal to "go forth, whether light or heavy," the possibility of a single battle was imaginable, especially when linked to epic struggles against Jews in and beyond Palestine. As he clarifies shortly after in the speech above, the "terror" against infidels sewn by Muslim liberators had spilled from Jerusalem to destinations east and west: "Praise be to God, Glorious and Exalted is He, terror spread elsewhere. If before the struggle we had thought of Jerusalem, now the first things to cross our minds were America and Russia with the Jews."

The theme of besieged Jerusalem was most productive, then, beyond its traditional territorial moorings. Exported to the fringes of the Arab world, beyond its connections to well-known towns, streets, and social networks, it afflicted the Islamic world like a debilitating plague. Bin Laden's formula to cure and revitalize Muslims consisted of action, ideally through radically violent means. "It is not our place to use reason in thinking through the texts, something called independent legal interpretation (*ijtihad*) of the texts' meaning." "Go forth," he solicits, for by assailing the cold war's greatest adversaries Muslims could smash their way to justice. Still, the audacity of his vision, if rooted in indignities shared by all Muslims alike, was curiously construed from the outset. In 1988, the United States and Muslim fighters struggling to liberate Afghanistan from Soviet occupation were on the same side. American taxpayers were contributing roughly $630 million annually to the Afghan cause, due most famously to the sway Texas congressman Charlie Wilson had on the U.S. House Appropriations Committee. Channeled through the Central Intelligence Agency, these funds were distributed to Afghan leaders rather than to Arabs, as historians keen to fend off charges that bin Laden was on America's payroll have taken pains to show. The ledger of what came to be known as "Charlie Wilson's War" nevertheless proved instrumental in American efforts to pressure the Saudis toward matching their war effort dollar for dollar. While the bulk of these matching contributions went to Afghans, the Saudi state's comfortable relation with wealthy private Arab donors ensured bin Laden's associates a steady stream of funds. Bin Laden's talents in deflecting questions about the convergence of American and Arab interests would need considerable refinement. When facing hard questions from the audience a year later about American funding and support for the Afghan cause, he would dismiss such reports as "rumor" and smoothly add that Saudi Arabia was providing "a large proportion of the weaponry."[6]

The excerpt above illustrates the formula that bin Laden would employ to rally support amidst enduring controversies about the enemies and allies of jihad. A top priority, bin Laden acknowledges, should be given to classical struggles against foreign infidels occupying Muslim lands. While supporting insurgencies in Kashmir, the Philippines, and the Central Asian republics would provide kindling for his diatribe in other speeches, none of these regions are evoked on this occasion.

Far more urgent is the Soviet occupation in Afghanistan, one that explicitly involves the United States, whatever has been said of bin Laden's lack of interest in America at the time.[7] Toward this end, preparation through combat training, front line experience and, most importantly, ideological discipline against Muslim complacency are imperative. "Praise be to God, there is a training camp (*mu'askar*), for without it how long would we continue to remain silent." Having just returned from the camp where, at the age of twenty-nine, he had participated in front line attacks against the Soviets, he could still lay claim to the youthful zeal of many a revolutionary. The rigors of this camp, and narratives of its legacy, would give his militant speeches an ascetic edge for years to come.

Although bin Laden had made regular trips to Pakistan after the Soviet invasion next door in 1979, his first journey into Afghanistan occurred in the summer of 1984.[8] A patchwork of Arab training camps had just been set up in the Khost and Paktia provinces, just over a mountainous saddle leading to Peshawar, Pakistan, where the Islamic opposition to Soviet occupation had taken root. Designed to mobilize Arab support for the Afghan mujahidin's struggle, the camps were established through the work of a powerful network of alumni and clients of the Pakistan-based Haqqani House of Islamic Sciences (*Dar Al-'Ulum Haqqaniyya*). Founded in 1947, the same year as Pakistan's independence from the British Raj, the madrasa sought independence from the Pakistani state and its perceived secular capitulations from the outset. The madrasa placed correct ritual observance at the center of its doctrinal mission and, over time, became Pakistan's premier school for Taliban leaders. While non-Muslims and the West occasionally featured in its Hanafi curriculum, teachings focused on reform within the Islamic world rather than beyond. Given Pakistan's historical relations with Britain and, during the cold war its strong economic and military partnership with the United States, however, students with political grievances against foreigners could find like-minds. One of these students, Jalaluddin "Haqqani," would develop a particularly strident anti-American message in his work as mujahidin commander during the years of Afghanistan's Soviet occupation. So too would he quietly prove middleman to some 12,000 tons of American supplies channeled annually to the mujahidin by the CIA during the 1980s.[9] A master of shell games involving repurposed products and loyalties, he would play ardent host to bin Laden from his earliest days in Afghanistan.

The camps were strung together just beyond the operating perimeter of a major Soviet outpost in Khost. By the late 1980s, they accommodated some 600 students and included Al-Badr 1, Al-Badr 2, Al-Faruq, Khalid Ibn al-Walid, Abu Jandal, and Salman Al-Farsi. Bin Laden was moved by the meager supplies and piecemeal infrastructure of the camps during his first visit. Upon seeing a band of Afghan mujahidin dropping four Soviet fighter planes from the sky, he is reported to have dashed back to Saudi Arabia where, war stories fresh in his mind, he raised between $5–10 million dollars, a sizeable chunk coming from his half-sister.[10] Back in Peshawar shortly later, the contribution delighted regional leaders. Bin Laden's first investments appear to have been educational: he helped found an enormous library of Arabic-language religious texts for the growing number of Arab volunteers who began arriving in the city, and organized classes in Islamic theology and history in the training camps.[11] At about the same time, he helped set up an Office of Services (*Maktab Al-Khidmat*) to formalize outreach efforts, housing, and training procedures. Still, bin Laden's brief encounter with the smoke of war left him unsatisfied with the business of finance, bureaucracy, and educational reform. Toward the latter half of 1986, he secured permission to set up his own camp near the others, some ten miles from the border of Pakistan.[12]

His site was originally labeled "Camp Madina" in homage to Islam's *axis mundi* and its ostensible openness to any who served its mission. Over time, the camp acquired a more specific moniker, as noted by bin Laden above: the "Lion's Den of the supporters" (*ma'sadat al-ansar*). Islam's early "supporters" (*ansar*) were the residents of Madina who welcomed the Prophet Muhammad after he had left Mecca in CE 632, the first year of the Islamic calendar. Their zeal for championing the Prophet's cause irrespective of tribe, status, or ethnic background marked them for distinction, hence one of the many names for Madina as the "Lion's Den" (*ma'asada*). Lofty ideals were strained from the beginning. Of the camp's original founders, six were bin Laden's childhood friends from Madina, where he had just moved with his family in order to oversee a new bin Laden Group construction project.[13] By October 1986, the roughly dozen men who were stationed at the camp were all Saudis, the bulk of new arrivals from bin Laden's own hometown. Volunteers from outside the cosmopolitan Hijaz region arrived only to discover a pronounced regional chauvinism: "I went to *Ma'sadat*

Al-Ansar," a Saudi Islamist later reported. "Most of the people there were from Jeddah. I didn't stay long because I didn't like it."[14]

If the camp's brawn was Saudi with a growing corps of Yemenis over time, its brain was Egyptian. The two top commanders, known by their *noms de geurre* as Abu Hafs Al-Masri and Abu 'Ubayda Al-Banshiri, were both former police officers who had been disillusioned by Egypt's swing toward Arab nationalism. In the late 1970s, they rejected the Muslim Brotherhood's rapprochement with the state and began making inroads with members of the Islamic Jihad, Egypt's most dedicated Islamic militant movement. After Abu 'Ubayda's brother helped assassinate Egyptian president Anwar Al-Sadat in 1981, he and Abu Hafs fled to Peshawar where they discovered a welcoming community of exiled revolutionaries. Even more prominent in the ranks of militant activists and intellectuals was Ayman Al-Zawahiri, a surgeon from a family of Egyptian notables who would become one of al-Qa'ida's most prominent spokespersons in future years. Around the time bin Laden and his colleagues struck forth across the Afghan border to pitch tents at the Lion's Den, Zawahiri set up shop in Peshawar's Kuwait-funded Red Crescent hospital. His reputation for steely diatribes against pro-Western Muslim regimes earned him respect among political dissidents, especially those from Egypt and North Africa. Others avoided him, especially the Muslim Brothers who found themselves the execrable subjects of a fiery treatise called *The Bitter Harvest* that he began circulating in Peshawar after his arrival.[15] Penned in the wake of his torture by Egyptian authorities for alleged involvement in Sadat's assassination, he accuses the Brotherhood of bartering the ideals of an Islamic state for a vocabulary of electoral democracy, man-made laws, and constitutions. Muslims who acquiesce to such betrayal serve material over spiritual interests. They are pronounced "disbelievers" (*kufar*) who, having fallen outside the pale of Islam altogether, can never be trusted. Al-Zawahiri met bin Laden for the first time shortly after his arrival from Jeddah, where he had secured employment for a while at a medical clinic.[16] Although no record is made of his visit to the Lion's Den, he was made a key supervisor over education and intellectual development at the nearby Al-Faruq training camp that was set up within two years. A more exclusive camp with advanced classes in weapons training, guerrilla combat, militant preparation, and religious instruction, Al-Faruq under Al-Zawahiri's leadership would leave a definitive stamp on al-Qa'ida's ideological legacy.

A decade later, Al-Zawahiri would come to be identified as al-Qa'ida's number two man, his name featuring next to bin Laden's on the organization's Declaration of War, published in the Arabic-language daily *Al-Quds Al-'Arabi* on 23 February 1998. Nowhere would al-Qa'ida's determination to attack what became known as "the far enemy," the United States and its allies, civilians as well as military personnel, be as clearly articulated as in that fatwa. In the late 1980s, Al-Zahawiri was focused on militant attacks against corrupt home rulers, foremost among them the Egyptian regime of Hosni Mubarak. Bin Laden stepped carefully around Al-Zawahiri's near-enemy discourse, especially since he enjoyed a robust flow of cash from Saudi coffers. Much as he would continue to do throughout his career, he preferred unifying maxims over remarks that might create dissension: "One should never ever demean anyone, especially oneself," he intoned repeatedly in his 1988 speech. This is not to say that bin Laden's priority was the far enemy, however. Even as he regularly trumpeted the idea of a united Muslim front against "America and Russia with the Jews," his vision of a purer, more ascetic Arabian Islam became the central leitmotif of his career as a propagandist.

Details of the composition and goals of the Lion's Den camp suggest much of the practical leverage of bin Laden's militancy at the time, as well as its shortcomings. A Saudi journalist who was invited to the Lion's Den in the months after its opening expressed shock at the juvenile state of the camp's strike force.[17] Despite bin Laden's wealth and international connections, the weapons arsenal consisted of poorly manufactured Egyptian Kalashnikov knockoffs, mortars, and some small anti-aircraft guns purchased in Peshawar. Although Afghan mujahidin had begun scoring dramatic reversals in the tide of the Soviet occupation through their use of American-made Stinger missiles, introduced to the region just a month earlier, bin Laden's attempts to obtain them through family connections were rebuffed.[18] His men made the most of Chinese rockets without launchers instead. To fire them off, the rockets were leaned against rocks, attached to a long fuse and lit from a distance. Shells regularly detonated far from their intended targets. Vehicles at the camp included a single bulldozer and a car, the latter of which was in constant use bringing food, supplies, and water from Pakistan. Later that year, bin Laden would manage to use family connections to import heavy construction equipment to build tunnels for the protection of men and supplies. At its inception, however, the camp's location at the timberline just three miles from a Soviet base provided ample grist for stories of human survival against all odds.

Battles with Soviet forces over the next year further illustrated the Arab-Afghans' scrappy determination. As word spread of bin Laden's setbacks, less ennobling narratives emerged about the hazards of improvising battle with few worldly resources. When approaching an Afghan government outpost near Khost in mid-April 1987, bin Laden's entire contingent of some 120 fighters was driven back by a single well-positioned Afghan sniper.[19] The tragedy of the defeat was amplified given the many months of planning that had gone into the attack and the advertising campaign that had been launched to recruit support in Peshawar. On 22 May, a smaller attack was organized by the camp's military commander Ali Al-Rashidi, known by his *nom-de-geurre* as Abu 'Ubayda Al-Banshiri, this time in the Jaji district of Paktia. Bin Laden seems to have been in Peshawar at the time, and after hearing of the attack rushed back to camp to experience heavy shelling by Soviet artillery and air bombardment.[20] Pitched battles ensued, often from freshly dug trenches, and in the course of combat bin Laden suffered the loss of some dozen comrades as well as his own foot injury. Nevertheless, after three weeks, as nearly 10,000 Soviet troops amassed in the area, the Arab-Afghans retreated. Before abandoning the Lion's Den, they set dynamite to their own installations to prevent hostile forces from making use of them.

Once safely back in Peshawar, surviving fighters had a ready audience among Arab journalists eager to paint the conflict in favorable hues.[21] In the period before the battles, bin Laden had often struck observers of the Afghan-Pakistan frontier as neither remarkable nor charismatic, especially when compared to the panoply of magnificent war heroes who jockeyed in Peshawar with established followings. Friends from Jeddah who visited him on the front lines report being shocked to see him playing the part of a militant on the front lines.[22] By 1988, bin Laden had begun using his contacts to pedal a new image. Saudi newspaper reporters seized on bin Laden's testaments of faith before an enemy with vastly superior firepower:

> We sometimes spent the whole day in the trenches or in the caves until our ears could no longer bear the sound of the explosions around us. War planes continually shrieked by us and their crazy song of death echoed endlessly.

We spent the days praying to God almighty…Reliance upon God is the main source of our strength and these trenches and tunnels are merely the military facilities God asked us to make.[23]

An Egyptian documentary producer was commissioned by bin Laden to present a more humanitarian angle. A fifty-five-minute film captures bin Laden in routine preparation rather than battle; he chats lightly with companions while reclining under blankets in a cave, paces summer pastures with a two-way receiver radio and tests out a gun at a shooting range.[24] In a book released around the same time, the producer commends the Arab-Afghans for struggling against "strong material and economic poverty," liberating Muslims from "slavery and oppression" and rejecting "an abased human condition" foisted upon people by twentieth-century dictators.[25] Audio-recorded speeches proved to be another important way to market bin Laden's message. As suggested by the excerpt above and explored later, their address to more discrete audiences and potential recruits captured an Arab-centrism that qualified bin Laden's broader, more ecumenical image in mainstream media channels.

Bin Laden would nevertheless feature very little in Arab-Afghans' most representative print publications in the years to come, despite assertions to the contrary.[26] These included those he himself funded such as the colorful monthly *Al-Jihad* magazine from Peshawar. Under the shadow of political heavyweights far more influential than he, bin Laden appeared comparatively puny. Still, his initiative in exploiting the media contacts available to him was well timed. If only a few dozen Arab fighters had ventured to Afghanistan before 1984, hundreds of volunteers began arriving between 1984–6, many of them from Saudi Arabia, Yemen, and Algeria.[27] They were largely young men in their twenties, most of them from middle-class families whose members had transnational connections with merchants, entrepreneurs, and Arab charitable associations providing humanitarian assistance to Afghan refugees. Foremost on their agenda was building a pan-Islamic community that might bring Muslims of diverse backgrounds together against the injustices of non-Muslim aggression. Upon arriving in Peshawar, they met the sobering reality of internecine Muslim strife. In such a context, a familiar Arab host was most welcome, the more so if appearing to be a fairly neutral mediator who shared one's national origins, language, and cultural history. "What caused your group of brothers to excel?" bin Laden was asked by observers. "Our brothers would come from their own countries, and they would be overwhelmed by their experience here and all the factors it included—such as the Struggle, the strange language, the harsh climate and hostile topography."[28] In addition to his growing media celebrity as a war hero, bin Laden had the wealth, social connections, and business acumen to help alleviate the culture shock felt by many young Arab men in the city.

Complicating Arab-Afghans' quest for a cultural *terra firma* in the region was the extraordinary influx of American dollars into the coffers of Afghan mujahidin. During the previous few years, the United States had increased its level of funding for the Afghan mujahidin to upwards of $630 million annually.[29] Part of President Jimmy Carter's "containment" strategy for drawing the Soviet Union into a costly quagmire on its southern borders, Operation Cyclone gave the highest priority to discretion since evidence of American support for the Islamic opposition would have given its cold-war enemy a massive propaganda boost. Funds were accordingly channeled through Pakistan's security apparatus, Inter-Services Intelligence, rather than directly to mujahidin leaders. In order to ensure "plausible deniability," arms suppliers on the CIA's payroll also tapped and fueled markets for Chinese and Egyptian weapons rather than relying on American manufacturers.[30] In case lines of credit were not complicated enough, the American government brokered an agreement with the Saudis to match their contributions year after year. Between 1979 and 1989, American and Saudi efforts to render the Afghan struggle adequately "Islamic" amounted to a tidy $6 billion dollars.[31] Islam's growing status as an equal opportunity employer gave rise to controversy if not outright cynicism among many in the region.[32] In light of such East-West collaboration, bin Laden's pitch to an authentic and discretely Arab asceticism found welcome ears. This was especially the case for the increasing number of Saudi volunteers who began arriving by 1989. More than any other group of Arab nationals, they knew the intimacy of American and Arab commitments. They could also appreciate the passion of those who sought to break them.

In his 1988 speech to Saudi audiences at home, bin Laden's emphasis on unleashing "terror" against the United States and Russia anticipate tensions that were emerging around this time with the celebrated icon of the Arab-Afghan struggle, 'Abdalla 'Azzam. If the emblem of bin Laden's heroism was an ascetic Arab fighter unleashing the bare-boned tactics of "massive and primeval emancipation" against global forces of economic and cultural extortion, 'Azzam's ideal hero sought to recapture lost Muslim territory on behalf of a pan-Islamic collective. Born in the Palestinian West Bank, 'Azzam was forced to flee with his parents and family to Jordan in 1967. In his late twenties at the time, he fought in the Palestinian resistance from Jordan under the military wing of the nationalist Fatah party. Disillusioned by the prospects of near-term victory against Israel, he turned to religious studies, acquiring his doctorate in Islamic law from Egypt's famous Al-Azhar University. He subsequently taught in Saudi Arabia and, after the Soviet invasion of Afghanistan in 1979, in Pakistan. 'Azzam appears to have rocketed to prominence as a leading intellectual and spokesperson for the Arab-Afghan jihad. By 1985, he directed the Islamic Coordination Council's main office in Peshawar, a conglomeration of about twenty charitable organizations and the principal institution for channeling state funding from both Saudi Arabia and Kuwait to the Afghan mujahidin.[33] Along with bin Laden, he raised an additional $200 million from private donors through the Office of Services. By the end of the decade, the bulk of this revenue came from the United States and Britain.[34] On tape no. 189, 'Azzam recounts stories of his trips to Detroit, Kansas City, Los Angeles, and dozens of other American cities between 1979–89. Rarely were audiences more generous than when 'Azzam linked his pitch for volunteers and financial contributions back to the needs of Palestinians and the good work of the Muslim Brotherhood and Hamas organizations. For 'Azzam, the extraordinary transnational nature of the struggle underway put Muslims at the gates of the greatest pan-Islamic community (*umma*) in modern history.

Bin Laden is reported to have met 'Azzam in Los Angeles during his first and only trip to the United States in 1979.[35] Five years later, their partnership was solidified when both met again in Peshawar to set up the Office of Services. As executive director, 'Azzam helped legitimize the pan-Islamic contribution of Arab volunteers and their financial backers. While a focus on Israel and the Middle East was paramount, regional ambitions were subordinate to the broader goal of struggling toward a global Muslim caliphate. Much of 'Azzam's work bore the marks of utopian aspiration. 'Azzam's theory of the caliphate was elaborated on at least one cassette in bin Laden's audio-library as well as in a book entitled *The Defense of Muslim Territories* published in the same year as the Office of Service's establishment. Despite the absence of a caliph in the modern Islamic world, 'Azzam considered armed struggle imperative given Judeo-Western assaults on Muslims.[36] On a tape entitled *Jihad Is An Individual Obligation (Al-Jihad Fard 'Ayn)*, he states:

> if disbelievers occupy a single hand width of Muslim land, jihad becomes an individual obligation incumbent upon every Muslim. If people in such a region remain indolent, neglectful, irresponsible, or hesitant, the individual obligation is passed on to a wider circle...to those behind them until the obligation spread across the entire earth: the woman would set out from her confines without permission from her husband, the son without permission from his father, the slave without permission from his master, the debtor without permission from the loaner. It is an obligation that none seeks to abandon being just as important as prayer and fasting.[37]

The tenor of such populist militancy was in many respects matched by other Afghan opposition leaders at the time, among them Jalaluddin Haqqani.[38] Delivered in Arabic, however, 'Azzam's fiery writings and audio-recorded speeches reached broader international audiences and were best sellers among supporters of the Afghan struggle worldwide. Bin Laden's house in Kandahar would later feature nearly seventy tapes by 'Azzam, making him the fifth most featured speaker in the collection. The Office of Service marketed his work from their ground-floor recordings and publications shop. Interviews and articles by 'Azzam were further available in pages of the Office's *Al-Jihad* magazine, most copies of which were dispatched to its fifty-two branches in the United States.[39]

Tensions appear to have emerged between bin Laden and 'Azzam, however, over the tactics, if not the larger architecture, of the struggle underway. Bin Laden complained of inadequate oversight of office accounts, $25,000 of which came from his pocket monthly.[40] By 1986, bin Laden had opened a separate dormitory for volunteers, "The House of the Supporters" (*Bayt Al-Ansar*), soon to be followed by guesthouses for more specific ethnic groups: the Saudis, the northern Arabs from Syria and its neighbors, the Algerians and so forth.[41] More ominous was the Saudi and Arab favoritism of bin Laden's training camp. In 'Azzam's opinion, Arab fighters needed to defer to the broader pan-Islamic goal of establishing a true Islamic state in Afghanistan. This objective required Arabs to split up into smaller groups so that they could train alongside the Afghan mujahidin and take direction from their leadership.[42] The Lion's Den was hardly conducive to such collaboration. Not only was its fixed target poorly suited to the hit-and-run guerilla warfare that the Afghans were waging. Its Hijazi favoritism and Egyptian command structure seemed to offer recruits a platform for mobilizing action back at home rather than abroad.

When bin Laden was asked about the origin of the term *"al-qaʿida"* just over a month after the 11 September attacks, he would downplay its significance:

> the situation is not as the West portrays it: that there exists a specific 'organization' with such a name. That particular name is very old and arose without our giving significance to it. Brother Abu ʿUbayda Al-Banjshiri created a training camp (*muʿaskar*) for young men to fight against the truly tyrannical, iniquitous, heretical, and terrorist Soviet Union. We used to call this place "the base" (*al-qaʿida*), as in a training base, and the name grew from this. We are not separated from the pious community, however.[43]

In many ways, the Lion's Den under Abu Ubayda's leadership expressed just such a "base," although as I discuss in chapter five, evidence of al-Qaʿida's organizational foundation leads more directly to the Al-Faruq camp and its platform of rebellion against Muslim rulers rather than non-Muslim infidels. By 2001, bin Laden had learned to repackage his controversial brand of Arabism under the broader framework of common Muslim resistance to infidel world superpowers. His skill in whitewashing the past is evident enough in his 1988 speech above: spreading "terror" was the hallmark of Arab warriors and not the "terrorist Soviet Union." In any case, ʿAzzam had a more idealized understanding of the concept. Around the time bin Laden began opening his own guesthouses, ʿAzzam circulated a pamphlet to Arab-Afghan recruits throughout Peshawar expounding the virtues of what he termed a "solid base" (*al-qaʿida al-sulba*).[44] Entitled *Join the Caravan*, the pamphlet conjured a utopian vision that brought together territorial reclamation, much in the fashion of Palestinian nationalism, with militant asceticism designed to unite Muslims everywhere. "Securing a solid base for the House of Islam," wrote ʿAzzam, begins with:

> the establishment of Muslim society on an area of land… [is] as necessary as water and air. This House will be reserved only for an organized Islamic movement that wages jihad through action as well as words, making combat its very warp and woof. Such a movement will establish Muslim society only through generalized popular jihad (*jihad shaʿbi ʿamm*). As a beating heart and thinking mind, the Islamic movement can be compared to a small detonator that triggers a massive bomb; it will free the Muslim community's

latent energy, releasing the good that is stored deep within. The Prophet's Companions, God be pleased with them, were few indeed when compared to the vast number of Muslims who overturned Chosroes' throne and tarnished Caesar's glory...The popular jihad movement, despite the length of its journey, the severity of its suffering, the magnitude of its sacrifices and the burden of its losses, can purify souls and elevate them high above the reality of this retreating earth. Such a movement helps us transcend our trivial obsession with cash, short-term interests, and frivolous commodities. As resentments are set aside and our spirits refined, the caravan climbs steadily from the retreating foot of the mountain to the lofty peak far beyond the putrescence of mud and contest of jungles! Qualities of leadership prevail along the road of jihad; qualifications emerge through generosity and sacrifice. True men are defined by courage and true commitment.[45]

For 'Azzam, as for bin Laden, establishing a "solid base" required securing actual territory to train and discipline Muslim fighters. While such territory would ideally be secured through a "generalized popular jihad," 'Azzam agreed with bin Laden that a small and dedicated leadership could prove instrumental in wresting victory from infidels. For both men, the passion and commitment of this minority evoked a certain romance with the lonely desert Arab and his ascetic ordeals. Later, 'Azzam would describe the solid base less in territorial terms than as a human "vanguard" (tali'a), preferable in his mind to bin Laden's "sect" (ta'ifa) and more assured of uptake by established Muslim reformers worldwide. For all their shared sentiments and ample Western attention to his origination of Al-Qa'ida, 'Azzam broke with bin Laden, Al-Zawahiri, and others who privileged revolt against Muslim tyrants in the Arab heartlands.[46] The vanguard's primary function, even in its most utopian cast, was military and not revolutionary. In light of repeated setbacks among Islamists across the Middle East, 'Azzam mocked the idea that a small clandestine group could mount a coup and establish an Islamic state.[47] Victory both near and far required patience, education in doctrine, self-abnegation (zuhd) and its ultimate expression of martyrdom.[48] However incendiary 'Azzam's militant rhetoric, "terror" was never invoked as a legitimate tactic in the art of war.[49]

Given 'Azzam and bin Laden's joint investment in the Office of Services, virtues of asceticism naturally enhanced their credibility. Brotherly differences aside, 'Azzam regularly praised the lifestyle of his partner. After visiting bin Laden in Jeddah, 'Azzam noted that "He lives in his house the life of the poor...I never did see a single table or chair.

Any Jordanian or Egyptian laborer's house was better than the house of Osama. At the same time, if you asked him for a million riyals for the mujahidin, he would write you out a check on the spot." Of bin Laden's involvement with the Afghan war effort, he wrote:

> The Afghans would see the Arab as a man who had left his commerce, employment and company behind in Saudi Arabia, the Arabian Gulf or Jordan, and had come to live a life of stale bread and tea on the peaks of mountains. They would see Osama bin Laden as a man who had left behind his business deal of expanding the Prophet's Mosque in Madina to his brothers, forfeiting his share of the proceeds—some 8 million Saudi riyals [U.S. $2.5 million]—in order to throw himself into the thick of battles.[50]

Through 'Azzam's mediation, bin Laden's reputation for austerity and generosity caught many an ear and helped put his estimable contacts among wealthy Saudi donors, family members, and bin Laden Group clients in their proper light.

In many ways, the urgency of clarifying the pious community's boundaries grew more, not less, urgent as the region's largest infidel horde turned heels and struck for home. On 15 February 1989, the Soviet army completed its withdrawal across Afghanistan's northern border. In its wake, the presiding Afghan government under Muhammad Najibullah declared emergency law, ousted party opponents and abandoned diplomacy in favor of buying off Afghan resistance leaders. As billions of dollars flowed into Najibullah's regime from Moscow, funding from older Saudi Arabia and the United States dried up, raising new concerns about the credibility of newly financed Muslim warriors. In March, a fierce battle erupted in Jalalabad pitching Muslim against Muslim. Under the rain of Scud missiles and cluster bombs, some 12–15,000 civilians were killed and thousands more injured. Hopes of conflict resolution among Afghans deteriorated from there. Although the Najibullah regime would fall to resistance forces in the spring of 1992, Kabul would see bleak and brutal years ahead as Pakistani-backed Hizbi Islamic forces under Gulbuddin Hekmetyar, the greatest beneficiary of CIA dollars just a few years before, shelled the city in hopes of wresting power from the reigning Islamic State of Afghanistan. In the turmoil of shifting battlefronts, a majority of Arab-Afghans found themselves backing Hekmetyar against the long hoped-for polity of their dreams. The costs of moral compromise were never more starkly manifest than on 24 November 1989. As 'Azzam and his two sons were approaching a mosque outside a Peshawar, a roadside bomb ripped through their vehicle, killing all three of them. Charges of foreign treachery naturally arose, although the hand of Egyptian Islamic Jihad leaders had been darkly played over the previous year in their public trial against ʿAzzam for his alleged mismanagement of Arab-Afghan funds. Rumors of Egyptians' complicity in the killing complicated ʿAzzam's legacy. Eulogies in praise of his worldly renunciation would be strained by controversy.

Arab volunteers continued to arrive in the region after the Soviets had left. By 1990, however, the celebrity of the Afghan cause in Arab countries would draw a lustier and less disciplined assembly of recruits to the region. Many sought to join in routing the communists from Afghanistan and positioning themselves as evangelicals at the gates of a crumbling Soviet Union. Others would arrive with an altogether different adversary in mind. On 7 August 1991, American military ground forces streamed into Saudi Arabia at King Fahd's behest, responding to the invasion of neighboring Kuwait by Saddam Hussein's million-man army. At the height of the war, a coalition of thirty-four nations from around the world joined the U.S. effort under authorization from the United Nations. To the consternation of pan-Islamists, over a third of coalition members were Muslim-majority states including Saudi Arabia, Egypt, Syria, Morocco, Kuwait, Oman, Pakistan, the United Arab Emirates, Qatar, Bangladesh, Niger, Senegal, and Bahrain. Arab public opinion weighed in favor of international involvement in the region as long as it was geared toward supporting a genuinely popular uprising against Saddam. As time drew on and regime change seemed unlikely, however, the long-term presence of an international coalition enforcing sanctions against Iraqis proved untenable for an increasing range of observers, especially when facilitated by an unprecedented scale of American military involvement in the region. Under these conditions, Afghanistan's new freedom offered volunteers an opportunity to overcome internecine division through a common fight against a "new world order," one that had begun with the Soviet invasion of Afghanistan and that would acquire its ultimate shape through American sovereignty over the Middle East.[51]

Anticipating a post-Soviet Afghanistan as early as 1988, bin Laden prepared himself to address the common bonds that would unite a disparate range of Arab volunteers. While the idea of reclaiming Jerusalem provides a poignant backdrop, bin Laden finds asceticism conducive to giving his envisioned holy warrior a more transnational mantle. Repeatedly throughout his concluding remarks, bin Laden cites the Qur'anic injunction "go forth, whether light or heavy." Giving substance to the verse, bin Laden cites the example of Yahya Shanyur of Jeddah, a young recruit who, admittedly "a bit overweight," defies all expectations by helping to mobilize "caravan loads and weapons" across the border from Pakistan to Afghanistan. He commends the steely discipline of such volunteers and their ability to put their sentimental peers back in Madina and Jeddah to shame. "Surplus wealth," he declares, is all well and good as long as one learns to heed religion's calling to shed one's mortal trappings and seek martyrdom in battle. Citing the verses of Ka'b Ibn Malik, an Arab poet who defended Islam's first community in Madina from an attack led by wealthy Quraishi merchants in the seventh century, bin Laden taunts the enemy: "Let them approach the lion's den/Her swords sharpened between the feeding trough and the newly dug trench." True warriors, it appears, inhabit a netherworld of martial discipline. Slightly earlier, bin Laden inclines his listeners toward proper ascetic virtues through the image of an Arabian Bedouin tent. "The main pole of Islam's tent is carrying weapons," bin Laden warns. Muslims who focus only on closing whatever "opening breach" (*thaghr*) might be closest at hand, to coin the idiom of his cosmopolitan Jeddah high school, endanger the community by privileging the defense of their own borderlands over the common good. Instead of a tent, one produces a mere "cloth on the ground." The integrity of Islam's "victorious and proclaiming sect," a phrase drawn from a *hadith* well known to militants, depends upon a tribalized defiance of worldly accumulation.

Bin Laden's strident Arabian imagery had mixed results among listeners. Some found his rhetoric of Bedouin tents, tribal austerity, and poetry alienating. Recruits from lower socioeconomic backgrounds who had experienced first hand the sour fruits of poverty, tribal conflict, and status discrimination found his romance with desert life overly elitist. At least one Saudi volunteer confessed frustration with the cosmopolitan Hijazi exclusivism at the Lion's Den and reportedly left shortly after his arrival.[52] The strained tenor of bin Laden's asceticism was never more prominent than when linked to his passion for purebred Arabian horses, a luxury few could afford. Wherever he lived, whether in Jeddah or the Sudan or Afghanistan, he kept active stables and repeatedly sought Arabians when possible. Throughout his career listeners would be struck by the ease with which bin Laden would shift from religious or political discussions to extended lectures about the minutia of horsemanship; as one close associate noted, "He is enamored with horses and speaks of them almost as he does of Islam."[53] Bin Laden's tribal asceticism came with a cultural baggage that spoke volumes of his privileged background.

Others found bin Laden's Arabian neo-tribalism highly politic. Images of horseback-riding mujahidin featured prominently in Arab-Afghan print media, just as they would later in al-Qa'ida's video and internet propaganda. For young men in their twenties looking for adventure, bin Laden tapped a vein of chivalry and heroism that made for good advertising.[54] Senior militant strategist Abu Mus'ab Al-Suri, though a critic of bin Ladin's ethnic parochialism, pitched the work of training Arab-Afghans in much the same romantic idiom, writing in his memoires that "we had to rely on the methods of training in houses and 'camps of nomadic mujahidin,' as I called them…Goat-hair dwellings (buyut sha'ir), two cars, a number of individuals, a camp in the desert and the wasteland. After the training program was implemented participants would leave…another group arriving at a different location and so forth."[55] If jihad was to transcend exclusive contracts of the nation-state and mobilize transnational audiences to take collective action against a corrupt global economic system, bin Laden's nomadism was serviceable. Gallant mounts aside, bin Laden's ascetic imaginary yielded special leverage against the Muslim world's own worst enemies. For Saudi and Gulf nationals who were fed up with entrenched tribal elites and political systems founded on nepotism, bin Laden's reconstructed tribalism offered hope. His own Yemeni father, after all, had faced stupendous hurdles when establishing social inroads with Saudi tribesmen.[56] The younger bin Laden offered lessons at once tested and ecumenical. North African militants, meanwhile, found bin Laden's pitch to asceticism a healthy corrective to what they perceived to be the overly comfortable and pliant lifestyles of wealthy Saudis, Gulf Arabs, and Yemenis.[57] As we will discover in chapter five when examining the foundations of the Al-Faruq training camp in Khost in 1989, such militants would need continued reassurance that bin Ladin, scion of a multimillionaire, could keep his ascetic priorities in order.

4

THE GENIE AND THE BOTTLE

ON AUTHORITY AND REVELATION
THROUGH AUDIOTAPES

(July 1989 recording of a genie (*jinni*) talking with Arabs in Afghanistan.[1] Cassette no. 1165.)

_____

Speaker A: So they cannot harm me in any other way? For example by using genies?

Jinni ʿAbdalla: If I was going to harm you, I would harm or enter you through your foot, by God, I would enter right into you. It would make no difference if you were willing or not.

Speaker A: For example, if we were continuously remembering God?

Speaker B: So Muslim genies cannot harm us?

Jinni ʿAbdalla: As a Muslim, I would not want to harm you. As for Muslims amongst us whose faith is weak, they do harm.

Speaker C: So, you can't really harm me?

Jinni ʿAbdalla: Of course I can harm you! Are you mad?

[Speaker C tries to interrupt.]

Jinni ʿAbdalla: In a moment of heedlessness or extreme laughter I can enter into you. Even if you were constantly remembering God, you could be inattentive and heedless for a single moment.

95

Speaker D [*in disbelief*]: Oh my son!

Jinni 'Abdalla: Liar, that's what you are! Whaaa! [*Genie screams, chasing the disbelieving bystander away.*] Leave the sick man alone [*referring to himself*]! Leave him! You're a wicked man! I am more informed about these things than you! Ahwooo!

Speaker A [*trying to intervene*]: Take it easy! Calm down!

Jinni 'Abdalla: There is no God but Allah! You ask me questions only to accuse me of lying, you wicked man! I'm a trustworthy Muslim!

Speaker A: Calm down! Relax!

Jinni 'Abdalla: The correct Muslim is considered trustworthy!

Speaker A: Say "There is no god but God alone."

Jinni 'Abdalla: There is no god but God alone! [*After an unclear comment from a bystander, the genie continues, calming himself.*] I seek refuge in God from the accursed Satan. I said that I'm sick. Don't cause me a lot of harm!

Speaker A: No no. Take a rest.

Jinni 'Abdalla: Are there any more questions? [*Pausing.*] Call the faithful to prayer, then, God's grace upon you.

[*Recording interrupted as the call to prayer is made. The genie's voice then cuts in.*]

Jinni 'Abdalla: They have given us their trust. [*He begins to recite a short prayer that often follows the longer public call to prayer*]: "O God, Lord of this perfect summons and firm prayer, grant Muhammad the means and favor." Right?

Speaker E [*adding another portion that customarily follows the word "favor"*]: "And the highest and most exalted stage of emanation."

Jinni 'Abdalla: No, that part is not correct! "And bestow upon him, O God, the praiseworthy station that You promised him."

Jinni 'Abdalla: [Now] I would like to make a comment. This madman who lacks understanding was saying: "You cannot! How could you have entered [the body of the possessed Muslim host] when he was in the middle of praying and remembering God?"

Speaker A: Right.

Jinni 'Abdalla: He doesn't understand! What is this stupidity?

Speaker F: That's right.

Jinni 'Abdalla: It is during moments of inattentiveness that I enter.

Speaker F: In a moment of inattentiveness!

Jinni ʿAbdalla: Yes. In a moment of heedlessness. This is why, all night long, one must remember and mention [God], not laughing a lot. Woo-ha-a-a-a-a-a-a! [*The genie imitates loud laughter.*] That's an easy way in!

Speaker F: Easy!

Jinni ʿAbdalla: What a devil (*shaytan*)! That ignoramus doesn't understand. May God bring blessings to you all.

[*Recording interrupted for prayer. The genie's voice resumes.*]

Jinni ʿAbdalla: Good. Bring another tape before this one runs out.

Speaker E [*talking to another bystander*]: Bring another tape, please.

Speaker G: We have one, right here somewhere.

Jinni ʿAbdalla: Good, but wait for this tape to run out. Now, I was speaking and you were suggesting that some righteous genies, on account of their extreme jealousy [of me], might visit you to learn about some of my lessons.

[*Interruption in recording.*]

Jinni ʿAbdalla: I need to rest, so hold off. Ahhh! I'm making you record this [on tape] so that the whole world believes what I'm saying and won't think that [this bodily host] is lying. Even the faithful can find his possession by a genie hard to believe, unless they already believe in the existence of genies. As for those who don't believe that genies can possess human beings, maybe they will become believers [after listening to the tape]. Ignoramuses!

If someone listening to cassette no. 1165 suspected bin Laden of having a genie at his command, it would not have been the first time. Roughly two years earlier, during battles with the Soviets from the Lion's Den, bin Laden's comrades grew suspicious of a bottle in his possession. As it so happened, that bottle was filled with glucose for bin Laden's low blood pressure at the time. With uncanny timing, the bottle seemed to bring on a Soviet air attack each time it was produced to feed a drip line. On the fifth occasion, ground trembling and walls collapsing, the brothers implored bin Laden's doctor to destroy the bottle for fear it contained a genie protecting a dark "secret." "Do not see it as an evil omen," bin Laden is reported to have replied, "for evil omens are forbidden in Islam." His reassurance seemed to mollify bystanders, even occasioning laughter about the absurdity of such a notion. Still, one of his countrymen chucked the bottle out the door just to be safe.[2]

Genies on audiotape prove somewhat more resilient. Unlike the genie in the bottle, they can speak for themselves. While granting wishes is not their forté, moreover, they can reveal what is hidden from believers, including the best paths to a more perfect community. In the excerpt above, the genie corrects Speaker E's style of prayer. When asking God to grant the Prophet Muhammad his favor, one should not commend Muhammad's worldly emanation (*daraja*), a quality much celebrated among Islam's Sufi mystics who believe they can employ the Prophet's intercession to access hidden knowledge of the divine. Genies have no earthly rivals: Muhammad's appointment to his proper station (*maqam*) in God's eyes is enough to wish for.

The edgy and assertive voice of the genie provides a commentary on the medium of the audiocassette itself, or at least what it afforded to upstarts like bin Laden and other militants committed to world transformation. An entire chapter devoted to the old-fashioned audiocassette may seem indulgent. Terrorism and our views of its sponsors are little, however, if not mediated by time, place and the curiously fashioned "bottles" that contain them. The audiotape library in bin Laden's Kandahar compound preserved the opinions and views of over two-hundred speakers from around the world, many of whom were linked by little more than coils of polyester recording tape stacked together under bin Laden's roof. While I provide an overview of some of the main speakers and their perspectives in the next chapter, my goal in this chapter is to unpack what is, in fact, a very messy archive.

From its invention in 1963 by the Netherlands-based Philips Company, the audiocassette technology seemed perfectly suited to creating mischief. Bucking the trends among recording companies at the time, Philips decided against a patent and instead allowed manufacturers around the world to mass-produce the technology as long as they honored the dimensions and design of the original prototype. As a result, home-grown cassette industries sprang to life across the world within a few years, quickly replacing the clunkier eight-track tape. For audiences seeking freedom in the Arab world, the timing could not have been better. During the 1950s and 1960s, most Arab states achieved independence from European colonial powers. Those revolutions had relied heavily on newspapers, radio, and vinyl record technologies to imbue audiences with nationalist sentiment. Still, the first post-colonial years of Arab states were not easy for nationalist leaders. During the shaky years of state consolidation, public culture was tightly monitored and censorship, along with new forms of repression, was often vigorous.

It was during these years, some five to fifteen years after Arab national-ists' benchmark achievements, that the 3.81-millimeter audiotape and its plastic cartridge found peculiar uptake. User-friendly, difficult to censor, and conducive to disseminating the views of marginalized actors, the audiocassette offered citizens a way to assess the nation's ideals through the sounds of a more conflicted auditorium.

At the center of debates over political representation, justice, and nationhood that were captured and amplified on audiocassette were, of course, questions about Islam. To what extent could classical Islam pro-vide guidance in a rapidly modernizing world? If top students seeking an Islamic education through the 1960s had been expected to memorize the entire Qur'an as his or her first step toward professionalization, increasing literacy across the Arab world by the 1970s diminished the urgency of by-rote memorization. With new study techniques came standardized educational curricula, a response deemed suitable in light of growing populations during the mid-twentieth century. As older face-to-face learning systems gave way to education for the masses, a new managerial class emerged to regulate the ways Islamic knowledge would be developed, tested, approved, and reproduced. The state's heavy involvement in such trends naturally found resistance among those who felt something was being lost in the rush toward modern forms of Muslim identity. Bigger questions arose about the continuity of Islamic tradition, culture, and proper respect for God's revelations to the Prophet Muhammad.

Audiocassette tapes, for all their plastic and commercialized market-ing, were providential for many Muslim reformers. In countries where literacy rates were low, foremost among them Afghanistan, Yemen and Saudi Arabia during the 1970s, cassettes amplified the voices of those who struggled to translate their concerns into the language of their middle and upper class compatriots. Every region and district had its home-grown cassette stars, including preachers, singers, musicians, and poets. Literate and highly educated audiences found cassettes equally compelling, however, no more so than when producers geared their craft to political commentaries that were otherwise edited or banned from mainstream media sources. During the 1970s, as Iranian dissent against the American-backed regime of Reza Shah Pahlavi built steam, audiocas-settes were used to smuggle the Ayatollah Ruhollah Khomeini's speeches into the country during his exile in Paris. The recordings lent momentum to a Shi'a revolution that would create shock waves across the world. In other Muslim countries, reformers speculated about the ways cassettes might be used in their own struggles, both large and small. In Egypt, Yemen, Bahrain, Saudi Arabia, Lebanon, Algeria, Morocco, Pakistan, India, Indonesia, and Malaysia, among other countries, burgeoning audio recording industries provided cultural depth to societies undergoing tremendous economic transformation. Popular Muslim preachers took pains to defend the utility of the technology for reformers, no more so than in Saudi Arabia, Iran's neighbor. In the wake of Khomeini's ascent, Salman Al-'Awda, Muhammad Al-Qahtani and 'Abd al-Wahhab Al-Turayri (all featured in bin Laden's collection) recorded specific lectures entitled "The Islamic Cassette." Their enthusiasm for the cassette lay precisely in its power to combat liberal cultural attitudes fueled in no small way by cassette-producers themselves, most of whom, according to the preachers, catered to all things low and licentious. Insofar as these trends were the results of Westernization, they drew rank with Al-Khomeini, commending his courage in defending Islam from its greatest foreign threat. Still, theirs was a Sunni revolution, its leaders and supporters relying on sound knowledge rather than the "misguided" and "seditious" claptrap of Shi'a. From their perspective, the cassette was a resource for education and guidance in learning, doctrine, and practice that, much in the tradition of Muhammad Ibn 'Abd al-Wahhab, could be developed quite apart from continuous Western perversion.

Speculations about the function and role of audiocassettes were not trivial. They implicated nothing less than revelation itself. Although God's words had found their way to the Prophet Muhammad's tongue more than fourteen centuries ago, Muslims understood only too well the living trust they had been given to transmit and abide by the scriptures to the best of their ability. Faith notwithstanding, the exercise of God's commands required clerical structures that could help believers resolve ambiguities and apply Qur'anic prescriptions in new contexts. Even as scholarly establishments were set up to guide Muslims, however, Islam's enormous geographical cast, reaching from southeastern China to Europe's western coastline within nearly one hundred years of Muhammad's death, greatly attenuated their influence. Concerns arose over the degree to which the singularity of Muhammad's message, conveyed in florid Arabic to a population of largely nomadic tribes, could be preserved in the face of extraordinary linguistic and cultural variation. One solution to these challenges was a heightened emphasis on verifiable oral transmission. If written texts could be mistranslated, damaged or even forged, oral recitation was considered an invaluable corrective when managed by credentialed transmitters and formal recitational styles. Within several generations, Muslims set precedent for committing the entirety of the Qur'an's 6,236 verses to heart. Memorizing other textual material, such as reports (*ahadith*) of sayings and deeds by Muhammad and his Companions, was quick to follow. Scriptural in its cast, Islam's vitality sprang from a disciplined tongue.

In light of Islam's historical emphasis on oral transmission, audiocassettes opened a new chapter in polemics over the merits and dangers of mechanical reproduction. Many appreciated the value of cassettes and, whatever ripples they might stir among those concerned with Islam's authenticity, commended the technology's service to spreading the faith. Others were less sure. What were pious Muslims to make of recordings that combined Qur'anic recitations with melodious popular anthems, political speeches, or studio-produced skits that dramatized ethical issues in the language of ordinary citizens? Should they support a recording technology that, by many measures, promoted folk-singers and corruptible poets over the words of the righteous? What was one to make of the commercial profits that increasingly came to define production values? What of the fitful and less accredited orators, preachers among them, who drew listeners toward thoughts of sedition? Such concerns drew attention to the poor regulation of recording industries worldwide but especially in Islamic societies where moral credibility was tightly linked to traditions of socially prescribed speech.

Many Muslim reformers have sought to ensure the proper uptake of cassette-recorded material by coaching audiences in the virtues of pious listening. The "mixed tape"—variously labeled "cocktail" (*kuktail*) or "sandwich" (*sanwish*) in Arabic—is a blessing, not a curse, for with a little self-discipline listeners can learn to hear with their heart. A cacophony of recordings in the urban metropolis, if a portal to debauchery and doubt, can be resisted through humility sharpened by pious fear (*taqwa*). The audio-recorded sermon itself is the classic genre for tuning in to God's will. Although varying widely in theme, content and style, sermons typically begin with verbal rituals, well rehearsed by those who know the bounds of proper devotion: "Praise be to God" (*al-hamdu li-llah*), followed by the testimonial declaration "There is no God but God alone and Muhammad is His Messenger" (*la illaha illa allah wa muhammadan rasulu-llah*) and capped by a conventional prayer for the Messenger, his Companions and Followers. Ears directed accordingly, listeners are encouraged to take active roles in aligning their bodies, minds and souls as well. Submission to God's order comes through channeling and refining one's senses while turning away from worldly affairs with divine remembrance (*dhikr*). Drawing listeners toward the original moment and very breath of revelation, the sermon invites believers to refine their ascetic sensibilities, especially through feelings of self-renunciation (*zuhd*), fear (*khawf*), timidity before God's majesty (*wara*) and trust in divine wisdom (*tawakkul*). However isolating the spiritual journey, for in the end Judgement Day concerns one's own soul alone, God's message is best mediated in this world through the preacher's pulpit, the community's anchor for all sounds good and true.

Other reformers have ventured into stormier acoustic frontiers. Jinni 'Abdalla's audio recording provides an illustration that, if extraordinary in some ways, underscores the controversy that can arise when transmitting God's revealed words. On the one hand, the Jinni defends his authority throughout the tape by recourse to Islam's well-established views on the existence of genies (*jinn*). Citing numerous Prophetic reports (*ahadith*), the Jinni finds ample support in the Qur'an, the most celebrated verse of which opens a separate *sura* on "The Jinn":

> Say: It has been
> Revealed to me that
> A company of Jinn
> Listened [to the Qur'an].
> They said, "We have
> Really heard a wonderful recital."

The Jinni instructs his audiences that his kind "hear, obey and [unlike humans] don't argue too much." Still, doctrinal evidence for Jinn notwithstanding, most of them remain invisible. Not only were they created, according to the Qur'an, from the "fire of a scorching wind" but they also typically gathered with their own kind in remote canyons, jungles and desert wastes. Speakers on the tape find the Jinni's bodily presence strange. They find it odd that he drinks water and eats food, questioning him about how a being made of fiery wind can feel thirst or hunger. They grill him about why he responds to questions from a sitting position, most Jinn preferring to speak from possessed bodies that remain lying down. They push him to explain why he behaves normally and doesn't fly off into the air, as he claims he could do if he wished. The Jinni's self-defense focuses on his respect for the body of his human host, a man who needs nourishment and comfort and would go crazy if lifted into skies. His answers stir more urgent questions. What about the person whose body he had possessed? "His name was Makarov," the Jinni admits. When pressed for biographical details, he adds only that the man had originated "from the Islamic republics that are occupied by the Soviet Communists." A good Muslim who regularly recited his prayers and remembered his Lord, the unfortunate soul was possessed when, according to the Jinni, "in a moment of inattentiveness, as he lay sleeping, I crept up and hit him here, on this side. The intensity of my blow caused him to awake in fright. At the moment he experienced fear, I entered into him through his left foot." Provoking audiences with threats of further violent hitting, screams, wild laughter and incantations in tongues human as well as strange, the Jinni conjures an untamed Afghan soundscape.

The audiocassette proves instrumental not only for broadcasting his capacity for violence, however. Much in the model of well-known cassette preachers, the Jinni professes using the technology for the higher aims of proselytizing: "Bring another tape before this one runs out," he implores a supportive bystander. "I'm making you record this [on tape] so that the whole world believes what I'm saying and won't think that [this bodily host] is lying. Even the faithful can find his possession by a genie hard to believe, unless they already believe in the existence of genies. As for those who don't believe that genies can possess human beings, maybe they will become believers [after listening to the tape]." On repeated occasions, he exhorts Muslims to uphold the tenets of their faith and devote themselves to learning, good manners, and the ascetic ideal: "Where is the true Muslim? Where is your concern for the brevity of this life (*qisar al-amal*)? You have been neglectful and have forgotten about the afterlife! Where is timidity (*wara'*) and self-abnegation (*zuhd*)? Where is your fear (*khawf*)? What of your duty to God? Listen to me!"

The cassette's function as a technology for instruction is also evident in the genie's responses to questions about global plots and conspiracies. His answers convey an authority hinging on worldly evanescence. "Was it you who killed [Muhammad] Zia Al-Haqq?" asks one speaker, referring to the former President of Pakistan who had died in a plane crash in August of the previous year. "No, we genies had nothing to do with the killing of Zia Al-Haqq…Listen, we know that there were plots between the West, Moscow, and hypocrite Muslims in Pakistan such as [Prime Minister] Benazir Bhutto. We don't know everything, busy as we are with many projects. I believe, however, that his death was a plot conceived late at night." A bystander probes the Jinni further about whether the United States was involved: "The American ambassador was also killed in the crash." "Indeed," the Jinni replies, "he was placed on that plane so that America would not be held suspect." "Aha! That way no one would suspect them!" "Yes yes. But the important thing is that while the conspiracy was huge, it worked ultimately to the benefit of Islam and jihad." If American plots against Muslims are far-reaching, even more sinister are threats from Iran:

These days the Shiʿa are plotting against you on a long term basis… Paying attention to this enemy is very important because they are eating away at your body. It is your obligation to face them. God knows best, but this is my view. You may think that some other approach is better, but I'm giving you my opinion by way of advice: I personally believe that Iran must be fought fiercely. If Iran was to gain control over Afghanistan, our struggle in Afghanistan would all be for naught. You need a long-term plan. After you're done with Afghanistan, you should spend a year or two, maybe three—whatever it takes—until things settle down and you are ready. You must not leap! Afghanistan may even take ten or fifteen years, so don't be hasty. "In the name of God," you exclaim, readying yourselves to go where? "Let's go liberate Palestine!" That's pointless [given Israeli and American suzerainty there]. You need ten or fifteen years to establish a well-trained standing army, okay? After that you can launch your attack. Having acquired a solid Muhammadan education, you would be able to unite the commanders and leaders of Afghanistan under one word. Unite the good ones, not the Sufis and those who are, shall we say, "onions." I won't mention names; you know them well enough. After building a strong Muslim army, then you can target Iran with its huge population. Those wicked people force Sunnis to the front lines of their wars so that they may get killed. Your own brethren led to their deaths!

The Jinni knows Muslims' true enemy well enough: Shiʿa, Sufis, and hypocritical Sunni "onions." These are the forces that, with perverse ascetic vehemence, "are eating away at your body." He lends support to his vision of militant world transformation elsewhere by alleging former nomination among Jinn to serve as their global caliph, a position that would have put him in command of an evil empire conspiring against

Muslims with assistance from Moscow and the West and even more sinister than global Freemasonry. His plans changed, however, once he possessed his human host. Now he commands only the good. Promising Muslims their own future caliphate, he coaches listeners in the more peaceable manners of communal harmony:

> Jinni 'Abdalla: You humans get so angry! You shouldn't let your anger enrage the Jinn, since their anger is much more severe than yours...You should be patient...Listen, my fellow Muslims, and correct your methodology. Do not anger me, God reward you.
>
> Speaker A: We love you.
>
> Jinni 'Abdalla: If you do love me, do not harm me. Listen and obey.
>
> Speaker A: God willing.
>
> Speaker B: In truth, we do love you.

The Living Archive

Did bin Laden ever listen to this tape? What would he have made of Jinni 'Abdalla's exhortations? Was the Jinni a member of al-Qa'ida? What was the significance of this recording to more practical discussions about the Arab-Afghan struggle under bin Laden's leadership? Was this a recruitment tape of some sort, to be distributed widely, or was it one of a kind? Who else knew about the tape? Why would it have been kept in bin Laden's house, and how did it get there?

Answers to such questions, important as they are to assessing the intelligence value of given cassettes in the collection, may never be known. The lack of reliable information does not prevent speculation. When I first heard about the collection in May 2003, I was consumed with the possibility of discovering the tapes to be a record of bin Laden's personal conversations. His son 'Umar, for example, had noted that during his father's stay in Tora Bora in 1996, he rarely parted with a Dictaphone mini-cassette recorder on which, "when frustrated at the recent changes in his life, he would thunder over past grievances or pose new ideas that he believed would alter the course of the world."[3] Were these tapes an extension of his audio-journal? Upon unpacking the cassettes from two cardboard DHL boxes sent from CNN's regional headquarters in Islamabad, I was sobered. Stripped of their original colorful casings to save space, the cheap plastic cartridges presented me with a jumble of post-invasion chaos. Roughly several dozen cassettes bore the name "Osama bin Laden" or the nickname attributed to him by virtue of his first-born son: "The Father of 'Abdalla" (*Abu 'Abdalla.*) The rest of the collection was a labyrinth. Some corridors were biographical: the names of over two-hundred featured speakers were written on cassette cartridges in an extraordinary range of scripts. They offered access to instances of authoritative dissertation by speakers across the political spectrum, including pro-Western reformers such as Kuwaiti entrepreneur Tariq Al-Suwaydan and establishment figures known for supporting the imprisonment of radicalized preachers such as Saudi Chief Jurist 'Abd al-'Aziz Ibn Baz. The titles of such tapes suggested an impressive range of intellectual concerns: "Poetic Magic Produced from Sorcery and the Evil Eye" by Tawfiq Al-Sayigh, "How to Spend Your Vacation" by Riyadh Al-Haqil, "The Truth about Extremism" by Salman Al-'Awda, "Exemplary Rules" by Abu Mus'ab Al-Suri. Other corridors of the labyrinth were geographical: Riyadh, Jeddah, Dammam, Sanaa, Doha, Al-Fuhayhil, and Peshawar were listed on many mass-produced commercial cassettes along with the names, addresses, and telephone numbers of specific production companies. Still other coordinates were visceral: cartridges worn smooth over many years of use, labels ripped off and new ones attached, coils of ribbon spilling out of their shells, spools stripped bare, tapes still glossy from the factory and others smudged with food stains, paint, and dust. Caught up in the details, I struggled to fathom how a single grand origin, personality, or event might represent the collection as a whole. Here were histories that could never be known, whatever the simplicity of the cassette's standard manufacture or the perfection of voice-recognition software.

Then, of course, came the sound. Sermons featured on the majority of cassettes, an oratorical genre much given to swings of passion, despair, and redemption. Delivered into microphones mounted on pulpits, their expression of a single preacher's intent was complicated by the routine surfacing of "backchannel" noises in much larger auditoriums including official sponsors, introductory and concluding speakers, audience responses, questions fielded after the sermons, and even street traffic. Speeches in more private and controlled settings abounded, many of them tailored to specific issues and events and sold afterward for profit by commercial recording companies. Professionally produced Islamic anthems offered lyrics upbeat and dolorous, while Qur'anic recitations directed listeners to inimitable words of God. Although most of the material was in Arabic, some recordings featured Farsi, Pashto, Urdu,

Bengali and Central Asian languages unfamiliar to me. Amateur recordings also loomed large in the collection, these featuring an array of oration and noise that was difficult to categorize: conversations in the cramped quarters of moving taxi cabs, classroom lectures and student-teacher interchange at Arab-Afghan training camps, interviews with well-known Muslim leaders and intellectuals, recorded telephone conversations, recorded radio broadcasts, collective anthem singing, creative radio-dramas about ordinary Muslims involved in combat, weddings, celebrations before and after combat missions, guest-house poetry competitions, and trivia games. If the audio-recorder was an instrument for proselytizing and propaganda, users seemed to find extraordinary urgency and even pleasure in capturing the ordinary sounds of life that threatened to get lost in the larger frame of things.

Much of the value of the collection lies, of course, in its connection with bin Laden himself, or at least with the house he occupied in Kandahar between 1997 and 2001. As diverse as the recordings in the collection are, they offer exceptional insight into the kinds of things bin Laden was listening to in the years leading up to the 11 September attacks in the United States. Tempted though we may be to link specific cassettes and their owner's own intellectual formation, however, influences must be qualified for at least one important reason: bin Laden appears not to have made a regular practice of listening to audiocassettes. In an interview I held with 'Umar bin Laden, who had lived with his father just outside of Kandahar through early 2000, 'Umar told me: "I can't remember one time that my father ever listened to such a tape."

'Umar's assertion could use a little unpacking. At the time, he lived with his father in the family's primary residential compound, located about eighteen miles outside Kandahar in the barracks of an old American-built agricultural base. He admitted to not traveling much with his father during Osama's many engagements and didn't know of the town house. Earlier reports suggest that Osama had at times been an avid enthusiast of audiorecording. During high school, he had cut a mixed-tape featuring Islamic anthems about piety, proper devotion, and Palestine and had distributed it among friends.[4] His talents in singing were later noted by Arab-Afghans.[5] Even during his years in and around Kandahar, Osama seems to have collaborated discretely with fans of audiocassettes. 'Umar's sister Fatima reports an incident in which a friend at their primary residence outside the city wanted to share

THE AUDACIOUS ASCETIC

cassette-recorded anthems with her but held off fearing that her father might adopt the much-reported Taliban practice of destroying audiocassettes and punishing their distributors. Fatima offered reassurance: "My dad is not going to destroy them…He's not really that hard. He just acts like that in front of the men."⁶ 'Umar's account of his father's abstention from listening to audiocassettes suggests less about his father's listening practices than about his well-known tendency to emphasize ascetic discipline among his sons. Even in the company of trusted Arab-Afghan colleagues, bin Laden was known to indulge. Former FBI agent 'Ali Soufan reports that bin Laden had the custom of listening to tapes while being driven around in his Hilux Toyota car:

> Bin Laden usually sat in the rear and listened to tape recorders of the Qur'an, religious lectures, or lectures on other Islamic topics. Other times, he just closed his eyes and relaxed. His repose was only disturbed if Zawahiri, Abu Hafs, Saif Al-'Adel, or another senior al-Qa'ida leader was riding with him, in which case a range of topics might need to be discussed, even operations.⁷

What kind of associations or opportunities for social exchange did this collection facilitate, then, either for bin Laden or for others under his roof? Notes from the collection's provenance may help provide a tentative answer. The residence housing the cassettes was not bin Laden's primary family home in the region but seems rather to have been a kind of guesthouse and office. Bin Laden had a handful of such facilities spread throughout Kandahar and its near vicinity; this one was not even the largest of the guesthouses, nor was it the most secretive. Its distinction lay in its strategic location in a lane directly across the street from the Taliban's foreign ministry office.⁸ It was al-Qa'ida's equivalent at the time of Capitol Hill, although esteemed institutions of statecraft bear poor resemblance: a headquarters and occasional dormitory for bin Laden's top brass during their liasons with Taliban leaders and elites in the city.⁹ Other guesthouses in the city were reserved for the rank and file; the so-called "Arabic House," for example, accommodated recruits from an increasingly diverse range of backgrounds, some of them English-speaking, as they prepared themselves for courses in weapons-training and special operations in camps outside the city.¹⁰ The foreign ministry house was of a higher intellectual order.

It is difficult to know just how much time bin Laden spent in the house. Souring relations with the Taliban haunted its halls from the beginning. Bin Laden's very move to Kandahar had been at the behest of Taliban leader Mulla 'Umar, a commander whose famously ascetic lifestyle made him little known to the outside world of flashing cameras and global news networks. 'Umar appears to have grown wary of bin Laden's tendency to recruit journalists in making grand declarations, drawing him to Kandahar in order to keep watch over him. Within two years of bin Laden's arrival, 'Umar's chief secretary and incumbent minister of foreign affairs Mulla Wakil Ahmad Mutawakkil made no secret of trying to restrict bin Laden's activities in the country.[11] In conversations around 1999, bin Laden complained that "two entities are against our jihad. One is the US, and the other is the Taliban's own foreign affairs ministry."[12]

Within the house itself, bin Laden's other pronouncements on the Taliban and any additional sounds would have been amply muffled: walls along the street were high and thick and the enormous residence itself was wrought of stone masonry.[13] A plethora of high-ranking Taliban families in the neighborhood would have enhanced the need for discretion. Listening to cassettes would have been done with care. "Walkman" players were condemned by Arab-Afghans, their sound being difficult to monitor by the larger social collective and therefore potentially subversive.[14] Speaker-equipped audiocassette players were preferable, although their volume had to be adjusted just enough to avoid raising alarms from conservative Taliban listeners. Listening would have mostly been conducted in small groups or by individuals in semi-private rooms. For the house's largely Arab guests and residents, a host's act of sharing audio recordings was not unusual. Personal cassette collections had been commonplace throughout the Arab world for decades, providing learning as well as enjoyment to owners and their friends. Still, the auditorium in Kandahar was somewhat peculiar. Outside the walls of the house, Taliban edicts banned public music and song and shut down cassette shops. Inside, the act of listening to recorded material would have been a gesture of the host's confidence and trust in listeners. The bond between listeners who could properly monitor their acoustic indulgence would have been pronounced not only due to the use of Arabic, so unusual in a sea of Pashto speakers, but also because of the language's associations with communities of speakers, singers, and listeners across the Arabic-speaking world generally. While present conditions cramped the ear and emphasized a certain withdrawal, listening also underscored a curious outreach to more sympathetic audiences, real or virtual, elsewhere. The cassette's ascetic edge was sharpened while also being qualified. However strange, extreme, or dystopic, recorded material was merely a station along the road to a grander and more public reclamation.

The technology's role in reinforcing social connections is evident on handwritten and printed material accompanying the tapes. Occasionally a relationship with bin Laden himself is made explicit. Side A of cartridge no. 1161 features the words "A Gift to Shaikh Osama bin Laden." While the message is in Arabic, the Islamic anthems featured on the tape, one praising bin Laden's courage in defying America, are in Bengali. Far more frequently, bin Laden proves marginal or altogether absent from the bonds or networks invoked on given tapes. On the back of a cassette jacket announcing a lecture by Saudi preacher Muhammad Al-Shaiha, one note reads "A gift to my honorable brother Ibn al-Mubarak 'Barry' from Muhammad Al-Shaiha." A number of tape cartridges feature more generic screenprinted messages reminding listeners of their fellowship with other listeners. Some are rife with militant symbolism. One cartridge reads "My gift to you" and on the back side "Jihad is the peak of Islam's camel hump" along with paired outlines of a handgun. Other messages are more suggestive of building camaraderie through pious inward struggle:

> Dear Muslim brother and sister: were you pleased by this tape? If your answer is "No" then stop listening to it. If your answer is "Yes" then pass it along as a gift to others in the interests of spreading the good that God desires for you. Youthful distraction, idleness, and all things new corrupt the mind with such scandalous evil.

Working as a kind of prophylactic against the cassette's potential abuse and controversy, the theme of gift-giving repeatedly frames the social relationships made possible by the technology. Whatever differences of opinion might arise when listening to its contents, cassettes express a spirit of generosity realized through reciprocal exchange.

Such evidence, when paired with the vast range of handwritten scripts, the diverse assortment of production companies and the multiple decades covered by recordings in the collection, suggest that the tapes had many histories and were not the result of bin Laden's one-time purchase. In all likelihood, bin Laden had assistants charged with acquiring select tapes and keeping his audio library well stocked. Many tapes seem to have had previous owners, their contributions evident in overlapping and often faded handwritten notes on cartridges: featured names and titles, typically, but also phrases such as "private meeting" (*jalasa khas*), "original" (*asl*), and "volume two." Not infrequently tapes seem to have been recycled: cartridges feature torn labels replaced with new ones, old names and titles scratched out and updated ones penciled in, recent audio recordings interrupted as sounds from other times and places suddenly cut in. The cassettes betray every sign of continuous and fluid exchange, a kind of "swap meet" fervor made personal through gifting, lending, and borrowing. On the day the collection was seized by an Afghan family after the fall of the Taliban, its ever-changing contents were arrested in time and subject to altogether different archival practices. The underground, temperature-controlled vaults at Yale University that now preserve the cassettes could not be further removed from the dusty, hot, and bustling world of Afghan-Arab Kandahar that once contextualized the collection.

It is perhaps obvious from the over 200 featured speakers in the collection that bin Laden himself was relatively marginal to the collection as a whole. The more important and difficult task is to recognize that while the historical value of the collection stems unquestionably from its former location in bin Laden's residential compound, his significance for listeners as an emblem for the Islamic cause at the time was always construed momentarily against a background of highly decentralized and open-ended listening practices. A single recording tells us less about what bin Laden heard or how he thought, in other words, than it does about a relationship that listeners long ago and far away would have been invited to consider, in particular buildings, social occasions and events, as they tried to make sense of bin Laden's aims and credibility as a leader. To grasp something of the way the archive once functioned, we need more than the usual methods for analyzing and translating militant worldviews. We need insights into the ways conjecture about the tapes and their significance was embedded in complex and ever-shifting social worlds.

Those who knew bin Laden well have left occasional notes into the ways such conjecture worked. Bin Laden's bodyguard Nasir Al-Bahri, for example, published memoirs about his experiences as an Arab-Afghan volunteer in which he mentions the significance of audiocassettes in helping him understand the struggle underway and his colleague's unique role as leader. During a three-day "media campaign" organized by bin Laden at the Khost-based Jihad Wal camp in 1997, Al-Bahri recalls being presented with a series of arguments designed to persuade potential recruits to take arms against the United States:

> [Bin Laden] explained to us just how bad things had become on the Arabian Peninsula and sought to persuade us that such affairs were due to American interference in the region…His observations were based on his own personal experience, and this powerful angle opened far-reaching and profound horizons for us concerning that issue. He shed new light on the [compromised] position of religious authorities in Saudi Arabia, the alliance that existed between the Saudi regime and the Islamic salafi movement, and the original call of Shaikh Muhammad Ibn 'Abd al-Wahhab [in the eighteenth century]. We became better informed about these topics thanks to Shaikh Osama and the way he talked.
>
> Given my salafi religious upbringing, of course, I did not agree 100 per cent with Shaikh Osama's words. Still, they suggested the need for further investigation. I began following up on certain matters, contacting people I knew and delving further into books and publications here and there, especially reports and material from the Saudi reform movement. We began to coordinate our thoughts on the case of Shaikh Salman Al-'Awda [who was imprisoned in Saudi Arabia at the time]. We went back and listened to his old recordings, the ones we used to hear in Saudi Arabia such as "From Behind Bars," "Steadfastness Until Death" and "The Inevitability of Confrontation." After that, we began to grasp the meaning of those tapes for the first time. Upon sitting down with one of the leaders of the Saudi reform movement as well as with Shaikh Osama, we began to receive these messages differently, appreciating the issues in new ways. We perceived things more keenly. Given our military backgrounds and experience with weapons, we said: 'What's America?! If we achieved victory against Serbs, Russians, and others through repeated bouts of armed confrontation and military campaigns, America is nothing new.' On many occasions we sat with brothers who had fought the Americans in Somalia. We heard about those who had struck the 'Aden hotel in the early nineties, and about those who had struck American facilities in Riyadh and Khobar. We became convinced that America was not a whit different from the powers that we had fought before. It had been assailed many times from adversaries of every stripe, and every one of its enemies had struck it from behind. So I decided to join Shaikh Osama bin Laden. That was the beginning of my work with the al-Qa'ida organization.[15]

Some militants depict cassettes as a kind of incendiary catapult, a technology that, once unleashed, destroys enemies with the force of collective retribution. Suruqa Al-Andalusi, killed fighting Americans in Tora Bora in December of 2001, writes in one poem:

THE GENIE AND THE BOTTLE

> Your life did change since you had heard
> The tape, "*In the Heart of Green Birds*"
> You sought then to invite others,
> "Jihad is the way my brothers!"
> Rise up and free Islamic land
> From the *kafir's* oppressive hand.[16]

Al-Bahri's narrative suggests, by contrast, that cassettes more often worked in subtler and less straightforward ways. Their significance and implications emerge through repeated stages of collaborative reflection, research, discussion, and listening. Al-Bahri's initial uncertainty about bin Laden and al-Qaʿida is said to have stemmed "from my salafi religious upbringing." Salafism is an instantiation of Muslim reform that emphasizes "unicity" (*tawhid*) and professes homage to the *salaf* or "pious forebears" thought mostly to have lived in the first three generations of Islam's earliest community. Al-Bahri acknowledges that he began to overcome his doubts when listening to Salman Al-ʿAwda's sermon "From Behind Bars," a recording that is featured on cassette no. 94 in the collection. The tape makes sense to Al-Bahri, however, only in relation to a host of other events in which he gathered and processed its contents. These events included hearing at least two other recordings by the same preacher, a three-day anti-American "media campaign" in Khost, close contact with bin Laden himself, bin Laden's "personal experience" and "the way he talked," discussions with colleagues, reading and personal research on the Saudi reform movement, and ongoing conversations with other militants, some of whom had been involved in combat operations against the United States in Somalia, Yemen, and Saudi Arabia. To complicate matters, the sermons he hears on cassette and finds so inspiring are not exactly new to him. He admits having heard them before, though never with such appreciation and clarity. The deeper significance of cassettes emerges only through repeated acts of listening. Their influence stems from having heard them on different occasions and re-evaluating them in light of his own changing circumstances.

Not all who heard the tapes featured in the collection had such immediate connection with bin Laden himself. In fact, very few likely did. Al-Bahri himself complains elsewhere that, even as his personal bodyguard, he found extremely few opportunities actually to sit down with his boss and talk at any length about the tactics of his platform or even the bigger political or moral issues at stake in the struggle.[17] Bin Laden was a busy man and none but his most trusted advisors knew his itinerary on any given day.[18] Reports from Kandahar guesthouses confirm the difficulties most volunteers had in securing an actual meeting with bin Laden, much less a heart-to-heart discussion. Some reported that when visiting his house in the city, they would be informed of his absence and instead directed to a room to watch videotapes of his interviews with CNN, Al-Jazeera, and other news agencies.[19] Others report that upon finally having the chance to converse with him, they hesitated when asked to "sacrifice" themselves for the larger cause, citing their need to deepen their religion first.[20] Even for potential recruits, it seems, a first encounter with bin Laden did not necessarily fuel desire for a second.

As volunteers in Kandahar sought to process bin Laden's point of view and its implications for their own lives, audiocassettes proved to be a valued educational resource. Before or in between training sessions in camps outside the city, volunteers would return to guesthouses for weeks and sometimes months at a time to re-examine their intellectual, ideological, and spiritual commitments, much in the fashion Al-Bahri describes above. In addition to conversations, lectures, and symposiums at guesthouses, audiocassettes proved instrumental, especially for addressing topics that were considered too controversial, parochial, or esoteric for public gatherings. Access to cassettes in guesthouses was especially valuable since camp rules forbade the use of tape recorders once on their premises, no doubt to focus trainees' attention on camp instruction and restrict quarrelling over "extracurricular" issues.[21] Audio recording did take place at the camps, as is evident from tape no. 1111, discussed in chapter eight, and from volumes in the collection featuring training camp instruction at Al-Faruq, among other locations. Volunteers managed such recording carefully, however, and most such recordings appear to be have been circulated in fairly restricted social networks.[22] Guesthouses protocol offered easier ways to sound out.

In trying to assess the significance of bin Laden's cassette collection, then, and gauge its function for Arab-Afghans in the city at the time, a host of factors complicate generalization. A single tape's presence in the collection, even if once housed under bin Laden's roof, provides no window into the man's mind or the attitudes of those who listened to the recordings. The tapes are valuable as historical records, however, and invite considerations of the collection's probable usage in a particular time and place. For Arab-Afghans in Kandahar from 1997–2000, the collection offered the possibility of a more personal and comprehensive understanding of bin Laden's views, interests, and leadership, one not available to the same degree from cassette shops in the city that marketed his speeches or other official media outlets. The archive promised glimpses into the real bin Laden's mission, however much this conceit lay obscured in the archive's many volumes and sounds. Still, it is the differences in bin Laden's figuration over time that I am interested in and they, to a large extent, have provided the central theme of this chapter. Whatever we may think of bin Laden now, it is important to remember the particular ways his influence was conceptualized during the heyday of his rise to power. Such difference is thrown into relief by the unique and easily overlooked technology of the audiocassette, the social dimensions of which are worth summarizing in six points.

First, cassette culture flourishes through collegial swapping. Whatever the collection reveals about bin Laden's listening preferences or worldview, specific tapes were deposited in the collection as loans and "gifts" to bin Laden as well as other individuals whose connections with him were loose or non-existent. The generic manufacture and presence of diverse handwritten labels on roughly four-fifths of tape cartridges suggests, moreover, the off-market origins of tapes, or at least their provenance from small-scale cassette shops marketing knock-offs of more expensive screen-printed originals. In this respect, the collection suggests less about bin Laden himself and his elaborate propaganda apparatus than about the interests and concerns of a broader Arabic-speaking community of volunteers in and beyond Kandahar, not all of whom shared bin Laden's views. Some featured speakers are known to have publicly denounced bin Laden and al-Qaʿida. They include the former Grand Mufti of Saudi Arabia ʿAbd al-ʿAziz Ibn Baz, for example, who openly backed the Saudi royalty's decision to solicit military and strategic assistance from the United States and Western powers after Saddam's invasion of Kuwait in 1990. They also include militants who later recanted, such as Salman Al-ʿAwda who, upon release from Saudi prison in 1999, renounced militancy and voiced strong condemnation of bin Laden and other jihadis who took up arms. The inclusion of such critics, even if through selective sampling, suggests the collection's indebtedness to multiple contributors. The range of voices and diverse provenance of the tapes situate bin Laden as a relatively minor player on larger intellectual battlefields. If anything, the collection conveys an image more of bin Laden as an aspiring guesthouse student than as a propagandist using the cassette medium to force his ideas on others.

Second, the audiocassette captures sound, especially speakers talking to live audiences. In this sense, cassettes invite audiences to associate with speech events that they didn't witness first hand, to envision themselves as part of a group of fellow listeners. Even when a single cassette is mass-marketed and sold in shops across the world, as was the case for many of 'Azzam's recordings as well as those of Ibn Baz and to an extent bin Laden himself, the sounds of given recordings are meant to engage listeners' sense of personal responsibility to a community that is "glocal" in essence: both global in its cast as a single pious community (*umma*) and localized in specific countries, towns, mosques, and streets. One studio-recorded conclusion, appended to a lecture by a Syrian theologian well-known among Arab-Afghans, illustrates the nature of this call:

> My brother Muslim: the Library of the Audible Qur'an in Abha [Saudi Arabia] greets you and hopes you found listening to this tape conducive to productive learning and good work. Please forgive any artistic lapses in the recording. Should you encounter them let us know so that we may fix them, may God accept our efforts. My honorable Muslim brother: the Islamic tape is a means to exalted ends. We need your support in reaching these ends. Should you learn of an impending Islamic lecture by one of the learned Muslim scholars, we urge you to inform us at least twenty-four hours before the event so that we can record the occasion in the service of all. With greetings from The Library of the Audible Qur'an in Abha, located in front of the Abu Bakr Al-Sadiq mosque in the Al-Manhal quarter. Telephone number 07–224–8192.

Wherever his actual location, the listening "brother" (the "sister" is heralded too on other tapes) is summoned to take up the cause not only as a pious receiver and activist but as a co-producer of communal audio recording. Rooted in Abha, Saudi Arabia, the community can imaginably be established anywhere, even through a single phone call.

Third, by virtue of the audiocassette's service to communally managed verbal exchange, whether real or imagined, the technology offers users a way to rally community activists along a different set of guidelines than those facilitated through other media technologies, especially visual electronic media such as the television and internet. At a basic level, the difference of cassettes from global visual media is a function of language: without accompanying visual cues, the technology's contents are of interest largely to those who can understand the languages featured on the tape. Even for native speakers, however, region-specific dialects, colloquial expressions, and references to speech events not readily appreciated by outside audiences require somewhat specialized or in-group knowledge, no more so than for amateur productions not designed to circulate widely. The implications of such opacity are evident in the ways CNN originally handled the tapes. In the months following the 11 September attacks, videotapes of training camp activities acquired in and around Kandahar were put to immediate use by the news agency, providing world audiences with their first glimpses of al-Qa'ida's activities in the region. The audiotapes, by contrast, sat on their shelves for over a year, and after being reviewed by American intelligence personnel, were sold to Williams College. Even after Yale University acquired the tapes in the summer of 2006, their digitalization for public researchers took over five years to complete, a delay largely due to the gap between the university library's high standards of archival preservation and the tapes' original dusty and sometimes warped condition. Throughout the technology's history, one can find cassette users taking advantage of the medium's "resistance" to uptake in broader circuits of print and visual media. Al-Qa'ida and other militant organizations have pressed the cassette into serving their own particular agendas. In his monumental opus *Call to Global Islamic Resistance*, the jihadi theoretician Abu Mus'ab Al-Suri, once top-level advisor to bin Laden and featured on at least eight tapes in the collection, acknowledges that until as late as 2004 he preferred disseminating his views through audiocassettes titled with aliases and pseudonyms. At that point, he changed his media strategy and began posting his lectures on the internet for one simple reason: the United States announced a $5 million dollar reward for information leading to his arrest. It was only once his name and influence had been broadcast to global audiences that he felt compelled to unpack his worldview for anyone outside his community of audio acolytes.[23] Bin Laden's own preference for releasing statements on audiotape rather than videos suggests that however much global media networks might broadcast and speculate on his global media presence, he too found the medium productive for signaling more covert forms of in-group solidarity.

Fourth, the built-in recording capacity on audiocassette players makes cassettes "user-friendly" by design. The effects of such utility are political as well as aesthetic. Available for use by people who are not usually represented on mainstream or state-controlled media networks, cassettes have long been a favorite medium for oppressed groups as well as minorities. Over multiple decades, cassettes presented considerable censorship challenges to authoritarian regimes. Political criticism set to lyrics and accompanying music was an especially tricky affair, both less serious for being "entertaining" as well as especially volatile given the ways popular songs could travel. Today, state censors have increasingly shifted their attention to monitoring digital and electronic media. To a great extent, however, cassettes had long presented a critical difference from other more public and "modern" mass-media technologies such as newspapers, printed books, television and, by the 1990s, the internet. In contrast to the authority of the visual, cassettes offered the possibility of noises without image, voices without visual identification, soundscapes devoid of conventional geographic markers. Even when compared to other strictly audio media technologies, from centralized state-run radio to garage band software programs, cassettes lend themselves to preserving especially complex "voice prints," a result of built-in recording mechanisms that, for all their attraction to non-specialists, also document a whole host of supplemental material. Aside from the fact that most recordings are made outside of professional studios, from crowded domestic spaces to mosque auditoriums to open-air settings teeming with midnight crickets, tapes also reflect the fumbling and incomplete tape-overs of previous users. Such material only heightens the listener's sense of participation in a collaborative and highly circumstantial community of fellow strugglers. Little wonder that when juxtaposed to the professional and seamless flow of Westernized global media programming, audiocassettes have provided a curious redoubt for resistance.

Fifth, in light of the cassette's gradual decline among world media technologies and, for some generations, absolute redundancy, cassette recordings are likely to evoke a certain edginess among audiences today. The cultural registers of edgy sound production are difficult to encapsulate; they include overlapping and sometimes contradictory sentiments of nostalgia, kitschiness, otherness, indigeneity, tenacity, authenticity, and fin-de-siécle promiscuity. In the case of bin Laden's collection, the edgy quality of the tapes was inflected as especially Arabic in Pashto-speaking heartlands, Saudi in an Arab-Afghan movement largely represented by Yemenis, Egyptians, and Algerians, boorish in a Wahhabi legal discourses overshadowed by establishment scholars from the Najd, transnational in narratives of modern identity emphasizing home-grown authenticity, dissident in the annals of Arab state authorities who had at some time imprisoned many of the speakers on the tapes, and extremist in the growth of international consensus about bin Laden's status as a prime financier of terrorism. For al-Qaʿida's supporters and would-be recruits who listened to the tapes, the collection offered a valued repository for recalling years of suffering and persecution. They also offered curious strains of hope that dramatized scenarios of survival against all odds, defiance in the face of crippling tyranny and fantastic self-actualization beyond all the constraints of humdrum mortal exigency. That these experiences were to be accessible largely through ascetic withdrawal toward a strangely primordial Arab community was not something to give pause. The necessity of practicing hatred and violence at the expense of others to defend this community seemed justified by its unparalleled victimization. Bin Laden played host to this wellspring of vitriol, giving body to its currents. His frequent absence from the house and from discussions about its deeper significance paradoxically enhanced this performance. Militant commanders and strategists who looked to bin Laden for guidance were well familiar with his lack of systematic ideology or organizational platform. He was the son of a multi-millionaire entrepreneur, after all: while an excellent business manager with a solid work ethic and an often generous purse, he also bore the marks of a heterogeneous intellect and a passion for wilderness survival. His voice conveyed the essence of the man. Stoic, monotone, and intimate, his oratory fell far short of the grandiloquent standards of preachers who had polished their craft speaking from pulpits to large audiences. Bin Laden instead conveyed the impression of addressing smaller, more reclusive audiences from private, informal, and even domestic spaces. The low-definition recording capacity of the audiocassette player, for all its archaicism, captured and broadcast this intimacy well. From the cassette's small cartridge, a voice produced from withdrawal and absence amplified the severity of Islam's modern struggles and the urgency for new political vocabularies.

Sixth and perhaps most telling, cassettes are not meant to last. Made of cheap plastic and affordably priced, the technology is typically handled and stored by customers in ways that suggest its limited half-life. In the Islamic world, written and printed documents tend to be preserved in folders and cabinets; books are a measure of erudition, their finer volumes embossed in leather and displayed for guests; digital media are kept stored on home computers that are gingerly treated and represent considerable investment. Cassettes, by contrast, often sold without accompanying plastic cartridges, are tucked on odd shelves around the house, clustered in cardboard boxes and sacks or wedged into dashboard compartments. Occasional rare recordings aside, cassettes fall well shy of the luxury item. If a single medium ever signaled asceticism, the cassette might be a contender were it not for its sheer mundaneness, its almost built-in immunity from anything suggesting the extraordinary. The Afghan stringer who worked for CNN at the time of the collection's acquisition originally found the tapes in a run-down Kandahari cassette shop. The owner of the shop had indeed found the cassettes useful, though not for their contents: he was planning to re-use their cartridges for Afghan pop songs, a genre of considerable more interest to his clientele in the wake of the Taliban's fall from power. The near complete erasure of bin Laden's archive underscores the extent to which cassettes of tremendous value to one community might, undervalued as historical records, be considered insignificant to another community nearby.

The cassette collection rests today in an underground storage facility in New Haven, Connecticut, home of Yale University's Sterling Library. Their contents are no longer so user-friendly. Any possibility of their over-recording or erasure has been eliminated by their digitalization and back-up on computer servers. Thanks to the investments of a distinguished American university, bin Laden's voice, along with many other pronouncements and sounds in the rest of the collection, are now permanently available for research and citation. As important as these recordings are to mapping the trajectory of bin Laden's intellectual world and changes in his rhetoric over the years, we would do well to remember their humble origins. The power of the audiocassette and its audible material never derived from its compatibility with global systems of data management or public record. Responsive to shifting social worlds, the cassette provided political communities with a platform for registering values and potential commitments that was effective because of its impermanence. Useful especially when consensus about identity or common purpose was difficult to achieve, the cassette provided users with a tool for building solidarity and trust precisely because, more often then not, it captured speeches and sound events that were not presumed equally germane to all listeners. The revolutionary potential of the cassette lay in intimating that local and occasional matters might become more permanent. Difficult to censor and notoriously indifferent to state-regulated hierarchies of authority, cassettes worked in favor of the genie: group identity and action might well transcend the logic of the master's voice or even the drift of history itself. The genie's magic came straight out from the bottle. When we forget his origins we grant wholly new dimensions to his power.

5

OUR PRESENT REALITY (*WAQIʿUNA AL-MUʿASIR*)

(Late summer/fall 1989 speech by Osama bin Laden in Saudi Arabia.[1] Beginning of cassette no. 507 along with concluding excerpts from nos. 504 and 493.)

———

[*Sounds of a trickling mountain brook. A young man begins speaking as the water track gradually fades.*]

In the name of God, the Compassionate and Caring. Peace and God's mercy and blessings upon you. My brother and sister listeners: we greet you and wish you beneficial knowledge and good deeds. We are happy to present to you the contents of this tape. With greetings from our brothers at Islamic Emigration Recordings in Al-Thuqba [Saudi Arabia]…

[*An anonymous speaker introduces bin Laden, mentioning that the talk is sponsored by the Saudi National Guard's Department of Religious Affairs. Bin Laden then steps up to the microphone.*]

Praise be to God who has guided us to this, and we would not have been guided had He not guided us Himself. Praise be to God who bestowed upon us the grace of Struggle in the path of God so we may defend this great banner, the banner of "There is no god but God alone, and Muhammad is His Messenger."

Today we will talk, God willing, about our present reality and the role of Struggle in defending this banner. The subject of today is a very dangerous one: never before has the Islamic world experienced such a time as this. Throughout the entirety of Islamic history, apostasy of such scale and design

123

has been unknown. The apostasy that occurred after [Muhammad's] death, God's blessings and salutations upon him, cannot be compared to that being committed today. We face a dangerous disbelief orchestrated by global apostasy from east to west. It was planned, decades ago, with the aim of subjecting the Islamic world to laws other than those revealed by God. Leaks from their documents indicate that the last of their raids will target the Land of the Two Holy Sanctuaries, may God guard and preserve it, with His permission.

Look around you. The Muslim must not be heedless of the fact that disbelievers surround us as they seek to spread the banner of heresy (*ilhad*). They want to substitute the banner of disbelief for the banner "There is no god but God alone."

The matter is very dangerous. Words do not permit me to describe its danger; it is even more dangerous than what I will be able to demonstrate to you. Look carefully around you.

[*Two gunshots are fired just outside the lecture hall, echoing through auditorium.*]

In the north...

[*Another gunshot stops bin Laden mid-speech. He hesitates as another voice remarks: "It's nothing." Sounds of a tapping microphone are then heard, and then bin Laden resumes.*]

Yes, today's disbelief has surrounded the Land of the Two Holy Sanctuaries like a bracelet coiled upon the wrist. We ask God to liberate Muslims everywhere and to protect our Two Holy Sanctuaries, a site from whence the Prophet, God's blessings and salutations upon him, set out on his Night Journey in full view and earshot of many of us who, upon reaching puberty, began penning writings about it afterwards.[2]

[*Long pause, a baby crying in the background.*]

Yes my brothers, I am not telling you secrets. The disbelief being considered today is one of extraordinary audacity and insolence. They openly declare their disbelief. From your east comes an open disbelief that declares its desire to rule the Land of the Two Holy Sanctuaries through [Shi'a] Rejectionism [*rafidiyya*]. We ask God to protect the Two Sanctuaries from them. Even though they lost their first military round, they continue to strive toward corruption on earth, spreading misguided principles and preparing themselves for other rounds to come.

[*Gunshot.*] And those empathetic with them [*gunshot*]; and those empathetic with them are also the ones who turn away from the oppressed, whether men, women, or children. They openly declare their disbelief. Their slogans? Tune into the media broadcasts, if you wish. Their slogans are: "One Arab community with an everlasting message: 'Unity, Freedom, Socialism'!" Open disbelief! They want to apply the principles of the red louts in Russia instead of the Book of God Almighty and the moral pathway of his Messenger, God's blessings and salutations upon him.

What does "one Arab community" mean? "One Arab community!?" They want this Arab community to be torn from the Islamic world and united under the rule of false freedom and disbelieving socialism. [*Gunshot.*] On this [*gunshot as a child bursts into tears*] On this they raise their children [*child crying*] and soldiers. This is their slogan in every administrative district and primary school. It's not simply that the oppressed in various countries, sons of Muslims, are compromised when practicing their faith every morning; sons of Muslims line up in school facing someone who directs them toward error and disbelief, reciting the slogan I mentioned to you as they repeat it and are taught that they bind this land together [*gunshot*], may God guard it. They desire to rule the Two Holy Sanctuaries, may God and their Lord disgrace them, and covet the oil of this land, oil that, we implore God, may allay the expenses of securing victory for this religion, as indeed it is the largest oil reserve in the world.

The entity that I am talking about has not crossed its arms idly. It is planning and doing what will facilitate its aims, spreading these destructive ideas in many parts of the Islamic world and in some of the countries that surround us. And then there are those who empathize with their style. Among those who empathize with them are Christians who want to rule Islamic lands with Christianity. Among those who empathize with them are Jews who remain undaunted by events of the past year. [*Gunshot.*] They threaten to gain possession over these lands; they threaten to bind these lands together. Their plots are well known. They sew them night and day, conducting their children toward military service while we conduct our children toward useless pursuits. As you well know, their path will not end until they have reached the city of God's Messenger [Madina], God's blessings and salutations upon him. We ask God to protect it from them.

If all of this lies before you, and disbelief is what they have envisioned, global apostasy working in their favor, then look around in wonderment. Is there not, on the Peninsula of the Arabs—the Peninsula of Islam on which no two religions can co-exist according to the text of the words of God's Messenger, God's blessings and salutations upon him—here, in the south of the Peninsula, open disbelief seeking to rule? There is no power or might except through God! When people abandoned the Struggle, they fell to the rule of Communism. Although they called it Socialism, they are the same people who wrote, in broad strokes across every administrative district and even on mountains: "No voice transcends the voice of the [Communist] party." We say "God is Greater!" They want to rule people by laws other than those revealed by God. The purest Arabs follow the red louts, disciples of Marx and Lenin—There is no power or might except through God!—and they now threaten to take possession of these lands too.

And I have said, the matter is even more dangerous than I have told you. If you follow the newspapers you would hear and read about the events covered by the press in these lands. Even our neighbors want to attack us until we are obliged to sign non-aggression pacts with them. Do you believe that they will keep their promises, those ephemeral Baʿathists? No, by God!

What have we done, then, by way of preparing to support this banner? The banner of "There is no god but God alone and Muhammad is his Messenger"? I need not tell you about the disbelief that is in the Philippines: it is an open disbelief that is far away, making it difficult for people to go there to support this banner. On the Arabian Peninsula, by contrast, we have no one left but you. They never stop thinking about you, though you remain negligent. Those Baʿathists who are north of you [in Iraq] drafted more than one million people for military service and enlisted more than six hundred thousand paramilitary troops. [*Several gunshots.*] Instead of recruiting from their own people, moreover, they brought in outsiders to do various jobs. They have been preparing for this. All sects of disbelievers are preparing for this while we remain heedless about what you [in fact] know already, except those upon whom God has shown mercy.

The people of this worldly life are immersed in this world. The people of Islam and good work [*gunshot*], by contrast, have practiced every good deed except protecting the integrity of this religion. No one mourns this! There is no power or might except through God. How then can we establish the truth after the paths to truth have become so obscured, especially given our issuance to a time in which every good deed is recognized except the loftiest summit (*dhirwat al-sanam*) of this religion? The path to good deeds now leads in every direction except toward the sword and spear, as on the day of Badr devoted to the support of this religion. Religion is advice, brothers and community of Islam. Our situation today is like those who are on a boat: if we keep quiet we will all drown, while if we give advice we would fulfill our duty.

So what is the path to establishing the truth, defeating falsehood, cutting off the roots of disbelievers and stopping their harm? What is the path? This religion has already been perfected. God had not left his slave abandoned or astray but has illuminated the path through clear verses in the Noble Qurʾan and through the customary acts of our Messenger, God's blessings and salutations upon him, as well as of the [first four] Rightly Guided Caliphs. Still, among the puzzles is expounding upon what is most clear. Is such heedlessness conceivable given that the matter is even clearer than the sun at its zenith?

One can be confused, but this is reality. I ask God, Glorious and Exalted is He, to bless Muslims and their efforts to protect the last of Islam's strongholds. They have planned for it to be the final stronghold, a place where, if a woman were to cry out in these lands saying "Oh, my Islam!" [*gunshot*] not a single savior from neighboring lands would hear! Our neighbors would have become the very people seeking our destruction, may God will it otherwise.

The path toward establishing the truth: this is our present reality. I need not decipher runes for you. You know that what I am saying is sound. [*Gunshot.*] The question is the easiest one could ask. [*Gunshot.*] Healthy recovery begins by asking it.

[*Gunshots ringing out in the background, bin Laden expounds on the urgency of armed jihad with a story of heroes who, despite their initial reluctance, fought the henchmen of seventh-century Meccan merchants in the battle of Badr. He continues with a story of the Prophet Muhammad's refusal to show clemency to non-believing hypocrites, and commends Abu Bakr for compelling apostate tribes to pay tithes. Having framed jihad as both an economic and military struggle, he returns to the issue of corruption on the Arabian Peninsula.*]

Let me say this: we have abandoned and neglected to take the path followed by God's Messenger, God's blessings and salutations upon him, along with the noble Companions in stopping the disbelievers' harm and bringing the apostates back to God's religion. There is no power or might except through God. Listen to what he did, may God be pleased with him. [Abu Bakr] said [of the fighters who fought the apostates] "By God, even had they bound me with a hobble, they still would have sought God's Messenger, God's blessings and salutations upon him, to struggle against them!" Abu Bakr was a witness: "to Struggle against them!" So the brigades followed him as he dispatched horse upon horse, soldiers upon soldier to the Peninsula of Islam. He reclaimed its farthest territories through struggle in the path of God.

Today, however, apostasy has returned without anyone recognizing it. We ask God to help us drive the disbelievers from Muslims' lands. You have been shown the path. Muslims must be prepared with these two great principles: true faith with no uncertainty or doubt, and struggle in the path of God by means of one's wealth and soul, one of the most notable characteristics of believers. God says, Glorious and Exalted is He, "Only the believers who have placed faith in God and His Messenger and have never since doubted, but have striven with their wealth and souls in the path of God: Such are the sincere ones."[3] The issue requires sincerity and trust in what lies in God, Glorious and Exalted is He, and in His promise that if we die we will be admitted into heaven. That is enough for the martyr (*shahid*) in the path of God, who looks toward God's mercy and satisfaction.

God says, Glorious and Exalted is He: "But those who are slain in the path of God: He will never let their deeds be lost. Soon will He guide them and improve their condition and admit them to the heaven that He has announced for them"[4]…

I have said what I have said. No Muslim should delude themselves in thinking that these lands, may God preserve them, lack enough power to bring the entire Islamic world back to the religion of God under this great banner. By God, there are real men here! People believe that those great men of the past, the Companions of the Messenger of God, blessings and salutations upon him, paid no attention to the [disbelieving] Arabs at the time until they began declaiming "There is no god but God alone and Muhammad is His Messenger" while raising their swords and spears in support of this religion. When they raised these weapons in faith and Struggle, nothing could stand in their way; neither the great states nor the small, Persians nor Byzantines. They all disintegrated before faith and the struggle. No Berber, Mongol, Turk, Sudani, or Frank: all of them disintegrated when your ancestors on this peninsula practiced their faith and undertook the struggle.

And today, may God reward the youth. I ask God to accept those killed among them as martyrs, to heal their wounded and ill, and to lend support to those standing up to struggle in support of this religion. They went there [to Afghanistan] not for this world or for a woman, desirous of marriage. They had no land there, no relatives, no commerce, or share in profits. All they had was tranquility in their hearts from their love of "There is no god but God alone." So they went to the rescue carrying weapons in support of this banner. No river or mountain constrained them! No quicksand, seas, or rivers! They went to the rescue, raising the heads of Muslims and spreading hope once again. How they remind us of those great men, may God be pleased with them. They are from this Peninsula. A person would never have thought this possible, given how these lands were distracted with such luxury that a man could almost be ashamed, by God, when traveling across these lands and seeing what was before him, when he left his house. Such corruption tarnishing the reputation of these pure lands! And if he raised issue with any of this, fingers would point at him, as still happens in this or that country, in those countries of disbelievers that are disposed to sin and debauchery, except those upon whom God has shown mercy. There is no power or might except through God. They changed the whole picture. They changed everything that people used to imagine was even possible…

[In order to provide further historical context for the terrible costs of Muslim hypocrisy, bin Laden details the thirteenth-century conquest of Baghdad by Moguls. Although Moguls were self-proclaimed Muslims at the time, bin Laden draws attention to the fact that an estimated 800,000 native Muslims died at their hands. He cites the following Prophetic report (hadith) to admonish listeners against pursuing their own material interests at the expense of military preparedness: "If people were to follow the deceptive way of dinars and dirhams and pledge allegiance [to a ruler] for material wealth and were to follow the tails of cows and let go of jihad, God would afflict disgrace upon them." Returning to the present, he laments the deaths of several of his closest camarades, Shafiq

OUR PRESENT REALITY (*WAQI'UNA AL-MU'ASIR*)

Al-Madani and Ahmad Al-Zahrani, during recent fighting against Afghan President Muhammad Najibulla's forces outside of Jalalabad.]

Talking about this could go on, and I can't summarize four years in a few minutes. I'll mention only a few examples. Among them, as I've mentioned, was the brother Shafiq [Al-Madani], and also our brother Ahmad bin 'Abdalla bin Yahya Al-Zahrani, a young man who was less than twenty years old. The likes of him are strolling in the streets of Muslim lands and elsewhere. He set forth, may God grant him mercy, to support this Struggle, and God, Glorious and Exalted is He, granted him exactly what he had requested. He had asked God, Glorious and Exalted is He, for the boon of martyrdom, and had asked to be struck in his chest. By the will of God, Glorious and Exalted is He, when we put him in his grave in the region where we had been: may God grant him mercy, by God I found his body intact and healthy, except for the one spot to which he had pointed. God grant him mercy. Their examples are many. I remember one of them, our brother Muhammad Al-'Azman, from the community in this very region. May God grant him a magnificent gain, along with eight of his brothers when they surrounded the "Commandos," once called the Russians' most elite forces. They saw themselves as invincible. The world media fed them this illusion, declaring that the Russians and Americans could never be defeated and that we should not even think about it. God allowed Muslims in Afghanistan to destroy this legend, however. This young man joined eight others, four of whom had memorized God's Book by heart. They set forth under the leadership of brother Abu 'Ubayda, a man who had also committed the Text to heart, may God honor him. They forced the Russians to a stop…

[*Shortly later tape 507 ends. Tapes 504 and 493 resume, however, completing the lecture.*]

And I remember a recent incident that occurred on the tenth of *Dhu Al-Hijja* in the year that just passed, 1409 [in the Islamic calendar; equivalent to CE1989]. One of our brothers was named Salih Al-Ghamdi. After driving back the disbelievers, he signaled that Muslims were low on ammunition—this is something that had to do be done—and he directed our brothers to securing the ammunition with the assistance of strong reinforcements. They then advanced to an exultant state of victory, having the good fortune to reclaim four kilometers of territory that contained a lot of rubble and a few trees, these being favorable to obstructing tank movement. After the [Afghan] strugglers and the [Arab] brothers had grouped together, they attacked from the rear once again. They drove the enemy back just one hour before dusk. That night the tanks were in an extremely compromised position, especially in the areas of ruins, trees, and mountains. They then assailed them from an area of dunes. At that point, we had a brother from Jeddah named Yusef Ba Khayda who was shouldering an 82mm anti-tank gun.

By the grace of God, he hit his target perfectly and the tank exploded. So too one of our Afghan brothers struck another tank with a MILAN rocket. Another struggler nailed a third tank, and it too exploded by the grace of God. The clashes continued late into the night, until about midnight. After the brothers performed their morning prayers, they conducted reconnaissance to locate other tank positions. They found these positions vacated, by God's grace, God having struck terror into the hearts of the disbelievers.

At that point, our brother Salih Al-Ghamdi, along with a brother from Egypt named Samir, managed to get on top of one of the tanks: a T-62 tank containing enemy soldiers that was parked on some rubble. They had just scaled this tank, by the grace of God—having previously trained themselves with captured tanks acquired earlier—and as they climbed quickly on top, they threw a hand grenade at the enemy. They were specialists and professionals, even if they had less than ten years experience. Brother Salih had been a student in a technical school, focusing on welding. God gave him good fortune, and he fired off a shot at the opponent. The opponent fired back. The brothers fired back again, and on the fourth shot, God gave our brother the good fortune of dropping a bomb down the barrel of the tank. The bomb did not finish them off, for it was a rapid-detonation device called the *Shifa* that was designed not to destroy the entire tank. With that, however, God struck terror into their hearts and the soldiers fled. The brother Salih Al-Ghamdi, God bless him, then went to this tank, carrying his Klashnikov. He then brought the T-62 tank to the brothers' camp, an outpost named Ahmad Al-Zahrani, war booty for the Muslims, by the grace of God.

There are many narratives like this. I don't want to go on since I want to leave time for questions. I only want to tell you this: there are Muslims everywhere who are killing and fighting, in Palestine, before our very eyes and ears, in the spot where our Prophet, blessings and salutations upon him, ascended on his Night Journey. We come together to fight for freedom, seeking to reclaim Palestine, and yet all this has come to naught. The path incites the entire pious community to struggle and preparation. Through this, with God's permission, we will be able to awaken victory against the siege on our brothers in Palestine. The dismemberment of Muslims has spread across the earth, their blood on every patch of land and field. The earth has exploded into flame from the sheer quantity of killing and slaughtering on it. So much so that if the earth defecated, it would find itself constipated from the bulk of blood and body parts.

The cheapest blood these days is Muslim. As one poet said, reminding us of our Muslim brothers across this earth. Despite the fact that the earth has been clogged, we have yet to meet our obligation. The poet says [*sighing*], reminding Muslims—as though he had been with us in Afghanistan, recalling the state of the brothers who were killed and injured—alongside us he says:

OUR PRESENT REALITY (*WAQI'UNA AL-MU'ASIR*)

The soil is drenched with the blood of victims
    While the battleground rages ablaze
As misguided soldiers conspire in the dark
    Their righteous confreres march forth
And lo! The Al-Aqsa Mosque [in Jerusalem]
    In imprisonment, the sincerest ones are shackled
Responding to their call, which resounds in every heart
    A believer thrusts forth the spear
[*Repeating the above four verses, he then continues.*]
Were I to cry out, I would ask the first of them:
    Don't you see how they hear my cry?
Then from the barren wastelands
    A spring of purest water appears
Gushing forth with the banners of men bent on sacrifice
    And of righteous champions
And it says: Should the initial offer fall short
    We will sacrifice ourselves for religion
Such victory! Victory for the blood-stained, their bodies soaked with wounds
    Refusing to forsake their homes for wanton bargains
Loathing life if one of humiliation and ruin[5]

The poet goes on as if to explain how some of our brothers were killed as they fought. Through most of the poem, he says:

They descend upon it pleasurably, like the wing-clipped falcon
    Their plunging wreaks destruction and thunder across the lands
I saw their vestments of blood as a sash most brilliant
    Their cleft visages a tale of battle for those nearby
Their incense infused the air like a flower at its prime
    My sympathy for his gushing nose-wound redoubled my own wounding
As if tears streamed across my cheek: O soul! O wine!
Have you not shown compassion to our hearts and accompanied us on this
        journey?
The courageous hero, beneath a shroud, answered me with a piece of advice:
    Hold back your tears, I find no comfort in your worthy gesture
This is a path: if you trust it with your love then pick up a weapon

I will not draw on. I've clarified for you how Muslims have been afflicted. I can't emphasize enough the extent to which you must rally to prepare yourselves to support this religion. May you give glory to God and praise Him. I attest that there is no god but God alone. We ask his forgiveness and repent unto Him.

[*A moderator steps up, elaborating briefly on bin Laden's call to arms. Bin Laden then begins to field questions from the audience. When asked whether a forty-five day training camp program could really equip Muslims with skills necessary for the longer fight, bin Laden defends the program in terms of its value for the individual recruit and not solely for the community. Through camp training, one could experience the kind of "purgation" (yatamahhas) described in the Qur'an: "God's object also is to purge those that are true in faith and to deprive of blessing those that resist faith."*]

[*Moderator, summarizing several questions fielded from the audience.*] Why do your speeches tend to focus on Afghanistan and overlook Palestine? The questioners urgently request more attention be given to the issue of Palestine, to support for the pious community, and to the 'Children of the Stones.' Please direct your discussion to the struggle in Palestine instead of to every other part of Muslim lands.

[*Bin Laden*] May God love you all, my brothers. We ask God to make us struggling believers, just as he granted such fortune to our Messenger, God's blessings and salutations upon him. With regards to the question, we have previously spoken about the situation of our brothers in Palestine and what afflicts them, and about our obligation to prepare ourselves for protecting what remains of the three mosques and for reclaiming what has slipped away, namely the site of our Prophet's Night Journey [in Jerusalem], God's blessings and salutations upon him. None of this will happen without combined efforts and continued preparation to lift the siege on our brothers. Muslims today must do everything they can to support their brothers in Palestine. From this perspective, the matter is very simple. Whoever doesn't help, well, I don't know what to say to them.

It is no secret to the discerning observer, no assault on the bounds of reason, that Americans, God shame them, are the ones who are supporting the Jews. Their treasury has unleashed weapons, enemies, and wealth to the Jew in Palestine. We must fight them as best we can. We must boycott their goods, from the perspective of economic war. America is one of our creditors. A man of discernment might say: how much does it matter if we purchase a $50,000 American car? No! Have you and your brothers not flourished by protecting this religion? This $50,000 puts their laborers to work! The American balance of trade is bolstered by taxes from this and other sales. In this way, they take our wealth, giving it to the Jews who slaughter our brothers. Boycott every one of their products! No one should require you to purchase an American car, air conditioner, clothes, or even American apples, food products, childrens' toys or such things. This is the least we can do, and is on the smallest scale. I advise all Muslims, and especially women, to remind their spouses to pay attention to these issues. By God's grace, God has given us the good fortune to have paid some attention to this matter for some time now. After we drew attention to this issue on the heels of the Intifada, may God protect and support them, American products have been boycotted. We don't buy American apples, pens, cars or other such things.

I think that this is the least we can do on the smallest scale. May God support and protect our brothers there…

[*Moderator summarizes another question.*] There are some questions being asked, although most of them are based on rumors fueled by newspapers and magazines. They suggest that the fighting going on in Afghanistan is between Muslims themselves and that what is happening is a civil war in the aftermath of the Russian departure. There are many rumors to this effect. Could you please comment?

[*Bin Laden*] We've discussed this before. It is not permissible to generalize judgment about a single tribe containing some members who are Muslim and others who are disbelievers or apostates. Some people suggest that the general judgment should be that all of the tribe's members are apostates. If this were so, what would we say of entire populations or tribes containing both Muslims and disbelievers, both those who follow in the footsteps of the Prophet, God's blessings and salutations upon him, and those who innovate and fabricate in matters of belief and practice? It is not appropriate to deliver a general judgment. Rather, our obligation is to fight the disbelievers and also the polytheists. God only knows [their destiny]…

[*Moderator summarizes another question.*] A lot of people who used to offer humanitarian assistance for orphans, or who used to send help or travel [to Afghanistan] are saying that some have stopped doing these things under the pretext, believed by some, that America and other nations are [already] helping the mujahidin and supplying them with funds and weapons. The questioner asks that you please clarify this matter: is this help real or simply a rumor?

[*Bin Laden whispers aside to the moderator.*] If you would, we need to take a little rest. I couldn't hear the most recent reply.

[*Moderator*] I should say to you all, as I've just told the brother, since he is growing tired, may God grant him goodness, Glorious and Exalted is He, may He alleviate this drowsiness. I should add though, brothers, that what you may have been hearing is not accurate: there is no direct help being provided by America, except, as was mentioned, in the matter of Stinger missiles, and that's it. And even these missiles, it appears, were actually purchased with monies from this blessed country and did not come directly from them [the Americans]. What you've heard about supporters, then, is by no means accurate. Although it is true that weapons were delivered, such work has been the product of beneficial revenues, God willing, Blessed and Exalted is He.

[*Bin Laden*] If I may add to this: although weapons have reached them, they have not been made in America but have rather come from the East. What is the American contribution? What share of support in the region comes from them? That I don't know. Is such and such true? I don't have any information on that; it is all rumor. As far as I know, however, this country, by the grace of God, is making a tremendous contribution by providing a large proportion of the weaponry used by the mujahidin. Muslims and their nations must partake in this [effort] so as to not put the mujahidin in a position where they would be forced to seek weapons from the enemies of God. God knows best.

In the late summer of 1989, bin Laden came home. As a young man first arriving in Afghanistan, he had been seen as a quiet, if persevering, millionaire's boy. Now, five years later, he was a thirty-one year old war hero. His accomplishments in driving the Soviet empire from Muslim lands, indeed, in smashing the very order of Communism itself, were touted amply enough by Saudi journalists and an Egyptian filmmaker. The lecture above resounded to his credit, selling over 250,000 copies in Saudi Arabia in the months after its release.[7] Given that cassettes are listened to in groups and copied off market and an estimate of the Kingdom's population at approximately five million at the time, roughly one in every six Saudis can be said to have heard the tape.

Something strange rung in the halls of victory, however. On the one hand, his lecture was sponsored by the Saudi National Guard, the monarchy's private military corps. Its Department of Religious Affairs seemed to be an ideal forum for trumpeting the Kingdom's achievements in balancing religious guidance with a muscular security apparatus. Having helped coordinate a diverse and fortified Arab-Afghan movement, bin Laden was the right man for contextualizing this experience in a broader vision of Saudi-supported Muslim reform worldwide. At the outset of the tape, sounds of a trickling brook suggest transcendent harmony. Quickly, however, the fruits of foreign struggles turn ashen. "Our present reality," bin Laden states "is a very dangerous one: never before has the Islamic world experienced such a time as this." He reiterates: "The matter is very dangerous. Words do not permit me to describe its danger; it is even more dangerous than what I will be able to demonstrate to you. Look carefully around you." If things looked alright enough, two gunshots exploding in the vaults of the auditorium suggested otherwise. Feigning nonchalance, bin Laden continues only to be stopped mid-sentence by a third report. "Is everything alright?" bin Laden gestures aside to an officiant near the podium. "It's nothing," he reassures him. A lone gunman, it seems, is testing out his equipment just outside the lecture hall. For the next twenty minutes, single gunshots echo continually, some of them so exquisitely timed after bin Laden's themes of apostasy at the gates that one would think they had been staged to dramatic effect. At several points, the tearful outbreaks of several babies and children lend further pathos to the idea of a human tragedy unfolding in the National Guard's inner hall.

Who threatens Islam's core? The enemy at the top of bin Laden's list is apostasy (*ridda*), betrayal of God's covenant with believers and the fundamental testimony to monotheism: "There is no god but God alone, and Muhammad is His Messenger." Shortly later bin Laden gets more specific. The threat is not from the West, whatever Western analysts have said of his objectives at the time.[8] The enemy heralds instead from the East. With homage to a book entitled *Our Present Reality* by Saudi scholar Muhammad Qutb, leader of the Saudi Awakening movement, bin Laden's lecture by the same title focuses on "heresy" (*ilhad*) in the "Land of the Two Holy Sanctuaries," Saudi Arabia itself with its two holy cities Mecca and Madina.[9] For Qutb, the ultimate foundation for worldly corruption is "political despotism" (*al-istibdad al-siyasi*). Sunni scholars who are overly lenient toward such an abuse of power (a group he likens to seventh-century Murji'ites) are given special opprobrium. For bin Laden, the principal source for heresy is instead Shi'ism. Drawing on ultra-conservative Sunni discourse, bin Laden labels Shi'a "Rejectionists" for denying the legitimacy of the first two caliphs who led the Islamic community after the Prophet's death. From the Shi'a perspective, authority over the affairs of the community should have been passed directly to the Prophet's blood-relative 'Ali, his nephew as well as son-in-law through Fatima, instead of to Abu Bakr followed by 'Umar and 'Uthman. For bin Laden, Iran's majority Shi'a population represents the wellspring of such heresy. Although "they lost their first military round" in a costly war with Iraq that had consumed most of the 1980s and ended just a year earlier, their antique perfidy suggested no resolution soon. Bin Laden's early and explicit fulminations against Shi'a and Iran would be routinely obscured by leading Western al-Qa'ida experts for years to come in favor of his allegedly far more pan-Islamic image among followers.[10]

Second on the scale of Islam's estimable foes are "those empathetic with them": Arab communists. Foremost in their ranks are socialists who have rallied under the leadership of Egyptian president Gamal 'Abd al-Nasir under the banner: "Freedom! Socialism! Unity!" Touted frequently on Egypt's far-reaching radio program *The Voice of the Arabs*, the slogan expresses the full extent of the enemy's inroads not only into religious belief but into Arab ethnic identity as well. What does "one Arab community" mean, exclaims bin Laden, if Arabs are "torn from the Islamic world"? Taking a cue from an especially loud crying infant in the audience, he extemporaneously vents at the threat to children "in every administrative district and primary school." He warns furthermore of Arab socialist ambitions to exploit the Peninsula's oil reserves for their "destructive ideas." Shortly later, he highlights a second and militarily more concerning front: Iraqi Ba'athism. Venturing an assertion that, by the summer of the following year, would prove prophetic, bin Laden states, "Even our neighbors want to attack us until we are obliged to sign non-aggression pacts with them. Do you believe that they will keep their promises, those ephemeral Ba'athists? No, by God!" Saudi listeners must defend Islam's heartland from invasions on all three fronts, for "we have none left but you."

Third and finally, bin Laden mentions Arab socialist "empathizers": Christians as well as Jews "who want to rule Islamic lands." Their plots vast, their persistence unflagging, little had they been swayed by the first Palestinian Intifada, the outbreak of which, discussed explicitly when responding to later questions, he glosses initially as "events of the past year." Their sights have been set instead on Madina itself, bin Laden asserts, a much greater prize for being "the city of God's Messenger." Still, even as non-Muslim conspiracies run deep and wide, bin Laden returns to the primary threat assailing his audiences as they speak: "Is there not, on the Peninsula of the Arabs—the Peninsula of Islam on which no two religions can co-exist according to the text of the Prophet's words—right here, in the south of the Peninsula (*huna fi janub al-jazira*), open disbelief seeking to rule?" Arab socialism, it appears, is a "religion" whose materialist designs undermine true faith. The location of his lecture gives further ecclesiastical profile to this religion. For inhabitants of the peninsula, "the south" refers to Yemen, the provinces of Najran, Jizan, and Asir that now form part of Saudi Arabia, and Dofar in Oman. In no place were the legacies of communism more visible than in the socialist-led People's Democratic Republic of Yemen. In no place were Shi'a more prolific than in its neighbor, the Zaidi-majority Yemen Arab Republic. The unification of the two Yemens in

1990 would, in fact, provide new grist for bin Laden's southern campaign. From the tape's introduction, of course, we know that bin Laden is in Saudi Arabia; his address to audiences in some of the Kingdom's most impoverished provinces, areas beyond his family's traditional influence, suggests that, for all his official sponsorship, he was also pressing his case to those outside the state's distinguished centers of power. Whatever we make of this fact, bin Laden's geography of heresy at the gates, captured poignantly in the image of a coiled "bracelet," prompts listeners to the fight ahead.

Origins of "The Base" (al-Qaʿida)

Nowhere in the speech does bin Laden mention the name of the al-Qaʿida organization that, according to conventional wisdom, he and several others founded the previous year. One could attribute this silence to diplomacy and his knack for discretion. Insofar as al-Qaʿida supported Islamist groups fighting insurgencies across the Islamic world, openly announcing its identity and objectives might make its members targets for reprisal by state authorities. Covert organization goes hand-in-hand with militancy.[11] Still, al-Qaʿida's earliest goals of providing material, tactical, and ideological support to Wahhabi-influenced Sunni militants across the world would not have been particularly controversial for Saudi officials or private donors long used to supporting such causes. According to Michael Scheuer, head of the Central Intelligence Agency's bin Laden unit from 1996–9, al-Qaʿida's primary focus at its inception was supporting Muslim insurgent groups in Kashmir, Tajikistan, Mindanao and Chechnya, all of which are known to have benefitted from Saudi financial largesse and ideological support.[12] If al-Qaʿida's principal goal was as ecumenical as "to lift the word of God, to make His religion victorious," as journalist Lawrence Wright has suggested, why would bin Laden not have wanted to inform listeners about the ideals of his organization?[13] Why so much fire and brimstone against fellow Muslims living on all four sides of the Kingdom's borders? What of his authority as a mediator between diverse Islamic factions, so prominent in Western accounts of his leadership as well as in the memoirs of militants themselves?[14] How does bin Laden's Saudi ethos square with what many have argued to be the ultimate goal of al-Qaʿida's head in chief: re-establishing a world-wide Islamic caliphate on behalf of Muslims everywhere?[15]

As a cosmopolitan construction magnate, bin Laden had long mastered the art of tailoring his projects to different audiences. Saudi reformers and their audiences perhaps expected a speech confirming their mission and sense of self-righteousness. Nevertheless, it is worth pausing briefly to re-evaluate the most authoritative accounts of al-Qaʻida's origins and goals in light of the jarring tones his 1989 lecture introduces to our understanding of the man and his leadership. I will do this through a closer reading of the source documents, some of them in Arabic, that are most frequently cited to support claims that bin Laden led al-Qaʻida from its inception. I will argue, in fact, that bin Laden's own authority was very much at issue in these documents. His audio-recorded lecture, far greater in the scale of its circulation and influence, reflects both the challenges that he faced in trying to lead a multi-national militant movement and the strategies he would develop for overcoming them.

Standard accounts of al-Qaʻida's formation rely on court documents from the USA v. Enaam Arnaout trial from 2002–3.[16] The essence of the narrative goes like this: on 11 August 1988, bin Laden met ʻAbdalla ʻAzzam, Abu Hafs Al-Masri, Abu ʻUbayda Al-Banshiri, and others in Peshawar to discuss the formation of an organization called "al-Qaʻida" with the aim of keeping jihad alive after the Soviets were gone.[17] Minutes for the meeting turned up in Bosnia and were subsequently used in the court case against Arnaout, former director of the now-banned Benevolence International Foundation. While details are sparse and original Arabic texts unavailable, bullet points include mention of a discussion "regarding the establishment of a new military group" along with the words "general camp," "special camp," and "*Qaʻida*" (left untranslated and in italics).[18] Wright concludes from these notes that "For most of the men in the meeting, this was the first time that the name al-Qaʻida had arisen."[19]

Shortly later, court documents report a meeting at bin Laden's house in Peshawar that led to the official formation of "*al-Qaʻida*."[20] Most of the meeting focused on selecting an advisory council, the head of which is said to have been bin Laden along with Saudi Red Crescent chief Waʼil Julaidan, Abu ʻUbayda, and Abu Hajir Al-Iraqi. Training of recruits was divided into sessions outlined as follows: "Limited duration (known), they will go to Sada camp, then get trained and distributed on Afghan fronts, under supervision of the military council. Open duration (long),·

they enter a testing camp and the best brothers of them are chosen, in preparation to enter *Al Qa'ida Al 'Askariya* ('the military base')."[21]

Other analysts have added further evidence to these accounts. In 2006, Westpoint's Combatting Terrorism Center released documents whose procurement prior to April 2002 suggests acquisition by American military or intelligence personnel operating in the Afghanistan-Pakistan regions after the fall of the Taliban. They are routinely cited to corroborate the story of al-Qa'ida's formation under bin Laden's leadership in 1988. One of the most popular documents is divided into two sections, one entitled "Al-Qa'ida's Structure and Bylaws" and the other entitled "Al-Qa'ida Goals and Structure."[22] The thirty-two page charter, heavily laden with bureaucratic details of executive, political, military, financial, media, and external relations committees, purportedly sets up the organizational coherence of bin Laden's world-wide vision. The document raises several important questions, however. First, no date is provided. Second, no mention is made of bin Laden, or any other specific individual for that matter. Oaths to "the amir" of al-Qa'ida are indeed mentioned as are the details of recruits' rights, obligations, and salaries. When reporting these details shortly after 11 September, however, former National Security Council directors Daniel Benjamin and Steven Simon insist that oaths given by recruits were made to bin Laden himself.[23] In subsequent years, leading al-Qa'ida experts such as journalists Peter Bergen and Lawrence Wright would follow suit. All would cite as evidence for their claims the testimony of one of bin Laden's associates in the Sudan, Jamal Al-Fadl, during USA v. Bin Laden court proceedings against bin Laden for his involvement in the American embassy bombings in East Africa in 1998.[24] Al-Fadl admits to receiving a document filled with committee details and membership stipulations that exactly resemble those outlined in the charter documents later released by Westpoint's CTC. He states in no uncertain terms, however, that oaths were given not to bin Laden but rather to three other individuals: Abu 'Ubayda and Abu Hafs, both Egyptian commanders in the group's military committee, and also an Iraqi Kurd by the name of Abu Ayyoub.[25] The latter, insisted the witness, was in fact the group's first amir, an assertion made elsewhere by others.[26] Al-Fadl suggests that while oaths were not given to bin Laden, he remained a kind of "general amir" to whom the others reported; his statements formed part of a plea bargain arrangement with prosecutors after having been convicted of conspiring to attack American military institutions. Whatever we make of Al-Fadl's testimony, the advisory council that drafted al-Qaʿidaʾs charter documents appears not to have wanted any explicit association with bin Laden. Contrary to what has been assumed from observations on the late August meeting in bin Laden's Peshawar home, the council took pains to make sure that bin Laden would *not* be the group's amir. In a section outlining the leadership's security apparatus, they add the following qualification, inaccessible in its English rendition due to garbled syntax: "Neither the commander of the guards nor his associates can be from any of the Gulf States or from Yemen."[27] With the addition of this single clause, peculiar for a document purporting to be a general charter for all Arab and Muslim militants, bin Laden's core Saudi and Yemeni supporters, those most likely to pledge their lives in his defense, were ensured no part in al-Qaʿidaʾs exceptional command structure. Rather than laying the foundations for bin Laden's future role in jihad, the document is more accurately a bid to marginalize him.

How are we to make sense of the fact that al-Qaʿidaʾs founding charter proves an impediment to bin Laden's leadership? We can begin with finer points of translation. In Arabic, *qaʿida* simply means "base" (as well as "rule" or "precept," as I suggest in later chapters). Defense Department translations, much in the fashion of documents produced by prosecutors in American court proceedings, repeatedly leave this single word in its Arabic original. By doing so, they give the impression that discussions of "the base" (*al-qaʿida*) are, in fact, about the organization that we have come to know since 11 September as bin Laden's brainchild. A closer reading suggests that the "base" being established is an organizational master-plan for the Al-Faruq training camp at Jaji in Afghanistan's Khost province (encompassed today in what is known as "The Greater Paktia Province"). This camp was established in 1989, a year after the August meetings in bin Laden's house, and pointedly under Egyptian leadership. My analysis suggests the need to revisit arguments made by prosecutors in the USA v. Enaam Arnaout trial, though our lack of original Arabic-language documents from the case prevents definitive conclusions. Before expanding on the implications of my claim, it is worth noting a few more details from the charter as well as corroborations from scholars and ex-militants who have been interviewed about what "al-Qaʿida" meant to those involved with bin Laden in the late 1980s.

In the months and years following 11 September, experts of diverse persuasions and experiential backgrounds have spoken of bin Laden's central role in establishing al-Qa'ida. In light of bin Laden's identification with the attacks, most prominent in a video released on the eve of United States presidential elections in 2004 in which he professes having had intimate knowledge of the hijackers' plans, these accounts help remind audiences of his impressive role as bankroller, organizational chief, warrior, and spokesperson for a struggle that would be turned against the United States in no uncertain terms. Given the generalizing and often breezy nature of narratives about bin Laden's role in history, however, it is important to recognize their inadequacy as records of the past, especially considering the desire of many interviewees to figure prominently in the unfolding drama of bin Laden's rise to notoriety. Countering assumptions that the al-Qa'ida we had come to know after 11 September could be projected backward for over a decade with little substantial change, others have emphasized the historical variability of the term, at least as it refers to a militant movement drawing strength from bin Laden's leadership. Bin Laden's closest associates reject outright the idea that al-Qa'ida signified bin Laden's movement from the outset. His bodyguard Nasir Al-Bahri states that "The practical jihadist beginnings of Shaikh Osama were not under the banner of anything called the al-Qa'ida organization."[28] Ahmad Zaydan, a Syrian journalist who attended the wedding of bin Laden's son Muhammad in 2001, states that al-Qa'ida was never a political organization, but only a term for practical military operations that had Arab-exclusive inclinations, even as the goal was to work roughly with the Afghan mujahidin.[29] Khalfan Khamis Muhammad, a militant sentenced for his role in the American embassy bombings in East Africa, has testified that at the time of the attacks in 1998 he had never heard of an organization called al-Qa'ida; the term was rather understood to be, in the words of his FBI interrogator, "a formula system for what they had carried out."[30] My review of bin Laden's tape collection to date has yielded only one cassette referring to "al-Qa'ida" as a militant organization or base associated with bin Laden: an al-Qa'ida propaganda tape produced in October 2000, an excerpt from which I examine in chapter fourteen.[31] More such references may be found in time. At the very least, however, these notes give pause to straightforward narratives of al-Qa'ida's organizational coherence over time.

One of the more substantial arguments for al-Qa'ida's early significance for Arab-Afghans suggests that the concept referred to a records database (*qaʿidat al-maʿlumat*) in Peshawar that was set up by bin Laden in 1988.[32] In coordination with the Office of Services, the database kept track of volunteers not only in Peshawar's guesthouses but in training camps and battle zones in Afghanistan as well, and was formalized on computer software in the following year.[33] In broad terms, the concept's links to an emerging bureaucratic infrastructure is sensible enough. In bin Laden's audio recorded speeches, however, bureaucratic renditions of "the base" prove poor currency for inspiring recruits. During the previous year, when speaking about Wa'il Julaidan's visit to the Lion's Den, bin Laden characterized him as a "bureaucrat" (*rijal idari*), adding that "while we are all to some administrators, his physique was weak because he spent most of his time at a desk."[34] As in the early lectures of top numerous militant strategists, foremost among them Abu al-Walid Al-Masri, as I show in chapter twelve, the intellectual as well as tactical leverage of "the base" inheres in more exuberant heroes and locales, ideally those situated beyond metropolitan centers of informational surveillance, control, and authority. On the one hand, there is the "training camp" or *muʿaskar* in Arabic. As multiple training camps are set up on the frontier of a battlefront, a more general operational base (*qaʿida*) becomes necessary, one that can supervise camp activities and coordinate logistics while at the same time remaining spatially redeployable should its headquarters come under attack. The importance of securing a well-fortified base that could remain in contact with battlefront operations, provide a physical refuge in times of duress, and also remain essentially de-territorialized, makes the base both physical and metaphysical, depending on circumstances. If "a formula system," as Khalfan Muhammad is reported to have said, the base could be conceptualized as a relationship between an agent and fields of perceived ethical contest and struggle. The base's credibility lay in its power to represent an individual or group to an established system of authority and, in the process, modify systemic practice. The idea of a computer database provides users with an interactive system of logistics; it fails to express the more disruptive potentials of the base for those grappling with corporations and their officiating councils. It also ignores the concept's roots in Islamic law, theology, linguistics, and culture, as I suggest in the final chapters of this book. For bin Laden, an iconoclastic rendition of *al-qaʿida* would become all the more essential if, as founding charter documents suggest, attempts were being made to obstruct his influence.

OUR PRESENT REALITY (*WAQIʿUNA AL-MUʿASIR*)

What evidence do we have that "the base" discussed in al-Qaʿida's charter is the Al-Faruq training camp and, should de-camping be necessary, its template? Aside from the fact that the words "training base/camp" make perfect sense every time *al-qaʿida* appears in the original Arabic text, the geographic specificity of the base/camp is clear in repeated discussions of its proximity to Peshawar. Scholars and militants corroborate al-Qaʿida's origins at Al-Faruq. Terror analyst Rohan Gunaratna suggested as much shortly after 11 September, though he later changed his views to fall in line with Bergen and Wright's emphasis on meetings in bin Laden's house the previous year.[35] The source for his first assessment was Al-Fadl's testimonial: Al-Faruq was the location in which he reports first meeting al-Qaʿida's first amir, receiving charter documents whose structure very much resembles those later posted online by the CTC, and giving an oath before the Egyptian-dominated military committee.[36] Al-Bahri goes into further detail elsewhere:

> With an increase in the number of Arab strugglers coming to Afghanistan, a training camp (*muʿaskar*) called Sada, meaning the "echo" (*sada*) of jihad, was established. It was located along the border between Pakistan and Afghanistan. After the arrival of many well-qualified militants from the Jihad Group and the Egyptian Islamic Group, bin Laden and his jihadi associates set up a new and more advanced training camp. It was called the Al-Faruq Camp or the Al-Faruq Military College (*kulliyyat al-Faruq al-ʿaskariyya*), and was effectively a military college…Of course, the college was later called the Al-Faruq Military College where military base training occurs (*bi muʿaskar al-qaʿida*), the understanding being that it was a military base for jihad.[37]

Al-Bahri's narrative suggests that the Al-Faruq camp was a qualitatively more advanced "college" for militant training, the significance of which I will discuss below. His account of bin Laden's leadership in setting up Al-Faruq corresponds with bin Laden's role as a financier and construction engineer, one whose combat experience the previous year would have put him in a solid position to exercise authority there. Charter documents, as I have shown, complicate this picture: bin Laden faced serious hurdles in extending actual command over the base and its activities. With respect to the foundations of al-Qaʿida, Al-Bahri's narrative proves illuminating in another respect: in mentioning the two-stage process of camp planning, the first consisting of basic introductory courses at the Sada camp and the second more advanced training at Al-Faruq, Al-Bahri sheds key light on the significance of conversations held in bin Laden's home the previous year. The discussion that day was about setting up plans to open the "special" Al-Faruq training camp, one whose distinction as a "base" (*qaʿida*) was conceptually different than other camps (*muʿaskarat*), as clarified in the previous meeting on 11 August. Wright's assertion that "for most of the men in the meeting, this was the first time that the name al-Qaʿida had arisen" is a historical canard.[38] Though his observation parallels conclusions drawn by prosecutors in the USA v. Enaam Arnaout trial, Al-Bahri's contextualization of training camp initiatives at the time suggests that the designation of *al-qaʿida* as "a group" under bin Laden's leadership would not yet have occurred. Bergen's notes from his own interviews suggest that something has been lost in translation: "Those with knowledge of the meetings at bin Laden's house say that some of those who participated only discussed dissatisfaction about how the Office of Services was being run, and were unaware that some of the other participants also discussed the founding of al-Qaʿida."[39] The very individuals present at the meeting, when asked about the meeting in a post-11 September era, profess being unaware of al-Qaʿida's foundation because no such event took place.

Asceticism in the Wake of Al-Faruq

What significance can be attributed, then, to al-Qaʿida's origins at the Al-Faruq camp rather than in bin Laden's residence in Peshawar? How would bin Laden begin to position himself to assert leadership in the organization? Before returning to clues from his 1989 speech, a brief review of the Al-Faruq camp's administrative and ideological priorities is in order. The camp's advisory council was composed of over a dozen members from across the Middle East and North Africa. Although Iraqis and Saudis were especially well represented, Egyptians outweighed the contributions of other members both numerically and intellectually.[40] They included the camp's chief instructors Abu Hafs as well as the self-styled Islamic scholars Ayman Al-Zawahiri and Sayyid Imam Al-Sharif (aka Dr Fadl), both surgeons by profession. Around the time of bin Laden's 1989 lecture, Al-Zawahiri and Dr. Fadl would be coaching audiences on the merits of breaking free from Egypt's largest Islamist organization, the Islamic Group (*Al-Jamaʿat Al-Islamiyya*). Founded by reform-minded university students in the 1970s, the Islamic Group had suffered attrition through the 1980s as it advocated militant solutions to state injustice. Sermons by the blind cleric 'Umar 'Abd al-Rahman, later imprisoned by the United States for his involvement in the 1993 World Trade Center attacks, provided much theological armament to members and would later feature on at least eight tapes in bin Laden's collection. According to Al-Zawahiri, however, the Islamic Group's aims were too parochial, their qualifications to represent the pious community (*umma*) too indebted to Egyptian nationalism. Accommodation with the infidel state held no appeal for true Muslims, and to support such a stance committed one to apostasy (*takfir*). Branding their movement Islamic Jihad (or "the Jihad Group"), the group's calling card became the assassination of Egyptian state officials, intellectuals and, by the 1990s, foreign tourists in the country. Although efforts were focused primarily on securing a true Islamic state in Egypt, the organization gained momentum and a wider range of recruits abroad. Following public backlash against militants in Egypt during the mid 1990s as well as set-backs for Islamists in Yemen and the Sudan, Jihad Group leaders gathering in Peshawar urged disaffected scholars across the Islamic world to help defend their mission in more transnational terms. In memos to group members, Al-Zawahiri seems to have tried to put a post-colonial stamp on the group's orientations: he spoke of the enemy as "foreign investors" and of operations as "commercial activities" designed to yield "joint profit," the assumption being that although Muslims were bound by their common hatred for Western global economic domination they could also, however self-consciously, turn its weapons to good use.[41]

Al-Faruq's instructors, most of them Egyptian, appreciated the need to combine exercises in military training with workshops on transnational jihadism that could discipline recruits in appropriate strains of reasoning and belief. Physical fitness courses in the morning were followed in the afternoon by classes on the use of light weapons, explosives, and anti-aircraft artillery.[42] Courses were also given on Islamic law, creed, and militancy.[43] The legacies of this militant institution have yet to be understood partly because it has been overshadowed by its more illustrious twin: a camp in Gharmabak Ghar near Kandahar, some 250 miles west of Khost, set up by bin Laden himself using the same name. The latter Al-Faruq, paired with a more advanced training camp near Kandahar's airport complex, provided a training ground for al-Qa'ida's recruits beginning in the late 1990s.[44] Geared toward preparing the faithful for al-Qa'ida's increasingly open war with the West, the camp hosted a second and less-experienced generation of fighters, many of them from Western countries. Its roster of guests and graduates included a host of 11 September hijackers such as Saeed Al-Ghamdi, Ahmad Al-Nami, and the brothers Wail and Waleed Al-Shehri, as well as a larger corps of militants who would later end up in Guantánamo, most infamous of them Khalid Shaikh Mohammad. As renowned as this second camp would become for minting al-Qa'ida's credentials under bin Laden, the first and older Al-Faruq must be distinguished from the second.[45] Inaugurated during a messy post-Soviet era, after the final remnants of the Red Army had left but before Kabul or Jalalabad had been wrested from the Communist sympathies of president Muhammad Najibullah, Al-Faruq 1 provided recruits with a curriculum for transnational militancy that remained unparalleled in sophistication and strategic vision. The Khost camp was al-Qa'ida's Ivy League campus through at least the late 1990s and likely up to 2001 as well.[46]

A survey of the lecturers featured on fourteen tapes labeled "Al-Faruq" in bin Laden's former collection gives rare insight into the ideological orientations that the camp sought to impart to its recruits. Of six individuals identified on tape cartridges, there are two Saudis ('Abdalla Al-Sabt, 'Abdalla Al-Hamad), two Egyptians ('Abd al-Rahman 'Abd al-Khaliq, Mustafa Hamid (aka Abu al-Walid Al-Masri)), one Kuwaiti (Ahmad Al-Qattan) and one Yemeni ('Abd al-Majid Al-Zindani). The majority of these figures are well-recognized jurists, some of them prominent state officials. While dates and locations for their speeches are difficult to identify, the likelihood of their appearance at Al-Faruq 1 is high given the controversy that their appearance at Al-Faruq 2 would have created by the time of its founding.[47] The contents of these tapes vary. Some are clearly lectures on combat and guerilla warfare. Cassette no. 338, for example, features Mustafa Hamid (aka Abu al-Walid Al-Masri) talking to recruits in 1998 about the tactics of fighting Soviet troops in Afghanistan's mountainous terrain and the lessons for turning the struggle against Americans. To these tapes might be added at least eight recordings by renowned theorist of global jihad, Abu Mus'ab Al-Suri; although his lectures tend not to mention locations or dates, he is known to have penned treatises on the legacies of modern Muslim militancy for world-wide jihad during his residence at the camp.[48] Such audio-lectures suggest the vanguard role of Al-Faruq 1 teachers in tailoring Muslim militancy to post-cold-war contexts of American geopolitical influence. Most of the tapes marked "Al-Faruq," however, dwell on topics that seem only obliquely related to armed jihad. Coaching audiences on commonalties among Muslims as well as virtues and morals that unify, these lectures shy from charges of apostasy (*takfir*) that camp recruits are reported to have indulged in when among Muslims of different sects and political affiliations back in Peshawar. However much instructors were known for sewing discord at home, their dissertation at Al-Faruq 1 is devoted to solidarity with fellow campmates and those who might be persuaded to join their ranks.

Why would the Al-Faruq founders have wanted to marginalize bin Laden at the time? To be brief, Al-Faruq's ideological orientation and courses in militancy focused primarily on supporting insurgent movements across the Islamic world that were fighting what were perceived to be corrupt Muslim states and their apostate rulers. Foremost among the advocates for such socio-revolution were Egyptians, notably Al-Faruq instructors Abu Hafs, Ayman Al-Zawahiri, and Dr. Fadl; they also included jihadi theorists from North Africa and Iraq, countries that had significant representations on Al-Faruq's advisory council. To be sure, a host of these individuals would later prove to be bin Laden's staunchest supporters; in the late 1980s, however, bin Laden was viewed by Arab-Afghans from non-Peninsular backgrounds as insufficiently committed to the kind of transnational, pan-Islamic radicalism required of camp leaders. Like many Saudis, Yemenis, and Gulf State nationals, bin Laden could return home after the Afghan jihad, unlike the majority of hard-core militants from Egypt or North Africa; the latter tended to view Saudis and their neighbors as inadequately steeled in the transnational jihadi cause, however valued their pocketbooks might be. The clause in al-Qa'ida's charter banning Saudis, Gulf State nationals, and Yemenis from the camp amir's security detail was, in fact, a strategic firewall against the potentially moderating influence of financial donors from those areas.[49] The implications for bin Laden himself were unambiguous. Through most if not all of Al-Faruq's existence as a camp, bin Laden abstained from funding assistance.[50]

Bin Laden's 1989 speech expresses just the kind of nationalism and Saudi-influenced charges of disbelief (*takfir*) that Al-Faruq camp instructors would have found counterproductive. Charges of apostasy (*ridda*) and heresy (*ilhad*) among Muslims themselves inaugurate his lecture. Conspirators' designs threaten not simply good Muslims everywhere but

Saudis most acutely of all. Asserting that "the last of their raids will target the Land of the Two Holy Sanctuaries," bin Laden expounds upon the treachery of Shi'a, Arab communists, and Ba'athists in particular before concluding, "We have no one left but you." Armed jihad, bin Laden recalls, proved just the fix for Arab forebears long ago when confronted by invading disbelievers. Since the eighth century, warriors from the Arabian Peninsula had not only defeated great civilizations in the north, notably the Persians and Byzantines, particularly among them the "Franks." They had also crushed vying ethnic groups within the Islamic world: "No Berber, Mongol, Turk, Sudani, or Frank: all of them disintegrated when your ancestors on this peninsula practiced their faith and undertook the Struggle." Arab-Afghans today, he continues, fight much the same enemy, a war he situates historically through reference to thirteenth-century conquests by Mongols who swept south to sack Baghdad. Struggling in former Mongol heartlands, such Arab warriors combat a new occupier: the Soviet Union, an enemy whose "legend," bin Laden assures, has been decisively crushed. Cued to Islam's impending post-Soviet challenges, bin Laden nods to the threat of America's own superpower status, one magnified by "the world media." Still, the dramatic highpoint of his speech, focusing on the perilous capture of a Soviet-made T-62 armored tank by Salih Al-Ghamdi in Afghanistan, highlights inter-Muslim struggle.

Bin Laden's focus on armed contest among Muslims elicits quick rebuke from several audience members in the ensuing question and answer period. Summarizing these questions diplomatically, a moderator asks: "Why do your speeches tend to focus on Afghanistan and overlook Palestine? The questioners urgently request more attention be given to the issue of Palestine, to support the pious community, and to the 'Children of the Stones.' Please direct your discussion to the struggle in Palestine instead of to every other part of Muslim lands." Implicit in the questions posed was a growing popular concern at the time that the Afghan jihad was now turning Muslims against Muslims. The moderator later reports an observation from another participant: "There are some questions being asked, although most of them are based on rumors fueled by newspapers and magazines. They suggest that the fighting going on in Afghanistan is between Muslims themselves and that what is happening is a civil war." Although implications of internal bloodletting are downplayed, bin Laden seems to devote special attention to martyrs who had died after the Soviet occupation, foremost among them Shafiq Al-Madani, Ahmad Al-Zahrani and Salih Al-Ghamdi, the latter of whom fell "on the tenth of *Dhu Al-Hijja* in the year that just passed, 1409 AH" (equivalent to 14 July, 1989). The combatants hiding from Al-Ghamdi inside their Soviet-made tank were, in fact, most likely other Muslims who had been rallied to defend Jalalabad by Afghan's premier at the time, Muhammad Najibulla, a full five months after the last Soviet troops had left the country. Speakers' questions have heated implications. Rather than turning weapons against other Muslims, bin Laden should rally the faithful toward non-Muslim aggressors, especially Israelis oppressing stone-throwing Palestinian youth.

The virtue of asceticism proves instrumental to bin Laden's self-defense. While gesturing toward the importance of every form of struggle for protecting "what has slipped away," bin Laden urges Muslims to discipline their spending habits above all. The principal target of cost-cutting should be American-made products, especially given that proceeds from their sale go directly to "the Jews who slaughter our brothers." Automobiles, air conditioners, clothes, toys, pens, food products and, repeatedly, the American apple: all must be boycotted in the interest of upsetting the United States' trade balance. Bin Laden's solicitation to use a form of non-violent protest to address injustice against Palestinians presents a striking contrast with his war poem just a few minutes earlier. There his poetic verses had hailed "the courageous hero" who "thrust forth the spear" to defend the Al-Aqsa mosque in Jerusalem. Now he appears to be backpedaling, his credentials as a reputable businessman and investor trumping whatever façade he might present as Islam's warrior in chief. In many ways, his bait and switch represents just the kind of treachery that Al-Faruq camp transnational militants had come to suspect of their well-heeled brothers from Saudi Arabia and neighboring oil states. Although fighting infidel occupiers of Islamic lands in Afghanistan had been their *cause celebre* and bolstered their credentials as defenders of the faith, bin Laden and his compatriots were suspected of lacking the resolve to bring the battle home and rally Muslims together against their deepest foes. Still, bin Laden's response highlighting the danger of American economic interests in the region anticipates the particular strain of asceticism that would come to define his leadership in the years ahead.

American unipolar dominance after the fall of the Soviet Union would, of course, provide a convenient backdrop against which Muslims of diverse persuasions could ostensibly find a common cause. By the following year, the presence of American troops in Saudi Arabia and neighboring countries lent special appeal to this cause among critics of Western intervention in the region. Bin Laden's rhetoric in this respect took its cue from conservative preachers who had been schooled in Muslim Brotherhood ideology, especially those who would be identified with the Saudi opposition movement. Bin Laden's distinctive contribution lay in how he figured American power. For bin Laden, America's threat in the Middle East stemmed more from its corrosive monetary influences on personal affect and culture than it did from actual territorial control, in the older post-colonial idiom. While bankrolling Israel's continued survival as a state with physical boundaries, America exercised more sinister forms of control through the consumption habits of Muslims themselves. Asceticism would be integral to the warrior's arsenal, then, insofar as it could coach Muslims on how to channel their most intimate desires and sympathies. Such discipline did not require the ideal struggler to be a luxury-averse Luddite. For bin Laden, the purchase of a $50,000 car was less concerning than its American manufacture. The measure of a believer's faith came from recognizing the attractions of the Chrysler, as the "man of discernment" (al-ʿaqil) might do, but choosing to buy something else. At the same time, the best of strugglers are those who seek distance from "the people of this worldly life" and those "immersed in this world." Reminding audiences of the virtues associated with putting one's wealth to God's service, he cites a Qur'anic verse: "Only the believers who have placed faith in God and His Messenger and have never since doubted, but have striven with their wealth and souls in the path of God: such are the sincere ones."[51] Relinquishing one's belongings expressed the spirit of martyrdom itself, and in this respect is the inseparable companion of armed jihad. Arab-Afghans exemplified such a spirit, venturing forth "not for this world or for a woman, desirous of marriage. They had no land there, no relatives, no commerce, or share in profits." If the rewards of death in combat would be a jingle, faith in ascetic devotion would become a mantra.

Even as bin Laden urged "economic war" against American companies, the rigors of asceticism in bin Laden's speech are to be practiced above all against Muslims who have been corrupted. Apostasy, he declares from the outset, is like "a bracelet coiled upon the wrist." The metaphor would reappear regularly in subsequent years. Expanding on its implications, bin Laden invokes a transmitted report (*hadith*) attributed to the Prophet Muhammad: "If people were to follow the deceptive way of dinars and dirhams and pledge allegiance [to a ruler] for material wealth and were to follow the tails of cows and let go of jihad, God would afflict disgrace upon them." The *hadith*'s emphasis on a subject's pledge of allegiance (*bai'*) to a ruler made explicit the revolutionary implications of bin Laden's wrath. Salafi firebrands straining at Al-Faruq to shake longstanding ties between political elites and clerical establishments would find bin Laden's pitch right on the mark. More questionable, though equally central to his vision, would be the depth of his romance with the Arabian desert warrior. The Arabian Peninsula's privilege as Islam's "final stronghold" is expressed through its "real men," warriors who, much in the fashion of Abu Bakr, might lead "horse upon horse, soldier upon soldier" against every non-Arab enemy. The cast of such a figure is made clearest in the concluding poem through an explicit contrast with Palestinians. Describing them as "shackled," bin Laden stages their rescue by a caravan of Arabian warriors sprung from an oasis:

Then from the barren wastelands
  A spring of purest water appears
Gushing forth with the banners of men bent on sacrifice
  And of righteous champions
And it says: should the initial offer fall short
  We will sacrifice ourselves for religion
Such victory! Victory for the blood-stained, their bodies soaked with wounds
  Refusing to forsake their homes for wanton bargains
Loathing life if one of humiliation and ruin.

The danger of bin Laden's Arabian prince lay not only in upstaging broader and more transnational efforts to secure justice for the Palestinians. As an emblem of Arabian purity, the warrior's virtues lay in a proud and ancient austerity that brooked little tolerance for "wanton bargains" in his homeland. With diplomacy, bin Laden carefully sidestepped the call to challenge the rule of his Saudi and Arabian hosts. The power of his rhetoric nevertheless tapped popular desires for cultural authenticity that would grow more vexed as Arab governments aligned themselves toward Western military and security objectives in the region.

6

DANGERS AND HOPES (*MAKHATIR W-AMAL*)

(February 1993 speech by Osama bin Laden in Sanaa, Yemen.
Beginning of cassette no. 498.)

[*Recording begins mid-sentence*] ...and we were not to be rightly guided,
unless guided by God. Our praise be upon Him for this magnificent grace,
the grace of faith. Praise be to God who bestowed upon this pious community the grace of Struggle in the path of God, the loftiest summit (*dhirwat
al-sanam*) of this religion. So we support the rituals of this religion. The
greatest fortune and share of Struggle in the path of God fell to our
Messenger, blessings and salutations upon him.

Today, our talk is about the dangers that envelope the pious community and
what remains of Muslim lands. Our talk is about a great matter that threatens the last of Islam's strongholds: the Land of the Two Holy Sanctuaries. A
great apostasy has occurred in this time. Never before has the Islamic world
passed through such a dark situation! There is no power or might except
through God.

The disbelievers—Crusaders and others—have laid plans to destroy and turn
off this great light. God will disappoint them, Glorious and Exalted is He.
They have planned to govern the lands of Islam through open disbelief, by
laws other than those revealed by God. Leaks from their documents, which
cover several decades, indicate that the last of their raids will target the Land
of the Two Holy Sanctuaries. We ask God to protect and secure these lands
from them. They have obtained what they sought. Very few Islamic lands
remain. Look around you carefully and reconsider: you will find that

153

disbelief is on the verge of surrounding these lands like a bracelet coiled upon the wrist. Arabs as well as non-Arabs one and all have committed heresy, excepting those who are shown God's mercy. As states, they govern Muslims in open disbelief, employing the most destructive and misguided principles. [*Recording cuts out, re-commencing in the second paragraph and continuing.*] They expound clearly on their blasphemy, delineating their plans to govern our lands with open disbelief. May God disgrace them.

Look to your east! I am talking about the states and forms of rule that they employ against people there. Look to your east at open disbelief: [Shi'a] Rejectionism arrives with open disbelief and seeks nothing more than the conflation of our religion with the legacy of their grandparents the Maji.[1] They want to bring Rejectionism to the Land of the Two Holy Sanctuaries. They expound this unambiguously! Past events have shown that their abhorrence and hatred for Muslims here is evident in the plainest terms: their shedding of sanctified Muslim blood in the sanctified month and on sanctified land. They think that we are disbelievers, greater infidels than even Jews and Christians. As for them, if they lost the first military engagement, they continue working and spreading deceptive ideas and rotten beliefs in most households across the Islamic world, from the Philippines, to Nigeria, to minority Islamic communities across the entire globe. There is no power or might except through God! [Those who] started this were especially Persian Muslims, many of whom do not distinguish between the people of the Prophet's moral pathway (*Sunna*) and people of other misguided interpretive tendencies who have attacked them. They began mixing and embracing the tendencies of those outrageously misguided off-shoots. It is the same for those who incline toward them in our borderlands, along the northern borders of this Peninsula. They too profess open disbelief.

As for the disbelief that produced Zionism and other tendencies including Communism, Socialism, Ba'athism, Secularism, the Freemasons, and other appellations that are misguided and destructive: if you examined [them] closely, they all surround us like the coiling bracelet. They practice open disbelief in their private chambers and courts of law, substituting the book of God Almighty, the Noble Qur'an, and the moral pathway of His Messenger, God's blessings and salutations be upon him, for writings by the red louts, followers of Marx and Lenin, God disgrace them all. Details are pointless: this affair is more dangerous than I can possibly relate. If you have been following these matters you should know about them. Only you are left! They never stop thinking about you, though you remain negligent. Turn on your radios, if you want: you [would] know the extent of the danger that surrounds you. And they, in their disbelief, in their audacity and insolence, openly declare such disbelief. Tune into media broadcasting and listen to the blasphemous slogans, some of which aim to unite Arab nations under false freedom and disbelieving socialism. We ask God to help us in protecting the last of Islam's strongholds, especially the Land of the Two Holy Sanctuaries, a site from which the Messenger—God's blessings and salutations upon him—set out on his Night Journey before our very eyes and ears.[2] Many of us, upon reaching puberty, were taken to the Sacred Mosque [surrounding the Ka'ba in Mecca] and began penning writings about it thereafter. I ask God to guide us along the right path so that we may reclaim the houses of Islam that slipped away from us, foremost among them our Messenger's destination [in Jerusalem], blessings and salutations upon him.

When the pious community abandoned the Struggle, it was struck with this humiliation, this loss and wandering. By your God, what kind of humiliation is greater and stronger than that which afflicted the Jews, those for whom humiliation and misery was written, those who, impure and deceitful, now occupy our Messenger's destination, God's blessings and salutations upon him. Almost everyday, a man among our brothers in Palestine is killed, a woman is pulled by her hair in those purest of streets, and the hands of Muslim children are destroyed. We don't budge, remaining silent and accustomed to humiliation and shame. There is no power or might except through God. [*Reciting a proverb*] "He who indulges in pleasure rests comfortably with shame, for the corpse feels not the pain of an injury."

How, then, can we find an escape from this loss and wandering, this compounded humiliation afflicting the entire community from the dutiful to the insolent, the knowledgeable to the ignorant, excepting those who receive God's mercy?

The people of Moses, blessings and salutations upon them, were stricken by God, Glorious and Exalted is He, with forty years of loss for a single sin that they committed: refraining from supporting this religion. They refrained from the Struggle, not bothering to even combine refraining with glorifying God but instead simply sitting. They replied, citing His words, Glorious and Exalted is He: "Depart with your Lord and fight together! We will sit here [and watch]."[3] Hence their punishment was loss, not for one or two years but for forty. God said, Glorious is He: "Therefore will the land be out of their reach for forty years. In distraction will they wander through the land; but do not sorrow over these rebellious people."[4] [The fourteenth-century scholar Isma'il] Ibn Kathir, may God have mercy upon him, notes that they walked all night long, and that when dawn came they found themselves back where they had begun, such was their punishment from God.

And yet, today, it is as though we live with the same loss and wandering that had once struck that nation. God demonstrates to us, Glorious and Exalted is He, that He does not guide those who tarry. He sends them neither His love nor that of His Messenger. He commanded us instead to struggle in the path of God, Glorious and Exalted is He. After detailing eight ways in which people abstain from defending the foundation of this religion, He also says,

Glorious is He, that the fathers, sons, and others who tolerated some of these obstructive maneuvers were disastrously afflicted, except those upon whom God has shown mercy. He clarifies afterwards that those who are afflicted will not be guided. Just like those who have been struck with loss, Muslims who refrain from supporting this religion when it is demanded of them will also not be guided by God, Glorious is He. He says, Glorious and Exalted is He: "Say: If it be that your fathers, your sons, your brothers, your spouses, or your kindred, the wealth that you have gained, the commerce that you fear may decline, or the dwellings in which you delight, are dearer to you than God or His Messenger, or struggling in His path, then wait until God brings about His decision; God guides not the rebellious."⁵ This, then, is the reason for the loss and wandering that have befallen us. The absence of guidance is due to abandoning the Struggle in the path of God. As has been narrated soundly in a report (hadith) about [the Prophet Muhammad], God's blessings and salutations upon him: "If people let their thoughts dwell upon the dinar and dirham, pledged allegiance [to rulers] for material gain, pursued the 'tails of cows' [the servants of the powerful] and abandoned the Struggle: God would inflict humiliation upon them."

This warning by the Messenger of God, blessings and salutations upon him, has already reached fruition among us. As you see before you, such humiliation! Muslims' blood and lands are lost every day. While they expound upon their [understanding of] religion, we remain submissive and silent, excepting those who have received God's mercy. The path, then, brothers in Islam? By His grace, Glorious and Exalted is He, this religion has already been perfected. He has not left us neglected, even as we are misled by scholars who invoke [faulty] legal opinions for the sake of expedience. He has demonstrated in clear and plain terms the exigency of struggle in the path of God. With the permission of God, I will cite for you clear and evidentiary verses from the book of God Almighty, from the deeds of our Messenger, God's blessings and salutations upon him, and from the deeds of the Rightly Guided Caliphs. [These verses show] how to stop the harm of disbelievers, how to repel apostates who commit heresy against the religion of Islam, and how, finally, to muzzle hypocrites who exist in Islamic lands.

To the people of Badr, God has spoken, Glorious and Exalted is He: they are the best of people.⁶ The best people in this pious community are the strugglers, for Badr was a land of Struggle. God be pleased with them, they are guiding luminaries in every legal science. They were the Companions of God's Messenger, God's blessings and salutations be upon him. They were the legal specialists, among them people who wrote about the revealed scriptures as well as those who took heed of God's noble book, may God be pleased with them. The most important characteristic mentioned of the Companions, may God be pleased with them, was this: their first-hand witnessing all events with God's Messenger, God's blessings and salutations be upon him. To be Badri was to have witnessed the battle of Badr and the treaty of Al-Hudaibiyya. Those people, may God be pleased with them, set forth on the day of the battle in search of the caravan, seeking the merchandise of Quraish. According to God's will, the merchandise was spirited away [by caravan leaders who were forewarned of the attack], although the Quraish set out [with an army from Mecca] to fight the believers. There was a group of believers, however, that was loath to fight, as [fourteenth-century scholar Isma'il] Ibn Kathir mentioned, may God have mercy upon him, when interpreting the following verse: "Behold! God promised you one of the two [enemy] parties, that it should be yours. You wished to take the one lacking might."[7] "Might" here means weapons; the caravan was unarmed. According to the text of the Qur'an, some of them sought only to take the [unarmed] caravan. God did not inspire this contingent, however, Glorious and Exalted is He. Rather, he sought to establish the truth, Glorious is He. He wanted to teach those seeking truth how truth is established. When God wanted to confirm the truth, He directed the others to Struggle in the path of God, Glorious and Exalted is He. He directed them to the fight [against the armed Quraish] on the day of Badr. It is through fighting in the path of God that the truth is established, and this is the meaning of His narrative, Glorious and Exalted is He...

[*Bin Laden expands on the failure of contemporary Muslims to match the commitment and valor of warriors who fought in several other early battles. After reminding audiences of the guidance God provides to those who fight and especially to martyrs, he turns to address present-day struggles.*]

I say that global disbelief lies behind the apostasy that unfolds today. Whatever you hear and read in the newspapers and on radios about dubious Arab alliances and unions is only a sign of the tremendous greed that exists for these lands, the Land of the Two Holy Sanctuaries. They strive to govern it in ways other than those revealed by God. They want us to cover [up the truth] like they have done, may God shame them. They strive for the greatest oil reserves in the world that rest beneath this very peninsula. Global disbelief lies behind them, monitoring this awakening (*sahwa*), this Islamic awakening. This is no more the case than with the vessel of crusades, America, God shame it, which monitors the Islamic world's awakening with its information apparatuses. Such apparatuses include sons of our own flesh who monitor the great awakening now spreading across the entire Islamic world, by the bounty of God. Whenever it has appeared and grown stronger, heretical tyrants have ordered it smashed. You may well have heard about these awakenings in the nations around us. And yet, whenever they have appeared and gained momentum, such tyrants have smashed them. They have killed its participants and thrown them in prisons, insulting and humiliating their scholars. There is no power or might except through God! The latest news, from this past week, reveals that in one of the many countries that inclines toward us—that of the land of Al-Kinana [Egypt]—the heretical tyrants, using their courts to govern with English and French laws in ways other than those revealed by God, incarcerated more than seventeen thousand young Muslim men. There is no power or might except through God! Against their pleasure and inclination, they were incarcerated by tyrants of global disbelief. Such hypocrites covet rulership over these lands. They want to assist global disbelief from abroad, employing hypocrites within to spread disbelief so that [they can] mess with our beards so pure...

[*Bin Laden elaborates further on the urgency of preparing to defend Saudi Arabia, "Islam's final stronghold," citing Saudi scholars Muhammad Ibn Salih Al-'Uthaimin and 'Abd al-Rahman Al-Dawsari's views on the importance of preparation "according to one's abilities" to support his cause. He then inaugurates the conclusion of his speech with the following recommendations.*]

Thus, I say: we cannot neglect preparing our selves to defend this religion. Our preparation should be continuous because the responsibility for defending this Land of the Two Holy Sanctuaries is the duty of every Muslim. By the grace of God, the matter has been made easier by the lands of the Afghanis. God has granted them the fortune. Through over ten years of fighting a so-called "superpower," they expelled the Russians through God's fortune, Glorious and Exalted is He. Despite pride and reluctance, the Russians' noses were forced into the dust.

The field there is wide open. The minimum preparation acquired by a man who completes, even if in a forty-five day program, is weapons training, from use of the Klashnakov, to the RPG, to the 82 mm armor-penetrating gun, to laying anti-tank mines. [By doing so], we can truly join those who prepare themselves to defend these lands.

If you have forgotten what plots are being sown against you, ask the people of the borderlands. Ask the people of the borderlands in the south, because hardly a week or two passes there without a communist attack. Open disbelief prevails on the southern Arabian Peninsula, the same Islamic Peninsula where the Messenger of God gave his final speech, God's blessings and salutations upon him. Among his final pronouncements, when he was severely ill, were words of advice, as it is relayed in sound reports (*hadith*) confirmed by [ninth-century scholars Muhammad] Al-Bukhari and Muslim [Ibn al-Hajjaj] through [Muhammad's cousin, 'Abdalla] Ibn 'Abbas. On Thursday—Oh what a Thursday!—Ibn 'Abbas began to cry, God be pleased with him. He was asked: Why are you crying? He replied: "On Thursday, the God's Messenger, God's blessings and salutations be upon Him, experienced severe pain." The pain experienced by God's Messenger grew so intense, he said. While [Muhammad] was laying on his death bed, blessings and greetings upon him—how my father and mother sacrificed for him!—he is reported to have given three commands to those attending. The first command, as witnessed by [Ibn 'Abbas], was: "Expel the polytheists from the Arabian Peninsula." Today, they are not scattered individuals, but groups, even leaders of idolatry, open disbelief. A state (*dawla*) on the Peninsula of the Arabs is being governed by laws other than those revealed by God, in open disbelief. There is no power or might except through God! Muslims from these communities who have experienced this particular miasma, along with whoever else might assist them, must understand that the aforementioned command is necessary: it is an individual obligation (*fard 'ayn*). They must prepare themselves to expel disbelievers and apostates from the Peninsula of the Arabs. We fight so that the word of disbelievers be made low as the word of God is made high. We fight so that all religion will be devoted to God. Already they have written, with broad strokes in their schools and institutions and on mountains with letters most vast: "No voice transcends that of the [Communist] party." [It is] open disbelief [to say] that the word of the party is higher! God blast them! We ask God to help us ensure that the word of disbelievers be made low as the word of God is made high. May I never be saved, even if others are given salvation, so long as a pulse beats or an eye blinks, until we expel all the disbelievers from the Peninsula of the Arabs in response to the command of God's Messenger, God's blessings and salutations upon him. For God, this is not a difficult matter.

I will say, brothers in Islam: you are supremely inattentive if you think that you are safe. Ask the people of the boundary lands in the south. Ask the people of the boundary lands in the north where things like this are also happening. A glance at newspapers from these lands indicates that something of this sort occurred there a few months ago. Fear God in your selves, then, and answer his command by preparing your selves to set forth on the Struggle. As I mentioned, the matter is facilitated by the grace of God. Whoever cannot [devote] a month and a half, then each man among you has a month-long vacation, so set forth and learn to struggle in the path of God. Keep garrison for a night, in the path of God. Stand guard for a night, in the path of God. Thrust a sword, in the path of God. Why did we forsake this magnificent reward? According to a report (*hadith*) about him, God's blessings and salutations upon him: "To keep garrison for a single night, in the path of God, is as sweet to me as spending the night of *Al-Qadr* [when the Prophet received his first revelation] at the foot of the Black Stone [in the Ka'ba in Mecca]." And I say, by the grace of God, Glorious and Exalted is He, that on this Peninsula—despite what I said to you about disbelief almost entirely surrounding it—there are men who remind us of those great men, the Companions of God's Messenger, God's blessings and salutations upon him. There are still men who—after many people thought this Peninsula had turned toward such abominable frivolity that no men would ever set forth again to sell themselves for the banner "There is no god but God alone"—set forth in numbers, by the grace of God, Glorious is He. More than 7,000 men set forth from this Peninsula. [Just] young men, striving for God's satisfaction, striving toward what God had promised, carrying their desire to those distant mountains. Having no land there, no relatives, no share in profits or merchandise, they strode through fields and mountains, oceans and rivers, shouldering their faith in support of the banner "There is no god but God alone and Muhammad is His Messenger." They sacrificed their future, their mundane future, because they confidently believed that what awaited them with God, Glorious and Exalted is He, would be greater, more blessed, and more lasting.

The heroism of Arab-Afghans resounded continuously in bin Laden's call to arms. By 1993, however, things had changed dramatically on the Arabian Peninsula. Over 600,000 Western coalition forces now operated in the region at the behest of Saudi Arabia, Kuwait, and other Gulf nations, all of whom reacted to Saddam Hussein's invasion of Kuwait in 1990 by seeking aid from the world's most advanced militaries and security corporations. The majority of coalition troops and security personnel were American. Another significant change by 1993, at least from the perspective of former Arab-Afghan volunteers, was bin Laden's new home address. He had taken up residence in the Sudan, his status with Saudi authorities uncertain. According to some accounts, he had been barred from traveling back to his homeland altogether.[8]

Bin Laden's decampment to Khartoum followed a series of setbacks in trying to keep the jihad going after the Soviets left Afghanistan. In the fall of 1990, after boasting of his ability to recruit 100,000 Afghan-trained warriors to expel Saddam from Kuwait, a sixty-page letter of solicitation to King Fahd met a cold rebuff.[9] Within weeks, his farm in Jeddah was raided by Saudi troops and approximately 100 Arab-Afghans working on the premises were arrested.[10] Although they were released later, bin Laden adopted the habit of carrying a semi-automatic gun with him wherever he went, traveling with bodyguards, and tinting the windows of his car. When his passport was seized in the following months, he acted quickly.[11] Employing his family's connections with internal security officials, he booked an air ticket out of the country while managing to recuperate all necessary documents. His homeland would henceforth be plagued with a motley crew of occupiers.

Bin Laden's first stop was familiar territory. From early 1991 through the following year he lived mostly in the neighborhood of Hayatabad in Peshawar.[12] There, no doubt sensing his precarious position as an organizational captain, he appears to have adopted the practice of taking signed oaths from followers who wished to recognize him as their amir. According to later assertions by bin Laden's associates at the time, second and third in command were Abu 'Ubayda Al-Banshiri and Abu Hafs Al-Masri, both well known to bin Laden from his earliest days at the Office of Services and later the Lion's Den camp.[13] These two would become key officers in what would later emerge to be al-Qa'ida's command structure in the Sudan. In 1991, the only "base" bin Laden can be said to have governed would have been his own Hayatabad household as well as the social and financial leverage it afforded elsewhere.[14]

Khartoum became his family's primary residence beginning in late 1991. The idea that bin Laden's presence in the Sudan catalyzed his image as Islam's holy warrior devoted to expanding Islam's pale against impious foreign aggression, especially from the United States, is advanced in the 9/11 Commission Report:

> In early 1992, the al-Qa'ida leadership issued a fatwa calling for jihad against the Western 'occupation' of Islamic lands. Specifically singling out United States forces for attack, the language resembled that which would appear in bin Laden's public fatwa in August 1996…While his allied Islamist groups were focused on local battles, such as those in Egypt, Algeria, Bosnia, or Chechnya, bin Laden concentrated on attacking the 'far enemy'—the United States.[15]

In line with this view are arguments alleging covert Saudi support for bin Laden's anti-American campaign.[16] By this measure, his residence in the Sudan was discretely promoted by Saudi benefactors; he could do little, after all, within Saudi Arabia itself given the King's clear alliance with American and Western countries at the time.

Whatever the intent of the 1992 fatwa, the text of which remains classified, evidence suggests that bin Laden was reticent about calls for jihad against secular Western powers, foremost among them the United States. Witnesses report that when packing up to leave for the Sudan, bin Laden and his closest advisors told audiences, "al-Qa'ida is finished."[17] To the consternation of others, bin Laden advised those who could return home to do so and urged young listeners to pursue university studies instead of combat.[18] Once settled in Khartoum, family members recall bin Laden waxing endlessly on new hybrids of corn, soybean, and sunflower seeds.[19] Saudi reformers who were enraged at the presence of American and Western troops in the region found bin Laden quiet on the issue; in the previous year, he had refused to sign a "letter

THE AUDACIOUS ASCETIC

of demands" to King Fahd aimed at securing democratic political reforms.[20] To be sure, militants from bin Laden's past were never far away in the Sudan. At his invitation, in fact, hundreds of Egyptian, Algerian, Syrian, and Iraqi veterans from the Afghan war, many banned from their own countries, settled in his neighborhood and relied upon his hospitality. In efforts to corral militant energies, the Egyptian Islamic Jihad under the leadership of Ayman Al-Zawahiri ran a smattering of training camps in Khartoum and its peripheries. Courses in espionage and the use of explosives were offered to recruits in preparation for over-throwing the regime of Hosni Mubarak in Egypt; in August of the fol-lowing year, recruits felled their first victims in a suicide motorcycle attack against Egypt's interior minister Hasan Al-Alfi, the first of its kind for Sunni militants. While Al-Alfi narrowly escaped, several officials nearby did not. Bin Laden's own involvement in such operations appears to have been muted, however. According to his former bodyguard, Nasir Al-Basri, he abstained altogether from training camp initiatives in order to avoid antagonizing the Sudanese government and jeopardizing his business relations.[21]

For many reasons, bin Laden stood to gain from the Sudan's bold new experiment in Islamic statehood. In 1989, a military coup by Colonel Omar Bashir had brought the Revolutionary Command Council for National Salvation to power. Implementing Islamic law had become the government's defining platform. The workings of justice were entrusted to members of the Muslim Brotherhood and especially the country's powerful National Islamic Front led by the ambitious and eclectic Islamist intellectual Hasan Al-Turabi. Having been raised in a pious religious family, studied law at college in Khartoum, secured graduate degrees in London and Paris, and traveled to America to slake his curios-ity about the world's most advanced industrial economy, Al-Turabi had developed a critique of Western secular materialism that had much in common with bin Laden's own. Inspired by Bashir's coup, Al-Turabi began organizing a series of "Popular Arab and Islamic conferences" (PAIC) in 1991 that were geared to make Sudan the center of a world Islamic revolution in which he would play lead man. The list of over 200 invited delegates included Muslim leaders who would sound alarm bells among terrorist watch-groups in the United States, Israel, and the West, including Hezbollah, Hamas, the Palestinian Abu Nidal organization, and the Abu Sayyaf movement from the Philippines.[22] Subsequent affiliates would include militant wings of the Jamiat-i Islami of Pakistan and India, the Hizb-i Islami and Jamiat-i Islami of Afghanistan, and the Hizb-ul Mujahideen of Kashmir.[23] Bin Laden's own activist cause paled in comparison to these, of course, though not for want of Al-Turabi's attention: in late 1990, Al-Turabi appears to have written a convincing letter to the Saudis in which he pledged the Sudan's offer of asylum to the black sheep that Osama had become.[24] Some have argued that bin Ladin's residence in the Sudan gave him, in fact, a kind of privileged status in the Saudis' own efforts to direct transnational jihad toward non-Muslims living outside the Islamic world.[25]

Bin Ladin's differences with Al-Turabi were apparent from the outset, however. Al-Turabi was an established religious scholar as well as one of Sudan's most influential politicians. With a pedigree of top state appointments that included minister of justice and foreign minister, he had polished his Islamist credentials by learning to reconcile competing sectarian interests and doctrinal shibboleths. At times, he took controversially populist positions on matters of Muslim authority: "Because all knowledge is divine and religious, a chemist, an engineer, an economist, or a jurist are all '*ulama*'," or men of learning.[26] Whatever the tenor of the PAIC series, moreover, Al-Turabi preached engagement with one's adversaries. Not only did he encourage his students to pursue graduate degrees in Western universities, something considered anathema among Saudi Awakening reformers; in the year preceding bin Laden's 1993 speech he had toured Europe, Canada, and the United States canvassing on behalf of creating a pan-Islamic movement for liberal, nonviolent Islamic states. Among his lecture points was a theme he had vociferously defended in Khartoum: Sunni and Shi'a Muslims must reconcile their differences.

While the Saudi expatriate's views contrasted sharply with the trajectory of a Turabi-inclined Sudanese state, bin Laden took important cues at the time from others in the country who were equally disillusioned with top-down Islamist reform programs. In the coup's aftermath, Bashir imposed a state of emergency banning independent newspapers and outlawing public demonstrations. While Sudan's Muslim Brotherhood viewed state consolidation favorably, their critics were less accommodating. In the venerable neighborhood of Omdurman, site of a battle against British-led forces in 1898 that led to the defeat of a massive army under the Sudanese leader 'Abdalla Ibn Muhammad, bin Laden regularly attended Friday prayers at a mosque run by the Sudan's indigenous

salafi organization, the Ansar Al-Sunna Al-Muhammadiyya.[27] Founded
initially in support of the 'Abdalla's father, a religious scholar proclaimed
mahdi by his students, the Ansar matured largely under British colonial
rule and before national independence in 1956. Wise to the repercus-
sions of what the British might perceive as political activism, the Ansar
shied away from the usual political vocabularies of Muslim nationalists.
Instead of calls for Islamic law and statehood, the Ansar focused on
proselytizing with the aim of improving society's moral foundations.
Political party activism, although tolerated, was considered secondary in
importance to "commanding the good and forbidding the wrong."
Proper governance (*hukm*) was not peripheral; indeed, it featured much
in Ansar discourse. Questions of sovereignty, however, were addressed
through debates about moral volition rather than statehood. Throughout
its history, the Ansar would remain suspicious of rulers' calls for militant
jihad, no more so than when such calls were leveraged against secular
foreign powers commandeered by non-Muslims.[28] The true "summons"
(*da'wa*) necessary for purging society of its ills and clearing the way for
Islam's worldwide rectification would focus on one's own co-religionists.
In the Sudan, one of the leading theoreticians of modern Ansar ideology
was Egyptian-born legal specialist 'Abd al-Rahman 'Abd al-Khaliq, a
figure whose lecture "The Rectitude of the Summons to God's Calling"
(*Maqam Al-Da'wa ila Allah*) would feature in bin Laden's collection.
Doctrine (*'aqida*) comes in many shades, instructs 'Abd al-Khaliq, and
while this-worldly politics has its place, virtue lies in confronting
Muslim believers' own errors and afflictions with heartfelt commitment
to destroying corruption (*fasad*). The cassette's accompanying jacket
suggests that proceeds from the tape's sale would go to the "Al-Faruq
camp's charitable endowment" (*waqf mu'askar al-Faruq*) in Khost, the
jihadi workshop that came to be known as al-Qa'ida's original base, as I
averred in the previous chapter.

Bin Laden's 1994 lecture, entitled "Dangers and Hopes" (*Makhatir
w-Amal*), suggests that the Ansar Al-Sunna's doctrinalism and focus on
struggling against the near enemy had made an impression. To be sure,
much of his oratory parallels his widely disseminated speech "Our
Present Reality," given five years earlier to the Saudi National Guard.
Shared themes, metaphors, even specific phrases suggest that bin Laden
had standardized his discourse and could readily call upon it when asked
to speak in public. In both speeches bin Laden begins by commending

"struggle in the path of God" (*jihad fi sabil allah*), foretelling "an apostasy" (*ridda*) of unprecedented proportions, warning listeners that Islam's enemies seek to "govern by laws other than those revealed by God," revealing that, according to "leaks from their documents…the last of their raids will target the Land of the Two Holy Sanctuaries," and declaring that Saudi Arabia is "the last of Islam's strongholds." Playing to his audiences' familiarity with Saudi-influenced doctrinal puritanism, he urges his audiences on both occasions to "look around you" at disbelief (*kufr*) and heresy (*ilhad*), each of which surrounds the pious community "like a bracelet coiled upon the wrist." As in 1989, moreover, the primary threat to Islam comes from not from the United States, whatever would later be avowed by chief of the CIA's bin Laden unit Michael Scheuer when reporting the substance of the lecture.[29] The danger came instead from from Muslims themselves: Shi'a "Rejectionism" (*rafidiyya*), above all, followed by mostly Sunni Muslims who have betrayed their religion for various strains of disbelief including "communism, socialism, Ba'athism, secularism, the Freemasons and other appellations that are misguided and destructive."

New additions to his stump speech, however, illustrate the depth with which bin Laden drew from the transnational emphasis of Ansar Al-Sunna's doctrinal mission even as he twisted the movement's suspicion of armed militancy toward his own goals. Shi'a Muslims, for example, are a threat not only to Saudi Arabia itself: bin Laden speaks, for example, of "their shedding of sanctified Muslim blood in the sanctified month and on sanctified land," an assertion that might be linked to a range of events including the 1979 Shi'a protests, clashes involving Shi'a during the 1987 *hajj* season, or any number of scattered outbreaks of violence between Shi'a activists and the Saudi state that occurred during the 1980s. Worse yet, they spread their "deceptive ideas and rotten beliefs in most households across the world, from the Philippines, to Nigeria, to minority Muslims across the entire globe."[30]

The majority of Sunni Muslims, meanwhile, are similarly yoked to a far-fetched amalgamation of transnational disbelievers that includes "Freemasons" as well as "Zionists." The propaganda from such enemies, according to bin Laden, reaches audiences through the "radio" as well as "media broadcasting," both of which "aim to unite Arab nations under false freedom and disbelieving socialism." In stark contrast with his 1989 speech, however, bin Laden cuts short a tirade against secular Arab states and Western infidels that would have been familiar territory for audiences used to Islamist calls for the application of *shariʿa*. Not only does he omit an extended narrative about Baʿathism, the brand of secular Arab nationalism long espoused by Iraq and Syria. He also omits mention of Christians who, according to earlier assertions, "empathized" with Communist ideologues seeking to rule the Arabian Peninsula; indeed, he drops reference to a *hadith* well known among Arab militants asserting that "no two religions can co-exist on the Arabian Peninsula," and sidesteps entirely a polished excoriation of American strategic objectives in the region. Where earlier he admonished his listeners to boycott American goods and reminded them that "American forces can be defeated," bin Ladin now takes an altogether different tack. With over a half-million coalition troops working, living, and fighting in his own homeland, he finds a renewed urgency in discussing his fellow Muslims' own humiliating "loss and wandering." Likening contemporary Muslims' humiliation to that of Moses' people, bin Laden attributes the shame to excessive this-worldly accumulation. After citing a Qurʾanic verse inciting strugglers to self-abnegation, he appends a *hadith* that was quickly becoming one of his favorites: "If people let their thoughts dwell upon the *dinar* and *dirham*, pledged allegiance [to rulers] for material gain, pursued the 'tails of cows' [the servants of the powerful] and abandoned the Struggle: God would inflict humiliation upon them." This, he reminds his audience, "is the reason for the loss and wandering that have befallen us."

Given that bin Laden was still a Saudi national in 1993, he was undoubtedly wise to downplay his anti-Americanism. He could still return to his homeland, despite his rebuff by King Fahd several years earlier. Serious penalties awaited any public speaker taking a principled stance against the Saudi administration's reliance on coalition troops to help defend the country from its Arab or Persian neighbors. Beginning in 1991, prominent Saudi Awakening activists such as ʿAʾid Al-Qarni, Salman Al-ʿAwda, and Safar Al-Hawali (three of the top ten speakers in bin Laden's tape collection) had been arrested, stripped of their pulpits, temporarily imprisoned, and, by 1993, had their audio recordings banned.[31] Accordingly, bin Laden confines his remarks on America to a brief sentence: as "the vessel of crusades," the United States presents a threat to Muslims primarily through "its information apparatuses." Still, bin Laden's speech provides clues to how he was learning to press doctrine toward far-reaching revolutionary goals. Having expounded upon the core values of ascetic self-abnegation for aspiring strugglers, bin Laden takes aim at Islam's religious establishment. Without naming specific countries, he laments, "While they expound upon their [understanding of] religion, we remain submissive and silent," and reminds listeners that "[God] has not left us neglected, even as we are misled by scholars who invoke [faulty] legal opinions for the sake of expedience." As in his 1989 speech, bin Laden finds recourse to the early Muslim battle of Badr in 624AD to expand upon the noble calling of those who take up arms against corrupt Meccan disbelievers. A verse from the Qur'anic *sura* The Spoils of War once again illustrates the nobility of following God's guidance. On this occasion, however, the people of Badr are described differently. Not only are they courageous and selfless warriors who privilege fighting in God's path to seizing booty, but they are also "guiding luminaries in every legal science" and "legal specialists" (*fuqaha'*). Their virtue lays as much in "witnessing" (*shahida*) the events of the Prophet Muhammad's day as in actual martyrdom (*shahada*). Embedded in bin Laden's narrative is a new exegetical message: field experience is worth more than bookish knowledge put in the service of corrupt Muslim states.

While the theme of Muslim hypocrisy figures as prominently on this occasion as it did in 1989, bin Laden sharpens his attack against "heretical tyrants" (*al-tughat al-mulhidin*) who suppress the "great Awakening (*sahwa*) now spreading across the entire Islamic world." Egypt deserves special mention, according to bin Laden. Identifying it as "the land of Al-Kinana," the name of an ancient tribal confederation in the region, bin Laden excoriates its use of European legal codes and its imprisonment of "more than 17,000 young Muslim men." His focus on Egypt would have sat well with members of the Egyptian Islamic Jihad such as Ayman Al-Zawahiri who had relocated from Peshawar with bin Laden and were living in Khartoum. Despite the group's emphasis on transnational militancy, their partnership with militant operatives in Egypt's larger Islamic Group (*Al-Jama'at Al-Islamiyya*) would claim over 1,200 victims inside Egypt itself by 1997, most of them intellectuals, writers, security personnel, and politicians.[32] Few preachers were as influential or unyielding in their chastisement of Muslim rulers who governed "by laws other than those revealed by God" than the Al-Azhar trained jurist Shaikh 'Umar 'Abd al-Rahman. Well known in the United States for his collaboration with 1993 World Trade Center bomber Ramzi Yousef and sentence of "seditious conspiracy" three years later, 'Abd al-Rahman had risen to acclaim among Islamists in the 1970s for breaking with clerics who warned audiences away from using violence to overthrow corrupt rulers. Bin Laden had met 'Abd al-Rahman in Peshawar during the mid-1980s after the shaikh had been released from prison in Egypt under charges of collaborating with members of the Islamic Group who had assassinated Sadat. At the time, the shaikh's vitriole against Egypt's Coptic Christian minorities as well as any who might capitulate to Jewish interests worldwide earned him esteem among those seeking to provide transnational armament to Islam's global mission. By the late 1990s, bin Laden and his associates had disseminated a propaganda card to audiences that featured one of 'Abd al-Rahman's fatwas on the permissibility of fighting Jewish and Christian civilians.[33] Confined to his American cell, the shaikh would become a poster child for those bent on turning al-Qa'ida's militant wrath against the American homeland. Still, the vast majority of 'Abd al-Rahman's tirades, as confirmed on at least eight recorded audiotapes in bin Laden's tape collection, would focus on the near enemy. In one lecture about Muslims who abandon the faith partly under the influence of American secular materialism, 'Abd al-Rahman's "satan" (*iblis*) refers not to the United States, as claimed by some Western analysts, but rather to Muslim rulers who turn from God's guidance with such vehemence that they cease to resemble humans at all.[34]

Staying on message, bin Laden directs the bulk of his invective not toward Muslim hypocrites generally but rather toward those in Saudi Arabia, "Islam's final stronghold." Preparing oneself to defend God's religion, in accordance with one's abilities, is a "duty," says bin Laden. In his earlier speech, given on the heels of the Soviet evacuation of Afghanistan, bin Laden had cited the support of the Saudi kingdom's chief jurist (*mufti*) 'Abd al-'Aziz Ibn Baz to illustrate those who supported the Struggle. On this occasion, Ibn Baz's name is omitted, his 1991 fatwa defending the monarchy's recourse to assistance from non-Muslims during the Iraqi invasion of Kuwait playing against bin Laden's hand.[35] Instead he cites two Saudi scholars whose tapes would figure prominently in his Kandahar house: the prestigious jurist Muhammad Ibn Salih Al-'Uthaimin, whose roughly sixty-seven tapes would make him the fifth most featured speaker in the collection, and 'Abd al-Rahman

Al-Dawsari, whose speeches would be recorded on over twenty tapes. Bin Laden's recourse to Al-'Uthaimin, imam at Mecca's Sacred Mosque for over three decades, and second only to Ibn Baz in intellectual gravitas throughout the kingdom, is construed in the broadest terms: the Muslim's duty, as set out in one of his many fatwas, is "to prepare himself to defend God's religion, himself, and his honor." Measuring his words carefully, bin Laden neglects to mention that Al-'Uthaimin had proven not only a staunch opponent of unlicensed jihad but also an outspoken critic of those who accuse rulers of disbelief. True apostasy, according to Al-'Uthaimin, remains a matter of the heart and as such lies beyond direct observation. Bin Laden's recourse to the conservative religious scholar, 'Abd al-Rahman Al-Dawsari, would likely have struck listeners as more aptly inspired. Although Al-Dawsari had died in 1979 a few months before the Soviet invasion of Afghanistan, he provided a model of activism for Arab-Afghans and Saudi reformers, especially in his willingness to challenge unbelieving rulers through newspaper articles, print publications, and audiocassettes.[36] Much of Al-Dawsari's energies were devoted to critiques of the Muslim Brotherhood. Commendable though the movement had been for its anti-colonialist origins and its opposition to Israel and the West, its leading proponents had lost sight of a far greater threat that Al-Dawsari called "Freemasonry" (*masuniyya*). A concept foreign to Wahhabi vocabularies, Freemasonry represented a hydra-headed amalgamation of polytheists that included Jews, secularists, communists, nationalists, materialists, existentialists, and any other tendency that might lurk in its shadow. Worse still, it bred in the thoughts, beliefs, and actions of Muslim hypocrites, foremost among them Saudi intellectuals who betrayed their compatriots' inclinations toward purified doctrinal practice. His lectures on "The Truth of Adversaries and Friendships under God's Sovereignty," "The Roots of Power in Islam," "Belief in Destiny and Divine Will," and "Contemporary Youth Movements," all of which can be found in bin Laden's collection, proved instrumental for lending a semblance of common grievance to the many pathways of Struggle that were emerging in a post-Soviet period.

After calling listeners' attention to a forty-five-day weapons training program in Afghanistan, bin Laden gives a face and geographical location to "the hypocrite" most dedicated to Islam's defeat: "If you have forgotten what plots are being sown against you, ask the people of the borderlands (*thughur*). Ask the people of the borderlands in the south because hardly a week or two passes there without a communist attack." Bin Laden refers here to Yemen, a country whose revolution against British colonial authority had swept in an avowedly Marxist-oriented People's Republic of South Yemen in 1967 and which, despite its unification with North Yemen in 1990, still glowed red in the eyes of Islamist reformers. Reminding listeners of aggressive educational and outreach campaigns that had been conducted in southern Yemen for decades, he laments, "Although they call it Socialism, they are the same people who wrote, in broad strokes across every administrative district and even on mountains: 'No voice transcends the voice of the [Communist] party.'" Citing a transmitted report (*hadith*) that would become well known among Western audiences in years to come, bin Laden admonishes his listeners to "Expel the polytheists from the Arabian Peninsula."

Yemen had long drawn bin Laden's attention. Aside from his father's roots in the country, bin Laden had long expressed admiration for the country's fiercely independent tribes. Many observers noted that during his years in the family business as well as in Afghanistan, bin Laden began particularly grueling work days by donning the classic Yemeni turban: a patterned headcloth (*kufiyya*) draping down the back and held in place by a tightly wound edge. Yemen's labor force was sizeable: with a population of over 14 million in the mid 1990s, roughly half of the Arabian Peninsula's entire population resided in the country, and its capacity to transform entire economies was heightened by the dearth of the country's oil reserves in comparison to its neighbors and the stark poverty of its citizens. Throughout the Arab-Afghan struggle against the Soviets, Yemenis had proven loyal volunteers.[37] Journalist Jonathan Randal suggests that "almost all the young men Osama had recruited in the mid-1980s belonged to southern landowning families dispossessed by the People's Democratic Republic of Yemen."[38] His assertion needs some qualification. As we have seen in chapter three, most of bin Laden's "Lion's Den" recruits were Saudis from the Hijaz; Saudi "Afghans" increased in ranks, moreover, through the late 1980s as highly placed scholars such as 'Abd al-'Aziz Ibn Baz sanctioned the Arab-Afghan cause in league with the state's massive commitments to the region. Still, the number of Saudi volunteers in Arab-Afghan camps, 45,000 during the 1980s by one journalist's reckoning, seems to be have been grossly inflated.[39] Thomas Hegghammer, a specialist on Muslim militant movements with extensive experience in Saudi Arabia, has estimated the total number of Saudi volunteers was between 1,000 and 5,000 individuals at most.[40] Yemenis, therefore, very well likely out-represented other nationalities through most of the Arab-Afghan era. The President of Yemen's own half-brother, Brigadier General ʿAli Muhsin Al-Ahmar, had recruited thousands of northern Yemenis for the Afghan struggle during the 1980s alone, setting up training camps in the Yemeni countryside to ensure that they could handle themselves once deployed abroad.[41]

Some of bin Laden's closest associates in Afghanistan report his commitment to armed jihad in Yemen during the 1980s. Reporting on his experience in Arab-Afghan training camps during from 1988–91, Abu Musʿab Al-Suri notes, "While the Afghan Struggle was under way, bin Laden was focusing on recruiting for the Struggle in the Arab peninsula, in Yemen. Osama's main passion was the struggle in South Yemen. He worked tirelessly to garner the support to struggle against the 'infidel' government there."[42] Mustafa Hamid, whose lecture on al-Qaʿida I discuss in chapter twelve, adds that:

> He talked frankly about the need to liberate South Yemen from the communist rule, the Afghan way. All his moves and preparations were within that framework. To him, the Afghanistan arena was just one for training, or preparing for the decisive confrontation on the land of Yemen…It is for this purpose that he established the al Qaeda [sic] organization to internationalize jihad. He meant specifically the internationalization of jihad in Yemen.[43]

While bin Laden himself traced the beginning of his tangible support for the anti-communist struggle in Yemen to the early 1980s, most associates move this commitment to Afghanistan's post-Soviet era a decade later.[44] Whatever the substance of these estimates, his meeting with Saudi Intelligence Director, Prince Turki Al-Faisal, in 1989 to discuss South Yemen proved a watershed. After proposing to employ Arab-Afghans in the overthrow of South Yemen, bin Laden met with Prince Turki's flat rejection.[45] Turki's colleagues in the interior ministry went further, warning bin Laden not to get involved in the region. When bin Laden was found shortly later recruiting and organizing fighters for the Yemeni struggle on an itinerary that stretched from southern Yemen to the kingdom's own southern province of Najran, his passport was seized.[46] Later, in the Sudan, he and his family members would receive Sudanese passports allowing them to move more freely.[47] Remarking on the period to Arab journalist, ʿAbd Al-Bari ʿAtwan, bin Laden later put it this way: "I delivered a series of lectures in the Yemeni mosques, inciting Muslims to rise up against the South Yemen regime. This prompted the Saudi government to ban me from preaching."[48] The date of the lecture featured in this chapter—by my estimates, given the mention of the Afghan Taliban by audience members in the question and answer period, early 1993—and his continuous impromptu references to "this peninsula" and its "borderlands," suggests that the location of the recording would very likely have been in one of these Yemeni mosques.[49] According to bin Laden's wife, Saudi authorities forbade bin Laden from traveling back to the kingdom at the onset of this same year.[50]

In keeping with bin Laden's established rhetoric, most of the speech focuses on the plight of the Saudi kingdom, "The Land of the Two Holy Sanctuaries" of Madina and Mecca. On this occasion, however, his Yemeni audience and their theater of conflict would have lent a more urgent, transnational inflection to bin Laden's call to arms. When delivering "Our Present Reality" in 1989, bin Laden addressed Saudi audiences who, even if supportive of armed militancy, brooked little tolerance for calls to overthrow rulers, a tendency that would endure among Saudis well through the 1990s.[51] Wahhabism, however critical of idolatry, had long granted indigenous Muslim rulers the luxury of acting with best "intention" (*niyya*), whatever the results. Yemenis were more demanding of their rulers. Inhabitants of a more fertile and mountainous country, they had long enjoyed more settled tribal confederations; as a consequence, their political vocabularies more easily challenged leaders in the interests of maintaining social order. Most of bin Laden's audience would likely have lived through two great revolutions in the country against much the kind of "heretical tyrants" identified in his speech. In 1962, Yemenis rallied across the country to unseat the centuries-old Zaidi Shi'a imamate whose authoritarian responses to pan-Arab sentiments at the time no longer earned the trust of a rapidly expanding population. Although Zaidis are a slight minority in Yemen and are widely recognized to be distinct from those labeled "Rejectionists" by virtue of the branch's founder, Zaid bin 'Ali, who, among other distinctions, pledged homage to caliphs Abu Bakr and 'Umar, memories of homegrown rebellion against powerful in-house corruption would have been acute enough. The Saudi monarchy, after all, had been one of the Imamate's strongest backers. Yemenis' second revolution was in many ways even more dramatic. Pitted against one of Britain's last remaining colonial outposts in the Middle East, Yemenis wrested control of the capital city Aden along with the rest of the country in 1967. To the dismay of those hoping for an Islamic state, counter-imperialist fervor at the time shifted the country farther left than any other Arab nation. In years to follow, the communist party killed, imprisoned, and exiled prominent religious families of diverse persuasions.

In 1990, as bin Laden launched his campaign in Yemen, the Soviet Union was lurching toward final dissolution. In step with these changes, North and South Yemen announced their formal unification, a sign for most Yemenis that old cold war rivalries between the two countries might be set aside. Old habits died hard, however. Within several years, tensions erupted between Yemen's old guard, led by long-time northern president General 'Ali 'Abdalla Saleh, and representatives from the country's southern governorates. Ominous for southerners was the president's appointment of the Islamist ideologue and doctrinal firebrand, 'Abd al-Majid Al-Zindani, to a five-member presidential council. For decades Al-Zindani had been the country's most strident voice against communism and socialism, his sermons and speeches broadcast through hundreds of audiocassettes. During Afghanistan's years of Soviet occupation, Al-Zindani had been a highly esteemed spokesperson for waging classical jihad against non-Muslim infidels; he would feature seventh among the most prominently featured speakers in bin Laden's tape collection. The breadth of his pan-Islamic dream found easy partnership with bin Laden's own inclination to lump disbelief, both "East" and "West," into a single amalgamation of enmity. On tape no. 508, recorded in Saudi Arabia in 1988 and discussed in chapter three, bin Laden would receive a ten-minute introduction by Al-Zindani in which he would be described as a "struggler (*mujahid*) giving his wealth and his soul" in service of true faith. Expanding on the nature of bin Laden's fight, Al-Zindani asks listeners to consider underlying commonalties between the Soviet invasion of Afghanistan, the Israeli occupation of Palestine, and America's own foreign wars, all of a piece under the grim cast of aggression against Muslims.[52] In the immediate wake of 'Abdalla 'Azzam's assassination one year later, the Office of Services' monthly *Al-Jihad* magazine would run a lead article entitled "Who Will Succeed Shaikh Al-'Azzam?: An Interview with 'Abd al-Majid Al-Zindani."[53] In 1990, celebrations underway in Sanaa for the country's unification, bin Laden would visit Yemen to meet up with Al-Zindani again, this time to arrange financial support for a militant training camp in Waoulia, along Yemen's northern border with Saudi Arabia.[54] Yemen was fast becoming the hot new destination for those bent on purging the Islamic world of communist remnants and any others who might loosely be associated with them.

Events in the evening of 29 December 1992, just a few months before bin Laden's "Dangers and Hopes" lecture, lent fodder to reports that Yemen's internal enemy was assuming a more transnational guise. Massive bombs were detonated at two of Aden's premier international hotels, killing an Australian tourist and a Yemeni hotel worker, and wounding seven others.[55] Since the attackers' motives were undisclosed at the time, varying accounts have emerged about the target and objective of the two bombings. Six years later, news of the al-Qaʿida organization having become a subject of public interest, bin Laden would allege that "this was the first al-Qaʿida victory scored against the Crusaders."[56] Western terrorism and security analysts have largely accepted the assertion at face value, noting that although no Americans were injured in the attacks, American military personnel were staying at a different hotel in the city a few days before the attacks and that, as a result of the bombing, all U.S. soldiers left Yemen.[57] Bin Laden's actual involvement appears to have been restricted to his role as a financial backer of northern Yemeni training camps, however, members of which, according to Yemen's own investigation unit, were associated with the bombing and were said to be linked most directly to the Egyptian Islamic Jihad.[58] Whoever was ultimately in charge of the attacks, this standard account suggests that the primary enemy was Western military and security personnel. One of the Egyptian Islamic Jihad's emerging battlefronts at the time, after all, was the international coalition of military and humanitarian forces converging on Somalia under the American-led famine relief effort Operation Restore Hope, launched just a few weeks before the bombings to ease the suffering of millions of Somalis.

By other measures, the primary objective of the attackers was far more familiar to Yemenis at the time, whatever multinational or even anti-American ideas might have filled their heads. From the first gasps of the fledgling republic, representatives of the Yemeni Socialist Party, the country's largest assembly of former southern leaders, suffered a string of assassinations. While state investigations into the killings yielded mixed results, other reports revealed that many of the assailants were among over 5,000 Arab-Afghan returnees who had, in fact, been welcomed into the country by President 'Ali 'Abdalla Saleh after being exiled from their homelands.[59] By 1992, the establishment of government-sponsored militant training camps in southern Yemen, notably in the governorates of Abyan (Jabal Al-Maraqisha), Lahej (near Dali'), and Hadramawt (near Al-Mukha), along with thousands of "scientific institutes" run by Al-Zindani to educate students on the errors of polytheism, did little to earn southerners' trust.[60] Evidence that assailants from these camps and institutes received assistance from northern security officials proved corroborative for many critics of the regime.[61] Talk began spreading of secession. From this perspective, the bombings were part of a government-orchestrated campaign of intimidation: dream of resurrecting Aden as the cosmopolitan capital of a southern Yemeni state and you shall awake to the taste of bitter ash. The bombing exacted its darkest toll in the next few years. In 1993, the Al-Faruq camp amir Abu Ayyoub Al-Iraqi advised bin Laden and others to move weapons from the Sudan's Islamic Jihad camps to Yemen.[62] By the following year over 150 YSP officials had been murdered and the country collapsed into a civil war. The conflict proved disastrous for southern secessionists. In the aftermath of the war, many Arab-Afghans and Islamists who had participated in the conflict were rewarded with key positions of leadership throughout the south. Two prime suspects in the Aden hotel bombings, bin Laden's associates from the 1989 Jalalabad battle, Tariq Al-Fadli and Jamal Al-Nahdi, were given posts in the President's General People's Congress and the political security apparatus.[63]

If bin Laden had any role in the Aden bombings, he makes no mention of it in this speech in early 1993. Not yet an international pariah known for inciting attacks on Western and American targets, he speaks of the United States as an indirect threat, a "vessel of crusades...which monitors the Islamic world's awakening with its information apparatuses" while leaving more direct interventions, notably among them exploiting oil reserves and imprisoning good Muslims, to "dubious Arab alliances and unions" that seek to govern "in ways other than those revealed by God." In 1996, after his much-publicized "declaration of war against Americans" from Tora Bora, Afghanistan, bin Laden would revisit the events in Aden and claim that the perpetrators, if not yet al-Qa'ida, were former Arab-Afghan militants and that their principal target had been United States military interests.[64] In this speech, the subject of his wrath is a doctrinal adversary whose aspects were far more malleable. At its broadest guise, the enemy is "apostasy" (*ridda*) and "open disbelief" that surround "the lands of Islam," and especially Saudi Arabia, "like a bracelet coiled upon the wrist." While playing upon his listeners' pan-Islamic sentiments with mention of "Crusaders," "Zionists," and "Freemasons," bin Laden devotes most of his attention to the doctrinal threat of Persian Shi'as, communists, and socialists, all of whom had long figured in the pantheon of dangerous adversaries of primary concern to conservative Sunni Arab regimes. From this vantage, his call to arms could be categorized as classical jihad against disbelievers occupying Muslim lands. While the loss of Muslim territory is a primary concern, however, bin Laden also refuses to identify neat battlefronts: "Arabs as well as non-Arabs one and all have committed, heresy, excepting those who are shown God's mercy. As states, they govern Muslims in open disbelief." From this perspective, the impending triumph of hypocrisy and "heretical tyrants" impels listeners toward revolution within their own societies. A more dangerous message to sound out, Yemen's unstable political situation lent itself to such strident oppositionalism. Bin Laden reached out to southern Yemenis in particular, many of whom, however supportive of northern Islamists at the time, also remained highly ambivalent about Saleh's regime. Not only was his administration committed to Arab socialist ideals, long central to the platform of the governing General People's Congress. Saleh's backers were also tribesmen who had grown deeply suspicious of southerners over decades of cold-war rivalry. Bin Laden's speech seemed auspicious for bringing change to Sanaa, if not in the form of an Islamic state then at least through a band of righteous brothers willing to defend the Arabian Peninsula from unprecedented harm.

Former American Federal Bureau of Investigation agent 'Ali Soufan suggests that upon bin Laden's arrival in the Sudan in 1991 he began lecturing on al-Qa'ida's far-reaching objectives. "Every Thursday after the sunset prayer, all al-Qa'ida members in Khartoum gathered at one of the farms the organization owned to hear a lecture given by bin Laden or someone else on jihad and on the organization's mission. At the first such meeting, bin Laden told his followers that their mission in Sudan would be to build al-Qa'ida, eventually turning it into an international network that would not only support others waging jihad but which would be capable of launching its own operations."[65] Bin Laden's

DANGERS AND HOPES (*MAKHATIR W-AMAL*)

Dangers and Hopes lecture gives important insights into the ways his views on al-Qaʿida's internationalism were qualified at the time. As I suggest throughout this book, the grouping of bin Laden's potential recruits under an entity named "al-Qaʿida" had not likely been made at this early date; certainly no reference to al-Qaʿida appears in this speech. More significantly, while "events such as the first Gulf War and the conflict in Somalia shaped the narrative of the terror network," as Soufan rightly suggests, the Yemeni context proved equally, if not more, important for bin Laden at the time for several important reasons. Not only did the struggle in Yemen better represent bin Laden's potential as a leader, highlighting his long commitment to fighting communists and his ongoing relevance to the Muslim world after the defeat of the Soviets in Afghanistan. Yemen also underscored the treachery of Muslims themselves, foremost among them, from bin Laden's regional perspective, the Saudi monarchy and religious establishment that was fast becoming his biggest problem. As his speech suggests, the primary battleground for bin Laden's holy warriors is the Arabian Peninsula itself, especially "the Land of the Two Holy Sanctuaries." While prompting listeners to prepare themselves through training in Afghanistan, bin Laden's lecture also coaches audiences on employing doctrinal vocabularies in the service of expedient militancy.

7

TAKING GANDHI TO JERUSALEM THROUGH
OSLO, NORWAY

(September 1993 speech by Osama bin Laden, probably in Saudi Arabia.[1] Opening remarks, cassette no. 494.)

_____

[*Recording begins mid-sentence*] ...we beseech Him for help and forgiveness. We seek refuge in God from the evil of our souls and our bad deeds. Whoever is guided by God will not go astray, and he whom He leads astray can have no guide. I testify that there is no god but God alone, who has no partners, and that Muhammad is His Servant and Messenger.

Thanks be to God. Thanks be to He who said: "How [can there be such a treaty] while, if they gain dominance over you, they do not extend any pact of kinship or covenant of protection toward you? [*Bin Ladin stutters several times as he reiterates the verse.*] They satisfy you with their mouths, but their hearts refuse, and most of them are obstinantly disobedient."[2] Truly by God. They appeared to our brothers, in Palestine and many other lands. They appeared as Jews, as Christians, as idolators and heretics.

They employed such machinations against us. As God, Glorious and Exalted is He, has said: "They hold no regard toward kinship or covenant of protection" with the believers.[3] They hold no regard toward a contract or covenant of protection with us and do not observe the basic principles of God who created us and them, Glorious and Exalted is He.

What is our duty today towards our brothers in Palestine? In the wake of the growing migration, the Jewish migration to the land of Palestine, the place to which our Prophet, God's blessings and salutations be upon Him, voyaged [during his mystical Night Journey from Mecca], the entirety of infidel forces have stormed the area, from East to West, bringing together camps of disbelief to gain control of Muslims in Palestine.

Do you hear today? Do you hear today what is being said about our brothers in Palestine, after America and Russia have come to agreement over the emigration of over one million Jewish occupiers from their countries, especially Russia, to occupy the land settled by our Palestinian brothers? In the wake of this terrible conspiracy, according to what we have seen and heard, we find a horrific silence descending upon the community, ignominy and disgrace extending like a canopy over the sons of Muslims. We must turn our silent abiding toward vocalization in support of our brothers there in Palestine. There is no power or might except through God!

What can we do about this enormous issue? It is an issue that incriminates Americans, may God shame them, since from dawn to dusk they adopt supportive positions [toward Israel] while the whole world listens and watches. As a member of the United Nations, America stands alone against the resolutions of all other nations in supporting Israel. They abet a crime that has resulted in the loss of blood among Palestinians in Palestine and the crushing of bones among our sons' children. There is no power or might except through God!

The matter has grown worse, exceeding all measures and reaching a climax. A few days ago [the United States] announced a financial aid package to Israel that is worth approximately $2.4 billion dollars and that will be used to provide newly arriving Russian Jews with housing. Even worse, just three days ago American spokesman [White House Chief of Staff] James Baker, may God shame him, announced that they endorse the unconditional and unrestricted migration of Jews to occupied Palestine. He even went so far as to denounce calls and warnings by some parties in Lebanon and elsewhere to punish air carriers for transporting Jews into Palestine. They censured these actions, condemning their sponsors for issuing such threats when, in truth, they are the greatest criminals of the age. They use a media disinformation campaign to drug Muslims' feelings with what they call The International [Oslo Accords] Peace Conference and with peace negotiations in the Middle East. What have we done to make them produce such nonsense? They are the ones slaughtering our brothers morning and evening in all places! Then they come along to tell Muslims that they best behave like sheep and chickens? There is no power or might except through God!

As we hear and see: how long will this silence last? We will be asked [by God] about our brothers on the Day of Judgment. We will be asked about those who have been slaughtered though they had drawn ranks with a single creed under the banner 'There is no God but God alone and Muhammad is His Messenger.'

How, then, must we act against this common enemy, especially the Jews and Christians? May God help us to clarify our obligation in this matter.

At this point, it is worth recalling the holy biography [of Muhammad] and the acts of the Companions of God's Messenger, God's blessings and salutations upon him, when they encountered barbarism (*jahiliyya*) among the Quraish, in all their hubris, when the latter oppressed sinless believers much as America and the Jews are doing today.[4] You are well aware of what they did to Bilal, may God be pleased with him, and what they did to Sumaya, may God be pleased with her. They killed her, though she was free of sin and wrongdoing of any kind, simply because she proclaimed "My Lord is God." [They killed her while] she was unarmed.

Unless we carry weapons, they will do exactly the same to us; indeed, they are already doing so to our brothers today. They will slaughter us just as they slaughtered our brothers in Sabra and Shatila [in Lebanon].[5] This business can no longer be covered up. With this massive emigration, officials in the enemy's government have clearly spoken. With this massive emigration, they are saying: "Now is the time to create a Greater Israel, one whose expansion won't cease until Tabuk has been taken along with Khaibar, Taima, and Bani Quraidah" in [Madina], the city of the Messenger of God, God's blessings and salutations upon him.

We recall what was done when the Companions of God's Messenger, God's blessings and salutations upon him, confronted the crimes and arrogance of *jahiliyya* in their time. The Quraish had been punishing faithful men and women, though they had remained sinless. They imposed a condition upon Muslims through the treaty of Al-Hudaibiyya stipulating that they not accept anyone among the Quraish who converted [to Islam] and sought to join them. This is the height of injustice.

In the wake of this treaty, Abu Basir, may God be pleased with him, traveled [from Mecca] to the town of God's Messenger [in Madina], God's blessings and salutations upon him. Two men from Quraish came, however, and took this Muslim back to Mecca to be tortured, binding him in shackles and chains. In keeping with the established contract, the Messenger of God, God's blessings and salutations upon him, relinquished him to the two polytheists, saying to [Abu Basir]: "Patience, for God will grant you an escape." So Abu Basir went [in compliance with his captors].

Take heed, O people of insight, how we should act. [Abu Basir] went along, thinking to himself along the way. This Muslim contingent [including the Prophet Muhammad] had delivered him to the Quraish who would interrogate him about his religion despite the fact that he was returning to his own people. He found no satisfaction in having to return to those houses of blasphemy. Indeed, he could find no rationale for lingering in these houses even though his Muslim companions had turned him away. No sooner did he arrive in the Al-Hudhaifa territory than he seized one of his journeymen's swords and slayed one of them. The other one immediately fled since barbarism (*jahiliyya*) does not understand dialogue.

In the same fashion they try to convince us that there is no place for fighting and bloodshed and that dialogue must be prioritized. As are you all well aware, Muslims in Palestine have been in dialogue for more than twenty years! They ask for dialogue on every occasion, demanding that United Nations resolutions be acknowledged; yet each time one resolution is adopted the Palestinians are told that they must comply with another. This is how it has all dragged on. At last they have entered into [protracted] negotiations with them and what comes of it? This massive and horrendous emigration, a response to abdication and to abandoning the Struggle in the path of God!

Have faith in God's Messenger, God's blessings and salutations be upon him, when he says: "If people let their thoughts dwell upon the *dinar* and *dirham*, pledged allegiance [to rulers] for material gain, pursued the 'tails of cows' [the servants of the powerful] and abandoned the Struggle: God would inflict humiliation upon them, never lifting them up again until they return to their religion."

[*Bin Laden stops to take questions from the audience. The first speaker's question is too difficult to hear, but bin Laden's response is clear.*]

Yes, Abu Basir killed the one who came to strip him of his religion, may God be pleased with him. He continued on until he reached Al-'Ais, here on the shores of the Red Sea, between Jeddah and Yanbu'. He refused to go back to the disbelievers, instead declaring jihad on that day. Those who were oppressed heard him in Mecca, and one after the other began to join Abu Basir, may God be pleased with him, until they formed a band. Did they sit still? No! Did they justify sitting still by pointing out how few they were in number and how scarce their resources? No and one thousand nos! [Abu Basir] did not declare "What can I possibly do about disbelievers when I am only one person?" may God be pleased with him. Many people today, by contrast, ask "What can we do with regards blasphemy?" even though we are pious nations! There is no power or might except through God! Be assured: there is nothing that fortifies the presence of Jews and Christians [in Muslim lands] more than our excuses for sitting still and not engaging in Struggle in the path of God.

After they formed a band, [Abu Basir] began to launch raids against the Quraish's trade routes, their very economy, may God be pleased with him, until the Quraish were overwhelmed and discovered fear entering their hearts. From thenceforth this unmitigated *jahiliyya*, having forbidden the believer from practicing his religion and having relied upon treaties to mitigate the burden of the ongoing economic attacks [against them by Muslims], began to dissipate, abased and humiliated. Indeed [the Quraish] appealed for help from God's Messenger, God's blessings and salutations upon him, to terminate the imposition [of such attacks] and to place Abu Basir, may God be pleased with him, as well as other Companions with him under the protection of the existing treaty [of Al-Hudaibiyya] so that they would no longer kill polytheists.

That's the disbelievers' principal: they understand nothing without painful strikes directly against their heads, their economy, and their selves. That's the case with America: she will not understand dialogue. These are a feeble people! For more than fifty or sixty years they were subjugated: first to the colonial British and then to the Jews. What kind of freedom is mentioned by America, in all its hubris, when it went to the peoples of the East, to Vietnam thousands of miles away, to bomb them in airplane sorties, slaughter them, and kill them. What freedom is this? The Americans left Vietnam only after they suffered terribly, these wretched people. More than 60,000 American soldiers died, their wealth having been spent and their resources exhausted, all of which caused the American people to raise a din in their homeland. Through numerous demonstrations they asked their criminal and despotic government to bring their sons home from Vietnam.

That's the situation today. America won't cease their support of Jews in Palestine who are killing Muslims until we smash them adequately and raise the banner of Struggle. They will not desist until we struggle against them. The malefaction of disbelievers will not cease except through Struggle; justice will not be achieved except through Struggle; the tails of apostates will never be severed except through Struggle; falsehood will never be eradicated except through Struggle.

This is all clear and sound. We are a nation with a Glorious history lasting more than fourteen centuries. God never neglected us, Glorious and Exalted is He; rather, he completed our religion for us, sending us his Messenger, blessings and salutations upon him, showing us how to act in these conditions. After [commissioning the Prophet], God also sent the Rightly Guided Caliphs, may God be pleased with them all. Clarifying this matter, Glorious and Exalted God says in the *sura* The Spoils of War: "You wished to take the one lacking might, but God sought to establish the truth according to His words and eradicate disbelievers. That He may establish the truth and abolish falsehood, even if criminals disliked it."[6] Establishing justice according to His words means that He commands you to Struggle in the path of God. Clarifying the means to stop disbelievers' malefaction and aggression, Glorious and Exalted God said to the Messenger, blessings and salutations upon him: "So fight in God's cause; you are held responsible only for yourself. And incite the believers [to do the same] that perhaps God will restrain the fury of those who disbelieve; for God is greater in might and stronger in punishment."[7]

This, then, is the path O brothers in Islam. We must prepare ourselves for the Struggle and train with weapons. The opportunity is now available, thank God, in Afghanistan. In such a way we may be truthful in supporting our brothers in Palestine. If we leave it all up to discussion and dialogue, we will never achieve results. Sixty years have passed and we have done nothing worth mentioning for our brothers there. On the other hand, if we learn to struggle and carry weapons we will be able to demand restitution, as will Islamic nations generally; the matter will be consequential and axiomatic in a way that lends support to our brothers.

This is one aspect. Another aspect is the following: it is extremely easy for us to accomplish this in these very lands; very easy for men, women, and even children to do what Abu Basir did, may God be pleased with him. They understand nothing unless we strike their economy. What is required is to launch an economic war against America and its sanctions just as it has been threatening Muslims by cutting off economic assistance [to them]. Today they threaten Pakistan saying that if you don't distance yourselves from the strugglers they will cut off economic assistance. Two weeks ago, they cut off aid to a neighboring Islamic country right here next to us, the Sudan, ordering the World Bank to stop its assistance to the Sudan because it has resolved to apply God's law. The disbelievers have scorned such efforts; indeed their former president Carter, God curse him, recently journeyed there to conceive plots in southern Sudan. What can make you apprehend the gravity of the danger approaching us if we remain as we are, unwilling to bear arms in these countries and in the Sudan specifically?

[Sudan People's Liberation Army leader John] Garang, God curse him, was supported through aid that was equivalent to ten times the national wealth of the Sudan. He is working from east to west as well as in the south to extend his influence. Pay close attention to this affair! When many people hear news from the Sudan about the rebellion going on in the south they think that the issue is very far removed from them. There is no power or might except through God! This issue is part of a global campaign orchestrated by America and the Jews to deprive Muslims of the very best of what they own! Western newspapers today state as much: Muslims have been overcome with elation and pride due to the triumph of their brothers in Afghanistan. As a result, they're observing a blessed Islamic Awakening [*sahwa islamiyya*] spreading everywhere: here, in Algeria, in Palestine, in Yemen, in the Sudan, in Jordan, and in most lands across the Islamic world, youth are returning to God. The Islamic revival's curve keeps climbing upwards [on the chart]. In their arrogance and vanity, they expound upon their intentions in no uncertain terms: they must work against Muslims until they are knocked down and until they return to their previous state.

Were I to elaborate on this business, describing what they are plotting against you, I believe that you would find little that was new. May God ensure the Sudan's deliverance should it collapse! Between the Sudanese shore and noble Mecca, may God protect it, is an expanse of less than 280 kilometers. Here [*Bin Laden pauses and can be heard directing the audience to a large map*], here just opposite Jeddah on the Sudanese coast is a prominent region called Ras Abu Shajara. From there to noble Mecca the distance is less than 280 kilometers. This means that if the Sudan falls into the hands of this zealous crusader Garang, the [enemy] will have the means to strike Mecca, should God will it, or threaten it with short-range SCUD missiles that have a range of 280 kilometers. With the escalation of pressure on us, including pressure from the East, people will forget Palestine and their brothers there. Jewish Israeli forces will thus seize the opportunity to secure a foothold and advance into what remains of Muslim lands including the Land of the Two Holy Sanctuaries. There is no power or might except through God!

My brothers: the matter is very dangerous. Struggle is obligatory. Do not be deceived in joining the many who sit back and desist from Struggle. The sheer magnitude of backwardness and complacency toward the Struggle has been unknown until recent times. In the era of the Companions of God's Messenger, blessings and salutations upon him, only strugglers were among them. The most distinguishing characteristic among them, may God be pleased with them, the first characteristic attributed to them: witnessing first-hand all events with God's Messenger, God's blessings and salutations be upon him. To be Badri was to have witnessed the battle of Badr and the treaty of Al-Hudaibiyya. We simply must incite the community to Struggle. We must boycott all American goods, inciting the Muslim community in this endeavor, especially the bulk of people in our country. If this happens, may God forgive whatever ensues. If we were to boycott these goods today, our enmity against those disbelievers would grow while their desire for withdrawal would increase. No longer would we confront the situation we have today in which the American, behaving as though he hasn't done anything against us, takes the wealth we have acquired to purchase goods and renders it to the Jews who kill our brothers. There is no power or might except through God.

So my brothers in Islam, take measure of yourselves. How have Jews today entered our countries? Have they not encouraged your brothers in the Sudan and in Palestine to collaborate with the Americans in commercial enterprises of this kind? [The tenth-century Andalusian scholar Abu Muhammad] Ibn Hazm has said, may God show him mercy: cooperation with the assailing infidel is illicit, in matters of sale and other things, if this lends itself to fighting Muslims. If we launch an economic boycott of their goods, unemployment there will grow and their people will speak before their representatives. They will go to Congress to protest that their own interests are being destroyed due to their support for Jews in Palestine.

This is what I wanted to say, then, to remind myself and my brothers what must be done for our brothers there.

THE AUDACIOUS ASCETIC

Let us not consider this matter lightly or philosophize about it. This is incumbent upon you. Consider the case of Great Britain, an empire so vast that, some say, the sun never set upon it. Britain was forced to withdraw from India, one of its largest colonies, when Gandhi the Hindu declared a boycott against their goods. Hindus began to stop wearing any clothing manufactured in Britain, their enmity for the British growing in their hearts. It reached such a point that if a British person wanted to walk freely in the street, he could not do so for fear of the ravenous looks cast upon him by Hindus. Enmity against them grew to such proportions that the British had to leave, by the grace of God, suffering tremendous losses in the process. We must do the same thing today.

We must tell any American we see about what is on our minds, about what distresses us, and about our hatred for their crimes in Palestine. We must explain that they are the reason for these crimes. We must also write to American embassies and consulates to express our condemnation of their criminal acts toward the children and poor women who are bound to us by a single religion and creed.

My brothers in Islam, we have been informed of what happened, as you know. By God, little heed will be given to us and we will be seen only as sheep tagging along like chattel as humiliation falls upon us like a canopy. If we don't bring new life toward our obligations to Struggle, we will forget all about Palestine, you can be assured. The drugged stupefaction underway works precisely in this way, much as it led people to forget how Bukhara and Samarkand were abandoned by Muslims [to Soviet occupation] only about sixty years ago. Today, people scorn anyone who stands up to talk about the ongoing need to struggle there. Such humiliation is odious even for those confused by the multitude of arrows.

Recall the words of [the early Islamic poet] Qatari Ibn Al-Fuja'a who said to himself on the battlefield:

To that part of me dismayed I speak
  Of heroes' ways: Woe should you not heed!
Patience, in the vaults of death such patience
  Not even those most capable can secure the everlasting
Seeking, as you might, but a single day's remove
  From the inviolable appointed hour
No benefit comes to a person in this life
  When his ledger tallies only the loss of worldly delights

That's our situation today. By God, no benefit comes of life except through the service of God and, as He has commanded, through Struggle in the path of God.

Roughly six months after his tough speech against the Saudis from a pulpit in Yemen, the subject of the last chapter, bin Laden seems to have had rediscovered certain merits in diplomacy. Absent from his speech is any reference to "hypocrites" (*munafiq*), a term mentioned over a dozen times earlier in the year and equally prominent in his famous speech to the Saudi National Guard in 1989. Although the location of his speech is unspecified, his presence back home in Saudi Arabia is suggested by a host of factors: his repeated references to Saudi territory and events "here" and "in our country;" his list of countries whose vibrant Islamic revival movements are contrasted with his present location, namely Algeria, Palestine, Yemen, the Sudan, and Jordan; and finally the Saudi and Peninsular Arabic dialects of respondents during a question and answer session following his speech.[8] Bin Laden's likely presence in the kingdom suggests the resilience of his connections with high-level supporters, however withering his critique of the Saudi state might be. Although the 9/11 Commission Report concluded that the Saudi Kingdom lent no assistance or material support to bin Laden as he mobilized audiences toward anti-American militancy leading to the infamous attacks, a Saudi platform at this late date would weaken this thesis.[9] Political scientist Joseph Kostiner has argued that the Saudis tacitly accommodated bin Laden well after 1994, most specifically by allowing him to channel money to terrorist causes as long as he didn't strike at the Kingdom.[10] Wherever the location of his pulpit, his soft handling of Saudi state capitulations, formerly so prominent in his earlier discourse, now marks an important shift in his rhetoric of enmity. Far more explicitly than in previous speeches, bin Laden addresses a topic familiar enough to twentieth-century populations in the Middle East: the Israeli state, or what he refers to as "Jewish migration to the land of Palestine." His exegesis provides a prelude to yet a further, even more serious issue: American economic power and its support for Jewish settlements and expansion under the mantle of the Oslo Peace Accords.

The timing of bin Laden's decidedly anti-American pitch suggests much about his knack for exploiting the news media to promote his interests among public audiences and Saudi state authorities alike. Beginning in early August, Arab and Israeli newspapers began circulating news of secret peace negotiations between long-time leader of the Palestinian Liberation Organization Yasser Arafat and Israeli delegates in Oslo, Norway. These reports were accompanied by the resignation of top PLO representatives in protest and by demonstrations by conservative orthodox Jews against any plan to strike a deal with the Palestinians.

Public hostility against peace negotiations had been conditioned by a violent summer of clashes in South Lebanon. In July, Israel had launched Operation Accountability in retaliation for attacks by both Hezbollah and the Popular Front for the Liberation of Palestine that had led to the deaths of five soldiers from the Israeli Defense Forces. In the course of a conflict that left 120 dead, some 300,000 Lebanese civilians from across the country were displaced and much of Lebanon's infrastructure was damaged or destroyed. The horrors of "the Seven-Day War" fresh in the memories of Arab audiences, distrust was at an all-time high even as international newspapers began heralding the negotiations as a crowning achievement for all parties involved. Just days before bin Laden's speech, news had begun breaking of the instrumental role played in the secret negotiations by then U.S. Secretary of State Warren Christopher; several weeks later, the peace accords would be formalized on the lawn of the White House and blessed by a capacious embrace from U.S. President Bill Clinton. In short, few occasions had been as ripe for bin Laden's critique of an emerging *pax Americana.*

The Saudi administration had been vigilant against overt demonstrations of anti-American and sectarian sentiments in the Kingdom, not only since the 1990 Gulf War and the United States' heavy military presence in the Kingdom. As early as the 1940s scholars no less formidable than 'Abd al-'Aziz Ibn Baz were met with short stints in jail for questioning the king's comfortable relationship with the United States.[11] In recent years, after the outbreak of the first Palestinian Intifada in 1987, the Saudi Ministry of Pilgrimage and Charitable Endowments issued an edict banning sermons making any reference to the destruction of Jews, Christians or the United States. The Saudi administration's wariness of preachers who used their pulpits to mobilize political opposition extended much deeper than censorship against hate speech directed to non-Muslims, however. In order to understand the broader contexts in which bin Laden's autumn lecture would have gained currency among his primary audiences at the time, we must situate his tirade against "outsiders" amidst members of a Saudi Awakening movement (*sahwa islamiyya*). By 1993, their defiance of the royal family was being expressed with unprecedented candor.

If the Saudi Awakening movement arose in the early 1980s among activists in the Muslim Brotherhood whose vocabularies of Western imperialism and its pan-Islamic antidote lay readily at their disposal, its principal leadership was drawn from a younger generation of preachers and intellectuals whose objective was nothing less than to splinter the old and comfortable relationship between the Saudi royalty and its clerical establishment. This relationship had estimable foundations. In 1744, tribal shaikh Muhammad Ibn Saʿud, the esteemed forebear of what would become the modern Saʿudi state, struck up an alliance with religious reformer Muhammad Ibn ʿAbd al-Wahhab in efforts to extend their sway among those who felt constrained by economic and cultural impositions foisted upon them by Ottoman Turks' regional delegates. Through a contract of political and moral expediency iconized later in the form of two crossed swords emblazoned on a national flag, the two men set the stage for what, in the twentieth century, would become ʿAbd al-ʿAziz Ibn Saʿud's claim to legitimacy as ruler over the "Kingdom of the Hijaz and of Najd and Its Dependencies." Capturing the capital city of Riyadh in 1902, ʿAbd al-ʿAziz would slowly consolidate control over the region's many tribes by empowering a tight circle of religious scholars who could trace descent to the Najd, homeland of Muhammad Ibn ʿAbd al-Wahhab. Loyalty to the crown was reinforced through collusion and select concessions. In 1926, King ʿAbd al-ʿAziz made appointments to a "Committee on Commanding the Good and Forbidding the Wrong" (*Hayʾat Al-Amr bi-l-Maʿruf wa-l-Nahi ʿan Al-Munkar*) at the same time that, with weapons and assistance supplied to him by the British, he conquered the Hijaz and changed his title from "sultan" to "king." In the decades that followed, the committee was steered by intellectual heavyweight Muhammad bin Ibrahim Al Al-Shaikh, the grandson of Muhammad Ibn ʿAbd al-Wahhab. Although a staunch critic of modernization, the scholar also navigated potential differences with the kingdom's ambitious rulers through loopholes designed to avoid charges of outright disbelief: rulers could violate God's laws in specific cases as long as they recognized their mistakes and understood that divine law was paramount.[12] Such was the mettle of the kingdom's religious establishment that scholars of non-Najd origin, those least schooled in the moral fabric of Wahhabi reasoning, faced almost universal exclusion from membership in the kingdom's highest offices.

At the onset of the late twentieth century, gradual changes occurred in the kingdom's university system to accommodate a wider range of theological and political debates. The Islamic University of Madina, founded in 1961, was established to provide career paths for non-Najdi students wishing to specialize in religious affairs. A decade later, faculty at the Umm Al-Qura University in Mecca would appoint Muhammad Qutb to teach creed ('aqida) in the Department of Islamic Law, an important signal that the Wahhabi monopoly over theological instruction in the kingdom was slowly eroding. Increasingly, faculty from across the Kingdom encouraged students to think about correct knowledge and behavior as psychological and cultural dispositions as much as strictly legal affairs. Literary clubs across the kingdom provided Awakening activists with an especially apt venue for addressing political advocacy through discourses on culture, tradition, authenticity, and the sour trajectory of all things contemporary.[13] Qutb's intellectual successors pioneered many of these debates. Foremost among them were his student Safar Al-Hawali, later dean of Umm Al-Qura's division of creed ('aqida) and the tenth most featured speaker in bin Laden's tape collection, as well as Salman Al-'Awda and Nasir Al-'Umar, the sixth and eleventh most featured speakers, respectively. Their lectures on "Modern Trends in Muslim Thought," "Jurisprudence Based on Social Reality" (fiqh al-waqi'), "Islam's Battle with Secularism," and "The Etiquette of Dialogue," all featured in bin Laden's tape collection, would make them intellectual superstars among young Saudis. Unlike the cloistered scholars of Riyadh whose arcane legal verbiage left most young Saudis confused, these new voices addressed widespread discontent that had built up as employment rates failed to keep pace with the kingdom's population growth and rapid development during the 1970s and 1980s. Theology students, approximately 40 per cent of whom enrolled in the kingdom's non-traditional Islamic universities, were especially well represented among these unemployed sectors.[14] Thoroughly woven into the rhetoric of disenchantment were aggressive new condemnations of Sufis and Shi'as, Muslim minorities in the country whose alleged susceptibility to psychological and cultural sickness provided far more convenient targets for discipline than did the Wahhabi establishment itself.

The kingdom's scholarly establishment was not immune from critique, however. The Gulf War of 1990 cleared the way for a new era of dissent when top scholars endorsed King Fahd's decision to invite non-Muslim forces under a U.S.-led coalition of armies into the kingdom to defend its borders from Saddam Hussein's advances into Kuwait. For critics of the West who had long warned of the dangers of an expanding American empire in the Middle East, the monarchy had played its hand.

Since direct or even oblique criticism of Saudi rulers was readily met with sanctions or imprisonment, preachers found it easier to focus on the Islamic heartland's assault by foreign infidels. As has been much reported by scholars and journalists both in the West and on the Qatar-based Al-Jazeera television station, Safar Al-Hawali was probably the most outspoken of these anti-American voices.[15] Drawing on his masters thesis on "secularism" and its Western origins, Al-Hawali released an audiocassette in September of 1990 entitled "Flee Thus To God" (*Fa-Farru ila Allah*) (no. 402 in the collection). Taking a page from the same Christian apocalyptic narratives that he denounced, most prominent among them those of the Reverend Jerry Falwell, Al-Hawali conjured up scenarios of Jesus' Second Coming followed by battle with the Antichrist: "those Ba'athists of Iraq are our enemies for a few hours, but Rome is our enemy until doomsday."[16] In a sermon shortly later on Christian Zionist influences on American foreign policies toward Palestine and the Arab world, he would give more immediate urgency to the impending battle by decrying "the imposition of Israeli and American hegemony over the entire area" (tape no. 417, entitled "Palestine: Between Promises Just and Empty"). Such diatribes would later prove inspirational to bin Laden, as noted by a chauffeur who recalled him listening to Al-Hawali's sermons on the way to interviews with Arab journalists in Afghanistan in late 1996.[17] Along with several other volumes later found in bin Laden's house, including "Lessons from the Crusader Wars" (no. 304) and "The Islamic World the Shadow of International Consent" (no. 413), these tapes would likely have proven engaging material for Osama as he rolled along the Afghan countryside. Still, back in Saudi Arabia, Al-Hawali's thesis on America's malevolence in the kingdom was spurned by Saudis across the kingdom for igniting "discord" (*fitna*), try as he might to substantiate his views through pamphlets, books, and letters to Ibn Baz.[18] Indeed, for all the attention he would receive for his focus on the American and Zionist enemies, Al-Hawali preferred to continue directing the bulk of his invective toward corrupt Muslim rulers themselves, the Saudis foremost among them. As noted by one of Hasan Al-Turabi's chief assistants in the Sudan, Ibrahim Al-Sanoussi, bin Laden:

> began to speak about what should happen in Saudi and the reformation that you have to have [there]. It was maybe '93/'94 when he began to speak about that. Before that he was just a contractor, but now these speeches of

Al-Hawali, they began to come all over the Arabic countries in cassettes, criticizing the [Saudi] royal family. And this [atmosphere] gave Osama bin Laden here in the Sudan the chance to speak.[19]

So vehement was Al-Hawali's advice to prioritize the near enemy that, in keeping with the views of other prominent Awakening clerics, he admonished Saudis and other Muslims against going to Afghanistan to fight the Russians, despite the Saudi state's support for the Arab-Afghan struggle.[20] Al-Hawali's dissertation, after all, had focused on the dangers of theological dissent on the Arabian Peninsula during Islam's nascence and their ideological legacies for modern Muslims. By his calculations, if Muhammad Ibn 'Abd al-Wahhab's indebtedness to the kingdom's predominantly Hanbali legal system set him on the right path, the vast majority of Muslims in Afghanistan and Pakistan who adhered to the Hanafi legal school were reprobates, evidence for which was amply supplied in their loyalty to Sufi lineages and unconstrained use of humanistic reasoning.[21] These and other points of orthodoxy are elaborated on at least twenty-five recordings by Al-Hawali in bin Laden's tape collection, roughly 80 per cent of which avoid any reference to the West or the United States. As one of the kingdom's leading creedal specialists, Al-Hawali held the most valuable form of jihad to be exercised through doctrinal studies and outreach (da'wa), not through use of the sword. Arab-Afghan leader 'Abdalla 'Azzam, bin Laden's co-founder at the Office of Services in Peshawar, deserved little attention and even less support: he was an American stooge embroiled in a war for the wrong cause.[22]

Shaikh Salman Al-'Awda proved to be another staunch adversary of the Saudi administration's drift after 1990. Along with Al-Hawali, Al-'Awda is widely considered to have been one of Osama's primary teachers, not least because bin Laden regularly cites Al-'Awda and Al-Hawali's arrests in the early 1990s as a rationale for turning to open militancy. Seeking to explain bin Laden's interest in Al-'Awda's thought, scholars have cited Al-'Awda's tendency to polarize contrasts between Islam's community of the faithful and modern Western secularism under the leadership of the United States, much in the fashion of Egypt's Muslim Brotherhood under its notorious maverick Sayyid Qutb.[23] Former militant colleagues of bin Laden's emphasize Al-'Awda's courage to break with the Saudi administration's conservative stance toward militant adventurism in foreign battles against disbelievers, especially in Bosnia and Tajikistan during the mid 1990s.[24] Once again, however, the topics and contents of Al-ʿAwda's audiotapes in bin Laden's former collection suggest that listeners valued his views on the need for Muslims to defend their faith mostly against corrupt governance within the House of Islam rather than against infidels beyond. His sermons, some of which filled soccer stadiums with an excess of 15,000 fans, exhort listeners on the importance of monitoring and improving their own religious comportment in the service of piety, education, and outreach, all aspects of what Awakening activists call "summoning" (*daʿwa*.) Released just a few months after the outbreak of the Gulf War in 1990, one of his most popular orations, "Sitting on the Sidewalk" (*Jalasa ʿala Al-Rasif*, no. 85 in the collection) exhorts youth to spurn "sleek fancy cars" and extravagant trips to "Bangkok, Casablanca, or France" and instead focus on the ascetic virtues of patience (*sabr*), modest contentment (*ridaʾ*), and humble comportment.[25] Other sermons and lectures underscore the subtle tactics of his political advocacy for change on the homefront.[26] A tape entitled "Let's Join the Struggle (*Hayya ʿala Al-Jihad*)" (no. 113) explains that strugglers can pursue multiple paths, employing their "wealth, soul, or tongue" in its service, as long as they prioritize seeking justice in their own communities over sallying forth to assist besieged Muslims in such far-away lands as Afghanistan or Palestine. A widely disseminated tape "From Behind Bars" (*Min waraʿ Al-Qudban*) (no. 95), released after the imprisonment of several Awakening preachers around 1992, seizes the moral high-ground rather than calling for mass demonstrations or militancy: states in the Islamic world have a responsibility to protect and promote due legal process for all citizens, equal rights to education, free speech, fiscal transparency, health care, and peoples' general quality of life as illustrated in the virtues of Islam's pious community. At least eight of Al-ʿAwda's cassettes feature excerpts from a twenty-nine-plus volume lecture series on transmitted reports (*hadith*) from a classic work of Sunni jurisprudence by fourteenth-century scholar Ibn Hajar Al-Asqalani (*Sharh Bulugh Al-Maram*), delivered from Al-ʿAwda's hometown of Buraida. In general, these and other recordings confirm what political scientist Stéphane Lacroix found to be a trend among religious activists in 1992–3: under Saudi administrative pressure to abide by royal decrees, religious groups competed with each other for legitimacy by organizing educational programs focusing on Wahhabi texts and demonstrating compliance with the kingdom's Islamic legal norms.[27] Al-ʿAwda's efforts to remain in the state's favor, however, proved mixed. His outspokenness on state corruption and occasional outbursts against collaboration with American military forces earned him temporary injunctions against preaching in 1991 and 1992 and then, with Safar Al-Hawali, a prison sentence in September of 1994.

Tensions among Muslim activists across the political spectrum were high, then, when bin Laden returned to the kingdom at the behest of sponsors whose organizational backgrounds and goals remain undisclosed on the audiotape. Still, the shifting terrain of political opposition movements at the time provides us with clues to how potential supporters and their audiences at the time would have construed Osama's past and potential future contributions. By most measures, the Awakening movement's heyday had passed, its most vociferous leaders jailed, cowed into silence, or, most typically, co-opted through institutional re-organization from above. In 1990, King Fahd responded to popular protests against American-led coalition forces in the kingdom by appointing a "Preachers Council" (*majlis al-du'at*) under the supervision of one of the most publicly esteemed senior clerics 'Abd al-'Aziz Ibn Baz. A "Committee of Five" in the following year, all top establishmentarians led by Ibn Baz, streamlined the process for disbarring preachers who strayed from the party line. A few months before bin Laden's speech, a new Ministry of Islamic Affairs, Pious Endowments, Proselytizing, and Guidance had been formed to regulate appointments and promotions across the entire field of religious professionals in the kingdom, a step that neatly complemented those taken for Saudi universities earlier that year.[28] By late 1993, then, Awakening activists who had mobilized over the last three years for serious political reform looked back at their efforts—petitions in the spring and fall of 1991, memorandums of "advice" to the king and Ibn Baz in 1992, renewed letters the subsequent year after a "Law of the Consultative Council" created a sixty-member advisory board staffed mostly by Saudis trained in Western universities and only nine specialists in Islamic law—with a jaundiced eye.[29] The vast majority of religious reformers in the kingdom were urging audiences to place scholarly commitments before further political agitation. In light of such accommodating currents, bin Laden would have to strike a chord among Saudi listeners that would galvanize political activism beyond traditional religious circles. Before examining his speech in closer detail, it is worth reviewing several currents in the Saudi opposition movement that would condition his appeal and shape the kind of leadership available to him among his primarily Arabic-speaking audiences.

By September of 1993, opposition to the monarchy had been fragmented into three notable groups. First among these was a small group of established Wahhabi scholars known among reformers as "the supporters" (al-munasirun). Beginning with the arrest and imprisonment of Shaikh Ibrahim Al-Dubayyan these scholars began to advocate for more open and direct contestation of the High Council of Scholars' monopoly over religious interpretation and law.[30] Key members of this group included Najd-born creedal specialist 'Abdalla Ibn Jibrin, a member of the Ministry of Islamic Affairs, Pious Endowments, Proselytizing and Guidance (no. 35 in the collection); jurist 'Abdalla Al-'Ubaykan (featured on at least four tapes), who urged Saudis to resist leaving the task of "commanding right and forbidding wrong" to establishment clerics themselves; and one of Riyadh's most senior preachers, 'Abdalla Ibn Qu'ud (featured on at least three tapes).[31] Whether due to their political views, their non-Najdi backgrounds or their status as non-tribesmen, such scholars advanced legal and theological arguments for dissent in ways that struck a chord among many Awakening activists who felt marginalized by the state and its ideological platforms. A second group of opposition activists mobilized audiences toward more overt militant activity. Known as the "Battalion of Faith" by late 1994, these individuals demanded the release of leading Awakening preachers, foremost among them Salman Al-'Awda. According to group communiqués, the state's failure to meet their demands would result in the kidnapping of royal family members, senior officers of the Saudi armed forces, and American and Western nationals working in the kingdom.[32] Over the next few years, their continued agitation, none of which appears to have led to specific known attacks, pushed the envelope on how extreme the opposition's rhetoric within the kingdom itself could go, and would lead to the arrests of 150–2,000 individuals.[33]

The third and most organized flank of the opposition was known as the Committee for the Defense of the Legitimate Rights of Arabia (Lajnat Al-Difa' 'an Al-Huquq Al-Shir'iyya). Founded in the spring of 1993 by a host of scholars and intellectuals in Riyadh, the Committee's chief representatives were immediately jailed or forced into silence. Most notable among these was Muhammad Al-Mas'ari, an intellectual and legal specialist whose imprecations against the Saudi administration and its chief legal representative ʿAbd al-ʿAziz Ibn Baz would force him into exile in London during the following year. From abroad, the CDLR would lead the Saudi opposition toward adopting a more fungible platform for political change in the kingdom. Instead of "Islamic legal rights," the ordinary translation of the Arabic phrase *al-huquq al-shirʿiyya*, the organization would translate its title as "legitimate rights" and emphasized its focus on human rights, civil reform, moral advocacy, and other objectives more palatable to multinational sponsors. Although the CDLR never endorsed militant operations in the Saudi homeland and would shy from any association with bin Laden after his public rise to notoriety in the late 1990s, Al-Masʿari's relocation to London would provide bin Laden with his first genuine opening to setting up an organization of his own in the West.[34] On 6 March 1994, the day after being stripped of his Saudi citizenship, bin Laden announced his establishment of an auspiciously labeled Committee for Advice and Protection of Legitimate Rights.[35] Terrorism, he stated to an Arab journalist a few days later, had no place in his group's mission.[36] Several months later, in homage to Al-Masʿari's exile, the Committee set up its headquarters in London as the slightly revised Committee for Advice and Reform (CAR) (*Hayʾa Al-Nasiha wa-l-Islah*).[37] The organization served, for the first time, to translate and publicize bin Laden's views worldwide and facilitate communications between those who might be inclined to his cause.

Bin Laden's September speech in the previous year can best be understood in relation to the unfolding charter of the Saudi opposition under the CDLR as its leaders faced increasing scrutiny and repression. At the very time that bin Laden took the podium, Muhammad Al-Masʿari was being tortured in Riyadh, a harrowing account of which would be preserved later in his audiotape library under the label "Muhammad Al-Masʿari and Imprisonment" (no. 1192). Bin Laden would certainly have been apprised of Al-Masʿari's plight and informed about the urgency of avoiding further retaliatory action by the state. His speech would have nicely complemented the opposition's campaign to mollify authorities at the time and secure breathing room while planning its next steps. Wherever the forum, bin Laden finds the occasion expedient for branding his image as a supporter of pan-Islamic unity, a theme that would come to play an increasingly pronounced role as he faced exile and continuous decampment in years ahead.

Citing Qur'anic verses originally delivered to remind the Prophet Muhammad's early followers of the treachery of pagan Arab tribes in the seventh century, bin Laden begins his speech by cuing listeners to a far more contemporary context of inter-faith conflict: "They appeared to our brothers, in Palestine and many other lands. They appeared as Jews, as Christians, as idolators (*mushrikun*) and heretics (*mulhidun*)… God, Glorious and Exalted is He, has said: 'They do not extend any pact of kinship or covenant of protection toward you.'"[38] Given the recently announced Oslo Accords, an event he likens to "a media disinformation campaign to drug Muslims' feelings," and in light of America's staunch advocacy for Israel despite "the loss of blood among Palestinians in Palestine and the crushing of bones among our sons' children," Muslims can no longer sit idly by, "a horrific silence descending upon the community." Returning to a well-rehearsed theme since his earliest days as an Arab-Afghan volunteer, bin Laden calls his audience to arms. The urgency of defending the homeland is underscored not only by the plight of Palestinians but by what bin Laden claims to be Greater Israel's designs on Saudi Arabia, including "Tabuk… Khaibar, Taima, and Bani Quraidah in [Madina]." Evidence for Israel's military threat to the kingdom lies in the Sudan. Reminding listeners of recent advances by John Garang, a U.S.-educated Sudanese Christian who was rallying forces against the Islamist regime of Colonel 'Omar Al-Bashir as leader of the Sudan People's Liberation Army, bin Laden notes that only 280 miles separated Mecca from the Sudan, an expanse easily bridged by SCUD missiles. Should the Sudan fall to Garang's troops, bin Laden exclaims, "Jewish Israeli forces will thus seize the opportunity to secure a foothold and advance into what remains of Muslim lands including the Land of the Two Holy Sanctuaries."

While the threat to Muslim heartlands is profoundly territorial and best illustrated by the suffering of Palestinians under an expanding Israeli state licensed by the Oslo Accords, bin Laden also suggests throughout his speech that the greater danger may, in fact, be economic. Slouching toward Jerusalem, its insidious presence a "ledger" that, in the words of bin Laden's sixth-century Arab poet, "tallies only the loss of worldly delights," financial profit corrupts Muslims through a logic that draws far and near enemies into one living tomb. For audiences who might wish to repel such a foe, bin Laden proposes a double-edged asceticism that might be deployed along multiple fronts.

First, rehearsing anti-American talking points that would draw much attention from Western and Arab media networks beginning in 1996, bin Laden frames Israel's ambitions as "part of a global campaign orchestrated by America and the Jews to deprive Muslims of the very best of what they own." To a far greater extent than in previous speeches, bin Laden identifies the United States as a primary instigator of Muslim oppression. Sidestepping the intimate relations between America and Saudi Arabia, mention of which could well have jeopardized the livelihoods of those in his audience at the time, bin Laden chooses his words carefully. American economic sanctions against the Islamic nations of Pakistan and the Sudan earn foremost opprobrium. When combined with its bankrolling of Israeli aggression against Palestinians and its venal hostility to "the Awakening" (*sahwa*) in "most lands cross the Islamic world," America can justifiably be targeted through armed resistance. Calling for "painful strikes directly against their heads, their economy, and their selves," bin Laden solicits listeners to prepare themselves by enrolling in militant training camps in Afghanistan. According to at least one individual who worked closely with him around this time, bin Laden seems to have explored the implications of his call by quietly reviewing plans to detonate car bombs outside American embassies and government buildings in Nairobi, Kenya just a few months later.[39]

When subject to public evaluation, bin Laden's argument for "striking" the American enemy was intrinsically fraught, of course. Aside from the support which governments across the Arabian Peninsula and Arab world gave to the United States in the wake of the Iraqi invasion of Kuwait, the newly founded post-communist Islamic State of Afghanistan keenly advocated for the United States' support in its campaign against rebels. In the Sudan, meanwhile, the Islamist regime of 'Omar Al-Bashir seemed by most accounts to be holding strong against Garang's forces, whatever pressure America might be applying against it at the time. To most of his listeners, as bin Laden acknowledges, the Sudanese conflict seemed "very far removed." Rather than attempting to bolster his case for violent attacks against the far enemy, bin Laden adopts a different tactic. He recruits Mohatma Gandhi, the world's most famous modern ascetic, to his cause. "Consider the case of Great Britain," he exhorts: "Britain was forced to withdraw from India, one of its largest colonies, when Gandhi the Hindu declared a boycott against their goods." Gandhi's lessons, according to bin Laden, include discarding the colonizer's fashionable clothes, cultivating enmity for the oppressor, and growing so "ravenous" that even one's looks might chase the enemy away.

The election of "Gandhi the Hindu" as chief emblem for bin Laden's war against Americans suggests the extreme to which bin Laden was willing to go in order to rally listeners against the far enemy. While the urgency of asceticism and boycotting American goods would continue to feature in his future speeches, notably among them his 1996 "Declaration of War" against the Americans and a sermon in 2003 excoriating Arab rulers for catering to Zionist-American interests, Gandhi's example would never again be mentioned. In late 1993, however, as bin Laden addressed a Saudi audience that was likely split about the Saudi Awakening's immediate and long-term goals for reform in the kingdom, bin Laden seems to have found Gandhi's legacy useful for putting a more ecumenical stamp on Muslims' struggles against foreign occupiers. For all his invective in support of armed militancy against the outsider, civil dissent at home may, in fact, be the nobler ambition. "We must boycott all American goods," he declares, "inciting the Muslim community in this endeavor, especially the bulk of people in our country." Elaborating further, he admonishes his listeners to put their mouths and pens to work: "We must tell any American we see about what is on our minds, about what distresses us, and about our hatred for their crimes in Palestine. We must explain that they are the reason for these crimes. We must also write to American embassies and consulates to express our condemnation of their criminal acts toward the children and poor women who are bound to us by a single religion and creed." Even if a stronger Muslim community was to be the goal of political activism, non-Muslims themselves might prove formidable allies. Indeed, while inaugurating his speech with reference to a "common enemy, especially the Jews and Christians," his turn to Gandhi's model of non-violent resistance at the end of his speech invokes an arsenal more secular and post-colonial than religious. In lieu of a pan-Islamic caliphate, bin Laden envisions a league of come-ye-may brethren who might steel their resolve against Western neoliberal economic policies and imperialism.[40] Much ink has been devoted to the tactical advantages of bin Laden's ecumenicalism for recruiting a rag-tag army of disaffected youth in a global Islamic jihad against the West. This speech illustrates, however, the extent to which a pitch to a more heterodox pool of activists might breathe new life into local opposition movements whose primarily religious vocabularies had exposed them to state repression or co-optation.

By some measures, bin Laden's big-tent approach corresponded with gains at the time among Saudi Awakening leaders in recruiting the support of a broader range of Saudi political activists. By late 1993, the state's heavy-handed meddling in professorial appointments at the Islamic University of Madina, long an Awakening stronghold, had produced a wider coalition of dissident voices among religious reformers, intellectuals, and even scattered Sufi brotherhoods accusing the state of exploiting a call for scholarly revival to repress any who contested its version of Wahhabi ideology.[41] When, in the following year, Ibn Baz issued his scholarly opinion in favor of the Oslo Accords and making peace with Israel, public outcry in the kingdom gave new fuel to the opposition. Bin Laden seized these occasions to release letters denouncing Saudi corruption and calling for regime change. The London-based Committee for Advice and Reform proved to be an ideal location for his activities: from its inception in 1994 until its closure in 1998, the CAR devoted the vast majority of its resources to coordinating opposition to the Saudi royalty.[42] Its distinction from other, more prominent London-based Saudi opposition groups at the time, such as the CDLR, lay in its recourse to more strident religious vocabulary when defending its mission. Muslim rulers who catered to ignorance and barbarism (*jahiliyya*), for example, deserved no part of an Islamic state's sovereign charter, and principles of accountability (*ihtisab*) were the bedrock of order for a markedly pious community (*umma*).[43] The CAR also distinguished itself through its occasional nod to the legitimacy of armed rebellion in struggles for regime change in the Muslim world, foremost among them the Battalion of Faith.[44]

However much bin Laden sought to couch his critique of the Saudis in a broader and more generic call for resistance to Zionist-American imperialism in the region, his efforts would come back to sting him. In the spring following his evocation of Gandhi as Islam's ideal warrior, bin Laden would wake up to find himself stripped of his citizenship, a highly unusual move even for Saudi authorities used to disciplining subjects. His September speech may well have raised alarms for urging audiences to take up arms against a foreign "colonial" who also happened to be the kingdom's primary military and economic benefactor. His rancor proved most damning, however, where his asceticism was given a classicized Arabian inflection. If bin Laden's call to administer "painful strikes directly against their heads, their economy, and their selves" implicated Americans explicitly, its rationale was to be grounded in Muslims' earliest struggles against Meccan disbelievers themselves. Much of the narrative anchor for his speech proved to be a history lesson about the ways a single valiant convert named Abu Basir had been persecuted and tortured by the Arabian Peninsula's most powerful ruling merchant family, the Quraish. Reserving roughly twice as much time to the narrative as in his earlier speech that year in Yemen, bin Laden asked listeners to consider Abu Basir's resolve in killing his infidel captors and waging armed combat against them from "Al-'Ais, here on the shores of the Red Sea, between Jeddah and Yanbu'." Before taking questions from the audience, he reminded them of Abu Basir's success in attacking the Quraish's economic livelihood and cited a transmitted report (*hadith*) that had regularly featured in his speeches since the late 1980s: "If people let their thoughts dwell upon the *dinar* and *dirham*, pledged allegiance [to rulers] for material gain, pursued the 'tails of cows' [the servants of the powerful] and abandoned the Struggle: God would inflict humiliation upon them, never lifting them up again until they return to their religion." Few who were aware of Al-Mas'ari's ordeals at the time would have missed bin Laden's cue to prioritize the battle on more familiar shores. Rounding off his response to the first question shortly later, he cites verses of Qatari Ibn Al-Fuja'a, a seventh-century poet renowned not only for his martial valor but for his loyalty to the Kharijites, a group of early Islamic iconoclasts who rejected claims to authority based on blood descent from the Prophet Muhammad. Greater than the thirst for martyrdom, depicted in much early Arab poetry as the warrior's desire to hasten death through combat, is the valor of a more ascetic forbearance: "Woe should you not heed!/ Patience, in the vaults of death such patience… No benefit comes to a person in this life/When his ledger tallies only the loss of worldly delights." Self-abnegation at home was the struggler's true path.

According to the 9/11 Commission report, bin Laden had begun reviewing operational plans to attack American targets in December of 1993, just three months after the speech that opens this chapter.[45] Although the assertion rests on unverifiable or questionable sources, more substantial evidence for bin Laden's operational involvement in planning attacks against the United States would certainly accumulate by the late 1990s.[46] However early we wish to push bin Laden's involvement in terrorist attacks against the United States, his speech in September of 1993 provides valuable insights into how he was crafting his image among public audiences at the time. My analysis of his speech and its historical context suggests that we must revise at least three widely spread assertions about bin Laden's views and al-Qa'ida's earliest strategic objectives.

First, the occasion for bin Laden's earliest and most developed speech against American influence in the Islamic world is not the 1990 Gulf War, as commonly professed.[47] The anchor for his anti-Americanism is instead the aftermath of the 1993 Oslo Accords that envisioned lasting peace between Israel and the Palestinians. Not until December of 1994, in his first open letter to Ibn Baz, does bin Laden raise the presence of U.S.-led troops on the Arabian Peninsula as a matter for public scrutiny.[48] Indeed, in 1992, when 107 Saudi clerics and intellectuals signed a "Memorandum of Advice" to King Fahd expressing their outrage at his decision to allow U.S. troops onto Saudi soil, bin Laden refused to sign. When addressing the topic of non-Muslim aggression in the Islamic world through the early 1990s, he would find most audiences far more receptive to either his accounts of fighting communists or his critique of Israel's treatment of Palestinians than to denouncing the United States, one of the most important allies of ruling Arab regimes across the region. As is evident in his September 1993 speech, bin Laden could draw amply from a trough of bilious religious discourse that coated Jews and Christians in ages of treachery and global conspiracy against Muslims. Still, Saudi preachers inclined to such demonization, most often in the service of some pan-Islamic ideal, were in ample supply in the kingdom and were featured by scores in bin Laden's tape collection. Audiences came to expect a different product from bin Laden than from the likes of Safar Al-Hawali, Nasir Al-'Umar, or Omar 'Abd al-Rahman. As noted by Pakistani journalist Hamid Mir, bin Laden's calling card was contemporary politics rather than Islamic law: "When he started quoting from the Islamic *shari'a* and Islamic books and Qur'an, that the Qur'an says to fight against the non-Muslims for the supremacy of the Islamic law, there was no thrill."[49] While the hallmark of his political critique would become a rant against America, this discourse emerged initially as a hydra whose heads assumed local guises. Abu Basir's fight against a "common enemy" proved exemplary because, much like Robin Hood, he had the courage to purge his native soil of its egregious materialists.

Second, bin Laden's most strident public speech against Americans is delivered first not from Afghanistan, the Sudan, Iran, Libya, or any other traditionally labeled "rogue" country but rather from a pulpit in Saudi Arabia, one of the United States' longest standing allies in the Middle East. The Oslo Accords were convenient for whipping up public sympathies. The pretext for his diatribe, however, was Saudi authoritarianism, no more so than under the glare of an emboldened and increasingly transnational Saudi opposition movement. However much the American FBI drew attention to his 1993 involvement in planning attacks on American targets in Kenya, Egyptian national ʿAli ʿAbdelsoud Mohammad, their chief informant, also insisted that bin Laden's main goal at the time was to train recruits to bring down the Saudi regime.[50] Bin Laden's public communiqués from the office of the Advice and Reform Committee between 1994 and 1996 focused above all on Saudi corruption. It is perhaps little wonder that the FBI found no reason to open a file on the Saudi renegade until his Declaration of War against Americans in August 1996. Indeed, by some accounts, American and British officials before that date found certain merits in bin Laden's rhetoric and advocacy for change.[51] Though it is easy to forget, consensus in Washington and London throughout the early 1990s was that pressure from Saudi reformers, including bin Laden himself, could help bring about much-needed reforms in the kingdom and prevent a volatile political system from collapsing into anarchy.[52] If my argument about bin Laden's Saudi podium is correct, certain high-level officials within Saudi Arabia itself agreed. Little imagination is needed to conjecture about the ways bin Laden's call to arms, ostensibly inflected with the right amount of civility, might play to the state's favor when countering its most vocal critics: Of course the presence of American troops on Saudi soil is a bone of contention! However played, the Saudi-centric pretext for bin Laden's animosity would be lost in translation when picked up after 9/11 and amplified in a theater of global sound bites. It was the proximity of the enemy, its resemblance to what was familiar more than to what was different, that rallied bin Laden's audiences and expanded his influence at the time. While bin Laden's speech was cued to the designs of a "Greater Israel" against Muslims across the world, his enemy was less a hydra, its heads bound by a single body, than a chimera of equal parts lion, goat, and serpent.

Third, bin Laden's path to militancy can be traced less to America's heavily expanded military presence in the Kingdom starting in 1990, as is commonly asserted, than to the Saudi administration's crack-down on Awakening activists in the early 1990s and its ongoing refusal to tolerate challenges to its autocratic style of governance. To restore these latter variables to the story of bin Laden's gradual maturation as the world's most wanted terrorist, we must move beyond his rhetoric about Americans, Jews, and non-Muslim infidels to consider his principal role for those seeking radical change in the region. Given the severity of censorship against those who would criticize the Saudi royalty itself, Saudi listeners clearly appreciated the way bin Laden could turn up the heat against their rulers indirectly. His denunciation of American interests in the region was all the more convincing given his family's long-established ties with American companies and the massive fortune assembled at the king's right hand. We may speculate about the ways history might have turned out differently had the Saudi administration implemented reforms addressing charges of autocracy and corruption in more productive ways. As it was, bin Laden's anti-Americanism provided the opposition with a voice that was otherwise easily quashed.

8

DAWN ANTHEMS (*ANASHID AL-FAJR*)

(Conversation among strugglers (*mujahidin*) in the kitchen of an Arab-Afghan training camp. Recording made by a cook named Abu 'Abd al-Rahman due to his affections for visiting senior Yemeni militant Abu Hamza.[1] Produced between mid-1989 and 2001. Excerpts from sixty-minute cassette no. 1111.)

Transcript 1: Egg Engineers (Side A, minutes 1:08–2:02)

[*Sound of kerosene stove*]

1. Cook: Air! Air! Air! Give it some air! Don't you notice that its voice is weak? It needs air...I mean...with force.

   [*Popping.*]

2. Cook: Yes!

   [*More popping.*]

3. Cook: Give it to him...Give it more, more, more...No, don't stop too early...Aaaaay! Too early, too early...Give it more...Give it more until... Heh! You see!

4. Speaker A [*admiringly*]: Oooooo!

5. Cook: Engineers are we!

6. Speaker A: Engineers of eggs.

7. Cook: No...We should put our [*unclear*] like this.

   [*Group laughter.*]

8. Abu Hamza: By God they're going to win your friendship!

9. Cook: Simple salt is what we have here. There you have politicians.
10. Abu Hamza: Where?
11. Cook: Over there... well actually, even here. In reality, we were going to make eggs in a way...mean...that would compel you and your crew to devour them ravenously.
12. Speaker B: All of you would devour the eggs, followed by your own fingers!
13. Speaker C: Tell them [*i.e. the politicians*]: 'You guys are the ones who made them.'

Transcript 2: Mister Hellfire's Desserts (Side A, minutes 2:04–4:09)

1. Abu Hamza: Is that meat, there? Is there any more left?
2. Cook: Huh?
3. Abu Hamza: Is there any more left?
4. Cook: I pray to God that there is some left, and if there is none left, I pray to God that a lamb comes our away... so we could roast it up.
5. Abu Hamza: Call out to them, Abu Hafiz...Tell them that [the lamb] is ready and waiting!
6. Cook: Yea yea! It is said "If something comes to you from Saudi Arabia..."
7. Speaker C [*interrupting*]: Tell them there is a storage facility here, like at the Badr Camp [a Saudi-funded camp in Eastern Afghanistan founded in the 1980s for Afghan Arabs fighting the Soviets].
8. Cook [*resuming*]: ..."then you should turn it into a gift."

[*Sound of kitchenware being moved around*]

9. Cook: Yes...I'll ask him about the desserts of Mister Hellfire.
10. Abu Hamza: Mister Hellfire?
11. Cook: We have someone nicknamed "Mister Hellfire" in Mecca. He makes *tahaniya* dessert. Of course, the dessert is a local delicacy; the better known Syrian desserts are different.
12. Abu Hamza: [*Unclear question about the dessert.*]
13. Cook: Not exactly.
14. Abu Hamza: Are they made with tahini?...Tahini?
15. Cook: They look like hair.
16. Abu Hamza: Ah!
17. Cook: They're like the red desserts that people call *harissa*.
18. Abu Hamza: [*Another comment on the dessert.*]
19. Cook: Look, it's made with homemade ghee. It is produced in Mecca and contains God's blessing (*baraka*).
20. Speaker D: God is Greater!
21. Abu Hamza: [*chuckles*]
22. Speaker E: Hey, let him finish eating. At this rate he'll need a thousand years!

[*Lull in conversation*]

23. Speaker D: Give me the knife, dear Shaikh…
24. Speaker E: That knife next to you there, Abu Hamza.
25. Abu Hamza: This one?
26. Cook: That's right.
27. Abu Hamza: Or this one [*alluding to a second knife*]?
28. Cook: It's that one there [*alluding to the first knife*].

[*Abu Hamza delays in jest*]

29. Speaker E: Will he ever hand us the knife!?
30. Cook [*laughing*]: They've downed too much tea! Drunk it down!

Transcript 3: Gathering Intelligence (Side A, Minutes 4:11–6:01)

1. Cook: He doesn't know the route.
2. Abu Hamza: To where?
3. Cook: To the square.
4. Abu Hamza: I'd like to go there because my house is there… Maybe we could bring back one of the roosters?
5. Cook: I tell you what. I'll get it [a rooster] for you.
6. Abu Hamza: Could you get me there and back on the same day?

[*Pause*]

7. Speaker B: You should bring your things with you.
8. Abu Hamza: He knows the route.
9. Cook: We'll go to Shaf [possibly Shaf-e Heyvanat, a village in the Helmand province], and bring a load of roosters back in the car.

[*Pause*]

10. Speaker F: By God, my Brother, perhaps they could go [to fetch the roosters] in the evening and bring the car back with them… After gathering intelligence, I mean. The alleged purpose for you brothers going… What could it be?
11. Speaker B: The car, perhaps.
12. Cook: Bringing the brothers.

[*Brief laughter*]

13. Speaker D: Bread!
14. Speaker E [*agreeing*]: For example!
15. Cook: I mean… it would have to be something strange.
16. Speaker E: We brought it for you, Abu Hamza!
17. Cook: Take it, my brother. The truth is…
18. Abu Hamza: A welcome gift indeed!

[*Group laughter*]

19. Cook: In truth, all this leads me to say things…

20. Speaker C: Don't betray us…we will eat the roosters.
21. Speaker E: Eat, eat, eat, eat Shaikh!
22. Cook: By God, it's not tasty enough…we need [*unclear*]
23. Abu Hamza [*protesting*]: It's tasty [*then exclaiming loudly as the cook adds something to his eggs*]: Oh!

[*Pause*]

24. Speaker G: Wait for tea.
25. Speaker D [*referring to Abu Hamza*]: Was he given just this much?
26. Cook: Huh?
27. Speaker D: Was his portion [*of eggs*] like this to begin with?…I mean, his portion couldn't have been this, by God!
28. Cook: It's fine, but, I mean, do you know what? To get this nice yolky part in the middle, you have to be an amir!
29. [*Brief laughter. Someone hiccoughs, causing more laughter.*]
30. Speaker E: What did you just say, my brother?!
31. Cook: I'll tell you. This middle portion always goes to Abu Hamza. Seriously…because he is crazy for taste.
32. Speaker D: That's right. And if not…you're doing him an injustice.

[*More stove pumping*]

Transcript 4: Dreams, High Heels, Coffee and Gas (Side A, minutes 17:17–21:12)

1. Cook [*laughing*]: What does he dream about?

2. Abu Hamza: Brother, what comes to me during sleep arrives unexpectedly.

[*Laughter*]

3. Abu Hamza: It's true…It's true, brother [*unclear*]…This [wakefulness] is not my disposition, even if circumstances require it. I never feel [the sleep coming on.]

4. Cook: It would have been better had you taken the first guard shift of the night. [*Laughter among others*]. Always.
5. Abu Hamza: Just to entertain the guests!
6. Cook: Why do you head to bed so early?
7. Speaker H [*to the cook*]: The situation you put yourself in: is it how you had anticipated it in your mind?
8. Cook [*drawing on a proverb*]: "I slept near hellfire, but he was right next to me." Say: Abu Hamza, wake up!
9. Speaker E: That's the night for you, the night.
10. Cook: Yep.
11. Abu Hamza: These days, when I wake up from sleeping, having gotten used to long stretches of sleep, I felt drowsy. One can say that these are the usual circumstances. But, for the most part, I come up with inde-

pendent lines of reasoning. When I rise after sleeping and begin to move around [*unclear*], I mean, all of it produces strange elucidation.

12. Cook: God is Greater!
13. Abu Hamza: That's right.
14. Cook: All of this is influenced by the trace of night. [*Laughs*]
15. Abu Hamza: Look. What is this indicative of? I never got any benefit from elucidation. [*Group laughter*] I would skew...I would skew my own analogical reasoning because such elucidation didn't seem to relate to anything. I just wanted to sleep. I'll say this: at one point, I used to spend in Aden, myself with my family. There was a female teacher there...
16. Speaker C: God is Greater!
17. Cook: Oh God! Oh God! Oh God! Watch out! Abu Hamza: who was studying what?
18. Speaker I: She must have been an elderly lady, mature in years.
19. Abu Hamza: Nope. She wasn't old.

[*Uproarious group laughter and muttering.*]

20. Cook: God help us!
21. Abu Hamza: She left her homeland, somewhere in the north. It was odd.
22. Speaker I: She must have been a doctoral student, I'm sure of it...for her to have left.

[*Laughter*]

23. Cook: Follow, follow the story, 'Abdalla.
24. Abu Hamza: She would walk in high, high ('*al* '*al*) heels...walk in high, high heels.
25. Speaker I: What are those?

[*Laughter*]

26. Abu Hamza: By God it's true.
27. Cook: "High high" ('*al* '*al*) is a brand of rice where I come from!

[*Laughter*]

28. Abu Hamza: By God! And when I used to do these math lessons, I would never pay attention, ever, and I didn't do the homework. One time I was reprimanded for not doing the exercises. I'd write down quick answers to the formulas and let her correct them.
29. Speaker I: God is Greater!
30. Speaker J: What was up with that teacher?...But what was your stance, Abu Hamza? What was the stance?
31. Abu Hamza [*laughing hard*]: We confused everything...[*Laughing*]... God help us!

[*Group laughter*]

32. Cook [*laughing*]: Wrap it up, wrap it up Abu Hamza!
33. Abu Hamza [*laughing*]: By God its true! How we confused things!

[*Group laughter*]

34. Cook [*laughing*]: Finish it up, finish it Abu Hamza!
35. Abu Hamza [*regaining control*]: So, I had written down an answer.
36. Cook: Yes.
37. Abu Hamza: And I made a gesture, saying: "Huh?" Blindly, I took no pleasure in it. So, it was suddenly all over, and she put a stop to it.

[*Pause*]

38. Abu Hamza: Ah! [*Suddenly bursting into laughter as he accidentally upsets a kerosene stove.*]
39. Cook: What have you done!

[*Group laughter.*]

40. Abu Hamza [*laughing hard*]: Good God!
41. Cook [*laughing*]: What have you made here, Abu Hamza!?
42. Abu Hamza [*perhaps referring to the upset kerosene stove*]: It won't be long before it starts singing!
43. Cook [*laughing*]: It happened here. Yes, from right here!
44. Speaker I [*clicking his tongue in disapproval*]: Take the glass from him.
45. Speaker E [*laughing in agreement*]: The glass! Yes good, brother.
46. Cook [*laughing*]: The glass!
47. Speaker H: Shut if off, shut if off! No, no, no! [*Laughter as gas from the stove spills into Abu Hamza's tea glass.*] Raisins!

[*Group laughter*]

48. Abu Hamza [*laughing hard*]: By God [*unclear*], there's some nice tea in the glass!

[*Group laughter*]

49. Abu Hamza: Raisins in the glass [*echoing Speaker C's comparison of the floating gas droplets to raisins*].
50. Speaker E: "Raisins with Gas," we'll call it.
51. Abu Hamza: Well, it's not exactly tea any more. It did have sugar, mind you.
52. Speaker E: No no!
53. Abu Hamza: If it was bagged up, it could be packaged [*and sold*] with other things!
54. Speaker E: It should absolutely be packaged!
55. Abu Hamza [*laughing*]: God be with us! [*Unclear*] What would we do with it!? Oh God!
56. Cook: We have conducted an experiment in having coffee with gas. It is a good thing! Yes [*laughing*]…if one of us gets diarrhea, this gas concoction will serve as medicine.

Transcript 5: Dinosaurs and Scary Dogs (Side A, minutes 23:14–26:08)

1. Speaker K: Oh Abu Hamza!
2. Speaker E: Did the raisins get into the glass, or not?
3. Abu Hamza: No. In the small one, you could say, there's a bit.
4. Cook: Look, let's test it out, Shaikh, it's still early.
5. Abu Hamza: This glass doesn't have any sugar in it?
6. Cook: No.
7. Speaker C: Sugar in the glass is good.
8. Cook [*to Abu Hamza*]: This one has it too, as you see. And now you don't need to light a fire or anything. [*Group laughter*] Just add sugar to your tea in the water, and that's it…Just pick it up and drink.
9. Abu Hamza: And you can leave me alone and content!

[*Group laughter*]

10. Cook: It's as if Abu Hamza has become a "dinosaur" [meaning a dragon]!
11. Speaker K: He begins to flap his wings, flames shooting out of his mouth!

[*Group laughter*]

12. Cook [*laughter*]: We'd send you to the bathroom (*dush*), to your own brood!
13. Speaker H: He would be in wretched places!
14. Cook: He'd leave from Bustuk [the nearest village] in quite a state!

[*Group laughter*]

15. Speaker K: Or rather, from far away he would blow flames on them… and everything would be incinerated! [*Laughing*] God is Greater! [*Pause*.] He'd blow flames on the tanks until they were all obliterated.
16. Cook: God is Greater!

[*Pause*]

17. Abu Hamza: As I was saying, I'll tell you: I would be sitting on the chair, and I'd want to sleep. [The female teacher would say]: "How is the sitting going for you my brother Abu Hamza?"

[*Group laughter*]

18. Abu Hamza [*laughing*]: "Excuse me! Excuse me!" [*Pause*] I mean, I would be sitting on the chair, of course. "Come here!" She used to say it like that to me.
19. Cook: I see.
20. Abu Hamza: Such a practice…Well, it was done in a way…All of us felt the same. It was difficult!
21. Cook: Yes.
22. Abu Hamza: Impossible!

[*Group laughter*]

23. Abu Hamza: So suddenly…Suddenly, I fell asleep!! What do you mean "I fell asleep"? What was my problem?! And then suddenly, I woke up from sleeping!

[*Laughter*]

24. Abu Hamza: I woke up to a peel of laughter all around me!
25. Cook: They were laughing at you?
26. Abu Hamza: They were all laughing. And the teacher said: "You're in big trouble Mister," and embarrassed me a lot.

[*Group laughter*]

27. Abu Hamza: Falling asleep was easy. Then I woke up: "When did I fall asleep?" [*Group laughter*] How they were laughing!
28. Speaker E: "A half hour ago. An hour." [*Group laughter*]
29. Cook: And then what?
30. Abu Hamza: After that, she asked me to get out and wipe off my face [having picked up smudges from the desktop]. I didn't want to. I didn't want to a bit!
31. Cook: To wipe your face against the blackboard or what?

[*Group laughter*]

32. Speaker E: Using an eraser?
33. Abu Hamza [*laughing*]: No, I was supposed to wipe it with running water. So, do you hear? I didn't want to. Why? When I had asked for permission to leave the classroom a previous time, I left, but was followed by a dog. And I began to run away, trying to escape! There was some free time, and by the will of God [*sighing*] there was the dog, roaming around and always coming at me. I would go another way and the dog would come running after me. When I returned to the class to recount what had happened, the whole class burst into laughter.
34. Cook: It was an experience full of lessons.
35. Abu Hamza: They thought I was scared.
36. Cook: They put a dog out there to keep people in class, huh?

[*Group laughter*]

37. Abu Hamza: The dog, the dog was normal…I mean, sure, it would issue commands on occasion.

[*Group laughter*]

Transcript 6: Eyeglasses and the U.S. Dollar (Side A, minutes 26:13–28:55)

1. Cook: See how they behave around him?

[*Pause*]

2. Speaker H [addressing Abu Hamza]: Those belong to you, do they [*referring to a pair of glasses*]?

3. Cook: What those? Yeah…they're excellent.
4. Speaker I: For when you wake up from sleeping.

   [*Pause*]

5. Speaker I: No laughing, now.
6. Speaker H [*jokingly*]: What are you hinting at!

   [*Group laughter*]

7. Speaker I [*laughing*]: My point is that people will tell stories. No, come on. He's deeply satisfied (*mukayyif*), deeply satisfied indeed.

   [*Group laughter*]

8. Abu Hamza [*laughing*]: "Deeply satisfied"!? How could that be?

   [*Pause*]

9. Cook: Has your eyesight been weak for a while?
10. Abu Hamza: Even my younger brother. It's the same even for my younger brother. His vision was weak. My father, and mother too…
11. Cook: God help us.
12. Speaker E: How much?
13. Abu Hamza: Huh?
14. Speaker E: How limited is it?
15. Abu Hamza: About half.

    [*Group laughter*]

16. Cook: God is Greater! Are you sure its half, Abu Hamza?
17. Speaker L: Do you mean five out of ten?
18. Abu Hamza [*using metrical units*]: Three out of six.
19. Speaker L: God is Greater!
20. Abu Hamza: The highest rating is six, and you subtract from that.
21. Speaker L: Where I come from, we measure eyesight on a scale of ten.
22. Speaker E: Of course, I find it strange that…
23. Abu Hamza [*interrupting*]: The standards differ from one place to another.

    [*Group laughter*]

24. Cook [*laughing*]: How does this happen!?
25. Abu Hamza: They differ! It's ten where he's from…what?
26. Cook: It varies according to the exchange rate of the U.S. dollar!

    [*Group laughter*]

27. Speaker H: It goes down and up.
28. Cook: That's why, in competition, he doesn't look out to see adversaries with his eyes but instead follows them [blindly] with his head.
29. Speaker H: He has to stand up.
30. Cook [*clarifying himself*]: Because his voice is stronger [than his vision].

    [*Pause*]

213

31. Abu Hamza [*yawning*]: The problem is that these are made with plastic lenses. They must be…Seeing through them…
32. Speaker G: They're difficult.
33. Cook: There are contact lenses that you can get, requiring a medical procedure.
34. Speaker G: Jihad is hard. One is always cleaning.
35. Cook: The contact lenses are mounted right on the eyeballs.
36. Abu Hamza: And with those the cleaning is done by blinking: that's what cleans them.
37. Speaker G: That kind of cleaning is troublesome. You'd need to take them out and have a case for them…
38. Abu Hamza: Take them out of your eyes? Do you need a medical procedure to get them out?
39. Speaker G: No, they come out on their own…they move.
40. Speaker L: You use your hands.
41. Abu Hamza: So, I would need a medical procedure every day!
42. Speaker H: Before he went to sleep, he would have to take his eyes out!

[*Group laughter*]

43. Speaker H: He'd have to set them down by his side!
44. Speaker E: Put them in a bag of water!
45. Speaker H: He'd get up in the morning, washing his eyes.

[*Group laughter*]

46. Speaker E [*laughing*]: He'd be looking around for his eyes!

[*Pause*]

47. Cook: Here's a spoon.
48. Abu Hamza: Is this one is clean? [*Pause*] Yes, it's clean.
49. Speaker E: Here's a spoon.
50. Speaker D: Eat up the eggs.
51. Abu Hamza: I don't want to…I don't want to.
52. Speaker E: Finish them up, finish them up.
53. Abu Hamza: I'm looking for the spoon that had been here.
54. Cook: Did you find it?

[*Pause*]

55. Cook: Glory be to God, Abu Hamza likes milk!
56. Abu Hamza: Very much so.

Transcript 7: Words Could Well Be Whispered (Side B, minutes 0–1:25)

1. Cook [*having just switched the audiocassette from side A to side B*]: It's good, this way.

[*Unclear*]

2. Speaker E: It's done, so let it be…

3. [*Speaker D makes an unclear comment about the recording underway. The switched tape has called attention to the fact that conversation is being taped.*]
4. Speaker I: No…no no…
5. Speaker D: But he has recorded the conversation here! A person should be left to his own path…It's dangerous. [*Unclear*] Words could well be whispered [*and thus not meant for recording.*]
6. Abu Hamza: What's this mention of whispering?! [*Laughs.*]
7. Speaker K: Believe me, everyone has a specific purpose, the small included. He plays a specific role.
8. Speaker I: [*Unclear*] That's a general viewpoint.
9. Speaker K: That's a general view alright. There are things…
10. Cook [*interrupting, as Abu Hamza accidentally upsets a glass of water*]: Abu Hamza! [*Laughter*]
11. Speaker K [*continuing*]: There are curves which that one [*Speaker D*] doesn't get.
12. Cook [*to Abu Hamza*]: What are you getting at? [*Laughter*]
13. Abu Hamza: God willing, to… [*Laughs*]

[*Speaker D and a few others withdraw momentarily.*]

14. Speaker K [*to the cook, Abu Hamza and others*]: What do you guys think? Should we move on?
15. Cook [*coldly*]: It's finished. You guys go. [*Pauses as speaker D can be heard complaining in the background.*] You're going with them?

[*Abu Hamza bursts into laughter.*]

16. Speaker K: Abu Hamza, what about you?

[*Pause*]

17. Cook [*returning to the spilled water*]: Abu Hamza! Like this, huh? You spill water on the place I sleep? Now I see…I see a wet dream!
18. Abu Hamza [*laughing*]: I seek God's forgiveness.
19. Cook: God willing…In the rivers of paradise…we'll see Abu Hamza swimming in the rivers of paradise.

Transcript 8: Why the Tape Recorder? (Side B, minutes 3:33–4:11)

1. Speaker M: Why the tape recorder?
2. Cook: [*Unclear.*]
3. Speaker D [*having now returned*]: It's forbidden to use an audio recording machine during the morning hours…except when it comes to recording Abu Hamza!
4. Abu Hamza: Excuse me?
5. Speaker D: Um, he's using an audiocassette recorder in the mornings… especially for you.

6. Abu Hamza: May your Lord grant you pardon! It's of no import whatsoever…
7. Speaker D: It's because of the power of what…He loves you greatly. He always brings out the tape recorder…

[*Abu Hamza tries to interrupt.*]

8. Speaker D: Always recording you…
9. Cook [*interrupting*]: Glory be to God.
10. Speaker D: Especially you.

[*Pause*]

11. Speaker K [*changing topic*]: It's seven thirty.
12. Speaker N: What's bothering that guy?
13. Speaker K: Yep, it's about seven thirty.

[*Pause*]

14. Speaker D: Don't be agitated, Abu Hamza. If I'm bothering you, just let me know.

Transcript 9: Osama's Seconds (Side B, minutes 5:52–9:38)

1. Cook: Abu Hamza, what is the best food you have ever had?
2. Abu Hamza: In truth, I tell you, the best food that I've ever had in my life has not been here.
3. Speaker I: I hate it.
4. Abu Hamza: I hate it too.
5. Speaker K: It's true.
6. Cook: Aaaah, Abu Hamza, my gentleman…It's not just about how one eats!
7. Speaker K: It's been two days.
8. Abu Hamza: I'm telling you, I'm telling you…
9. Speaker K: We've only been here two days so far, and all the…
10. Abu Hamza: No no no! I haven't finished, I haven't finished…
11. Cook: Okay okay, go ahead.
12. Abu Hamza: During one week, a guy invited us…
13. Speaker K: Did they bring you food?
14. Abu Hamza: It was with ʿAbdalla [*mumbles last name*]
15. Cook: [ʿ*Abdalla*] ʿAzzam?
16. Abu Hamza: No. Another guy, living in Jeddah. He invited us over… [*Unclear*] I'm no fan of the food in Peshawar, Pakistan. The food there is tasteless and doesn't suit a man. Rice and such…
17. [*Unclear comment by one of the speakers about Saudi cuisine.*]
18. Abu Hamza: It's true! In Saudi Arabia…in Saudi Arabia they wake up every morning to varied and nuanced dishes.

[*Unclear*]

19. Abu Hamza: It's even that way with their honey, which you can really consume and taste… [*Unclear; continued laughter.*] Choosing is difficult…It's a bit like having to choose between one's own children! It's difficult. One may be pious, another not very upstanding, another not especially good, but still…

20. Cook: God is Greater!

21. Speaker K: Come on, it's only logical!

22. Cook: How beautiful is your explanation and its details, Abu Hamza!

[*Brief silence*]

23. Speaker K: Aside from food, what else do you have a craving for?

24. Abu Hamza: In this place here, you know them [*unclear*]…

25. Cook: You don't know them?

26. Speaker K: With Osama [*Bin Laden*]?

27. Abu Hamza: Huh?

28. Speaker K: You haven't gotten to know Osama yet?

29. Abu Hamza: Mmm…Unfortunately, no. I know a second Osama…

30. Cook: Who's that?

31. Abu Hamza: He is also Saudi…

[*Unclear*]

32. Abu Hamza: He is Saudi, Saudi…

33. Cook: Do you mean [Osama] Abu Khalid?

34. Abu Hamza: Abu Khalid, that's right.

35. Speaker K: The one from The Illuminated City [*a moniker for Madina*]?

36. Abu Hamza: Yeah.

[*Unclear*]

37. Speaker K: But that is his pseudonym.

38. Abu Hamza [*joking*]: What? You mean I haven't learned his real name!? He was originally with us among the guests invited to the feast. [*Unclear*] But he went back for seconds. I mean, what was really gained by that?

39. Speaker K: He should have…

40. Cook [*interrupting*]: What was the benefit in that!?

41. Speaker K [*switching topic, speaking to Abu Hamza*]: We'd like to invite you over for dinner.

42. Abu Hamza: Where?

43. Speaker K: It's set then, Abu Hamza. God willing, it will happen.

44. [*Abu Hamza assents, laughing.*]

45. Speaker K [*returning to the etiquette of second helpings*]: One needs to have years of experience with these things, really.

46. Cook [*steering conversation back to haut cuisine*]: But in Lahore, Abu Hamza, it can't get any better than that! In Lahore, no food can compare to it! In Peshawar, there's no food there…

47. Abu Hamza: It's the soil there.
48. Speaker N: Where's the good soil? There are tomatoes, sure… they're rich in them.
49. Cook: It's known that in poor rural areas, the most common thing is tomatoes, from sunrise to sunset. From the morning to the night, even until three or four o'clock in the morning…
50. Speaker K: The restaurant that is behind the [unclear]…when it opens, it is actually not too bad.

Transcript 10: The Excesses of Raiding (Side B, mins 9:53–11:49)

1. Cook: I will tell you a little story. It's about some brothers who had come to work [unclear]…I had gone down to that restaurant with the brother [Osama] Abu Khalid. Of course, they didn't know him. Everything that they put in front of him disappeared. Half of every main dish that was served was consumed…Even the potatoes [on the side] that he tasted, he still wolfed them down right away. [Unclear]
2. Abu Hamza: The restaurant that was down below street level?
3. Cook: Yes, like the one we're in here.
4. Abu Hamza: Ah, okay.
5. Cook: Then he gobbled up some raw onions.
6. Abu Hamza: What!?
7. Cook: Yes, he ate everything they brought!

[Group laughter]

8. Cook: Then the other brothers began to eat. The staff began to take their orders… [The cook briefly attends to someone who enters the kitchen, and then resumes.] The staff began to take their orders: Abu Hudhaifa, Abu Anis, Abu Hanifa…
9. Abu Hamza: Oh yea?
10. Cook: Yes. As for Abu Anis [unclear]… whenever he ate, would look around for a sheep, always hungry. They said to him: Be satisfied!

[Group laughter]

11. Abu Hamza [laughing]: You are most praiseworthy!

[More laughter]

12. Cook: So he replied "I am following the Prophet. I begin with the shoulder. This is *Sunna.*" He would approach the lamb…"In the name of God"…And he'd begin with the shoulder, eating it ravenously. He raided (*ghara*) the lamb! All the way up to the eyes…no bone or meat was left! At that point, there were no more orders placed.
13. Abu Hamza [correcting the cook's grammar]: Look here…I believe that when one says ghara, it's from the verb ghira [meaning "to be zealous"]… To say "he raided" you would use a different verbal root [as in aghara.]

14. Cook: Oh my God! [*After a short chuckle, he resumes.*] So, further orders weren't taken. The brothers were told: "There's no more shoulder left." The staff had a talk with several of them.
15. Speaker K: And did they ask for more, in addition to what they'd eaten?
16. Cook: Yep.
17. Speaker K: And did they serve it up?
18. Cook: Yep. The orders kept coming.
19. Speaker K: By God, they should be respected for eating all that food!
20. Cook: The owners of the restaurant, all of them, were in a state of panic whenever these brothers arrived! They were afraid of them. They considered them a strange picture indeed.

[*Group laughter.*]

In the late 2000s, I had the opportunity to share thoughts on some of bin Laden's former tapes with Osama's fourth son 'Umar. Knowing of his appeal for political asylum in the West since abandoning his father in April of 2001, I contacted him through journalists. Despite years of suffering under his father, he agreed to hear digitalized excerpts from roughly a dozen recordings. At our first meeting, 'Umar was dressed in jeans and a studded leather jacket. With his goatee and short black pony tail, he sported a goth image that had won him considerable press coverage in the West. Still, listening with 'Umar was not easy. Although we were able to hear and talk about the excerpts in the comfort of his home, I was asked not to divulge the place or circumstances of our meetings. He showed great patience in sharing his thoughts, though several days into our interviews his wife Zaina confided to me that he was falling into depression. The sound of his father's tirades and of incendiary militant preaching left him sickened. He could hear no more. His only request was to receive a copy of no. 1111 so that he could listen to the tape with friends.

I had not expected this recording to leave 'Umar with such a favorable impression. None of its topics seemed notable. Speakers on the tape were unidentifiable other than by occasional pseudonyms such as "Abu Hamza," "Abu Ra'd," and "'Abdalla." The handwritten cassette titles "With the Mujahideen" (*Ma' Al-Mujahidin*), on side A, and "Dawn Anthems" (*Anashid Al-Fajr*), on side B, were equally vague, and no dates were mentioned anywhere. When hearing to the tape for the first time, however, 'Umar's behavior changed. No longer watchful and edgy, he grew entranced and waved off attempts to solicit verbal feedback. After roughly ten minutes I was able to elicit his response. "The tape was made before the Soviets had left," he said.[2] When I asked how he was able to date the recording, he stopped the tape and replied matter of factly: "In those days, the strugglers knew how to speak. They were intelligent and respectful of one another. That was the way they were. They never slung insults or shouted at each other. They were incredibly dignified (*mu'addab*). If you met them, you would have loved them." Conversations nearly lost to the passage of time had found new voice.

'Umar's effort to link strugglers' demeanor to a cultural shift among Arab fighters in post-Soviet Afghanistan was not his alone. Scholars of al-Qaʿida have made similar arguments.[3] Combining sociological data with their own interviews, they highlight a gap between al-Qaʿida's "first generation" of fighters during the mid–late 1980s and a "second generation" that emerged after the Soviet departure from Afghanistan in February 1990. Earlier fighters arrived in Pakistan and Afghanistan when jihad in the region was not viewed as negatively by Arab regimes. Many were young men in their early twenties who ventured to the region less for armed militancy than to help thousands of refugees fleeing from Afghanistan's brutal conflict. They often had a university education and were of urban middle-class backgrounds. The second generation, by contrast, confronted a less coherent enemy and, accordingly, espoused a broader range of goals. Many of these men were more familiar with labor migration, having come from families enjoying fewer social advantages. Although much enamored with the pan-Islamic discourses of the first generation, a higher proportion of them knew imprisonment and exile at the hands of their own state regimes. While they admired the first generation of Arab-Afghans, many of whom had become heroes, they also sought guidance from more cosmopolitan leaders who could lead them in the multi-pronged struggles of a post cold-war Arab world. In April 1992, when the last vestiges of communist leadership in Kabul fell to the Afghan mujahidin, their support and presence was no longer necessary or wanted.[4] 'Umar's date for the company of mujahidin on tape no. 1111 expressed a growing sense after that time that relations among Arab-Afghans were not as they had once been. The chapter order in the book reflects this perspective.

'Umar spoke about the lamentable decline of the Arab-Afghan cause once the Soviets had departed. After listening to a recording of a wedding celebration in which his father was praised as "the sun shining with light most radiant," as discussed in chapter fourteen, he admitted that sycophancy toward Osama had bothered him most. Returning again to "With the Mujahideen/Dawn Anthems," he acknowledged that something quite different was going on. Given that speakers' identities were not readily known, he seemed reluctant to venture thoughts on their views or goals. His hesitancy changed when hearing a comment in turn nine of the first transcript. Whereas I and my native Arabic-speaking research assistants had heard the word "politicians" (*siyasiin*) in the sentence "Simple salt is what we have here. There you have politicians," 'Umar heard mention of a long lost friend "Yasin" (*Yasiin*). The phrase was a bit garbled, but after another listening 'Umar was convinced. Yasin had been one of his father's close associates while fighting against the Soviet occupation in Afghanistan. In 1987, as Arab-Afghans withdrew from one battle to regroup, Yasin stayed behind to hold off Soviet pursuers. While monitoring the young fighter's movements from afar through binoculars, his father had watched Yasin be killed by tank fire. Listening with a sense of such loss, 'Umar found himself connecting with the recording in a very personal way. The experience pushed 'Umar toward withdrawal.

In presenting excerpts from tape no. 1111, I have sought, in keeping with the rest of the book, to understand how bin Laden's ascendency to world attention came at the cost of supporters who could lend his struggle prolonged coherence. In particular, the tape demonstrates asceticism's conflicted stakes for Arab-Afghan militants. Recorded voices sound forth not from a training camp podium or lecture hall, as in chapters four, twelve, and fourteen, nor from a mosque, as in many other chapters. They emanate instead from a makeshift kitchen at an unidentified Arab-Afghan training camp.[5] In translating and assessing the contributions of at least sixteen speakers who drift in and out of the recording, I aim to demonstrate how views of the strugglers' ascetic goals and pursuits, their "jihad" as one speaker puts it, emerge less from transmitted doctrine or rational deliberative processes than by social encounters filled with exuberance and contingency.[6] While an interest in gastronomy shared between a kitchen cook named Abu 'Abd al-Rahman and a senior Yemeni militant named Abu Hamza gives a sustained consistency to the conversations, the steady turn-over of strugglers dropping in to eat, drink, listen, and chat provides rare insight into the ways collective sensibilities are formed in settings that are at once culturally specific, defined by everyday rituals such as ethical eating, and extremely versatile. The sound studio at hand is a multipurpose room used for sleeping as well as food preparation, dining, and casual interchange. Hierarchies of learning and militant experience no longer command obvious deference. The chief officiant, as suggested in transcripts seven and eight, is in fact the cook himself, one of the youngest participants in the room. From atop his own mattress, he monitors group morale and behavior. As master of ceremonies responsible for getting food to diners, his primary challenge lies in managing the presence of the hungry and much-venerated Abu Hamza. Toward the start of side B (transcript 8), we learn of the cook's profound love for his guest. We also discover troubles that arise when he and others witness the effects of Abu Hamza's age on his agility, vigilance, and health. In order to help manage the leader's physical lapses and turn them into opportunities for reflection, the cook uses humor. In the process, he leads kitchen diners toward a strain of asceticism that reinforces group solidarity at the expense of bin Laden himself.

A sense of collective purpose builds slowly. At the tape's outset, not even the gas stove has been lit. The stove's primer needs pumping, a task delegated by the cook to a languid assistant. With coaching, the assistant succeeds and is met with light-hearted congratulations from the cook: "Engineers are we!" Another speaker takes up his joke, adding that they are "Engineers of eggs!" Within a few seconds sounds of laughter are heard from a handful of other participants nearby. It is at this point that we hear Abu Hamza, who offers unabashed praise for the cook. The cook's deference to Abu Hamza is immediate: "Simple salt is what we have here. There you have politicians." With the elegant turn of a phrase, the cook cues his associates to a high-stakes game. This is no ordinary breakfast, nor are these ordinary engineers. What unfolds is the work of making allies where resources are scarce. The primary recruits to be won over in this contest are Abu Hamza and his influential colleagues, as revealed in the use of turn 11's second-person plural enclitic pronoun (-*kum*). So ravenous would they be for the cook's meal that they would be driven to self-abnegation, consuming their own fingers in their zeal for salty eggs. They might even lay claim to such mastery, loath to admit its provenance from a mere sous-chef.

Within less than a minute, hungry strugglers poised for breakfast, a much larger drama is in the offing. The work of recruiting Abu Hamza's loyalties requires appealing to a gourmand sensibility. The tactics of such appeal unfold in transcript two. Drawn forth with talk of delicious eggs, Abu Hamza confides his desire for meat. At this point, he invites ready association with epicureanism, meat at the Arab-Afghan camps having been famously absent for all but the most special meals.[7] To the delight of others in the kitchen, Abu Hamza shows that he can poke fun at himself. When informed of the stiff odds involved in procuring an alternate protein source, Abu Hamza suggests they engage in a bit of sport by shouting to anyone nearby that roast lamb is being served: "Call out to them, Abu Hafiz…Tell them that [the lamb] is ready and waiting!" Although the playful nature of his jest is recognized, the cook and others indulge Abu Hamza with stories of Saudi Arabia's rich and ample fare. So rewarding are desserts by one "Mister Hellfire" (*Abu Nar*) of Mecca that, according to the cook, they grant God's blessing (*baraka*) to the consumer. The idea that a talented pâtissier might create anything so divine draws mild rebuke from speaker D: "God is Greater!"

Over the next several minutes (transcript 3), Abu Hamza's audience discovers the seriousness of his desire for good meat. He lays plans to redirect the entire day's activities toward satisfying his hunger. Upon overhearing the cook talking of a brief trip to a nearby town, probably in order to restock supplies, Abu Hamza asks whether he might come along for the ride. His own local house appears, after all, to lie near the town square and he confides ownership of several roosters. When the cook attempts to decline the request, saying that he'll swing by Abu Hamza's house himself, another man renews the bid to ensure the realization of Abu Hamza's wish (turn 10). He proposes that several brothers in the kitchen accompany him under the false pretense of "gathering intelligence." Suspecting the proposal to be half in jest, the cook asks for a more serious pretext for using group resources and manpower in the pursuit of Abu Hamza's whimsy. He kicks off a new round of proposals that ends with group laughter (after turn 18). However hilarious the idea that committed strugglers might upend operational priorities for worldly passions, the cook moves the group toward ethical considerations. Cueing his colleagues to the "truth" (*haqiqa*) of such matters (turns 17 and 19), he invites them to consider Abu Hamza as an "amir" who, although "crazy for taste," might also suffer "injustice" if not allotted the egg yolk.

Aside from the deference given by kitchen diners to Abu Hamza, the latter's experience in militancy is suggested on several occasions. He uses a pseudonym rather than his real name, in the fashion of Arab-Afghan fighters, and speaks of his associates doing the same. He is a "bomb fanatic" (*mawlaʿ bi-l-qanabil*) according to one speaker, while others speak, albeit jokingly, of his confrontation with "tanks" (*dabbabat*) and "the enemy" (*al-ʿaduw*). From the cook's perspective, Abu Hamza may have dined with ʿAbdalla ʿAzzam and met bin Laden himself. Whether or not the featured speaker on this tape is the same as the alleged al-Qaʿida operative Abu al-Hamza "the Yemeni" who was captured in Karachi in 2003 while hiding in an Islamic Group women's dormitory may never be known.[8] What matters to the strugglers having breakfast with Abu Hamza is less his martial prowess than his guidance in preserving moral ideals amidst an onslaught of everyday bodily needs and desires. "Jihad is hard," admits one young man. "One is always cleaning" (transcript 6, turn 34). Grander battles lie ahead. The strugglers in the kitchen mostly seek Abu Hamza's help in reflecting on the business of managing life's incessant material demands with dignity. In transcripts 4–7, Abu Hamza's leadership is conveyed through self-deprecating humor. He focuses on his own aging, especially his compromised sensory faculties and deteriorating body.

Topics of sleep and dreaming provide a consistent theme beginning in transcript 4. Abu Hamza, it appears, dozed off while serving on guard duty. At the outset, the cook comes to Abu Hamza's rescue with a joke. Perhaps he was given over to dream. In Islamic mysticism, dreams provide believers with true insight on divine pathways otherwise unknown to mankind. According to one transmitted report (*hadith*), they are one forty-ninth of prophecy. The cook alludes to such traditions, though partly tongue in cheek: sleep can also lead toward hellfire (turn 8). After much laughter among the strugglers, Abu Hamza takes up the cook's novel possibility with a twist. Dreaming can be dangerous. It becomes so, however, not through fantasies one produces in sleep but rather because it "produces strange elucidation" (*sharh ʿajib*) when waking up and lingering in a state of drowsiness (turn 11). To the amusement of his audience, he likens such elucidation to skewed "analogical reasoning" (*qiyas*) in Islamic law and his delusion of having become a scholar qualified to exercise independent legal reasoning (*mujtahid*). He illustrates the perils of dreaming as well as the ironic benefits of sound sleep through a succeeding and even more uproarious narrative about learning math in an Aden high school from a sexy Levantine Arab teacher. Abu Hamza's lesson to listeners, continued in transcript 5 (turn 17) after brief interruption, is that sleep, along with practiced blindness, sitting, and persistent stupor, can be a form of moral tenacity. When presented with the "confusion" (transcript 4, turns 31–3) of wholly foreign command structures—whether in the form of Westernized teachers in high heels or aggressive dogs that bark commands—sleep and withdrawal can offer an effective means of resistance. Far more so, indeed, than direct confrontation.

In the midst of his edifying comedy, Abu Hamza inadvertently creates another opportunity to reflect on the merits of bodily debilitation. He upsets a nearby kerosene stove. Although convulsed in laughter, others in the room scramble to aid their senior militant camarade. As they reach out to take his glass, Abu Hamza only makes things worse, spilling gas into his tea glass. Awkward though the situation is, the strugglers collaborate together in making an asset of dysfunction. Intoxication, in this case, normally a sign of moral weakness, becomes salubrious. Speaker C initiates this narrative by comparing the floating gas bubbles in Abu Hamza's tea to "raisins" (transcript 4, turn 47). The product, others joke, might be marketed for consumption under the label "Raisins with Gas." Rather than toxic poisoning, the brew might be an antidiarrheal medicine. The cook's summary of the event as an "experiment in having coffee with gas" (turn 56) portrays the diners as entrepreneurs as well as engineers. In substituting the word "coffee" (*qahwa*) for tea, he evokes a commodity far more celebrated for its origins on the Arabian Peninsula. According to Arab tribal custom, coffee is often served to guests as a gesture of hospitality and honor. With appropriate flavoring, the danger of overproducing natural gas might be turned into a blessing. Such a concoction might even turn the tables on enemies. In transcript 5, the cook suggests that Abu Hamza's so-called firewater might burst from his mouth like flames from a dragon or fanciful "dinosaur" (*dinusur*) (turn 10). When venturing further that such eruption risked shooting out his backside, another leaps to his succor: "Or rather, from far away he would blow flames on them…and everything would be incinerated. God is Greater! He'd blow flames on the tanks until they were all obliterated."

Abu Hamza's handicaps are never more evident than when the topic of his weak eyesight is raised (transcripts 6 and 7). The cook once again draws attention to his troubles while creating opportunities for empathy. When the group discovers the severity of Abu Hamza's visual impairment and its link to genetic preconditions in his family, the cook

THE AUDACIOUS ASCETIC

employs humor once again to direct attention to shared vulnerabilities and goals. Varying scales of visual acuity are not the result of differing national standards among Arab countries, the cook suggests, but are rather the result of "the exchange rate of the U.S. dollar" (transcript 6, turn 26). Confusion arises, much as in the presence of high-heeled math teacher, from irrational standards of Western and global knowledge and power. Mujahideen from across the Arab world and South Asia knew the troubles of fluctuating currencies linked to an American-dominated global market. Abu Hamza's vigilance, in such contexts, comes not from his vision, the cook suggests further, but rather from his voice. "Adversaries" can be vocally addressed by Abu Hamza even as they remain ephemeral. Compromised vision, like sleep, might even be an advantage. The absurdity of such an idea is entertained in subsequent talk about Abu Hamza's removable eyes (transcript 6, turns 31–46). When the hazards of Abu Hamza's uncoordinated body manifest themselves in his spilling yet another glass, the cook depicts the mistake as an act of generosity (transcript 7, turns 10 and 17–19). The cook has received a "dream" or hierophanic vision (ru'ya) through his master's tutelage, in the idiom of mystical Sufi apprenticeship. Ever the joker, the cook gives the concept a bawdy inflection: Abu Hamza's spill produced a "wet dream" (ru'ya muballala) well exceeding the bounds of manly decorum.[9] Any discord produced by Abu Hamza's actions is quelled, however, by the cook's final assertion. Their leader has drawn them closer to "the rivers of paradise," a destination of countless martyrs.

Toward the end of "Side A/With the Mujahideen," the cook and his crew gradually finish eating. The simplicity of their fare, consisting of tea with sugar, eggs, and milk, has heightened their sense of life's many compromises. Faced with their own deficiency, they use humor to expose the ironies of jihad on Islam's Arab-Afghan frontier. Ascetic pilgrims no doubt, they also yearn for dessert, homemade ghee, lamb, and grilled chicken. So zealous is their kitchen-room commander, in fact, that the group considers upending tactical priorities in order to satiate his hunger. While Abu Hamza's passions elicit a great deal of satire, the diners also work together to reflect on how his material needs reinforce ethical commitments shared by all. Satisfying one's hunger is not sign of weakness but rather an opportunity to establish new social bonds. Sleep is not a rebuke to the pious but rather a pathway to sensory withdrawal and vigilance. Human beings are all strugglers when it comes to the aging process or empowerment as consumers in a global marketplace. Whatever Muslims' differences, their responses to these basic human conditions are surely what most unite them. Abu Hamza's strength as a leader lies precisely in his status as a diminished man.

The handwritten label "Dawn Anthems" (*Anashid Al-Fajr*) on side B suggests that listeners were to view the contents of the recording as having religious import. Few genres of chanting were more popular across the Islamic world, after all, than religious anthems. What unfolds, instead, are continued humorous exchanges about the pleasures of fine dining. Unlike on side A, the actual preparation and consumption of breakfast has been completed. The conversation leads accordingly toward memories of good food, and, with them, more sober reflection on the perils of gastronomic excess. It is amidst these reflections that the example of bin Laden's own ascetic bent is brought up for consideration.

"In truth," Abu Hamza tells the cook when pressed, "the best food that I've ever had in my life has not been here" (transcript 9, turn 2). As others leap to offer assent, the cook retorts: "Aaaah, Abu Hamza, my gentleman...It's not just about how one eats!" At risk of offending the chef, Abu Hamza quickly changes tack: "No no no! I haven't finished, I haven't finished..." He continues with a story about an especially memorable feast at the house of a man named "'Abdalla." For the Arab-Afghan cook, steeped as he is in traditions of patronage and aware of Abu Hamza's broad social network, there can only be one such doyenne. "['Abdalla] 'Azzam?" he asks, referring to the giant among militant leaders who, by many accounts, co-founded al-Qa'ida with bin Laden.[10] Abu Hamza deflates the cook's excitement. He speaks of a Saudi rather than Palestinian host. Having broached the possibility that life's pleasures might lie beyond cuisine, the group entertains another question (turn 23): "Aside from food, what else do you have a craving for?" asks speaker K. Abu Hamza responds obliquely: "In this place here" (*fi hadha al-makan*) there are people "who you know" (*ta'rifhum*). Surprised to hear Abu Hamza deferring to the speaker's own social network, others in the kitchen attempt to clarify. "You haven't gotten to know Osama yet?" asks a speaker. "Unfortunately, no," replies Abu Hamza. He knows "a second Osama," a Saudi national. Better known by his pseudonym Abu Khalid, the man betrayed weakness by exceeding the bounds of gustatory indulgence: having also been a guest at 'Abdalla's epic feast back in Jeddah, he returned for second helpings. The cook's ensuing narrative about witnessing the extravagant appetite of the same man and his friends (transcript 10) underscores the dread inspired by "raids" from such audacious consumers. Islam's moral pathway (*Sunna*) became an excuse for gluttony.

Among Arab-Afghan camp fighters, the first Osama was known to keep a spartan table. When men complained of having nothing more than eggs, bread, and tea, he confided to his bodyguard that "we have not yet reached a condition like that of the Prophet's Companions, who placed stones against their middles and tightened them around their waists. The Messenger of Allah used two stones!"[11] The virtues of asceticism (*zuhd*) were the topic of at least one sermon by bin Laden in the late 1990s.[12] "May God be praised," bin Laden declared to supporters, "We are eating, but there are millions of others who wish that they could have something like this to eat."[13] Those in his entourage who shared meals with him at weddings or banquets found no lack in his taste for fine cuisine. As the son of a multimillionaire, "he was not a McDonalds guy."[14] While Syrian dishes were a favorite, he also expressed relish for traditional Saudi fare, no more so than when among recruits from the Arabian Peninsula. During a workshop outside Jalalabad devoted to rallying support for his anti-American message, he wooed his future Yemeni bodyguard with promises of a popular Hijazi dish called *ma'suba al-qarmushi*, a fritter made from flour, bananas, and sugar.[15] Tactical indulgences aside, however, he worked assiduously to commend his audiences to martial asceticism. As acknowledged by Abu Hamza and his companions, bin Laden's campaign led toward goals "aside from food" altogether.

The dilemma for bin Laden's would-be supporters was that, beginning in late 1996, bin Laden's growing media celebrity as the world's most strident anti-American militant led him to assume a role that yielded diminishing returns. As I show in the next and following chapters, the marketing of his image by CNN, American Broadcasting Company, and Al-Jazeera, while augmenting his perceived relevance to Western strategic objectives across the Arab world and especially in Iraq, came at the price of his alienation from indigenous struggles that engaged most fighters. For the Arab-Afghan diners building rapport with each other, the seeds of bin Laden's peripheralism are already evident in a short-circuit that occurs at his mention. When Abu Hamza mentions that "unfortunately" he has not met bin Laden, none of the others venture accounts of greater intimacy with the leader. It is unclear, in fact, if any of them have ever actually met the man. Leaving encounters with bin Laden to speculation, speakers switch to discussing what does, in fact, unite them: a repudiation for the lifestyle of a "second Osama," one whose indebtedness to Saudi affluence is far more egregiously displayed. It is through difference from this fighter and his men that the strugglers, in all their material and bodily cravings, express solidarity. In the years ahead, bin Laden's election to the U.S. Justice Department's "most wanted" list would make him only more extrinsic to such discussions. Attention given to his declarations would evoke new and more absolute scenarios of bodily disintegration.

In the next chapter, I revisit bin Laden's famous "Declaration of War against the Americans," delivered from Tora Bora, Afghanistan in August 1996. Rather than focusing on its best-known opening and middle sections, as I do in chapter one, I attend instead to the rousing poetry that constitutes its final twenty minutes. I argue that hearing the speech delivered orally provides key insights into its significance among bin Laden's primary audiences at the time, and explore why the speech's faxed, printed, and electronic renditions fail to do so, especially when translated into English. Much as on that tape, the "Dawn Anthems'" recording proves valuable to its producers as an aural product. It is by sounding out their conversation to a potentially much broader listening audience that strugglers can convey the true spectrum of their efforts. The utility of audiocassettes for this end becomes a subject for discussion in transcripts 7 and 8 by virtue of the built-in design feature of most tape recorders: in order for users to take advantage of both sides of a tape, cartridges must be manually flipped once side A has ended. On the morning of this recording event, we hear the cook verbally approving the tape's flip at the start of side B (transcript 7, turn 1), followed by several others. Not all are pleased, however. One of the less jocular speakers protests as he tries to stop the recording machine. Angry at not being alerted in advance to its presence, he erupts, "But he has recorded the conversation here! A person should be left to his own path…It's dangerous. [*Unclear*] Words could well be whispered." Abu Hamza leaps to the cook's defense: "What's this mention of whispering?!" Another speaker expands: "Believe me, everyone has a specific purpose, the small included. He plays a specific role" (turn 7). Despite overlap from an adjoining conversation, the speaker continues once the offended speaker has withdrawn: "There are curves (*munhanayat*) which that one doesn't get" (turn 11).

229

Insofar as audio recording provides users with a way to assert communal attachments in a relatively public way, not all who participate in such activity are likely to feel the same way. Disagreements can arise over the substance of such attachments and the implications of social or political alliances invoked. Tracks etched into magnetic recording tape can preserve a record of such disputes and provide a resource for later review and analysis. In this case, a dissenting voice meets with collective reprobation and is forced into withdrawal. According to one critic, the speaker represents an unjust establishment that has little tolerance for open and honest discussion. The path to righteousness may well begin with those, such as the cook, considered too "small" (*saghir*) to make much difference. Just as audio recording exposes friction in the ranks, however, so too does it lend itself to collaborative reconciliation. Differences between strugglers may give way to a more "general view" (*nazra 'amma*) of the common good. Several minutes later, we hear the offended speaker return along with a disapproving colleague (transcript 8, turns 1 and 3). The speaker tries, at first, to defend himself, expressing his reason for indignation: rules at their base-camp forbid the use of audio recorders, especially "during the morning hours" (transcript 8, turn 3.)[16] The cook and others have made an unfair exception to such rules "when it comes to recording Abu Hamza!" When confronted more vehemently by Abu Hamza, he adopts a more conciliatory tone: "It's because of the power of what…He loves you greatly. He always brings out the tape recorder…Don't be agitated Abu Hamza. If I'm bothering you, just let me know" (turns 7 and 14). He and his colleague appear to have learned their lesson. Rules and their qualifying exceptions are matters for in-house negotiation, even, and perhaps especially, at a training camp.

It is hard to say exactly what this recording was doing in bin Laden's former Kandahar tape collection. No other copies of the tape are found in the archive. The cook made the recording for his own personal use, perhaps to recall the pleasures of his brief time with Abu Hamza before life's vicissitudes erased them. It was not unknown, after all, for Arab-Afghan cooks to die on the front lines. In the fourth issue of the Office of Services' flagship magazine *Al-Jihad*, none other than 'Abdalla 'Azzam wrote a piece commemorating the life and contributions of one humble chef, a Palestinian man from Ramallah who had come to work at eastern Afghanistan's Badr camp.[17] He was, according to 'Azzam, "the first Muslim Arab to mix with the Afghans to such a degree, living with patience amidst the agonies of their life, the severity of their circumstances, and the roughness of their food and clothes." His manner was the essence of civility: "he would carry food and tea, offering them to us and then sitting with dignity (*adab*) waiting until the meal was finished in order to gather the dishes and wash them. When in his presence, each of us grew shy around him due to the vehemence of his devotion to his brothers." Such was his cause that, according to 'Azzam, he won God's favor as the very first Arab-Afghan martyr. His pseudonym, it turns out, was Abu Hamza, a testimonial to the Prophet Muhammad's uncle who also died in battle. The latter Abu Hamza suffered the indignity of having his liver eviscerated and eaten by a female Meccan warrior. "With the Mujahideen/Dawn Anthems" certainly offered a brighter vision of the inevitable struggle with death.

9

I HAVE SCORNED THOSE WHO REBUKED ME

(August 1996 speech by Osama bin Laden. The Hindu Kush mountains, Afghanistan. Beginning of Side B, cassette no. 506.)

———————

[*Recording begins mid-sentence*] … in particular, we remind them of the following: the wealth you devote to the purchase price of American goods will be transformed into bullets shot into the breasts of our brothers in Palestine, in the Land of the Two Holy Sanctuaries, and elsewhere. In buying their goods we strengthen their economy while exacerbating our own poverty and weakness.

Our struggle against these occupiers is aided enormously by cutting them off from the enormous revenues generated through trade with us. Such action expresses our anger and hatred of them in significant and important ways. We will have participated in cleansing our sacred places of Jews and Christians and forced them to leave our lands defeated, routed, and forsaken, with the permission of Exalted God.

We expect the women of the Land of the Two Holy Sanctuaries and elsewhere to carry out their role by practicing asceticism from the world, and by boycotting American goods. If economic boycotting is combined with the strugglers' military operations, then the defeat of the enemy would be even nearer, by God's permission. The opposite is also true: If Muslims do not cooperate with the struggling brothers, supplying them with assistance in curtailing economic collaboration with the American enemy, then they are supplying them with wealth that is the mainstay of war and the lifeblood of armies. In effect, they extend the period of war and abet the oppression of Muslims.

Every security and intelligence bureau in the entire world cannot force a single citizen to purchase the enemy's goods. The economic boycotting of American goods is an especially effective weapon for weakening and hitting the enemy, particularly since it is a weapon whose power is not subject to states' repressive institutions.

My Muslim Brother in the Land of the Two Holy Sanctuaries: is it fathomable that our country is the world's largest buyer of arms from America and that we provide its citizens with their largest trading partner in the region even as America occupies the Land of the Two Holy Sanctuaries? Is this conceivable given how they use their wealth, weapons, and manpower to support their Jewish brothers in occupying Palestine and in killing and evicting Muslims there?

Before concluding, we have some important words, important indeed for the young men of Islam, men of the brilliant future of the pious community of Muhammad, God's blessings and salutations upon him.

Our talk with the youths is about their obligation during this most difficult period of history for our pious community, a period in which only youths, may God preserve them, are stepping forward to carry out the great variety of duties. Some youths, wagging their fingers, had procrastinated in preparing themselves as necessary to defend Islam, largely in order to protect themselves and their wealth from state tyranny, injustice, and oppression and because the pious community had been subject to brainwashing by state media. Other youths advanced, however, may God preserve them. They raised the streaming banner of struggle against the American-Jewish alliance occupying Islam's sacred places. Even as this occupation was occurring, conspirators stepped forth [to foil these youth], whether in response to their own states' use of terrorism or to their desire for the fleeting rewards of a material world. Stumbling and succumbing, they concocted legal justification for this tremendous betrayal, this enormous calamity that had befallen the Land of the Two Holy Sanctuaries when it suffered occupation. There is no might or power except through God.

The audacity of the youth is neither wondrous nor surprising. Were not the Companions of Muhammad, God's blessings and salutations upon him, young? These youths are the successors of these pious predecessors. Was the pharoah of this pious community, Abu Jahl, killed by any other than these youth?[1]

'Abd al-Rahman Ibn 'Awf, may God be pleased with him, said "I was at the frontline on the day of Badr.[2] When I turned my head, I noticed on my right and left two adolescents, both young in years. I could hardly believe how similar they were to each other. One of them said to me, aside and beyond earshot of the other: 'O uncle, point Abu Jahl out to me.' I replied: 'What will you do with him?' The boy answered 'I have been informed that he insulted God's Messenger, God's blessings and salutations upon him.' He said: 'I swear by He who holds my soul in His hand that if I see him, I'll not let my shadow leave his until the more worldly of the two is dead.' I marveled at this." He said that the other youth signaled to him and stated something similar. "Without hesitation, I saw Abu Jahl strolling around among the people and said: 'Do you boys not see? Here is the very fellow you were asking me about.'" He said: "Then they began to show him their swords, striking him until he was dead." God is Greater. Such was the ardor of the two youths, may God be pleased with them. Such was the ardor of our forefathers. While those two adolescents were few in years, they were old in ardor, courage, discernment, and zeal for God's religion. Each of them asked for the most important battlefronts against the enemy, even if they involved killing the pharaoh of the community, the leader of the disbelievers in Badr, Abu Jahl. The role of 'Abd al-Rahman Ibn 'Awf, God be pleased with him, was to direct the two youths toward Abu Jahl. That is the role required of people who have knowledge and experience in fighting the enemy. They should guide their sons and brothers in this matter. Were they to do so, our youths would repeat what their forefathers said: "I swear by He who holds my soul in His hand that if I see him, I'll not let my shadow leave his until the more worldly of the two is dead." This is the story of 'Abd al-Rahman Ibn 'Awf.

The story of Umayya Ibn Khalaf on the day of Badr also illustrates the extent of Bilal [Ibn Rabah]'s persistence, may God be pleased with him, in killing the leader of disbelief. Bilal said: "The leader of disbelief is Umayya Ibn Khalaf. I shall not live if he survives."[3]

A few days ago news agencies released a statement from the Secretary of the Occupying Crusader American Defense Force saying that he learned one lesson from the explosions in Riyadh and Al-Khobar.[4] The lesson was never to withdraw from "cowardly terrorists." We say to the Secretary of Defense that this talk provokes laughter from the bereaving mother whose child died without her. It exposes the extent of fear that afflicts you all. Where was this false courage of yours when the explosion in Beirut took place in 1403 AH, [1983 CE] an explosion that made you [*recording interrupted*] injurious, pieces and body parts of 241 killed soldiers. Where was this false courage of yours in Aden when two explosions occurred and drove you to leave Aden without pause less than twenty-four hours later!

But your biggest disgrace was in Somalia. After a vigorous, multi-month propaganda campaign about the power of America after the cold war and its alleged leadership of the New World Order, you moved tens of thousands of international forces, including twenty eight thousands American soldiers into Somalia. After a couple of skirmishes, though, when a few scores of your soldiers were killed and an American pilot dragged through one of

Mogadishu's streets, you left the country defeated and disappointed, carrying your dead and dragging your tail with defeat, loss and disgrace. While Clinton appeared afterward, threatening us and promising the whole world that he would seek revenge, these threats were merely a preparation for withdrawal. Having been disgraced by God, you withdrew; the extent of your impotence and weakness became very clear. Your scenes of your defeat in these three Islamic cities—Beirut, Aden and Mogadishu—brought joy to the heart of every Muslim and cured the chests of believing nations.

I say: just as the sons of the Land of the Two Holy Sanctuaries had set forth to fight the Russians in Afghanistan and the Serbs in Bosnia Herzegovina, today they have become strugglers in Chechnya—having been granted success and victory, through God's permission, against your current allies the Russians—and also in Tajikastan, through God's favor.

I say: while the sons of the Two Holy Sanctuaries have strong feelings and faith in the necessity of struggle against disbelievers everywhere, their numbers, power and zeal are even greater in their own land. They were born to defend the greatest of their sanctuaries, the noble Ka'ba, the direction of prayer for all Muslims. They know that Muslims across the entire world will assist and support them in their great cause, a cause of every Muslim: the liberation of their sanctuaries.

I say to you, William [Perry, the Secretary of Defense under the Clinton Administration]: these youths love death as you love life. They have inherited dignity, pride, courage, generosity, sincerity, daring, and the will to make sacrifices, from father to father. They are steadfast at war, and sincere in the encounter. They have inherited these qualities from their ancestors from the time of the pre-Islamic Age of Ignorance (*Jahiliyya*). Islam came and firmly established these praiseworthy morals, and perfected them, as the Prophet said, God's blessings and salutations upon him: "Verily, I was sent to perfect beneficial morals," as has been relayed in the *Small Collecting Work*.[5]

When the King 'Amru Ibn Hind sought to humiliate 'Amru Ibn Kulthum, the latter cut the head of the king with his sword, rejecting aggression, humiliation and indignation.[6] He then produced a *qasida* poem about this:

> If the king exceeded all disgrace among people
>> We give shame no sanctuary among us
> By what volition, O 'Amru Ibn Hind
>> Do you want the land to be so pliant?
> By what volition, O 'Amru Ibn Hind
>> Do you subject us to betrayal and slight us?
> In truth, O 'Amru, our spear vitiated
>> The enemies even before your pliancy

These youths believe in paradise after death. They believe that staying behind will not advance them audaciously to the fight, and will not postpone their final hour. As the Exalted has said: "Nor can a soul die except by God's leave, the term being fixed like writing."[7] They also believe in the report of God's Messenger, God's blessings and salutations upon him, as relayed in the *Small Collecting Work*: "I shall teach you a few words, my lad: if are mindful of God, He will be mindful of you; if are mindful of God, you will discover him right before you; if you make a request, request it of God; if you seek assistance, seek it from God. Know that if the pious community gathered together to help you, they can grant you nothing that God has not pre-scribed for you. If they gathered to harm you, they can do nothing that God has not prescribed for you. On this matter, the pens have been lifted and the papers dried!"

They take example from the words of the poet:

If there is no escape from death
  Dying cowardly is an expression of impotence[8]

And another [poet] who said:

Whoever dies not by the sword will die for some other reason
  Many are the causes of death, but death is singular[9]

These youth believe in what they have been told by God and His Messenger, God's blessings and salutations upon him, with regards the magnificence of the reward for the struggler and martyr. Exalted God says: "But those who are slain in the way of God, He will never let their deeds be lost. Soon will He guide them, and improve their condition, and admit them to the Garden which He has announced for them."[10] The Exalted also says: "And say not of those who are slain in the way of God 'They are dead.' Nay, they are living, though ye perceive it not."[11] And as related in the *Small Collecting Work*, God's Messenger says, God's blessings and salutations upon him: "There are a hundred levels in paradise, and God prepared two levels for the strugglers along God's path that resemble those between heaven and earth." The [ninth-century] compendium by the Imam Ahmad [Ibn Hanbal] also relays the report: "The most favored martyrs are those who meet the battlefront without turning their faces until they are killed. Those are the ones who prance in the highest chambers of paradise. Your Lord sends them his laugh-ter, and should your Lord laugh to his servant while he remains in the world, no final reckoning need be made." As related in the *Small Collecting Work*, [the Prophet] also says: "The pain that a martyr discovers in death is merely like a pinch felt by any one of you." And as related in the Compendium of the Imam Ahmad [Ibn Hanbal], the Prophet says, God's blessings and salu-tations upon him: "For God, the martyr is endowed with a special charac-teristic: he is to be forgiven at the first gush of his blood, shown his seat in paradise, festooned with the jewels of faith, married to heaven's dark-eyed beauties, exempted from the tribulations of the grave, given protection from the terrifying Day of Judgment, adorned with a crown of dignity upon his head—a single ruby of which is better than this world and anything in it—married to seventy-two of heaven's dark-eyed beauties, and given the right to intercede on behalf of seventy relatives [on Judgment Day]."

These youths know that the reward for fighting you is double that for those who are not People of the Book. Their only interest is to enter paradise by killing you, for the disbeliever and his executioner will never meet in hell. They reiterate and chant the words of the Exalted: "Fight them, and God will punish them by your hands, cover them with shame, help you [to victory] over them, heal the breasts of believers."[12] So too [they recall] the words of the Prophet, God's blessings and salutations upon him, when he was inciting Muslims at Badr: "I swear by He who holds the soul of Muhammad in His hand: no man shall fight them today, be slain even as they are patient and pious, advance and not retreat, without being admitted into paradise by God." After this, [the Prophet] told them: "Ascend to paradise, for its width comprises both the heavens and the earth!"

They also chant the words of the Exalted: "Therefore, when you meet the disbelievers [in fighting], smite their necks."[13] These youths do not enjoy speaking with you. The tongues of every one of them say, rebuking you:

The only rebuke between me and you
   Is a stab to the kidneys and the striking of necks[14]

And they repeat to you what their grandfather, the Commander of the Faithful Harun Al-Rashid, said to your grandfather, [the Byzantine Emporer] Nicephorus, when he threatened and railed against the Muslims in his letter to Harun Al-Rashid.[15] Harun Al-Rashid replied to him in a letter in which he said: "From Harun Al-Rashid, Commander of the Faithful to Nicephorus, the Byzantine dog: You will see, not hear, my answer." Then he went with the Islamic troops to meet Nicephorus and his army, where God struck Nicephorus with an odious defeat. May God honor the people of Islam and break the people of the Cross.

These youths whom you call "cowards" say to you:

They cannot deafen us with their clamor
   They cannot flatten us with their spears
You will see, not hear, my answer

The youths vie among themselves to kill and fight you, just as [the tribes of] 'Aws and Khazraj, God be pleased with them, vied to fight the disbelievers [during the early Islamic expansion].[16] As one of them has said:

The Crusader army retreated in vain on the day we blasted Khobar [towers]
   With the youths of Islam, the meekest of them fearing no danger

I HAVE SCORNED THOSE WHO REBUKED ME

If told 'the tyrants will kill you,' they reply 'my death is a victory'
  I betrayed no king, though he betrayed the horizon of our prayers
Exposing that sacrosanct land to the evil of humans most filthy
  I swear by Great God to fight whoever rejects the faith[17]

For ten years they carried weapons on their shoulders in Afghanistan and
they have vowed to God to continue their campaign against you until you
leave disappointed, defeated, and banished by God's permission. As long as
a pulse beats and an eye blinks, their tongue expresses their state:

Tomorrow, William, you will discover which young man
  [Will] confront your brethren, who have been deceived by [their own] leaders
A youth, who plunges into the hazards of war, smiling
  He hunches forth, staining the blades of lances red
May God not let my eye stray from the most eminent
  Humans, should they fall, Genies, should they ride
[And] lions of the jungle, whose only fangs
  [Are their] lances and short Indian swords
As the stallion bears my witness that I hold them back
  [My] stabbing is like the cinders of fire that explode into flame
On the day of the stallions' expulsion, how the war-cries attest to me
  As do stabbing, striking, pens, and books[18]

Your imbalance is demonstrated by your insult to the grandsons of the
Prophet's Companions, may God be pleased with them, when you called
them "cowards" and by your threat not to withdraw from the Land of the
Two Holy Sanctuaries. This display of madness is [simply] medicine for the
youths of Islam, who say:

My soul and everything within my right hand have been sacrificed
  Knights, entrusted in my deepest beliefs
Knights never tired by death
  Even as the savage mill of war grinds on
The furnace growing hot, they care not a whit
  They cured the madness from further madness[19]

Terrorizing you, while you are carrying arms on our land, is truly an obligatory and righteous command, a product of good discernment, a legitimate
right according to the customs of humans everywhere and even non-human
creatures.

Our relationship with you is like that of a man who killed a snake entering
his house. Only a coward lets you walk across their land while armed, secure,
and protected. These youths differ from your soldiers: while your problem
will be how to convince your troops to advance to war, ours will be how to
convince our youths to wait for their turn to fight and conduct important
operations. These young men champ at the bit for the sake of God.

These youths are commendable and praiseworthy. They stood up to defend religion on a day when the [Saudi] state subdued the most prominent scholars, deriding them by issuing legal opinions founded in neither the book of God nor the pathway of His prophet, God's blessings and salutations upon him. [The state] handed over the Al-Aqsa Mosque [in Jerusalem] to the Jews and exposed the Land of the Two Holy Sanctuaries to Christian armies. Twisting and throttling the holy scriptures can change truth not a wit.

As for the shame of those who stay behind, and the praise of the strugglers, the poet says:

> I have scorned those who rebuked me
>> Who have strayed from the path of righteous guidance
> Who, gathered in their clubs around crackling fireplaces, have quibbled endlessly
>> Who, delusional and despite the wilderness around them, think that they have arrived
> [But] I commend those who have pressed on, asking no questions about hardships faced
>> Or their goals. Despite the turmoils of the path, they have never relented
> In the darkness of confusion, a torch has been kindled from their blood
>> O lively colt! How you excel in all measures, never graying with exhaustion!
> O honorable skiff! How you move against the swelling wave
>> As a sword, a bolt of lightning flashing from its origin
> I have seen you clearly while others linger at the gates and allege
>> For my part, the wound of Jerusalem still festers in my sides
> The source of its affliction like fire ablaze in my intestines
>> I have not betrayed my covenant with God. Why have the nation-states done so
> After I struggled on their plains, the most illustrious of their mortals falling short?[20]

As their grandfather 'Asim Ibn Thabit said, may God be pleased with him, responding to disbelievers who sought to negotiate and who called for a cessation of fighting, insisting instead on fighting them:

> What is this illness of mine? Is not my flesh that of the archer
>> My illness but a bow whose string is taut?
> Death is true, life but a falsehood
>> If I do not fight you, my mother will mourn my loss.[21]

The youths consider you responsible for everything your brothers the Jews are perpetrating in the lands of Palestine and Lebanon; for the killing, expulsions, and violations against Muslims' protected sanctities. Openly and every day you supply them with wealth and weapons. Meanwhile, the children in Iraq have suffered more than six-hundred thousand deaths due to the shortage of food and medicine, the result of your unjust sanctions on Iraq and its people. They are our children. You and the Saudi regime bear responsibility for the bloodshed of these innocents. All of this invalidates every treaty that has been made with you. The Prophet Muhammad, God's blessings and salutations upon him, considered the treaty of Al-Hudaibiyya [with the Quraish] null and void after the Quraish helped Banu Bakr undermine the Khuza'a, allies of the Prophet, God's blessings and salutations upon him. So he fought the Quraish and liberated. He also considered the treaty with Banu Qaynuqa' null and void since, among other reasons, one of their Jews attacked a woman in the marketplace. How, then, are we to react to your killing hundreds of thousands of Muslims and seizing their sanctuaries? It has become clear through such events that those who claim as inviolable the blood from soldiers of the American enemy occupying Muslim lands are merely repeating the most despicable views given to them by the regime; they do for fear of its oppression and their desire to live peacefully.

[*Recording interrupted*]...Every tribe on the Peninsula of the Arabs must struggle on the path of God and cleanse the land from those occupiers. God knows that their blood can be spilled with impunity and their wealth seized. Whoever kills one of them can take the spoils. Exalted God has said: "But when the forbidden months are past, then fight and slay the pagans wherever you find them, and seize them, beleaguer them, and lie in wait for them in every stratagem [of war]."[22] Our youths know that this humiliation now plaguing Muslims due to the occupation of their sanctuaries will not be eliminated or struck down without struggle and explosions. They repeat the words of the poet:

> The walls of humiliation fall only through a rain of bullets
> He who is free does not abandon leadership to every disbeliever and sinner
> Without the shedding of blood, disgrace cannot be wiped from the brows[23]

I say to the youth of the Islamic world, who fought in Afghanistan and Bosnia Herzegovina with their wealth, selves, tongues and pens that the battle did not end. I remind them about the talk between [the angel] Jibril and our Messenger, God's blessings and salutations upon him, after the raid of Al-Ahzab, as narrated by [the ninth-century scholar Muhammad] Al-Bukhari. When God's Messenger, God's blessings and salutations upon him, proceeded to Medina, he immediately began to set down his sword. Jibril came to him and said: "Have you set down your sword? By God, the angels did not set down their swords after the fray. Wake up and take whoever is with you to fight Banu Quraiza.[24] I will journey ahead of you to shake their fortresses and strike fear into their hearts." Jibril then traveled with his band of angels, and God's Messenger, God's blessings and salutations upon him, followed in their footsteps with a band of emigrants and supporters.[25]

These youths know that whoever does not fight dies, and that the most honorable death among us occurs while killing in the path of God. They repeat the words of their forefather, the noble Companion, 'Abdalla Ibn Rawaha, may God be pleased with him—especially in the wake of the four heroes who died while bombing the American headquarters in Riyadh, those youths who raised the head of the pious community high, debasing the occupying American enemies with these courageous operations. Expressing their condition, their tongues repeat:

> O soul, if you do not fight, you will die
>> This is the pool of mortality, destination of your prayers and hopes
> Should you be able to match the actions of your predecessors
>> You will have been rightly guided[26]

They also repeat the words of Ja'far, may God be pleased with him, when he was at Mu'ta:

> Lovely is paradise and its nearness
>> Good and cold is its ambrosia
> The Byzantines are Roman, their torment has drawn near me
>> If I meet them I shall smash them[27]

As for our mothers, sisters, women, and daughters, they take example from the revered female Companions, may God be pleased with them. Their model follows the Prophet, God's blessings and salutations upon him, as they emulate the Companions' penchant for courage, sacrifice, and generosity in support of God's religion, Exalted and Glorious is He. They remember the courage and resolve of Fatima, daughter of al-Khattab, may God be pleased with her, when she justly encountered her brother, 'Umar Ibn al-Khattab, before he converted to Islam. When he learned of her conversion, she challenged him saying: "'Umar, have you not seen what would happen if justice lies somewhere other than your religion?" They also remember the position of Asma', daughter of Abu Bakr, on the day they set out to emigrate to Madina. [They recall] how she cut her belt in two pieces, using one piece to tie up the cloth food bag that was to be taken during the journey by God's Messenger, God's blessings and salutations upon him, as well as Abu Bakr. [When the Prophet blessed her, saying she would receive two belts in paradise for the one she gave up,] she became known as "She of Two Belts." They also remember the position of Nusaiba bint Ka'b who helped defend God's Messenger, God's blessings and salutations upon him, on the day of Uhud. She suffered twelve wounds, the deepest of which stayed with her the rest of her life. They also remember the female Companions' willingness to barter and sell their jewelry to help Muslim troops prepare for raiding in the path of God.

In this era, our women have shown tremendous example through generosity in the path of God, and through inciting their sons, brothers, and husbands to struggle in the path of God, including in such countries as Afghanistan, Bosnia Herzegovina, and Chechnya. We ask God to recognize their endeavors and to grant solace to their sons, fathers, husbands, and brothers. May God strengthen their faith and make them steadfast on this road, a road of sacrifice and selfless devotion to the supremacy of God's word. Our women mourn only for men who have fought in the path of God. As the poet has said:

> Lament only for the lion of the jungle, courageous in burning wars
> They have summoned me to wars in order to die beloved, for honorable death is far better than my life[28]

Our women incite their brothers to struggle in the path of God, taking example from the words of the poet:

> Prepare yourself like a contender, this issue is far greater than play
> Are you going to abandon us to wolves of disbelief who feast upon our wings?
> Wolves of disbelief, once adolescent, work as a pack,spawn of iniquity from motley plains
> Where, among the sons of a religion, is the free man who defends the free with weapons?
> Better is death than a life of humiliation, the burning of even a little shame cannot be erased[29]

My Muslim brothers across the world: your brothers in the Land of the Two Holy Sanctuaries and in Palestine are calling upon your help and asking you to take part in struggling against their enemy and yours as well—the Israelis and Americans, in their offense—in every context you can until they are expelled in defeat and exile from the Islamic sanctuaries. Everyone must struggle according to his or her ability. The Exalted has said: "But if they seek your aid in religion, it is your duty to help them."[30]

O stallions of God ride on! This is a straining time, so be passionate! Know that your assembly and cooperation toward liberating the sanctities of Islam is a correct step toward unifying the word of the pious community under the word of monotheism.

Three months before this speech, under pressure from the United States, officials in Khartoum stripped bin Laden of his Sudanese passport. For the first time, he and his family had become stateless. Employing connections with associates in Afghanistan, bin Laden made a hasty departure in a battered old Soviet aircraft for lands that had once been his frontier for combat against the "far enemy." In chapter one, I lay out the extent of his desperation in the summer of 1996. With the militant initiatives of Islamist groups across the Middle East losing ground to broad-based coalitions for political reform, bin Laden's own survival depended on further radicalizing his vision of Islam's call to arms. As I suggested in that chapter, Islamic asceticism (*zuhd*) proves an important idiom for attempting to justify his pitch against the United States and its interests across the world. On Side B of his audiocassette recorded speech, at the outset of this chapter, bin Laden admonishes listeners to boycott American products: "The wealth you devote to the purchase price of American goods will be transformed into bullets shot into the breasts of our brothers in Palestine, in the Land of the Two Holy Sanctuaries, and elsewhere." The urgency of "practicing asceticism (*zuhd*) from the world" remains paramount, no more so than for the pious Muslim woman, a model for how Islam's decentralized struggle might begin on the home front.

Much attention has been devoted to bin Laden's statement against Americans in February 1998 as chief representative of the newly formed "World Islamic Front."[31] Along with five Muslim scholars including Ayman Al-Zawahiri, bin Laden would call upon Muslims to defend their lands in stark and unconditional terms: "To kill the American and his allies—civilian and military—is an individual duty incumbent upon every Muslim in all countries…" Given the media attention that bin Laden had managed to generate by that time, the statement would quickly be picked up by global news networks and cited thereafter as his first declaration of war against the United States. However galvanizing the announcement appeared to Western audiences in the wake of 9/11, its release provoked great controversy in the Islamic world, no more so than among bin Laden's own Arab and Muslim audiences and supporters. Of twenty jihadi groups operating in Afghanistan when the declaration was announced, only three signed on.[32] In following months, Arab militants fighting and training for deployment across Central Asia, North Africa, and the Middle East saw their Afghan camps shut down by bin Laden's Taliban critics, many of whom had expressed scorn for the dangerous provocateur upon his first arrival.[33] After witnessing repeated setbacks and retractions from former supporters, bin Laden confided to an Arab journalist several months later that his portrait of Islam's geopolitical target had perhaps been too one dimensional.[34]

In this chapter, I'll suggest that bin Laden's speech from Tora Bora roughly a year and a half earlier not only proved more important at the time than we have hitherto assessed but also better anticipates the directions and ultimate legacy of al-Qaʿida under the mantle of bin Laden's leadership as well as beyond. Contrary to the 9/11 Commission's report of the 1996 Declaration as a "long, disjointed document," an audio recording of the original speech, formerly deposited in bin Laden's tape collection, reveals a careful exposition on the value of targeting multiple enemies, even as the United States looms large among them.[35] The craft of bin Laden's message would prove instrumental not only for recruiting purposes but also for smoothing his path to Kandahar in the fledgling state of Taliban-led Afghanistan. I'll suggest, furthermore, that translators and journalists in the West ignored key facets of bin Laden's message in their efforts to highlight the global ambitions of his anti-American pitch. However much they rightly sought to depict bin Laden as an international pariah, they abetted his capacities for terrorism by producing a set of talking points that could be digested more easily by public audiences, especially in the West, and by bestowing upon him an alleged singularity of purpose.

Most Arabic-speaking audiences first heard of bin Laden's speech from the weekend issue of the popular newspaper *Al-Quds Al-'Arabi* (*Arab Jerusalem*), published from London and wired to major cities across the world. Recognized, if peripheral, in the Arab press, bin Laden's name flashed across the front page as the leading story: "Bin Laden Calls for Guerrilla War To Expel 'The American Occupiers' from Saudi Arabia" (*Bin Ladin Yad'u li-Harb 'Isabat li-Ikhraj 'Al-Muhtallin Al-Amrikiyin' min Al-Sa'udiyyah*).[36] In light of his post 9/11 image as a global spokesperson for Muslim terrorists fighting the American enemy, several points are worth noting about the way his speech struck mainstream audiences at the time. First, bin Laden is identified from the outset not as a religious figure, organizational leader, financial executive, or even a proponent of global jihad against the West. Rather, he is "one of the most prominent members of the Saudi Opposition." His role as head of the London-based Committee for Advice and Reform had clearly advanced his cause in this regard, though his leadership on that front remained unmentioned.[37] His political and religious discourse is couched, accordingly, for a more parochial audience than the entire Muslim community (*umma*) to which he frequently made appeal: "He has called on his supporters in Saudi Arabia to launch a guerilla war against American forces and to 'expel the polytheists from the Arab Peninsula.'" If rallying attacks on the American enemy is the primary objective of his speech, according to the article, his rationale for doing so is decidedly local: outrage against the Saudi regime and a wider crew of "polytheists" that support its corrupt moral fabric. "Is it right," the article reports him saying, "that we are the largest oil-exporting country and that, at the same time, we [in Saudi Arabia] feel that this is a punishment from God since people must remain quiet about the regime's injustice and non-Islamic behavior?"

In keeping with the terms of bin Laden's speech, the *Al-Quds* article depicts his call to war against the United States not as a license to unleash indiscriminate violence against civilians, a theme that would prove one of the most alarming aspects of his 1998 declaration. He calls instead for attacking American military "forces" and directs ordinary Saudi citizens to do so by "whatever means available to you," from indirect support for combatants to boycotting American products. In their 2001 book *The Age of Terror: America and the World After September 11*, former Deputy Secretary of State Strobe Talbott and Nayan Chanda would call bin Laden's speech a "fatwa," an idea that would be amplified in a popular Public Broadcasting Service documentary a few years later.[38] Aside from the problem of bin Laden's lack of training and credentials for issuing fatwas, his speech dispenses with telltale features of the fatwa tradition, most notably an opinion formulated as a narrow response to a specific question. Bin Laden takes pains, moreover, to repudiate those who might express their opinions according to the terms of corrupt state religious establishments: "their fatwas," he insists, "lack any basis either in the book of God or in the *Sunna*"—that is, the moral path of the Prophet Muhammad. Popular accounts of bin Laden's influence as a religious demagogue would later make much of PBS's designation of bin Laden's speech as a "fatwa," misconstrued by many Western audiences as an imperious edict to be obeyed at the risk of some terrible punishment and not as a single "legal opinion," as commonly understood in the Islamic world.[39] The parentheses around "American Occupiers" in the title of the *Al-Quds* report expresses exactly the kind of controversy that most Arabic readers would have associated with bin Laden's opinions, among them aggressive opposition to an American military presence in the heart of the Arab world.

The *Al-Quds* article likens bin Laden's speech not to a fatwa but to a very different rhetorical genre: a "memorandum" (*mudhakkira*), the idiom of choice for a generation of Saudi political activists when giving their royal leaders "advice" (*nasiha*) in the most dignified manner possible. As a "memorandum," bin Laden's speech illustrates a tradition of Muslim counsel and advice in the Middle East that had long been conducted through written letters. For Arabs, epistles became a defining medium of eloquence during the ninth century in the Abbasid court of Baghdad. Although the exchange of elegant prose would become popularized with the spread of literacy, the epistle had never quite lost its associations with long-established traditions of *belle-lettres* in which colorful pleasantries, competitive verbal jousts, and political wrangling are all of a piece. Bin Laden deploys the genre with his own rhetorical flourishes. His epistle first reached Arabic audiences in a more artful and emotional idiom than many Western audiences would later understand it to be. Beginning his speech with an opening supplication to God in the manner of a bonafide preacher (the text of which is in chapter one), he addresses listeners initially in the deliberative fashion of a political orator, introducing key talking points and laying out the circumstances of his call to arms. Much of this early salvo focuses on a "Judeo-Christian alliance" that has conspired with the United Nations and its allies to plunder the wealth of Muslim societies, especially in the Arabian Peninsula, and massacre their inhabitants everywhere. After announcing that he has secured a "safe base" on the summit of the Hindu Kush in Afghanistan, his voice reaching its highest pitch, he adopts a more solicitous tone for his "memorandum." Comprising roughly a third of the speech, he excoriates ruling Saudi leaders for corruption, fiscal mismanagement, human rights abuses, and especially for its alliance with "American Crusader forces" since the Gulf War of 1990. Such accusations gain religious significance for bin Laden as apostasy (*shirk*) insofar as Saudi leaders are represented as recurring to man-made state law instead of to true Islamic law (*shariʿa*), the latter of which remains confidently underspecified. Overall, the pious tenor of bin Laden's epistle is consistently maintained as an act of remembrance (*dhikr*), so central to Islam's message that mankind is essentially forgetful and thus in need of constant reminding.

When framed as a memorandum, bin Laden's anti-Americanism is contextualized by the *Al-Quds* article as the desperate pitch of a social revolutionary. His long-term strategic priority, in other words, is less driving non-Muslim occupiers from Muslim lands, as classical jihadi treatises might have it, than rectifying the deterioration of economic and political conditions inside Saudi Arabia and alleviating state repression against the Islamic Awakening, especially its scholars and preachers. His call to focus on "the greater apostasy," namely the "American-Jewish" enemy, is depicted as a tactical step in the longer in-house struggle: by focusing on an ostensibly common cause, Muslims can at last stop quibbling among themselves and take action. As bin Laden remarks when discussing Saudis' reluctance to take their rulers to task and demand substantive political reform:

> In the shadow of these discussions and arguments, truthfulness is lost to falsehood while partisanship and personal feuds that erupt between people only augment the pious community's division and frailty. In such circumstances, our priorities in Islamic work are lost as blasphemy and polytheism continue paralyzing and controlling the community. We must be alert to the ways the [Saudi] Ministry of Interior facilitates this atrocious business. The correct response, then, is to adopt the path taken by knowledgeable scholars, as recommended by [thirteenth-century scholar Taqi al-Din] Ibn Taymiyya, God's mercy and blessings upon him: 'People of Islam should all join forces to work toward repelling the greater apostasy that has gained control over the lands of the Islamic world. They must tolerate the nearer danger while on the path to repel the greater danger, otherwise known as the greater apostasy.'

As noted in the *Al-Quds* piece, the "greater apostasy" bin Laden refers to is perpetrated above all by the "American Jewish enemy." However construed, bin Laden's jihadism against American forces reached Arabic readers as a pitch that was conditioned unambiguously by Saudi rulers' own actions. Unlike mainstream American audiences several years later, most Arab audiences did not initially believe bin Laden's religious fervor called for an unqualified fight against the West until the span of the earth was subject to a single worldwide caliphate.

While giving bin Laden headline coverage, *Al-Quds* framed bin Laden's speech as relatively parochial in one further respect. Contrary to the allegations of PBS and many other analysts before and after its documentary, the newspaper never actually published bin Laden's hour-long speech, instead releasing a seven-hundred fifty word report that merely summarized its contents. Several months later the paper published an interview with bin Laden conducted by chief editor 'Abd Al-Bari 'Atwan, but even there bin Laden's objectives were depicted through his identity as "Saudi Oppositionist" and his speech against the United States left unpublished.[40] The lackluster response of Arab newspapers and print media to bin Laden's bold declamation might strike us as odd were it not for the fact that a large chunk of this industry was owned by Saudis, most notably the two leading newspapers *Al-Sharq Al-Awsat* and

Al-Hayat, published from London and Beirut, respectively. To the royal family's benefit, wealth ensured a certain consistency to what was considered newsworthy. Censorship aside, important questions remain about the effects of his speech at the dawn of al-Qaʿida's most coherent mobilization in Afghanistan in the years leading to 11 September. When, in particular, did his speech become known primarily as a "declaration of war against the Americans?" How did copies of his oratory reach audiences? Most importantly, what did they make of it, especially those most inclined to rally under its banner?

In his volume on Islamic jihad published before news of bin Laden's tape collection had broken, historian Rudolph Peters reports the influential role of the audiocassette in circulating bin Laden's 1996 speech among his primary Arabic-speaking audiences.[41] The presence of such a cassette in bin Laden's former residence confirms his findings. Given the volume of commercially licensed and underground Arabic audiocassettes produced at the time and disseminated across the Islamic world, we may safely assume that the tape reached listeners numbering in the tens of thousands. In years to come, internet distribution would extend the reach of this recording.[42] As I suggest below, the acoustic delivery of the speech, orchestrated by bin Laden in measured syllables that crescendoed with dramatical flair and gained intensity as the speech progressed, appears to have been instrumental to its first and primary audience of Arabic speakers. The most widely cited translator of the speech, for example, Saudi opposition leader Muhammad Al-Masʿari, appears to have relied on an audio recording to supplement his work when translating the original Arabic printed version for English speaking audiences: verbiage clipped off on the original recording, the result of having to flip the tape cartridge from side A to side B, is likewise omitted from his translation. For Al-Masʿari, as for others, listening provided cues that risked being lost in print.

The audio recording itself provides no clear title to indicate how listeners might refer to the speech or caption its main points. The cassette cartridge originally in bin Laden's collection reads only "Shaikh Osama bin Laden," while an internet version of the recording I found on a jihadi website in 2010 advertised the speech as "Struggle Against Occupiers in the Land of the Two Holy Sanctuaries" (*Jihad ʿala Al-Muhtallin fi Bilad Al-Haramayn*). Its identity among English speakers as a "declaration," then, proves something of a misnomer, especially insofar as it suggests that bin Laden was the ratified leader of some organization, delegated on its behalf to issue proclamations that committed its members to a single and unambiguous cause. As I argue in later chapters, the idea of al-Qaʿida as an entity under bin Laden's sole leadership had yet to be established or even acknowledged by bin Laden's primary audiences, and any mention of his main organizational headquarters at the time, the London-based Advice and Reform Committee, is absent from copies of his speech. The analogy to a "declaration" may partly have been the result of Al-Masʿari's decision to square his translation with a faxed Arabic copy of the speech, sent to *Al-Quds Al-ʿArabi*. That fax, redactions of which were published shortly later in a London-based opposition newspaper *Al-Islah* and ultimately posted online by Westpoint's Combatting Terrorism Center, bears the expansive title "Declaration of Struggle against the Americans Occupying the Land of the Two Holy Mosques: Expel the Polytheists from the Arabian Peninsula. An Epistle from Osama bin Muhammad bin Laden to His Muslim Brothers in the Whole World and Especially in the Arabian Peninsula." The framing of his discourse as a "declaration" (*iʿlan*) bears an even earlier imprint, however.

The previous month, Robert Fisk, reporting for the British daily *The Independent*, interviewed bin Laden upon his return to Afghanistan from the Sudan. Fisk's account goes as follows:

> In Saudi robes—and sitting next to his two teenage sons, Omar and Saad— bin Laden revealed that he had arrived here from Sudan on 18 May with his fighters, after the Saudis and Americans had put pressure on the Khartoum military government to expel him. He claimed that he would carry on a campaign from Afghanistan to set up a 'true' Islamic state under shariʿa law in Saudi Arabia which, he said, had been turned into 'an American colony.' When I asked if he was declaring war on the West, he replied: 'It is not a declaration of war—it's a real description of the situation. This doesn't mean declaring war against the West and Western people—but against the American regime which is against every Muslim.

As one of Britain's best foreign correspondents, Fisk takes pains to convey bin Laden's bitter hatred of the Saudi regime. He notes that, upon arriving in Afghanistan, bin Laden's primary objective was to carry the fight back to Saudi Arabia in the interests of setting up a "true" Islamic state. Upon hearing this, Fisk follows up with a provocative question that sets his interlocutor on edge. Asking if he was "declaring war on the West," Fisk gets a quick retort: "It is not a declaration of war—it's a real description of the situation." On second thought, as if caught up with the idea that a formal "declaration" might just enhance the credibility of his admonishments to millions of Western readers, bin Laden accepts Fisk's characterization of his discourse with a qualification: his "war," to borrow Fisk's term, is with the American regime and not with Western peoples generally. To back up his alleged threat to the United States, he cites two recent attacks on its military forces and security contractors in the kingdom—the first in November 1995 at the Saudi National Guard Headquarters in Riyadh and the second on 25 June of the following year at the Khobar Towers in Dhahran—the pair of which resulted in twenty-four American casualties and many more wounded. Historical records suggest that bin Laden's links to either attack were insubstantial, though efforts would be made in subsequent years to finger al-Qaʿida operatives under his direction.[43] Over the following month, as bin Laden followed international news speculating on the identity of the Dhahran-bombing perpetrators and experienced an unprecedented shortage of cash reserves, the idea of a "declaration" (*iʿlan*) would be promoted to ascendency in drafts of the speech that had previously labeled his performance a mere "epistle" (*risala*).[44]

After 11 September, Americans would come to read translations of the "declaration" produced by the Central Intelligence Agency's Foreign Broadcast Information Service (FBIS). That version, however, would be doctored to emphasize the primacy of bin Laden's American adversary over its Saudi equivalent. In a section of the speech following bin Laden's description of the "greater apostasy" and Ibn Taymiyya's advice to tackle the greater of two evils, the FBIS omits his criticism of Saudi banks that "deal in usury" and that "vie for wealth with the Two Holy Mosques, raising their voices in war against God." Shortly later, as bin Laden hails the courage of Saudi youth in defending their homeland against disbelieving co-religionists, the FBIS translator excises a much larger section of the speech due to what appeared at the time to be an irregularity in the original faxed draft sent to *Al-Quds Al-ʿArabi*.[45] The translator notes that "a portion of the text is missing at this point; if pagination of fax copy is correct, this suggests two pages, approximately 1,600 words, are missing." The lament, although technically sound, is disingenuous: a fuller English translation of bin Laden's speech, along with the missing section, was widely available at the time and was in fact consulted by the translator as a supplement, as evident in the use of words and phrases used in that translation and found nowhere else.[46] This translation was by the leading Saudi opposition figure in London, Muhammad Al-Mas'ari. It would be the first English rendition of bin Laden's speech produced and eventually, when posted online, the most widely cited of its kind. To be sure, Al-Mas'ari's work had many faults: its syntax proved at times impenetrable and a host of Arabic words unfamiliar to non-native speakers—"*Kufr*" (disbelief), "*Riba*" (usury), "*Da'ees*" (preachers), and "*Umma*" (pious community)—are preserved in ways that make parts of the text nonsensical. Indeed, in some respects Al-Mas'ari's word choice accentuates bin Laden's focus on the United States even more blatantly than does the FBIS rendition, as when he consistently renders "the Israelis and the Americans" as "the Americans and the Israelis" and "Jews and Christians" as "crusaders and Zionists." Still, Al-Mas'ari preserves roughly two thousand words from the most impassioned section of bin Laden's speech while the FBIS translator fails to see their relevance. This section, richly wrought with symbols of militant asceticism, underscores more clearly than any other the centrality of the nearer Muslim enemy to bin Laden's late summer tirade.

How could this missing section convey anything other than what Western readers have been led to conclude about Osama's primary directive: his unambiguous and relentless call on Muslims of all persuasions to target the United States and the West? The crux of difference lies in bin Laden's recourse to a verbal idiom altogether enigmatic for Western audiences and their interpolators. This idiom is Arabic poetry. Excerpts from no less than fifteen poems anchor the imagery and heightened emotional pitch of the entire final third of the speech, a section addressed specifically to Arab and especially Saudi youth. Bin Laden's English-language translators would give short shrift to such material: Al-Mas'ari, in his haste to get a digestible political communiqué into the hands of global audiences, skipped or badly mangled verses, sometimes simply rendering them as prose, while the FBIS translator dropped all but five poems from record altogether. Leading Islamic scholars in the West would later issue popular editions of bin Laden's key speeches, the "1996 Declaration" among them, with even greater discretion, omitting any reference to the poems entirely.[47] A review of this material, re-translated and given its rightful due at the start of this chapter, restores something of the flavor of bin Laden's acerbic summons. Bin Laden's primary audience would have understood the full measure of his political radicalism through his poetry.

The foil for bin Laden's first poem, in keeping with the outset of his speech, is the headless corpse of a monarch:

If the king exceeded all disgrace among people.
We give shame no sanctuary among us
By what volition, O 'Amru Ibn Hind.
Do you want the land to be so pliant?

Composed by a sixth-century Arab poet, the short rhymed couplets present regicide as justifiable when a king cannot defend his own people from external aggression. In the context of a speech devoted to rallying listeners primarily against the United States and its interests in the Arab world, the chilling vignette is made personal for Americans through its ostensible address to one individual in particular: William Perry, the Secretary of Defense serving in the Clinton administration at the time. "I say to you, William, that these youths love death as you love life," bin Laden exclaims in response to Perry's characterization of the perpetrators of the Riyadh and Al-Khobar bombings in 1995 and 1996 as "cowardly terrorists." Much of the substance of his initial rebuke to Perry focuses on Islam's valorization of martyrdom in battle and the bombers' courage in facing certain death. Casting his venom against "People of the Book," Christians and Jews, in particular, bin Laden ignores admonitions from even Islam's most battle-tested religious scholars that they first be invited to convert through education and, if unresponsive, subject to the Islamic state through poll-taxes and treaties. Instead, he directs listeners to "fight" and expect a double reward in paradise.

Bin Laden's use of poetry to bolster his claims suggests much about his skill as an orator in appealing to the emotions of his audiences. As "the public register of the Arab people," according to a tenth-century grammarian, Arabic poetry has long bridged divisions of ethnicity, religion, gender, and background by appealing to a shared historical memory of Glorious deeds and their champions. As all good poets know, memory proves selective. Bin Laden's champions exhibit all the marks of Arab warriors through the ages, as discussed below. Bin Laden's preference for the *qasida* genre proves telling: as the ambassador of Arabic poetry, known even before the rise of Islam for its rhymed couplets and formal meters, the *qasida* represents his controversial views in standards of literary eloquence recognized widely by Arabic speakers across the world. Lacking the credentials of a religious scholar, bin Laden stood to gain from the ennobling mantle of poetry. In many of the countries representing bin Laden's primary recruiting grounds in years to come, including Saudi Arabia, Yemen, and Egypt, poetry would be a familiar tool for militants, as would it be for their detractors.

Still, if bin Laden's recitation of poetry elicits powerful emotions and stirs cultural memories, what is its content? What exactly is it that audiences are being invited to feel? Much of poetry's magic comes, of course, from its difference from everyday speech. The poet can express things that are difficult or even impossible to be said in other ways, a skill that political dissidents in the Arab world had long used to their advantage. What is it that, from the peaks of the Hindu Kush, bin Laden had trouble putting into ordinary diction? The inexpressible subject is not exactly fighting the United States, though this proved controversial enough at the time for both mainstream and core militant audiences, as suggested in other chapters. This directive had been unpacked in no uncertain terms earlier in the speech. Let us consider, rather, how poetry advances the rationale for taking the fight to the far enemy. Couched in verses that had been memorized and transmitted by Arabic speakers for generations, the rationale for engaging Americans and their "Crusader-Jewish" conspirators in battle is that, for all their foreign iniquity, they resemble the nearer Arab enemy too well.

In initial and concluding poems, the archetypal crusader (*salibi*) so often invoked by bin Laden is depicted as thoroughly "other" as possible. The image of this adversary is the Byzantine Christian, a figure that loomed large in the modern pan-Islamic vocabulary insofar as clashes between the U.S.-backed Israeli state and its Arab-majority neighbors could be portrayed as an extension of conflicts in the early Levant. Much of this poetry emphasizes the warrior's thirst for martyrdom. Composed as early as the sixth and seventh centuries, verses by 'Amru Ibn Hind as well as the Prophet Muhammad's Companions 'Abdalla Ibn Rawaha and Ja'far Ibn Abi Talib are cited to express the modern young militant's kinship with those who fought Byzantine troops long ago: "This is the pool of mortality, destination of your prayers and hopes/ Should you be able to match the actions of your predecessors/You will have been rightly guided." Ninth-century caliph Harun Al-Rashid, emblem of stately Arab honor in the *Tales of One Thousand and One Nights*, gets special mention for calling the Byzantine Emperor Nicephorus I, the eponymous ancestor of Secretary Perry, a "Byzantine dog." His alleged threat to Nicephorus, "You will see, not hear, my answer" would appear later, along with thrusting spears, in al-Qaʿida videos celebrating the 11 September attacks.[48]

So too, however, are the villains of bin Laden's poems depicted as Arabs themselves who have gone astray. In the first poem, King ʿAmru Ibn Hind and his assailant ʿAmru Ibn Kulthum share more than similar names: both were from a noble lineage of Peninsular Arabs, the latter chief of a tribe much feared for wreaking vengeance against its neighbors. As online listeners would recall, the sorry object of "two-handed stabbing and smiting necks" in the fourth poem was none other than ʿAli Ibn Abi Talib, the Prophet Muhammad's own nephew, though he had fallen out at the time with the governor of Syria who drafted the challenge.[49] Their battle at Karbala shortly later would go down in history as the icon of Shiʿa persecution at the hands of Sunnis. A theme of righteous mutiny against Arab leaders themselves is elaborated more explicitly after the Harun Al-Rashid episode. After describing Al-Rashid's rejection of any further dialogue with Nicephorus (himself of Arabian descent), bin Laden introduces five poems that illustrate not only the valor of his young Muslim knights but also their experience with ruthless tribal violence exercised against their own. The first of them, attributed to bin Laden himself, conveys much of the double voicing that inflects this verse. Once again claiming credit for the Khobar Towers bombings, he celebrates a retreat by the "Crusader army" only to take up arms against a more proximate heretic:

> If told 'the tyrants will kill you,' they reply 'my death is a victory'
>   I betrayed no king, though he betrayed the horizon of our prayers
> Exposing that sacrosanct land to the evil of humans most filthy
>   I swear by Great God to fight whoever rejects the faith.

The Saudi monarch can expect much the same treatment as ʿAmru Ibn Hind. Next come gory verses describing the rigors that await Arab rulers who stray from indigenous codes of honor. While performed for the ostensible education of William Perry, the famous verses also remind Arab youth, bin Laden's primary audience, of martial exploits by early Arabian warriors such as the legendary ex-slave ʿAntar Ibn Shaddad, an Arab Sparticus whose adventures in battle as well as in romance had long been recorded in popular tales. The origins of such men heralded not from an Islamic community but rather from a lustier race of pre-Islamic tribesmen who lived in the *Jahiliyya*, the "Age of Ignorance." In his initial volley to Perry, bin Laden extols the "praiseworthy morals" of those living in that early twilight period, a time maligned by Muslim reformers across the board for its obstinent paganism. From "father to father," he states, their values of "dignity, pride, courage, generosity, sincerity, daring, and the will to make sacrifices" have been passed down to modern Muslim youth. In his later, post 9/11 writings, bin Laden would reiterate the "strength," "loyalty," and "warriorship" of those who lived in the *Jahiliyya*, a position echoing arguments by many nineteenth-century Arab nationalists that bonds of ethnicity and culture could complement or even supplant those defined by religion.[50] In this case, bin Laden also sees religion as having been compromised by a corrupt Saudi state, an in-house perfidy described clearly just before the onset of a contemporary poem beginning with the strophe "I have rejected all who scorn me." Bin Laden's valiant youth are said to have "stood up to defend religion on a day when the [Saudi] state subdued the most prominent scholars, deriding them by issuing legal opinions (*fatwas*) founded in neither the book of God nor the pathway of His prophet." Deriding wealthy Saudi monarchs for their ostensible capitulations to Jews and Christians as early as the 1930s, he exclaims that "twisting and throttling the holy scriptures can change truth not a whit." The subsequent *qasida*, pitting those who "gathered in their clubs, have quibbled endlessly around crackling fireplaces" against sword-wielding Arab tribesmen, is embellished with even greater historical antiquity in the closely paired poem afterward. In that case, the traitors are Mecca's ruling merchant family, the Quraish, along with its allies when, in CE 624, they fought Muslims at the battle of Badr.

For audiences in the West reading truncated versions of bin Laden's speech meant to be easily digestible, the Saudi exile's objective is unmistakable: he declared war on the United States and in doing so rallied his primary Arab audiences toward a common enemy. As national security experts considered the implications of his speech in the years ahead, the possibility that bin Laden might have used his anti-American pitch to advocate for war against Muslim rulers themselves, much less that he did so through the subtle art of poetry, seemed outlandish. The events of 9/11 would help make such a reading anathema. Restoring bin Laden's poetic voice does not diminish his radicalism or make him a more sympathetic character, but rather illustrates the devastating extent of his double game. For his anti-American militancy to hold any credibility among militants, he would first need to lay out a rationale premised on no uncertain savagery against Muslim authorities in the Arab world. The role of bin Laden's verse in highlighting the Arab enemy is suggested not only in the ways poems were mangled or dropped entirely by CIA translators and Saudi oppositionists seeking global news coverage. The localizable wrath of his poetry is also evident in the way bin Laden's online jihadi supporters in the West would follow suit after 9/11. In 2010, an audio recording of the speech was posted on one of the most popular militant websites for non-Arabic speakers *Minbar Al-Tawhid wa-l-Jihad* ("The Pulpit of Monotheism and Jihad").[51] The recording features the first half of bin Laden's speech but eliminates all poems along with any reference to bin Laden's call for "guerrilla war" inside Saudi Arabia. Instead, the speech appears to end with bin Laden's outline of seven reasons against internecine Muslim infighting.

In subsequent chapters, I show how militant Muslim theologians and their supporters employ the Arabic term *al-qaʿida* to advance claims of confessional unity that are belied by destructive tendencies to anathematize their fellow co-religionists. In his 2004 book *Globalized Islam: The Search for a New Ummah*, political scientist Olivier Roy offered a pioneering account of global jihadism in which he explored how such apparently contradictory ambitions are reconciled by Islamic militants. Citing bin Laden as a case in point, he notes that:

> For the sake and pleasure of Allah (*reza*), for the sake of self-achievement (in death), for escaping a corrupt world…There is a strange mix of deep personal pessimism and collective millenarianist optimism among this type of terrorists: they do not trust the people they are fighting for (they are also indifferent to killing Muslims), they are sure to die, and as political scientist Farhad Khosrokhavar pointed out in the case of the Iranian martyrs of the Iran-Iraq War, they know that, even if they succeed, in the future society will not match the ideals for which they are fighting.[52]

In important ways, bin Laden's poems convey just such strained exuberance. While bin Laden's youths herald the "brilliant future of the pious community of Muhammad," so too are they represented as exhibiting little of the generic pan-Islamic sentiments so often touted by corrupt states. As they line up against a presumably common foe, they do so more as Arabian tribesmen than as a global caliph's legates. Bin Laden's solution for the "failure of political Islam," as Roy put it some years earlier, is not an appeal to traditional jihadism, long the idiom of state rulers and scholars and rarely a topic for popular uptake.[53] Rather, he produces a more eclectic rhapsody advocating for an all-out front against the Arabian Peninsula's most egregious representative of secular materialism: the United States. The consequences of bin Laden's adventurous rhetoric would be evident not only in his nomination by Western counter-terrorist agencies as a most dangerous adversary. As the *Tawhid wa-l-Jihad* omission suggests, bin Laden's discourse had a dangerously Janus-faced quality whose threat to pan-Islamic unity required close monitoring.

According to Roy, the effects of bin Laden's disenchantment speak volumes about the ways Islamic militancy has been shaped by the globalization of Islam, and exhibit the corrosion of traditional ties between social groups bound by specific territories. For terrorists such as bin Laden, their heads filled with visions of paradise, any prospect of negotiation with the enemy is off the table; after all, Roy insisted, "his fight, as we have seen, is not directly linked to the various conflicts in the Middle East."[54] Such views of al-Qaʿida's essential unmooring from local conflicts, I suggest, need revisiting. From his redoubt in Tora Bora, bin Laden advanced a rationale for fighting the Americans that was grounded in his proven resolve to purge the Arabian Peninsula, and Saudi Arabia specifically, of its own ruling infidels. To do so, he had to dance with the devil, merging the face of the American enemy so thoroughly with his own Muslim adversaries that al-Qaʿida's holy warriors would be forced to create new visions of primordial ethnic ties to sustain them. Among bin Laden's would-be supporters, such a socialized model of Islamic revolution faced detractors from the outset. In his memoir, Yemeni militant Nasir Al-Bahri recalls how he and his colleagues tried to avoid bin Laden when first arriving in Afghanistan in late 1996. Having come to the region for training and redeployment in support of Muslim insurgents in neighboring Tajikistan, Al-Bahri reports being wary of bin Laden's focus on bringing the revolution back to the Arabian Peninsula, a place to which he hoped to return: "we knew that if he got hold of us, we would not be able to get away…our evasion was not out of fear, but we felt we would not be able to meet some of bin Laden's requirements."[55] Participants at bin Laden's three-day workshop near Jalalabad shortly later felt the same way. Although the conference was ostensibly devoted to outlining reasons that the United States should be considered Islam's principle threat, some of the militants, especially those who were not Arab, departed early with a sense that bin Laden's incessant focus on the Arabian Peninsula revealed his true colors.[56] It was during this same period, Al-Bahri reports, that bin Laden revived the idea of opening headquarters for his operations back at home, especially in Saudi Arabia and Yemen.[57]

Bin Laden's near-enemy focus did not bode well for his own survival. Within a few weeks of his arrival in Jalalabad in May of 1996, he was forced to withdraw for security reasons to an old fortress five miles outside the city.[58] By the spring of the next year, he had experienced three assassination attempts, at least one of them sponsored by the Saudis.[59] If he was to gain leverage at all in his new surroundings, he would need to enhance his image as a more ecumenical spokesperson for Muslims of diverse backgrounds. The task required walking a fine line. As a public speaker in an Afghan Hanafi heartland whose customs of prayer and reverence for families of Sufi saints had long drawn rebuke from Arab recruits used to Wahhabi-style salafi doctrine, he had to avoid being drawn into divisive polemics about theology and Islamic law. Close associates of bin Laden's complained at the time of not being able to engage him on pressing religious and ethical matters, even when in private settings.[60] Such obtuseness risked impugning his credibility given that the bulk of his oratory had profoundly religious content, namely, justifying the merits of Islam's prescriptions for armed struggle against some of the Islamic world's most esteemed leaders and their allies. He faced the challenge of having to demonstrate leadership in a community of explicitly religious authorities, then, while absolving himself from their traditional standards of evaluation and approval.

It was at this time that bin Laden discovered a key resource for promoting his image as a religious chief, however maverick. In late March of 1997, holed up in his Tora Bora cave, he would give his first interview for a Western television network. Produced by CNN's Peter Bergen and aired on 10 May, the program broadcast bin Laden's own words to millions of viewers along with the following narrative:[61]

> We begin with the story of a shadowy multi-millionaire who has declared a holy war against the United States. To some in the Islamic world he is a hero. To the United States government, though, he is a terrorist, a real threat to the lives of U.S. troops. He is Osama bin Laden, and *Impact's* Peter Arnett takes us into his hideaway and into his mind with this first-ever television interview.
>
> [*The caption "Holy Terror?" appears on the screen. After describing bin Laden's presence in Afghanistan, Arnett's voice continues.*]

The U.S. state department calls him one of the most significant financial sponsors of Islamic extremism in the world…The State Department links the forty-one-year-old bin Laden to Ramzi Youssef, alleged mastermind of the World Trade Center bombing, New York, an attempted bombing of U.S. troops in 1992, Yemen, terrorist training camps in Sudan and Afghanistan, Islamic terrorist groups in Egypt and Algeria.

[*Al-Quds Al-'Arabi editor in chief 'Abd al-Bari 'Atwan*]: Younger generation Islamists, especially those Islamic fundamentalists, they are looking for a hero. And Mr Bin Laden fits the bill.

In Western intelligence circles bin Laden is best known for this document [*A picture of the Arabic fax sent to Al-Quds Al-'Arabi scrolls across the screen*]: a call for jihad, or holy war, against the thousands of U.S. soldiers now stationed in Saudi Arabia. That call to jihad came out to two bombings of U.S. troops in Saudi Arabia: the first in Riyadh in 1995. Seven dead. The second in Dhahran in 1996. Nineteen dead and hundreds injured. [*Pictures show wounded American soldiers and blasted buildings.*]

To support his holy war, sources estimate bin Laden has up to half a billion dollars. [*Picture of bin Laden in a Sudan house sitting in front of shelves stacked with expensive leather-bound Arabic books and a machine gun.*] To execute his jihad, bin Laden has thousands of committed followers inside Saudi Arabia.

[*Saudi Opposition leader Saad Al-Faqih in London*]: They are either direct followers taking command, direct command and order from bin Laden, or they are small cells and groups who believe bin Laden is a godfather. His message is almost like a religious order…

[*The documentary continues, discussing the Arab-Afghan jihad against the Soviets, his years in the Sudan and then his move to Afghanistan. Peter Arnett is then shown asking bin Laden questions about his plans. Bin Laden responds with the following.*]

We have focused our declaration of jihad on striking at the U.S. soldiers inside Saudi Arabia, the country of the Two Holy Places, Mecca and Madina. In our religion, it is not permissible for any non-Muslim to stay in Arabia. Therefore, even though American civilians are not targeted in our plan, they must leave. We do not guarantee their safety.

[*Former CIA senior official Graham Fuller*]: When this guy delivers his statements attacking the U.S. presence or his call for jihad, he is justifying these actions in very explicit Qur'anic Islamic terms—it's like a careful legal brief.

[*The documentary continues, discussing bin Laden's support for terrorism in the Middle East and views on the suffering of Palestinians.*]

[*Arnett*]: What are your future plans?

[*Bin Laden*]: You'll see them and hear about them in the media, God willing.

If bin Laden's emphasis on attacking the American enemy was thematized consistently in his speech the previous fall, his message to English-speaking audiences was more explicit and comprehensive. "Our main problem is the U.S. government" bin Laden would explain in the longer interview. "By being loyal to the U.S. regime, the Saudi regime has committed an act against Islam. And this, based on the ruling of Islamic jurisprudence (*shari'a*), casts the regime outside the religious community. Subsequently, the regime has stopped ruling people according to what God revealed…"[62] Whereas in previous speeches the American presence in Saudi Arabia had always been a symptom of the larger illness that plagued the House of Saud, namely governance through "man-made" rather than divine law, this time bin Laden turns the vector of causation about face. He embellishes his accusation with yet further threats unprecedented for their global cast: "it is our duty to make jihad so that God's word is the one exalted to the heights and so that we drive the Americans away from all Muslim countries." In light of 9/11 and ensuing fears about al-Qa'ida's global capabilities, such statements appear portentous, no more so than his final remark to Arnett about future plans: "You'll see them and hear about them in the media, God willing." In retrospect, it seems clear that CNN was setting the pace among global news networks for telling it like it was.

The benefit of hindsight also provides us with a more sobering perspective on the ways a leading Western news network, while justly calling public attention to the danger of an international pariah, could provide leverage to dark ambitions. CNN's report of his access to "up to a half billion dollars" overlooked widespread speculation about the depleted state of bin Laden's financial holdings at the time. CNN was hardly alone in magnifying bin Laden's fortunes. In the spring of 1996, the U.S. State Department called bin Laden "one of the most significant financial sponsors of Islamic extremist activities in the world today."[63] According to *New York Times* reporters Judith Miller and Jeff Gerth, bin Laden's net worth was around $250 million, a figure that would be adjusted in the mid 2000s to a more realistic $20 million.[64] When the CIA produced its first biographical profile of bin Laden shortly after the Khobar Towers attacks in June of the same year, terror experts concluded that most of bin Laden's fortune remained intact after his move to Afghanistan, though whether in Swiss bank accounts, Islamic charities, or the vast system of local commercial brokers known as *hawala*, none could say for sure.[65] Bin Laden had certainly risen to super-donor status during the 1980s and 1990s among a host of militant groups and extremist movements willing to use violence and terror to further their causes. Some reports suggested that he sent tens of millions of dollars annually to such benefactors, most notably Yemen, the Sudan, Algeria, Egypt, Lebanon, Afghanistan, Pakistan, Chechnya, and the Philippines.[66] It is important to note that with the exception of the last country, however, bin Laden's largesse was confined to Muslim-majority countries mostly in the Arab world. So marginal was his threat to Western countries, in fact, that when the United States put out a list of the most wanted terrorists in 1997, the same year as CNN's interview, neither bin Laden nor al-Qa'ida was on it.[67]

CNN's first-ever interview by a Western television network amplified bin Laden's menace for millions of Western viewers in two important respects. First, focusing on worries among U.S. State Department and intelligence experts that bin Laden's cash reserves may have survived his move to Afghanistan, CNN neglected to mention demonstrable steps that had been taken in previous years by the United States as well as international and state agencies to clamp down on bin Laden's accounts and cripple his financial empire. In 1994, his family's disinheritance put a notch in his access to bin Laden Group ventures and board members' annual distribution of $1 million. In 1995, President Clinton passed the Omnibus Counterterrorism Act that froze the accounts of terrorist groups, a measure whose effects, though considered limited at the time, opened avenues to more concerted transnational monitoring efforts. After his move to Afghanistan in 1996, the Saudis froze the bulk of his assets, estimated to be $2–300 million.[68] Colonel Omar Bashir's regime in the Sudan, meanwhile, presented bin Laden with a debtor's lament: none of the $165 million he put in to building the country's roads, infrastructure, and businesses would be returned to him. Bin Laden's own supporters in the Sudan had known of his financial woes from their first months in the country. In 1992, Jamal Al-Fadl and Abu Rida Al-Suri, bin Laden's closest financial advisors, informed their boss that his Sudanese investments made little business sense and were rapidly depleting his reserves.[69] At the end of 1994 bin Laden told his closest employees that he would have to reduce their salaries because he had "lost all my money."[70] Several years after 9/11, the story of bin Laden's impoverishment upon arriving in Afghanistan in 1996 would be confirmed by the Congressional Research Service's resident Middle East expert Kenneth Katzman.[71] Summarizing findings by the 9/11 Commission report as well as several other independent inquiries, Katzman found that "He left Sudan with practically nothing." The idea that al-Qaʿidaʾs financial wherewithal had ever rested principally on bin Laden's own fortune was a red herring; in fact, support from a much wider array of donors proved far more instrumental. Persistence of the myth could be traced to the fact sheets by the U.S. State Department and CIA and especially to growing public fascination with bin Laden fueled by such news stories as that by CNN.

CNN further personalizes bin Laden's threat for viewers by emphasizing his circumstantial ties to the World Trade Center bombing in New York City in February 1993. At the time, the only substance to this link was a report by Pakistani investigators that Ramzi Yousef, one of the main perpetrators of the attack, resided at a guesthouse in Peshawar partly funded by bin Laden.[72] Four years later, in early 2001, further evidence for bin Laden's possible involvement would be produced by former CNN investigative reporter and terror expert Steven Emerson: a bomb manual found in the possession of one of the attackers and invoked during the original trial proceedings was, in fact, produced by bin Laden's organization, as evident in the manual's title, "The Base" (*Al-Qaʿida*), incorrectly translated earlier as "The Basic Rule."[73] Emerson's much-cited re-translation proves impossible to corroborate given that the bomb manual in question appears not to be publicly available; his assertions about the 1993 attackers' connections with bin Laden's group deserve scrutiny given his lamentable record in seeing Muslims of all persuasions as being united by the same ideology of hatred: even the anti-terrorism fatwas of North American Muslims, it appears, were "bogus" and a public relations trick.[74] However construed, CNN's early accentuation of bin Laden's possible links to terrorism within the United States ran counter to reports by other Western journalists who interviewed bin Laden in the mid-1990s.[75] The Khobar Tower bombings would supply bin Laden with a mise-en-scène that he exploited assiduously whenever speaking to Western audiences, as evident in his August 1996 oration. His statements to Peter Arnett about the attacks would be even more provocative and become a standard reference for Western reporters seeking evidence for his possible involvement: "What they did is a great job and a big honor that I missed participating in."[76] What gave teeth to CNN's allegations of bin Laden's involvement in terrorist strikes targeting Americans was his speech from Tora Bora and its uptake in the West over the previous year.

In a letter written later to Taliban leader Mulla ʿUmar, bin Laden would emphasize the importance of a well planned media strategy for projecting the image of a common front: "It is obvious that the media war in this century is one of the strongest methods; in fact, its ratio may reach 90% of the total preparation for the battles."[77] According to bin Laden, an image of the Arabian Peninsula under American occupation could rally sympathies among Muslims in ways few other causes could. CNN's 1997 report suggests how well bin Laden's strategy worked when parleyed into the hands of Western journalists and their interviewees. Most alarming, bin Laden's story would hinge on his own alleged role as a leading religious authority, and a pan-Islamic commander in chief. According to Saudi Opposition activist Saad Al-Faqih, bin Ladin is "a godfather" to his admirers and "his message is almost like a religious order." In fact, religious scholars far more influential among bin Laden's Arab salafi followers had already denounced him explicitly and expressed revulsion at the Khobar Tower attacks. Not only did they include Saudi chief jurists such as ʿAbd al-ʿAziz Ibn Baz who, in a prominent Arabic newspaper article published just a month after bin Laden's 1996 Tora Bora speech, wrote that "Bin Laden is among the earth's most corrupted individuals, spewing on about paths both evil and corrupt."[78] They also included far more dissident voices such as Yemen's leading salafi traditionalist Muqbil Al-Wadiʿi who, just two weeks after the Khobar bombing, inveighed against the attackers for privileging their own views over the reasoned opinions of established scholars (*ulama*) and chastised "the kind of discord recently fomented in Yemen by Osama bin Ladin."[79] Instead of depicting bin Laden as a man whose religious views were widely considered deficient, CNN features former CIA senior official Graham Fuller testifying to his scholarly discipline: "When this guy delivers his statements attacking the U.S. presence or his call for jihad, he is justifying these actions in very explicit Qurʾanic Islamic terms—it's like a careful legal brief." As I suggest in this chapter as well as others, bin Laden's appeal to listeners was founded in aligning himself not with scholarly convention but rather in sustained tension with it. Far more central to bin Laden's message was a reconstituted Arabian homeland whose ancestral claims trumped whatever accommodations an Abrahamic faith might make for its various adherents.

CNN's failure to recognize or acknowledge the deeply factionalized aspects of bin Laden's rhetoric for Muslims themselves signaled a grander logic in global media reportage on bin Laden that he and those standing behind the al-Qaʿida brand in years to come would routinely exploit: a coherence in identity could mask an incoherence of ideology. As long as bin Laden's message among audiences could be construed as primarily anti-American or, even better, anti-West, ideological disagreements between those rallying under his banner could always be muffled. The problem of how to keep America in the news would be the main challenge in years to come. The task would become especially controversial after attacks on the American embassies in East Africa in 1998 and the events of 11 September. Global media coverage provided a convenient solution: especially where bin Laden was consistently portrayed as the Islamic leader that he could never be.

10

NEW BASES NEAR AN ANCIENT HOUSE

(18 May 1998 speech by Osama bin Laden.[1] A training camp outside of Kandahar. Opening remarks, cassette no. 1035.)

———

Praise be to God. We show Him gratitude, seek His help and ask for His pardon. We take refuge in God from the evils within us and our wrongful deeds. Who ever is guided by God will not be misled, and who ever is misled will never be guided. I bear witness that there is no god but God alone, Who has no associates, and that Muhammad is His Slave and Messenger.

Now then. Thanks be to God for the blessing of Islam. Thanks to God, Glorious and Exalted is He, for this complete religion conferred upon us. Through this religion He has led us from darkness into the light. Thanks be to God who commanded us to struggle for the good of his creation, in accordance with our Prophet, God's blessings and salutations upon him. May the word leading to disbelief be brought low and the word of God raised most high.

On the likes of this day, eight years ago, the Arab Peninsula experienced a tragedy whose enormity has had no precedent. On the likes of this day, in the year 1411 [CE 1990], on the first of [the Islamic month of] Muharram, the Arab Peninsula was invaded by a Christian horde. They advanced with tanks and with ships that bore into the waters of Islam in the peninsula, the Red Sea, and the Arabian Sea. They circled with planes in Islam's skies over the Arab Peninsula. Never since its creation by God, Glorious and Exalted is He, had this peninsula—with all its deserts, wadis, and encompassing seas—suffered such animosity as this. There is no power and might except

267

through God! It was then that more than 760,000 Americans advanced. They were followed by Christians who were British, French, and other nationalities. In this Peninsula, whose history had never known the mark of submission or surrender to Christians, ever! The one exception was when there was an attempt by Christians before our Prophet was sent down, God's blessings and salutations upon him. At that time the Christian Abraha from the Horn of Africa tried to replace the Ancient House by destroying it and driving people instead to a house and church that he had constructed.

Sixty thousand Christians from the Horn of Africa set out. They entered Yemen and advanced onward from Sanaa in ordered ranks seeking to demolish the Ancient House built by Ibrahim and Isma'il, may God grant them peace. The Arabs were polytheists, though there remained among them those of the Religion of Abraham as well as those who glorified the Ancient House.

How these Arabs, even in their polytheism, set forth to fight Abraha and protect this house! Abraha defeated them on that occasion due to their small number of troops and piecemeal organization. He advanced, in fact, until he reached Ta'if. A man in Ta'if known as Abu Righal came forth to direct Abraha to the trail leading to the Ancient House. For that, God killed Abu Righal between Ta'if and Mecca, Glorious and Exalted is He.

The Arabs, even as they were polytheists, would learn to pelt Abu Righal's grave with stones. Such an offense had he committed against God! Why did he guide those Christians to the Ancient House? History never recorded an event of this sort. The one exception has been in these more recent days of ours. There is no power and might except through God. The previous event, as we mentioned, occurred before the Muhammadan mission of our prophet, may he be granted the finest blessings and salutations.

Abraha set out with sixty thousand troops in the direction of the honorable Ka'ba in venerable Mecca. As he approached, God sent a flock of birds to torment those who sought to assail the Ancient House, Glorious and Exalted is He. Just before that, moreover, He commanded beastly elephants to crouch immovable on the earth when threatened with the destruction of the House. This event was indeed a splendid miracle though the hearts of those who had turned away from God and committed polytheism could take no lesson from this sublime miracle. Indeed the elephantine beasts thwarted them from moving toward the Ancient House! They lashed these beasts. When trying to move north, they moved that way. When trying to move east, they moved that way. When trying to move toward Yemen [in the south], they moved that way. Try though they may to unleashed their iron against the beasts when approaching the Ancient House, however, they were thwarted, unable to move but a single hand width.

At this point, there were none left in the sacred house who could mount a defense. Despite this, 'Abd al-Mutallib, in his polytheism, made an effort to defend the house. He met with no success, however. With no way to repel advances against the house, he went directly to the Ancient House, as early biographies relate. He pledged responsibility for the site as he implored God, Glorious and Exalted is He, to abandon Abraha and his army. His fellow Quraishis took their women and sons to the peaks of the surrounding mountains. They waited to learn how God would respond.

God sent forth a flock of birds, Glorious and Exalted is He. It was a Glorious sign! Those who had assailed the Ancient House were suddenly paralyzed before the very House that led people to resurrection on the final Day of Judgement! For God accepts no Muslim, pure or honest, nor any of his deeds, supererogatory or obliged, unless he directs his prayer toward the Ancient House at least five times every day. From above the seven heavens God would later send a complete *sura*, Glorious and Exalted is He, the *sura* of the Elephant, in order to clarify what summoned believers to the glory of this House. God's ardor for his Ancient House becomes apparent in this *sura*, Glorious and Exalted is He. The story is told of what the beasts did to those polytheist disbelievers who distorted their scriptures and transgressed against their prophets. God clarified that should any of them ever attack the Ancient House in the manner of those before them, they would face punishment, Glorious and Exalted is He. May God give them what they deserve.

We Muslims have never before experienced such sedition as this. Never before have Muslims abandoned the honorable Ka'ba. Since the time of our Prophet's mission, may God's blessings and salutations be upon him, this honorable Ka'ba has never suffered an attack from Jews and Christians except in these recent years, as you know.

[*After discussing the leadership of Saudi clerics such as 'Ali bin 'Abd al-Rahman Al-Hudhayfi and Safar Al-Hawali in calling upon the Saudi administration to rid the Arabian Peninsula of "American Jews and Christians," among other polytheists, bin Laden calls attention to a large map nearby.*]

If we look at this map, we can see the extent of the occupation in the Arab Peninsula. The Arab Peninsula today consists of land and water. The waterways surrounding it are Islamic. In the past, infidel powers of a military capacity were not allowed entry into these waters, whether in the case of the Red Sea or in the Islamic Gulf. In Muslims' history, moreover, no exception was made even for merchant ships requesting access to this enclosed area, the Red Sea. Such ships were obliged to drop anchor near the Bab Al-Mandab [an ocean gateway separating Yemen from Djibouti]. There, they unloaded their charge and were afterwards escorted out of these Islamic waters by Islamic vessels.

In the region today, more than 120,000 American troops are stationed in Kuwait, the Land of the Two Holy Sanctuaries, Bahrain, Qatar, the Emirates, Oman, and Egypt. Today, they use the Aden airport as a base whose purpose is said to be naval support. If we look further, we see how their presence has extended across the Land of the Two Holy Sanctuaries from the north to the south, the east to the west. In the east, as you have heard by the grace of God, an explosion in Khobar killed nineteen American soldiers and injured hundreds of other Americans by the grace of God on high, Glorious and Exalted is He. That was in the east, where they are located in Khobar, but they are also found in Dhahran and Dammam where military bases are also located. So too they have a large base in Hafar Al-Batin. During his visit to the region, President Clinton did not venture to Riyadh, Jeddah, or Dhahran, but instead went to hail the importance of the occupying soldiers, asking the governor of Riyadh to come to him for a meeting there. So too in Tabuk there is a large American base that even Saudi soldiers are forbidden from entering. They cannot go into these bases. There is a base in Jeddah as well. This one is a naval base located south of the city that harbors aircraft carriers moving through the region. There is also an air base just east of the city airport's civilian runways. So too in Ta'if. As you know, some sixty kilometers separate Ta'if and Mecca, and in Ta'if there is an American military air base. Roughly seventy kilometers lie between Mecca and Jeddah, so Noble Mecca is fairly well hemmed in from both the east and the west. Then we have the Hormuz Straits, also in the hands of American and British forces, and French Crusaders patrol the Bab Al-Mandab. Their ships do exactly as they please, behaving like kings in their kingdom. Whether in the Gulf or the Red Sea, they search any ship belonging to an Islamic or Arab nation. There is no power or might except through God!

They have stationed more than supplies in these bases. These bases house more than 760,000 American troops. Should a war break out, they can deploy their tanks and appropriate weapons from these bases. They have pre-positioned them in attempts to confront and drive out any Islamic movement in these countries. Within a single week, they can mobilize upward of 130,000 American soldiers in the Land of the Two Holy Sanctuaries, this great land chosen by God, Glorious and Exalted is He, as the site for his Ancient House, for our Messenger's birthplace, blessings and salutations be upon him, for his final resting place and mosque.

Despite this enormous presence, Muslim souls have experienced a rising power by the grace of God, Glorious and Exalted is He. This power stems from faith in God, Glorious and Exalted is he, while He remains greater as the supremely powerful savior. The youth of Islam have succeeded in bombing an American center in Riyadh where American troops witnessed their tremendous vulnerability. Newspapers and other media broadcast photographs of them crying in fear and dread of the soldiers of Islam, may God favor them. So too, after the bombing of their center in Khobar, they cried and asked to be relocated back to their country. Every time a television reporter or journalist asked them about their hopes, they would say "My hope is to return to America."

At the end of March, a few weeks before this speech, bin Laden moved from Jalalabad in eastern Afghanistan to Kandahar in the west. The new location would be providential for al-Qaʿida. It was in here, between 1997 and 2001, that bin Laden's influence in planning, orchestrating, and carrying out terrorist strikes against the United States and the West would reach proportions unmatched either before or after this period. In a memoir, ʿUmar bin Laden would later write: "My father finally had his own military base."[2]

"On the likes of this day, eight years ago, the Arab Peninsula experienced a tragedy whose enormity has had no precedent," bin Laden began. Speaking to supporters and family members most likely at a compound near Kandahar's airport, bin Laden directs his venom at the outbreak of the Gulf War of 1990. "More than 760,000 Americans advanced" into Saudi Arabia on the occasion, "followed by Christians who were British, French, and other nationalities." In perhaps no other speech had bin Laden's animosity against the United States been spelled out with more clarity. Repeatedly emphasizing the unprecedented nature of the threat from non-Muslim occupiers, bin Laden speaks of Muslims' "rising power" to repel such invaders. As in previous speeches, he gives special commendation to those who orchestrated attacks on Saudi National Guard headquarters in Riyadh and in Khobar in 1995–6 that killed American servicemen. Even as the danger to an "Arab Peninsula" bears no historical parallel, bin Laden notes one exception. Before the Prophet Muhammad's day, Arabians of a wilder compact drew ranks against another Christian foe. "At that time," he recounts, "the Christian Abraha from the Horn of Africa tried to replace the Ancient House by destroying it and driving people instead to a house and church that he had constructed."

In his interview with CNN several weeks earlier, discussed in the previous chapter, bin Laden had first made mention of God's "Ancient House" (*al-bait al-atiq*). The Arabian flavor of its pious inhabitants was unmistakable.

[*Peter Arnett*]: Can you tell us now about your expulsion from Saudi Arabia and your time you spent in Sudan and your arrival here in Afghanistan?

[*Bin Laden*]: I was, by the grace of God, praise and glory be to Him, in the great spot that is dear to God, praise and glory be to Him: the Hijaz region and Venerable Mecca in particular, where lies God's Ancient House. However, the Saudi regime imposed on the people a life that does not appeal to the free believer. They wanted the people to eat and drink and celebrate the praise of God, but if the people wanted to encourage what is right and forbid what is wrong, they can't. Rather, the regime dismisses them from their jobs and in the event they continued to do so, they are detained in prisons. I have rejected to live this submissive life, by God's favor, praise and gratitude be to Him, that is not befitting of man let alone a believer…

Omitting any mention of Jeddah or Madina, where he had lived through the late 1980s, bin Laden traces his pre-exile days in Saudi Arabia to Mecca, the most important of Islam's holy sites. He speaks in particular of the city's "Ancient House," a Qur'anic phrase for the shrine of black granite that is believed to contain the foundations of a dwelling originally built by the Prophet Abraham (or Ibrahim in Arabic). Prior to CNN reporter Peter Arnett's interview, bin Laden had never made much of his connection with Mecca. Although his family had lived in the city during the five years preceding their move to Khartoum and the importance of the metropole was implicit in his designation of Saudi territory as "The Land of the Two Holy Mosques," bin Laden spoke far more frequently of the cosmogony of early Madina, the founding city for Islam's first community of believers. If anything, Mecca was the home to the idolotrous ruling Quraish clan that routinely assaulted Muslims and tempted them with worldly remunerations. Bin Laden's new origin story, floated during his interview, seems to have provided a better match for the expectations of CNN's global viewers.[3] Non-Muslim Westerners who knew little about Islam or the significance of Madina were likely to know at least something of Mecca's centrality for Muslims. Accordingly, Mecca and its "Ancient House" are re-aligned as the *axis mundi* of his political activism, a sacred territory where he first grasped the extent of the Saudi regime's corruption and refusal to tolerate dissent. On that occasion, Arnett appears to have felt that enough was said. The correspondent switched back to bin Laden's views on a worldwide "Islamic movement" and the phenomenon of his ascendance to militant leadership, topics that his host appeared eager to speak about. Several weeks later, when bin Laden ascended the podium before a very different crowd outside of Kandahar, the significance of the "Ancient House" and its global legacy for Muslims would be expanded. The virtue of this House would stem less from its pan-Islamic merits, however notable they might be to outsiders, than from its power to qualify them in radical ways.

Directing listeners to the supposedly shared heritage available to them through connection to the Ancient House, bin Laden lauds its original construction by Ibrahim and Isma'il, two of the Arab peoples' most important progenitors. He ventures further by reminding audiences of the house's significance in Muslim prayers: "God accepts no Muslim, pure or honest, nor any of his deeds, supererogatory or obliged, unless he directs his prayer toward the Ancient House at least five times every day." As bin Laden develops his case for attacking the United States, however, the implications of Islam's essentialized Meccan origins grow messy. A stage for in-house dissent is set when bin Laden likens the American presence in Saudi Arabia to an invasion by sixth-century Monophysites led by Abraha Al-Ashram, an Ethiopia-born viceroy for the powerful kingdom of Aksum in East Africa. The Qur'an depicts Abraha's defeat just two years before the Prophet Muhammad's birth as a lesson for the wealthy Quraish clan on how not to spurn Arabia's emerging monotheist faith. Traditional custodians of the Ka'ba, the Quraish had long supervised worship at "the Ancient House" in what had been an animist and polytheist Arabia. As Abraha and his "Companions of the Elephant" advanced, some of them astride the lumbering subjects of their namesake, the Qur'an describes how they were rendered "like an empty field of stalks and straw" through divine intervention: an enormous flock of birds armed with pebbles of "baked clay" came to the defense of retreating Meccans and smashed their enemy to bits. According to bin Laden, Americans face a similar Meccan conglomerate. While drawing upon the Qur'anic narrative, bin Laden also adds his own twists. Instead of depicting Abraha and his followers as polytheists, he calls them "Christians." He chastises them, further, as "People of the Book," a phrase used consistently in the Qur'an to portray Jews and Christians as Abrahamic peoples worthy of admiration and respect. The Quraish, meanwhile, are no longer people to be admonished for pagan inclinations and pre-Islamic "ignorance" (*jahili-yya*). Instead, they are courageous tribesmen, heroes who although outright "polytheists" also "glorified the Ancient House." The stalwarts who defend the Arabian Peninsula from darkness could certainly benefit from religious sentiments introduced or perfected through Muhammad's revelations. Some of them had already expressed homage to the "Religion of Abraham." Their collective moral fiber, however, comes from Arab family descent.

Bin Laden's praise for the "Religion of Abraham" (*Millat Ibrahim*) evokes common themes in Saudi neo-Wahhabism. Juhaiman Al-ʿUtaibi, leader of the insurgents who stormed Mecca's Sacred Mosque in 1979 and a well known proponent of the concept, described its tenets as unfolding in three stages: disavowal of idolatry (*shirk*), emigration (*hijra*), and struggle (*jihad*), preferably with weapons.[4] In the mid 1990s, Jordanian militant Abu Muhammad Al-Maqdisi, founder of the popular pro-al-Qaʿida website *Minbar Al-Tawhid wa-l-Jihad*, would publish a volume entitled *Millat Ibrahim* that would push Al-ʿUtaibi's call to arms even further by arguing that the Saudi regime itself could legitimately be fought since they had committed sins disqualifying them as Muslims altogether. In Al-Maqdisi's formulation, members of the Religion of Abraham were bound by a commitment to "worship" (*iʿbada*) so broadly construed as to move fundamental questions of "loyalty and disavowal" (*al-walaʾ wa-l-baraʾ*) wholly beyond the religious sphere alone.[5] Bin Laden's discourse is much of a piece with these ideas. Bin Laden enters new territory, however, when weaving in the story of Abraha's sixth-century invasion and defeat by a rag-tag assembly of godly Arab idolators. By this account, the enemies of Abraham's pious community are not the forebears of Saudi citizens gone awry. The primordial threat to the region's spiritual, legal, and political integrity, as voiced for the first time in his CNN interview a month earlier, is the far enemy.

The concept of a "base" (*qaʿida*) provides bin Laden with valuable leverage when justifying his switch from assailing the Saudi administration to mobilizing armed opposition against Americans. A map of the Arabian Peninsula and neighboring territories helps bin Laden give the concept at least a dozen territorial coordinates. In none of these cases does he use the term to signify a global Islamic organization dedicated to militancy under his leadership, as it was construed by American federal prosecutors at the time and alleged to be a shibboleth among operatives working at his behest. The bases all converge, instead, as the institution for America's own transnational network of military operations bent on controlling the Middle East and oppressing Muslims specifically. "In the region today," he states, "more than 120,000 American troops are stationed Kuwait, the Land of the Two Holy Sanctuaries, Bahrain, Qatar, the Emirates, Oman, and Egypt." Continuing on to the Arabian Peninsula, he notes how "they use the Aden airport as a base whose purpose is said to be naval support. If we look further, we see how their presence has extended across the Land of the Two Holy Sanctuaries from the north to the south, the east to the west." Three years later, in January 2000, bin Laden would once again recall Abraha's invasion for a large crowd of supporters at the Tarnak Farm camp outside of Kandahar.[6] By that time, stories of his al-Qaʿida organization much in the news, he found no need to complicate public perceptions of the idea. Accordingly, he dropped the term and its territorial specifics from his speech altogether. On this occasion bin Laden appears to have felt that a concrete lesson on America's imperial geography was warranted. Audiences needed reminding that, however cosmopolitan he might be, the context and ultimate goal of his wrath was to purge his homeland of foreign infidels.

Bin Laden's big tent approach to the Muslim world's problems would present him with new obstacles. Righteous reclamation under an anti-American banner jeopardized his personal security like never before. Multiple assassination attempts by the Saudis and possibly other Muslim state powers, detailed in previous chapters, were complemented by the Central Intelligence Agency's discussions about a possible raid on his airport compound around the time of his speech.[7] So too, however, did blanket condemnation of a monolithic enemy leave bin Laden with dissension in his own ranks. As one Saudi Afghan would recall, his growing status as world pariah led to the recruitment of "everyone, seasonal dropouts, Wahhabis, yesterday's drunk, salafis, last year's adulterer, Tahrir [Palestinian Islamists], even Takfiris [who have been anathematized from Islam], you name it."[8] By late 1998, after being fingered as a prime suspect for involvement in the U.S. Embassy attacks in Kenya and Tanzania, an increasingly young and disparate crew of renegades would rally to his cause in Afghanistan, many of whom lacked the religious credentials or training of bin Laden's senior colleagues.[9] At the time, however, the costs to bin Laden of a more consistent message against Americans and a global anti-Muslim conspiracy under their leadership were balanced by several key factors.

First, much in keeping with bin Laden's role as a well-connected mediator who might bring competing Islamist factions into dialogue, a staunch counter-West platform supplied shared coinage for recruits whose deeper political commitments were not always aligned. On tape no. 1290 in bin Laden's former collection, an unidentified training camp teacher reminds listeners of how the bombing of the U.S.S. Cole in Yemen on 12 October 2000 provided militants with a clear blueprint for attacking the "new world order" spoken of in bin Laden's August 1996 Tora Bora speech. Though mechanisms of the West's economic and political power over Muslims were diffuse and had begun, in fact, from the East when the Soviet Red Army invaded Afghanistan over two decades earlier, Muslims could re-energize their cause by focusing on social and economic ills that could be traced to American influence, especially if backed by its military. Although most Arabs who reached Afghanistan's training camps in the mid- to late 1990s did not arrive thinking of the United States as a primary destination for operatives, their sights instead on Central Asia's fledgling Muslim republics or the Middle East and North Africa, bin Laden's reputation for an increasingly anti-American position had organizational advantages where political and doctrinal goals remained diffuse.[10]

On a strategic level, bin Laden's vision of consolidating Arab support for Muslim insurgents fighting American forces stood much to gain if given regional inflections that could complement one another without necessarily overlapping. Modern peninsular Arabs, for example, had never fought pitched battles against American occupiers in their own homelands. Given the strength of commercial, political, and strategic commitments shared by the United States and its allies in Saudi Arabia and the Gulf, moreover, any narrative dramatizing actual historical confrontation with American forces would prove fleeting at best, at least if situated on Arabian soil. Just across the Red Sea in East Africa, however, things were conceivably different, as bin Laden's narrative of Abraha's invasion suggested. While in the Sudan during the 1990s, bin Laden had regularly lent support to the Egyptian Islamic Jihad's expanding theater of operations, among them Somalia in the wake of American military and humanitarian intervention in late 1992. One of the leaders of this Somalian mission had been Egyptian flight lieutenant Abu Hafs Al-Masri, a veteran Arab-Afghan who had not only been appointed to leadership in the Khost-based Al-Faruq camp in the late 1980s, but had also been selected by bin Laden to run militant operations upon his return to Afghanistan in 1996.[11] By most accounts, Abu Hafs failed in securing a foothold for Arab militants in the country. In 1992, he composed a sour letter that reported Somali clan chiefs' scant regard for dreams of a global Islamic brotherhood, especially when spun by Arab exiles.[12] Four years later, bin Laden's bodyguard Nasir Al-Bahri would report that little had changed.[13] Revisionary accounts of al-Qaʻidaʼs impact in the country would certainly ensue. In interviews with bin Laden conducted by CNN in 1997 and the National Broadcasting Company in 1998, reporters would invite bin Laden to expand on statements he had made to Arab newspaper journalists boasting of his menʼs courage in fighting American soldiers in the infamous battle of Mogadishu in 1993. Bin Laden would wax expansively:

> Our boys were shocked by the low morale of the American soldier and they realized that the American soldier was just a paper tiger…After a few blows, it forgot all about those titles and rushed out of Somalia in shame and disgrace, dragging the bodies of its soldiers. America stopped calling itself world leader and master of the New World Order.

Helicopter pilot Mark Bowden, author of the acclaimed memoir *Black Hawk Down*, would later help call bin Ladenʼs bluff.[14] While bin Laden may have been involved in the financing and training of militants under the flag of Somalia warlord General Mohammad Farah Aidid, no al-Qaʻida personnel were involved in combat leading to the withdrawal of American and United Nations forces in the following year. Facing glaring disparities between militantsʼ own internal reports of failure in their Somalian efforts and stories of their success in both Arab and Western news media, bin Laden would have faced audiences in Kandahar very eager to hear about the ways more generous accounts of his influence over operations in East Africa could translate into historical experiences most considered factual or at least feasible with a bit of divine help. If the termination of U.S. military involvement in Somalia might be read as a victory for Muslims, a distinctly Arab and Saudi history behind the coup would be welcome. Devastating attacks by mostly Arab militants on the American embassies in Kenya and Tanzania a year later would make the credibility of bin Ladenʼs manufactured account convincing to many like never before.

Finally, with regards to bin Ladenʼs financial status, some evidence suggests that well endowed Saudi state officials may have been encouraged by a change of tone in his 1997 Kandahar speech. With America firmly in the cross hairs, bin Laden had turned, after all, from calling for their own violent deposition to depicting them as pawns in a more sinister Judeo-Christian conspiracy. According to Taliban intelligence chief Muhammad Khaksar, Saudi Intelligence Chief Turki Al-Faisal sealed a deal with bin Laden in 1998: as long as he refrained from attacking Saudi targets, the Kingdom would provide funds and material assistance to the Taliban, cease supporting bin Laden's extradition from Afghanistan, and stop exerting pressure to close the Arab-Afghan training camps.[15] Similar pledges from Saudi state officials may indeed have occurred several years earlier, as noted by several Western intelligence and government officials.[16] Saudis would naturally reject these allegations. Continued attacks in the Kingdom by Arab-Afghan militants from 1996–2001, though under-reported in the West, suggest that Saudi riyals were small guarantee of any favorable influence from bin Laden, however generously supported.[17] Indeed, according to some of bin Laden's close associates, Saudi authorities responded in kind, targeting bin Laden in yet more assassination attempts as late as 2000.[18] Whatever the substance to stories of bin Laden's reassembled donor base, the sheer possibility of such a network, especially when directed to fighting a more powerful American adversary, provided bin Laden with a key ally essential to his long-term survival in Afghanistan: Taliban leader Mulla 'Umar. At the time, 'Umar's credentials as a viable political leader for a broader swath of Afghanistan's southern populace needed considerable rebuilding. Since his rise to leadership in Kandahar in 1994, a civil war had erupted in the newly minted Islamic State of Afghanistan between U.S.-backed Northern Alliance troops and Taliban-backed southern fighters led by Gulbuddin Hekmetyar. Much to his chagrin, 'Umar was on record as having supported American commercial interests in the region at the time. In the mid 1990s, the Union Oil Company of California (UNOCAL) had submitted a bid to build a natural-gas pipeline extending from Central Asia to Western-bound ships on the Indian Ocean. Since the pipeline would inevitably have to pass through southern Afghanistan, 'Umar had been included in discussions about compensation and revenues for Afghanis. 'Umar's American allegiances, much touted by UNOCAL executives and U.S. officials concerned about Iran and China's expanding influence in the region, proved a serious liability. Conveniently for bin Laden, 'Umar was in need of someone to help him rework his image as America's man in Afghanistan.[19] Bin Laden's continued access to the pockets of Arab multi-millionaires, even if hearsay, did much to assuage other Taliban chiefs, many of whom had heard of bin Laden's financial woes and thought his presence in the country was putting an unnecessary strain on foreign relations efforts.

Bin Laden's move to Kandahar in April 1997 suggests how closely the Taliban leadership felt he needed monitoring. Most Taliban leaders had considered the Saudi exile's presence in the country tolerable as long as he directed his anti-American fulmination to local Arabic-speaking audiences.[20] Global saber rattling was another matter altogether, however. Mulla 'Umar appears to have flown into a rage when hearing of bin Laden's interview with CNN in the previous month.[21] By relocating him in Kandahar, the seat of command as "Leader of the Faithful" among Taliban supporters, 'Umar stood a better chance of being able to manage bin Laden's growing romance with global news networks. His efforts appear to have been welcomed by operatives in close touch with bin Laden. Several months later, Fazul 'Abdulla Muhammad, a militant in Nairobi, Kenya who had helped plan an attack on a United Nations office in Mogadishu, wrote a letter to bin Laden expressing deep concern. According to Muhammad, his "declaration of war" and March CNN interview had exposed his associates to unprecedented surveillance by local state security forces:

> The fact of these matters and others leave us no choice but to ask ourselves are we ready for that big clandestine battle? Did we take the necessary measures to avoid having one of us fall in the trap?...As you know, the decision to declare war on America was taken and we only know about it from t[h]e news media and we should have known about that decision (and the decision only) and not the plans so that we could take the necessary precautions...[22]

Muhammad appears to have pressed on and would later be indicted for his involvement in the U.S. Embassy bombing in the city in the following year. Some months later another letter of complaint and advice would be dispatched to "Abu 'Abdalla" by top Syrian operatives Abu Mus'ab Al-Suri and Abu Khalid Al-Suri who were working alongside him in Afghanistan:

> The strangest thing I have heard so far is Abu 'Abdalla's saying that he wouldn't listen to the Leader of the Faithful when he asked him to stop giving interviews...I think our brother has caught the disease of screens, flashes, fans, and applause...Abu 'Abdalla should go to the Leader of the Faithful with some of his brothers and tell them that...the Leader of the Faithful was right when he asked you to refrain from interviews, announcements, and media encounters, and that you will help the Taliban as much as you can in their battle, until they achieve control over Afghanistan...You should apologize for any inconvenience or pressure you have caused...and

commit to the wishes and orders of the Leader of the Faithful on matters that concern his circumstances here.[23]

Echoing the sentiments of Muhammad, the authors expressed serious reservations about bin Laden's obsession with global television audiences. His lust for screen time not only jeopardized local battles for meaningful political change but also threatened Arab-Afghans' hard-won relations with their Taliban hosts.

In the next few chapters, I consider how bin Laden's increasingly globalized media persona and the idea of al-Qaʿida under his leadership would be received and processed by followers and supporters. In the years ahead, thousands of new foreign recruits would flock to Southern Afghanistan for militant training and education on struggles both large and small. Bin Laden would not be the only director for these trainees. Quite apart from other top Arab leaders whose credibility among recruits rivaled that of bin Laden, some thirteen other jihadist organizations and camps operated in Taliban-held territory by 1999.[24] While many of these temporary migrants were Arab, mostly from Saudi Arabia and Yemen, many more were from other parts of the world, especially Uzbekistan. Confronting widespread speculation about the true direction of his leadership, bin Laden learned the art of dancing between two fires. Renowned in the global media for his imprecations against the United States, he ensured that video footage of his interviews with CNN, Al-Jazeera, and other news networks would run continuously on television monitors in Arab-Afghan guesthouses in Kandahar as well as in training camps nearby.[25] Although recruits complained of never being able to meet or see bin Laden in person, the videos offered promise that they might yet encounter the holy warrior any day. Meanwhile, bin Laden worked diligently to address questions about how his far-enemy focus would contribute to more urgent priorities including military operations in local settings. In Afghanistan itself he appears to have rallied some two thousand fighters to the aid of Taliban forces struggling against Northern Alliance troops for control of the country.[26] One day after the U.S. Embassy bombings in East Africa, news footage streaming across the world, he would reserve several hundred of these men for deployment by the Taliban as they slipped through the cotton fields of Mazar-e-Sharif and slaughtered some 5–6,000 Hazara Shiʿa compatriots. Then, too, al-Qaʿida chief Ayman Al-Zawahiri would be suspect number one in the execution of famed Northern Alliance commander

Ahmad Shah Massoud, a strike carried out with more tactical precision just four days after 9/11. As for struggles beyond Afghanistan, bin Laden laid the groundwork for a longer campaign of terror and violence in the Arabian Peninsula. According to FBI agent Ali Soufan, he began taking a hand in planning terrorist attacks on American interests in the region starting in early 1998.[27] Yemen featured centrally in his operational plans. Nasir Al-Wuhayshi, future leader of al-Qa'ida's Yemen branch representing the organization's most vigorous presence in the Arabian Peninsula, was appointed head manager of a key training camp at the Kandahar airport and kept in close contact with his patron.[28] After failing to get into Tajikistan to fight Russians, 'Abd al-Rahim Al-Nashiri also began working with bin Laden soon after his arrival in Kandahar.[29] He would later be sought and captured by U.S. authorities for his alleged involvement as mastermind of the U.S.S. Cole bombing in Yemen in 2000.

To bin Laden's supporters, a "Religion of Abraham" it may all have seemed. In reality, Kandahar's iconoclasts were united less by a shared set of religious standards than by their experience workshopping a catch-bag of political ideals with the vision of an enemy at their gates. Some families who shared living quarters with the bin Laden family at the Arab-Afghan training camp were said to share reflections on how the site had originally been built by Americans under the auspices of a Helmand Valley agricultural project in the 1950s.[30] On colder nights, bin Laden made allowances to his usual ascetic discipline by wearing an American-made military field jacket to keep warm.[31]

11

AN INTIMATE CONVERSATION (*JALASA*)

(Early May 1998. Arab-Afghan militants Salim Hamdan, Nasir Al-Bahri, and Khaled Al-Masah with American Broadcasting Company Nightline News personnel John Miller, Rick Bennett, and Tarik Hamdi. Recorded in a pickup truck en route to the ABC team's interview with bin Laden. Near the Al-Faruq training camp in Khost, Afghanistan. Cassette no. 1105.)

———

Transcript 1: Getting to Know You (Side A, Minutes 38:00–38:25)

Hamdan: Where are you from?

Hamdi: I'm originally from Iraq.

Hamdan: Where in Iraq?

Hamdi: From Baghdad…the Al-A'zamiyya neighborhood.

Hamdan: Welcome.

Hamdi: God give you life. Have you been to Iraq before?

Hamdan: By God, I'd love to see it, but conditions aren't good.

Hamdi: Yeah, right…Oh Iraq! [*Unclear.*]

Hamdan: When did you leave Iraq?

Hamdi: I left…Let's see…It's been about twenty years.

Hamdan: Where did you go?

Hamdi: I went to the Emirates for five years. I was sixteen years old, really…I went with my father and worked at the University of the Emirates. I studied at the university. Then, after graduation in 1983, I went to America.

Transcript 2: An Interest in Evidence (Minutes 43:50–end of Side A, then 0–1:00 Side B)

Hamdi: There's tremendous interest in political, media, intelligence, and

283

military circles these days. All of them keep up with the issue of our brother.

Hamdan: What interests them most?

Hamdi: They're interested in getting more information about him, his group, and who he knows. It appears…well, now they're busy with court proceedings…and it appears that they are trying to [*unclear*] bin Laden with the events in Riyadh.

Hamdan: Yeah?

Hamdi: They issued an arrest warrant, I mean…

Hamdan: Yeah.

Hamdi: The strategists are taking a path of confrontation with him and his group. As to the American people, they don't do anything.

Hamdan: Yeah.

Hamdi: I mean only the specialized circles are attending to this stuff.

Hamdan: So, they want evidence incriminating Abu 'Abdalla?

Hamdi: Exactly. Evidence to prove…I mean…his involvement in that operation. It seems that they're on their way to getting proof. There is talk now that someone is confessing…Chatter, I mean…Rumors, no more…

Hamdan: Right.

[*End of tape; recording resumes on Side B*]

Hamdi: [*Inaudible.*] So, if they obtain a confession, there will be further proceedings.

Hamdan: So, they are now coming to get evidence?

Hamdi: Sorry?

Hamdan: Now they are coming to…

Hamdi: Who?

Hamdan: The group who are with you. Have they come to get…

Hamdi: No, No, sir.

Hamdan: [*Laughs briefly.*]

Hamdi: This is not related…These guys are reporters. We're talking secular satellite news agencies. These, of course…their role is…like when CNN came…Their role is to show an image of the person himself stating what he believes in.

Hamdan: Yeah.

Hamdi: So that the American public gets a perception of the difference between what their administration is saying about him and what he has to say about himself.

Hamdan: Yeah.

Hamdi: This is the role of the press, I mean.

Hamdan: Yeah.

Hamdi: And of course, this is beneficial for them from a practical standpoint…letting them get to know his personality in a good way.

Hamdan: Yeah.

Transcript 3: They're Taking Abu 'Abdalla Very Seriously (Side B, Minutes 2:13–3:20)

Hamdi: Regarding the issue of…I mean…our brother Abu 'Abdalla…and his activities…and what Americans are saying…As a Muslim of course, I try with my abilities and in the position I'm in, to show why it got to this extent…how it came that a man like our brother Abu 'Abdalla and his group could take such a stern position against Americans.

Hamdan: Yeah.

Hamdi: Because regarding Americans and their foreign policy over the last twenty, thirty, forty years, they took a supportive position toward the Zionist nation…its injustice and oppression in the region. They destroyed an entire country like Iraq and invaded many other countries such as Somalia and Saudi Arabia.

Hamdan: Yeah.

Hamdi: So, it appears that…one has to look at this man as someone who wants to liberate his country and people just as Americans once waged war against the British…

Hamdan: Yeah.

Hamdi: They weren't considered terrorists. They were considered harbingers of freedom for their country…I mean…and they unleashed violence and killing against the British as well as everything else.

Hamdan: Yeah.

Hamdi: This is the picture that I want to convey when there is talk or portrayals of him.

Hamdan: Yeah.

[*Brief silence*]

Hamdi: They're taking him very seriously…I mean, to an unimaginable extent.

Hamdan: Who?

Hamdi: They're taking our brother Abu 'Abdalla very seriously.

Transcript 4: His Understanding Is Superficial (Side B, Minutes 9:30–12:47)

Hamdan: What about them [sitting next to you]? What's their personal opinion? Ask them.

Hamdi: I already know. I'll tell you: the guy on my [far] right is a cameraman [*i.e. Richard Bennett*]…he doesn't understand [*inaudible*]. As for the one on his left [*i.e. John Miller*], his personal opinion is…that all of this is comparable to the context of American revolutionary soldiers. That's one aspect. On the other hand, of course…as an American, also…he doesn't want this thing to escalate…I mean…the confrontation…

Hamdan: How come he doesn't understand given that he knows what America did in Cuba? It killed hundreds of children!…For what sin did

285

it kill them? What did they do to deserve to be killed...these children? What was their sin? What was the sin of [*inaudible*]...and they kill people. So, what would he say, the one on your left?

Hamdi: With respect to him in particular, he says... his understanding of international affairs is still superficial. He's the one who does the interviewing. The one who does the interviewing is called the [*inaudible.*] Still, he's a man who has a good sense about international issues and has had a lot of experience. He was in the Iraq war...and he has a very balanced perspective...so much so that some viewers in America have accused him of treason...

Hamdan: Yes.

Hamdi: As for this other guy, he's just taken on a new assignment...a foreign affairs position. His work had mostly focused on criminal activity in America...So, this is why his awareness is very superficial. I tried, I mean...to explain many of the issues to him, but they still rub him the wrong way.

Hamdan: You weren't able to clarify things for him?

Hamdi: I explained everything to him! Everything! The issue of Iraq, the embargo, Israel, the Zionist regime...

Hamdan: And what does he say? What does he say?

Hamdi: Okay, [he says] that's one viewpoint...but there is another side: Arab governments' own absolutist mentality.

Hamdan: Yeah.

Hamdi: He observes that the issue is not just America and imperialism...

Hamdan: Yes.

Hamdi: But that the problem has domestic facets...In fact, there's a truth to what he says, I mean...There are tyrannical regimes that are supported by the West, but these tyrannical regimes are...I mean, the West benefits from them, but they also exist due to an internal condition.

Hamdan: Yeah.

[*Long silence.*]

Many are the words and deeds of terrorists captured for the record. One sound never survives translation, however. Preserved on several of the audiotapes in bin Laden's former collection, this sound is listening itself. Most of what can be heard on tape no. 1105 is knocks and clanking from a stick-shift vehicle on a country road. Like snagged wool on an old fence post, this material is tenacious. Ten minutes can pass before a human voice intervenes. When I first heard the tape I wondered: why did someone make this recording? What story did it tell? The cassette cartridge itself is stripped of its original labels. Hints of a recording once filled with poetry and song can be detected on occasional moments when the newer sounds of the truck and its passengers do not quite line up. Scrawled across the plastic cartridge in letters of blank ink is the Arabic word *jalasa*, something equivalent to "an intimate conversation." Scattered words and occasional bouts of conversation suggest the presence of a handful of passengers. Some speak in fluent English. An Iraqi Arabic speaker is especially garrulous. As travelers reflect on their journeys and exchange views, a man in the front-seat speaks of "bin Laden" and "his group" (*jama'atuh*). The topic proves fertile. Mention is made of an effort underway by American prosecutors to indict "Abu 'Abdalla" for the bombing of Saudi National Guard headquarters in Riyadh, Saudi Arabia in 1995. The conversation turns to evaluating the man's "stern position" toward America and assessing broader perceptions of his influence.

Intrigued by the recording, I made a copy of the tape and listened to it on repeated occasions with Arab-Afghans who had known bin Laden well. One of them, bin Laden's son 'Umar, told me that none of the voices sounded familiar. Most likely they were among the thousands of often polyglot Arab-Afghan volunteers who passed through the region fighting one cause or another as they speculated about the nature of bin Laden's leadership. When I shared the recording with Abu Jandal, better known as Nasir Al-Bahri and bin Laden's bodyguard from 1997–2001, I got a different response.[1] The quieter of the two Arabic voices was that of Salim Hamdan. A Yemeni national, Hamdan had served as one of bin Laden's personal drivers in Afghanistan during the late 1990s and would later be captured and imprisoned at Guantánamo from 2002–8. The other voices in the truck were members of the ABC Nightline television network en route to interview bin Laden at the Al-Faruq training camp in May of 1998. The precision of Al-Bahri's voice recognition surprised me. After listening to tapes in the collection with dozens of native Arabic speakers across the world, I had become wary of attempts to pin specific voices to people whose names or identities could not be confirmed in other ways. Speculation was a handmaid to who's-who accounts among interviewees. Two years later, Al-Bahri would provide further details of ABC's trip to bin Laden's camp. In his memoir, he would disclose that he had been in the very same truck himself at the time:

> The next day Osama gave an interview to an American journalist with the ABC News network accompanied by an Iraqi translator and a Canadian cameraman. The three men were brought together at the Khost camp. Osama sent me to fetch them with Salim Hamdan and Khaled Al-Masah.

We began our screenplay by giving them a rough frisk down. After confiscating their camera, we put them in a truck and intentionally took them on a very long detour to convey the impression that our camp was hard to access.[2]

According to former ABC reporter John Miller, Al-Bahri would have been positioned in the front passenger seat with the others while he sat in the back flanked by Canadian cameraman Richard Bennett and Hamdi.[3] Hamdi would thus have been leaning forward over the front seat as he spoke with Hamdan, an arrangement confirmed by him on the tape: "the guy on my [far] right is a cameraman" and the "American" who is to conduct the interview is sitting "on his left." The microphone and cassette recorder seem to have been concealed somewhere near the driver's seat, a tactic known to have been used by al-Qaʿida operatives on other occasions when trust among fellow passengers had yet to be established.[4] The entire arrangement bears witness to careful orchestration. Hours before bin Laden was videotaped for his biggest exposure yet to American television audiences, a secret audio recording was being made to gain a better measure of the ABC news team's objectives. Even before bin Laden spoke, he and his colleagues were listening. In order to tailor their message to Western audiences, they sought a transcript of what they really wanted to hear.

What is it that Salim Hamdan and fellow conspirators hoped to learn from this clandestine tape? As early as the 1890s, anthropologist Franz Boas made an important discovery: no two listeners ever hear exactly the same thing.[5] Perceptions differ according to what people have heard before. Despite challenges due to the cultural and psychological variability of received sound, however, we can take something else from the recorded conversation: a measure of how well our own sense of history lines up with the past. In discussing bin Laden's leadership and al-Qaʿida's larger goals, Hamdan and Hamdi also produced a transcript offering access to historical events at the time that may have been lost to the drift of what seems so obvious to us today. These events had everything to do with bin Laden's perceived significance, whether for core supporters or for audiences who knew little more about him than what flashed across their screens during the six-o'clock evening news. Their particular depiction by Hamdi also suggests much about the role that American news journalists, and with them a vast range of Western law-enforcement, intelligence, and counterterrorist officials, could play in shaping history.

As introductions unfold at the tape's outset, Hamdi's background as an Iraqi national provides Hamdan with a natural topic for discussing the news team's goals and America's objectives in the region broadly. While Hamdi reports a positive experience in the United States during his years there pursuing higher education and a career in journalism, he expresses more ambivalence about the country's role in Iraq itself. By the late spring of 1998, Iraqis had suffered nearly eight years of devastation under Saddam Hussein's rule, despite the heavy involvement of the United States to dislodge the dictator in the Gulf War of 1990. International economic sanctions, applied from the earliest days of Iraq's invasion of Kuwait, had been imposed to force Saddam to pay war reparations as well as abide by inspectors' efforts to monitor the country's alleged development of weapons of mass destruction. "Oh Iraq!" exclaims Hamdi at one point, lamenting the state of a country that had once been able to support aspiring professionals like himself. For many observers attuned to the suffering of ordinary Iraqis, the rationale for sanctions proved increasingly difficult to sustain. With reports in 1996 that some half a million children had died from starvation and a lack of access to medicine, United Nations Security Council members France and Russia changed their positions and advocated an immediate end to the embargo. While media outlets in the United States featured a range of views on the crisis, most Americans backed their administration's stance: a poll taken a few months before ABC's visit to Afghanistan showed 65 per cent of respondents favoring continued sanctions and even military action should Saddam persist in defying United Nations resolutions.[6] Observers in the Arab world could hardly understand such vehemence of support for the sanctions. In contrast with their Western counterparts, every Arab political figure during this period felt the need to declare open and unconditional sympathy with the Iraqi people. No medium was more effective in tapping the Arab public's sentiments on Iraq than the Al-Jazeera satellite news network run out of Qatar, as I discuss later in this chapter. Given such polarization in public views of America's involvement in Iraq, the story of bin Laden's rise to world notoriety was sure to have more than one version.

Other events surface concerning bin Laden's own status as an international pariah. They tell us much about how his leadership was being construed by different audiences at the time. When pressed by Hamdan to clarify the nature of his and others' "tremendous interest," Hamdi mentions a trial underway in the United States to investigate bin Laden's alleged connections to the 1995 bombing of the National Guard Headquarters in Riyadh. Around the time of bin Laden's "declaration" against Americans and Saudis just two years earlier, attorneys in the Southern District Court of New York had begun assembling an indictment against bin Laden much as they had done for militants involved with the 1993 World Trade Center bombing. Central to the prosecution's argument was the story that bin Laden had founded a terrorist organization called al-Qaʿida in 1988 and that, by virtue of family wealth and extensive financial investments, he was fast to becoming the common link behind a host of terrorist attacks threatening Americans and American interests across the Middle East, North Africa, South East Asia, and other regions. Hamdi reveals little knowledge of this narrative, much of which I examine critically in chapter five. He drops reference to the Riyadh bombings, an attack that prosecutors were trying to link to bin Laden despite American intelligence officials' conclusions to the contrary.[7] He notes that "someone is confessing," likely a reference to prosecutors' star witness Jamal Al-Fadl, a figure whose identity as "Confidential Source No. 1" had been disclosed to news reporters in preliminary court documents during the previous year. Underscoring progress in the case, Hamdi asserts that they issued "an arrest warrant" (*hukm bi-ilqa qabd*) for bin Laden's capture and that "strategists are taking a path of confrontation with him and his group." Hamdan appears jarred by the news. In probing further about whether the ABC crew is in fact an extension of the prosecutors' office, having come to gather evidence and a "confession" of bin Laden's guilt, he receives a chuckle from the newsman. Journalists, he is told, are a more sympathetic crew.

Hamdi's assertion of bin Laden's status as a wanted man in the United States packs more of a blow than it deserved. In fact, the only warrant for bin Laden's arrest at the time had come from not from Washington but rather from Interpol at the behest of one of America's longtime adversaries: Muammar Al-Qaddafi of Libya.[8] Issued a few months before the American news team's arrival in Afghanistan, the warrant reflected the dictator's fury at bin Laden for providing assistance to Libyan veterans of the Afghan jihad who had led operations to assassinate him.[9] That bid to stop bin Laden received quick response in the West. Given that Britain's MI6 was collaborating with members of the Libyan Islamic

Fighting Group to overthrow Al-Qaddafi, its London headquarters a
natural home for coordination among dissidents including bin Laden's
own Advice and Reform Committee through 1998, British and French
intelligence agencies quashed the notice. At the time of the ABC interview, America's leading criminal investigators had followed suit and
taken the opposite stance to that communicated to Hamdan. Although
the Federal Bureau of Investigation acknowledged Interpol's warrant in
the same month, its own call to arrest bin Laden would be put off until
November, the effects of East Africa's U.S. embassy bombings much in
the air.[10]

Hamdi's account of American officials' impending stand-off with bin
Laden certainly draws on a familiar arsenal of accusations, whatever
technicalities he gets wrong. Echoing the perspective of Arab and
Muslim audiences troubled by America's unswerving allegiance to Israel,
Hamdi berates the United States' for its "supportive position toward the
Zionist nation" and for having "destroyed an entire country like Iraq and
invaded many other countries such as Somalia and Saudi Arabia." Facing
such an assault, Hamdi explains, bin Laden can be considered a freedom
fighter. John Miller would suggest just this analogy shortly later, likening
bin Laden to "the Middle East version of Teddy Roosevelt," a man who
had set aside his own wealth and privilege, "put together his own men…
and went to battle." Miller would also grill his host on charges of terrorism, however, including the accommodation of 1993 World Trade
Center bomber Ramzi Yousef in one of his guesthouses, his collaboration
with Uzbek national Wali Khan Amin Shah in planning assassinations
of President Clinton and Pope John Paul II during their visit to the
Philippines in early 1995, his leadership of the bombings in Riyadh and
Al-Khobar in 1995–6 that left twenty-four Americans dead, and his
followers' victories in taking down American troops in Somalia. To all
allegations bin Laden would respond as he had done in previous interviews. He denied involvement while lavishing praise on the attackers and
welcoming suggestions that he had inspired them.

However scripted the ABC team's exchanges, the American public
would receive a portrait of bin Laden and his organization that differed
in several important respects from what they had learned of him before.
The news network's depiction, tailored to emerging legal narratives that
had begun to surface in preliminary trials underway in Manhattan, set
important precedents for his representation in Western and global media

networks over the years ahead. For the first time, bin Laden is viewed as a man whose indictment and capture by American authorities are only a matter of time. Hearing from John Miller that "there is word that the American government intends to put a price on your head—in the millions—when you are captured," bin Laden replies, "Americans heap accusations on whoever stands for his religion or his rights or his wealth…no matter how much pressure American [*sic*] puts on the regime in Riyadh to freeze our assets and to forbid people from contributing to this great cause, we shall still have God to take care of us; livelihood is sent by God; we shall not want." News stories across South Asia had also focused on the depletion of bin Laden's financial resources. By some accounts, Osama had become an object of satire, a man who replied to hard questions about his meager reserves with the quip "My heart is rich and generous."[11] ABC broke ground among Western news networks in foregrounding the possibility of bin Laden's recent impoverishment. "You come from a background of wealth and comfort to end up fighting on the front lines," Miller remarks to bin Laden at the outset of the interview, only to receive the reply: "We believe that this is the call we have to answer regardless of our financial capabilities." For ABC, however, bin Laden's steely asceticism makes him more rather than less of a threat. Miller remarks later to Ted Koppel, host of the *Nightline* program, "terrorism by its nature, conventional terrorism, is a very low-tech business… It allows him to fund many of these projects without putting out a great deal of money for any single one." Introducing the program, video footage of victims being carried from the World Trade Center Towers in 1993 suggests just how devastating his attacks could be.

ABC producers contextualize bin Laden's threat beyond the concerns of security officials alone. Three months earlier, bin Laden had advocated unambiguous support for attacking civilians in a legal opinion co-authored by four mid-rank Islamist jurists. Issued before a gathering of international reporters at the same Al-Faruq location, the delegation used the occasion to announce the formation of "The World Islamic Front for Jihad Against Jews and Crusaders" and included future al-Qa'ida chief Ayman Al-Zawahiri. Accordingly, *Nightline* begins with a review of procedures being undertaken in Saudi Arabia to protect an estimated 31,000 American personnel, military as well civilian, from terrorist attacks of the sort promised by the front. Heightened security concerns in the Kingdom came not just from terrorist attacks, however, but from an obstinate Saudi administration that refused to allow American investigators free rein in pursuing leads that could result in the arrests of suspects involved in the Al-Khobar Towers attacks a few years earlier. For the Saudis, according to military analyst Anthony Cordesman, "The image of the FBI is a forensic bull in an Arab China shop—a bull that can't speak the language and doesn't understand the culture." Saudi implacability had the potential to stoke American viewers' anger toward a long-time strategic ally in the region, especially given the United States' role in driving Saddam Hussein's forces from neighboring Kuwait during the Gulf War of 1990. The story of bin Laden's open enmity, by contrast, supplies producers with a cleaner narrative for identifying and diagnosing the nature of resistance to America's policies in the region. Preliminary hearings and grand jury indictments provided valuable material for narrating the extent of bin Laden's financial, logistical, and strategic influence in a war directed primarily against the United States. As I suggest in chapter five and outline further below, prosecutors' focus on the "al-Qaʿida" brand became essential to this narrative, though the name for this organization would not surface in American news coverage until September.

Hours before ABC's arrival at the Al-Faruq camp, the original "base" (*qaʿida*) for Arab-Afghans' global ambitions since its founding by Egyptian militants in 1988, news of American legal proceedings reaches the ears of those riding in bin Laden's truck. "They're interested in getting more information about him, his group, and who he knows," Hamdi is heard to explain. When Hamdan voices concerns that the ABC team might be an extension of the prosecutor's office, Hamdi reassures him that he too views bin Laden as a freedom fighter. Shortly later, Hamdan's doubts can be heard resurfacing: "What about them [sitting next to you]? What's their personal opinion? Ask them." At issue are profoundly differing views on the objectives, ideology, and moral constitution of "his group" (*jamaʿtuh*). Once again, Hamdi appears to align himself with his listener. Rick Bennett "doesn't understand," he insists, and John Miller's "understanding of international affairs is still superficial." When Hamdan expresses shock that the higher moral imperatives of bin Laden's group could not be conveyed, the journalist shoots back, "I explained everything to him! Everything! The issue of Iraq, the embargo, Israel, the Zionist regime." These protestations, however, appear to pall when he is pressed further to unpack Bennett's sense that bin Laden and his group have somehow missed the mark. There is "another side" Hamdi confides to his listener: "Arab governments' own absolutist mentality." His voice betrays sympathy for Bennett's viewpoint: "the problem has domestic facets…In fact, there's a truth to what he says, I mean…There are tyrannical regimes that are supported by the West, but these tyrannical regimes are…I mean, the West benefits from them, but they also exist due to an internal condition." After weak assent from Hamdi, several long minutes feature only the noise of the clattering vehicle. An important lesson offers itself to listeners. To acknowledge that "the problem has domestic facets" is to taint the anti-Western and anti-imperialist messages of bin Laden's group with the scent of expediency. American accountability for crises in Iraq, Israel, Palestine, and other regions might just prove less than absolute. The strength of bin Laden's appeal was best served by sticking to a rigid binary. His group could only lock horns with one behemoth.

It was certainly not the first time that such a Manichaean imperative arose for bin Laden and his associates. What does define this interaction, however, as I suggest earlier and explore in more detail in the following few chapters, is a shifting terrain of American-led arguments about the identity of "al-Qaʻida" that, especially by 1998 onward, would leak back to Arab militants in a range of locales and be exploited to the best of their abilities. For bin Laden and his supporters, the concept of "al-Qaʻida" proved felicitous where it could be branded as an organization defined both by the clarity of its anti-American platform and by its hierarchy of command under one amir. We might wonder that no mention of this term is made by Hamdan as he rallies to defend his patron or indeed his Iraqi passenger when mentioning legal proceedings underway in the United States. As I discuss elsewhere in this book, however, none of the audiotapes in bin Laden's former collection appear to evoke the term when describing bin Laden's group before October 2000, a full year after its first usage in this sense by Western journalists. Little significance might be given to its absence on the tapes. In alignment with American intelligence reports, the general consensus among al-Qaʻida analysts is that this name was known among core supporters from its first mention by bin Laden in 1988 and that, in the years following, it served as a secret code-word for inside operators to communicate that bin Laden was in charge without having to squabble about who was really on top. By this logic, Hamdan surely knew of the term's more restricted usage, whatever else might be said by the ABC personnel of bin Laden's significance for an American public and his chief culpability as construed by U.S. prosecutors. While no leader, he had spent countless hours driving bin Laden and his closest advisors across the country and would have been privy to intimate discussions.

If the story of al-Qa'ida's links with bin Laden is absent on any audiotape before late 2000, the narrative gained early traction through documents produced in English, no more so than by chief U.S. federal prosecutors seeking to indict bin Laden for terrorist involvement in the years following his August 1996 Tora Bora speech against the Americans and Saudis. As I show in chapter five, however, textual evidence submitted by prosecutors to substantiate al-Qa'ida's history under bin Laden's sole command fails to hold up under scrutiny. The "al-Qa'ida" charter and meeting notes presented to grand jury members are documents corresponding to the foundation of a very different "base" than bin Laden's terrorist organization, namely the Egyptian-led Al-Faruq training camp that tried to marginalize the operational influence of Arabs from the Gulf States, including Saudi Arabia, as well as Yemen. By leaving the Arabic word for "base" (*al-qa'ida*) untranslated and capitalized, translators provided jury members with a clean history for prosecutors' arguments. The Southern District of New York appears not to have been the only dupe to such sleight of hand. In future years, intelligence and security analysts would cite another Arabic-language document as referring "explicitly, repeatedly, and unambiguously to the activities of 'al-Qa'ida' *as an organization* in 1993 and 1994 in Peshawar, Khartoum and Somalia."[12] Posted on-line by Westpoint's Combatting Terrorism Center in 2007, the memo by one "Sword of Islam" reports the experiences of Arab-Afghan militants who traveled to Kenya and Ethiopia to assist members of the Somalia-based Islamic Union to set up a pan-regional Islamic state. Once again, ten mentions of the Arabic word spill across the document as notes are provided on the challenges of coordinating operations in the region. According to translators, the objective and outcome of such work is clear:

> It appeared that the leaders of the Islamic Union wanted to have a discussion with Abu Fatima about building upon their strengths with the help of al-Qa'ida …One of the matters we agreed upon with 'Abd al-Salam was that I would have the right to represent al-Qa'ida in political discussions with the Islamic Union, to coordinate military affairs, and to send the results to the brothers in al-Qa'ida.[13]

Omitted from the English prose are at least six other references to the "base" at issue, all of which clarify that the "al-Qa'ida" being discussed here is a "rear base" (*qa'ida khalfiyya*) in the Ogaden region of Ethiopia located about sixty miles north of a key meeting location for Islamic Union leaders. The logic of partial translation is consistent. When Islamic Group bases are discussed, the Arabic word *al-qa'ida* (*qawa'id* in the plural) disappears or is rendered into an altogether different form such as "their constituents" (*qawa'idhum al-shababiyya*). When the word lends itself to the story of Arab-Afghans on behalf of bin Laden's worldwide terrorist organization, the term is transliterated: "young men at the base" (*shabab al-qa'ida*) thus becomes "al-Qa'ida members." On several occasions the word "al-Qa'ida" is simply added extraneously to make the text more coherent for English-speaking lay readers.

Such observations on a possible *tromp l'oeil* in Western accounts of al-Qa'ida's emergence might well be dismissed by those who insist that the organization's goals and influence, manifest enough by the late 1990s and after 9/11, defined the group's coherence from the outset. People later identified as key al-Qa'ida operatives such as Egyptian commanders Abu 'Ubayda Al-Banshiri, Abu Hafs Al-Masri, and Sayf Al-'Adl, all of whom are mentioned in the Ogaden file memo, ensure the credibility of earlier records vouchsafing bin Laden's singular command and the organization's uppermost goal of launching global jihad against America. As I have suggested throughout this book, such narratives are prone to misleading inferences, historical fictions from which not even reasonably balanced legal proceedings are immune. Charter documents from the Al-Faruq base, discussed in chapter six, committed signatories to waging jihad within the Islamic world rather than to carrying the fight to America and stipulate command structures betraying as much fission as unity in the ranks. If the struggle in Ogaden in 1993–4 could be framed by visiting Arab-Afghans as a launching pad for assailing the greater American threat to Muslims worldwide, its chief leaders Abu 'Ubayda and Abu Hafs, both founding officers at Al-Faruq, had resumés that spoke volumes of their ambition to support insurgencies closer to home. Osama may well have been involved with the trip at some level, though he is nowhere mentioned in the memo. While busy at the time trying to staunch the loss of several tens of millions in the Sudan, he is reported to have retained enough leverage to have offered some material support to his associates, if not strategic and operational as well.[14] So, too, for that matter did many other wealthy Gulf patrons and organizations committed to the perceived aid of Muslims suffering under Ethiopia's ruling socialist coalition.

In reassessing narratives about al-Qa'ida's organizational coherence through the mid 1990s, I suggest we recall not so much the weakness of particular legal arguments as some of reasons why American officials and terror analysts had much at stake in their telling. It is for no small reason that English translators examining such Arabic documents as the Ogaden memo took care when managing the appearances, effects, and omissions of a single Arabic word for "base." Among top-ranking officers in the Central Intelligence Agency, such textual work would have supplied valuable justification for building a file on bin Laden given how little actual data they were able to gather about his aims, plans, and co-conspirators. According to Michael Scheuer, former head of the CIA's bin Laden unit, from 1992 until 2004 "we worked side by side with the Egyptians, the Jordanians—the very best Arab intelligence services—and they didn't recruit a single person who could report on al-Qa'ida."[15] When Western intelligence circles did finally recruit Moroccan spy Omar Al-Nasiri to report on bin Laden's activities in Afghanistan during the mid-late 1990s, he produced only disappointing news: he never found anyone at his top training camps using the term in any organizational sense.[16] American federal prosecutors working out plea-bargain arrangements with Sudanese national Jamal Al-Fadl and others had more success. For the CIA, though, the deciphering of confiscated Arab-Afghan documents had especially important intelligence value.

After 9/11 and America's response in Iraq, the work of back-dating and substantiating al-Qa'ida's strategic threat to the United States would become even more urgent. Despite Vice-President Richard Cheney's arguments to the contrary, bin Laden and his cohort had no significant leverage in the country before America's invasion in 2003. An increasingly futile search for Saddam Hussein's weapons of mass destruction deflated the administration's credibility across the world, nowhere more so than at home. Scrambling to justify a whirlwind of foreign military interventions and legislation passed to restrict civil liberties, a whole new generation of experts appeared to reassure the American public that their executive and legislative leaders got the war on terror right. Their task was herculean given the war's many tendrils. The job was all the more excruciating given bin Laden's persistence in avoiding capture alongside many of al-Qaʿidaʾs top operatives. During this heady period of post-cold war anxiety, the story of al-Qaʿidaʾs rise to power obviously lent itself well to accounts of primaeval origins, dark oaths, and unswerving ideologies of hatred. Even before the attacks in 2001, however, the image of a well-financed network of Arab warriors dedicated to the ultimate goal of ending American influence in the Islamic world found ready uptake by a range of observers in the West. Quite aside from those who saw opportunity in using the story to influence American foreign policy, a coterie of law enforcement agents, intelligence officials, and security analysts found the coherence of the al-Qaʿida narrative useful when seeking accountability for a host of anti-American attacks by Islamic militants through the early to mid-1990s, notably among those in New York in 1993 and in Saudi Arabia in 1995–6. For this counter-terrorist community, an argument in favor of conspiracy under bin Laden was worth making, however sketchy its details. Given the events of 9/11, their perseverance can only be commended in the highest terms.

America's own implication in creating a narrative of al-Qaʿidaʾs coherence and death-defying power would be nothing, however, without its uptake by Arab-Afghan veterans including bin Laden himself. As early as 1992, before moving to the Sudan, bin Laden appears to have begun searching for ways to found his own "base" (*qaʿida*) in the model of the Al-Faruq camp, though more firmly within his purview. According to Arab-Afghans living in Peshawar at the time, bin Laden asked guests in his own Hayatabad residence to sign oaths attesting to his leadership as "amir" followed by co-deputies Abu ʿUbaida Al-Banshiri and Abu Hafs.[17] It is difficult to assess how this idea of an organizational command structure led by bin Laden fared among competing claims to Arab-Afghan leadership in Peshawar at the time, much less how well they traveled with his own person. On the eve of their departure for the Sudan, bin Laden and his close associates are said to have advised supporters to scrap battle-field ambitions and instead seek higher education back at home if they could.[18] One can imagine how such a proposition struck his most adventurous admirers. Reports of a quietist turn aside, what does appear to have received a fairly good uptake were copies of the nearly twenty-page founding charter for the Al-Faruq training camp in Afghanistan. Signed in triplicate and distributed for study among recruits at the camp, the charter shows every mark of a tiered organization defined by a command structure, organizational committees, salaries, and a clear ideological focus on militancy and Muslim reform worldwide. More importantly, multiple editions of the charter were issued with what appears to be a sustained effort to produce a more abstract and deployable prototype on which future bases could be modeled.

Careful analysis of several charter editions circulating among Arab-Afghans shows just how the Al-Faruq camp prototype was tailored to promote bin Laden's cause. Translated into English by American intelligence or military personnel in April of 2002, just three months before the CIA began covert operations in Iraq in preparation for the war against Saddam, the documents were posted in 2006–7 with titles representing fixed organizational coherence: "Al-Qaʿida's Structure and Bylaws," "Interior Organization," "Al-Qaʿida Goals and Structure," and "Al-Qaʿida: Constitutional Charter."[19] Differences between the editions tell a messier story. In an initial revision of the Al-Faruq camp charter, Arabic remarks scrawled across the pages betray a deep concern about the institutional independence and resilience of "the base" beyond its particular Afghan setting. The resemblance of penmanship to bin Laden's own might elicit knowing recognition were the draft's significance premised on the work of original authors.[20] As this chapter suggests, the making of bin Laden transcends his own person. "Should the amir and/or his deputy die," one comment reads, "the office of the amir shall be entrusted to members of the council who will convene a three-day meeting to choose the next amir and his deputy."[21] Notes elsewhere attempt to bolster the amir's authority: his one-year term is adjusted to two, and a potential loophole around strict chains of command is eliminated with a single bold line drawn through item seven in the section on the camp's "internal organization": "Complaints. If the infraction comes from the immediate supervisor and cannot be feasibly brought to his deputy the plaintiff has the right to bypass the supervisor's authority and bring the matter to the deputy."[22] The support such editing would have lent to bin Laden is suggested further by modifications in the financial section designed to improve fiscal transparency as well as the elimination of clause no. eleven, so crucial to the Al-Faruq camp charter, stipulating that none of the amir's security guards could be from the Gulf States or from Yemen.[23] "The base" becomes radicalized for a new era of open confrontation with host governments. Stricken from this second edition, for example, are several paragraphs underscoring the importance of local coalition building and diplomacy. As if in illustration, a bold line is drawn through a clause that reads, "Our politics with regard to the Afghan jihad is to offer advice and assistance in battle as well as through cooperation with trustworthy jihad organizations [and] to align ourselves with Islamic institutions in fields of struggle relating to our own politics."[24] Emblazened on the title page with a new bold font, "Al-Qa'ida" should no longer subordinate itself to the goals and ideologies of established Islamic entities. The writing depicts a base-camp with far more autonomy and ambition, one dedicated less to supporting pre-existing Muslim insurgencies than to "achieving righteousness, defeating injustice, and establishing an Islamic state."[25] To date, we have no record to suggest that any of these proposed amendments were ever formalized in a third edition or distributed for consideration among bin Laden's would-be supporters. Nevertheless, on paper, al-Qa'ida had the semblance of a political project that could rival state powers with its own universal ideals.

The challenge facing bin Laden and his most ardently militant supporters in the early 1990s would have been to win broader support for the revised version of "the base" and its charter. As shown in previous chapters, bin Laden worked assiduously to propagate his views of militant insurrection. From pulpits in Saudi Arabia and Yemen as well as headquarters in Pakistan, the Sudan, and London, he used his words and wealth to mobilize support for his insurgency. Despite these efforts, his views grew more controversial among audiences in the Arab and Islamic world. It is perhaps little surprise that, at this time, murmurs began surfacing in the West of bin Laden's rising star under the al-Qa'ida label. In 1992, according to American intelligence officer Billy Waugh, the CIA station chief in Khartoum alerted his staff to rumors of "outfits called al Qaeda" working under bin Laden's protection.[26] The next year several Jordanian militants arrested for plotting to "set Jordan ablaze" reported to the *Agence France-Presse* that they had been trained "by al-Ka'ida [sic], a secret organization in Afghanistan" financed by bin Laden.[27] An Egyptian militant located the organization in the Sudan and told FBI officials that bin Laden's real target was the Saudis.[28] By early 1994, an outline of al-Qa'ida's history surfaced when the U.S. State Department issued a cable describing bin Laden's work with Ayman Al-Zawahiri and members of the Islamic Group (*Al-Jama'at Al-Islamiyya*) in Peshawar to set up "the 'Base,' a guest-house for those desiring to participate in the Afghan Jihad."[29] Such reports likely mirror conversations taking place among Arab-Afghan veterans during this period as they evaluated various editions of the Al-Faruq camp charter and speculated on the true measure of bin Laden's influence. Where they differed was in likening al-Qaʿida to a full-fledged organization given operational life by bin Laden himself. This image would be drawn most clearly in the 1996 CIA biography of bin Laden released days after the Al-Khobar bombings. By 1985, the report states, "Bin Ladin had drawn on his family's wealth, plus donations received from sympathetic merchant families in the Gulf region, to organize the Islamic Salvation Foundation, or al-Qaida [sic]."[30] No longer was the "base" a specific guest-house established in the early 1990s, as the earlier State Department cable had suggested. Al-Qaʿida was now the darker side of an official organization founded by bin Laden with his brother Khaled to provide assistance to Afghan groups and Arab volunteers favored by the Saudis. Given the charity organization's global outreach in some thirteen countries, the report describes the presence of "a network of al-Qaʿida recruitment centers and guesthouses in Egypt, Saudi Arabia, and Pakistan." Over the next two years, American federal prosecutors, intelligence analysts, and scholars alike would focus much on the organization's network capacities. Key to this composite vision was the idea of a "base" that was abstract enough to transcend the limits of specific locales, while concrete enough to coordinate terrorist attacks against Americans and the interests of their government.

In the wake of the twin bombings of U.S. embassies in Kenya and Tanzania on 8 August 1998, bin Laden's identity as a prime suspect was broadcast to audiences across the world. Within two weeks, President Clinton responded by ordering the dispatch of sixty-six cruise missiles to key militant training sites in Khost, including the Al-Faruq camp where he had held his interview with ABC earlier that spring. A similar strike that day on a Sudanese chemical factory proved later to be an imbroglio for the administration given faulty intelligence about the presence of chemical weapons. The Khost bombings, however, were deemed successful and precipitated a flurry of news stories the following month introducing global audiences to an international terrorist organization called al-Qaʿida, allegedly headed by bin Laden.[31] Once again, speculation on bin Laden's tremendous financial holdings received much attention, especially given the U.S. Treasury's announcement shortly after the strikes that bin Laden had been placed on their list of suspected terrorists. Arab-Afghan veterans paint a dire scenario of bin Laden's financial capabilities especially after the attacks, though ensuing financial restrictions imposed on American companies and donors played little part in their accounts. Given the large number of Muslim casualties in both embassy bombings, many of bin Laden's former supporters responded vehemently to him when first hearing of his association with the attacks. How could he possibly justify killing innocent Muslims even if in battle with a known enemy? According to some of bin Laden's close advisors, such controversy further harmed his financial leverage for operations, although by some estimates, his cash supply had shrunk to a mere $55,000 even before the attacks.[32]

The ABC interview in May suggests much about the ways bin Laden would find leverage in the media by riding his growing reputation as the world's most wanted man. His withdrawal to faraway Afghan caves presented viewers with a figure of extraordinary power, given assertions by top American officials and intelligence analysts about his ongoing global influence and wealth. Bin Laden's asceticism now presented a threat less to ruling regimes in Arab and Islamic worlds than to America's power in an international economic order dominated by the West. Given the increasing militarization of America's sanctions efforts in Iraq, this message traveled well. Among Arab television audiences, bin Laden's status as a virtual poster-boy for anti-Americanism found no greater uptake than on Qatar's Al-Jazeera network. Founded in 1996, shortly after a coup in Qatar brought in a regime more willing to do business with Washington, Al-Jazeera offered satellite subscribers across the Arab world a spectrum of programming and chat shows airing controversial political viewpoints. Integral to the channel's mission was a sustained attention to the emergence of a new Arab public whose identity was stylized in collective opposition as much to misguided Western policies in the region as to repressive authoritarian regimes such as those of Saudi Arabia and Bahrain, the tiny neighboring oil-rich state. When America's Operation Desert Fox in Iraq began with a seventy-hour aerial bombing campaign in November of 1998, the network found its voice like never before. As viewers themselves expressed outrage at the bombings through popular call-in shows, bin Laden too weighed in during his first interview with the network in December.

Despite their shared interest in bin Laden's anti-Americanism, however, Al-Jazeera and American television networks differed from one another in several ways. First, for the latter, public support for bin Laden's position in the Arab world had nothing to do with Iraqi sanctions or escalating Western militarization in the region. His antipathy stemmed instead from the Gulf War of 1990, when the Saudis and other Peninsula rulers allowed Americans to station troops in the region, as well as from U.S. support for Israel. Although bin Laden comments repeatedly on the suffering of Iraqis both on camera and in his February World Islamic Front declaration, Peter Arnett and John Miller would both, like their Western counterparts, steer clear of Iraq altogether. The idea that the punitive effects of U.S.-led sanctions in Iraq could be fueling support for bin Laden appears to have been unsayable. For Al-Jazeera's chief correspondent, by contrast, this possibility was outlined for viewers in an explicit opening question: "Do you think that the British-American attacks against Iraq will increase the popularity of uprising people against America, or will such attacks subdue them into desisting from any actions militarily or otherwise against the U.S. and its interests?" From its earliest inception, for most Arab audiences, bin Laden's stripe of anti-American militancy arose as a tactical response to external aggression widely perceived to be morally bankrupt. Downplayed by the network were the divisive implications of his Saudi-influenced salafism and Arabian ethnic privileging that had long proven a toxic mix for pan-Islamists of diverse backgrounds.

Al-Jazeera's spin on bin Laden's defiance would come with its own baggage. Critics in the West would later call the network "inexcusable" for encouraging sympathetic views of bin Laden's anti-American cause. Others would argue that Al-Jazeera was simply doing what leading news channels around the world were doing best: selling news to primary audiences as American military involvement in the Islamic world reached an unprecedented scale. By the mid 2000s, the network had become the most watched news source across the Arab world, especially among Jordanians (62% of whom identified the network as their top choice), Moroccans (54%), Lebanese (44%), citizens of the United Arab Emirates (46%) and Saudi Arabia (44%).[33] Loyal to viewers' desire for an image of Arab and even Islamic unity, the network adopted an altogether more qualified understanding of the notion of bin Laden's "base" as the term was popularized following the East Africa attacks. In the Arab world's first documentary on al-Qaʿida, aired in June 1999 and entitled *Osama bin Laden: The Destruction of the Base* (*tadmir al-qaʿida*), the topic of analysis was not a worldwide militant network but rather the Al-Faruq camp in Khost struck by cruise missiles the previous summer. The program made sure to voice American officials' concerns about the global reach and power of bin Laden's terrorist objectives. According to former U.S. intelligence officer Larry Johnson, "he has killed and wounded more American citizens than any other group involved in terrorist attacks in the past seven years. No individual or group has killed as many Americans or foreigners." Implicit in the report was bin Laden's involvement in the East African embassy bombings a year earlier. These views provided anchor, however, for a more redeeming view of bin Laden as an anti-establishment idealist and even a victim. Innocent of accusations linking him to the Khobar and Riyadh attacks, bin Laden's greatest threat to Americans was at that point verbal fulmination. Most illustrative was the World Islamic Front fatwa calling on Muslims to kill American civilians. Paralleling bin Laden's rationale, though, producers framed such provocations as matters of reciprocity in a war marked by the deaths and suffering of millions in Iraq, Palestine, and elsewhere in the Islamic world. If bin Laden's rage on these fronts had been growing, the spark for committing himself to real action lay in the destruction of his Khost camp in August 1998. This base, according to producers, was the first and original *qaʿida* by American authorities' own admission.

In the following chapters, I examine the ways in which Arabic-speaking audiences tried to make sense of the very different ways mainstream news represented al-Qaʿida under bin Laden. For Western audiences, beginning in late 1998, al-Qaʿida was the Arabic name for bin Laden's worldwide terrorist network. Its ideology, goals, and membership were tightly linked to bin Laden himself, a Saudi multimillionaire whose struggle against his own king had led him to more radical confrontations with the West and the United States in particular. From this perspective, al-Qaʿida was what at least one leading observer called "an armed political party."[34] Most simply called it the latest form of "global Islamic insurgency," one whose purpose was defined by its common hatred for the United States.[35] For Arabic speaking audiences, whether mainstream or among bin Laden's closest advisors, these designations were evidence enough of the West's maleficent typecasting. Even if recognizable as the tradecraft of criminologists and intelligence analysts, such framing propagated dangerous essentialisms about Islam and the

Arab world. Attuned to many currents of Muslim political discourse employed by national leaders as well as their critics, they found discussions of bin Laden's al-Qa'ida filled with conflicting accounts of the locations, circumstances, and significance of specific bases. In an effort to counter such discrepancies, bin Laden would lay public claim to leadership over a more general and abstract "base" just three months before 9/11: his followers would merge with members of the Egyptian Islamic Jihad to form "the Jihad Base" (*Qa'idat Al-Jihad*). From this point on, the West's sense of al-Qa'ida would be mirrored in bin Laden's own discourse. For most media audiences in the Arab world, such affinities would only grow more pronounced after the September attacks.

As early as September of 1998, bin Laden's efforts to match the expectations of the world's leading television networks had made a substantial difference in his position. As news of the Khost missile strikes reached global viewers, those most inclined to open their pockets to America's most wanted terrorist appear to have done so with gusto. Before the strikes, an Islamist commentator remarked wryly, "there was no al-Qa'ida." When Saudi Prince Turki visited Afghanistan a month after the bombing, he found the Taliban to have changed their attitude toward bin Laden "180 degrees." Mulla 'Umar, he reports, was "absolutely rude," insulting the Saudi royal family as American "lackeys" and refusing to discuss bin Laden's hand-over. Constraints on bin Laden's media interviews were likewise swept off the table.[36]

12

A PRAGMATIC BASE (*AL-QAʿIDA*)

(October 1998 lecture on Yemen by Mustafa Hamid, also known as Abu al-Walid Al-Masri. A training camp in Afghanistan. Excerpt from cassette no. 1113).[1]

In terms of geography, it is very important that work in the Arabian Peninsula be focused on the base (*qaʿida*) of Yemen. This accords with rules (*qawaʿid*)—the geographical truths of the place, as a chain of mountains that extends from the middle of the Peninsula down to Yemen. We must focus the work of jihad on these mountains, and create jihadi posts in this extensive mountain range so that Yemen can be established, as a base. This is the case for commanders in liberated places as well as in their posterior areas. Just as the posterior base of the jihad in the Arabian Peninsula can't be completed except in Yemen, or in the borderlands near Yemen, inside Saudi Arabia, but on the shared borders. Just as you see, now, in places that are a struggler base for leaders in Pakistan: Even though part of [the base] is in the posterior areas of Iran, part of it is also, in truth, in Pakistan, as well as in Afghanistan.

We must organize mountain bases (*qawaʿid jabaliyya*) for our brothers. They will be used for training, operational planning, storing weapons and ammunition, medical treatment, and harboring those on the run. All of this work must be conducted over there. Training must be transferred to the Arabian Peninsula. Talk of training here no longer has any meaning due to security dangers and prohibitive costs. You hear me?…

There are many issues. How do we win the support of the Yemeni society? How do we win the support of the tribes? How do we deal with the government? Or how do we win a round against the government so that it doesn't trick us like the Algerian regime did when deploying a group of strugglers against the country's own citizens and causing the whole population to turn against them. How do we avoid a calamity like that one? In truth, this is a lengthy topic. It is also a very interesting one and requires brothers to really think about it. What are the rules of engagement specific to Yemen? Strugglers there should launch offensives in accordance with their own circumstances. As we said before, in every place strugglers should have their own specific rules of engagement. These are separate from the general rules of war and are specific to every locale. What are the specific rules for Yemen?

If military operations were to be launched only in the Arabian Peninsula without focusing on Yemen, they would be insufficient since, without a doubt, the operations will ultimately have to be launched from Yemen. Without such support, such operations will be weak, a mere scrap of paper blown about by the wind. In fact, the movement to liberate the Arabian Peninsula must proceed from Yemen. The liberators and freedom fighters must be deployed from Yemen, and their base must be in Yemen with assistance from Muslims nearby as well as those far away from larger urban areas. In cities, the spirit of fighting is almost totally extinguished due to lifestyle and Western cultural influences such as television, media norms, newspapers, magazines, pressure from the state, and so on. For this reason, people living in the mountains and the countryside must be strugglers' first allies in Yemen. Good folks living in the cities should, of course, also carry out work inside urban areas so that operations can unfold both inside cities and from bases distributed in the mountains…

[*Follow-up question from a student.*] Hey Abu al-Walid.

[*Hamid*] Yes.

[*Student*] Let's say we establish a base inside Yemen's borders. How then can we win the support of the Yemeni government so that it turns a blind eye to the base as we prepare to conduct operations inside the Arabian Pensinsula? How can we stop the Yemeni government, in other words, if it attempts to shut down the base?

[*Hamid*] There's no doubt that the Yemeni government will mobilize against you! Let's not deceive ourselves: they will never agree to such a thing. President 'Ali Saleh is not a Muslim ruler. Across the entire Arab world, there is no ruler who would agree to have a base in his country for staging operations against the state and its allies. You know how international law governs these things. Borders were established and each country was asked to abide by them. Under the auspices of international law we were forced to comply with borders drawn for us on paper. You see what I mean?

One of the consequences, then, is that we must sidestep the Yemeni government or at least isolate it. You see what I mean? We have to isolate the government from the people. How do we make people trust the strugglers rather than the government? This is a crucial question. When a problem arises, the people need to be standing side by side with the strugglers and not with the government. We can't begin by stirring up trouble with the government. Right now, the Yemeni mainstream supports the government. A lot of the brothers work for the government, either in the army or the police force. A lot of the state's scholars don't even think about questions of jihad. Whether directly or indirectly, the most renowned Islamist luminaries are already under the government's control. So how do we sidestep all of this?

There is a general rule (*qaʿida ʿamma*). If you want to sidestep all the obstacles that a ruling government puts before you—its pressure on you and the support given to it by the people—you can challenge it by targeting a common enemy. Let's take an example. In Egypt, we have a case in which people are all afraid of the government. You know what I mean? There is a small minority who sympathizes with the government but the rest are afraid of it. If you want to wage jihad in Egypt and win support from the people, then, you have to target a common enemy whom everyone dislikes. Jews serve this function well, as do Americans: there is a general consensus against them, at least among most Egyptians. If you start targeting these people, then, and do so consistently for a while, you will earn the sympathy and support of Egyptians.

When the government rises against you, for they surely will, you must tolerate the offensive for a while and only then retaliate. At that point, the people will say that your response against the government is justified. They will see how you patiently tolerated the government's absurd behavior. They will say: whenever the strugglers have targeted Jews or Americans, the government has cracked down; at last, the strugglers can stand it no longer and have defended themselves against the state's aggression. This reaction is good and justified.

In Yemen, with respect to the Hunaish islands, we have a case of land occupied [by Eritrea in 1996]. This is actually a blessing for the strugglers. Occupied territory makes the Yemeni government a sell-out. The whole world, at least all Yemenis, know that their government has sold off Hunaish. What is more, they have no interest in reclaiming it. Anyone venturing to claim his taken land does not go to disbelievers to file a claim [with the Permanent Court of Arbitration in the Hague]. This is a well-known fact! The strugglers now have a case in which they can challenge the government. They should show the world, then, that they will kick the Eritreans out off the islands, so eager are they to reclaim Hunaish. This is an example of a way to challenge the Yemeni government, isolating it while gaining the support of the Yemeni people. You see what I'm saying? We begin with Hunaish and the Eritrean issue and then move on to address European investments there as well as American interests in Yemen generally…

Regarding Yemen, grappling with the Yemeni regime through the Eritrean issue is the best conceivable solution. After that, strugglers can turn to affairs in the Arabian Peninsula and to its residents. With respect to targets and operations, there are Jewish and American targets inside Yemen. They can be struck in the name of the Peninsula and the holy lands. Such action would constitute a great embarrassment for the government however it responds, whether by choosing to fight back or abstaining from engagement. They would be able to neither target the strugglers nor leave them alone—it's a lose-lose situation. How many American Jewish targets are there in Yemen? They exist. There are plenty of targets. Launch operations against these targets and claim responsibility for the attacks in the name of the Land of the Two Holy Mosques, then let the government see what it can do.

Success will depend on public relations with the region's various tribes as well as other Islamists, even if they criticize you. And criticize you they will, telling you things like "You're trying to spread corruption in Yemen" or "This is nothing but mischief," as they did in Algeria, or "You are rising against a legitimate [Muslim] ruler," and so on. We must prepare answers to such accusations and stay vigilant. In no cases, however, should we raise a gun against our Muslims brothers. Never. If so-and-so issues a *fatwa* against us, or so-and-so produces an audiotape against us, or some spread propaganda against us, we should still never go kill such people. Doing so only causes a severe deviation in our battle. And, of course, our enemies are brilliant at luring into distractions like these. Sometimes they assassinate some of our members or those of competing Islamic parties. If you are jihadi, for example, they may go and kill a member of the Muslim Brotherhood just to fuel internecine conflict between the Brothers and jihadis, salafis and jihadis, different movements. This is exactly what happened in Pakistan. For twenty years now, the fight has been raging between Shi'as and Sunnis. This fight is directed by the government itself in compliance with orders from the America…

[*Shortly later Hamid resumes his discussion of bases and how to establish them.*]

You've got to think about how to take your money from the enemy. Before launching jihad, let this sit in your mind: The raid of Badr. Wherever the enemy's money is found, go take the money. Not only do you kill the enemy, then, but you also take money. Wealth can be built not only through such direct means as war booty, however. You may also gather it from your enemies through extortion. The obligation to extract "dues" (*itawa*) from your enemies exists across the Muslim world and is an excellent one given so many competing interests. Such extraction is one of the easiest things to do! First, you have to establish your credibility, showing that you have carried out attacks and that we have the ability to take their money. Then, you ask them whether they prefer beating or paying dues. They'll pay us, of course, and from that point on there is no need to beat them. After hitting them two or three times, they'll get the point that our beatings are severe and that we don't joke around. The master is telling you to pay, so you're going to pay…

Three weeks after the August bombings of the American embassies in East Africa, news of bin Laden's likely involvement reached audiences across the world. Through an Associated Press release followed by reports by CNN and other global news agencies, the picture that emerged was that of a secret terrorist network known among its hard-core followers as al-Qaʿida and committed above all to attacking America and its interests across the world. No safer haven was afforded this entity than by the Taliban in Afghanistan.

In October, Arab-Afghan leader Mustafa Hamid, better known by his *nom-de-guerre* Abu al-Walid Al-Masri, took the opportunity to debrief listeners about operational priorities and the longer war for those most closely associated with bin Laden. In a chilly Afghan training camp, "the base" (*al-qaʿida*) received much attention, though not as most audiences understood it then or ever since. Hamid was no sideshow to bin Laden's operational and strategic plans at the time. Born in Egypt and having fought with the Palestinian Fatah movement to liberate South Lebanon from Israeli occupation, he traveled to Afghanistan in 1979 to join ranks with Afghan commander Jalaluddin Haqqani in fighting the Soviets. He quickly became recognized not only for his tactical skills and courage in combat but for his savvy as a war correspondent. By the mid 1980s, he filled a post in Islamabad as bureau chief for the *Al-Ittihad* daily, one of the United Arab Emirates' largest government-run newspapers with wide circulation throughout the Arab world. At the time of the audio recording featured in this chapter, he had recently signed on as the Kandahar-based supervisor of *Al-Imara* ("The Islamic Principality"), a newsletter regarded as the mouthpiece of Mulla ʿUmar with its own English-language version for non-Arabic speakers.[2] Knowing of Hamid's skill in coordinating media operations for global audiences, bin Laden warmed to him from their earliest meeting. By 1990, Hamid was lecturing at Arab-Afghan training camps. Within a few years he filled a position of executive authority among bin Laden's closest allies.

The audio recording conveys no clues to the location of Hamid's lecture. Given his presence in Kandahar at the time, Hamid was mostly likely at the Abu ʿUbaida training camp at Kandahar's international airport, chief residence for bin Laden and his family. A clean definition of voices suggests the presence of some ten to fifteen students in a small

311

room. Hamid's fluid oratory leaves room for student uptake. While most reply with questions, some students express views of their own that, when aptly defended, earn Hamid's gentle praise. To most of the world, bin Laden was al-Qaʿida's uncontested leader, his strategy and tactics a guiding signpost for recruits like none other. To a narrower crew of those most familiar with the halls of Afghanistan's Arab camps, Hamid was the man to follow. According to Fazul ʿAbdulla Muhammad, an East African militant who had become director of Arab militant operations in the Horn of Africa a few years earlier, no al-Qaʿida theoretician was the "architect of the strategy" like Hamid through the 1990s.[3] After 11 September, thousands of pages of his writing would be collected and posted online at the Combatting Terrorism Center in Westpoint. As of yet, this and other copies of his audio-lectures from bin Laden's former tape collection have yet to be examined.

For Hamid, the base for present and future armed struggle cannot be in Afghanistan. "Training must be transferred to the Arabian Peninsula," he insists. "Talk of training here no longer has any meaning due to security dangers and prohibitive costs. You hear me?" Yemen is the favored location for redeployment. "It is very important that work in the Arabian Peninsula be focused on the base (*qaʿida*) of Yemen." Still, as an abstract concept as well as a destination, the base is anything but stable. Not only are there to be multiple bases (*qawaʿid*), but the notion of the base itself is qualified by a whole range of variables. Describing bases as "geographical truths" (*haqaʾiq jiyughrafiyya*) befitting specific locales, Hamid likens the Arabic word for "base" to its homonym: a rule (*qaʿida*). As rules go, so too bases take on life not in isolation from their particular contexts but rather through them. In the excerpt of his lecture above, Hamid provides his listeners with a succession of at least sixteen modifying contexts that give meaning to the working of the base when construed as a rule. Beginning with the base's geographic setting, Hamid continues to explain how bases change according to conditions that are topographic, territorial, military, medical, social, strategic, tactical, rhetorical, linguistic, legal, financial, cultural, temporal, administrative, and ethical. Whatever ʿAbdalla ʿAzzam is reported to have emphasized, no base can exist by virtue of a rigid structure to be applied in the same way everywhere. However much al-Qaʿida had become a hallmark sign among global audiences of bin Laden's organizational purview, such a designation finds no leverage among those closest to bin Laden during the time of his allegedly unprecedented operational sway.

A PRAGMATIC BASE (*AL-QA'IDA*)

How can we explain such a stark gap between discussions about a relatively generalizable "base" among these diehard Arab-Afghan militants and those in the West who were calling public attention to their threat? Let us abandon, for a moment, the quest for a specialized usage of the term among an even more committed group of operatives seeking to brand their work as the orchestration of a single commander. A more plausible explanation can be found in basic conventions of discourse, conduct, and action evoked by the concept across the Islamic world. Beginning as early as the eighth century, Muslim grammarians and legal specialists identified conventions of speech and signification that could be expressed as founding rules, what we might more accurately call "precepts" (*qawa'id*). Such men were brilliant and bold pioneers. Their goal was nothing short of formalizing Arabic so that, however imperfectly spoken by an increasingly diverse Muslim populace, traditions of rhetoric could be identified linking communities up with the essence of Islamic law and morality as practiced by the Prophet Muhammad and his Arabic-speaking community. Through the centuries, their daunting work was taken up by many others.

Before considering Hamid's lecture on the base in greater detail and its implications for our understanding of the trajectories of militancy under bin Laden's shadow at the time, it is worth devoting a few pages to the ways the concept is expounded by two leading jurists whose speeches are featured in bin Laden's former tape collection. Although not responsible or even indirectly linked with the particular stripes of militancy espoused by such figures as Hamid or bin Laden, these speakers were luminaries for Arab-Afghans as they struggled on many fronts. Saudi Shaikh Musa Al-Qarni, the first of these men, had been a superstar among camp recruits since the 1980s. In the wake of 'Abdalla 'Azzam's assassination in 1989, the Office of Services' *Jihad* magazine considered Al-Qarni second only to Yemeni cleric 'Abd al-Majid Al-Zindani as 'Azzam's likely successor.[4] In a lecture entitled "Salafi Precepts in Matters of Summoning" (*Al-Qawa'id Al-Salafiyya fi Al-Masa'il Al-Da'wiyya*) recorded on tape no. 644, Al-Qarni provides his audience with an updated outline of Islam's core precepts. "General precepts (*qawa'id kulliyya*)," he explains, "like Islam's most general stipulations, are not subject to differences of opinion. Scholars unanimously agree upon them because they are among the certitudes of our religion. These precepts can only be derived from the principles of the

Prophet's moral pathway (*Sunna*), the Holy Book, and the methods of pious predecessors (*manhaj al-salaf*) forged through the guidance of revelation." Al-Qarni reviews over a dozen precepts. All focus on ways to prioritize unity and prevail over dissension: "Summon others toward unity," "Highlight what is good in people and forgive their deficiencies," "God never lets his prophets persist in error," "The Muslim is accountable for what he sees, strives to do, and believes and not for what others see, though they be the most knowledgeable of people." Muslims are not always of the same opinion, of course. The art of disputation (*ikhtilaf*) is integral to salafi methodology. A fundamental respect for differing viewpoints, expressed through "aspectual disputation" (*ikhtilaf al-tanawwu'*), is essential to the community's preservation against arguments that are merely "contradictory" (*tadadd*). Al-Qarni warns listeners to remain vigilant against the "authoritarian retort" (*al-radd al-mutlaq*), an opinion advanced with such vehemence and alleged religiosity that dialogue is shut down rather than enabled.

As Al-Qarni expounds on the value of social collaboration and unity in Islam, he attends equally to the nature of threats against the community and those who would sow discord. He takes the recent Gulf War of 1990 as his prime case study:

> One consequence of this crisis was that leaders and scholars voiced different opinions on what was happening... Some began accusing others of certain lapses. These disputes lead from specialist questions about Islamic legal precedent to matters in other fields entirely. The result was growing enmity and antagonism.

Al-Qarni commends a recent "statement of clarification" (*bayyan*) by Saudi chief jurist 'Abd al-'Aziz Ibn Baz for helping to resolve some of the trouble. Some have said that the statement and media attention surrounding it were a "defining summit (*dhurwa*)," he reports. "Still, others have said: Let's talk a little more about the statement. Isn't this an occasion for fostering dialogue and conversation about it? Some of those calling for such action are criticized as 'fundamentalists' (*usuliyun*), in a derogatory sense, as well as 'narrow minded,' 'extremist,' and so forth." Siding with scholars of the Saudi Awakening (*sahwa*), Al-Qarni exclaims that such browbeating "is far removed from the discourse of our righteous predecessors" and betrays poor understanding of the ways Islamic precepts can be used to achieve justice for all. Precept number four, Al-Qarni reminds his listeners, is the "forbiddance of injustice, hatred and enmity." So imperative is this command that, according to the much revered thirteenth-century scholar Taqi al-Din Ibn Taymiyya, "A just state can be established even if it is a disbelieving one while an unjust state can wither even if Islamic." Rooting out hypocrisy proves the first and most foundational of Al-Qarni's precepts. Transcending conventions of mere religiosity, precepts are ethical resources that allow Muslims to reflect on the self (*dhat*) and empower the soul (*nafs*), "very different methods than directing enmity toward the outsider." Taking the early Caliph ʿUmar Ibn al-Khattab as an example, Al-Qarni makes patience in this work his fifth precept.

Further lessons on the ethics and politics of pretexts are supplied by a second preacher in bin Laden's tape collection, Kuwaiti jurist Tariq Al-Suwaidan. Known to millions not only through publishing and media appearances but also as one of the Arabian Peninsula's most successful Western-style entrepreneurs, Al-Suwaidan entitles his early 1990s lecture an "Introduction to Islamic Jurisprudence: Defining versus Declaratory Law" (*Taʿrif Usul Al-Fiqh: Al-Hukm Al-Taklifi wa-l-Hukm Al-Wadʿi*). How, begins Al-Suwaidan, can Muslims know God's plan for them? His answer lies in developing techniques for reading Islam's founding texts closely. After outlining the approaches of several schools of Muslim law, Al-Suwaidan underscores the importance of orally transmitted narratives (*hadith* in the singular) of the Prophet Muhammad's words and deeds. Much in keeping with Sunni reformers who emphasize the historical value of independent legal reasoning (*ijtihad*), Al-Suwaidan returns to the scene of early Medina, the site of Islam's first established community, to illustrate the value of such intellectual work. Proceeding with a discussion of Islam's core doctrinal pretext (*hujja*), Al-Suwaidan recommends four primary sources for cultivating one's understanding of God's will. These sources are, in order: the Qurʾan, technical terms (*mustalahat*) in Islamic law and discussions of belief, Arabic, and disciplined reasoning (*ʿilm al-mantaq*). Between the Qurʾan, on the one hand, and careful legal reasoning, on the other, lies a proficiency in Arabic and its terminological apparatus. In drawing attention to the medium of language, Al-Suwaidan introduces variables of ethnicity, lifestyle, and cultural origin that would provide militants such as Hamid with rich narrative fodder. As I suggest below, confidence could be instilled in students by helping them to realize that every precept is partly a social construct. Some individuals, by virtue of their experience and commitment, can understand and implement precepts better than others.

Knowledge of God's plan, Al-Suwaidan continues, requires learning what he terms "applied ethics" (*hukm faraʿi*). The discipline required of good Muslims is best understood by situating Islam historically in its emergence from the natural habits of native Arabic speakers:

> In the beginning, there were no foundational principles (*usul*). As Arabs did at the time, Muslims moved along with Arabic and its precepts (*qawaʿid*), naturally. They didn't have principles or grammar—these were lacking. Their nature was like that. It was the same even for legal scholars: they moved along according to the principles of their natures, even the most esteemed jurists among them. Then came documentation, first by the Imam Ahmad Al-Shafiʿi…and then others…They began to follow the legal opinions of Abu Hanifa…and at this point they gained a path…[5]

Islam's applied ethics have been cultivated through a centuries-long process of language acquisition and refinement. Insofar as religion has a social history, Muslims' founding principles were formulated first as linguistic "precepts" (*qawaʿid*) that eventually consolidated into a "path" (*nahaj*). This historic path gained coherence over time not through state standardization, as modern reformers might have it, but, rather, given the wide geographical compass of Islam's historical networks of learning, through chains of Arab legal scholarship. Indeed, Al-Suwaidan reminds listeners shortly later, a single consensus or "pretext" (*hujja*) among Muslims has emerged. This common bond is available not only through well-tuned language but through the legacy of something deeper and more instinctive: the pre-grammatical "nature" (*tabiʿa*) of early Arabs. An ethics of expression has been passed on from the bodily habits of Arabs who lived and spoke as a community.

At the time of the recording, Al-Suwaidan was speaking to group of university students in Canada who were members and guests of a group called the Arab Society. Comments and questions after his talk suggested listeners' grave concerns about their community's poor understanding of Islamic doctrine as well as about sectarianism between Muslims worldwide. Dressed in his white cloak and Gulfi *ghutra* headdress, and lecturing in flawless Arabic, Al-Suwaidan would have made quite an impression. His tremendous charisma had no doubt preceded him, especially among younger television audiences who had not grown up in the Arab world and whose familiarity with customs in the homeland paled in comparison to that of their parents. For these listeners, Al-Suwaidan's lecture would have carried the imprint of orthodoxy mixed with something a bit more exciting. On the one hand, his views of language as a natural and instinctive characteristic of early Arab speakers reflected a common understanding that while the Qur'an was the inimitable ideal for Arabic speakers, so too could recourse be made to the linguistic usage of Arabic by ordinary speakers most familiar with traditions of eloquence and public oratory. As early grammarians had professed, the best models for such discourse were central Arabian nomads sharing blood ties with the Prophet Muhammad's own tribe of Quraish. On the other hand, Al-Suwaidan embellished his account with idioms of Arabian pastoral nomadism that, perhaps especially for his young Western listeners, carried with them a certain romance. Describing the ways that early Muslim scholars used language, he explained that "Like the Arabs, they were moving along," and, later, he reiterated how "they were moving along" (*kanu mashiyin*) according to the principles of their natures. Ultimately, he explains, their journeys made it "possible to move along a path." Along with Al-Suwaidan's reasoned pedagogy come lessons both on language as well as on a way of moving through a spatialized Arabian homeland. Invoked initially as a temporal return ("in the beginning"), this founding imaginary and its precepts spring to life in itineraries known not only by anonymous early nomads but also by path-finding legal personalities. Figures of note include the Gaza-born Imam Muhammad Al-Shafi'i, widely considered to be one of the most important early theorists of Islamic law, and Abu Hanifah Al-'Anbari, an eighth-century Persian jurist who promoted the use of common sense reasoning in Islam. Proper legal reasoning, it appears, could reconnect Arabic language users with Arabian ways of life wherever they might live.

The idea of the precept receives more concerted attention as Al-Suwaidan unpacks the ways exemplary individuals can use Arabic to reconstitute authentic Muslim communities in the fashion of Arabia's predecessors. When reading the Qur'an, he continues, one can discover what God considers to be obligatory for Muslims by looking for imperative verbs. Verbs that command Muslims to do things help one to know what is considered obligatory. Attention to grammatical mood is only a first step, however. Such an exegetical technique is a *qa'ida*, a flexible rule or precept, and in this regard is conditional. A *qa'ida* has pragmatic exceptions: The precept applies "except if its associated context (*qarina*) is separated from it." If another piece of evidence appears to call the imperative verb into doubt, its obligation is accordingly conditional. How is such evidence assembled? First, Al-Suwaidan explains, by relying upon Arabic, and he adds: "We use this precept that was given to us by linguists: they have linguistic evidence that has been gathered from the imperative verb's usage by Arabs." Second, however, evidence for the *qaʿidaʾs* applicability in any given situation must be gathered from the inner comportment of those best qualified to speak Arabic morally, especially jurists and those familiar with Islamic law, whatever their ethnic origins. In the practice of discovering God's plan, linguistic evidence is not enough, since linguistic precepts can be fully internalized. "When [legal experts] use Arabic precepts," Al-Suwaidan continues, "they consider them intuitive. This [intuition is granted to them through] the work of language, and, thus, they are able to decide whether the imperative verb satisfies what is needed to be obligatory." The logic of the *qaʿida*, is, thus, unmistakably attached to one's intimacy with Arabic, and with an intuition that comes through full conversance with using language in particular social and cultural settings. The *qaʿida* is a product of expressive acculturation.[6] In short, Al-Suwaidan gives strong credence to the esteemed purveyors of Muslim knowledge in the Arabic-speaking world, even as listeners are offered exegetical lessons by which they might participate in moral reasoning themselves.

Much more could be said about Muslim scholars' weighty cogitations on the idea of the *qaʿida* as Islam spread to distant shores within just a few generations of its birth. By the tenth century, legal scholars had penned entire treatises on the topic. They distilled the essence of thousands of transmitted reports of Muhammad's words and deeds, culled through dusty archives of legal cases, and reviewed what consensus had been established in order to supply jurists with a set of overarching maxims for the application of Islamic law. Phrases such as "Acts are judged by the intention behind them," "Custom is the basis of judgment" and "The norm of *shariʿa* is that of non-liability" became affixed in jurists' minds and attached to vast taxonomies of subtle distinction.[7] Due to their generality, precepts such as these gave broad license to reversal in specific cases. As stated by thirteenth-century scholar Taqi al-Din Ibn Taymiyya, founding father of an entire school of legal pragmatism, "There is no entity that is free from any qualification in the external world" (*la yujad fi-l-kharij shayʾun mawjudun kharijun ʿan kulli qayd*).[8]

Every rule has its contingencies. Guiding precepts and their caveats were not only the tradecraft of legal experts, however. A wider range of scholars also produced governing maxims, perhaps no more so than those challenging authoritarian regimes in the modern period. "Whatever exists can be seen" (*kullu mawjudin yuraa*), states one Sufi scholar in rebuke to Saudi jurist ʿAbd al-ʿAziz Ibn Baz's fatwa that the Prophet Muhammad can never be seen in a daydream.[9] Theology too, it appears, could have precepts, some of them conducive to mass prophetic witnessing. The metaphysical dimensions of precepts lent themselves to critiques of oppressive bodily convention. "Violence after the fact," states a twenty-first-century Muslim feminist about precepts governing spatial separation between the sexes in traditional Moroccan households. "The *qaʿida*, the invisible rule, often was much worse than walls and gates. With walls and gates, you at least knew what was expected from you."[10]

Arab-Afghan militants, no strangers to opprobrium against scholarly establishments, would also come to appreciate the subtler tactics of precepts. Rather than perpetuating forces of oppression, however, precepts could upend and explode them. This capacity for worldly change seemed imminent when construed within religious vocabularies highlighting global agents of conspiracy and sedition. Never would revolution appear more realizable, though, than when coordinated with the precept's homonymic twin: the base (*al-qaʿida*), an actual territorial headquarters for staging insurgency. As an outpost guiding both faith and heartfelt work, the precept in this sense achieved its most radical instantiation as a workshop for alternative histories, geographies, and ways of speaking and being.

Bin Laden first models the value of the precept for listeners when orating his defiance against American and Saudi regimes from Tora Bora in August 1996. After denouncing Saudi and American collaboration in assassinating and imprisoning preachers and legal scholars in "the Land of the Two Holy Sanctuaries," his own birthplace, he casts himself as a victim to this injustice and outlines his vision of global jihad. A new "safe base" (*qaʿida amina*) has been established, he explains. Its power derives from its historical location in territory marked by extraordinary conquests and speech acts alike:

> After this injustice, we have suffered by being prevented from speaking publicly to Muslims. We have been exiled from Pakistan, the Sudan, and Afghanistan, hence a prolonged absence on my part. But by the Grace of God, a safe base has now been found in Khurasan, on the summit of the

THE AUDACIOUS ASCETIC

Hindu Kush—this summit where, by the Grace of God, the largest infidel military force in the world was destroyed, and where the myth of the superpower withered before the mujahidin's cries of "God Is Greater." Today, from atop the same summit of Afghanistan, we work to lift the iniquity that had been imposed on the Muslim community by the Jewish-Crusader alliance, particularly after they have occupied the Land of the Two Holy Sanctuaries.[11]

Part of the force of his "declaration," as it was later called, comes from bin Laden's principled stance against Muslim states that have tried to silence him. These include Saudi Arabia but also "Pakistan, the Sudan, and Afghanistan." Through divine grace, he has at last found a podium back in Afghanistan. Located on a specific territorial "summit," however, the base's significance and primary objectives multiply along several different fronts. As a launching point in Khurasan, the base evokes memories of eleventh-century Muslim expansions in which valiant frontier warriors tested their mettle against ruinous infidel tyrants. By some accounts, the term "Hindu Kush" was Persian for "Hindu killer." From the same summit, an even greater assemblage of enemies clashed with Muslim forces in the twentieth century: the Soviet army, "the largest infidel military force in the world." It too dissolved, along with an entire myth of Communist cold-war supremacy, "before the mujahidin's cries of 'God is Greater' (*Allahu Akbar*)." Today the base faces yet another foe, a "Jewish-Crusader alliance" that is both antique and resurgent since the Arabian Peninsula's occupation in 1990. In their broadest cast, such a panoply of enemies reminds Muslims of what they share in common. Within a few short breaths, bin Laden reiterates three times that the base is located on a "summit" (*dhurwa*), a word recalling an aphorism printed on cassettes in his collection and well known among militants: "Jihad is the summit of religion's camel-hump" (*jihad dhurwa sanam al-din*). Struggle in God's cause might just be the bond that keeps the pious community together. At the same time, the territorial conditions so pivotal to the idea of the base pull bin Laden toward contexts more Arabian than pan-Islamic. If struggle is likened to a "camel hump," religious though it may be, so too must Islam's warriors be mobilized in the defense of Mecca and Madina, above all.

Few jihadi theoreticians would be as skilled at helping recruits think through the operational and strategic prerogatives of base training as Hamid. Like bin Laden, Hamid views the *qaʿida* primarily as an institution for challenging or disrupting the territorial and security regimes of

320

a modern nation state system. The base's strength lies in its flexible capacity for redeployment across borderlands. Rugged mountains provide the optimal topography for such bases. Although Yemen is the favored destination, a state considered "liberated" (*muharrar*) much like Pakistan and Afghanistan, its chief strategic asset is a chain of mountains that cuts across the two states of Yemen and Saudi Arabia. The power of such a base, in fact, lies in its twin presence as a location in territories that are "liberated" and also in "posterior" (*khalfi*) areas that have yet to be secured. The latter include Saudi Arabia, where large numbers of American and Western military forces were stationed at the time, and also Iran, where Shi'a Muslims have long been the majority. The "base," thus, acquires power by linking places that are primary and sacrosanct to those that remain embattled.

Later, perhaps in an effort to motivate his listeners, Hamid searches for an image of the kind of person best suited to negotiating such a trans-national topography. He arrives at the figure of a transhumant Arab nomad. The nomad's ability to survive depends in part on his competences in metropolitan settings. Corrupt though urban areas may be "due to lifestyle and Western cultural influences such as television, media norms, newspapers, magazines, pressure from the state, and so on," cities are also key targets for conducting raids and extortion. Reminding listeners of the Prophet Muhammad's attack on a wealthy Meccan caravan in CE 624, Hamid suggests that "Before launching jihad, let this sit in your mind: the raid of Badr. Wherever the enemy's money is found, go take the money." Shortly after the longer excerpt cited above, he elaborates on the ideal topography for building wealth through war and extortion while remaining an ascetic at heart:

> Whoever finances operations in cities, the operations that are called terrorist operations in cities, he has with him posts in the mountains for strugglers. When a brother gets suspicious or is discovered, or when someone is injured and people are captured and taken away, he immediately undertakes a nomadic journey to the mountain on high. You've got to establish a base (*qa'ida*) on the high mountain. That is the first command. The people who live in the city, among those who have been downtrodden, go to such a base, then, if they want to get better. They go draw from the base, if they want to train, or get a salary, or money. They go to the base, taking from the mountain on high. That center effectively becomes the new headquarters, just as happened the Enlightened City (*madina munawwara*) of Madina [in the seventh century]. The people of Madina were essentially administrators of

jihadi work as well as of the Muslim society surrounding the city. You can establish an Enlightened City yourselves in Yemen. I mean, Muslims' issues on this matter have long been in accordance with the Prophet Muhammad's moral pathway (*Sunna*): You must found an enlightened city on the model of the enlightened city, as an Enlightened Base (*qaʿida munawwara*), an Enlightened Jihadi Base, an Islamic base that can direct the work of jihad. This is the city. By applying our Islamic law, we apply Islamic law inside the base as well as around it. And keep in mind: we always apply Islamic law in areas that we control.

So, this is the jihadi base. The Enlightened City is an expression of the struggle. Whether inside or outside Yemen, or around it, this City must be established. As for the number of people required to set it up, there are no specifics. Five, ten, maybe more than that. The important thing is that the heart must work with faith.

In explaining the modern tactics required of the armed militant, Hamid finds the notion of the base instrumental. Initially, the exemplary moral tactician is one who can imaginatively journey back in time to the raid of Badr. Wealth having been secured, the tribal warrior can protect his assets by taking "a nomadic journey" (*yishidd al-rahala*) from troubled cities into the safer highlands, to the "*qaʿida* on high." The community to be established there is envisioned not as a rural backwater but rather as a utopian city itself. In calling the location a "Shining City" (*madina munawwara*), Hamid refers to the moniker by which Muslims have long known Madina, where Islam's first Muslim community was founded by the Prophet Muhammad in CE 622. By securing new territories with homage to the past, listeners can found a "shining jihadi base" (*qaʿida jihadiyya munawwara*) to direct the work of their brethren. As creative work by base leaders improves the financial stability of operations, urban militants work as a kind of service class for their more inspired highland brothers. Religion itself emanates from the base through its perceived ethical calling: "By applying our Islamic law, we apply Islamic law inside the base as well as around it." Such a message would have resonated well with disenfranchised youth from the Arabian Peninsula who represented the majority of new volunteers arriving in Afghanistan after 1998.

A comparison between Hamid's use of the term *qaʿida* and that of the jurists Musa Al-Qarni and Tariq Al-Suwaidan reveals similarities, as well as important differences. As for the legal scholars, the resourcefulness of the *qaʿida* derives not from its fixed and timeless structure. Rather, the *qa'ida* acquires value in relation to contexts that are conceptually "separated" from it. As for the scholars, too, the relation between the "base" or "precept" and its contextual deployment is to be determined through a particular spatial and temporal mooring: one must seek recourse to the communities, social customs, and instincts of exemplary Arab leaders in and around the Arabian Peninsula. It is precisely on matters of authority, however, that Hamid as well as bin Laden differ from the jurists. Perhaps not surprisingly, from the formers' perspective the *qa'ida*'s leverage works in relation to a system of modern states engaged in geopolitical struggles. Invoking tactical maneuvers both within, but also, crucially, across territories of state jurisdiction, the militants use the concept of the *qa'ida* to create new stories of primordial acts and topographies. The unfolding deeds of this cosmogony are exemplified, in particular, by canny utopian warriors rather than by legal specialists or statesmen. According to Hamid, one's "first command" (*awwal amr*) or obligation is only indirectly related to God's will as conveyed through a Qur'anic exegesis of imperative verbs; instead, the most important command is to secure a safe territorial zone, to "establish a base (*qa'ida*) on the high mountain." The populist flavor of such work is evident enough in his assertion that "in every place strugglers should have their own specific rules of engagement (*qawa'id khassa li-l-qital*). These are separate from the general rule of war (*al-qa'ida al-'amma li-l-harb*) and are specific to every locale." Whatever license to anarchy such a formula might entail, Hamid offers listeners his vision of an ethical center in the final portion of his lecture. In exhorting that "You [too] should create a radiant city that is a Shining City," he ratifies each listener as a prophetic activist. Empowerment comes less from formal education than from an ability to perceive "geographical truths" that belie the artificial boundaries of states and nations. As with bin Laden, the heroes of this order are the kinds of deterritorialized migrants, workers, and youth who have so often formed the bulwark of militant movements across the world.

In late October, at the time of this lecture, Hamid reports in a memoir that he had grown troubled by growing friction among Arab-Afghan volunteers who had begun arriving *en masse* after the 20 August cruise missile strikes. A growing array of training camps, each led by its own amir, fostered in-house quarrels as each camp competed for limited resources. With an eye toward improving the situation, Hamid approached bin Laden, Ayman Al-Zawahiri, and leaders of the Egyptian

Islamic Jihad with a proposal. Solidarity between groups could be enhanced by pledging allegiance to Taliban chief Mulla 'Umar. The reply he received was cold and short: Only Afghan nationals could pledge loyalty of this sort. Roughly a week later, fearful of rising dissension in the ranks, he pressed on, contacting Mulla 'Umar's deputy to help arrange a meeting. On 2 November, Hamid met with Omar and pledged an oath. Returning to bin Laden and others with good news of his example, Hamid found his colleagues enraged.[12]

Students who had attended Hamid's lecture on base-camp operations and the Arabian Peninsula might well have found dissension among commanders puzzling. Hadn't bin Laden openly praised the Taliban in the previous year, calling them "the legitimate rulers" of Afghanistan and commending their "total support for all Islamic causes"?[13] Wasn't the most important goal, a "general rule" (qa'ida 'amma) as Hamid put it, targeting a "common enemy whom everyone dislikes"? Didn't a Judeo-Crusader alliance spearheaded by the United States fit this bill for all Muslim leaders in Afghanistan? By some accounts, the urgency of confronting the American adversary had been no more clearly articulated than by Hamid; according to one top militant, Hamid was in fact responsible for convincing bin Laden and Zawahiri to confront the United States as ardently as they did.[14] One audiotape in bin Laden's former collection, a recording of a lecture in the spring of 1998 at the Al-Faruq camp in Khost, seems to support this claim. While reading portions of Saudi firebrand Safar Al-Hawali's newly revised treatise *Kissinger's Promise*, much of which, released in 1991, focuses on American military and strategic ambitions in the Arabian Peninsula, Hamid reiterates the author's lament that scholars had yet to produce a single fatwa commending youth's uptake of armed rebellion against the infidel occupiers. "During the Apocalypse, when the False Messiah sees the Messiah [Jesus], he will melt like salt just at the sight of him, by God. This is what will happen in that battle. If Americans were to face the Islamic army, no matter how weak it may be, you too would see what would happen on the battlefield."[15] How could bin Laden and others possibly fall out with Hamid over his decision to strengthen group solidarity in league with Afghanistan's most defiant anti-American chief?

As a general precept, confrontation with a common enemy was riven with qualifications. For their part, bin Laden and leaders of the Egyptian Islamic Jihad were loath to relinquish control over strategy and operational command to a non-Arab, even one in charge of an Islamic state. For Mulla 'Umar and associates, oaths from their Arab guests were a poisoned chalice: welcome if substantive but a potential liability for building relations with other Taliban leaders, most of whom thought the Arab-Afghan presence was a tinderbox. As Hamid discovered when meeting with Omar, the ritual of oath-giving was shockingly deficient and nothing was put in writing. For his part, Hamid expressed his views on confronting Americans and Jews through lectures more about public relations and media priorities than about operational tactics. "We must sidestep the Yemeni government or at least isolate it," Hamid notes to his students in Kandahar. "We can't begin by stirring up trouble with the government. Right now, the Yemeni mainstream supports the government…So how do we sidestep all of this?" As in Egypt, the answer is to target "a common enemy whom everyone dislikes. Jews serve this function well, as do Americans: there is a general consensus against them, at least among most Egyptians. If you start targeting these people, then, and do so consistently for a while, you will earn the sympathy and support of Egyptians." State crackdowns against militants following such attacks can only be "a great embarrassment for the government," he claims, "a lose-lose situation." Success, he adds, "will depend on public relations with the region's various tribes as well as other Islamists, even if they criticize you." Hamid's campaign against the outside enemy is a short-term tactical card played in a battle for Muslims' own hearts and minds. The war is not for a global Islamic caliphate bending the West to its rule but rather for something much more familiar to generations of Muslim reformers: true Islamic law at home. Few other Arab-Afghans had met with as much success in marketing this cause not only to audiences worldwide but also to official cadres in countries hosting their operations.

The substance of Mustafa Hamid's difference from bin Laden over al-Qa'ida's ideology and goals is manifest in his lecture in the very halls of bin Laden's cloistered Arab-Afghan world. Little future remained for his students under bin Laden's command in Afghanistan. Listeners should prepare to return back to their homelands or, if exiled, the closest equivalent, and work to re-engage broader populations with their message. In a revision of an early 1990s journal published around this time, Hamid puts *al-qa'ida* in quotes when discussing bin Laden's leadership.[16] The Saudi exile's focus on taking the war to the far enemy was too much the product of sensational media coverage. Especially if this adventure came at the expense of actual security in specific Islamic polities.

13

LISTEN, PLAN, CARRY OUT *"AL-QAʿIDA"*

(Lecture by ʿAbd al-Rahim Al-Tahhan delivered in Taʾif, Al-Qarʿa and Abha, Saudi Arabia during the 1980s. Recorded originally as a three-volume audio-tape series, the lecture was repackaged by a Riyadh audiocassette shop after 1998 in support of bin Ladenʾs efforts. Excerpt from cassette no. 906.)

If there are both obedience and disobedience [to God] in a person, we shall love him to the extent of his obedience and dislike whatever disobedience and violations he is guilty of. Thus, in our hearts there would be love for him from one perspective, and hatred (*bughd*) towards him from another perspective.

This matter [of love and hatred]—just as they exist simultaneously in us, they also exist concurrently in our Lord, may He be glorified and exalted. They co-exist within each of us, moreover, by virtue of a particular matter to which we are subject. It is relayed in a sound report (*hadith*) by [the ninth-century scholar Muhammad] Al-Bukhari and elsewhere by [the seventh-century Companion of the Prophet] Abu Hurayra, may God be pleased with him, that the Prophet said, God's blessings and salutations upon him:

> Exalted God has said: 'I declare war on whomever shows enmity towards an ally of Mine. My servant will seek to draw near to me through what I have required of him. Indeed nothing is more beloved to Me than his pursuit of the obligatory. My servant will also continue to seek to draw near to me through voluntary actions, persevering until I love him. Once I do, I shall have blessed the hearing through which he has heard, the sight through which he has seen, the hands though which he has acted, and the feet that have born him. If he requests some-

327

thing of me, I shall grant him his wish. If he seeks refuge in me, I shall give him respite. I hesitate in nothing so much as intending to take the soul from my faithful servant. He dislikes death and I dislike displeasing him. And yet it is inevitable.'

Glory be to my Almighty Lord! God conjoined two opposite matters here. God's dislike of death accords with that of the believer. God thus grants the believer a great station indeed. Whatever the believer loves, God too loves; whatever the believer dislikes, God too dislikes. In the same manner, whatever his Lord loves, the believer loves and whatever his Lord dislikes, the believer too dislikes.

Since the believer is repulsed by death and does not want it, the will of God, may He be glorified and exalted, requires that He too dislike this matter. "I hesitate in nothing so much as intending to take the soul from my faithful servant." He hates death! Mutual accord between the lover and the beloved, the Godly believer and God the beloved, has a necessary consequence: God dislikes death. "I hate displeasing him!" [says God.] In other words, my dislike of death accords with that of the believer so that he may not be displeased. Then He added: "And yet it is inevitable." The upshot is: I love death from a different perspective, since in death there lies, in fact, enormous happiness for the human being. He becomes liberated from the sufferings and anguish of this worldly life. He experiences great comfort when meeting He who loves him and in turn beloved: God [himself], may He be glorified and exalted. Thus [He says]: I love death from one perspective, since many great felicities result for the believer, and I dislike it from another perspective since the believer dislikes it. However, I give precedence to that which advantages the believer even if he may not fully appreciate what is done. "And yet it is inevitable." "And yet it is inevitable."

Co-existing in our Lord, Glorious and Exalted is He, are two opposing wills (iradatan). This is the reality of hesitation (taraddud): that two wills oppose each other. Then, God—Glorious and Exalted is He—grants precedence to one of the two matters due to its benefits (masalih) for the believer both now and in the future. It is inevitable.

And you, my faithful brother, when you see obedience and disobedience in your brother, you [should] love him from one perspective and from another perspective hate the acts of disobedience in which he engages. You [should] give precedence to that which is more just than the other. Thus, he whose obedience is greater [than his disobedience], our love for him shall be greater [than our hatred], and vice versa. We must acquire this attribute. God, may He be glorified and exalted, has this attribute and it is a matter which happens to us—and that is death.

For these two reasons, I wish to talk about this great topic: "The Position of the Astute on People's Dispute."

In the spring of 2000, questions posed by Afghan militant training camp students to top al-Qa'ida leaders were recorded in a notebook that appears to have been authored anonymously by a secretary for Osama bin Laden. While most questions focus on the strategy and tactics of sustaining the militant movement worldwide, a segment entitled "Questions Section" considers dissension among Muslims themselves, especially in Arab and Afghan contexts. Among these questions is the following, notable for its pronounced vocabulary of Islamic law:

> You know that every dissension (*furqa*) involves disputation (*ikhtilaf*) but every dispute does not involve dissension, because there are various types of dispute (*khilaf*) from contradictory (*dadd*) to comprehensional (*ifham*) to aspectual (*tanawwu'*). As you know, comprehensional and aspectual disputes are healthy for one's consciousness—scientific, political, legal, and practical (*al-wa'i al-'ilmi wa-l-siyasi wa-l-shar'i wa-l-waqi'i*). Yet dissension still lingers among the ranks of Arab strugglers. Are we to understand that such dissension results from contradictory disputes [disputes, that is, which are] knotty (*'aqdi*), whether accompanied by good evidence or by wild fantasy?[1]

Scholars who study Muslim militant movements, including al-Qa'ida, frequently recur to the writings of the Egyptian thinker Sayyid Qutb (discussed in chapter two) or the Pakistani reformer Abu al-'Ala Al-Mawdudi, a giant among twentieth-century Muslim political leaders, to narrate modern Islam's turn from classical to socio-revolutionary jihad. If classical jihad focused on a legitimate Muslim ruler's call to arms against infidel forces occupying Muslim lands, socio-revolutionary militancy aims to overthrow corrupt Muslim leaders themselves, especially those influenced by the West, in the interests of just Islamic rule. Much attention has been drawn to the ways Qutb and Al-Mawdudi invoked the "age of ignorance" along with concepts of "servitude" (*jahiliyya*) and divine sovereignty in worship (*hakimiyya*) to license charges of excommunication (*takfir*) and bolster arguments for killing apostates. My analysis of the concept of *al-qa'ida* in the last chapter should give pause to studies of militancy that begin and end with soaring polarities between holy warriors and their infidel aggressors. If socio-revolutionary jihad is to stand any chance against the world's most oppressive enemies, those likely to take up its call must be convinced to set aside what they are doing and re-evaluate their closest allies: neighbors, associates, group leaders, friends, even lovers. For top al-Qa'ida operative Mustafa Hamid and his training camp students, classical jihadi treatises about the validity of taking up arms against one's oppressors were less important than conversations about how to turn basic "precepts" (*qawāʿid*) of Islamic law, Arabic, and morality against one's own unjust authorities and to win public acclaim for doing so. Questions about "disputation" (*ikhtilaf*), whether "contradictory" or "aspectual" in particular, were not peripheral to *al-qāʿidaʾs* strategists and tacticians. Founded in long-established religious discourse, these nuances were elemental to identifying the true fault-lines of global political coalitions and building resources to exploit them.

In this chapter, I examine the ways in which theological matters of creed (*ʿaqida*) are pressed into service by speakers in bin Laden's former audiotape collection as they unpack the legacies of Islamic precepts for broader audiences.[2] I focus on the works of the top-featured speaker in the collection, the Syrian preacher and jurist ʿAbd al-Rahim bin Ahmad Al-Tahhan. One set of recordings draws my attention for the white printing label affixed to several cartridges: "My brother struggler: Listen—plan—carry out ʿal-Qaʿida'" (*Akhi Al-Mujahid: Ismaʿ—Dabbir—Iʿmal "al-Qaʿida."*). When first encountering the tapes, I assumed that they would relate much about bin Laden's organization and the machinations of a group working under its purview. After all, with the exception of a wedding tape featuring a speech by bin Laden from late 2000, examined in the next chapter, no other material in the collection featured as explicit a reference to an entity called "al-Qaʿida." A puzzle arose for me when listening, however. The shaikh's nearly four-hour lecture, recorded on three separate audiotapes, makes no mention of bin Laden, much less the tactics or strategies of militancy. Instead, Al-Tahhan lays out ethical groundwork for enabling a more disparate range of political discourses that include, but do not necessitate, militant uptake. With respect to "*al-qaʿida*," he situates the concept within a set of arguments about the urgency of religious creed (*ʿaqida*) and Islamic law to political action. In particular, he invites listeners to consider the implications for mankind of God's own experiences of hesitation and death. These matters, some of which seemed almost existential, left me wondering about just how such a label could be associated with the tapes. There could be no mistake: six recordings of the shaikh's lecture could be found in the collection, and the same leading label was found on every copy of volumes two and three, though curiously absent from those of volume one.[3]

Wanting to learn more about Shaikh Al-Tahhan's work and get help understanding his influence, I traveled to Doha, Qatar in 2010 to interview him. Qataris who had long known of Al-Tahhan's sermons told me that he had withdrawn entirely from public life and no longer entertained guests. He expressed, in the words of some, the epitome of asceticism (*zuhd*). Other forces had also played a hand in his withdrawal. In 1995 Shaikh Hamad bin Khalifa seized power from his father in a coup and set a course for rapprochement with the United States. After Al-Tahhan criticized the country's swing toward the West, singling out the amir's passion for flashy soccer stadiums, he was stripped of his pulpit and barred from giving any more tutorials to the head of the country's Ministry of Religious Endowments.[4] Within five years, his books and audiotapes were available only on a website that routinely switched servers. Officials in the country told me that Al-Tahhan would be unavailable for an interview.

Whatever we make of Al-Tahhan's run-in with the Qatari administration, the trajectory of his outspoken political discourse remains a heated topic of debate among those familiar with his work. Some commend him for reminding fellow Muslims of Islam's fundamental commitment to unity and non-violence. One ardent Somali student I interviewed in Qatar told me that Al-Tahhan's lectures were a cornerstone for his father's refusal to harbor weapons during years when their Somali village was wracked by tribal conflict and war in the 1990s.[5] His perspective aligned well with reports among Egyptian members of the Muslim Brotherhood a decade earlier. If thrown in prison and confronted by interrogators with evidence of extremist sympathies, members were told to insist that they listened to Shaikh Al-Tahhan's audio-recorded sermons. Security officials would be mollified.[6] At the same time, other students vouchsafed Al-Tahhan's formidable legacy for militants.[7] Abu Mus'ab Al-Suri, for example, one of the most influential theoreticians of global armed jihad and a speaker featured on at least nine recordings in bin Laden's former tape collection, commends Al-Tahhan in no uncertain terms. In a chapter of his book *Call to Global Islamic Resistance* (2006) entitled "The First Arena of Education: Creed and Legal Learning (*Al-'Aqida wa-l-'Ilm Al-Shar'i*)," Al-Suri recommends reading classic accounts of creed by such figures as Abu Ja'far Al-Tahawi and Taqi al-Din Ibn Taymiyya as well as more contemporary militant theoreticians such as 'Abdalla 'Azzam, 'Umar 'Abd al-Rahman, Ayman Al-Zawahiri and Abu Muhammad Al-Maqdisi. Turning to readers more attuned to affairs on the Arabian Peninsula and the growing strength of the Arab-Afghan movement in particular, he adds: "I also suggest listening to the lectures and recordings of the symbols of the Awakening (*al-sahwa*) in the Land of the Two Holy Sanctuaries that were published between 1980–95. They contain outstanding material on creed and legal learning and jihadi movement ideology, especially the tapes of Shaikhs ʿAbd al-Rahim Al-Tahhan…"[8] While Al-Suri refrains from providing further details on how exactly Al-Tahhan could provide militants with guidance, bin Laden himself provides a glimpse in a handwritten letter to the shaikh thanking him for providing him with "advice" (*nasiha*) on drafts of his first open letter to the Saudis. The letter, sent to the kingdom's chief jurist ʿAbd al-ʿAziz Ibn Baz in 1994, excoriates the Saudi administration for allowing American, "Jewish," and Western military forces to expand operations on the Arabian Peninsula.[9] Assessments of Al-Tahhan's influence elicited more questions for me than answers.

Summary accounts of Al-Tahhan's legacy are no easier given the total absence of attention given to his life or work by Western scholars. Any attempt to categorize his thought as the product of a religious sectarian militant—violence justifies the ends when levied against infidel aggressors and has no place among co-religionists—meets with obstacles given Al-Tahhan's consistent fulmination against Muslims who veer toward secularism. In a lecture entitled "The Separation of Religion from the State" (tape no. 909), Al-Tahhan declares that the Antichrist himself is less frightening than "errant Imams" who mislead their own flock. Citing transmitted reports of the Prophet Muhammad's words and deeds (*hadith*), Al-Tahhan argues that as few as three individuals can constitute a group (*jamaʿa*), appoint their own amir, and re-establish righteous Muslim governance through the "text and the sword" (*al-mushaf wa-l-sayf*). Venturing that enemies' "eyes be plucked out and throats cut," he summarizes more dispassionately that, at the very least, they should be fought, taken captive, chained by the neck, and forced to convert or else remain in bondage. The chief targets of Al-Tahhan's wrath are secular Muslims swollen with the platitudes of Western nationalism and humanism, especially those who claim leadership of the Muslim Brotherhood in Egypt. Critics charge Al-Tahhan with "sectarianism," "excessiveness" (*ghuluww*), "Wahhabism," "Shiʿism," and "Sufism."

To some extent the florid controversy surrounding Al-Tahhan's legacy can be attributed to his upbringing and education. Social convention seems to have been a consistent whetting stone. Born in Aleppo, Syria in the early 1950s, Al-Tahhan's Al-Nuʿaymi clan traced descent to the Prophet's cousin ʿAli bin Abi Talib. Although his father was not a religious scholar, he sought to enhance what status came through blood by prioritizing his sons' religious education. First came a more conservative primary school in Saudi Arabia, where the family lived during ʿAbd al-Rahim's early adolescence. Later came more advanced training back in Aleppo where, following regional custom, the legacy of Naqshbandi Sufism weighed heavily in his sons' studies.[10] Immersed in heated debates about the value of Sufi allegiances to modern Islamist reform, Al-Tahhan spurned the more accommodating vocabulary of most Syrians. After completing secondary school, he returned to Saudi Arabia to pursue higher education at the Islamic University in Madina. There he studied Islamic law under Maliki jurist Muhammad Al-Amin Al-Shanqiti, one of the most influential non-Saudis to have risen through the ranks of the traditional Riyadh-based Najdi clerical establishment. He seems to have taken special inspiration from Al-Shanqiti's willingness to think outside the box. In a class on creed (*ʿaqida*), hackles raised by one young lecturer's tired review of the many ways deviant groups misinterpret God's divine names and attributes, he is reported to have quipped: "We have not come to the Kingdom from abroad to study Wahhabism!" Shortly later, when being forced to report his comments to ʿAbd al-ʿAziz Ibn Baz, the university's chief rector at the time, he was told, "Review your lessons again, my son," whereupon he replied to Ibn Baz, "But you are the grandmaster of Wahhabism!"[11] Critics report his prompt expulsion from the university.[12]

Al-Tahhan's courage in confronting the Saudi establishment on matters of creed and, more broadly, subservience to state ideology ensured further stages in his transnational education. By the 1970s, he had matriculated at Egypt's renowned Al-Azhar University and was soon to complete a graduate degree in exegesis (*tafsir*) with highest marks. Committed to returning to the Kingdom but unable to secure appointments in the country's more prestigious institutions of learning and worship, he accepted employment in Abha, a city in the southern ʿAsir province known for its political preachers. There he taught at a branch of the Imam Muhammad Ibn Saʿud University as well as at a religious college for women. While in Abha, he is reported to have taught a number of students from non-Najdi families who would become prominent reformers during the 1980s.[13] Toward the end of the decade, Al-Tahhan's credentials were called into question once again. Lectures supporting tomb visitation and intercession from the dead, both anathema to the Saudi Wahhabi establishment, earned him expulsion from the Kingdom.[14] Subsequently, he taught at branches of the Imam Muhammad Ibn Saʿud University in the Emirates as well as in Jakarta, Indonesia. In 1993 he moved to Doha, where his lectures kept pace with the city's frenzied construction boom. Through his use of audiotapes as well as the internet, by the end of the decade his audiences had expanded considerably.[15]

A tumultuous educational and career history is in keeping with the profile of many modern Arab revolutionaries, of course, perhaps especially Islamic ones. The truer measure of Al-Tahhan's radicalism would come from his formidable intellect, one expounded for followers on some six-hundred audio recordings and over one hundred print publications. Armed struggle and its legal armature would not loom large in his work, though these topics would have been much in currency around him. Far more important, instead, are theological matters of creed (ʿaqida). In previous chapters I have outlined the origins and concerns of Muslim reformers known as salafis, literally those who pay homage to "pious predecessors" (aslaf) who typically lived during the Prophet Muhammad's lifetime as well as the two succeeding generations. Some Muslims I spoke with in Doha considered Al-Tahhan a salafi insofar as he holds creed to be central to Islam's political objectives. In part, salafism has been defined through legal vocabularies, including discussions about the legitimate use of violence configured within discourses of "commanding right and forbidding wrong" (al-amr bi-l-maʿruf wa-l-nahy ʿan al-munkar). Managing in-house disputes (ikhtilaf) has been part of this legal fabric. Such work has also long exceeded the formal boundaries of law, however.[16] In efforts to re-animate the events and deeds of predecessors long ago for contemporary audiences, salafi thinkers have had to offer bold new accounts of world transformation and the ways forces both great and evil impinge on daily life. Lessons on creed have proven a valuable resource for narrating this drama. What core beliefs define the path of God's true servants? How can Islam's central message of monotheism—God is singular, divine ordinance comes through prophecy, revelation is conveyed through scripture, and so forth—illuminate the complexities of an often tormented human existence? When daily rites and actions don't meet the mark, what higher order comforts the Muslim and preserves life's purpose? Salafis regularly eschew the idea that they engage in theological debate (kalam), a practice condemned by the Sunni establishment due to internecine conflicts fueled by their rubrics in the tenth century. Theology also comes through broad inquiry into the nature of the divine and its relation to human lifeworlds, however. Such inquiry has long engaged salafi reformers and their audiences because it invites answers cast in far more ordinary and accessible terms than those in Islamic jurisprudence. Al-Tahhan would come to master the art of creedal exposition. His students were regularly moved to tears when contemplating the majesty to be witnessed through everyday struggles with norms of identity, community, and selfhood.

In what follows, I examine one of Al-Tahhan's most explicit lectures on "the base" (*al-qa'ida*) with an aim of understanding how he situates Muslim activism at the intersections of law and theology. As I have argued in previous chapters, the concept of "the base" is only obliquely related to the militant frameworks of computer databases, military or terrorist bases, or even ideologically "solid bases" (following popular interpretations of 'Abdalla 'Azzam's concept) that are frequently cited by theoreticians of jihad, whether Muslim or non-Muslim.[17] Rather, the concept is far more flexible, conditional and redeployable, its foundations in legal theory as well as Arabic linguistics highlighted by speakers as they explore the contingencies of general ethical precepts. In what follows, I move beyond the narrow legal terminology of salafism to explore how potential ruptures in legal arguments (such as varieties of "contradictory disputation" mentioned at the chapter's outset) grant militants license to invoke supra-legal foundations of human agency, some of which espouse violence.

The cassette cartridge label reading "My brother struggler: Listen—plan—carry out 'al-Qa'ida'" represents a selective redeployment of Al-Tahhan's speech. As explored below, the label is affixed only to the second and third cassettes of a three-part series featuring a lecture delivered in the 1980s under a more auspicious title: "The Position of the Astute on People's Dispute" (*Mawqif Al-Akyas min Ikhtilaf Al-Nas*). After considering the lessons of this talk, I explore the implications of this selective labeling for understanding the intellectual arsenal of those supporting bin Laden's anti-American militancy in the years leading up to 11 September.

In the first of the three cassettes, Al-Tahhan's lecture draws from standard elements of a salafi treatise on "loyalty and disavowal" (*al-wala' wa-l-bara'*). Much as other authors have done when employing the genre, Al-Tahhan lays out his vision of the ways the doctrine of God's oneness (*al-tawhid*), so key to salafi credal works, can be preserved amidst the influences of polytheists, including Jews, Christians, and especially fellow Muslims.[18] Of foremost importance is the matter of independent legal reasoning in Islamic law (*ijtihad*), a subject which, although occasionally grounds for dispute among Muslims, should be understood as a framework for accommodating pluralism above all. Postponing elaboration on the topic until the second tape, however, Al-Tahhan moves to what he considers to be the more serious threat to Islam: the question of "love" or "friendship" (*al-mahabba*). Some Muslims befriend Islam's sworn enemies, foremost among them Western-influenced Muslim intellectuals who pedal theories drawn from modern psychology to defend their expositions of "things as they really are."[19] The hubris of human secularism, then, imperils the Islamic community by implanting into Muslims a false sense of friendship. After elaborating upon the nature of this threat by recourse to the concept of radical "ignorance" or rebellion against God's sovereignty (*jahiliyya*), so marked in the writings of Sayyid Qutb and Pakistani reformer Abu al-A'la Al-Mawdudi, Al-Tahhan strikes upon a wholly different and more Saudi-influenced path by moving to the core theological assertion of his lecture: believers must learn to cultivate "two wills" (*iradatan*) that inform their life as modern Muslims. First, he asserts, they must learn to love properly; second, they must learn to hate in equal measure. The necessity of coming to terms with these two wills, moreover, is made manifest by the fact that God, too, shares this experience of opposing wills; indeed, it is one of his "essential attributes" (*sifat*). The name for this characteristic is "hesitation" (*taraddud*). Drawing from a *hadith* narrated from Abu Hurayra in which God is depicted as conflicted over taking the human being's life,[20] Al-Tahhan states:

> If there are both obedience and disobedience [to God] in a person, we shall love him to the extent of his obedience and dislike whatever disobedience and violations he is guilty of. Thus, in our hearts there would be love for him from one perspective, and hatred (*bughd*) towards him from another perspective. This matter [of love and hatred]—just as they exist simultaneously in us, they also exist concurrently in our Lord, may He be glorified and exalted, regarding a particular matter which we're subject to.

The central premise of Al-Tahhan's lecture is that God's attribute of hesitation is defined by what humans experience: death.[21] This charac-

teristic is perfectly expressed by God, of course, and Al-Tahhan, along
with other established Saudi jurists, defend this characterization of God
from critics' charges of anthropomorphism by saying that human "hesitation" is altogether different, since they lack a knowledge of what is to
come in the future and thus hesitate because they are uncertain.[22] Critics
such as Grand Mufti Ahmad Al-Khalili of Oman, however, remain
unconvinced, and view such positions on God's "two wills" as indicative
of Wahhabi tendencies to liken God to humans (*tashbih*), a profound
violation of divine unicity (*tawhid*) founded in dangerous theological
arguments that God changes "states."[23]

As Al-Tahhan's lecture continues, he further elaborates the ways ethical action is to be grounded in humans' experience with the conflicts
and contradictions of sentiment and sensory observation. In the struggle
to recognize that, within each of us, love and hatred both vie for
supremacy, the Muslim's task lies in balancing the two sentiments
together while giving a slight advantage to love. The challenge of keeping love and hate proportionally balanced is exacerbated by Western
orders of secular humanism—especially psychologists, "callers at the
Gates of Hell"—who accentuate and pervert older forms of Islamic
theological rationalism (*'ilm al-kalam*). Still, Al-Tahhan's focus on fac-
tionalism is directed primarily to inter-Muslim strife, a discord that is
informed by a more profound ontological condition: Muslims are a
fallen people, and the knowledge once held by the pious predecessors
(*salaf*) during the Prophet's time and in the two generations that followed has been irretrievably lost forever. Having succumbed to whims
of desire, Muslims can best repair their moral community by showing
absolute loyalty to rulers lest dissension further erode their unity.
Indeed, the surest ethical anchor for Muslims is not public involvement
and action but rather seclusion and hesitation accompanied by physical
and sensory asceticism (*al-zuhd*). Much in the manner of sleep, labeled
elsewhere the "small death," such retraction from the commonsense
world opens access to the far more powerful experience of "spiritual
insight" (*ru'ya*), in which visions of divine authority grant Muslims a
practical means for combating injustice in this world.[24]

Such abstinence proves to be a preparatory stage, then, an "initial
fortification" best exemplified by seventh-century Arab Companions of
the Prophet. With Apocalyptic themes of hellish gatekeepers ("psychologists"), earthquakes, deformations, and End Times, Al-Tahhan says

"loners" (*ghuraba'*) can rebuild the community.[25] In fact, to undertake such action in a contemporary world marked by greater perversions of desire and liberal intellectualism than the Muslim community has ever known is to invite divine rewards grander than even the Prophet's own Companions could have enjoyed.[26]

The second of the three tapes focuses on Islamic law, especially the question of disputation (*ikhtilaf*). First, he continues discussion of a small vanguard of loners—a small group (*jama'a*) can be formed of several persons or even one individual—and argues that this group can form its own "majority" upon which consensus over Islamic law and *Sunna* can be assembled. The model for such a path-breaking collective is the Persian "Imam, Godly scholar, and Shaikh of Islam" Muhammad bin Aslam Al-Tusi, a contemporary of Ahmad Ibn Hanbal's, who challenged the vainglorious Khurasani amir 'Abdalla bin Tahir and was condemned to suffer in prison for his impudence.[27] From withdrawal and seclusion, then, comes extraordinary political redemption, first and foremost against errant fellow Muslims. The weapons for such redemption are ideally forged not through militant training but rather through Islamic law. Al-Tahhan cites the importance of prayer, in particular, but moves quickly to matters of managing disputes (*ikhtilaf*), a healthy and necessary element of Islamic law that ensures a tolerance for pluralism as expressed and defended through reasoned debates about concrete legal norms (*al-furu'*).[28] Striking a more optimistic tone, Al-Tahhan devotes the entirety of the second and third cassettes to managing *ikhtilaf* both intellectually and emotionally. In summary, disputes arise primarily from differing methods of independent legal reasoning (*ijtihad*). Disputes can be "aspectual" (*tanawwu'*), focusing on statements or reasoning methods that, while ostensibly incompatible, are reconcilable by virtue of their relation to each other within broader classes and types of knowledge (historical, legal, exegetical, linguistic, dispositional). In contrast with aspectual disputation, contradictory disputes (*tadadd*) involve two positions that are not mutually correct. Al-Tahhan states that while this is the most dangerous form of dispute, it may still be tenable and sustained if no conclusive evidence from *hadith*s and consensus can be provided to reject one of the two views. Comprehensional disputes (*ifham*), noted by bin Laden's secretary as mentioned at the outset of this chapter, occurs when *hadith* interpreters take recourse to personal and cultural knowledge that does not impinge on correct legal practice, and so is not addressed by Al-Tahhan.[29]

The conditions and qualifications for disputes hinge on a key concept, as the label appended to volumes two and three of Al-Tahhan's trilogy suggests: the *qaʿida*, a flexible "base" or template of attunement that steers Muslims toward what they share in common. While the concept is deployed indirectly in a range of narratives about the contingency of sacred law, it is mentioned explicitly twice during the lecture, both times on the second cassette. In the first instance, reference to the *qaʿida* follows a defense of the allegorical interpretation (*taʾwil*) of Qurʾanic verses that are deemed ambiguous (*mutashabihat*). Portraying such reasoning as integral to legal interpretation (*tafsir*) based on personal opinion (*raʾy*), an especially important concept for Hanafi scholars, Al-Tahhan urges his listeners to ground their insights in a mastery not only of Islamic legal texts but also of Arabic:

> Legal interpretation based on [personal] opinion: is it permissible or not? If one looks into the books of later authors, one would see strange things. [Some authors] say that scholars considered it permissible, providing evidence for their stance, while other scholars say it was not considered permissible, providing other evidence. Take it easy, my man, and be fair with scholarly issues! There is no need to provoke a difference of opinion on an issue when there is no difference of opinion.

> Legal interpretation based on [personal] opinion has two possible conditions. Each of the two conditions is agreed upon by our scholars with no differences of opinion. Interpretation based on opinion which is done in accordance with precepts (*qawaʿid*) of Arabic and Islamic legal texts is unanimously considered permissible. Interpretation relying on [personal] opinion based on whims, however, not drawing upon either [the Arabic] language or a legal text is unanimously prohibited.

In this instance, the *qaʿida* (plural *qawaʿid*) is obtained through recourse to the established conventions of Arabic discourse and signification that have been identified and standardized by Islam's earliest grammarians and legal specialists. Many of these individuals worked from the eighth century onwards to formalize Arabic rhetoric so that Islamic law and the *Sunna* (the moral pathway based on the Qurʾan and *hadith* traditions) could be developed in accordance with what were perceived to be the original utterances of the Prophet Muhammad and his Arab community. In the previous chapter, I explored the ways militants such as bin Laden and Mustafa Al-Hamid differed from established jurists over the interpretation and use of "precepts." In this case, Al-Tahhan avoids potential tensions between the legal derivation of "personal opinion" (*ra'y*) and privileged competences in Arabic by invoking a contrast with the kind of "opinion" that ostensibly marked pre-Islamic Arabs and that—driven by "desire" (*hawa*) and egotistic intellectualism—has culminated in Western psychology influenced by "Freud, Hegel, and Hitler."

In the concept's second invocation, Al-Tahhan is already deep into a discussion about the ways in which legal specialists may approach given cases through different processes of reasoning, arrive at dramatically different judgments, and yet still be considered to have performed meritorious ethical action founded on a common "base." After reviewing several legal rulings that involve differences over "general" (*'amm*) and "particular" (*khass*) applications, Al-Tahhan asserts the following:

> This is a precept (*qa'ida*) of theirs which [the legal specialists] believe in and support through considerable evidence. I don't want to say that one or another is stronger, but rather, that each of the two opinions relies upon well-established evidence from the Prophet, praise be upon him. There is no need to accuse one another of misguidance, wrongdoing, or heresy. There is no need for conflict or disagreement. He who thinks that a given position is stronger should act accordingly and should leave the other to act as he wishes. He should not cry out: 'You are violating the *Sunna*.' No! If he were to desert others because of this, he would be the one who actually violates the *Sunna*, threatens the unity of Muslims and creates dissension (*yufarriq*) in their communities.

The function of the rule or "precept" (*qa'ida*) here proves central to Al-Tahhan's narrative of the unifying foundations of creed (*'aqida*) for all Muslims. Indeed, to split with other Muslims over differences of sustained legal argument proves grounds for the charge of sectarianism. In Al-Tahhan's formulation, then, the concept of the *qa'ida* is intended to be a unifying one, and is not meant to license the kinds of isolationist or extremist mandates that are frequently associated with the term al-Qa'ida by those who would designate bin Laden's group as a religious or ideological "off-shoot."

The third tape in the series extends the discussion of managing *ikhtilaf*. The most scholarly of the three tapes, it gives strong emphasis to legal reasoning and the dangers of ossified legalism in established schools of Islamic law. This discussion is accompanied by strong condemnations of those who excommunicate other Muslims for differences of ritual practice or belief that cannot be conclusively defended through recourse to *hadith* and consensus. Overall, the formalization of Islamic law for

Al-Tahhan contains a seed of alienation of religion from its practitioners. He advocates re-discovering an earlier purity of knowledge that marked Hanbali thought, especially as transmitted through Hanafi legal scholars' more ecumenical horizons.

Given Al-Tahhan's overt lack of militant incitements, how might his lecture have been appropriated by those seeking to brand bin Laden's movement as "al-Qaʿida" for a wider audience before 11 September? How might Al-Tahhan's careful legal and theological excurses have been distorted and re-deployed toward violent scenarios of world transformation? The marketing of Al-Tahhan's lecture on audiotape provides tentative answers. Given the ninety-minute limit on standard commercial audiotapes, Al-Tahhan's roughly four-hour lecture had to be split into three separate volumes.[30] Originally, a recording studio in Jeddah grouped the three volumes together and sold them as the inaugural lectures in a thirty-eight volume series of Al-Tahhan's recordings.[31] During the late 1990s, propagandists in Riyadh, seeking to legitimate bin Ladin's controversial strain of militancy, affixed the "al-Qaʿida" message to only the latter two volumes and marketed them through a studio in the city called Islamic Pious Fear Recordings (*Tasjilat Al-Taqwa Al-Islamiyya*). The result of such marketing is that the emphasis in volumes two and three on legal reasoning is branded under the rubric of a "base" or "precept" that should accommodate and also discipline diverse Islamic movements, while the more radical theological strains of volume one, including God's "two wills" as well as the broader discourse on "loyalty and disavowal," Western-influenced secularism, and the necessity of isolation from one's own errant co-religionists, is bracketed separately.[32] As the integrity of Al-Tahhan's lecture is fractured, the relation between legal and theological disciplines becomes perilously strained. On the "al-Qaʿida" cassettes, leadership is portrayed as a moral enterprise founded in a comprehensive understanding of Islamic legal reasoning and exercised through doctrinal practice, including testimony (*shahada*), prayer, Qurʾanic recitation, exegesis of the Qurʾan and transmitted *hadiths*, and independent legal reasoning (*ijtihad*). The ethics of such leadership are expressed in the concept of the *qaʿida*, a term which, as outlined in the last chapter, signifies legal principles that have been deduced from Prophetic sayings or from important rulings and consensus by jurists. Crucially, such principles are easily qualified in practice, given their generality; indeed, it is their contingency in relation to culturally situated ethical practices that makes knowledge of them essential for defending a broader range of Muslim interpretations. Militants such as bin Laden who argue for indiscriminate violence against non-combatants, a position rejected by even the most conservative legal scholars,[33] take the contingencies of the *qaʿida* as a license not only to abrogate previous legal rulings and consensus about "commanding right and forbidding wrong" but also to assert their inspired authorization to dictate legal norms afresh. Bin Laden's own attempts to justify such exceptionalism led him to elaborate narratives of continuing onslaughts on the Arabian Peninsula, whether from sixth-century Abyssinian Monophysites or from a twenty-first century "Jewish-Christian Crusader Alliance" worldwide. As narratives of cosmic war against non-Muslims are mobilized territorially and historically through reference to the privileged claims of Arab leaders in particular, bin Laden and other al-Qaʿida militants would naturally take recourse in theological accounts of mankind's privileged relationship with God, especially if exemplified by the Prophet's early Companions. Volume one of Al-Tahhan's lecture not only focuses on this relationship but also gives it a radically existential turn that derives an essential characteristic of God from mankind's own struggles with hatred and death, especially those launched by a minority group or even a single individual taking action under assault from Western secular aggression. The volatile implications of such a position are dramatized, objectified, and subject to a more maverick range of interpretations when distributed on a cassette that is marketed and sold separately from its accompanying volumes. In effect, "al-Qaʿida" becomes a bid for unity which, while ostensibly privileging an umbrella framework for diverse currents in Islamic activism, coaches listeners on how to manage a far more exclusionary set of claims to knowledge and justice. For Al-Tahhan, the tactics of such critical reform begin with scholarly training, and even in their ultimate end must be fully compatible with the living tradition of Islamic law; for militants armed with branding strategies, the tactics of reform begin with more accessible repertoires of technological and media manipulation.

Between 1999 and 2001, when I estimate the re-branding of Al-Tahhan's lecture to have occurred, bin Laden found himself walking a fine line between his new status as an international terrorist financier bent on attacking the United States and his older reputation as an Arab-Afghan veteran capable of purging Muslim lands of their occupiers. The rhetorical compass and erudition of a tape series labeled "Listen, Plan, and Carry Out 'al-Qa'ida'" was likely to have aided recruitment in several ways. First, from 1999 onwards, Saudi militants began to outnumber Egyptian militants at the camps, a phenomenon largely attributable to the Egyptian state's co-optation of extremist elements through electoral and political reform.[34] Al-Tahhan's lecture not only coached young Saudis on the tenets of salafist activism attuned to their own national context but also gave them a more ecumenical vocabulary for mobilizing support for controversial causes beyond their Arabian intellectual milieus. Especially valuable in this regard was Al-Tahhan's training in Hanafi jurisprudence, a school of Islamic legal interpretation that, while under-represented in the Kingdom, is the most common among Muslims worldwide and in Afghanistan and Pakistan specifically. Over a decade earlier, bin Laden and 'Abdalla 'Azzam had overseen the marketing of Al-Tahhan's lectures on an audiotape series exceeding fifty volumes distributed from the media shop of their Peshawar-based Office of Services.[35] Al-Tahhan's recordings would subsequently dwarf the piecemeal contributions of other Hanafi scholars represented in bin Laden's own tape collection. Featuring discussions of everything from Islamic legal practice to divine sovereignty, his tapes gave attention to topics regularly considered anathema by the Saudi salafi establishment, such as the defensibility of tomb visitation along with experiences of hierophanic witnessing (*ru'ya*), intercession (*shafa'a*), and blessings (*karamat*). For Saudi preacher Safar Al-Hawali, such visitation was evidence enough of Arab-Afghans' "errancy" and susceptibility to deployment as "American stooges" in battles not their own.[36] Through the 1980s and again at the turn of the millennium, Al-Tahhan's lectures offered refreshing new perspectives to Saudi and Arab activists looking to build bridges with fellow Muslims in the Hanafi heartlands. Most Saudis who arrived in Afghanistan after 1999 for training and deployment, after all, cited Hanafi-majority Chechnya as their cause célèbre and preferred combat locale.[37]

Second, the tape series would also have done much to reassure wealthy Arab donors, most of them from Saudi Arabia and the Arab Gulf States, that bin Laden was primarily in the business of supporting guerrilla insurgency rather than terrorist operations against civilians. Given media coverage of bin Laden's activities at the time, this message would have involved considerable marketing and presentation skills.[38] By 1999, bin Laden began hosting hunting trips for wealthy Arab elites from the Gulf in the hill country around Kandahar. Al-Tahhan's tape, when segmented into three volumes and repackaged to foreground a far less controversial pan-Islamic legal vocabulary, would have made a fine parting gift. Far more so, indeed, than a reprint of the 1998 Declaration of Jihad Against Jews and Crusaders.

Memoires by Arab-Afghan veterans attest to the power of theology in recruitment. Moroccan-born militant "Omar Nasiri," who worked as an undercover agent for British and French intelligence services, held theological training to be a litmus test defining al-Qa'ida's true leaders. While in London in the late 1990s, Nasiri wrote of his first impressions of the Egyptian militant cleric Abu Hamza Al-Masri, currently in prison in the United Kingdom for using his sermons to incite racial hatred:

> I was even more amazed when I heard Abu Hamza speak. He knew nothing at all about theology, which seemed odd for someone who had gone through the camps. He was very loud and very passionate, but to me he also seemed very stupid. He was trying to defend the GIA [Algeria's Groupe Islamique Armée] in terms of Islamic law, but it was clear to me that he didn't know what he was talking about. It was clear to Abu Qatada and Abu al-Walid as well; they demolished every argument he put forward…I came out of that meeting understanding two things very clearly: Abu Qatada was a true scholar, and Abu Hamza was nothing more than a demagogue.[39]

When Nasiri tried to explain to British intelligence officers that Abu Qatada and Abu al-Walid al-Filistini were far more dangerous figures, he was waved off and re-assigned the task of monitoring Abu Hamza Al-Masri at the Finsbury Mosque, a decision he laments in his book given the far more transnational militant influence of the first two since that time. Under the newly coined al-Qa'ida label, Al-Tahhan's work, too, slipped much under the radar.

14

'UMAR'S WEDDING

(Official recording by al-Qaʿidaʾs Publicity Committee. Afghanistan. Produced in March 2001.[1] Opening remarks, cassette no. 1164.)

Al-Qaʿidaʾs Publicity Committee presents this release to you:

[*Song excerpt*]

> Good fortune appears suddenly, singing of desires
>> Good tidings volley forth: Congratulations!
> As birds perched in branches chant joyfully
>> Such fortune and felicity on the wedding night

[*Song fades out as another fades in.*]

> These days of yours are sweet
> For God is Most Beautiful
> Oh! Oh!…

[*The song continues as more upbeat wedding songs and Islamic anthems follow. After roughly seven minutes, a new recording excerpt begins with introductions by a wedding officiant.*]

[*First Officiant*] Peace and God's mercy and blessings be upon you. May God reward you all.

We welcome all honorable guests who are here to participate with us in this notable celebration. We bring your attention to the fact that the revelry will begin after lunch, God willing. Bon appétit!

Oh honorable participants: we greet you one by one. Especially your chiefs and leaders, the virtuous Shaikhs and honorable guests who are with us in this celebration. God's salutations and congratulations upon you, along with His mercy and blessings. In this wedding celebration dedicated to our brother 'Umar Ibn Abu 'Asim, we celebrate a new program and build a new home for the family of the struggling emigrants (*al-muhajirin al-mujahidin*). The finest way to begin this celebration and to listen with one's ears before hearing people's words is through attending to the words of the Almighty and All-Knowing as set forth in the Holy Qur'an as delivered by our brother Abu al-Ma'ali. Please proceed.

I seek refuge in God from the accursed devil.

[*Qur'anic recitation from the* sura *of Jonah: 57–65.*]

O humankind! There hath come to you a direction from your Lord and a healing for what is in your hearts, and for those who believe, a guidance and a mercy.

Say: "In the bounty of God and in His mercy, in that let them rejoice": it is better than all [the wealth] that they may amass!

Say: "See what things God has sent down to you for sustenance? Yet you hold forbidden some things thereof and make some things lawful." Say: "Has God indeed permitted you, or do you invent [things] to attribute to God?"

And what think those who invent lies against God of the Day of Judgment? Verily God is full of bounty to humankind but most of them are ungrateful.

In whatever condition you may find yourself, and whatever portion you may be reciting from the Qur'an, and whatever deed you may be doing, we are witnesses thereof when you are deeply engrossed. Nor is hidden from your Lord [so much as] the weight of an atom on the earth or in heaven. And not the least and not the greatest of these things happen but they are recorded in a manifest Book.

Behold! Verily on the friends of God there is no fear, nor shall they grieve;

Those who believed and had been God-fearing;

For them are glad tidings, in the life of the present and in the hereafter: no change can there be in the words of God. This is indeed the supreme triumph!

Let not their speech grieve you: for all power and honor belong to God: It is He who hears and knows all things.

[*Recitation ends, and the officiant resumes.*]

[*First Officiant*] Yes, in the bounty of God let them rejoice. The bounties of God upon us are numerous. The bounties of God, Glorious and Exalted is He, are countless and inestimable. It is through His bounty that we convene here today in this blessed gathering, united in this place of honor and empowerment.

The following is a group of sayings from the Chosen One [the Prophet Muhammad], God's blessings and salutations upon him. May they perfume our ears. He says, God's blessings and salutations upon him:

Whoever humbles himself, God will elevate him.

Whoever grows arrogant, God will humiliate him.

Whoever does not thank people will not be grateful to God.

Whoever shows the path to the good will be rewarded as if he had performed the good deed himself.

Whoever does not invoke God will incur God's wrath.

Whoever steals from the spoils of war is not of us.

Whoever carries a weapon against us is not of us.

He also says:

Whoever remains silent [in times of tribulation] will be saved.

Whoever belittles His blessings will be deprived of all good.

Whoever imitates a people is indeed one of them.

Whoever struggles to support a fighter on the path of God, it is as though he himself fought.

Whoever looks after a fighter's family, it is as though he himself fought.

Whoever prays in my name once, God blesses him tenfold.

Pray to the Prophet of God. Blessed be your wedding, 'Umar. All your struggling brothers in this blessed land send you their congratulations. We say to you: may God bless you and your wife, and may he bring you two together in goodness. Typically in weddings, grooms usually feel pretty constrained, especially during the wedding ceremony itself. It's like the groom is in a military drill, I mean: he's totally disciplined, neither laughing nor smiling, moving neither right nor left. He just looks forward, sometimes carrying a sword weighing between three to five kilograms on his shoulders, as is the custom in Yemen. He can't move a muscle as the ceremony draws on for hours. You find him in a condition known only to God, Glorious and Exalted is He. We ask God, Glorified and Exalted is He, to ease his burden. It all lasts just one night and it shall pass.

Honorable brothers: it is bizarre to read the news and follow newspapers and magazines. It is hilarious, I mean, to read about the "bat camp"! Have you heard about the bat camp? Anybody heard about this camp? It is a camp that is found in caves belonging to bin Laden. It is called "Bat Camp." Its graduates never laugh. Their hearts are hardened. Our brother, the groom today, I mean, is a graduate of this camp. Here's the strange thing, though: the brother is laughing, praise the Lord! People who live in societies far removed from jihad, its strugglers, and the land of true bonds often imagine the strugglers to be monsters. They think of these guys as vicious, as thirsty for blood and knowing only destruction, killing, and theft. This, they say, is part of an affliction that has struck Muslims in this day and age. If they only knew how the strugglers are a people of goodness and generosity. If they only knew how they ease the tribulation of all nations whether disbelieving or Muslim.

THE AUDACIOUS ASCETIC

We give you an anthem, if only to keep me from blabbering. We don't want to leave you thinking that we are people of idle talk! Here are some brothers who will sing an anthem by the band called "Criterion" [Al-Furqan, *an epithet for the Qur'an.*]

[*Chorus of singers*]

> My trench is my paradise, whoever attacks it meets with hellfire
>> Take up arms, my brothers, we embrace death in the trench
> Come O Salman, with spirit sally forth among us
>> The [enemy] confederation has returned and is headed for Madina[2]

[*Refrain*]

> Say it, for whoever does so is made sincere
>> Say it, the solution is in battle
> Say it and go forth as men!

> Victory shines upon us from those mountains
>> The oath of death is here! Greatness awaits, O men!
> These are the Confederates, inclining toward disgrace
>> Etching shame in faint letters

[*Refrain*]

> Ask history: Did the ranks of men sleep?
>> O world, say: Who is it that does no harm?
> Should conspirators plot against them, God's plotting proves mightier
>> Slowing their clusters and granting them delays indeed

[*Refrain*]

[*First Officiant resumes*]

May God reward you. Again, we congratulate Abu Mustafa [the bride's father] and Abu 'Asim [the groom's father]. We congratulate you all on the occasion of this honorable wedding and great celebration. We ask God, may He be glorified and exalted, to let it proceed in goodness.

The moral path (*Sunna*) of marriage, especially for the emigrant and struggler, punishes enemies. For this reason it is desirable and even recommended by Islamic law. Many who have abandoned their religion think, in their state of flight, that they cannot get married. They think this because they lack stability, moving from one place to another in fear, always traveling and filled with terror. In fact, the opposite is true. Consider the story of Moses, salutations upon him, and how he fled from the pharaoh and his people and became a wanted man. When Moses arrived in the villages of Midian [east of Mount Sinai], he watered the flock of two women who were holding back [from a well, since they were crowded out by the flocks of older male shepherds]. He uttered his famous supplication: "O Lord! Truly am I in need of

348

any goodness that You can send me!"[3] One of the two women then approached him, walking bashfully. The story is well known, but its point is this: Moses at this time, in the very hour he had become a wanted man, married and found himself greatly improved. After this blessed marriage, what came to him but revelation (al-wahy), for God, Glorious and Exalted is He, spoke to him on the right side of Mount Sinai.

[*Recording briefly interrupted.*]

This is what grabs the attention of the youth! If you just lay things out straight up, or whatever, they instantly [get embarrassed and] say "God is Greater!" since the issue is, I mean [somewhat sensitive.] This is why we can't separate something called "marriage" from something else called "politics." Can we say there is no marriage in politics or politics in marriage? We can't separate [the two], really, so we need to combine the two issues. We are people of a holistic methodology.

All due apologies, 'Umar. People like me will talk freely. The issue, though, is that we must get involved in politics. We absolutely must be involved in politics. If we really look at this issue, I mean, our Islamic peoples have voiced complaints against the governance of rulers. The Egyptian people especially are natural jokers. It is said that the president in their country gets involved in every project, becoming partners with the whole nation in every project, big or small. [For this reason] he always takes a cut of 50 per cent, and sometimes more than that. Once, a Bedouin tribesman from the Sinai Peninsula came to Cairo and went into a café. When he entered, he saw a poster, or rather three posters on the wall. He asked the manager of the café [*the officiant switches into Egyptian Arabic*]:

"Whose poster is this?"

[The manager] said to him: "Don't you know him? This is the late president, Gamal 'Abd al-Nasir. Such an example! This is the founder of a community and the founder of this and that."

He said to him: "Excuse me, son. I'm a Bedouin who doesn't know about these things." He then said to him: "Okay, now whose poster is this one?"

[The manager] said: "This is the poster of the believing president, Anwar Al-Sadat. Don't you see the raisin-like mark on this forehead, the result of prostrating himself in prayer so many times?"

"Good enough. Hey, sorry about that, my son. Okay, so whose poster is this one?"

"La la la la la! You don't know him!" [said the manager.]

"Who is he?"

[*Speaker imitates the manager's astonished stuttering*]: "This…this…this is Hosni Abu 'Ala, the owner of the restaurant!"

[*Audience laughter heard in the background.*]

THE AUDACIOUS ASCETIC

[*First Officiant*] It's all for the best, God willing. We're going to leave you now with an anthem by Abu Salman called "And the Stories Circulate on the Ground."[4]

[*Singer greets the audience.*] Peace and God's mercy and blessings upon you.

Listen, for we are creators
  Our stories circulate on the ground
About a great matter in jihad
  Its heroes are hardened Arabs
They struck forth, a community of the Prophet most praiseworthy
  Until they reached the peaks and camel humps
They struck forth as equals in a line
  Beseeching the Merciful in the heavens
In exile from their land
  Their souls having compelled them to flee
Forced to flee from exile itself
  Extending their lifespans
Recite these stories from the tear's pen
  Its writing just a sad slave
Trails drawn with fingertips
  That once touched the best of companions
The best of companions, strugglers
  Whose names have become stories and poems
A lion and admonisher from among the noble-born
  A victor and father of Hussain
To those who ask questions: he sought aggression
  How he bore his wings
In the final days of the noble month
  'Your mount set forth, O martyr!'
They came, and upon their shoulders
  They carried the wounded one, that martyr
Carried the wounded one in his sadness
  Carried the martyr in his happiness
As the bird set out alone, wrapped in silence
  Beautiful is that recompense from the Almighty
How Kandahar knows the suffering of Mecca's Sacred House.

[*New anthem begins.*]

For the region of Shakardara [near Kabul], how my heart clings to what happened
  It now sees the entirety of life as grief
Ahmad, then Najm al-Din, then 'Azam followed by Hasan
  You'll find them with the dark-eyed beauties of paradise, sitting without grief
Adolescents as sweet as sugar, as fragrant as ambergris their remembrance
  Greater yet is my affliction, for in their departure I carry such grief

[*First Officiant resumes*]

May God reward you. You have reminded us of some of our brothers who have preceded us into the gardens of eternity. Our brothers have revealed the unfolding of history to us. They were not harmed by their critics or fearful, for God's sake, of those who might blame them.

Honorable brothers [*recording interrupted*] with Shaikh Abu 'Abdulla [Osama bin Laden]. Anyone with a question on their mind, whether about reality or fiction, the near or far, the antique or contemporary—go ahead and ask it of the Shaikh directly. This is an open meeting between all of you and Shaikh Abu 'Abdalla. Please proceed, may God reward you all.

[*Newly recorded excerpt features the first question by a young man.*]

Peace be upon you. Honorable Shaikh: why do you direct your strikes toward America only and not toward the Jews in Palestine?

[*First Officiant*] May God reward you.

[*Bin Laden responds in a very quiet voice.*] Praise be to God. Blessings and salutations on Muhammad, his family, and all his companions. Now then: it is no secret that the Crusader-Zionist alliance is like two banknotes of the same currency. We must strike them both. Breaking the back of Zionism will come from breaking the back of the Crusaders, with God's permission, Glorious and Exalted is He. America is foremost among them. Striking Zionism will set limits on the Crusader-American advance. We ask God, Glorious and Exalted is He, to assist us in striking them both. I give you glad tidings that we are about to hear news of both of them, God willing. We ask God to grant our brothers success.

[*Second Officiant shouts out*] Say God is Greater!

[*Audience shouts*] God is Greater!

[*Recording interrupted, then the voice of an audience member is heard mid sentence.*] … to surrender to a new administration, and has attacked Iraq, I mean, without any justification. What is your analysis with regards Islam and Muslims? What directions are we moving in, as strugglers?

[*Bin Laden*] Praise be to God. With regards to the latest strike that was carried out against Iraq, it is a very powerful indication of the weakness and utter folly of American politics at present.[5] The American regime and the new administration wanted to "turn up the heat" and divert some attention from Palestine by attacking Iraq before Colin Powell, the Secretary of State, undertook his latest tour. [This tour was designed] to seek support and lend credibility to the idea that the [American] administration wants to take down the Iraqi regime. So it was one of the most unsuccessful visits that has occurred in the last decade. It was the first visit for this secretary, and the visit met with severe opposition in the region beginning with Egypt and the Gulf States. Even international radio coverage, including the *Voice of America*, reported Gulf newspaper headlines condemning this attack and refusing this policy. It is no secret that newspapers in the Gulf are governmental controlled, and [as such are] indirect mouthpieces for official governments. [Secretary Powell] returned, then, empty-handed and having accomplished nothing. Whoever follows statements made on many occasions by the new American administration will notice the weakness of its political capacities and its ability to continue putting pressure on the region. They are constrained or are beginning to be constrained, praise be to God. Our affairs look promising, by contrast. The enemy didn't move a finger after God granted victory to the strugglers in Nairobi [Kenya] and Dar Al-Salam [Tanzania], Glorious and Exalted is He. After God granted the strugglers victory in smashing their destroyer in Aden, [the Americans] avoided direct finger-pointing even though they know which of the brothers God led in this operation, Glorious and Exalted is He. They are weak, while as I've mentioned before, our own matters proceed well, with steadfastness and promise. We ask God to give us and you resolve and to grant victory to our struggling brothers. Praise be to God.

[Recording interrupted, then a third question is posed by an audience member.] What can you say about the influence of having destroyed the U.S.S. Cole, both locally and internationally?

[Bin Laden] With regards to the attack on the Cole, there is not enough time here to discuss its influence. The more time that passes, though, and the more people become aware, the more likely they will learn someday about the magnificence of this attack. May God grant them martyr status to the honorable brothers who were guided [on this attack], Al-Midrar Ibrahim Al-Thawr and our brother Hasan ['Awad Al-Khamri.][6] We ask God to receive them. We are at a dangerous juncture in the history of our pious community, as it ascends higher. At the same time, it is a downhill juncture for our opponent. This greater idolater legislates for people by laws other than God's own as it beholds the countenances of Arab and non-Arab rulers turning toward him. How they listen and obey him godlessly, far away from the Lord of the Ancient House [the Ka'ba], Glorious and Exalted is He. This same idolater threatens the whole region with its weapons and great destroyers. Tyrants render their submission accordingly. The only exceptions are people of true faith and righteousness, though God alone will be their final judge. Such people refuse to trade their religion for a lowly life. With the help of God, Glorious and Exalted is He, they destroyed the greatest destroyer on the surface of the sea. The consequences of this attack have had a tremendous political, economic, and even psychological effect on Americans. Even they have been overcome with humiliation and submission. In the wake of the attack, they commissioned an admiral and general to lead an investigation committee. Praise be to God. The committee wrote a report about the aftermath and made recommendations on avoiding such an incident in the future. Following a press conference after they returned home, their own radio service, the *Voice of America*, declared that they found the magnitude of the destruction highly disturbing. Praise be to God. Since the

strike, as I've mentioned, the scale of press coverage has increased as journalists try to understand what is on our minds. Among their questions has been: is your enmity directed against the West in general or against America in particular? Is there anything in the West, I mean, that can be reconciled with your views or that you consider to be good? Anything at all? I mean, they want to study the psychology of those who struggle against the West in an attempt to contain the healthy phenomenon [of jihad] that God, Glorious and Exalted is He, has bestowed upon us! We ask God to make us and you steadfast...

[*First Officiant*] May God reward Shaikh Abu 'Abdalla for his good contribution. These are indeed very special messages for 'Umar Ibn Abu 'Asim. His brothers in the personal security detachment (*al-hirasa al-lasiqa*) greet and congratulate him. They say: may God bless you and your marriage and may He accept your acts of obedience. We know that the heart is saddened because you are leaving the detachment, 'Umar. We ask Him to give you righteous offspring. Sincerely, your guardian brothers.

Another special message comes from the brother "The Northerner" (*Al-Shami*). He says: I tell you, dear brother and companion, may God bless you and your marriage and unite the two of you on good terms. We ask God, may He be glorified, to give you righteous children who will carry out the struggle and keep the enemy's wounds from healing. May God guard and protect you.

[*Representative of the Athletics Committee*] May God reward the Shaikh, our brother Abu 'Ubaida [*likely the name of the First Officiant*]. Oh dear ones: the athletics committee insists on a competition between the bachelors and those who are married. Since our married brothers are off the hook today given their obligations to attend the wedding of our brother 'Umar 'Asim, the onus is upon them to show up tomorrow at ten o'clock in the morning. Their bachelor-team cheer will be: beat us and you'll get to marry us off!...

[*On the opposite side of the tape, another officiant begins by introducing a poem.*]

[*Third Officiant*] Here are a few verses of poetry, my beloved ones. I present them to the Imam of the Strugglers in these sad times, may God preserve and guide him: our Shaikh, Osama bin Muhammad bin 'Awad bin Laden, may God preserve him with His protection, Glorious and Exalted is He.

> A star twinkles in our radiant sky
> > As at the outset of night, in our moonlit darkness
> He appears to us as the generous shaikh
> > Like the sun shining with light most radiant
> Unyielding piety descends to our horizons
> > While his place climbs toward heaven, perfuse with ambergris

THE AUDACIOUS ASCETIC

For he dwells in the passion of our hearts like a guest
   Our open spaces and platforms lift him aloft
Welcome to the assembly, Shaikh
   Bringer of prosperity and good tidings
By God, I ask that his reward be multiplied
   For God acknowledges those who borrow and return his favor

Oh God's beloved ones: in a recent monthly issue of the [Egyptian run] *Al-Sharq Al-Awsat* newspaper, the front page discussed a state (*dawla*) founded by Shaikh Osama, may God preserve him. This state is called Jihadistan, though it lacks borders and a population estimate.

[*Second Officiant shouts out*] Say God is Greater!

[*Audience shouts*] God is Greater!

[*Third Officiant*] We ask God, Glorious and Exalted is He, to delight us with the victory of His loyal subjects, for He is sovereign and most capable of this.

[*First Officiant*] This state consists of a small number of strugglers. What do you think if the entire pious community went forth to struggle? What would be the condition of the disbelievers? Imagine the situation! And now: a contribution from our brothers from the northern Arab lands, our brother Abu Osama the Palestinian, may God reward him. Please proceed.

My brother, how our thoughts have been comforted
   By the promise of God, the All-powerful and Steadfast
The prison fueled nothing but our tenacity
   The shackle nothing but our certitude
The torture of our brothers
   And murder of preachers by the hundreds
Fanned nothing but the flag of our faith
   Showing righteousness and the unity of monotheism
Our Islam will raise your banner
   With the summit of men and unflappable patience
Hoist them high, despite the violence of tyrants
   Show and dispatch them across the worlds
Like Suhayb [Al-Rumi], brother of the pious ones
   Selling his life to make a profit of religion
And Mus'ab [Ibn 'Umayr] who left his comfortable life
   Dwelling as a martyr in the eternal heavens
Hundreds of thousands of sincere believers
   Departed with tenacity, departed with certitude
Even as travelers venture forth in their wake
   With God's assistance, for the victory of religion.

May God reward you all.

[*Second Officiant shouts out*] Say God is Greater!

[*Audience shouts*] God is Greater!

[*First Officiant*] May God bless and reward you all. [*Introducing a new speaker*] Haydara: how could you possibly sum up Haydara? He is in a pious community all to his own. He would like to participate, God willing, may He be praised and exalted. Please proceed.

[*Haydara and a chorus of male singers*] In the name of God, the Compassionate and Caring. This is a poem about camels.

[*Chuckles from the chorus*]

It is entitled "The Camel's Playing Card Has Fallen," and it's an elegy about the condition of camels in our day and age. The meaning of "The Camel's Playing Card Has Fallen" is—I mean, for those who don't know what it means—[the camel's] card has dropped, because these days it is no longer used for transportation.

> If indeed it happened as it happened: [It's like] two slices of onion
>> You can't even work with the fresher of them
> The camel's playing card has fallen
> [*Group chorus*] The camel's playing card has fallen
>
> With a chicken sandwich, *shawarma*, or flatbread,
>> One's mood will get straightened out
> [*Group chorus*] The camel's playing card has fallen
> [*Group chorus*] The camel's playing card has fallen
>
> And Ahmad, the Berber, most pleasing to the foreigner
>> His wound has yet to heal
> [*Group chorus*] The camel's playing card has fallen
> [*Group chorus*] The camel's playing card has fallen
>
> The struggle is [now carried out] through the machine gun, cannon, and tank
> [*Group chorus*] The camel's playing card has fallen
> [*Group chorus*] The camel's playing card has fallen
>
> Trips are [now] by taxi, ship, and plane
> [*Group chorus*] The camel's playing card has fallen
> [*Group chorus*] The camel's playing card has fallen
>
> As many greetings to the guests as there are storm clouds, knots of wool
>> And sheep trotting by
> [*Group chorus*] The camel's playing card has fallen
> [*Group chorus*] The camel's playing card has fallen
>
> Peace be upon you…

[*Shortly after, Side B begins with an anthem that echoes the following* [*refrain:*]]

> Our son's master is death
>> By You, God! Hey, hey, hey

THE AUDACIOUS ASCETIC

By God, martyrdom is a gift
    May its blessedness be mine, my Lord

As I began to take leave
    They said "The final separation is near at hand"
I said "Love will carry on
    With sincerity and intention"
[*Refrain*]

Oh you who carries the toxic Bika rocket launcher
    [Say] God is Greater!
Strike America
    With a cruise [missile] and a tank
[*Refrain*]

Saddam, O Saddam [Hussein]!
    Oh rubbish of the rulers!
You who replaced the Prophet's moral path (*Sunna*)
    With Ba'athist decrees
[*Refrain*]

Oh you who climb up to Ta'if [*the summer residence of wealthy Saudis*]
    My heart is afraid of you
From among Al Al-Sa'ud gang
    A band of criminals
[*Refrain*]

Oh Hosni [Mubarak]! Oh cow!
    Oh pillow for the disbeliever!
You who banished that most fresh
    And killed that most righteous

[*Refrain along with more anthems. A new piece ensues with the following refrain:*]

    La la la la la la la, I lodge complaint with those who have wronged me

Our groom is Ibn 'Asim, may your wedding be completed
[*Refrain*]

They called me a fundamentalist
[*Refrain*]

Pray every day, Oh Muslim, for your recompense is with God
    Oh Shaikh bin Laden, your love travels like the astral phases
[*Refrain*]

Oh tree, incline
    My inclination is toward your side
[*Refrain*]

Pray every day, Oh Muslim, for your recompense is with God

[*First Officiant*] Good. Now brothers, before we reach the final round of this celebration, we need to honor the poets. Their compositions won audiences' admiration on the whole, as we've mentioned, and have garnered prizes for this [honorable] purpose. The number one entry winning first prize—a sum of ten million Afghani [*$2,100 U.S. dollars at the time*]—is a poem about the [U.S.S. Cole] destroyer by Shaykh Abu Hafs the Mauritanian.[7] Say "God is Greater!"

[*Audience shouts*] God is Greater!

[*First Officiant*] The prize for second place goes to the poem of our brother Al-Muhannad and comes with five million Afghani. Say "God is Greater!"

[*Audience shouts*] God is Greater!

[*First Officiant*] There's another second-place award for our brother Hazim whose poem receives a prize too. God willing, let's say "God is Greater!" [*Moderate audience response.*] There's also third poem by Abu al-'Abbas Al-Najdi that won. He presented it yesterday and earned third place, winning two-and-a-half million Afghani. May God reward them all.

We close with a few words by our Shaikh Abu 'Abdalla Osama bin Laden, God willing. Please proceed. Many thanks and may the benefits be gainful.

[*Bin Laden*] Praise be to God. Blessings and salutations on Muhammad, his family and all his companions. With regards to honoring the authors of the poems: although they are symbolic matters, God has made some of these poems very influential, Glorious and Exalted is He. They have been broadcast by international news agencies as God brings cheer to the hearts of believers and the nascent pious community experiences a flood of momentum and pride in this religion. May God receive our praise. To conclude this blessed wedding, we repeat our congratulations for our brother 'Umar, asking God, Glorious and Exalted is He, to complete their marriage and bestow upon them righteous offspring that can wage the struggle. And we say: may God bless you, bless your marriage, and unite both of you on good terms.

On occasions like this happy one, in days of contentment, we must take special care to control the tongue. The human being's tongue may slip when in a state of anger or even joy. We ask God to strengthen our piety and the propriety of our speech in states of both anger and of joy, Glorious and Exalted is He. Of the brothers who contributed to this gathering, I mention some in particular, if only as a cautionary measure, may God reward them: some of these brothers speak without giving due consideration to some of their more extemporaneous poetic verses and to some words that praised the poor slave [*referring to himself*]. So, I hope that God, Glorious and Exalted is He, will forgive those of what they know not and that He will make me better than what they think of me. I hope, too, that they will desist from this practice, may God reward them all. We ask for God's forgiveness if some words uttered during this gathering were not properly controlled due to states of joy and cheerfulness. In conclusion, we give blessings and salutations on our Prophet Muhammad, his family and all his companions. Exalted are You, O God, [beyond anything that might be falsely attributed to You], all praise belongs to You. I testify that there is no god but God alone. I seek Your forgiveness and I repent to You…

[*After several more songs, the tape concludes with a studio-recorded voice announcing the final poem to the accompaniment of heavy reverb. The poem is then recited by Osama's son Hamza.*]

> O my father, wither the escape?
> When will we have a stable home?
> Alas, my father, have you not seen the circle of danger?
> You have prolonged my journey, Father, between the wastelands and the settled
> You have prolonged my journey, Father, in every wanton valley
> Until you have forgotten my tribe, the sons of my uncles and human beings all
> Why has our residence disappeared from us without a trace?
> Why has my mother not been able to wonder at the delight of travel?
> My dear brother, sacrificed to the passage of time, appears no more
> Why is it that we see nothing but obstacles and holes along our path?
> Now America has come from beyond to perpetrate defilement. And the news?
> You emigrated as a stranger to the land where the Nile flows down:
> Khartoum, how I yearn for its fragrance! Yet my residence there was denied
> I then journeyed east, to where men were the finest of people:
> Kabul! Kabul! How it raises its head despite all poverty and danger
> The borderlands of Kabul smile, sheltering and aiding whoever comes
> Shaikh Yunis [Khalis] appeared [*the tape ends mid verse*][8]

In March 2001, plans for the 11 September attacks were well under way. By the previous winter, Saudi hijackers Khalid Al-Mihdhar and Nawaf Al-Hazmi had already been in the United States for over a year taking courses in flight training and making preparations. Others would begin joining them in May. In Afghanistan, Kandahar's camps were busy. Amidst long days of weapons training, fitness drills, course work on militancy, and religious studies, an occasion to celebrate arose. One of bin Laden's personal body guards, 'Umar Ibn Abu 'Asim, had at last decided to get married. Weddings were an ideal forum for publicity, bin Laden had recently confided to an Arab journalist.[9] They were a way to get out messages to a broader world audience under tight surveillance by the Taliban and restrictions on his media interviews. Marked only with the handwritten words "Original Copy" (*al-asl*), the audio tape begins with an announcement of sponsorship by "al-Qaʿidaʾs Publicity Committee" (*al-lajnat al-iʿlaniyya li-l-qaʿida*).

Aside from several audiocassettes featuring the cartridge label "Listen, Plan, and Carry Out 'al-Qaʿidaʾ," discussed in the previous chapter, tape no. 1164 is the only recording in bin Ladenʾs former collection branded with the hallmark sign of his own worldwide organization dedicated to militancy and terror. Unlike the other cassettes, al-Qaʿidaʾs professed commander-in-chief does make a guest appearance. A question and answer session is arranged so that audience members can query the amir "about reality or fiction, the near or far, the antique or contemporary." The first question comes at bin Laden like a hornet: "Peace be upon you. Honorable shaikh: why do you direct your strikes toward America only and not toward the Jews in Palestine?" The amir responds quietly, his voice betraying fatigue and disappointment. He evokes the image of paper currency while urging himself toward steely resolve: "it is no secret that the Crusader-Zionist alliance is like two banknotes of the same currency. We must strike them both. Breaking the back of Zionism will come from breaking the back of the Crusaders, with Godʾs permission, Glorious and Exalted is He. America is foremost among them." Following the lead of a drill instructor, audience members give assent with the cry "God is Greater!" (*Allahu Akbar!*). A second question concerns Iraq under American-led sanctions and air strikes. Bin Laden delivers a formulaic response about Americaʾs perceived weaknesses and gloats over the two of the most spectacular attacks by al-Qaʿida against American interests in the last several years: the twin bombings of the American embassies in East Africa on 7 August 1998 and the attack on the U.S.S. Cole destroyer in Aden, Yemen on 12 October 2000. A follow-up question about the Aden bombing grants bin Laden a platform for asserting his repugnance for the West. "They want to study the psychology of those who struggle against the West in an attempt to contain the healthy phenomenon [of jihad] that God, Glorious and Exalted is He, has bestowed upon us!"

Throughout the ceremony, bin Laden is presented as a tribal warrior bent to the task of a holy crusade. "He appears to us as the generous shaikh," declares one rhapsode at the start of the tapeʾs second side: "Like the sun shining with light most radiant/Unyielding piety descends to our horizons/While his place climbs toward heaven, perfuse with ambergris." In an idiom of tribal honor in which shaikhs are generous and their guests well protected, bin Laden earns additional praise for seeking the status of a martyr. A second poem hails martyrdom, torture, and imprisonment as vapors for the "flag of our faith" and commends the pathways of early Muslim ascetics Suhayb Al-Rumi and Musʿab Ibn ʿUmayr.[10] Bin Laden extols such compositions when prizes and cash are distributed to the most popular poets. "Although they are symbolic matters, God has made some of these poems very influential." He also advocates greater sobriety: "On occasions like this happy one, in days of contentment, we must take special care to control the tongue. The human being's tongue may slip when in a state of anger or even joy." As God's "poor slave," bin Laden admonishes his listeners not to let mirth or good cheer privilege the human spirit, even if for a moment, over the divine. Victory against the United States, the "greater idolater," begins with self discipline.

Listeners attuned to the events at hand discover tensions at the heart of bin Laden's ascetic vision, however. Arab-Afghans have gathered, after all, not to celebrate ʿUmar's wedding to a virgin in paradise. The groom is destined for an earthlier bed. What becomes apparent, moreover, is that ʿUmar has chosen life with his new family back in Yemen over the virtues of service under bin Laden abroad.[11] A letter read aloud to the audience from bin Laden's fellow bodyguards expresses sadness "because you are leaving the detachment, ʿUmar" and asks God to "give you righteous offspring." Al-Qaʿida's official propaganda tape provides bin Laden's closest militant associates with an opportunity for this-worldly escape. Qurʾanic verses at the tape's outset give sanction to this path:

O humankind! There hath come to you a direction from your Lord and a healing for what is in your hearts, and for those who believe, a guidance and a mercy.

Say: "In the bounty of God and in His mercy, in that let them rejoice: it is better than all [the wealth] that they may amass!"

Say: "See what things God has sent down to you for sustenance? Yet you hold forbidden some things thereof and make some things lawful." Say: "Has God indeed permitted you, or do you invent [things] to attribute to God?"

Mercy is provided to those who choose God's bounty in this life. However absolute the divine, He is also permissive. God makes allowances for sustenance.

Much of the celebration dramatizes a clash between the ascetic habits of die-hard warriors and the propensities of a more affable people. A narrative about "Bat Camp" (*mu'askar al-witwat*), introduced by the chief officiant at the start of the event, signals to listeners the farcical nature of mainstream news coverage of al-Qa'ida and its recruits. At issue is the gap between fantasies of a global organization dedicated to terror and darkness and its alleged realization in specific places and communities.

> Its graduates never laugh. Their hearts are hardened. Our brother, the groom today, I mean, is a graduate of this camp. Here's the strange thing, though: the brother is laughing, praise the Lord! People who live in societies far removed from jihad, its strugglers, and the land of true bonds often imagine the strugglers to be monsters…If they only knew how the strugglers are a people of goodness and generosity. If they only know how they ease the tribulation of all nations whether disbelieving or Muslim.

Throughout the celebration, humorous stories, jokes, and songs in vernacular Arabic offer audiences unabashed levity. Feelings of desperation and withdrawal characterize mainstream society rather than al-Qa'ida. "Bat camp" graduates are not so selfish as to privilege their own religious community at the expense of others. They seek instead to alleviate the suffering of all people.

Yemeni colleagues of mine who listened to this tape during the mid 2000s expressed surprise at the range of voices featured on the tape. One of these respondents, whom I will call Muhsin, marveled at how "complete" (*shamil*) the world of militants on the tape seemed to him.[12] "They draw not solely on traditional wedding customs but also on sports, nationalism, tribalism, and Islam. From many countries, no less! They create something new, something that's distinctly modern (*hadith*.)" I pressed Muhsin further on how such a maelstrom of associations would have appealed to such recruits. He replied that, having known young Yemenis who had left for Afghanistan and Iraq to fight with al-Qa'ida, they would likely have appreciated the recording because it offered something more than practical training:

> Finding work ranks among the top reasons that Yemenis have left for these fronts. Under-employment or the inability to secure a job leaves such men with little to hope for. They want their lives to amount to something. To a certain extent, these camps offer professionalization—technical training, time management skills, courses on religion and international politics, and,

most importantly, access to social networks—that can enhance their employment prospects. These camps also offer something more, however. They offer their participants a kind of dignity (*sharaf*). Many of these young men have experienced marginalization within their tribes (*tahmish qabaliyya*). Their families lack position and influence and may be from lower status groups. Such camps offer them the chance to improve their situation.

Muhsin's comments were perhaps less empathetic than they seemed. As a professor of philosophy at Aden university, he had experienced years of criticism from salafi students for teaching what they perceived to be lessons contrary to those espoused by conservative Muslim leaders, among them luminaries of the Afghan jihad. His reputation at the university and candidacy for promotion had suffered as a result. His remarks nevertheless provide insight on the multiple and complex rationales that drew young recruits to Afghanistan at the time.

There are many ways of becoming modern. Getting a job, improving ones' standard of living, getting an education or adopting a contemporary lifestyle seem the most obvious paths. Learning to fight against entrenched systems of power or perceived exploitation can also be a path to modern sensibility. As a set of cultural aptitudes, however, becoming modern requires sustaining a meaningful connection with the past, however outdated it may seem. In the case of young Yemeni militants such as 'Umar Ibn Abu 'Asim and those described by the philosophy professor, aspirations to "something distinctly modern (*hadith*)" were conjoined to a sense that tribal tradition might still provide a moral compass to its adherents. "Dignity" (*sharaf*) is one of the most salient virtues in tribal discourse. Achieved through decorum, self-presence, and prowess in managing one's own affairs, *sharaf* communicates social aptitudes that travel well even as they remain grounded in the history of a given community. Quality of life being more essential than sheer material accumulation, *sharaf* fits well with the orientation of what sociologists have termed "new social movements" that mobilize supporters through struggles for cultural identity and self-realization rather than promises of control over traditional political establishments.[13] The idiom of *sharaf* proves especially valuable insofar as it defies social hierarchy. When first introducing bin Laden to his audience, the chief wedding officiant emphasizes the speaker's availability to all participants: "Anyone with a question on their mind, whether about reality or fiction, the near or far, the antique or contemporary—go ahead and ask it of the Shaikh directly." Chief officer of a hierarchical terrorist organization he may have been, at least by some accounts, but the amir could also exhibit a more demotic profile. Camp life promised training in open public debate, meaningful political participation, even civic engagement on a global stage defined by universal principles. "We are people of a holistic methodology" (*manhaj shamuli*), boasted the officiant shortly earlier. The godfather of such etiquette was the exiled tribesman Moses.

The order of performances during the celebration situates conventions of martial asceticism in relation to a more contemporary and discriminating *ésprit de corps*. After the liberal sentiments of the Bat Camp anecdote, for example, a chorus of singers belts out a war song in honor of Islam's earliest defenders of the faith. Although Bat Camp graduates struggle for "all nations whether disbelieving or Muslim," adversaries who defy their prerogative shall meet with hellfire. This act is followed by the chief officiant's narrative of Moses's gentler ways. While he too "punishes enemies," he does so through the pursuit of nuptial bliss. His quest is amply rewarded not only through marriage but also through a gift of prophecy bestowed upon him on Mount Sinai. A follow-up narrative dramatizes Moses's political acumen through a fourth performance. Focusing on a more contemporary Son of Abraham, the narrative is delivered in vernacular Egyptian and is structured as a joke. Once, the officiant begins, "a Bedouin tribesman from the Sinai Peninsula came to Cairo and went into a café…" The punch line reveals much about the problem with everyday "politics" as waged by modern nation-state establishments. Politics, in this idiom, is simply a matter of getting food on the table for loyal constituents. To laugh at the joke is to recognize that greater virtues await those who struggle for something beyond material pandering. The path toward airing "voiced complaints against the governance of rulers" begins with Islam rather than with pan-Arab nationalism, in the style of Egyptian President Gamal 'Abd al-Nasir, or Westernized secularism, in the style of his successor Anwar Al-Sadat. Audiences can appreciate the merits of reclaiming Muslim dignity, moreover, through a tribal imaginary that is at once antique and modern. Two final poems toward the end of side A offer eulogies to Muslim warriors through the ages. As "hardened Arabs" whose faith brought them to "peaks and camel humps," many of them died as martyrs. Others remained in this world as living ascetics, commemorating their comrades through stories and the burdens of memory. Prefacing bin

THE AUDACIOUS ASCETIC

Laden's own remarks in the ensuing question and answer period, a singer intones, "How Kandahar knows the suffering of Mecca's Sacred House (*al-bait al-haram*)."

Six months before 11 September, bin Laden stepped onto the podium to declare that "breaking the back of Zionism will come from breaking the back of the Crusaders…America is foremost among them." His foreknowledge of impending attacks is conveyed with brevity and mirth: "I give you glad tidings that we are about to hear news of both of them, God willing." Hijackers who had pledged themselves to martyrdom could rest assured. An acclaimed amir had vouchsafed their mission and would continue broadcasting their goals to the world. From the sound studio of al-Qaʿida's media committee, however, their venture was slated for appearance alongside others. Warriors who chose an "oath of death," as one poet exclaims, shared the stage with those who resigned from bin Laden's service, acknowledged the Qurʾan's estimation for a "life of the present," and undertook more plebian work. "Whoever struggles to support a fighter on the path of God, it is as though he himself fought," declares an opening poem: "Whoever looks after a fighter's family, it is as though he himself fought." Toward the end of the cassette, a rousing anthem urges listeners to "Strike America with a cruise [missile] and a tank." So too are militants directed to more familiar and long-term battles at hand. Struggles against the Iraqi president Saddam Hussein, the Saudi royalty and Egypt's premier Hosni Mubarak earn select attention. When the anthem is performed in November of the same year, this time on the one recording in the collection dated after 9/11, the same verses are again sounded out. On that occasion, chanting against America occurs only after an even lengthier fulmination against Arab premiers, Libya's Muammar Al-Qaddafi now thrown in to boot.[14]

In the years ahead, al-Qaʿida's grim toll would claim the lives of many victims. Americans were caught in al-Qaʿida's headlights on 11 September. Audiences across the world expressed shock at the attacks, of course, and demonstrated profound sympathy for those who suffered incalculable losses on that day. A study published in 2009 showed that al-Qaʿida's wrath not only preceded 9/11, however, but also precipitated years of devastation far beyond America's shores. Of twenty-six attacks by al-Qaʿida from 1995–2003, 88 per cent were in Muslim-majority countries, the vast majority of whose victims were non-Westerners.[15] While the highest number of al-Qaʿida's victims before 2003 were Americans, the

364

result of casualties on 9/11 itself, the ensuing Iraq war beginning in 2003 would begin changing this legacy. From 2004–8, the proportion of Westerners among al-Qaʿidaʾs 3,010 new victims was 15 per cent. In the latter years of this period, as southern Afghanistan too descended into hellish conflict under the Taliban, this figure dropped to 2 per cent.[16] In Iraq alone, more than one thousand people were being killed every month in al-Qaʿida attacks by the spring of 2008, according to United Nations estimates.[17] Pakistan and Afghanistan, meanwhile, also experienced a growth of al-Qaʿida attacks and recruitment efforts through the mid-2000s, despite drone attacks meant to eliminate top leaders.[18] Shiʿa Muslims in these countries, as in Iraq, fared especially badly. Ordinary Sunnis repulsed by al-Qaʿidaʾs extremism, however, also found little respite from the group's steady appeal to hatred and violence. After a string of plots and assassinations broke out in Saudi Arabia during this time, Sunnis found special cause to denounce bin Laden's legacy.[19] Beginning in 2011–12, Syria's descent into open war, followed more recently by Yemen, only extended al-Qaʿidaʾs shadow across Arab heartlands.

Given the bloody prospects of al-Qaʿidaʾs brand for Muslims themselves as well as non-Muslims, those rallying under its banner had much work to do when soliciting supporters and recruits to their cause. The many voices and performances on tape no. 1164 express the challenges involved in such a task. Faced with a death-defying summons to fight Americans wherever they might be, ceremony organizers choose to sound out bin Laden's proposition in a host of ways. The notion of the "base" or "rule" (*al-qaʿida*), announced at the start of the tape, headlines their efforts. After initial supplications and a welcome speech, however, the chief officiant invites audiences to reflect on the concept's links to militancy, violence, and asceticism through the image of a fictionalized "camp" (*muʿaskar*). Much like traditional Yemeni grooms, recruits understand that disciplined ritual activities are to be experienced less as actual exercises in self-denial, as mainstream media coverage might suggest, than as skillful performances of asceticism that allow one to experience something different than what is typically expected. Longer wars accommodate diverse inclinations. Beneath overwrought images of the struggler's grave and hardened demeanor, ʿUmar knows the pleasures of mirth, love, and humanitarian sentiment. From bin Laden's viewpoint, al-Qaʿida is a militant organization dedicated to fighting non-believers through recourse, if necessary, to unconditional violence. Jews and

Christians under America's flag are especially accountable. More urgent is a critical engagement with the Muslim world's own oppressive conventions. Corrupt state rulers and their carefully groomed religious establishments provide natural targets. On the occasion of 'Umar's wedding, a more diffuse adversary is identified as mainstream Arab "newspapers and magazines." However much Egyptian dailies such as the *Al-Sharq Al-Awsat* ridicule bin Laden and his political ambitions as the toxic products of "Jihadistan," such a state might well be just fare for murderous tyrants. At the start of the tape, audiences are reminded to "listen with one's ears before hearing people's words." Rumor and calumny only amplify the need to close ranks with those who "believe and guard against evil."

Al-Qa'ida and its supporters find natural recourse to Islam when justifying armed struggle against oppressors. A summons toward asceticism, conveyed most notably in poetry, commends listeners to an abstemious and patient temperament. As I have suggested throughout this book, however, Islamic discourse on *qawā'id* creates space for considering differences between co-religionists as much as it identifies common ground, especially when concerning matters of jihad. Asceticism proves all the more appealing to activists for this very reason. As a vigilant discipline waged against the seductions of material excess, asceticism offers moral rectitude hewn from mundane and secular struggles more expansive than those typically evoked in religious discourse alone. Toward the end of side A, after a poem offering tribute to the martyrs of "Jihadistan," a poet named Haydara steps up to lead a brawny chorus in a song about card playing. Entitled "The Camel's Playing Card Has Fallen," the song depicts modern life as a sad state of despair. To be sure, globalization has provided consumers with access to extraordinary products. Consumers now enjoy fast-foods such as the chicken sandwich and Middle-Eastern *shawarma*, weapons technologies such as the machine gun and tank, and transportation options including taxis, ships, and airplanes. Ultimately, though, something rings hollow in the rush toward modern existence. If consumers are empowered, they still face having to choose between "two slices of onion." Luxury items promising that "one's mood will get straightened out" also substitute Arabian authenticity for a lesser and debilitated self. Nicknamed "Ahmad, the Berber, most pleasing to the foreigner," this character, at once familiar and strange, finds its destiny paralleled by the camel, the traditional lifeblood of Arabian society.

Ahmad and the camel, figures of potential compassion, emblematize the ways modernization can violate whatever contracts of sociality might be established between strugglers. Like playing cards adrift in a sea of chance, wedding participants' greetings become mere "storm clouds, knots of wool and sheep trotting by." Amidst these heavy meditations, Haydara's song offers redemption. Performed in a raw vernacular Arabic, its verses highlight potential merits in a more ecumenical critique of global economic progress. Conventional religious discourse, rendered in classical Arabic, may not be contemporary enough to address jihadis' dilemmas. Striking tensions with such discourse, Haydara has probably entered "a pious community all to his own," as the wedding officiant puts it. The poet nevertheless finds a chorus and backers on stage. Dignity may yet be in the offing.

Like the poet Haydara, bin Laden too sought to hedge his bets by expanding the terms of his struggle beyond religious convention alone. An Arabian and tribal sensibility had long been integral to his speeches in favor of armed jihad. Over time, his references to Bedouin tents, camel humps, Arabian horses, and clipped-wing falcons had gradually ceded to a more consistent message about targeting "Crusader-Jewish" interests rather than those of the Arab "Quraish." Some audiences held bin Laden's amalgamated enemy to be warranted. As political strategy alone, shifting focus to combatting something outside "the system" made sense when victories on one's own home turf had been fore-closed.[20] The trouble was, of course, that this solution belied the ongo-ing efforts of millions who, whether due to circumstances beyond their control or deeply held convictions, could not leave the system. For them, casting the threat as a "far enemy" proved false coin. They contin-ued to wage excruciating battles against religious and moral adversaries on a daily basis. Desperate for advice and skills, they found bin Laden's strategic shift toward combatting American geopolitical influence counter-productive to their efforts. According to top al-Qa'ida leader Mustafa Hamid, whose contributions I explored in chapter twelve, bin Laden "was not even aware of the scope of the battle he had opted to fight, or was forced into fighting." He ventured further: "It may be that the Islamic movement had already suffered from an intellectual as well as an organizational defeat before it had even started its battle against America. Jihad is a broad and serious issue that should not be left to the jihadist groups alone. Jihad is more than just an armed battle."[21]

For Hamid, as for others, the opportunity costs of attacking America were too high.

Recruits who received training at the Arab camps were only occasionally deployed by commanders in actual combat or commissioned to undertake terrorist operations. Selection for such operations was competitive and priority was given to those with the right experience, fitness, age, background, and ethnicity. Of the estimated 11,000 militants who passed through the camps before 11 September, the vast majority returned home without commission. Although these veterans had stories to tell, they regularly faced difficulties in finding employment and translating their skills into gainful activity. With limited options, many eventually joined the armies of their respective states, defending the very regimes that had so often been objects of scorn. Ruling authorities eagerly hired these young activists. Such a policy not only helped keep them out of trouble but also gave the state a decided advantage in elections: days before voting, entire army units could be redeployed to districts that risked falling to opposition candidates, their votes used to tip local outcomes.[22] Camp recruits were well familiar with their deployment as pawns in such games. When arriving in Afghanistan or Pakistan to receive training and education, they looked to their leaders for guidance in how to manage assured humiliation and defeat when confronting powerful state establishments. Tape no. 1164 shows how the concept and branding of al-Qaʿida was relevant for these individuals. However wondrous or inspiring bin Laden's lonely base, victory was more likely to be secured through the more collaborative rule-books of Haydara or ʿUmar. Fighting forces of injustice and oppression began not with enmity toward the outsider. This path risked hypocrisy, as suggested by bin Laden's own son, Hamza, through a poem at the end of side B: "You have prolonged my journey, Father, in every wanton valley/Until you have forgotten my tribe, the sons of my uncles and human beings all." True victory begins instead with subordinating one's desires to the standards of a more ideal community at hand. Marriage, eating, travel, and pleasure itself were not sideshows to this larger battle. They were its heart and blood.

EPILOGUE

In 2004, Naval strategist Thomas Barnett's book, *The Pentagon's New Map*, offered a summary of America's post cold-war security priorities. As a former analyst in Secretary of Defense Donald Rumsfeld's Office of Force Transformation, Barnett's message was clear. The U.S. military needed to join hands with global market forces. After the collapse of the Soviet Union, the Pentagon had already begun re-gearing for shorter-term conflicts spread across more diverse locales. As a consequence of such changes, military strategists worried about the dwindling of federal and public support for longer-term engagements that could ensure America's continued global leadership. Barnett had a solution. Labeled the "Evernet," his paradigm appealed to the attractions of a "universal rule set" based on Western principles of free-market competition, happiness, education and women's rights. Following the logic of *New York Times* journalist Thomas Friedman, Barnett suggested that wherever there was "connectivity," the fruits of this rule-set would be enjoyed. These parts of the world were called "The Core." Wherever threats arose to connectivity and its rewards, people suffered and yearned to be admitted to the club. These areas were marked by chronic poverty, wars, dictators, and religious theocracies. They were collectively labeled "The Gap."[1]

Drafting his paradigm for the first time in 1996, the same year as bin Laden's infamous Tora Bora speech as well as the first U.S. court proceedings against bin Laden, Barnett made "radical Islam" the primary threat to a functioning Core. While acknowledging in his book that Islamic extremism was a straw man at the time, Barnett nevertheless describes 9/11 as a "gift" that resolved conflicts between the military and market security strategists. On the one hand, the attacks presented Americans with "the Big One," a single, unified and hierarchically organized threat in the form of a global terrorist network that rivaled those from states such as China. On the other hand, the attacks exposed the workings of an extremely decentralized adversary whose defeat required continued militarization and security outlays in numerous conflict zones across the world. What was needed were further details about the nature of this amalgamated enemy.[2]

The problem that would come to face Barnett, as many others, was that "the base" proved too diffuse to respond as predicted to the kinds of militarized intervention marshaled by the United States after 11 September. Al-Qaʿidaʾs rejuvenation in 2014 in such places as Iraq's Anbar province is a sad testimony to how little Barnett's paradigm lent itself to improving security in the region. Its legacies have been costly on many fronts. What I have offered in this book is a better way to study and assess threats to established systems of order, security, and well-being among those who fall under al-Qaʿidaʾs shadow. My approach calls for contribution from a broader range of experts than those typically considered qualified to speak on matters of national security. More challenging, I have suggested, is that greater scrutiny devoted to the ways narratives of Islam's clash with the West essentializes the threat of Muslims who struggle in far more ordinary ways against the adverse effects of globalization and modernity. With bin Laden as poster boy, such narratives not only pre-empt opportunities to address forms of political and economic injustice shared by Muslims and non-Muslims alike. They also offer false remedies.

Bin Laden certainly fit the bill of the super-empowered wild-man in the hills, never more so than when decrying American aggression before world television audiences. Obscured from screen time are the ways his outbursts reflected and deepened his isolation as the Muslim world's icon of extremism. During the late 1990s and 2000s, popular Arab and Muslim audiences expressed fascination with his audacity. As polls suggested, his staunch opposition to Western intervention in Islamic lands commanded respect, even as his terrorist methods were roundly denounced. So much did some supporters rally to his cause that a core group of several dozen men pledged themselves to an attack inside America's national territory unprecedented since the British invasion of Washington in the Battle of 1812.[3] Confronting such an enemy, law enforcement and intelligence officials were well employed doing what they could to intervene. What was jeopardized in the focus on a single man and his network was a better understanding of how to situate such efforts within a more comprehensive strategy for enabling political reform in the Arab world without undermining regional stability and prosperity. The ensuing wars in Iraq and Afghanistan were certainly responsive to America's troubled history with Saddam and the Soviets as well as to public outrage after 9/11. They also obscured lessons on what was needed to fight a longer, multi-pronged battle against al-Qaʿida. My book offers guidance by exploring the intellectual and institutional mechanisms that have given al-Qaʿida resilience. I have focused on two different but overlapping domains: modern Muslim reform and state power largely within the Arab world, and Western security ambitions as channeled through counter-terrorism efforts, especially those in the United States. A brief synopsis is in order.

In attending to tensions between bin Laden's views and methods, and those of other Arab-Afghan militants as well as Muslim reformers generally, I have shown that al-Qaʿida is less a non-state entity, as it is so frequently depicted in counter-terrorist discourses, than it is a relation to state power. As a religious discourse about "rules" or "bases," *qawaʿid* (singular *qaʿida*) invoke precepts of Islamic law and ethics that have been codified since the tenth century CE. Since its most articulate theorists were typically Muslim jurists rather than statesmen, such discourse was not homologous with state power. Many legal specialists employed *qawaʿid* discourse toward keeping state abuses in check. Given the importance of deferring to consensus and a legal establishment's heavy precedent, however, *qawaʿid* also provided constraints on zealotry. In this respect, they were a valued resource for state leaders as they struggled for legitimacy, the more so for being responsive to local cultures and histories. *Qawaʿid* were avenues to civility as defined by the community rather than outlets for hostility or isolation.

The principal current of Muslim reform that I have examined in this book can broadly be labeled Saudi-influenced salafism. This categorization reflects top speakers in bin Laden's former audiotape collection, the bulk of whom, though not Saudi-born, received substantial schooling at its premier institutions of learning. Salafi thought emphasizes homage to God's absolute indivisibility (*tawhid*) as professed and practiced by *salaf*, or "pious forebears," thought mostly to have lived in the first three generations of Islam's earliest community. Speakers inclined to salafism find discussions about *qawāʿid* beneficial insofar as they emphasize unity under a single creed (*ʿaqida*) and warn against sectarianism. In the eighteenth century, Saudi Arabian reformer Muhammad Ibn ʿAbd al-Wahhab moved such thought in new directions in order to contest burdensome taxes imposed by the Arabian Peninsula's ruling Ottoman authorities. He encouraged the use of independent legal reasoning (*ijtihad*) by Muslims of a much wider intellectual cast, not just those with scholarly accolades. The Ottomans and their supporters branded Wahhabism as vile desert contumacy. In fact, ʿAbd al-Wahhab, a townsman at heart, spurned Bedouin asceticism. Like other salafi reformers, he envisioned a productive relationship between civil political authorities and a community of abstemious believers pan-Islamic in their calling. As long as believers pledged obedience to just rulers, they should be free to practice their monotheistic faith without fear of hypocrisy. Social, economic, and ideational "connectivity," in Friedman's sense, was integral to defending this mission.

ʿAbd al-Wahhab's universal ambitions had a distinctly Arabian caste. Hanbali legal scholars, predominant on the Arabian Peninsula like nowhere else, had not traditionally given much attention to *qawāʿid* literature, certainly when compared to Hanafi jurists who represented most Muslims in the world. ʿAbd al-Wahhab's theological bent proved toxic, moreover, when levied against Muslims not sharing his own cultural background. Shiʿa Muslims found little comfort in his depictions of them as "rejectionists" (*rawafid*) and suffered persecution over generations by those rallying beneath his banner. Despite their potential for division, ʿAbd al-Wahhab's writings nevertheless won the day in early twentieth-century Riyadh due to circumstances he could never have foreseen. A tribal shaikh seeking regional dominance through help from non-Muslim Westerners found valuable leverage in his plea to obey just leaders. That man was ʿAbd al-ʿAziz Ibn Saʿud, the founder of the modern Saudi state. Initially, Ibn Saʿud's allies were British. Their supply of guns and ammunition after World War I was followed, in 1927, by a treaty unique in the history of British-Arab relations for recognizing the power of a single man rather than a state. Six years later, employees of Standard Oil of California broke ground in the interests of a more lasting Saudi-American relationship. In the decade following World War II, through assistance from Standard Oil's successor, the Arabian American

Oil Company (ARAMCO), the Saudi royal family came into such wealth as it had never before experienced. With the Eisenhower Doctrine established to fight communism in 1956, Saudi Arabia became America's chief ally in the region and the beneficiary of hundreds of millions of dollars of military and economic assistance. In exchange, Saudi consumers supported a growing American work force: by 1978, the Kingdom was the U.S.'s seventh-largest export market, importing $4.4 billion annually. Given these and many other contracts of mutual support, Saudi citizens grew accustomed both to royal absolutism, as traditional Saudi merchant families were deprived of the ability to negotiate on behalf of their constituencies, and to increasing public support for a homegrown Islamic opposition movement. Reacting to charges of hypocrisy, King ʿAbd al-ʿAziz and his successors tried to burnish their religious credentials. They cultivated a tightly knit clerical establishment devoted to ritual observance and doctrine. They founded institutions for transnational Muslim solidarity in the fields of education, economics, and governance. Given constantly deepening ties with the United States, Saudi Arabia expressed the adaptability of Islam's loyalties like no other country. Not all were pleased.

In chronicling the ascendency and controversy of al-Qaʿida, I have attended throughout the book to the ways audiences—Arab as well as American, Muslim as well as non-Muslim—confronted the paradoxes of Saudi power through bin Laden's ascetic figuration. At least three narratives of asceticism came into play; each had its own sonority. First, during the years of Soviet-occupied Afghanistan, bin Laden was a pious and wealthy devotee of classical jihad, a multimillionaire who forsook the luxuries of his Saudi upbringing to drive infidel invaders from Muslim lands. Numerous were his stories of Arab-Afghan martyrdom, recounted to audiences during question and answer periods after audio-recorded lectures. This narrative played well to diverse Muslim audiences and found ready public uptake. Second, and overlapping with his role as frontier warrior, bin Laden was a disciple of self-abnegation (*zuhd*), one whose frustration with corrupt in-house governance led him toward political action in step with the Saudi Awakening movement. Like many Saudi reformers, he emphasized discipline at the expense of Shiʿa Muslims, Arab communists, and Muslim leaders given over to perceived excesses in material pleasure. This was an asceticism given prominence in his prepared speeches. Its rigors were made ambivalent, however, by their double edge. While bin Laden could be seen as a voice for regime change within the kingdom, as opposition supporters often highlighted, so too did calumny against Persian Shiʿa and Arab socialists mirror the state's own legitimizing discourse. Bin Laden's fine English safari boots, worn during trips to Peshawar's hospitals for Afghan refugees, raised eyebrows among Sunni Arab militants committed to true revolution at home. Third and finally, bin Laden came to represent an ascetic battle pitched against "Crusader-Jewish" interests broadly writ. After being stripped of his Saudi citizenship in 1994 and losing his fortune in the Sudan, this scenario featured regularly in his speeches. Such asceticism was anti-American in essence. Evoked as early as 1989 to rally support for boycotting American goods in the name of beleaguered Palestinians during their first Intifada, such asceticism had become, by 2000, simply a means to cultivate enmity for American Christians and Jews wherever they lived. Never was bin Laden's ascetic bent more detached from specific national or territorial conflicts than when amplified on American television news networks under the mantle of al-Qaʿida. His audacity became pronounced through more restricted and globally managed sound bites.

Those who study al-Qaʿida must restore plurality to narratives of bin Laden's asceticism. This book offers insights and guidance on how to do so. The urgency of accounting for asceticism's very different political functions is evident when considering how much the Western image of his non-state capacities, so integral to counter-terrorism discourse, obscured al-Qaʿida's operative dynamics. Al-Qaʿida remains a potent source of radicalism because it is so closely intertwined with the management of state authority in messy contexts of global interaction. As audiotapes reveal, discussions about the workings of specific militant base-camps prioritize the cultivation of relations with state authorities. Within host states, as was evident in Mulla ʿUmar's Afghanistan, authorities need reassuring that militant activities will serve their interests. In neighboring or client states, as is evident from bin Laden's speeches, leaders, donors, and potential recruits need regular briefing about shared values and goals. The concept of *al-qaʿida* in Islamic jurisprudence proves even more responsive to state security imperatives. Consider the Arabian Peninsula, for example, intellectual powerhouse for the top speakers in bin Laden's former tape collection. As evidenced by the dramatic Arab revolutions beginning in 2010, Arabian Gulf states are marked by relative stability by virtue of security regimes that devote a lot of attention to tightly controlled religious establishments. Within the borders of these states, jurists' lectures on foundational ethics award a vital role to minority dissent, as long as it is couched in an appropriately Sunni vein. Audio recordings by ʿAbd al-Rahim Al-Tahhan, Musa Al-Qarni, and Tariq Al-Suwaidan, as discussed in chapters twelve and thirteen, illustrate how such discourse works. State credibility relies on citizens' sense that room exists for discussion and debate about important political issues. More expedient still, *qawaʿid* discourse can be deployed to enhance regime survival where regional power imbalances threaten state sovereignty. In few countries is the value of such discourse more evident than in the smaller "late rentier" Gulf states such as Qatar and other members of the United Arab Emirates.[4] Hemmed in by much more powerful states, such as Saudi Arabia, Iraq, and Iran, these states look out at their regional neighbors as well as at dominant economic powers with an appreciation for "confrontational competition."[5] On the one hand, planning for what will come after oil, state rulers have diversified their economies and developed huge foreign exchange investment portfolios that increasingly align them with global economic norms. On the other hand, as discussed by political scientist Mehran Kamrava, they seek deliberately to change the rules and norms that underlie the international system.[6] Qatar, then, while heavily invested in the West and a key U.S. ally, has gradually shifted its import policy toward China and now exports almost all of its oil there. Over the past decade, Qatar has also continuously maintained active relations with Khamenei's Iran, Hamas, and a host of Islamic reform and militant movements, among them the al-Qaʿida associated Jabhat Al-Nusra front in Syria. A U.S. State Department cable in 2009 called Qatar the "worst in the region," in fact, when it comes to cooperation with American counterterrorism efforts.[7] Qatar, like other rentier states, plays up such rivalry between states in order to give it leverage along multiple and shifting fronts. *Qawaʿid* discourse supplies a framework for managing such tensions. Through the early-mid 1990s, as explained in chapter thirteen, the Syrian jurist ʿAbd al-Rahim Al-Tahhan held sway in Qatar's Ministry of Religious Endowments. His lessons on *qawaʿid* and the exceptional virtues of asceticism appear to have been conveyed through personal tutelage to the minister himself, ʿAbdalla bin Khalid Al Thani.[8]

Al-Qaʿida's activities can easily be linked to the region's poorer and more conflict-ridden nations: Yemen, Somalia, Iraq, Syria, and so on.

Where security regimes lack the funding and centralization enjoyed by powerful states, militants thrive, as do their insurgencies. In these cases, *qawāʿid* discourse tips in favor of maverick minority opinion and no longer accommodates different points of view under a shared tradition or social charter. The real challenge lies in recognizing that salafi discourse about al-Qaʿida exceeds the vocabulary of disenfranchised militant rebels. New questions must be asked about how al-Qaʿida has been managed within salafi discourse as challenges arise to the legitimacy of Muslim states. Focusing only on al-Qaʿida's most vociferous anti-American exponents has at least two serious drawbacks. First, excessive attention to self-styled rogue actors risks giving warrant to militarized solutions that can undermine efforts to address deeper structural problems. When in early 2013 American intelligence officials licensed drone strikes against the Syrian group Jabhat Al-Nusra, identified as an al-Qaʿida affiliate by the State Department, the fringe group was provided with global publicity and a rallying cry. Newly licensed in its combat against extremism, the regime of Bashar Al-Assad ramped up its atrocities. Despite opposition from the Syrian National Coalition, such strikes continued, giving pause to an international community weighing the benefits of intervention against growing fractures within the opposition. A half-year later, desperate to reassemble at least one common front against the Syrian army, opposition moderates defected en masse to Jabhat Al-Nusra's flanks, magnifying the very threat that U.S. policy makers had sought to contain.[9] Second, inordinate focus on Arab Sunni militants' long-term fight against the American enemy misses what gives al-Qaʿida resilience. Al-Qaʿida is less a single organization, network, or set of affiliates united by a common ideology than it is a tactic for winning battles within Muslim-majority societies. Relegating this tactic to scenarios of global cultural or ideological confrontation only deflects attention from the concentrations of authoritarian power that have enabled it. The history of such power can be understood only from the vantage of specific states as they grapple with transnational security orders in which America remains a dominant partner.

APPENDIX A

TOP THIRTY-FIVE SPEAKERS IN AUDIOTAPE COLLECTION

(arranged by approximate number of audio recordings)
'Abd al-Rahim Al-Tahhan
'A'id Al-Qarni
Ahmad Al-Qattan
Muhammad Ibn Salih Al-'Uthaimin
'Abdalla 'Azzam
Salman Al-'Awda
'Abd al-Majid Al-Zindani
Muhammad Salih Al-Munajjid
Sa'd Al-Barik
Safar Al-Hawali
Nasir Al-'Umar
Osama bin Laden
'Abd al-Rahman Al-Dawsari
Sa'id bin Musaffar Al-Qahtani
'Abdalla al-Hamad
Muhammad Nasr al-Din Al-Albani
Abu Bakr Jabir Al-Jaza'iri
Mustafa Hamid (aka Abu al-Walid Al-Masri)
Muhammad Qutb
Ibrahim Al-Duwaish
Abu Mus'ab Al-Suri (aka Mustafa bin 'Abd al-Qadir Al-Rifa'i)
Ahmad Al-Mawra'i

'Abd al-Rahman Al-'Ashmawi
'Abd al-'Aziz Ibn Baz
Sa'id bin Mubarak Al Zu'ir
'Umar 'Abd al-Rahman
Musa al-Qarni
'Abd al-Hamid Al-Kishk
'Ali 'Abd al-Rahman Al-Hudhaifi
Nabil Al-'Awdi
Tariq Al-Suwaidan
'Abd al-Wahhab Al-Turayri
'Umar bin 'Umar (aka Abu Qutada Al-Filistini)
Riyad Al-Haqil
'Abdalla Ibn Jibrin

NOTES

INTRODUCTION

1. ʿAbdalla heralded from a nearby training camp in Abyan that was Osama bin Laden's favored training camp in Yemen at the time. Scheuer, Michael (Anonymous), *Through Our Enemies' Eyes: Osama bin Laden, Radical Islam, and the Future of America*, Washington, D.C.: Brassey's, 2002, p. 34. The Jabal Hattat camp officially belonged to the Islamic Jihad organization, a hybrid between the Egyptian Islamic Jihad and the Aden-Abyan Islamic Army. ʿAbdalla's self-disclosure as "leader" (*qaʾid*) of the World Islamic Organization (*Al-Munazmat Al-Islamiyyat Al-ʿAlamiyya*) conveyed a more diplomatic image of the World Islamic Front (*Jabhat Al-Islamiyyat Al-ʿAlamiyya*) announced by bin Laden, Ayman Al-Zawahiri, and others just two months earlier in Khost, Afghanistan. Militants in Yemen appear to have been indignant at not being consulted before the front's declaration, a lapse that bin Laden sought to patch up in June by visiting Abyan and working with colleagues there to ratify the statement. See Tawil, Camille, *Brothers in Arms: The Story of al-Qaʿida and the Arab Jihadists*, London: Saqi, 2010, pp. 153–4. After the camp was bombed by Yemeni government forces around the time of bin Laden's June visit, al-Qaʿida's principle southern base moved further east near Mawdiyya.
2. Anderson, C., "FBI Reports Jump in Violence against Muslims," *Associated Press*, 25 Nov. 2002.
3. "Public Remains Conflicted Over Islam," Pew Research on Religion and Public Life, 24 Aug. 2010, http://www.pewforum.org/2010/08/24/public-remains-conflicted-over-islam/
4. "Impressions of America," The Arab American Institute Foundation/Zogby International, Washington, D.C., 2004, http://www.aaiusa.org/page/-/Polls/ArabOpinion/ImpressionsOfAmerica_2004.pdf

5. Dufour, Jules, "The Worldwide Network of U.S. Military Bases," Montreal, Canada: Centre for Research on Globalization, (2007), http://www.globalresearch.ca/the-worldwide-network-of-us-military-bases/5564

6. Coll, Steve, *Ghost Wars: The Secret History of the CIA, Afghanistan, and bin Laden, from the Soviet Invasion to September 10, 2001*, New York: Penguin Press, 2004, pp. 271–2.

7. Friedman, Thomas, "Foreign Affairs; Angry, Wired, and Deadly," *The New York Times*, 22 Aug. 1998.

8. Garamone, Jim, "Rumsfeld Says Link Between Iraq, al Qaeda 'Not Debatable,'" *American Forces Press Service*, 27 Sept, 2002, http://www.defense.gov/News/NewsArticle.aspx?ID=43413

9. Jackson, Richard, "Bin Laden's Ghost and the Epistemological Crises of Counter-Terrorism," In *Covering bin Laden: Global Media and the World's Most Wanted Man*, (eds) Susan Jeffords and Fahed Al-Sumait, Bloomington, IN: The University of Indiana Press, 2015.

10. See, for example, Gunaratna, Rohan, *Inside Al Qaeda: Global Network of Terror*, London: C. Hurst, 2002, pp. 56–7; Benjamin, Daniel and Steven Simon, *The Age of Sacred Terror: Radical Islam's War Against America*, New York: Random House, 2002, p. 104. This definition emerged from American legal proceedings against transnational Muslim militants including bin Laden, as I detail later in the book, and remains foundational in Western counter-terrorism efforts; see, for example, "The Future of Al Qaeda," Canadian Security Intelligence Service, 2013, https://www.csisscrs.gc.ca/pblctns/cdmctrch/20130401_th_ftr_f_lgd-eng.asp

11. See, for example, Johnstone, Mark A., "A Proposed Grand Strategy for Defeating bin Laden and His Al Qaeda Network," U.S. Army War College, Carlisle Barracks, PA, report no. 20020806–354, 2002, p. 7; Hoffman, Bruce, "Al Qaeda, Trends in Terrorism, and Future Potentialities: An Assessment," RAND Center for Middle East Public Policy and Geneva Center for Security Policy, Third Annual Conference on the Middle East After Afghanistan and Iraq, Geneva, Switzerland, 5 May 2003, p. 12; Ranstorp, Magnus, "The Virtual Sanctuary of Al-Qaeda and Terrorism in an Age of Globalisation," in *International Relations and Security in the Digital Age*, (eds) Johan Eriksson and Giampiero Giacomello, London: Routledge, 2006, pp. 31–3; Sageman, Marc, *Leaderless Jihad: Terror Networks in the Twenty-First Century*, Philadelphia: The University of Penn Press, 2008, p. 24.

12. See, for example, Bergen, Peter L., *The Longest War: The Enduring Conflict Between America and Al-Qaeda*, New York: Free Press, 2011; Gerges, Fawaz A., *The Far Enemy: Why Jihad Went Global*, Cambridge: Cambridge University Press, 2005.

13. See, for example, Burke, Jason, *Al-Qaeda: Casting a Shadow of Terror*, New York: Palgrave, 2003, pp. 12–22; Martin, Gus, *Understanding Terrorism*, Thousand Oaks, CA: Sage, 2003, p. 234; Vertigans, Stephen, *Militant Islam: A Sociology of Characteristics, Causes and Consequences*, New York: Routledge, 2008, p. 53. Hellmich, Christina, *Al-Qaeda: From Global Network to Local Franchise*, London: Zed Books, 2011, p. 14. Abdel Bari Atwan reflects general consensus that al-Qaʿida was a hierarchical organization before 9/11 but mostly an ideology afterward. *After bin Laden: Al Qaeda, The Next Generation*, New York: The Free Press, 2012, pp. 13–14.

14. The tapes were deposited with the Williams Afghan Media Project run by anthropologist David Edwards.

15. See, for example, Ryan, Michael W. S., *Decoding al-Qaeda's Strategy: The Deep Battle Against America*, New York: Columbia University Press, 2013.

16. See also Pankhurst, Reza, "The Caliphate, and the Changing Strategy of the Public Statements of al-Qaeda's Leaders," *Political Theology*, 11 no. 4 (2010), p. 550.

1. THE MESSAGE (*AL-RISALA*)

1. This was the original title of the Declaration of War, found in a draft document by the Federal Bureau of Investigation on a computer file dated 31 July 1996 and owned by bin Laden's associate in London, Khalid Fawwaz. Soufan, Ali H., *The Black Banners: The Inside Story of 9/11 and the War Against al-Qaeda*, New York: W.W. Norton, 2011, p. 101.

2. *Sura* of The Family of ʿImran: 102.

3. *Sura* of The Women: 1.

4. *Sura* of The Confederates: 70–1.

5. *Sura* of Hud: 88.

6. *Sura* of The Family of ʿImran: 110.

7. English-language reports on bin Laden prior to his speech include Fisk, Robert, "Anti-Soviet Warrior Puts His Army on the Road to Peace," *The Independent*, 6 Dec. 1993; Fisk, Robert, "Arab Rebel Leader Warns the British: 'Get Out of the Gulf'," *The Independent*, 10 July 1996; Macleod, Scott, "Osama Bin Laden: The Paladin of Jihad," *Time Magazine*, 6 May 1996; Coughlin, Con, "Tempting Array of Strike Targets for Pentagon," *The Sunday Telegraph*, 4 Aug. 1996; Gerth, Jeff and Miller, Judith, "Funds for Terrorists Traced to Persian Gulf Businessmen," *The New York Times*, 14 Aug. 1996. I contextualize these reports further in chapters ten and eleven.

8. Storer, Cynthia, "Working with al-Qaeda Documents: An Analyst's View before 9/11," in *9/11 [Ten Years Later]: Insights on al-Qaeda's Past and Future through Captured Records*, (eds) Lorry M. Fenner, Mark E. Stout and Jessica L. Goldings, National Defense University: The Johns Hopkins University Center for Advanced Governmental Studies, 2012, p. 38.
9. Wright, Lawrence, *The Looming Tower: Al-Qaeda and the Road to 9/11*, New York: Alfred A. Knopf, 2006, pp. 4–5.
10. Sasson, Jean, Najwa bin Ladin and Omar bin Ladin, *Growing Up bin Laden: Osama's Wife and Son Take Us Inside Their Secret World*, New York: St. Martin's Press, 2010, p. 224.
11. Former U.S. Assistant Secretary of State for South Asian Affairs Robin Raphel held a meeting with top Taliban officials in Kandahar in April 1996 after having made a case to the United Nations that the best way to combat Taliban extremists was to engage with them. Rashid, Ahmed, *Taliban: Islam, Oil, and the New Great Game in Central Asia*, London: I.B. Tauris, 2002, p. 240.
12. Coll, Steve, *Ghost Wars*, pp. 192–3. Mustafa Hamid, who worked closely with bin Laden, served as Islamabad bureau chief for a United Arab Emirates newspaper at the time and published newspaper editorials on the disastrous campaign; see *Tharthara Fawq Saqf Al-ʿAlam, v. 10*, available in English translation from Westpoint's Combatting Terrorism Center under the file no. AFGP-2002–600088.
13. Bergen, Peter, *The Osama bin Laden I Know: An Oral History of al Qaeda's Leader*, New York: Free Press, 2006, p. 275; Brown, Vahid, *Cracks in the Foundation: Leadership Schisms in Al-Qaʿida 1989–2006*, West Point, NY: Combating Terrorism Center, 2007, p. 13.
14. Bergen, *The Osama bin Laden I Know*, p. 118; Al-Bahri, Nasir, *Dans l'ombre de Ben Laden*, Neuilly-sur-Seine: Michel Lafon, p. 105.
15. Bergen, *The Osama bin Laden I Know*, p. 106.
16. Brown, *Cracks in the Foundation*, p. 2.
17. See Tawil, Camille, *Brothers in Arms: The Story of al-Qaʿida and the Arab Jihadists*, London: Saqi, 2010, pp. 28–9; Randal, Jonathan, *Osama: The Making of a Terrorist*, New York: Alfred A. Knopf, 2004, pp. 92–3, 99–100.
18. Bergen, Peter L., *Holy war, Inc.: Inside the Secret World of Osama bin Laden*, New York: Free Press, 2001, pp. 177–8; Fishman, Brian, *Bombers, Bank Accounts, and Bleedout: Al-Qaʿida's Road In and Out of Iraq*, Westpoint's Combating Terrorism Center, 2008, p. 106.
19. Hegghammer, Thomas, *Jihad in Saudi Arabia: Violence and Pan-Islamism since 1979*, Cambridge: Cambridge University Press, 2010, pp. 64–5, 135. Hegghammer reports that views toward Americans changed by 2000 with the outbreak of the second Palestinian Intifada in 2000. A surge of Saudis occurred thereafter in Afghanistan's training camps (pp. 80–1, 109).

20. After Feb. 1998, when bin Laden co-founded a World Islamic Front targeting Jews and "Crusaders," Al-Suri is reported to have told bin Laden that "we are in a ship that you are burning on false and mistaken grounds." Stenersen, Anne, "Blood Brothers or a Marriage of Convenience? The Ideological Relationship between al-Qaida and the Taliban," Paper presented at the International Studies Association 50th Annual Convention, New York, Feb. 2009, p. 14, http://citation.allacademic.com/meta/p_mla_apa_research_citation/3/1/2/5/2/pages312525/p312525–1.php

21. Lia, Brynjar, *Architect of Global Jihad: The Life of al-Qaida Strategist Abu Mus'ab al-Suri* London: Hurst, 2007, pp. 397–400.

22. Arabic text available at http://www.aljazeera.net/channel/archive/archive?ArchiveId=90841

23. Islamic Fundamentalist Audio Recording Collection, Yale University, tape no. 1160.

24. *Sura* of The Narration: 77.

25. *Sura* of Those Who Tear Out: 40.

26. The hadith is recorded in Sahih Muslim, book 42 no. 7148.

27. In addition to narratives by bin Laden and Mustafa Hamid discussed in this book, see the symbolism of a "white mountain" in the martyrology of Suraqa Al-Andalusi, an Arab-Afghan who died in Afghanistan in Dec. 2001. Al-Andalusi, Suraqa, "Suraqa Al-Andalusi: From the Friend and Companion," http://www.islamicawakening.com/viewarticle.php?articleID=713&pageID=233&pageID=234& last accessed 20 Feb. 2014.

2. HEART PAINS

1. *Sura* of The Cow: 120.

2. *The 9/11 Commission Report: Final Report of the National Commission on Terrorist Attacks upon the United States*, Washington, D.C.: Norton, 2004, p. 67.

3. Two of these attempts were made while bin Laden was in the Sudan, the first in 1994 and the second, known to have been sponsored by Saudis, around the time of the Riyadh bombing in 1995. See http://www.historycommons.org/context.jsp?item=a1195yemeniassassins. In Afghanistan, the first attempt was in January 1997 and was also sponsored by Saudis. See Al-Bahri, Nasir, *Dans l'ombre de Ben Laden*, Neuilly-sur-Seine: Michel Lafon, 2010, p. 76. Michael Scheuer reports two other assassination attempts in March of the same year. *Through Our Enemies' Eyes*, p. 153. At least one more Saudi attempt to kill bin Laden occurred in Kandahar in 2000. Al-Bahri, Nasir, "Tanzim Al-Qa'ida Min Dakhil," *Al-Quds Al-'Arabi*, 25 Mar. 2005 [Part 7/9], p. 17.

4. Stenersen, Anne, "Blood Brothers or a Marriage of Convenience? The

Ideological Relationship between al-Qaida and the Taliban," Paper presented at the International Studies Association 50th Annual Convention, New York, Feb. 2009, p. 7, http://citation.allacademic.com/meta/p_mla_apa_research_citation/3/1/2/5/2/pages312525/p312525-1.php

5. Further details of bin Laden's increasingly controversial position among Arab-Afghan fighters are provided in chapters ten and twelve.

6. See Lacroix, Stéphane, *Awakening Islam: The Politics of Religious Dissent in Contemporary Saudi Arabia*, Cambridge, MA: Harvard University Press, 2011, pp. 148–9. Foremost among such critics was Safar Al-Hawali, the tenth most featured speaker in the tape collection.

7. Sasson, Jean, Najwa bin Ladin and Omar bin Ladin, *Growing Up bin Laden: Osama's Wife and Son Take Us Inside Their Secret World*, New York: St. Martin's Press, 2010, p. 166.

8. Wright, Lawrence, *The Looming Tower: Al-Qaeda and the Road to 9/11*, New York: Alfred A. Knopf, 2006, p. 73.

9. Sasson et. al., *Growing Up bin Laden*, p. 42.

10. Ibid., p. 190.

11. Ibid., p. 167.

12. Ibid., pp. 169–71.

13. Bergen, *The Osama bin Laden I Know*, p. 26.

14. Randal, Jonathan, *Osama: The Making of a Terrorist*, New York: Alfred A. Knopf, 2004, p. 58.

15. Sasson, *Growing Up bin Laden*, p. 169.

16. Coll, Steve, "Letter From Jedda: Young Osama," The New Yorker, 12 Dec. (2005). Ten audiotapes featuring English lessons for beginners were later found in his Kandahar house and suggest that bin Laden may have tried to improve his speaking skills in private. The recordings (nos. 1128–30, 1185–7, and 1275–8) were produced by the Boston-based Heinle and Heinle Publishers, an excerpt of which can be found on the website associated with this book.

17. Sasson, *Growing Up bin Laden*, pp. 121,166.

18. Journalist Stephen Coll reports that students at Jeddah's Al-Thaghr high school would entrust valuable items to bin Laden for the day to prevent them from being stolen. "Letter From Jedda," (2005).

19. Bergen, *The Osama bin Laden I Know*, p. 14.

20. Coll, Steve, *The bin Ladens: An Arabian Family in the American Century*, New York: The Penguin Press, 2008, p. 230.

21. Sasson, *Growing Up bin Laden*, p. 177.

22. Bin Laden's call to attack American economic interests for the sake of Muslim struggles against Israel is conveyed repeatedly in his speeches, no more so than on the eve of the Oslo Accords in Sept. of 1993, as discussed in chapter eight.

23. The indebtedness of Nusayri ideology to Christianity and Judaism is outlined by Syrian jihadist Abu Musʿab Al-Suri. Lia, Brynjar, *Architect of Global Jihad: The Life of al-Qaida Strategist Abu Musʿab al-Suri*, New York: Columbia University Press, 2007, p. 274.
24. Bergen, *The Osama bin Laden I Know*, pp. 4–5.
25. Coll, "Letter From Jedda."
26. Ibid.
27. Ibid.
28. Bergen, *The Osama bin Laden I Know*, p. 15.
29. Ibid., p. 21.
30. Ibid., p. 19.
31. Qutb, Sayyid. *Milestones*. Cedar Rapids, IA: The Mother Mosque Foundation, 1964, p. 8.
32. Ibid., p. 19; Lacroix, *Awakening Islam*, p. 44.
33. An illustration of the Qurʾan's characteristic allowances toward Jews and Christians is found in the two verses that follow Qutb's selective citation of the *sura* of The Family of ʿImran: 112, neither of which he mentions: "Not all of them are alike: of the People of the Book are a portion that stand (for the right); they rehearse the signs of God all night long; and they prostrate themselves in adoration. They believe in God and the Last Day; they command what is right and forbid what is wrong; and they hasten (in emulation) in (all) good works: they are in the ranks of the righteous" (verses 113–4).
34. Bergen, Peter L., *Holywar, Inc.: Inside the Secret World of Osama bin Laden*, New York: Free Press, 2001, p. 51.
35. Al-Bahri, Nasir, "Haris Sabiq li-Zaʿim Al-Qaʿida," (2010), http://alwatan.kuwait.tt/ArticleDetails.aspx?Id=108707&YearQuarter=20112, last accessed 8 May 2014.
36. Randal, *Osama*, p. 88.
37. Bergen, *The Osama bin Laden I Know*, p. 11.
38. ʿUmar bin Laden's wife Zayna told me of bin Laden's Oxford course in a personal interview in the mid 2000s. Photographs of bin Laden's time at Oxford and Western-style clothes are available at Macintyre, Ben, "Osama bin Laden: The Mummy's Boy Who Found Refuge in Radicalism," *The London Sunday Times*, 3 May 2011.
39. Sasson et. al., *Growing Up bin Laden*, p. 302; Zernike, Kate and Michael T. Kaufman, "The Most Wanted Face of Terrorism," *The New York Times*, 2 May 2011, http://www.nytimes.com/2011/05/02/world/02osama-bin-laden-obituary.html
40. Al-Bahri, Nasir, "Haris Sabiq li-Zaʿim Al-Qaʿida."
41. Sasson et. al., *Growing Up bin Laden*, p. 301; also personal communication with Zayna bin Laden.

42. Ibid., 54.
43. Ibid., 60.
44. Bergen, *The Osama bin Laden I Know*, p. 22.
45. Sasson et. al., *Growing Up bin Laden*. p. 62.
46. Ibid., 116.
47. Ibid., 72.
48. Ibid., 61–2.
49. Sasson et. al., *Growing Up bin Laden*, p. 60.
50. Ibid., 19, 165.
51. Ibid., 115–16.
52. Ibid., 43.
53. Lacroix, Stéphane, *Les Islamistes Saoudiens: Une Insurrection Manquée*, Paris: Presses Universitaires de France, 2010, p. 61. The 2011 English translation omits reference to the concept of free spaces.
54. Ibid., 61.
55. Bergen, *The Osama bin Laden I Know*, p. 15.
56. Wright, *The Looming Tower*, p. 77.
57. Ibid., 97.
58. Al-Bahri, Nasir, *Dans l'ombre*, 2010, p. 99 (author's own translation).
59. Ibid., 87.
60. Sasson et. al., *Growing Up bin Laden*, p. 61.
61. Mustafa Hamid emphasizes this adage, for example, in a lecture on militancy on tape no. 338 in Yale University's Islamic Fundamentalist Audio Recording Collection.
62. Lacroix, *Awakening Islam*, pp. 111–2.
63. Kechichian, Joseph, "Islamic Revivalism and Change in Saudi Arabia: Juhayman Al-Utaybi's Letters to the Saudi People," *The Muslim World*, 80, 1 (1990); Hegghammer, Thomas and Stéphane Lacroix, "Rejectionist Islamism in Saudi Arabia: The Story of Juhayman Al-'Utaybi Revisited," *International Journal of Middle East Studies*, 39 (2007).
64. Kechichian, Joseph, "The Role of the Ulama in the Politics of an Islamic State: The Case of Saudi Arabia," *International Journal of Middle East Studies*, 18, 1 (1986), pp. 65–6.
65. Wright, *The Looming Tower*, p. 91.
66. Kechichian, "Islamic Revivalism," (1990), p. 16.

3. REMEMBERING THE LION'S DEN

1. This recording, originally at Williams College, appears to be missing or filed under a different number in Yale's Islamic Fundamentalist Audio Recording Collection. I relied upon a duplicate I made of the tape while it was at

Williams. My estimated date of the recording comes from bin Laden's reference at one point to the "eighth year" of the Afghan struggle against occupying Soviet forces.

2. Qur'anic verse: "Go forth, whether light or heavy, and strive and struggle with your goods and your persons, in the cause of God. That is best for you, if you but knew" (*sura* of Repentence: 41).

3. Ka'b bin Malik is said to have declaimed these verses on the day when the trench was dug around Madina to defend it from Quraishi-supported tribes. The Battle of the Trench outside Madina occurred in CE 627. A nickname for Madina at the time was "The Lion's Den."

4. Reuven Paz argued that bin Laden's interest in Palestine was only a belated strategic ploy. "Qaidat al-Jihad," The International Policy Institute for Counter-Terrorism, 7 May 2002. Also see Doran, Michael, "The Pragmatic Fanaticism of al Qaeda: An Anatomy of Extremism in Middle Eastern Politics," *Political Science Quarterly*, 117, 2 (2002), p. 187; Roy, Olivier, *Globalized Islam: The Search for a New Ummah*, London: Hurst, 2004. p. 53. Egyptian author and early Al-Qa'ida documentarian 'Isam Diraz comes closer to the mark when suggesting that bin Laden's concern with Palestine began in earnest in 1990. See interview with Diraz on 19 Mar. 2002, "Sadiqi bin Ladin: Laysa Irhabiyyan," http://islamtoday.net/nawafeth/artshow-14–15817.htm, last accessed 14 May 2014.

5. Interview with bin Laden by the magazine *Nida' Al-Islam* in Oct./Nov. 1996. "New Powder Keg in the Middle East" at http://www.fas.org/irp/world/para/docs/LADIN.htm, last accessed 14 May 2014.

6. See chapter five.

7. Lawrence Wright asserts that "the United States was not yet on anyone's list." *The Looming Tower: Al-Qaeda and the Road to 9/11*, New York: Alfred A. Knopf, 2006, p. 131. Peter Bergen places bin Laden's first anti-American speech in 1990. *The Osama bin Laden I Know: An Oral History of al Qaeda's Leader*, New York: Free Press, 2006, p. 110. Michael Scheuer notes that Al-Qa'ida's 1988 meeting specified support for Islamic movements in Kashmir, Tajikistan and Mindanao, but none in the Arab world itself or against the United States. *Osama bin Laden*, New York: Oxford University Press, 2011, p. 73. Tactical directives differ from broader ideological fronts, however. At least one recording in the collection suggests that as a recruiter, bin Laden found leverage in linking jihad in the Arab heartlands to a global conspiracy fomented by the United States and Jews in particular. Islamic Fundamentalist Audio Recording Collection, Yale University, no. 505.

8. Wright, *The Looming Tower*, p. 101.

9. Brown, Vahid, and Rassler, Don, *Fountainhead of Jihad: The Haqqani Nexus, 1973–2012*, London: Hurst, 2013, pp. 5–6.

10. Wright, *The Looming Tower*, pp. 101–2.
11. Scheuer, *Through Our Enemies' Eyes*, p. 98.
12. Bergen, *The Osama bin Laden I Know*, 2006, p. 49.
13. Diraz, 'Isam, "Impressions of an Arab Journalist In Afghanistan," In *The Lofty Mountain*, ed. 'Abdallah Azzam, London: Azzam Publications, 2003, p. 95.
14. Hegghammer, *Jihad in Saudi Arabia*, p. 67.
15. Wright, *The Looming Tower*, 2006, p. 122.
16. Ibid., p. 122.
17. Ibid., 112.
18. Coll, Steve, *The bin Ladens: An Arabian Family in the American Century*, New York: The Penguin Press, 2008, p. 290.
19. Wright, *The Looming Tower*, 2006, pp. 115–16.
20. Diraz, "Impressions," 2003, p. 106.
21. Bergen, Peter L., *Holywar, Inc.: Inside the Secret World of Osama bin Laden*, New York: Free Press, 2001, p. 57.
22. Bergen, *The Osama bin Laden I Know*, 2006, p. 51.
23. Ibid., pp. 58–9, citing Jamal Khashoggi's article in the Saudi magazine *Al-Majalla*, 4 May 1988.
24. Excerpts from the film *Al-Ansar Al-'Arab fi Afghanistan* are shown in Michael Moore's *Fahrenheit 9/11* and are discussed by Steve Coll. Coll, *The bin Ladens*, 2008, p. 303.
25. Diraz, 'Isam, *Usama bin Ladin Yarwi Ma'arik Ma'sadat Al-Ansar Al-'Arab Bi-Afghanistan (Osama bin Laden Recounts Arab Al-Ansar Lion's Lair Battles in Afghanistan)*, Cairo: Al-Manar Al-Jadid, 1991, p. 5.
26. Peter Bergen states that bin Laden was "lionized" by the Office of Services' *Al-Jihad* magazine and provides a quote about bin Laden in the April 1989 issue that I could not find in the original. *The Osama bin Laden I Know*, 2006, p. 50. I also found no evidence to support R. Kim Cragin's assertion that bin Laden was first mentioned in the June 1987 issue. "Early History of al-Qa'ida," *The Historical Journal*, 51, 4 (2008), p. 1055–6. It can safely be said that bin Laden features very little if at all in any of the magazine's seventy-two volumes.
27. Bergen, *Holywar, Inc.*, 2001, p. 55.
28. Diraz, "Impressions," 2003, pp. 97–8.
29. Bergen, *Holywar, Inc.*, 2001, p. 68.
30. Ibid., p. 68.
31. Ibid., p. 104.
32. Some Arab-Afghan critics even slandered the Office of Services as a CIA front and 'Azzam himself as an American spy. Wright, *The Looming Tower*, 2006, p. 134.

33. Hegghammer, Thomas, "Abdallah Azzam, The Imam of Jihad," in *Al Qaeda in Its Own Words*, (eds) Gilles Kepel and Jean-Pierre Milelli, Pascale Ghazaleh, Cambridge: Belknap Press of Harvard University Press, 2008, p. 95.

34. Gunaratna, Rohan, *Inside Al Qaeda: Global Network of Terror*, London: Hurst, 2002, p. 18.

35. Sasson, Jean, Najwa bin Ladin and Omar bin Ladin, *Growing Up bin Laden: Osama's Wife and Son Take Us Inside Their Secret World*, New York: St. Martin's Press, 2010, p. 302.

36. See, for example, Chapter Four, "Second Question" in ʿAzzam, ʿAbdallah, *Defence of the Muslim Lands: The First Obligation After Iman*, (1984–5 [1405–6 A.H.]), http://www.religioscope.com/info/doc/jihad/azzam_defence_1_table.htm. Armed jihad under the leadership of an ad-hoc amir "is the right way to reform the divided authorities to the ultimate authority of the caliphate."

37. Islamic Fundamentalist Audio Recording Collection, Yale University, tape no. 1160.

38. Rassler, Don and Vahid Brown, *The Haqqani Nexus and the Evolution of al-Qaʿida*, Harmony Program: The Combatting Terrorism Center at Westpoint, (2011), pp. 20–1.

39. Bergen, *The Osama bin Laden I Know*, 2006, p. 33.

40. USA v. Enaam Arnaout (Government's Evidentiary Proffer Supporting the Admissibility of Coconspirator Statements), Chicago: no. 02 CR 892, 2003, p. 36. For the estimate of bin Laden's monthly contribution, see Kepel and Milelli, *Al Qaeda in Its Own Words*, 2008, p. 41.

41. Tawil, Camille, *Brothers in Arms: The Story of al-Qaʿida and the Arab Jihadists*, London: Saqi, 2010, p. 21; Zaydan, Ahmad, *Bin Ladin bi-la Qinaʿ*, Beirut: Al-Sharikat Al-ʿAlamiyya li-l-Kitab, 2003, p. 71.

42. Hegghammer, Thomas, "Abdallah Azzam," 2008, p. 93.

43. Interview with Al-Jazeera, 20 Oct. 2001, translated and reprinted in *Messages to the World: The Statements of Osama bin Laden*, ed. B. Lawrence, New York: Verso, 2005, p. 120.

44. On the distribution of *Join the Caravan* (Ilhaq bi-l-Qafila), see Kepel, Gilles, *Jihad: The Trail of Political Islam*, Cambridge, MA: Harvard University Press, 2002, p. 146, ftn.28.

45. *Ilhaq bi-l-Qafila*, available in Arabic from http://www.hanein.info/vb/showthread.php?t=113466&page=1, last accessed 14 May 2014.

46. Western scholarship has routinely traced bin Laden's ideas about al-Qaʿida to ʿAzzam's notion of a "solid base" (*al-qaʿida al-sulba*) rallied against non-Muslims across the world, especially Americans. ʿAzzam, ʿAbdalla, "Al-Qaʿida Al-Sulba," *Al-Jihad*, Apr. 1988. The inception of this argument can be attributed to writings by former head researcher for the Israel Security Agency

Reuven Paz shortly after 11 September. Paz, Reuven, "Islamists and Anti-Americanism," *Middle East Review of International Affairs*, 7(4), 2003. Early al-Qaʿida scholar Rohan Gunaratna, for example, acknowledges indebtedness to Paz for this argument. Gunaratna, Rohan, *Inside Al Qaeda: Global Network of Terror*, London: Hurst, 2002, p. 3. The "solid base" idea was not ʿAzzam's alone. Muhammad Qutb, a jurist with greater scholarly credentials than ʿAbdalla ʿAzzam and familiar to bin Laden from his adolescence in Jeddah, published a book on the Afghan jihad around the same time as ʿAzzam's article in which he discusses the concept. Qutb, Muhammad, *Al-Jihad Al-Afghani Wa Dalalatahu*, Jeddah: Mu'assasat Al-Madina Li-l-Sihafa Wa-l-Tibaʿa Wa-l-Nashr, 1989, p. 48. According to Qutb, the "solid base" was a theological precept, not a territorial one, and was to be deployed through renewed commitment to monotheism when confronting economic and material self-interest (*jahiliyya*).

47. Hegghammer, "Abdallah Azzam," 2008, p. 100.
48. "Al-Qaʿida Al-Sulba," *Al-Jihad*, Apr. 1988, pp. 4–6.
49. "Jihad... La Irhabiyya," *Al-Jihad*, Feb. 1987, pp. 4–7.
50. *The Lofty Mountain*, available at http://islamic-empire.synthasite.com/resources/The%20Lofty%20Mountain%20-%20The%20Last%20Book%20By%20Abdullah%20Azzam.pdf, last accessed 14 May 2014.
51. This vision of the Soviet-American collaboration in a "new world order" is expounded by one unidentified speaker in the collection in a lecture given in late 2000 or 2001. Islamic Fundamentalist Audio Recording Collection, Yale University, tape no. 1296.
52. Hegghammer, *Jihad in Saudi Arabia*, 2010, p. 67.
53. Al-Bahri, Nasir, *Dans l'ombre de Ben Laden*, Neuilly-sur-Seine: Michel Lafon, 2010, p. 99 (author's own translation).
54. Hegghammer, *Jihad in Saudi Arabia*, 2010, p. 194.
55. Al-Suri, Abu Musʿab, *Daʿwa ila Al-Muqawamat Al-Islamiyyat Al-ʿAlamiyya*, (2006), pp. 1425–6, http://www.megaupload.com/?d=D1Q8JDR1, last accessed 27 Aug. 2009
56. Lacroix, Stéphane, *Awakening Islam: The Politics of Religious Dissent in Contemporary Saudi Arabia*, Cambridge, MA: Harvard University Press, 2011, p. 28.
57. Al-Bahri, *Dans l'ombre*, 2010, p. 52.

4. THE GENIE AND THE BOTTLE: ON AUTHORITY AND REVELATION THROUGH AUDIOTAPES

1. Jinni ʿAbdalla cites the date during the recording.
2. Diraz, ʿIsam, "The Battle of the Lion's Den," In *The Lofty Mountain* ed. ʿAbdallah Azzam, London: Azzam Publications, 2003, p. 91.

3. Sasson, Jean, Najwa bin Ladin and Omar bin Ladin, *Growing Up bin Laden: Osama's Wife and Son Take Us Inside Their Secret World*, New York: St. Martin's Press, 2010, p. 165.
4. Wright, Lawrence, *The Looming Tower: Al-Qaeda and the Road to 9/11* New York: Alfred A. Knopf, 2006, p. 77.
5. Burke, Jason, *Al-Qaeda: Casting a Shadow of Terror*, New York: Palgrave, 2003, p. 56.
6. Wright, *The Looming Tower*, 2006, p. 253.
7. Soufan, Ali H., *The Black Banners: The Inside Story of 9/11 and the War Against al-Qaeda*, New York: W.W. Norton, 2011, pp. 78–9.
8. The house's proximity to the foreign ministry building was identified for me in a personal interview with the Afghan stringer who helped CNN locate and purchase the collection (June 2003, Williamstown, MA.)
9. After Sept. 1996, the Taliban's capitol in Afghanistan was officially Kabul. Kandahar's Foreign Ministry building retained its importance through the late 1990s, however, due to its proximity to the Taliban's founding leader Mulla 'Umar and to its location in the historic Pashtun heartlands. Foreign delegations routinely privileged Kandahar over Kabul through 1997. The city was especially important for Arabs in Afghanistan given their far greater concentration and influence in the southeast.
10. Bergen, *The Osama bin Laden I Know*, 2006, pp. 262, 326, 353, 412.
11. Ibid., p. 250.
12. Ibid., p. 250.
13. Bodansky, Yossef, *Bin Laden: The Man Who Declared War on America*, New York: Random House, 1999, p. 312.
14. The Walkman's association with corrupt Western social mores is mentioned by those who lived with bin Laden in Afghanistan during the late 1990s. See Bergen, *The Osama bin Laden I Know*, 2006, p. 174.
15. Al-Bahri, Nasir, "Tanzim Al-Qa'ida Min Dakhil," *Al-Quds Al-'Arabi*, 22 Mar. 2005 (*author's own translation*.) The Jihad Wal location is mentioned by former FBI agent Ali Soufan in his memoir. *The Black Banners*, 2011, p. 65.
16. Azzam, 'Abdallah, *The Lofty Mountain*, London: Azzam Publications, 2003, http://islamic-empire.synthasite.com/resources/The%20Lofty%20Mountain%20-%20The%20Last%20Book%20By%20Abdullah%20Azzam.pdf, p. 121, last accessed 16 June 2011
17. Al-Bahri, *Dans l'ombre*, 2010, p. 87.
18. Bergen, *The Osama bin Laden I Know*, 2006, p. 265.
19. See Fouad Al-Rabia's testimony in ibid., 278–9.
20. Ibid., p. 266.
21. Ibid., p. 406.

22. In contrast with the commercial recordings of well-known preachers, this material rarely surfaces on the internet in later years, particularly since the tapes lack accompanying visual footage.

23. Lia, Brynjar, *Architect of Global Jihad: The Life of al-Qaida Strategist Abu Mus'ab al-Suri*, New York: Columbia University Press, 2007, p. 323.

5. OUR PRESENT REALITY (*WAQI'UNA AL-MU'ASIR*)

1. The approximate date of the speech is suggested by bin Laden's reference to "the year 1409 AH that has just passed." The last day of 1409 AH was 2 Aug. 1989.

2. Muhammad's mystical journey from the Ka'ba in Mecca to the "farthest mosque," a location conventionally associated with Islam's third holiest site, the Sacred Noble Sanctuary or "Temple Mount" in Jerusalem, occurred in around CE 612.

3. *Sura* of The Inner Apartments: 15.

4. *Sura* of Muhammad: 4.

5. Verses by Jordanian professor of Islamic law Yusif Muhy al-Din "Abu Hilala."

6. *Sura* of The Family of 'Imran: 141.

7. Amba, Faiza Saleh, "Sources Say bin Laden Lives Spartan Life, Friends Claim Radical Saudi Lacks Millions," *The Sunday Patriot News (Associated Press)*, 30 Aug. 1998.

8. Citing an unavailable 1989 sermon by bin Laden in Jeddah, Lawrence Wright argues that bin Laden never thought of targeting repressive Arab regimes at the time and that he instead focused on getting the Soviet infidels out of Afghanistan and punishing America through economic boycotting, p. 127. R. Kim Cragin also provides insubstantial evidence when asserting that al-Qa'ida leaders in the early 1990s focused on the United States. "Early History of al-Qa'ida," *The Historical Journal*, 51, 4 (2008), p. 1066.

9. Muhammad Qutb's audiotape by the same title summarizes his book and is featured in the collection. Islamic Fundamentalist Audio Recording Collection, Yale University, tape no. 778. Whereas Qutb frames his rage in more explicitly unifying terms, bin Laden focuses his charges of apostasy on Muslims who refuse to take up arms.

10. As late as 2006, Peter Bergen continued to insist that "While bin Laden and Al-Zawahiri, both of whom are Sunni fundamentalists, may privately consider Shias to be heretics, they have never said this publicly." "Bin Laden Might Find Relief in Al-Zarqawi's Death," 8 June (http://www.cnn.com/CNN/Programs/anderson.cooper.360/blog/2006/06/bin-laden-might-find-relief-in-al.html). Informing bin Laden's alleged aversion to anti-Shi'a dis-

course, according to other American analysts, was his ongoing relationship with Iran. Scheuer, *Through Our Enemies' Eyes*, p. 186; "A Biography of Osama bin Laden," *Frontline* PBS, April 1999 (http://www.pbs.org/wgbh/pages/frontline/shows/binladen/who/bio2.html). For another recording featuring bin Laden's prominent vitriole against Shiʿa, see his 1993 lecture "Dangers and Hopes" (*Makhatir W-Amal*), discussed in chapter six.

11. According to CIA analyst Cynthia Storer, al-Qaʿida remained secret since its inception by bin Laden and ʿAzzam in the 1980s. "You have to try to figure out they're there when they're trying to deny even to their friends that they exist." As such, al-Qaʿida remained a covert organization unknown to the US government until she deciphered its name and ultimately revealed its objectives in a brief written for former president George Bush before 11 September. *Manhunt: The Search for bin Laden*, director Greg Barker, Home Box Office, Inc., 2013.

12. Scheuer, Michael, *Osama bin Laden*, New York: Oxford University Press, 2011, p. 73.

13. Wright, *The Looming Tower*, 2006, p. 133.

14. For a typical Western account of bin Laden's role as a unifier among Islamists after ʿAzzam's death, see Bodansky, Yossef, *Bin Laden: The Man Who Declared War on America*, New York: Random House, 1999, p. 49.

15. Gunaratna, *Inside Al Qaeda*, p. 55; Riedel, Bruce, *The Search for Al Qaeda: Its Leadership, Ideology and Future*, Washington, DC: Brookings Institution, 2008, p. 121; Ryan, Michael W. S., *Decoding al-Qaeda's Strategy: The Deep Battle Against America*, New York: Columbia University Press, 2013, p. 96.

16. The grand jury charges read as follows: "In or about 1988, Usama Bin Laden began directing resources to train mujahideen for eventual deployment to places outside Afghanistan. In or about August 1988, Usama Bin Laden and others (including Mamdouh Salim, a/k/a ʿAbu Hajer al Iraqi') held a series of meetings in Afghanistan during which the *al Qaeda* (the "Base") organization was formed. Members of *al Qaeda* pledged an oath of allegiance (called a 'bayat') to al Qaeda. Thereafter, Usama Bin Laden used the *al Qaeda* organization, as well as affiliated organizations, to provide financial and logistical support to mujahideen in various areas of the world. Al Qaeda had a command and control structure which included a *majlis al shura* (or consultation council) which discussed and approved major undertakings, including terrorist operations…In addition to participating in armed confrontations in Afghanistan, *al Qaeda*, acting on its own as well as in concert with other groups, also participated in armed confrontations and violence in other locations, including Bosnia-Herzegovina and Chechnya." USA v. Enaam Arnaout (Special April 2002 Grand Jury Charges), Chicago: no. 02CR892, 2002, p. 2. In the late 1990s, Mamdouh

Salim was an employee of the now banned Benevolence International Foundation, hence his connection with the trial of Enaam Arnaout, the BIF's former director. He was later indicted for co-founding al-Qaʿida and for planning the 1998 bombings of U.S. embassies in East Africa. He was ultimately sentenced for several crimes while in custody, including attempted murder, and is currently serving a life sentence at the ADX Florence facility in Colorado.

17. Wright, *The Looming Tower*, 2006, p. 131. *USA v. Enaam Arnaout* documents mention only the presence of bin Laden, Muhammad Bayazid and unnamed others at this meeting. USA v. Enaam Arnaout, 2003, pp. 34–5.

18. Ibid., p. 34.

19. Wright, *The Looming Tower*, 2006, p. 133.

20. USA v. Enaam Arnaout, 2003, p. 35.

21. Ibid., p. 36.

22. My analysis suggests that these two files are part of a single larger document, despite their separate titles and cataloguing. In scholarly literature they are often referred to as AFGP-2002–600178 ("Structure and Bylaws," at one time also catalogued as 2002–600048), portions of which are featured in its abridged and annotated version AFGP-2002–000080, the latter of which, as noted in the English translation, is paired with its second section AFGP-2002–000078 ("Goals and Structure," absent from the more complete version). These documents are not to be confused with the similarly labeled "Al-Qaʿida: Constitutional Charter, Rules and Regulations" (AFGP-2002–600175). The latter text displays hallmark characteristics from al-Qaʿida's official releases in the very late 1990s or early 2000s, including introductory Qurʾanic verses, a definition of "al-Qaʿida" that emphasizes its identity as an "Islamic group devoted to jihad," prominent mention of the group's "doctrine" (*ʿaqida*) and goals of setting up a worldwide Islamic caliphate.

23. Benjamin, Daniel and Steven Simon, *The Age of Sacred Terror: Radical Islam's War Against America*, New York: Random House, 2002, p. 104.

24. Much in the fashion of Benjamin and Simon though with more detail, Bergen and Wright both insert bin Laden's name when mention of oath-taking arises: "New recruits filled out forms in triplicate, signed their oath of loyalty *to bin Laden* [my italics], and swore themselves to secrecy" Wright, *The Looming Tower*, 2006, p. 141; "When the Russians decide to leave Afghanistan, bin Laden he decide to make his own group. Al-Qaeda [*sic*], it's established to do jihad. You have to make bayat. 'Bayat' means you swear [*an oath of allegiance to bin Laden*] [my italics]." Bergen, Peter, *The Osama bin Laden I Know: An Oral History of al Qaeda's Leader*, New York: Free Press, 2006, p. 86. The first reference I have found of someone claiming to

have made an oath (*bayʿa*) to bin Laden, other than Jamal Al-Fadl, is the Palestinian operative in East Africa Muhammad Odeh, who dates his pledge to 1992 (cited in ibid., pp. 138–9).

25. Abu Ayyoub Al-Iraqi appears to have been killed in Pakistan in the early-mid 1990s.

26. See, for example, Camille Tawil's interview with Libyan Arab-Afghan militant Noman Benotman. *Brothers in Arms: The Story of al-Qaʿida and the Arab Jihadists*, London: Saqi, 2010, p. 28. In an early volume, Rohan Gunaratna clarifies Abu Ayyoub's appointment as the first amir but adds that the name "al-Qaʿida" was bin Laden's brainchild and that its leaders, such as Abu Ayyoub, were his immediate deputies. Gunaratna, *Inside Al Qaeda*, p. 56.

27. "Al-Qaʿida's Bylaws," Combatting Terrorism Center's Harmony Database document no. AFGP-2002–600178 (entitled "Al-Qaʿida's Structure and Bylaws" through late 2013), p. 33, http://www.ctc.usma.edu/wp-content/uploads/2010/08/AFGP-2002–600178-Orig-Meta.pdf (author's own translation).

28. Al-Bahri, Nasir, "Tanzim al-Qaʿida min Dakhil," *Al-Quds Al-ʿArabi*, 22 Mar. 2005 [Part 4/9], p. 19.

29. Zaydan, Ahmad, *Bin Ladin bi-la Qinaʿ*, Beirut: Al-Sharikat Al-ʿAlamiyya li-l-Kitab, 2003, ibid., pp. 70–1.

30. Transcript day 19 of the USA v. Usama Bin Laden, et. al. trial, 19 Mar. 2001, p. 2810.

31. One tape in bin Laden's former collection, produced by "The Media Department of al-Qaʿida" in October 2000, features a recording of a wedding celebration in Afghanistan involving one of bin Laden's bodyguards. Islamic Fundamentalist Audio Recording Collection, Yale University, tape no. 1164. Additionally, one cassette jacket in the collection reads "A political course on bin Laden's base (*qaʿida bin Laden*)." Since jackets were separated from their original cassettes during shipping, however, a tape associated with this jacket has not yet been identified. No other recorded material yet found mentions the concept in this way.

32. Jason Burke suggests this possibility based on interviews with Saudi intelligence. *Al-Qaeda: Casting a Shadow of Terror*, New York: Palgrave, 2003, ftn. 3, p. 251. Tawil adds that, according to his reports, the base encompassed Arab-Afghan camps and battle zones. *Brothers in Arms*, 2010, p. 25.

33. For the "computer database" derivation, see Bunel, Pierre-Henri, *Proche-Orient, une guerre mondiale?: des derives de la finance internationale*, New York: Carnot, 2004; also see Randal, Jonathan, *Osama: The Making of a Terrorist*, New York: Alfred A. Knopf, 2004, p. 90.

34. I discuss cassette no. 508 in chapter three.

35. Gunaratna, *Inside Al Qaeda*, 2002, p. 56. The author's change of opinion is noted in *Beyond al-Qaeda: The Global Jihadist Movement*, Santa Monica, CA: RAND Corporation, 2006, ftn. 15, p. 27.

36. Transcript for day 2 of the USA v. Usama Bin Laden trial, 6 Feb. 2001, p. 191. Al-Fadl's description of the documents he received closely matches the core structural components of the CTC's charter documents, particularly the outlining of camp goals, the delineation of "advisory," "military," "financial" and "media" councils, and the clarification of duties expected from amirs and recruits (Ibid., pp. 192–209.)

37. Al-Bahri, "Tanzim al-Qaʿida Min Dakhil," 22 Mar. 2005 [Part 4/9], p. 19.

38. Wright, *The Looming Tower*, 2006, p. 133.

39. Bergen, *The Osama bin Laden I Know*, 2006, p. 80.

40. Jamal Al-Fadl reports four Egyptians, three Iraqis, two Saudis, and single delegates from Yemen, Oman, Algeria and Libya. Transcript for day 2 of the USA v. Usama Bin Laden trial, 6 Feb. 2001, pp. 205–7.

41. Cullison, Alan, "Inside al-Qaeda's Hard Drive," *Atlantic Monthly*, Sept. (2004).

42. Testimony of L'Houssaine Kherchtou in USA v. Bin bin Laden trial as cited in Bergen, *The Osama bin Laden I Know*, 2006, pp. 101–2.

43. Transcript for day 2 of the USA v. Usama Bin Laden trial, 6 Feb. 2001, p. 186.

44. For Al-Faruq's Gharmabak Ghar location and operations see Gunaratna, Rohan, "The Terrorist Training Camps of al Qaida," In *The Making of a Terrorist: Recruitment, Training and Root Causes Volume II: Training*, ed. James J. F. Forest, 2, Westport, CN: Praeger, 2006.

45. See Gunaratna for a discussion of Zhawar Kili, a region in Khost hosting a military complex that was built during the Soviet occupation and that later accommodated the addition of Al-Faruq. "The Terrorist Training Camps of al Qaida," 2006. He does not mention Al-Faruq, however, or discuss the profiles or orientations of specific camps within the complex.

46. Al-Faruq 1's dates of operation are difficult to pinpoint. Based on my re-reading of USA vs. Enaam Arnaout documents, I calculate that ground was broken on around 10 Sept. 1988, i.e. before the last Soviet troops had officially left the country in Feb. 1989. Administrators welcomed the camp's first class of recruits, however, only in the summer of 1989, following a disastrous defeat at Jalalabad in May in which Shafiq Al-Madani, one of bin Laden's closest friends, was killed. Wright, *The Looming Tower*, 2006, pp. 140–1. From this perspective, assertions that Al-Faruq was founded in Soviet-occupied Afghanistan, frequently found in militant narratives, hold primarily symbolic significance. Cassette no. 338 in Yale University's Islamic Fundamentalist Audio Recording collection, recorded at the camp in 1998

NOTES

by leading militant theoretician Mustafa Hamid, suggests that al-Qaʿida's top cadres continued to teach there at that time. In Aug. 1998, Al-Faruq 1, as part of the larger Zhawar Kili complex, was the target of United States cruise missiles strikes in retaliation for embassy bombings in East Africa. These strikes were not very devastating, however, since the camps appear to have been operational again within two weeks. Bergen, Peter L., *Holywar, Inc.: Inside the Secret World of Osama bin Laden*, New York: Free Press, 2001, p. 122.

47. Saudi Arabia is perhaps the most important index of such controversy. As early as the fall of 1994, attacks by Arab-Afghan returnees on Saudi officials resulted in heightened crackdowns on preachers supporting armed jihad even in foreign countries. Hegghammer, *Jihad in Saudi Arabia*, pp. 70–1. By 1999, two years after Al-Faruq 2's founding, Saudi superstar Salman Al-ʿAwda openly denounced the jihad in Afghanistan. In the years following 2000, only the most openly militant clerics, such as Hamud Al-Shuʿaybi, defended the Taliban and encouraged Saudis to go fight in the region. Lacroix, Stéphane, *Awakening Islam: The Politics of Religious Dissent in Contemporary Saudi Arabia*, Cambridge, MA: Harvard University Press, 2011, p. 253.

48. For example, see "Book by Mustafa Hamid," (http://www.ctc.usma.edu/wp-content/uploads/2010/08/AFGP-2002-600087-Trans.pdf)

49. Thanks are due to Cynthia Storer, former analyst in the CIA's bin Laden unit, for this reading.

50. A memo from the CIA around 1996 reports that, since the late 1980s or early 1990s, the only camp benefitting from bin Laden's financial support was a "Kunar camp" for Arab-Afghans located north of Jalalabad. Interviews with Hizb-i Islami and Sayyaf activists confirm this memo. Burke, *Al-Qaeda*, 2003, pp. 97–8.

51. *Sura* of The Inner Apartments: 15.

6. DANGERS AND HOPES (*MAKHATIR W-AMAL*)

1. "Rejectionism" (*al-rafidiyya*) is a derogatory term for Shiʿa who, in jingoistic Sunni parlance, reject the legitimacy of the first two Muslim caliphs, Abu Bakr and ʿUmar, claiming instead that ʿAli should have been the Prophet's immediate successor.

2. Muhammad's mystical journey from the Kaʿba in Mecca to the "farthest mosque," a location conventionally associated with Islam's third holiest site, the Sacred Noble Sanctuary or "Temple Mount" in Jerusalem, occurred around CE 612.

3. *Sura* of The Table: 27.

4. *Sura* of The Table: 28.

5. *Sura* of Repentence: 24.

6. Muslims' raid on a Quraishi caravan passing through the plains of Badr occurred in CE 624. The treaty of Al-Hudaibiyya four years later proved key to the Muslim community's sanctuary against Quraishi attacks.

7. *Sura* of The Spoils of War: 7.

8. Sasson, Jean, Najwa bin Ladin and Omar bin Ladin, *Growing Up bin Laden: Osama's Wife and Son Take Us Inside Their Secret World*, New York: St. Martin's Press, 2010, p. 104.

9. Bin Laden's claim to command one-hundred thousand fighters was made to Prince Sultan. Wright, Lawrence, *The Looming Tower: Al-Qaeda and the Road to 9/11*, New York: Alfred A. Knopf, 2006, p. 157.

10. Sasson, Jean, et. al., *Growing Up bin Laden*, 2010, p. 83.

11. Coll, Steve, *The bin Ladens: An Arabian Family in the American Century*, New York: The Penguin Press, 2008, pp. 375–6.

12. Bergen, Peter, *The Osama bin Laden I Know: An Oral History of al Qaeda's Leader*, New York: Free Press, 2006, p. 104.

13. Associates include L'Houssaine Kherchtou and Hasan Abd-Rabbuh Al-Surayhi. Ibid., pp. 101–2, 83.

14. Don Rassler and Vahid Brown state that bin Laden had established two earlier camps in Afghanistan called Abu Bakr Al-Sidiq (in the Zhawar district of Khost) and Jihad Wal. *The Haqqani Nexus and the Evolution of al-Qaʿida*, West Point, NY: Combatting Terrorism Center, 2011, p. 26. Former FBI agent ʿAli Soufan states, however, that the Al-Sidiq camp was run by Saudi militant Khalid Fawwaz. *The Black Banners: The Inside Story of 9/11 and the War Against al-Qaeda*, New York: W.W. Norton, 2011, p. 129. With regards to Jihad Wal, bin Laden's bodyguard Nasir Al-Bahri states that the camp was an early name for the Khost-based Al-Faruq camp. "Tanzim al-Qaʿida Min Dakhil," *Al-Quds Al-ʿArabi*, 22 Mar. 2005 [Part 4/9], p. 19. As noted earlier (ftn.50, chapter five,) a CIA memo from around 1996 states that the only training base funded by bin Laden in these early years was a "Kunar camp" outside of Jalalabad.

15. *The 9/11 Commission Report: Final Report of the National Commission on Terrorist Attacks upon the United States*, Washington, D.C.: Norton, 2004, p. 59.

16. Summers, Anthony and Robbyn Swan, *The Eleventh Day: The Full Story of 9/11 and Osama bin Laden*, New York: Ballantine Books, 2011, pp. 250, 393, 420.

17. Arab-Afghan veteran Osama Rushdie, interviewed by Paul Cruickshank in 2005 as cited in Bergen, *The Osama bin Laden I Know*, 2006, p. 106.

18. Ibid., p. 110.

19. Sasson, Jean, et. al., *Growing Up bin Laden*, 2010, pp. 97–8.
20. Lacroix, Stéphane, *Awakening Islam: The Politics of Religious Dissent in Contemporary Saudi Arabia*, Cambridge, MA: Harvard University Press, 2011, p. 194.
21. Al-Bahri, Nasir, "Tanzim al-Qaʿida Min Dakhil," *Al-Quds Al-ʿArabi*, 21 Mar. 2005, p. 19.
22. Burr, J. Millard and Robert O. Collins, *Revolutionary Sudan: Hasan al-Turabi and the Islamist State, 1989–2000*, Leiden: Brill, 2003, p. 59.
23. Ibid., p. 62.
24. Ibid., p. 68.
25. Summers, Anthony and Robbyn Swan, *The Eleventh Day: The Full Story of 9/11 and Osama bin Laden*, New York: Ballantine Books, 2011, p. 249–50.
26. Esposito, John L., *Voices of Resurgent Islam*, Oxford: Oxford University Press, 1983, p. 245.
27. Wright, *The Looming Tower*, 2006, p. 192.
28. Saloman, Noah, "The Salafi Critique of Islamism: Doctrine, Difference and the Problem of Islamic Political Action in Contemporary Sudan," In *Global Salafism: Islam's New Religious Movement*, ed. Roel Meijer, London: Hurst, 2009, ftn. 19, p. 152.
29. Scheuer remarks of the talk: "Pretty dry stuff, but probably a fair description of the content of most visits. It is certainly in character for bin Laden to promote unity among Islamist groups and listen more than talk. Bin Laden did, however, take advantage of his status as the world's best-known Arab Afghan to meet Islamist leaders, contribute to their activities, *preach Muslim unity and anti-U.S. actions* [my italics], and generally lay the groundwork for future cooperation and coordination." Scheuer, *Through Our Enemies' Eyes*, pp. 129–30.
30. As a practical organizer, bin Laden was apparently not averse to meeting with Shiʿa militants when common goals could be identified. During the early 1990s, for example, he is reported to have met with Hezbolla officials in the Sudan. Wright, *The Looming Tower*, 2006, p. 173. When speaking publicly, however, as his 1989 and 1993 speeches suggest, bin Laden found ready recourse to demonizing Shiʿa in the service of his Sunni-inflected ethnonationalism. Such vitriol was well in keeping with the rhetoric of other Saudi Awakening preachers, notably Shaikhs Salman Al-ʿAwda and Ahmad Al-Qattan, the third and sixth most prominently featured speakers in bin Laden's tape collection.
31. Lacroix, *Awakening Islam*, 2011, p. 203.
32. Wright, *The Looming Tower*, 2006, p. 258.
33. Bergen, *The Osama bin Laden I Know*, 2006, p. 204–5.
34. Islamic Fundamentalist Audio Recording Collection, Yale University, tape

no. 16.   For the loose association of ʿAbd al-Rahman's "Great Satan" with
America, see Friedman, Robert I., "Sheikh Abdel Rahman, the World Trade
Center Bombing and the CIA," Westfield, NJ: Open Media, pamphlet
no. 27 (1993), p. 4.

35.   On 22 Sept. 1996, after bin Laden's "Declaration of War Against the United
States," the leading Arab newspaper *Al-Sharq Al-Awsat* reported Ibn Baz's
assertion that bin Laden "strives toward paths of evil and corruption and
has deviated altogether (*kharaja*) from the principle of due obedience to a
ruler (*wali al-amr*)." "Fatawa Al-ʿUlamaʾ Fi Usama bin Ladin," (n.d.), www.
sahab.org/books/book.php?id=423, last accessed 8 Apr. 2014. Muslim
affairs magazines such as *Al-Muslimun* widely circulated this statement.

36.   Fuchs, Simon, *Proper Signposts for the Camp: The Reception of Classical
Authorities in the Jihad Manual al-ʿUmda Fi ʿImad al-ʿUddah ("The Essential
Guide of Preparation for Jihad")*, Wurzburg: Ergon-Verlag, 2011, p. 114,
ftn. 300.

37.   During a decade of its publication (1984–95), the *Al-Jihad* magazine, run
by the Office of Services, features a small but steady supply of articles about
Yemeni volunteers and martyrs in Afghanistan (see issue nos. 31, 32, 42,
97, 110, 112.)

38.   Randal, Jonathan, *Osama: The Making of a Terrorist*, New York: Alfred
A. Knopf, 2004, p. 100.

39.   Atwan, Abdel Bari, *The Secret History of al Qaeda*, Berkeley: The University
of California Press, 2006, p. 153.

40.   Hegghammer, *Jihad in Saudi Arabia*, p. 47. Saudi recruits escalated their
ranks considerably during the late 1990s. Khalid Shaikh Muhammad would
later state that approximately seventy per cent of the recruits in any given
Arab-Afghan camp were Saudis. Hegghammer, *Jihad in Saudi Arabia:*,
p. 117. These were followed by twenty per cent Yemenis and ten per cent
other nationalities. Gerges, Fawaz A., *The Far Enemy: Why Jihad Went Global*,
Cambridge: Cambridge University Press, 2005, p. 179. A September 2001
report in *Jane's International Security* stated that camp membership during
the late 1980s and early 1990s was primarily Saudi (around 5000 fighters),
followed by Yemenis (3000), Algerians (2800), Egyptians (2000), Tunisians
(400), Iraqis, and Libyans. Gold, Dore, *Hatred's Kingdom: How Saudi Arabia
Supports the New Global Terrorism*, Lanham, MD: Regnery Publishing,
2003, p. 129. Hegghammer's observations suggest that Saudi fighters were
fewer than this report estimated.

41.   Erlanger, Steven, "At Yemen College, Scholarship and Jihadist Ideas," *The
New York Times*, 18 Jan. 2010. http://www.nytimes.com/2010/01/19/
world/middleeast/19yemen.html?pagewanted=1

42.   Bergen, *The Osama bin Laden I Know*, 2006, pp. 108–9.

43. Ibid., p. 109.
44. Interview with bin Laden by the magazine *Nidaʾ Al-Islam* in Oct./Nov. 1996. "New Powder Keg in the Middle East" at http://www.fas.org/irp/world/para/docs/LADIN.htm, last accessed 14 May 2014. For the later date, see Al-Bahri, Nasir, *Dans l'ombre de Ben Laden*, Neuilly-sur-Seine: Michel Lafon, 2010, p. 29. Abdel Bari Atwan's strange postponement of bin Laden's commitments in Yemen around 2000 reflects the tenuousness of his argument that al-Qaʿida's focus on the "near enemy" was a late manifestation of the organization's ideology. *After bin Laden: Al Qaeda, The Next Generation*, New York: The Free Press, 2012, p. 89.
45. Wright, *The Looming Tower*, 2006, p. 153.
46. Bonnefoy, Laurent, *Salafism in Yemen: Transnationalism and Religious Identity*, London: C Hurst, 2011, p. 167.
47. Personal interview with ʿUmar bin Laden, mid 2000s.
48. Atwan, *The Secret History*, 2006, p. 161.
49. The date is suggested by the fact that this cassette title is mentioned in bin Laden's September 1993 speech (discussed in chapter seven). A reference to the Afghan Taliban during the question and answer period suggests that the recording was made no earlier than 1993. Most accounts date the Taliban's formation to the spring of 1994, citing Mulla ʿUmar's confirmation as "commander of the faithful" in Kandahar; by these accounts, public media only picked up news of the Taliban in the fall of that year, especially after the capture of Kandahar in October. See Zaeef, Abdul Salam, *My Life with the Taliban*, New York: Columbia University Press, 2010, pp. 64–5. Afghan photographer Khaled Hadi, however, took a rare photo of Mulla ʿUmar in 1993, suggesting that he was a recognized leader by then (http://www.vanityfair.com/politics/features/2003/02/mullah200302). This recording confirms that reports of the Taliban's formation were circulating among Arab Muslim diasporas before Aug.–Sept. 1993. Two other sources corroborate the Sanaani location of this speech and suggest a February date: Al-Jawjiri, ʿAdil, "'Terrorist' bin Laden Returns to Yemen," *Al-Watan Al-ʿArabi*, 20 Mar. 1998, pp. 32–4; Scheuer, *Through Our Enemies' Eyes*, 2002, p. 129.
50. Sasson, Jean, et. al., *Growing Up bin Laden*, 2010, p. 104.
51. Hegghammer, *Jihad in Saudi Arabia*, 2010, p. 47.
52. This recording is the only source I have found for Al-Zindani's explicit ideological support of bin Laden. U.S. Treasury Department officials evidently assembled enough support for this conclusion to designate Al-Zindani as a "Specially Designated Global Terrorist" in 2004. The Yemeni government has since consistently tried to get his name removed from the list; their refusal to allow for Al-Zindani's extradition has led to ongoing tensions between the regime and the United States.

53. *Al-Jihad*, vol. 64, 1990, pp. 24–6.
54. Al-Bahri, *Dans l'ombre de Ben Laden*, Neuilly-sur-Seine: Michel Lafon, 2010, p. 29. Bin Laden also allegedly met with Muqbil Al-Wadiʿi, an ideological heavyweight at the Waoulia camp. (Ibid., p. 29). Al-Wadiʿi would condemn bin Laden for having turned to weapons to resolve this-worldly conflict. Audio recording *Man Waraʾ Al-Tafjirat Fi Bilad Al-Haramayn?*, 1996 (in author's collection). Such a stance was in keeping with his regular condemnation of violence used to rectify injustice against Muslims. Al-Jamhi, Saʿid ʿUbaid, *al-Qaʿida fi-l-Yaman*, Sanaa: Maktabat Al-Haḍara, 2008, p. 236. Despite his position against militant action, Al-Wadiʿi's publications favor a discourse of such radical militancy that Saudis would accuse him of being the ghost writer for Juhayman Al-ʿUtaibi's letters against the monarchy.
55. Wright, *The Looming Tower*, 2006, p. 174.
56. Interview with bin Laden published by *Pakistan* magazine on 20 Feb. 1999, cited in Scheuer, *Through Our Enemies' Eyes*, p. 135.
57. Ibid., p. 135.
58. Bin Laden's role in supplying cash to the camps has been noted by former associates of his from the 1990s. Wright, *The Looming Tower*, 2006, p. 153. For the Yemeni government's conclusions about the identity of the bombers, see Scheuer, *Through Our Enemies' Eyes*, 2002, p. 135. Yossef Bodansky argues that bin Laden supported and financed one of the prime suspects for organizing the 1992 Aden attacks, Abyan-based Tariq Al-Fadli. *Bin Laden: The Man Who Declared War on America*, New York: Random House, 1999, p. 71. As noted by Scheuer, however, Bodansky's decision not to include sources for his assertions leaves his account very difficult to corroborate.
59. Worth, Robert F., "Ex-Jihadist Defies Yemen's Leader, and Easy Labels," *The New York Times*, 26 Feb. 2010.
60. *Intelligence News Letter* (no. 309, 17 Apr. 1997), released by an unidentified Arab intelligence agency. See http://www.danmahony.com/binladen2.htm, last accessed Feb. 2014
61. Brehony, Noel, *Yemen Divided: The Story of a Failed State in South Arabia*, New York: I.B. Tauris, 2011, pp. 188–9.
62. Burke, Jason, *Al-Qaeda: Casting a Shadow of Terror*, New York: Palgrave, 2003, pp. 133–4.
63. *Al-Watan Al-ʿArabi*, 27 Dec. 1996.
64. A report of bin Laden's assertion appeared in *Al-Watan Al-ʿArabi*, 27 Dec. 1996. Bin Laden is alleged to have referred in his statement less to the hotel bombings than to a sub-plot by Arab-Afghans on the same day near the Adeni airport in which several men were arrested by Yemeni officials for

possessing rocket-propelled grenades. An American C5 Galaxy transport plane was parked on the airport's runway.

65. Soufan, *The Black Banners*, 2011, p. 34.

7. TAKING GANDHI TO JERUSALEM THROUGH OSLO, NORWAY

1. The date is suggested by bin Laden's reference to the United States' announcement on 18 Aug. 1993, "two weeks ago," of its decision to cut off aid to the Sudan, and also to American President Jimmy Carter's visit to the country, occurring in Aug. of the same year.
2. *Sura* of Repentence: 8.
3. *Sura* of Repentence: 10.
4. The Quraish was a powerful Meccan tribe that had long controlled mercantile activities in the region. They were traditional custodians of the Sacred Mosque and its House (*Ka'ba*).
5. In Sept. 1982, during Israel's occupation of Beirut and the Lebanese civil war, Christian Lebanese forces massacred approximately 700–3,500 Palestinians and Lebanese Shi'a in the two refugee camps of Sabra and Shatila.
6. Verses 7–8. As in his earlier speeches, discussed in chapters five and six, bin Laden finds verses about the Badr raid inspiring insofar as they indicate God's preference for testing one's faith in armed combat. On this occasion, he downplays the theme of fighting Meccan disbelievers and instead emphasizes training in Afghanistan in preparation for combat against Israeli Jews and Americans.
7. *Sura* of The Women: 84.
8. His possible presence in Pakistan or Afghanistan is discounted by the fact that respondents ask him about ways to travel to these two countries. Although there is a remote possibility that bin Laden was speaking from Qatar, where he is known to have traveled on at least one occasion through the mid 1990s, or Brunei, where he is reported to have conducted a short visit in 1993, his continuous reference to his presence on Saudi territory makes these locations highly unlikely.
9. The report only criticized the Saudi government for inadequately supervising Islamic charities within the Kingdom. Kostiner, Joseph, "The Rise of Jihadi Trends in Saudi Arabia: The Post Iraq-Kuwait War Phase," in *Radical Islam and International Security: Challenges and Responses*, (eds) Efraim Inbar and Hillel Frisch, Routledge, 2007, p. 87.
10. Ibid., p. 81.
11. Lacroix, Stéphane, *Awakening Islam*, p. 75.
12. Ibid., p. 26.

13. Ibid., pp. 19–22,136–7.
14. Dwailibi, Georges Jawdat, *La Rivalité entre le Clergé Religieux et la Famille Royale au Royaume d'Arabie Saudite*, Paris: Éditions Publibook, 2006, p. 32–3.
15. See Fandy, Mamoun, "The Hawali Tapes," *The New York Times*, 1990; Steinberg, Guido, "The Wahhabi Ulama and the Saudi State: 1745 to the Present," in *Saudi Arabia in the Balance: Political, Economy, Society, Foreign Affairs*, (eds) Paul Aarts and Gerd Nonneman, London: Hurst, 2005; *Al-Jazeera* interview with Hawali on 10 July 2002, http://www.aljazeera. net/channel/archive/archive?ArchiveId=90841. In light of more contemporary scholarship on Saudi reform and opposition, Mamoun Fandy's thesis that "the Saudi oppositional discourse is determined more by exogenous variables, such as the Gulf War and American's role in the Middle East, than it is by domestic variables," proves to have been ambitious. *Saudi Arabia and the Politics of Dissent*, New York: St. Martin's Press, 1999, p. 62. See Hegghammer, *Jihad in Saudi Arabia: Violence and Pan-Islamism since 1979*, Cambridge: Cambridge University Press, 2010; Lacroix, *Awakening Islam*, 2011; Alshamsi, Mansoor Jassem, *Islam and Political Reform in Saudi Arabia: The Quest for Political Change and Reform*, New York: Routledge, 2011.
16. Al-Hawali, Safar, "Infidels, Without and Within," *New Perspectives Quarterly*, 8 (1991); for Al-Hawali's indebtedness to Christian apocalypse narratives, see Filiu, Jean-Pierre, *The Apocalypse in Islam*, trans. M. B. DeBevoise, Berkeley: The University of California Press, 2011, p. 108.
17. Bergen, Peter, *The Osama bin Laden I Know: An Oral History of al Qaeda's Leader*, New York: Free Press, 2006, p. 169.
18. Al-Qahtani, Saʿud ʿAbdalla, *Al-Sahwa Al-Islamiyya Al-Saʿudiyya*, Maktaba Dar Al-Nadwa Al-Alaktruniyya, 2004, p. 11.
19. Bergen, *The Osama bin Laden I Know*, 2006, p. 150.
20. Al-Rasheed, Madawi, *Contesting the Saudi State: Islamic Voices from a New Generation*, Cambridge: Cambridge University Press, 2007, p. 93; Lacroix, *Awakening Islam*, 2011, pp. 111–12.
21. Ibid., p. 135.
22. Ibid., p. 136.
23. Commins, David, "Contestation and Authority in Wahhabi Polemics," in *Religion and Politics in Saudi Arabia: Wahhabism and the State*, (eds) Mohammed Ayoob and Hasan Kosebalaban, Boulder, CO: Lynne Rienner, 2008, p. 40; Pollack, Josh, "Anti-Americanism in Contemporary Saudi Arabia," *The Middle East Review of International Affairs*, 7, 4 (2003), pp. 33–4. Neo-salafi websites frequently categorize Al-ʿAwda as a "Sururi," referring to the writings of Syrian-born Muslim scholar Muhammad Surur,

a militant theoretician frequently associated with Sayyid Qutb. See, for example, "Al-'Ulama' Alladhina Qadhafahum Ada'iyya' Al-Salafiyya," http://www.qassimy.com/vb/showthread.php?p=7372918, last accessed 15 May 2014.

24. Ibrahim Al-Sanoussi interview in Bergen, *The Osama bin Laden I Know*, 2006, pp. 149–50; Al-Bahri, Nasir, "Tanzim al-Qa'ida Min Dakhil," *Al-Quds Al-'Arabi*, 18 Mar. 2005 [Part 1/9], p. 17.

25. He would elaborate his views on asceticism (*zuhd*) over the next several years in sermons on "So Where is Asceticism?" (*Ayna Al-Zuhd, Idhan?*), delivered from his hometown of Burayda in 1992, as well as "Pious Reserve and Asceticism" (*Al-War' wa-l-Zuhd*) and "Affirmative Asceticism" (*Al-Zuhd Al-Ijabi*).

26. For additional examples in Yale University's Islamic Fundamentalist Audio Recording Collection, see: "The Obligations of the Pious Community toward Its Scholars" (*Wajib Al-Umma Tujah 'Ulama'ihi*) (nos. 87, 98), "The Tongue and Silence" (*Al-Lisan wa-l-Samt*) (no. 81), "On the Etiquette of Dialogue" (*Adab Al-Hiwar*) (no. 84), "The Truth About Extremism" (*Haqiqat Al-Tatarruf*) (no. 123), and "O People of Kuwait!" (*Ya Ahl Al-Kuwait*) (no. 119). To date I have not found the most strident of Al-'Awda's attacks against U.S. troops on the Arabian Peninsula, released in the early 1990s under the title "The Workmanship of Death" (*Sina'at Al-Mawt*) and discussed by Bodansky. *Bin Laden: The Man Who Declared War on America*, New York: Random House, 1999, p. 118.

27. Lacroix, *Awakening Islam*, 2011, p. 218.

28. Ibid., pp. 246–7.

29. Al-Rasheed, Madawi, "Saudi Arabia's Islamic Opposition," *Current History*, 95, 597 (1996), pp. 16–17.

30. The date of Al-Dubayyan's arrest and the establishment of a Committee for Aid Relief and Rights is discussed in "Muhammad Al-Mas'ari and Prison" (*Muhammad Al-Mas'ari wa-l-Sijn*), Islamic Fundamentalist Audio Recording Collection, Yale University, tape no. 1192.

31. For a fuller discussion of leaders, see Lacroix, *Awakening Islam*, 2011, pp. 175–7.

32. Al-Rasheed, "Saudi Arabia's Islamic Opposition," (1996), p. 20.

33. Prados, Alfred B., "Saudi Arabia: Post-War Issues and U.S. Relations," Congressional Research Service [CRS] Report by the Federation of American Scientists [FAS], Washington, D.C., report no. 93113, 1996. http://www.fas.org/man/crs/93-113.htm

34. Yossef Bodansky claims that the CDLR supported armed militancy against the Saudis. See Leitner, Peter, *Unheeded Warnings: The Lost Reports of the Congressional Task Force on Terrorism and Unconventional Warfare* Washington,

D.C.: Crossbow Books, 2007, pp. 376–7. Evidence he provides from a CDLR newsletter, however, does not demonstrate the committee's support for armed jihad. As noted by Al-Rasheed, the CDLR explicitly denounced the Battalion of Faith. Al-Rasheed, "Saudi Arabia's Islamic Opposition," (1996), p. 20.

35. Lacroix, *Awakening Islam*, 2011, p. 195.
36. The interview was with *Al-Quds Al-'Arabi* on 9 Mar. 1994. See *Report of the Joint Inquiry into the Terrorist Attacks of September 11, 2001*, House Permanent Select Committee on Intelligence and the Senate Select Committee on Intelligence, 2002, Appendix A, p. 7.
37. Scheuer, *Through Our Enemies' Eyes*, p. 145.
38. *Sura* of Repentence: 10.
39. Ali Abdelsoud Mohamad's testimony, reported in Benjamin, Daniel and Steven Simon, *The Age of Sacred Terror: Radical Islam's War Against America*, New York: Random House, 2002, pp. 129–30.
40. As Faisal Devji explains, popular understandings of Gandhi's resistance movement as primarily religious misconstrue the extent to which he focused on a broad-based, ecumenical vocabulary for global coalition building against Western imperialism and neo-liberal economic policies. While Gandhi supported the idea of an Islamic caliphate, his goal was less to give Muslims their own state than it was to draw rank with Muslims in the fight against Western imperialism's localized territorial ambitions. Devji, Faisal, *The Impossible Indian: Gandhi and the Temptation of Violence*, London: Hurst, 2012, pp. 125–6.
41. Lacroix, *Awakening Islam*, 2011, pp. 211–25.
42. Cragin, R. Kim, "Early History of al-Qa'ida," *The Historical Journal*, 51, 4 (2008), p. 1062. Bin Laden's letters from these years were acquired and translated in 2006 by the Rand Corporation's Early History of Al Qaeda Working Group. They are accessible as part of its "Harmony" collection.
43. Al-Rasheed, "Saudi Arabia's Islamic Opposition," (1996), pp. 19–20.
44. Ibid., pp. 19–20.
45. *The 9/11 Commission Report: Final Report of the National Commission on Terrorist Attacks upon the United States* Washington, D.C.: Norton, 2004, p. 68.
46. These sources include classified reports by the Federal Bureau of Investigation as well as the agency's interview with Ali Abdelsoud Mohammad, notes from which, according to the Defense Department, were lost. Wright, Lawrence, *The Looming Tower: Al-Qaeda and the Road to 9/11*, New York: Alfred A. Knopf, 2006, p. 182. They also include the FBI's interview of Moroccan double agent L'Houssaine Kherchtou in Morocco, Aug. 2000, a man whose credibility as an informant has been subject to reasonable sus-

picion. Hirsch, Susan, *In the Moment of Greatest Calamity: Terrorism, Grief and a Victim's Quest for Justice*, Princeton: Princeton University Press, 2006, p. 117.

47. See, for example, Talbott, Strobe and Nayan Chanda, *The Age of Terror: America and the World After September 11*, New Haven: Basic Books, 2001, p. 40.

48. A text of this letter on "The Betrayal of Palestine" can be found in Lawrence, Bruce, *Messages to the World: The Statements of Osama bin Laden*, New York: Verso, 2005, pp. 3–14.

49. Bergen, *The Osama bin Laden I Know*, 2006, p. 201.

50. Wright, *The Looming Tower*, 2006, p. 182.

51. For a summary of the British government's collaboration with bin Laden's ARC through 1998 in efforts to destabilize Libya's Moammar Qaddhafi, see Curtis, Mark, *Secret Affairs: British Collusion with Radical Islam*, London: Profile Books, 2010.

52. Coll, Steve, *Ghost Wars*, p. 270.

8. DAWN ANTHEMS (*ANASHID AL-FAJR*)

1. Abu 'Abd al-Rahman remains the "cook" in the transcript by virtue of his estimation by 'Umar bin Laden even without being named.

2. Soviet troops completed their withdrawal from Afghanistan on 15 Feb. 1989. Since one speaker on the tape mentions the death of Arab-Afghan militant Ahmad Al-Zahrani, which occurred in May during fighting near Jalalabad, the recording was technically produced after the Soviets had left. 'Umar did not have a chance to hear this mention of Al-Zahrani.

3. See Roy, Olivier, *Globalized Islam: The Search for a New Ummah*, New York: Columbia University Press, 2004, pp. 99; Hegghammer, Thomas, *Jihad in Saudi Arabia: Violence and Pan-Islamism since 1979*, Cambridge: Cambridge University Press, 2010, pp. 59–60.

4. Ibid., p. 46.

5. Given mention of the Badr camp and the martyr Ahmad Al-Zahrani (ftn. 2), both prominent among Arab-Afghans during the late 1980s and early 1990s, the camp was likely located in eastern Afghanistan. The cook's reference to the village of "Shaf" (transcript 3), an unusual place name, raises the possibility that the location was near to Shaf-e Heyvanat, a village outside the capital city of the Helmand province in the southwest. Elsewhere on the tape, mention is made of "Bustuk Square," a place I have been unable to identify.

6. My challenge of linking voices to speakers A–N was made all the more formidable by what appears to have been warped audiotape toward the middle

of side B (mostly beginning with transcript 8.) Special thanks are due to assistant co-translators Mohamed Amin and Nour-Eddine Mouktabis.

7. Sasson, Jean, Najwa bin Ladin and Omar bin Ladin, *Growing Up bin Laden: Osama's Wife and Son Take Us Inside Their Secret World*, New York: St. Martin's Press, 2010, pp. 214.

8. *Al-Sharq Al-Awsat*, 11 Jan. 2003; see http://www.aawsat.com/details.asp?section=4&article=146387&issueno=8810.

9. The cook's neologism differs from the standard Arabic term for "wet dream" (*ihtilam*).

10. See chapter three for a fuller discussion of 'Azzam's contributions.

11. Wright, Lawrence, *The Looming Tower: Al-Qaeda and the Road to 9/11*, New York: Alfred A. Knopf, 2006, p. 248.

12. Al-Bahri, Nasir, "Haris Sabiq li-Za'im al-Qa'ida," (2010), http://alwatan.kuwait.tt/ArticleDetails.aspx?Id=108707&YearQuarter=20112, last accessed 8 May 2014. No copies of this sermon appear to have surfaced.

13. Wright, *The Looming Tower*, 2006, p. 248.

14. Zaydan, Ahmad, *Bin Ladin bi-la Qina'*, Beirut: Al-Sharikat Al-'Alamiyya li-l-Kitab, 2003, p. 155.

15. Bergen, Peter, *The Osama bin Laden I Know: An Oral History of al Qaeda's Leader*, New York: Free Press, 2006, p. 187.

16. For restrictions on tape recording at Arab-Afghan camps, see ibid., p. 406.

17. "Al-Tariq," *Al-Jihad*, vol. 4, Mar. 1985, pp. 37–8.

9. I HAVE SCORNED THOSE WHO REBUKED ME

1. 'Amr Ibn Hisham, nicknamed "Mr. Ignorance" (*Abu Jahl*), was responsible for Islam's first two martyrs. A member of one Mecca's wealthiest tribes, the Banu Makhzum, and a vocal critic of Muhammad's growing influence, he was killed in the battle of Badr.

2. The battle of Badr occurred in CE 624 after Muslims attempted to seize a merchant caravan bound for Mecca. Bin Laden's narrative of Badr underscores the determination of the early Companions of the Prophet to fight Quraishi merchants and give them no refuge, whatever the bonds of previous friendship or mutual interest.

3. Umayya Ibn Khalaf was a Quraish leader in Mecca who owned Bilal, an Abyssinian slave, until his emancipation by the Prophet's father-in-law Abu Bakr. He later fought and died at Badr.

4. The Riyadh attack on the Saudi National Guard headquarters, conducted by Saudi militants, occurred on 6 Nov. 1995. Five Americans and two Indians were killed. The bombing of the Khobar Towers near Dhahran, where foreign military personnel were housed, occurred on 25 June 1996. Nineteen

American servicemen were killed along with over 370 killed or wounded from many other countries. Subsequent investigations have concluded that the operation was conducted by Shi'a extremists rather than al-Qa'ida or its Sunni affiliates.

5. The *Small Collecting Work* (*Al-Jami' Al-Saghir*) was written by the Hanafi scholar Muhammad Al-Shaybani in the eighth century. It remains among the most authoritative summations of early Muslim doctrine, and contains a large assemblage of sound *hadith* reports.

6. 'Amru Ibn Kulthum Al-Taghlibi was the leader of a powerful Arab tribe before the advent of Islam. His opponent, 'Amru Ibn Hind, was not only a Nestorian Christian regent but was of a dynasty that had made capitulations to Persian conquerors.

7. *Sura* of The Family of 'Imran: 145.

8. Verse of the famed tenth-century poet Abu Tayyib Al-Mutanabbi, a poet whose chief patron, Saif al-Dawla of Aleppo, led constant raids against the Byzantines. Saif al-Dawla was descended from the same Arab tribe as 'Amru Ibn Kulthum.

9. Anonymous aphorism.

10. *Sura* of Muhammad: 5–6.

11. *Sura* of The Cow: 154.

12. *Sura* of Repentence: 14.

13. *Sura* of Muhammad: 4.

14. Attributed to the seventh-century governor of Syria Mu'awiyya Ibn Abi Sufyan, these verses were allegedly sent to the caliph 'Ali Ibn Abi Talib when the latter demanded that he abdicate leadership. Mu'awiyya is reviled among Shi'a for having rejected 'Ali's claim to succession and plunged the Islamic community into internecine warfare that would mar Islam's legacy ever after.

15. In CE 806, some 135,000 Muslim troops advanced into Asia Minor under Harun Al-Rashid's command after the Byzantines, under Emporer Nicephorus I at the time, had stopped paying tribute to the Muslim caliphate. The advance began with a decisive victory against the Byzantine army in the previous year in Phrygia, modern-day Turkey.

16. The 'Aws and Khazraj tribes of Madina were some of Muhammad's first supporters. They ultimately fell into fierce conflict with resident Madinan Jews.

17. Verses are attributed by commentators to bin Laden himself. http://www.hajrcom.com/hajrvb/showthread.php?t=402813659, last accessed 30 July 2013.

18. Verses by 'Antar Ibn Shaddad, a pre-Islamic slave of the Arabian Banu 'Abs tribe whose adventurous life and eventual emancipation provides material for many well-known stories of heroism, romance, and courage in battle.

19. Pre-Islamic poet Abu Al-Ghawl Al-Tahawi.
20. Verses by Jordanian professor of Islamic law Yusif Muhy al-Din "Abu Hilala."
21. 'Asim Ibn Thabit was a companion of the Prophet who fought against the Quraish in the battle of Badr.
22. *Sura* of Repentence: 5.
23. Verses are attributed by commentators to bin Laden himself. http://www.muslm.net/vb/archive/index.php/t-332127.html, last accessed 30 July 2013
24. Muslim tradition holds that the Banu Quraiza were a tribe of Madinan Jews who conspired with the Quraish in the battle of "The Confederates" (*Al-Ahzab*) in CE 627. In the conflict's aftermath, they were expelled from the city, enslaved, or killed.
25. "Emigrants" (*muhajirun*) are typically understood as the Arabs in and around Mecca who converted and accompanied Muhammad on his journey to Madina. "Supporters" (*ansar*) are those from Madina who joined his cause.
26. These verses were recited by 'Abdalla Ibn Rawaha at the battle of Mu'ta in CE 629, Islam's first against the Byzantines. Muslim commanders were Zayd Ibn Haritha, Ja'far Ibn Abi Talib, and 'Abdalla Ibn Rawaha, each of whom was killed in succession. The "predecessors" referred to here are Zayd and Ja'far.
27. Verses by Ja'far Ibn Abi Talib (see ftn. 20).
28. Verses by the pre-Islamic hero 'Antar Ibn Shaddad (see ftn. 13).
29. Poem attributed by commentators to bin Laden himself. http://www.ksaislam.com/vb/showthread.php?t=12333, last accessed 30 July 2013.
30. *Sura* of The Spoils of War: 72.
31. The speech was first published in full by *Al-Quds Al-Arabi*, a London-based Arabic newspaper, under the title a "Declaration of the World Islamic Front for Jihad against the Jews and the Crusaders" on 23 Feb. 1998.
32. Brown, Vahid, "Al-Qa'ida Central and Local Affiliates," in *Self-Inflicted Wounds: Debates and Divisions within Al-Qa'ida and Its Periphery*, (eds) Assaf Moghadam and Brian Fishman, Westpoint: Combatting Terrorism Center, 2010, p. 93.
33. According to Anne Stenerson, the Taliban's deputy Minister of the Interior Mulla Khakshar met bin Laden in 1996 and told him flatly: "It is time for you people to leave our country," Stenersen, Anne, "Arab and Non-Arab Jihadis," in ibid., p. 141. After 1998, the Taliban's Foreign Minister and Mulla 'Umar's secretary Mulla Wakil Ahmad Mutawakkil made repeated attempts to restrict bin Laden's activities. Bin Laden remarked around this time that "Two entities are against our jihad. One is the US, and the other is the Taliban's own Foreign Affairs Ministry." Bergen, Peter, *The Osama bin Laden I Know: An Oral History of al Qaeda's Leader*, New York: Free Press, 2006, p. 250.

34. Brown, "Al-Qaʿida Central and Local Affiliates," 2010, p. 94.

35. *The 9/11 Commission Report: Final Report of the National Commission on Terrorist Attacks upon the United States*, Washington, D.C.: Norton, 2004, p. 48.

36. *Al-Quds Al-ʿArabi*, 31 Aug./1 Sept. 1996, p. 1.

37. I discuss this committee in chapter seven.

38. Talbott, Strobe and Nayan Chanda, *The Age of Terror: America and the World After September 11*, New Haven: Basic Books, 2001, p. 102.

39. See, for example, Talbott and Chanda, *The Age of Terror*, 2001, p. 102; Gunaratna, *Inside Al Qaeda*, Hurst & Co., 2002, p. 116; or the Wikipedia entry "Fatawa of Osama bin Laden" (as of July 2013).

40. *Al-Quds Al-ʿArabi*, 27 Nov. 1996, p. 1.

41. Peters, Rudolph, *Jihad in Classical and Modern Islam*, second edition, Princeton: Marcus Wiener, 2005, p. 174.

42. In addition to the *Minbar Al-Tawhid Wa-l-Jihad* audio recording of the speech discussed later in this chapter, a full Arabic transcript of the speech would be published online in a comprehensive encomium of bin Laden by Saudi militant Faris Al-Zahrani, also known as Abu Jandal Al-ʾAzdi. *Usama bin Ladin: Mujaddid Al-Zaman wa Qahir Al-Amrikan*, Minbar Al-Tawhid wa-l-Jihad, n.d., http://www.tawhed.ws/dl?i=2v5pw774, last accessed 15 May 2014.

43. See Porter, Gareth, "Khobar Towers Investigated: How a Saudi Deception Protected Osama bin Laden," (2008), https://deeppoliticsforum.com/forums/showthread.php?1674-quot-Khobar-Towers-Investigated-How-a-Saudi-Deception-Protected-Osama-bin-Laden-quot. Focusing on the Khobar bombings, Porter's account of al-Qaʿida's involvement largely debunks allegations of Iranian sponsorship that were floated at the time by the Saudis and the United States. For a counter-assessment of al-Qaʿida's non-involvement in the attacks, see Hegghammer, Thomas, "Deconstructing the Myth about al-Qaʿida and Khobar," *Combatting Terrorism Center Sentinel*, 1, 3 (2008).

44. A draft of the speech entitled "The Epistle" (*al-risala*), dated 31 July 1996, was found by the Federal Bureau of Investigation on a computer owned by bin Laden's associate in London, Khalid Fawwaz. Soufan, Ali H., *The Black Banners: The Inside Story of 9/11 and the War Against al-Qaeda*, New York: W.W. Norton, 2011, p. 101. For bin Laden's chronic cash deficit when returning to Afghanistan in July, see Sasson, Jean, Najwa bin Laden and Omar bin Laden, *Growing Up bin Laden: Osama's Wife and Son Take Us Inside Their Secret World*, New York: St. Martin's Press, 2010, p. 224.

45. The *Al-Quds Al-ʿArabi*'s report on the speech suggests that editors received a complete facsimile. Since the newspaper refused to hand over the fax to

other news services, the FBIS had to rely on an incomplete version that was published several weeks later in a newsletter by the Movement for Islamic Reform in Arabia, led by London-based Saudi Opposition exile Saad Al-Faqih. Al-Faqih's inability to appreciate the ethical nuances of poetry is suggested in his CNN interview in 1997, featured later in this chapter.

46. Al-Mas'ari's text features the addition of a clause, for example, found nowhere in bin Laden's original speech in any of its versions but also found in the FBIS translation. After criticizing the United States for burning Middle Eastern oil wells during military conflicts so that they are unserviceable either by its enemies or its own European or Asian allies, bin Laden is alleged to have added the phrase: "particularly Japan, which is the major consumer of oil in the region." His freewheeling translation led assiduous scholars at the Middle East Research Institute of Japan to post on-line one of the earliest available copies of bin Laden's speech, courtesy of Al-Mas'ari. This example is only one dozens of unique clauses and words that appear exclusively in translations by both Al-Mas'ari and the FBIS.

47. See, for example, and Kepel, Gilles and Jean-Pierre Milelli, *Al Qaeda in Its Own Words*, Pascale Ghazaleh, Cambridge: Belknap Press of Harvard University Press, 2008.

48. See al-Qa'ida videotape accompanying bin Laden's Mar. 2008 statement about the Danish newspaper *Jyllands-Posten's* cartoons depicting the Prophet Muhammad.

49. In 2005, a jihadi chatroom participant noted bin Laden's use of the poem and redeployed it in his own savage critique of Shi'a Muslims' theological errancy. http://sh.rewayat2.com/ansab/Web/3897/003.htm, url no longer available.

50. See "Tactical Recommendations" as cited in Saghi, Omar, "Osama bin Laden, the Iconic Orator," In *Al Qaeda in Its Own Words*, 2008, p. 30.

51. Accessed on 29 Jan. 2010.

52. Roy, Olivier, *Globalized Islam: The Search for a New Ummah*, New York: Columbia University Press, 2004, pp. 56–7.

53. Roy, Olivier, *The Failure of Political Islam*, Cambridge, MA: Harvard University Press, 1994. On the traditional restrictions of discourse about the obligations of jihad, see chapter four of Kelsay, John, *Arguing the Just War in Islam*, Cambridge, MA: Harvard University Press, 2007.

54. Roy, Olivier, *Globalized Islam*, 2004, p. 57.

55. Al-Bahri, Nasir, "Tanzim al-Qa'ida Min Dakhil," *Al-Quds Al-'Arabi*, 22 Mar. 2005 [Part 4/9], p. 19.

56. Al-Bahri, Nasir, *Dans l'ombre de Ben Laden*, Neuilly-sur-Seine: Michel Lafon, 2010, p. 75.

57. Al-Bahri, Nasir, "Tanzim al-Qa'ida Min Dakhil," *Al-Quds Al-'Arabi*, 18 Mar. 2005 [Part 1/9], p. 17.

58. Burke, Jason, *Al-Qaeda: Casting a Shadow of Terror*, New York: Palgrave, 2003, p. 146.
59. The first assassination attempt was in January and was also sponsored by Saudis. Al-Bahri, *Dans l'ombre*, 2010, p. 76. Michael Scheuer reports two other assassination attempts in March. Scheuer, *Through Our Enemies' Eyes*, 2002, p. 153.
60. Al-Bahri, *Dans l'ombre*, 2010, p. 87.
61. The video is available at http://www.youtube.com/watch?v=dqQwnqjA-6w under the title "Exclusive Osama Bin Laden—First Ever TV Interview," last accessed 15 May 2014.
62. Interview available at http://www.informationclearinghouse.info/article7204.htm
63. Macleod, Scott, "Osama Bin Laden: The Paladin of Jihad," *Time Magazine*, May 6, 1996.
64. Gerth, Jeff and Miller, Judith, "Funds for Terrorists Traced To Persian Gulf Businessmen," *The New York Times*, 14 Aug. 1996, p. A1; for later revisions see Randal, Jonathan, *Osama: The Making of a Terrorist*, New York: Alfred A. Knopf, 2004, p. 203; Bergen, *The Osama bin Laden I Know*, 2006, p. 10.
65. According to investigative journalist Gareth Porter, the CIA's report was a product of inter-agency tensions at the time. Produced by head of the bin Laden unit Michael Scheuer and his team, long at work on the Riyadh bombing investigation, the report was an opportunistic gambit that was released when they were told by agency chief Winston Wiley and FBI director Louis Freeh that links between bin Laden and both the Riyadh and Khobar bombings were officially no longer tenable. Porter, Garth, "Khobar Towers Investigated." The CIA's report is available at http://www2.gwu.edu/~nsarchiv/NSAEBB/NSAEBB343/osama_bin_laden_file01_transcription.pdf
66. See, for example, Habib, Randa, "Jordanian Militants Train in Afghanistan to Confront Regime," *Agence France-Presse*, 30 May 1993, and Kifner, John, "Wealthy Force Behind Murky Militant Group," *The New York Times*, 14 Aug. 1998.
67. Zernike, Kate and Michael T. Kaufman, "The Most Wanted Face of Terrorism," *The New York Times*, 2 May 2011. http://www.nytimes.com/2011/05/02/world/02osama-bin-laden-obituary.html
68. Atwan, Abdel Bari, *The Secret History of al Qaeda*, Berkeley: The University of California Press, 2006, pp. 51–2.
69. Wright, Lawrence, *The Looming Tower*, p. 196.
70. Ibid, pp. 196–7.
71. "Bin Laden No Longer Seen as Main Al-Qaida Financier," *Associated Press*, reported by MSNBC on 2 Sept. 2004, http://www.nbcnews.com/

id/5896423/ns/us_news-security/t/bin-laden-no-longer-seen-main-al-qaida-financier/#.UhPIbGTF1G4

72. The results of this investigation are mentioned in the CIA's 1996 biographical profile of bin Laden.

73. Pyes, Craig, Judith Miller and Stephen Engelberg, "One Man and a Global Web of Violence," *The New York Times*, 14 Jan. 2001.

74. Nacos, Brigitte L., "Covering bin Laden," in *After bin Laden: Global Media and the World's Most Wanted Man*, (eds) Susan Jeffords and Fahed Al-Sumait, Bloomington, IN: The University of Indiana Press, 2015.

75. Robert Fisk's article in July 1996 reported that bin Laden was gaining notoriety for his role as the "'financier of an Islamic international army,' training fighters to oppose the governments of Algeria and Egypt as well as Saudi Arabia." "Arab Rebel Leader Warns the British: 'Get out of the Gulf,'" *The Independent*. In May of the previous year, *Time* reporter Scott Macleod admitted that, despite bin Laden's possible role in financing terrorist attacks in Saudi Arabia, Egypt, Afghanistan, the Sudan, Yemen, and France, "so far, no one has produced conclusive evidence of bin Laden's involvement with terrorism." "Osama Bin Laden: The Paladin of Jihad," *Time Magazine*, 6 May 1996.

76. In the wake of the 1998 bombings of U.S. embassies in East Africa, his lament would supply the *New York Times* its best evidence for linking him to previous anti-American terrorist activity. "Rescuers and Investigators Sent by US Begin to Arrive," *The New York Times*, 9 Aug. 1998.

77. "Letter to Mullah Mohammed 'Omar from bin Laden," available on the Combatting Terrorism Center's Harmony Program database as document no. AFGP-2002–600321.

78. Ibn Baz's article was published in the *Al-Sharq Al-Awsat* newspaper on 22 Sept. 1996 as well as in the magazine *Al-Muslimun*. "Fatawa Al-'Ulama' Fi Usama bin Ladin," n.d., www.sahab.org/books/book.php?id=423, last accessed 2004

79. Al-Wadi'i, Shaikh Hadi Muqbil, *Man Wara' Al-Tafjirat Fi Bilad Al-Haramayn?*, 1996.

10. NEW BASES NEAR AN ANCIENT HOUSE

1. The date is written on the cassette cartridge.

2. Sasson, Jean, Najwa bin Ladin and Omar bin Ladin, *Growing Up bin Laden: Osama's Wife and Son Take Us Inside Their Secret World*, New York: St. Martin's Press, 2010, p. 208.

3. Bin Laden continued foregrounding his Meccan origins in later television interviews with Al-Jazeera. See, for example, "Bin Ladin Yatahaddath," December 1998, http://www.youtube.com/watch?v=oDmp-lM5hL0

4. Wagemakers, Joas, "The Transformation of a Radical Concept: al-wala' wa-l-bara' in the Ideology of Abu Muhammad al-Maqdisi," in *Global Salafism: Islam's New Religious Movement*, ed. Roel Meijer, London: Hurst, 2009, p. 90.

5. Ibid., p. 92.

6. This speech is featured on cassette no. 1233 in Yale University's Islamic Fundamentalist Audio Recording Collection as well as on a video tape released by al-Qa'ida's Al-Sahab media department in 2007 (in author's collection).

7. Formulated by the CIA with the assistance of Afghan tribal leaders in early 1998, a raid into the Kandahar airport complex was set to take place in June before being deemed too prone to injuring or killing innocent bystanders. Coll, Steve, *Ghost Wars*, pp. 395–6.

8. Randal, Jonathan, *Osama: The Making of a Terrorist*, New York: Alfred A. Knopf, 2004, p. 91.

9. Hegghammer, Thomas, *Jihad in Saudi Arabia: Violence and Pan-Islamism since 1979*, Cambridge: Cambridge University Press, 2010, pp. 130–1.

10. Ibid., p. 135.

11. Tawil, Camille, *Brothers in Arms: The Story of al-Qa'ida and the Arab Jihadists*, London: Saqi, 2010, p. 151.

12. Soufan, Ali H., *The Black Banners: The Inside Story of 9/11 and the War Against al-Qaeda*, New York: W.W. Norton, 2011, p. 41.

13. Al-Bahri, Nasir, *Dans l'ombre de Ben Laden*, Neuilly-sur-Seine: Michel Lafon, 2010, p. 61.

14. Bowden, Mark, "The Truth about Mogadishu," *The Philadelphia Inquirer*, 8 Oct. 2006, http://articles.philly.com/2006–10–08/news/25417846_1_al-qaeda-mogadishu-bin. Bowden's conclusion of bin Laden's peripheral role in Somalia is backed by the State Department's former counterterrorism chief Robert Oakley, who had intimate knowledge of the battle, as well as Jason Burke and Lawrence Wright. Loeb, Vernon, "A Global, Pan-Islamic Network; Terrorism Entrepreneur Unifies Groups Financially, Politically," *Washington Post*, 23 Aug. 1998; Burke, *Al-Qaeda: Casting a Shadow of Terror*, New York: Palgrave, 2003, pp. 134–5; Wright, *The Looming Tower: Al-Qaeda and the Road to 9/11* New York: Alfred A. Knopf, 2006, pp. 188–9.

15. Summers, Anthony and Robbyn Swan, *The Eleventh Day: The Full Story of 9/11 and Osama bin Laden*, New York: Ballantine Books, 2011, p. 393.

16. Ibid., pp. 393–4.

17. Hegghammer, *Jihad in Saudi Arabia*, 2010, pp. 114–16.

18. Al-Bahri, Nasir, "Tanzim al-Qa'ida Min Dakhil," *Al-Quds Al-'Arabi*, 25 Mar. 2005 [Part 7/9], p. 17.

19. Bergen, Peter, *The Osama bin Laden I Know: An Oral History of al Qaeda's Leader*, New York: Free Press, 2006, pp. 177–8.

20. Mustafa Hamid, on-line narrative entitled *Qissat Al-Bayʾat Al-ʿArabiyya*, p. 15, as discussed in Brown, Vahid, "The Facade of Allegiance: bin Ladin's Dubious Pledge to Mullah Omar," *CTC Sentinel*, 3, 1 (2010), p. 3.
21. Brown, Vahid, *Cracks in the Foundation: Leadership Schisms in Al-Qaʿida 1989–2006*, West Point, NY: Combating Terrorism Center, 2007, p. 16.
22. Fazul, Haroun, "The Letter from El Hage's Computer," Frontline, Public Broadcasting Service, 1997. http://www.pbs.org/wgbh/pages/frontline/shows/binladen/upclose/computer.html
23. Email dated July 1998, found on an al-Qaʿida computer purchased by the *Wall Street Journal* in 2001. See Cullison, Alan, "Strained Alliance: Al Qaeda's Sour Days in Afghanistan—Fighters Mocked the Place; Taliban, in Turn, Nearly Booted Out bin Laden—A Fateful US Missile Strike," *Wall Street Journal*, 2002. Mention of the date "1999" in a later, breezier, article in *The Atlantic Monthly*, Sept. 2004, appears to be a typo.
24. Tawil, *Brothers in Arms*, 2010, p. 169.
25. Bergen, *The Osama bin Laden I Know*, 2006, pp. 278–9.
26. Gunaratna, *Inside Al Qaeda*, p. 59.
27. Soufan, *The Black Banners*, 2011, p. 256.
28. Al-Bahri, *Dans l'ombre*, 2010, pp. 103–4.
29. Hegghammer, *Jihad in Saudi Arabia*, 2010, p. 114.
30. Zaydan, Ahmad, *Bin Ladin bi-la Qinaʿ*, Beirut: Al-Sharikat Al-ʿAlamiyya li-l-Kitab, 2003, p. 120.
31. Ibid., p. 154.

11. AN INTIMATE CONVERSATION (*JALASA*)

1. I was able to share the recording with Al-Bahri and hear his account through collaboration with documentary film director Laura Poitras who visited Yemen in 2009 during the making of her film *The Oath*.
2. Al-Bahri, Nasir, *Dans l'ombre de Ben Laden*, Neuilly-sur-Seine: Michel Lafon, 2010, pp. 88–9 (author's translation from French.)
3. Personal communication with Deputy Commissioner John Miller, 13 Feb 2015.
4. See mention of such a practice by Peter Bergen, *The Osama bin Laden I Know: An Oral History of al Qaeda's Leader*, New York: Free Press, 2006, p. 281.
5. Boas, Franz, "On Alternating Sounds," *American Anthropologist*, 2,1 (1889).
6. Moore, David W., "Public Ready for War with Iraq," Gallup News Service, 18 Feb. 1998. http://www.gallup.com/poll/4252/Public-Ready-War-Iraq.aspx
7. See Porter, Gareth, "Khobar Towers Investigated: How a Saudi Deception Protected Osama bin Laden," (2008), https://deeppoliticsforum.com/forums/

showthread.php?1674-quot-Khobar-Towers-Investigated-How-a-Saudi-Deception-Protected-Osama-bin-Laden-quot#.U3EJK61dURw

8. Yemen is reported to have approached Interpol with a request to arrest bin Laden as early as 1994, as noted by the CIA in 1996. "Usama bin Ladin: Islamic Extremist Financier," Central Intelligence Agency, 1996. http://www2.gwu.edu/~nsarchiv/NSAEBB/NSAEBB343/osama_bin_laden_file01_transcription.pdf. The intelligence organization appears to have been unresponsive.

9. Among these veterans was Anu Anas Al-Liby. Curtis, Mark, *Secret Affairs: British Collusion with Radical Islam*, London: Profile Books, 2010, chapter thirteen.

10. File nos1998/20232, from May, and S(2) 98CR.1023, from Nov., are available on the FBI's website: http://vault.fbi.gov/osama-bin-laden/osama-bin-laden-part-1-of-1/view

11. Yusufzai, Rahimullah, "In the Way of Allah," *The News* (Islamabad), 15 June 1998. *FBIS Report: Compilation of Usama Bin Laden Statements 1994–January 2004*, pp. 72–4, http://www.fas.org/irp/world/para/ubl-fbis.pdf, last accessed 15 May 2014

12. Brown, Vahid, "Al-Qaʿida Central and Local Affiliates," in *Self-Inflicted Wounds: Debates and Divisions within Al-Qaʿida and Its Periphery*, (eds) Assaf Moghadam and Brian Fishman, Westpoint: Combatting Terrorism Center, 2010, ftn. 221, p. 73.

13. "The Ogaden File: Operation Holding (Al-Msk)," available on the Combatting Terrorism Center's Harmony Program database as document no. AFGP-2002–600104 (English version.)

14. Stenersen, Anne, "Arab and Non-Arab Jihadis," In *Self-Inflicted Wounds: Debates and Divisions within Al-Qaʿida and Its Periphery*, (eds) Assaf Moghadam and Brian Fishman, Westpoint: Combatting Terrorism Center, 2010, p. 135. For reports of bin Laden's financial connections with African diamond and gem mining industries, see Pirio, Gregory Alonso, *The African Jihad: bin Laden's Quest for the Horn of Africa*, Trenton, NJ: The Red Sea Press, 2007, pp. 136–8.

15. Whitlock, Craig, "After a Decade at War With West, Al-Qaeda Still Impervious to Spies," *The Washington Post*, 2008. http://articles.washingtonpost.com/2008-03-20/world/36926605_1_al-qaeda-qaeda-european-intelligence-officials

16. Nasiri, Omar, *Inside the Jihad: My Life with Al Qaeda*, London: Hurst, 2006, p. 285.

17. Testimonies of L'Houssaine Kherchtou and Hasan ʿAbd-Rabbuh Al-Surayhi as reported in Bergen, *The Osama bin Laden I Know*, 2006, pp. 83, 101–2.

18. Ibid., p. 110.

19. Posted on the Combatting Terrorism Center's Harmony Program database, these four documents are numbered as follows: AFGP-2002–600178 (though under the new title "Al-Qaʿida Bylaws" as of late 2013; note that the same document without interspersed blank pages is filed as no. AFGP-2002–600048), AFGP-2002–000080, AFGP-2002–000078, and AFGP-2002–600175. The second and third of these files are part of a single paginated edition. While none of the charters are dated, the fourth document is likely of a much later provenance (by my estimate 1999–2001) given its explicit designation of al-Qaʿida as a global terrorist organization. Additionally, along with a discussion of clandestine cells operating in non-Muslim-majority societies and extensive Qurʾanic citation absent from earlier editions, this document foregrounds a definition of "al-Qaʿida" worthy of a latter-day apologist: "An Islamic group (jamaʿa) whose path is jihad because jihad is the matter that brings individuals together."

20. A sample of bin Laden's handwriting is found in Al-Daghidi, Anis, Bin Ladin…wa Alladhina Maʿhu, Cairo: Matkabat Jazirat Al-Ward, 2005, p. 55.

21. AFGP-2002–000080 (author's own translation from the Arabic version), p. 6.

22. Ibid., (author's own translation from the Arabic version), p. 3.

23. AFGP-2002,000078, pp. 21–2, available at https://www.ctc.usma.edu/wp-content/uploads/2010/08/AFGP-2002–000078-Orig.pdf

24. AFGP-2002,000078, p. 13; AFGP-2002–000080, p. 3. Note that with the deletion of the term "Afghan jihad," the Al-Faruq camp charter becomes stripped of any attachment to a specific place or history.

25. AFGP-2002–000080 (author's own translation from the Arabic version), p. 2.

26. Waugh, Billy and Tim Keown, Hunting the Jackal: A Special Forces and CIA Soldier's Fifty Years on the Frontlines of the War against Terrorism, New York: Avon Books, 2004, p. 132.

27. Habib, Randa, "Jordanian Militants Train in Afghanistan to Confront Regime," Agence France-Presse, 30 May 1993.

28. Wright, Lawrence, The Looming Tower, p. 182.

29. The cable is posted on the internet at http://intelfiles.egoplex.com/1994-02-16-Qassem-Interview.pdf, last accessed Feb. 2014. Two months later, the Egyptian English publication Al Ahram Weekly reported the establishment of an Arab-Afghan support base in Pakistan in 1985 called Al Qaʿida. "Part 2, History of al Qaida," (anonymous author, n.d.), http://www.oss.net/dynamaster/file_archive/091213/2adb31631131c668f1a8257035d7 34c5/Part%202,%20History%20of%20al%20Qaida%20(NXPowerLite). doc, p. 13, last accessed 15 May 2014

30. "Usama bin Ladin: Islamic Extremist Financier," Central Intelligence

Agency, 1996. http://www2.gwu.edu/~nsarchiv/NSAEBB/NSAEBB343/
osama_bin_laden_file01_transcription.pdf

31. The story broke on 17 Sept. in the Associated Press and was picked up on the same day by CNN.

32. Al-Bahri, *Dans l'ombre*, 2010, p. 169. In a video posted online on 3 June 2012, Ayman Al-Zawahiri cites bin Laden's pre-attack finances as having been roughly $55,000. Whatever we make of such posturing, journalist Jason Burke notes that from 1998–2001, radical groups more often approached al-Qaʿida with their plans and budgetary outlays for conducting attacks rather than vice-versa. *Al-Qaeda: Casting a Shadow of Terror*, New York: Palgrave, 2003, p. 208.

33. Lynch, Mark, *Voices of the New Arab Public: Iraq, Al Jazeera, and Middle East Politics Today*, New York: Columbia University Press, 2006, p. 45.

34. Gunaratna, *Inside Al Qaeda*, 2002, p. 240.

35. Morris, Michael, "Al-Qaʿida As Insurgency," US Army War College, Carlisle Barracks, Pennsylvania, 2005, www.dtic.mil/cgi-bin/GetTRDoc?AD=AD A434874, p. 1.

36. Cullison, "Strained Alliance," 2002.

12. A PRAGMATIC BASE (*AL-QAʿIDA*)

1. Mustafa Hamid's identity is suggested by the resemblance of topics discussed on this tape to those he has published elsewhere, his strong Egyptian accent, and a student's reference to him by his *nom de guerre* "Abu al-Walid." The date is suggested by Hamid's reference to recent headlines about a ruling by "the international court" in Europe about the conflict between Eritrea and Yemen over the Red Sea island of Hunaish. This decision was by the Permanent Court of Arbitration in the Hague, and was first announced on 9 Oct. 1998. The location is suggested by the fact that Hamid was in close contact with bin Laden throughout late 1998, and references to Yemen suggest that speakers are not inside the country.

2. Gerges, Fawaz A., *The Far Enemy: Why Jihad Went Global*, Cambridge: Cambridge University Press, 2005, p. 192.

3. Brown, Vahid, "Al-Qaʿida Central and Local Affiliates," in *Self-Inflicted Wounds: Debates and Divisions within Al-Qaʿida and Its Periphery*, (eds) Assaf Moghadam and Brian Fishman, Westpoint: Combatting Terrorism Center, 2010, ftn. 258, pp. 82–3.

4. *Al-Jihad*, vol. 64, 1990, pp. 31–3.

5. Islamic Fundamentalist Audio Recording Collection, Yale University, tape no. 1232.

6. In summing up before moving to his next topic, Suwaidan reminds listen-

ers that there are three types of evidence: "We have [situational] evidence (*dalil far'i*) for applied ethics, we have general evidence (*dalil kulli*), and we have a precept (*qa'ida*)." The *qa'ida*, in other words, provides an interpretive medium for comparing idealized norms of moral behavior with the ethical complexities of situated social interaction.

7. For an overview of the legal literature on *qawa'id*, see Kamali, Mohammad Hashim, "Legal Maxims and Other Genres of Literature in Islamic Jurisprudence," *Arab Law Quarterly*, 20, 1 (2006).

8. Ali, Mohamed M. Yunis, *Medieval Islamic Pragmatics: Sunni Legal Theorists' Models of Textual Communication*, Richmond, Surrey: Curzon Press, 2000, p. 89.

9. Haddad, Gibril Fouad, "Sheikh Ahmadu," 9 May 1999, https://groups. google.com/forum/#!topic/soc.religion.islam/jVDrPJ1EXNU, last accessed 14 Sept. 2008.

10. Mernissi, Fatima, *Dreams of Trespass: Tales of a Harem Girlhood*, New York: Addison-Wesley Publishing Company, 1994, p. 63.

11. Islamic Fundamentalist Audio Recording Collection, Yale University, tape no. 506.

12. Hamid, Mustafa, "*Qissat Al-Bay'a Al-'Arabiyya Li-Amir Al-Mu'minin Al-Mulla Muhammad 'Umar* (The Story of the Afghan Arabs: From the Entry to Afghanistan to the Final Exodus with the Taliban)," first published in *Al-Sharq Al-Awsat*, 8 and 9 Dec. 2004, http://www.muslm.org/vb/ showthread.php?354320, last accessed May 2014.

13. Reported in a Pakistani newspaper called *The Muslim* on 15 Mar. 1997. *FBIS Report: Compilation of Usama Bin Laden Statements 1994—January 2004*, pp. 39–41, http://www.fas.org/irp/world/para/ubl-fbis.pdf, last accessed May 15 2014.

14. According to Fazul Abdullah Muhammad, it was actually Mustafa Hamid "'whose great merit it was to have convinced the al-Qa'ida leadership to confront the United States of America' during secret meetings in Peshawar in 1991." Brown, "Al-Qa'ida Central and Local Affiliates," ftn. 258, pp. 82–3. Whatever the substance of Muhammad's assertion, the speeches by bin Laden I examine in earlier chapters show how little bin Laden spoke in public of identifying the United States as his primary enemy before 1996.

15. Islamic Fundamentalist Audio Recording Collection, Yale University, tape no. 338.

16. "A Mother's Deep Sorrow/The Airport Project," Combatting Terrorism Center's Harmony Database document no. AFGP-2002–600092, p. 13 (English version; Arabic version p. 10). For an estimated document date of 1998 see Brown, Vahid, *Cracks in the Foundation: Leadership Schisms in Al-Qa'ida 1989–2006*, West Point, NY: Combating Terrorism Center, 2007, p. 5.

13. LISTEN, PLAN, CARRY OUT "*AL-QA'IDA*"

1. "Various Admin Documents and Questions," available on the Combatting Terrorism Center's Harmony Program database as document no. AFGP-2002–801138, p. 215 (Arabic version; p. 52 in English version), http://www.docexdocs.com/mc/AFGP-2002–801138.pdf, last accessed 15 May 2014.

2. For fuller discussion of the intellectual debates and policy implications of material in this chapter, see Miller, Flagg, "Listen, Plan and Carry Out 'al-Qa'ida': Theological Dissension in Usama bin Ladin's Former Audio-cassette Collection," in *Contextualising Jihadi Thought*, (eds) Jeevan Deol and Zaheer Kazmi, London: Hurst, 2011.

3. There are three copies of the middle volume in Yale University's collection (nos. 857, 896 and 905), two copies of the first volume (nos. 868 and 906) and one copy of the final volume (no. 921).

4. "La'ib Kharaj Al-Mal'ab," Arab Times, http://mms.zain.sd.arabtimes.com/writer/05.htm

5. Interview held in early Apr. 2010.

6. Personal communication with Omar Ashour, senior lecturer at the University of Exeter, in Sept. 2009. Al-Tahhan's association with the Muslim Brothers is suggested by the first location of his original lecture, as announced on one of the volumes: a summer camp for memorizing and reciting the Qur'an located in Ta'if, Saudi Arabia. Summer camps at this time were heavily sponsored by the Muslim Brotherhood.

7. Among these militant students was Qatar's first suicide bomber. An Egyptian computer engineer named 'Umar 'Abdalla 'Ali, he was completing a book manuscript on his teacher at the time that he drove a truck loaded with explosives into the British-sponsored Doha Players Theater during a performance of Shakespeare's *Twelfth Night*. Conducted on 19 Mar. 2005, the attack left one British citizen dead and twelve others wounded. http://www.aawsat.com/details.asp?section=4&article=290218&issueno=9615

8. Al-Suri's mention of Al-Tahhan is followed by other figures better known in the West such as Safar Al-Hawali, Salman Al-'Awda, Nasir Al-'Umar, and 'Abd al-Wahhab Al-Tariri. *Da'wa ila Al-Muqawamat Al-Islamiyyat Al-'Alamiyya*, (2006), pp. 1129–30, https://archive.org/details/Dawaaah, last accessed 15 May 2014.

9. Combatting Terrorism Center document AFGP-2002–800073. In a two-page letter, bin Laden thanks Al-Tahhan for his advice in confronting the Saudi authorities and clerical establishment: "We have taken the advice that it would not be suitable to quote any scholars serving. We have decided to omit those quotes from this letter and only mention other available evidence." Most of the letter is devoted to a point-by-point defense of his ratio-

nale for having waited until the mid 1990s to present the Saudis with such a heated communiqué. Overall, the letter positions Al-Tahhan as a public relations advisor to bin Laden, one specially attuned to the tactics and diplomacy of maneuvering within the Saudi clerical establishment. Although the letter is undated, it appears to have been written in 1994 or 1995, just after the establishment of the Advice and Reform Committee in London.

10. 'Abd al-Rahim's own training in Syria, acknowledged abstractly on several of his tapes, seems to have been expurgated from biographies. His elder brother Mahmud Al-Tahhan (confirmed through personal communication with his students in Doha) is a *hadith* scholar and professor at the University of Kuwait with a wide following, and studied jurisprudence from Jum'a Abu Zalam, a student of the renowned Syrian scholar 'Isa Al-Bayanuni of the Khalidi brotherhood. His brother's training would have set a formidable precedent for the family, even if as a source of differentiation for 'Abd al-Rahim.

11. See "Al-Shaikh 'Abd al-Rahim Al-Tahhan bayn Al-Sunna wa-l-Sufiyya faila Ayyahuma Aqrab?" (1995), http://www.d-sunnah.net/forum/printthread.php?t=43521, last accessed 13 July 2008.

12. By contrast, supporters allege that his name is still featured on a list of the university's "most honored graduates." See chatroom entry dated 29 June 2006 at http://www.almanhaj.com/vb/showthread.php?t=167748, last accessed 17 January 2008.

13. These include 'Awad Al-Qarni, 'A'id Al-Qarni (a preacher with the second highest number of tapes in the collection), Sa'id bin Musaffar Al-Qahtani (the thirteenth highest number of tapes), and 'Ali bin 'Abd al-Khaliq Al-Qarni.

14. The question of tomb visitation was especially contentious among Arab-Afghans since the Taliban widely accommodate its practice. Abu Mus'ab Al-Suri, also from an Aleppan family with prominent historical links to Sufi brotherhoods, was one of the most outspoken apologists for the Taliban in this regard, though he lacked the deeper theological and legal vocabularies to defend tomb visitation. Al-Tahhan's competence in situating tomb visitation within the purview of salafi doctrine suggests an important reason for his support by Al-Suri and other training camp leaders as they sought to bridge fierce ideological divisions among transnational jihadis.

15. Al-Tahhan's website is available at http://s.sunnahway.net/altahhan/2012/11/27/, last accessed May 15 2014. Between the years 2006–8, his name and recordings were removed from one of the largest on-line databases for Islamic recordings, www.islamway.com, a conservative Saudi site operated out of 'Asir, where Al-Tahhan lived for sixteen years.

16. Masud, Muhammad Khalid, "Ikhtilaf al-Fuqaha: Diversity in Fiqh as a

Social Construction," in *Wanted: Equality and Justice in the Muslim Family*, ed. Zainah Anwar, Kuala Lumpur: Musawah/Sisters in Islam, 2009.

17. Miller, Flagg, "'Al-Qaʿida' as a Pragmatic Base: Contributions of Area Studies to Sociolinguistics," *Language and Communication*, 28, 4 (2008).

18. Muhammad bin Saʿid Al-Qahtani's well-known book *Al-Walaʾ wa-l-Baraʾ* launches a diatribe against fellow Muslims who seek means (*tawassul*) to ameliorate their condition through supplication and intercession. Al-Tahhan's *ikhtilaf* narrative leads this discourse toward Hanafism's greater tolerance for Muslim pluralism even as he moves to draw ranks against a common enemy.

19. Al-Tahhan asserts that the roots of modern psychology are in Greek-influenced Islamic theology (*ʿilm al-kalam*), the errors of which were expounded by twelfth-century philosopher Abu Hamad Al-Ghazzali. The ultimate source of Muslim errancy, then, hails more from within the Muslim community rather than from the West. Such an argument situates Al-Tahhan's narrative of "loyalty and disavowal" closer to a tradition of Saudi-influenced religious discourse than to political treatises on the topic by such militants as Abu Muhammad Al-Maqdisi or Ayman Al-Zawahiri. See Wagemakers, Joas, "Framing the 'Threat to Islam': Al-Walaʾ wa al-Baraʾ in Salafi Discourse," *Arab Studies Quarterly*, 30, 4 (2008).

20. Al-Tahhan narrates the *hadith* as the following: "It is reported in Al-Bukhari's compendium and elsewhere that Abu Hurayra—may God be pleased with him—[said] that the Prophet, praise be upon Him, said that God, glory be to Him, said: 'I declare war on whoever shows enmity towards an ally of Mine. My servant will not seek my nearness through anything that is more beloved to Me than that which I have made obligatory on him. And my servant will continue to seek my nearness through voluntary actions until I love him. Once I love him, I shall bless the hearing with which he hears, sight with which he sees, hands with which he acts, and feet with which he walks. If he asks of me, I shall grant him that which he asked for. If he seeks refuge in me, I shall grant him refuge. I do not hesitate in anything that I intend to do as much as I hesitate in taking away the soul of my faithful servant; he dislikes death and I dislike displeasing him, but it is necessary for him.'"

21. The Qurʾan not infrequently characterizes God in a state of suspended decision, having a "wait-and-see attitude" that is resolved only through human initiative, as noted by Rahman, Fazlur, *The Philosophy of Mulla Sadra Shirazi*, Albany: State University of New York Press, 1975, p. 180. The concept of *al-taraddud* is richly elaborated in traditions of "mystical" or esoteric knowledge, including Sufi narratives of "the perfect human being" (*al-insan al-kamil*) that were perfectly familiar to Aleppan scholars who influenced

Al-Tahhan's early intellectual development. Such narratives center on a half-divine, half-human mediator who connects man with God through his own bridge of love, and who, in the process of migrating between experiences of God's majesty and God's beauty, can intervene in creation. The mediator's intervention is enabled through hesitation (*taraddud*) as his heart vacillates between four experiences: ignorance, doubt (*shakk*), probability (*zann*), and knowledge (*'ilm*). Jassemi, Bahram, "The Dimensions of the Mystical Journey," Ibn Arabi Society, (n.d.), www.ibnarabisociety.org/articles/mysticaljourney.html

22. See explanations by Salih Al Al-Shaykh and others at http://www.ahlalhdeeth.com/vbe/showthread.php?t=5817

23. For Al-Khalili, Al-Tahhan represents the quintessence of Wahhabi zealotry, particularly with regards to unquestioning allegiance to thirteenth-century jurist Taqi al-Din Ibn Taymiyya. The principle error of Ibn Taymiyya, as well as his student Ibn al-Qayyim Al-Jawziyya, is their anthropomorphic tendency to assign God attributes resembling those of the human being. Defending such a likeness leads them toward Trinitarian perspectives notorious among Christians and Jews. Ultimately, Al-Khalili finds Al-Tahhan especially dangerous because his arguments for divine insight favor a strain of interpretive activism that has long eschewed the conventions of religious establishments. See Al-Khalili, Ahmad bin Hamad, *Wa Saqat Al-Qina' (And the Weapons Fell)*, (1997), available at http://istiqama.net/books/all-books.htm, last accessed 14 May 2014.

24. While the term *ru'ya* is not explicitly mentioned on "The Position of Astute," Al-Tahhan evokes it explicitly in his subsequent discussion of Muhammad bin Aslam Al-Tusi's exemplary act of self-abnegation (*zuhd*) in which he directs his vision toward the heavens rather than at the "changing faces" of the unjust Muslim tyrant 'Abdalla bin Tahir.

25. The reference to "strangers" expounds on a well-known *hadith*: "It is narrated on the authority of Abu Hurayra that the Messenger of Allah, praise be upon Him, said: Islam began as something strange, and it would revert to its being strange—so good tidings for the stranger."

26. Excluded among the Companions, in this respect, are those who participated in the battles of Badr and Uhud and in the Al-Ridwan pledge of allegiance. Additionally, the reward of "companionship" will never be as great for modern activists as it was for the Companions.

27. The role of such a small group (*jama'a*) in leading the Muslim community is elaborated in militant terms on Al-Tahhan's audio lecture "The Separation of Religion from the State" (*Fasl Al-Din 'an Al-Dawla*). Discussing the legitimate uses of violence in jihad, he argues that a group consisting of as few as three individuals can appoint its own amir and re-establish righteous Muslim governance through the twin forces of the "text and the sword"

(al-mushaf wa-l-sayf.) Drawing upon *hadiths* to argue that the Antichrist himself is less frightening than "errant Imams," Al-Tahhan ventures to suggest that enemies' "eyes be plucked out and throats cut," and in a less impassioned portion of the lecture, falls back to the position that they should be fought, taken captive, chained by the neck, and forced to convert or else remained chained. In most of the lecture, the enemies concerned are secular Muslims, especially Egypt's Muslim Brotherhood leadership, who have been misled by Western secular nationalism and humanism.

28. A weak but well-known *hadith* states, "The disputation of my community is mercy."

29. Ibn Taymiyya's *Majmu' Al-Fatawa* treats aspectual and contradictory disputes but not comprehensional. Al-Farm, Nawf bint Majid, "Al-Farq bayn Al-Ikhtilaf Al-Tanawwu' w-Ikhtilaf Al-Tadadd," 2008, *Muntada Al-Difa' 'an Al-Sunna* website, ftn22.

30. Internet copies of the lecture reflect the same compartmentalization, digital versions having been made from audiotape.

31. Evidence for this assertion comes from handwritten numbering on the first volume along with a screen-printed advertising label by the Jeddah-based studio The Audio-Brigade Library (*Maktabat Al-Liwa' Al-Sam'iyya*). No tapes from this studio feature the leading "al-Qa'ida" labels while those that do all feature initial audio-recorded announcements that advertise the Riyadh cassette shop Islamic Pious Fear Recordings.

32. Both volumes two and three feature a studio-recorded announcer informing the listener that material on those tapes "completes" lecture points presented on a previous tape.

33. Kelsay, John, *Arguing the Just War in Islam*, Cambridge: Harvard University Press, 2007 pp. 142–9.

34. Sageman, Marc, *Leaderless Jihad: Terror Networks in the Twenty-First Century*, Philadelphia: The University of Pennsylvania Press, 2008, pp. 49–50.

35. Evidence comes from a cassette jacket in the bin Laden tape collection that was designed and marketed by the Office of Service's media wing.

36. Lacroix, Stéphane, *Awakening Islam*, 2011, p. 112.

37. Hegghammer, Thomas, *Jihad in Saudi Arabia*, p. 79.

38. Ibid., pp. 124–5.

39. Nasiri, Omar, *Inside the Jihad: My Life with Al Qaeda*, London: Hurst, 2006, p. 275.

14. 'UMAR'S WEDDING

1. Bin Laden refers on the tape to the United States' Secretary of State Colin Powell's recent first tour to the Middle East. This tour occurred on 24–28 Feb. 2001.

2. Salman was a Persian Christian convert who led Arabs in digging a trench around the city of Madina in preparation for a battle against a confederation of tribes led by the Quraish. The ensuing conflict in CE 627 became known as the "Battle of the Trench."

3. *Sura* of The Stories: 24.

4. The poem was dedicated to the memory of four mujahideen who had fallen as martyrs.

5. The air strike on 16 Feb. 2001, just a week before Secretary of State Colin Powell's tour, was the first outside Iraq's "no fly" zone.

6. The U.S.S. Cole attack occurred on 12 Oct. 2000 and resulted in the deaths of seventeen American sailors and thirty-nine injuries. While Al-Thawr's involvement in the bombing is clear, most sources identify the second bomber as a Yemeni national named 'Abdullah Al-Misawa. For Saudi bomber Hasan Al-Khamri's involvement, see *The 9/11 Commission Report: Final Report of the National Commission on Terrorist Attacks upon the United States*, Washington, D.C.: Norton, 2004, p. 191.

7. Abu Hafs Al-Mauritani, also known as Mahfuz Walad Al-Walid, was one of bin Laden's key lieutenants, serving with him during his years in the Sudan and afterward. He has been sought by the United States since the 1998 embassy bombings in East Africa, and his assets were frozen three days after 11 September. Along with Sayf Al-'Adl, he opposed the 11 September attacks two months before they occurred. Ibid., p. 251. He is now reportedly living in Iran. Unlike on this occasion, bin Laden personally recited his poem about the Cole bombing two months earlier, on 10 Jan., at his own son Muhammad's wedding in Kandahar. Zaydan, Ahmad, *Bin Ladin bi-la Qina'*, Beirut: Al-Sharikat Al-'Alamiyya li-l-Kitab, 2003, p. 134. Since the poem was to be broadcast to world audiences by global television networks, bin Laden recited the composition twice in efforts to produce a flawless performance.

8. Muhammad Yunis Khalis was a prominent mujahidin commander during the Soviet occupation of Afghanistan and provided important sanctuary for bin Laden when he returned in 1996. *The New York Times* is alone in attributing this poem to a well-known jihadi poet and colleague of bin Laden's 'Abd al-Rahman Al-'Ashmawi. Rohde, David, "Verses From bin Laden's War: Wielding the Pen as a Sword of the Jihad," *The New York Times*, 7 Apr. 2002.

9. Zaydan, *Bin Ladin bi-la Qina'*, 2003, p. 129.

10. Al-Rumi was a companion of the Prophet Muhammad whose piety and asceticism qualified him to lead the Muslim community in prayer. The prophet's companion Al-'Umayr renounced his family's mercantile wealth and died as chief standard-bearer in the battle of Uhud in CE 625.

11. I have not found record of ʿUmar Ibn Abu ʿAsim's service. His return to Yemen is suggested both by reference to Yemeni wedding rituals and to the fact that, after the 1998 East Africa bombings, almost all of bin Laden's ten chief bodyguards were Yemenis, the majority of them unmarried and from the Taʿizz governorate. Al-Bahri, Nasir, *Dans l'ombre de Ben Laden*, Neuilly-sur-Seine: Michel Lafon, 2010, p. 105.

12. Interview in Aden, Dec. 2005. I have changed the informant's name to preserve his anonymity.

13. Vertigans, Stephen, *Militant Islam: A Sociology of Characteristics, Causes and Consequences*, New York: Routledge, 2008, pp. 37–9.

14. Islamic Fundamentalist Audio Recording Collection, Yale University, tape no. 1253. Yale archivists report that the cassette was recorded on 18 Nov. 2001. The singer's reflections on worldly demise encompass even al-Qaʿida's alleged mastermind himself. In an earlier poem on the tape, he depicts bin Laden as having entered paradise as a martyr: "Dream, my believers, dream! As if one has perished just like him: Osama bin Laden. Perished, my God show mercy upon him! Hark, whatever youth may be listening!" Along with demoting the United States' significance as a target, the singer infers that rumors of bin Laden's death were circulating even before the US-led war in Afghanistan beginning in December.

15. Helfstein, Scott, Nassar Abdulla, and Mohammad Al-Obaidi, "Deadly Vanguards: A Study of Al Qaeda's Violence Against Muslims," The Combatting Terrorism Center's Occasional Paper Series, Dec. 2009, pp. 52–5.

16. Ibid., p. 2.

17. Lewis, Jessica D., "Al-Qaeda in Iraq Resurgent," Institute for the Study of War, Washington, D.C., Middle East Security Report, 14 Sept. 2013, p. 7.

18. Hussain, Zahid, "Pakistan's Most Dangerous Place," *The Wilson Quarterly* (2012), http://www.wilsonquarterly.com/essays/pakistans-most-dangerous-place

19. See Hegghammer, Thomas, *Jihad in Saudi Arabia*, pp. 199–226. Intensifying between 2002 and 2006, operations targeted both Westerners and native Saudis, especially those associated with security and oil industries.

20. Comment by interviewee Saad Eddin Ibrahim, as noted in my introduction. *Osama bin Laden: The Destruction of the Base* (Tadmir Al-Qaʿida). Doha, Qatar: Al-Jazeera. Arabic transcript at http://www.elismaily.tv/forum/topic/19054, last accessed Oct. 2013.

21. See Gerges, Fawaz A., *The Rise and Fall of Al-Qaeda*, Oxford: Oxford University Press, 2011, p. 96.

22. For such electoral chicanery in Yemen, see Lackey, Sue, "Yemen: Unlikely Key to Western Security," *Jane's Intelligence Review*, 11, 7 (1999), p. 27.

EPILOGUE

1. Barnett, Thomas, *The Pentagon's New Map: War and Peace in the Twenty-First Century*, New York: G.P. Putnam's Sons, 2004, pp. 82, 122–4, 153–4, 216, 300–15.
2. Ibid., pp. 109, 34, 103–5. The political expediency of arguments about an amalgamated Islamic enemy employed by terror analysts and their American "neo-conservative" allies during the mid-1990s is discussed by Stampnitsky, Lisa, *Disciplining Terror: How Experts Invented Terrorism*, Cambridge: Cambridge University Press, 2013, pp. 140–6.
3. Comparisons of the 9/11 attacks to those by Japanese air forces on Pearl Harbor are not as apt. The Hawaiian Islands were referred to by US authorities at the time as "territories," a designation reflecting a half-century of American colonial history in the Asia-Pacific. Pearl Harbor was a military base, moreover, and civilian deaths were far fewer than those of servicemen.
4. The term "late rentierism," coined by Middle East scholar Matthew Gray, describes states marked by the professional operation of state-owned industries, continued state control over strategic industries, preferential treatment of certain actors, the weakening of traditional merchant families, and the emergence of new, state-dependent classes. Kamrava, Mehran, *Qatar: Small State, Big Politics*, Ithaca: Cornell University Press, 2013, p. 132.
5. Tammen, Ronald et. al., *Power Transitions: Strategies for the 21st Century*, New York: Chatham House, 2000, p. 10.
6. Kamrava, *Qatar*, 2013, p. 28.
7. Ibid., p. 80.
8. Al-Nu'aimi, Sa'd Muhammad, *Amir Qatar: La'ib Kharij Al-Mal'ab: Intihaziyya Mahsuba am Tab'iyya Mufida?*, Paris: Dar Al-Wakra li-l-Nashr, 2003, p. 6. In 1994, the same minister is reported to have officiated a meeting in Doha between bin Laden and Egyptian Islamic Group leaders Ayman Al-Zawahiri, Muhammad Shawqi Al-Islambuli, and Mustafa Hamza. 'Issam al-Din, Jamal, "Al-Alfi Claims Doha Connection," *Al-Ahram Weekly*, 8 Jan 1998, p. 3, cited in Scheuer, *Through Our Enemies' Eyes*, p. 129.
9. Allam, Hannah, Jonathan S. Landay, and Mitchell Prothero, "US Syria Plans Face Setback as Key Rebels Break from Coalition," *McClatchy DC*, Washington, D.C.: 25 Sept. 2013.

SOURCES CITED

The 9/11 Commission Report: Final Report of the National Commission on Terrorist Attacks upon the United States, Washington, D.C.: Norton, 2004.

Ali, Mohamed M. Yunis, *Medieval Islamic Pragmatics: Sunni Legal Theorists' Models of Textual Communication*, Richmond, Surrey: Curzon Press, 2000.

Allam, Hannah, Jonathan S. Landay, and Mitchell Prothero, "US Syria Plans Face Setback as Key Rebels Break from Coalition," *McClatchy DC*, Washington, D.C.: September 25 (2013).

Alshamsi, Mansoor Jassem, *Islam and Political Reform in Saudi Arabia: The Quest for Political Change and Reform*, New York: Routledge, 2011.

"Al-'Ulama' Alladhina Qadhafahum Ad'iyya' Al-Salafiyya," http://www.qassimy.com/vb/showthread.php?p=7372918, last accessed 15 May 2014.

Amba, Faiza Saleh, "Sources Say bin Laden Lives Spartan Life, Friends Claim Radical Saudi Lacks Millions," *The Sunday Patriot News (Associated Press)*, 30 Aug. 1998.

Al-Andalusi, Suraqah, "Suraqah Al-Andalusi: From the Friend and Companion," http://www.islamicawakening.com/viewarticle.php?articleID=713&pageID=233&pageID=234&, last accessed 20 Feb. 2014.

Anderson, C., "FBI Reports Jump in Violence against Muslims," *Associated Press*, 25 Nov. 2002.

Atwan, Abdel Bari, *The Secret History of al Qaeda*, Berkeley: The University of California Press, 2006.

'Atwan, 'Abd al-Bari, "Ayyam Fi Imarat Al-Afghan Al-'Arab Fi Jibal Afghanistan," *Al-Quds Al-'Arabi*, 27 Nov. 1996.

'Azzam, 'Abdallah, *The Lofty Mountain*, London: Azzam Publications, 2003, http://islamic-empire.synthasite.com/resources/The Lofty Mountain—The Last Book By Abdullah Azzam.pdf, last accessed 16 June 2011.

———, *Defence of the Muslim Lands: The First Obligation After Iman*, 1984–5, http://www.religioscope.com/info/doc/jihad/azzam_defence_1_table.htm

SOURCES CITED

Al-Bahri, Nasir (Khalid Al-Hamadi), "Al Qaʻida from Within, as Narrated by Abu Jandal, bin Laden's Personal Bodyguard," *Al-Quds Al-ʻArabi*, 2005 (first four sections only available in English at http://groups.yahoo.com/group/cmkp_pk/message/2497, last accessed May 7 2014).

———, "Tanzim al-Qaʻida min Dakhil," *Al-Quds Al-ʻArabi*, 18–29 Mar 2005 (a nine-part series).

———, *Dans l'ombre de Ben Laden*, Neuilly-sur-Seine: Michel Lafon, 2010.

———, "Haris Sabiq li-Zaʻim al-Qaʻida," (2010), http://alwatan.kuwait.tt/ArticleDetails.aspx?Id=108707&YearQuarter=20112, last accessed May 8, 2014.

Barnett, Thomas, *The Pentagon's New Map: War and Peace in the Twenty-First Century*, New York: G.P. Putnam's Sons, 2004.

Benjamin, Daniel and Steven Simon, *The Age of Sacred Terror: Radical Islam's War Against America*, New York: Random House, 2002.

Bergen, Peter L., *Holywar, Inc.: Inside the Secret World of Osama bin Laden*, New York: Free Press, 2001.

———, *The Osama bin Laden I Know: An Oral History of al Qaeda's Leader*, New York: Free Press, 2006.

———, *The Longest War: The Enduring Conflict Between America and Al-Qaeda*, New York: Free Press, 2011.

Beyond al-Qaeda: The Global Jihadist Movement, Santa Monica, CA: RAND Corporation, 2006.

Bin Ladin, Carmen, *Inside the Kingdom: My Life in Saudi Arabia*, New York: Warner Books, 2004.

Bin Laden, Osama, *Nidaʼ Al-Islam* in Oct./Nov. 1996. "New Powder Keg in the Middle East" at http://www.fas.org/irp/world/para/docs/LADIN.htm, last accessed 14 May, 2014.

"Bin Ladin Yadʻu Li-Harb ʻIsabat Li-Ikhraj ʻAl-Muhtallin Al-Amrikiyin' Min Al-Saʻudiyyah," *Al-Quds Al-ʻArabi*, 31 Aug./1 Sept. 1996.

"Bin Ladin Yatahaddath," *Al-Jazeera Satellite Channel*, December 1998, http://www.youtube.com/watch?v=oDmp-lM5hL0, last accessed 15 May 2014.

"Bin Laden No Longer Seen as Main Al-Qaida Financier," *Associated Press*, reported by MSNBC on 2 Sept. 2004, http://www.nbcnews.com/id/5896423/ns/us_news-security/t/bin-laden-no-longer-seen-main-al-qaida-financier/UhPIbGTF1G4

Boas, Franz, "On Alternating Sounds," *American Anthropologist*, 2, 1 (1889), pp. 47–54.

Bodansky, Yossef, *Bin Laden: The Man Who Declared War on America*, New York: Random House, 1999.

Bonnefoy, Laurent, *Salafism in Yemen: Transnationalism and Religious Identity*, New York: Columbia/London: Hurst & Co., 2011.

Bowden, Mark, "The Truth about Mogadishu," *The Philadelphia Inquirer*, 8 Oct. 2006, http://articles.philly.com/2006–10–08/news/25417846_1_al-qaeda-mogadishu-bin

Brehony, Noel, *Yemen Divided: The Story of a Failed State in South Arabia*, New York: I. B. Tauris, 2011.

Brown, Vahid, *Cracks in the Foundation: Leadership Schisms in Al-Qaʿida 1989–2006*, West Point, NY: Combating Terrorism Center, 2007.

———, "Al-Qaʿida Central and Local Affiliates," in *Self-Inflicted Wounds: Debates and Divisions within Al-Qaʿida and Its Periphery*, (eds) Assaf Moghadam and Brian Fishman, Westpoint: Combatting Terrorism Center, 2010, pp. 69–99.

———, "The Facade of Allegiance: Bin Ladin's Dubious Pledge to Mullah Omar," *CTC Sentinel*, 3, 1 (2010), pp. 1–6.

———, *Fountainhead of Jihad: The Haqqani Nexus, 1973–2012*, Oxford: Oxford University Press, 2013.

Bunel, Pierre-Henri, *Proche-Orient, une guerre mondiale?: des derives de la finance internationale*, New York: Carnot, 2004.

Burke, Jason, *Al-Qaeda: Casting a Shadow of Terror*, New York: Palgrave, 2003.

Burr, J. Millard and Robert O. Collins, *Revolutionary Sudan: Hasan al-Turabi and the Islamist State, 1989–2000*, Leiden: Brill, 2003.

Coll, Steve, *Ghost Wars: The Secret History of the CIA, Afghanistan, and bin Laden, from the Soviet Invasion to September 10, 2001*, New York: Penguin Press, 2004.

———, "Letter From Jedda: Young Osama," *The New Yorker*, 81, 12 Dec. 2005, pp. 48–61.

———, *The bin Ladens: An Arabian Family in the American Century*, New York: The Penguin Press, 2008.

Commins, David, "Contestation and Authority in Wahhabi Polemics," in *Religion and Politics in Saudi Arabia: Wahhabism and the State*, (eds) Mohammed Ayoob and Hasan Kosebalaban, Boulder, CO: Lynne Rienner, 2008, pp. 39–53.

Corman, Steven R. and Jills R. Schiefelbein, "Communication and Media Strategy of the Jihadi War of Ideas," Arizona State University, Phoenix, AZ, report no. 0601, 2006.

Coughlin, Con, "Tempting Array of Strike Targets for Pentagon," *The Sunday Telegraph*, 4 Aug. 1996.

Cragin, R. Kim, "Early History of al-Qaʿida," *The Historical Journal*, 51, 4 (2008), pp. 1047–67.

Cullison, Alan, "Strained Alliance: Al Qaeda's Sour Days in Afghanistan—Fighters Mocked the Place; Taliban, in Turn, Nearly Booted Out bin Laden—A Fateful U.S. Missile Strike," *Wall Street Journal*, 2002.

————, "Inside al-Qaeda's Hard Drive," *Atlantic Monthly*, Sept. 2004, pp. 55–70.

Curtis, Mark, *Secret Affairs: British Collusion with Radical Islam*, London: Profile Books, 2010.

Al-Daghidi, Anis, *Bin Ladin…wa Alladhina Ma'hu*, Cairo: Matkabat Jazirat Al-Ward, 2005.

Devji, Faisal, *The Impossible Indian: Gandhi and the Temptation of Violence*, London: Hurst and Company, 2012.

Diraz, 'Isam, *Usama bin Ladin Yarwi Ma'arik Ma'sadat Al-Ansar Al-'Arab bi-Afghanistan* (Osama bin Laden Recounts Arab Al-Ansar Lion's Lair Battles in Afghanistan), Cairo: Al-Manar Al-Jadid, 1991.

————, "The Battle of the Lion's Den," In *The Lofty Mountain*, (ed.) 'Abdallah Azzam, London: Azzam Publications, 2003, pp. 88–92.

————, "Impressions of an Arab Journalist in Afghanistan," in *The Lofty Mountain*, (ed.) 'Abdallah Azzam, London: Azzam Publications, 2003, pp. 87–120.

Doran, Michael, "The Pragmatic Fanaticism of al Qaeda: An Anatomy of Extremism in Middle Eastern Politics," *Political Science Quarterly*, 117, 2 (2002), pp. 177–90.

Dufour, Jules, "The Worldwide Network of US Military Bases," Montreal, Canada: Centre for Research on Globalization, 2007, http://www.globalresearch.ca/the-worldwide-network-of-us-military-bases/5564

Dwailibi, Georges Jawdat, *La Rivalité entre le Clergé Religieux et la Famille Royale au Royaume d'Arabie Saudite*, Paris: Éditions Publibook, 2006.

Erlanger, Steven, "At Yemen College, Scholarship and Jihadist Ideas," *The New York Times*, 18 Jan. 2010.

Esposito, John L., *Voices of Resurgent Islam*, Oxford: Oxford University Press, 1983.

Fandy, Mamoun, "The Hawali Tapes," *The New York Times*, 1990.

————, *Saudi Arabia and the Politics of Dissent*, New York: St. Martin's Press, 1999.

Al-Farm, Nawf bint Majid, "Al-Farq bayn Al-Ikhtilaf Al-Tanawwu' w-Ikhtilaf Al-Tadadd," 2008, *Muntada Al-Difa' 'an Al-Sunna* website, last accessed 15 May 2014.

"Fatawa Al-'Ulama' fi Usama bin Ladin," (n.d.), http://www.sahab.org/books/book.php?id=423, last accessed June 2004.

Fazul, Haroun, "The Letter from El Hage's Computer," Frontline PBS documentary *Hunting bin Laden*, 1997, http://www.pbs.org/wgbh/pages/frontline/shows/binladen/upclose/computer.html

FBIS Report: Compilation of Usama bin Laden Statements 1994–January 2004, (1994–2004), http://www.fas.org/irp/world/para/ubl-fbis.pdf

SOURCES CITED

Filiu, Jean-Pierre, *The Apocalypse in Islam*, trans. M. B. DeBevoise, Berkeley: The University of California Press, 2011.

Fishman, Brian, *Bombers, Bank Accounts, and Bleedout: Al-Qaʿidaʾs Road In and Out of Iraq*, Westpoint's Combating Terrorism Center, 2008.

Fisk, Robert, "Anti-Soviet Warrior Puts His Army on the Road to Peace," *The Independent*, 6 Dec. 1993.

———, "Arab Rebel Leader Warns the British: 'Get Out of the Gulf,'" *The Independent*, 10 July 1996.

Friedman, Robert I., "Sheikh Abdel Rahman, the World Trade Center Bombing and the CIA," Westfield, NJ: Open Media, pamphlet no. 27 (1993).

Friedman, Thomas, "Foreign Affairs; Angry, Wired, and Deadly," *The New York Times*, 22 Aug. 1998.

Fuchs, Simon, *Proper Signposts for the Camp: The Reception of Classical Authorities in the Jihad Manual al-ʿUmda Fi ʿImad al-ʿUddah ("The Essential Guide of Preparation for Jihad")*, Wurzburg: Ergon-Verlag, 2011.

"The Future of Al Qaeda," Canadian Security Intelligence Service, 2013, https://http://www.csis-scrs.gc.ca/pblctns/cdmctrch/20130401_th_ftr_f_lgd-eng.asp

Garamone, Jim, "Rumsfeld Says Link Between Iraq, al Qaeda 'Not Debatable,'" *American Forces Press Service*, 27 Sept 2002, http://www.defense.gov/News/NewsArticle.aspx?ID=43413

Gerges, Fawaz A., *The Far Enemy: Why Jihad Went Global*, Cambridge: Cambridge University Press, 2005.

———, *The Rise and Fall of Al-Qaeda*, Oxford: Oxford University Press, 2011.

Gerth, Jeff and Judith Miller, "Funds for Terrorists Traced To Persian Gulf Businessmen," *The New York Times*, 14 Aug. 1996.

Gold, Dore, *Hatred's Kingdom: How Saudi Arabia Supports the New Global Terrorism*, Lanham, MD: Regnery Publishing, 2003.

Gunaratna, Rohan, *Inside Al Qaeda: Global Network of Terror*, London: C. Hurst, 2002.

———, "The Terrorist Training Camps of al Qaida," in *The Making of a Terrorist: Recruitment, Training and Root Causes Volume II: Training*, (ed.) James J. F. Forest, Westport, CN: Praeger, 2006, pp. 172–93.

Habib, Randa, "Jordanian Militants Train in Afghanistan to Confront Regime," *Agence France-Presse*, 30 May 1993.

Haddad, Gibril Fouad, "Sheikh Ahmadu," 9 May 1999, https://groups.google.com/forum/#!topic/soc.religion.islam/jVDrPJ1EXNU, last accessed 14 Sept. 2008.

Hamid, Mustafa, *Tharthara Fawq Saqf Al-ʿAlam*, v. 10, (n.d.), Westpoint, NY: Combatting Terrorism Center, file no. AFGP-2002–600088.

———, "A Mother's Deep Sorrow/The Airport Project," (1998), Westpoint, NY: Combatting Terrorism Center, file no. AFGP-2002–600092.

————, "*Qissat Al-Bay'a Al-'Arabiyya Li-Amir Al-Mu'minin Al-Mulla Muhammad 'Umar* (The Story of the Afghan Arabs: From the Entry to Afghanistan to the Final Exodus with the Taliban)," first published in *Al-Sharq Al-Awsat*, 8 and 9 Dec. 2004, http://www.muslm.org/vb/showthread.php?354320, last accessed May 2014.

Al-Hawali, Safar, "Infidels, Without and Within," *New Perspectives Quarterly*, 8 (1991), p. 51.

Hegghammer, Thomas, "Terrorist Recruitment and Radicalization in Saudi Arabia," *Middle East Policy*, 13, 4 (2006), pp. 39–60.

————, "Deconstructing the Myth about al-Qa'ida and Khobar," *Combatting Terrorism Center Sentinel*, 1, 3 (2008), pp. 20–2.

————, *Jihad in Saudi Arabia: Violence and Pan-Islamism since 1979*, Cambridge: Cambridge University Press, 2010.

————, "Abdallah Azzam, The Imam of Jihad," in *Al Qaeda in Its Own Words*, (eds) Gilles Kepel and Jean-Pierre Milelli, Pascale Ghazaleh, Cambridge: Belknap Press of Harvard University Press, 2008, pp. 81–101.

Hegghammer, Thomas and Stéphane Lacroix, "Rejectionist Islamism in Saudi Arabia: The Story of Juhayman al-'Utaybi Revisited," *International Journal of Middle East Studies*, 39 (2007), pp. 97–116.

Helfstein, Scott, Nassar Abdulla, and Mohammad Al-Obaidi, "Deadly Vanguards: A Study of Al Qaeda's Violence Against Muslims," The Combatting Terrorism Center's Occasional Paper Series, Dec. 2009, pp. 52–5.

Hellmich, Christina, *Al-Qaeda: From Global Network to Local Franchise*, London: Zed Books, 2011.

Hirsch, Susan, *In the Moment of Greatest Calamity: Terrorism, Grief and a Victim's Quest for Justice*, Princeton: Princeton University Press, 2006.

Hoffman, Bruce, "Al Qaeda, Trends in Terrorism, and Future Potentialities: An Assessment," RAND Center for Middle East Public Policy and Geneva Center for Security Policy, Geneva, Switzerland, Third Annual Conference on the Middle East After Afghanistan and Iraq. 5 May 2003, http://www.rand.org/content/dam/rand/pubs/papers/2005/P8078.pdf

Hussain, Zahid, "Pakistan's Most Dangerous Place," *The Wilson Quarterly*, (2012), http://www.wilsonquarterly.com/essays/pakistans-most-dangerous-place

"Impressions of America," The Arab American Institute Foundation/Zogby International, Washington, D.C., 2004. http://www.aaiusa.org/page/-/Polls/ArabOpinion/ImpressionsOfAmerica_2004.pdf

Jackson, Richard, "Bin Laden's Ghost and the Epistemological Crises of Counter-Terrorism," In *Covering bin Laden: Global Media and the World's Most Wanted Man*, (eds) Susan Jeffords and Fahed Al-Sumait, Bloomington, IN: The University of Indiana Press, 2015.

Al-Jamhi, Sa'id 'Ubaid, *Al-Qa'ida fi-l-Yaman*, Sanaa: Maktabat Al-Hadara, 2008.

Jassemi, Bahram, "The Dimensions of the Mystical Journey," Ibn Arabi Society, (n.d.), http://www.ibnarabisociety.org/articles/mysticaljourney.html, last accessed 15 May 2014.

Johnstone, Mark A., "A Proposed Grand Strategy for Defeating bin Laden and His Al Qaeda Network," U.S. Army War College, Carlisle Barracks, PA, report no. 20020806 354, 2002.

Kamali, Mohammad Hashim, "Legal Maxims and Other Genres of Literature in Islamic Jurisprudence," *Arab Law Quarterly*, 20, 1 (2006), pp. 77–101.

Kamrava, Mehran, *Qatar: Small State, Big Politics*, Ithaca: Cornell University Press, 2013.

Kechichian, Joseph, "The Role of the Ulama in the Politics of an Islamic State: The Case of Saudi Arabia," *International Journal of Middle East Studies*, 18, 1 (1986), pp. 53–71.

———, "Islamic Revivalism and Change in Saudi Arabia: Juhayman al-Utaybi's Letters to the Saudi People," *The Muslim World*, 80, 1 (1990), pp. 1–16.

Kelsay, John, *Arguing the Just War in Islam*, Cambridge, MA: Harvard University Press, 2007.

Kepel, Gilles, *Jihad: The Trail of Political Islam*, Cambridge, MA: Harvard University Press, 2002.

Kepel, Gilles and Jean-Pierre Milelli, *Al Qaeda in Its Own Words*, Pascale Ghazaleh, Cambridge: Belknap Press of Harvard University Press, 2008.

Al-Khalili, Ahmad bin Hamad, *Wa Saqat Al-Qina' (And the Weapons Fell)*, 1997, http://www.alfida.jeeran.com/wasqtl.htm—25, last accessed 9 Oct. 2008.

Kifner, John, "Wealthy Force Behind Murky Militant Group," *The New York Times*, 14 Aug. 1998.

Kostiner, Joseph, "The Rise of Jihadi Trends in Saudi Arabia: The Post Iraq-Kuwait War Phase," in *Radical Islam and International Security: Challenges and Responses*, (eds) Efraim Inbar and Hillel Frisch, Routledge, 2007, pp. 73–92.

Lackey, Sue, "Yemen: Unlikely Key to Western Security," *Jane's Intelligence Review*, 11, 7 (1999), pp. 24–9.

Lacroix, Stéphane, *Les Islamistes Saoudiens: Une Insurrection Manquée*, Paris: Presses Universitaires de France, 2010.

———, *Awakening Islam: The Politics of Religious Dissent in Contemporary Saudi Arabia*, Cambridge, MA: Harvard University Press, 2011.

Lawrence, Bruce, *Messages to the World: The Statements of Osama bin Laden*, New York: Verso, 2005.

Leitner, Peter, *Unheeded Warnings: The Lost Reports of the Congressional Task*

Force on Terrorism and Unconventional Warfare Washington, D.C.: Crossbow Books, 2007.

Lewis, Jessica D., "Al-Qaeda in Iraq Resurgent," Institute for the Study of War, Washington, D.C., Middle East Security Report, 14 Sept. 2013.

Lia, Brynjar, *Architect of Global Jihad: The Life of al-Qaida Strategist Abu Mus'ab al-Suri*, New York: Columbia University Press, 2007.

Loeb, Vernon, "A Global, Pan-Islamic Network; Terrorism Entrepreneur Unifies Groups Financially, Politically," *Washington Post*, 23 Aug. 1998.

Lynch, Mark, *Voices of the New Arab Public: Iraq, Al Jazeera, and Middle East Politics Today*, New York: Columbia University Press, 2006.

Macintyre, Ben, "Osama bin Laden: The Mummy's Boy Who Found Refuge in Radicalism," *The London Sunday Times*, 3 May 2011.

Macleod, Scott, "Osama Bin Laden: The Paladin of Jihad," *Time Magazine*, 6 May 1996.

Manhunt: The Search for bin Laden, director Greg Barker, Home Box Office, Inc., 2013.

Martin, Gus, *Understanding Terrorism*, Thousand Oaks, CA: Sage, 2003.

Masud, Muhammad Khalid, "Ikhtilaf al-Fuqaha: Diversity in Fiqh as a Social Construction," in *Wanted: Equality and Justice in the Muslim Family*, (ed.) Zainah Anwar, Kuala Lumpur: Musawah/Sisters in Islam, 2009, pp. 65–93.

Mernissi, Fatima, *Dreams of Trespass: Tales of a Harem Girlhood*, New York: Addison-Wesley Publishing Company, 1994.

Miller, Flagg, *The Moral Resonance of Arab Media: Audiocassette Poetry and Culture in Yemen*. Camridge, MA: Harvard University Press, 2007.

———, "'Al-Qa'ida' as a Pragmatic Base: Contributions of Area Studies to Sociolinguistics," *Language and Communication*, 28, 4 (2008), pp. 386–408.

———, "Listen, Plan and Carry Out 'al-Qa'ida': Theological Dissension in Usama bin Ladin's Former Audiocassette Collection," in *Contextualising Jihadi Thought*, (eds) Jeevan Deol and Zaheer Kazmi, London: Hurst & Co./ Columbia University Press, 2011, pp. 69–97.

Mir, Hamid, "The Taliban Will Never Surrender," *The Friday Times*, 14–20 Sept. 2001.

Moore, David W., "Public Ready for War with Iraq," Gallup News Service, 18 Feb. 1998, http://www.gallup.com/poll/4252/Public-Ready-War-Iraq.aspx

Morris, Michael, "Al-Qa'ida As Insurgency," U.S. Army War College, Carlisle Barracks, Pennsylvania, 2005.

Nacos, Brigitte L., "Covering bin Laden," in *After bin Laden: Global Media and the World's Most Wanted Man*, (eds) Susan Jeffords and Fahed Al-Sumait, Bloomington, IN: The University of Indiana Press, 2015.

Nasiri, Omar, *Inside the Jihad: My Life with Al Qaeda*, New York: Basic Books, 2006.

Al-Nuʿaimi, Saʿd Muhammad, *Amir Qatar: Laʿib Kharij Al-Malʿab: Intihaziyyah Mahsubah Am Tabʿiyyah Mufidah?*, Paris: Dar Al-Wakrah li-l-Nashr, 2003.

Pankhurst, Reza, "The Caliphate, and the Changing Strategy of the Public Statements of al-Qaeda's Leaders," *Political Theology*, 11, 4 (2010), pp. 530–52.

"Part 2, History of al Qaida," (anonymous author, n.d.), http://www.oss.net/dynamaster/file_archive/091213/2adb31631131c668f1a8257035d734c5/Part%202,%20History%20of%20al%20Qaida%20(NXPowerLite).doc, last accessed 15 May 2014.

Paz, Reuven, "Qaidat al-Jihad," The International Policy Institute for Counter-Terrorism, 7 May 2002, http://www.freerepublic.com/focus/news/763378/posts, last accessed 15 May 2014.

———, "Islamists and Anti-Americanism," *Middle East Review of International Affairs*, 7(4), 2003.

Peters, Rudolph, *Jihad in Classical and Modern Islam*, Second Edition, Princeton: Marcus Wiener, 2005.

Pirio, Gregory Alonso, *The African Jihad: bin Laden's Quest for the Horn of Africa*, Trenton, NJ: The Red Sea Press, 2007.

Pollack, Josh, "Anti-Americanism in Contemporary Saudi Arabia," *The Middle East Review of International Affairs*, 7, 4 (2003), pp. 30–43.

Porter, Gareth, "Khobar Towers Investigated: How a Saudi Deception Protected Osama bin Laden," (2008), https://deeppoliticsforum.com/forums/showthread.php?1674-quot-Khobar-Towers-Investigated-How-a-Saudi-Deception-Protected-Osama-bin-Laden-quot, last accessed 15 May 2014.

Prados, Alfred B., "Saudi Arabia: Post-War Issues and U.S. Relations," Congressional Research Service [CRS] Report by the Federation of American Scientists [FAS], Washington, D.C., report no. 93113, 1996, http://www.fas.org/man/crs/93–113.htm

"Public Remains Conflicted Over Islam," Pew Research on Religion and Public Life, 24 Aug. 2010, http://www.pewforum.org/2010/08/24/public-remains-conflicted-over-islam/

Pyes, Craig, Judith Miller and Stephen Engelberg, "One Man and a Global Web of Violence," *The New York Times*, 14 Jan. 2001.

Al-Qahtani, Saʿud ʿAbdalla, *Al-Sahwa Al-Islamiyya Al-Saʿudiyya*, Maktaba Dar Al-Nadwa Al-Alaktruniyya, 2004, http://www.daralnadwa.com/books/download/saud.pdf, last accessed 8 Mar 2005.

Qutb, Muhammad, *Al-Jihad Al-Afghani Wa Dalalatahu*, Jeddah: Muʾassasat Al-Madina Li-l-Sihafa Wa-l-Tibaʿa Wa-l-Nashr, 1989, p. 48.

Rahman, Fazlur, *The Philosophy of Mulla Sadra Shirazi*, Albany: State University of New York Press, 1975.

Randal, Jonathan, *Osama: The Making of a Terrorist*, New York: Alfred A. Knopf, 2004.

Ranstorp, Magnus, "The Virtual Sanctuary of Al-Qaeda and Terrorism in an Age of Globalisation," in *International Relations and Security in the Digital Age*, (eds) Johan Eriksson and Giampiero Giacomello, London: Routledge, 2006, pp. 31–56.

Al-Rasheed, Madawi, "Saudi Arabia's Islamic Opposition," *Current History*, 95, 597 (1996), pp. 16–22.

———, *Contesting the Saudi State: Islamic Voices from a New Generation*, Cambridge: Cambridge University Press, 2007.

Rassler, Don and Vahid Brown, *The Haqqani Nexus and the Evolution of al-Qaʿida*, Harmony Program: The Combatting Terrorism Center at Westpoint, (2011), http://www.ctc.usma.edu/posts/the-haqqani-nexus-and-the-evolution-of-al-qaida

Report of the Joint Inquiry into the Terrorist Attacks of September 11, 2001, House Permanent Select Committee on Intelligence and the Senate Select Committee on Intelligence, Dec. 2002.

"Rescuers and Investigators Sent by U.S. Begin to Arrive," *The New York Times*, 9 Aug. 1998.

Riedel, Bruce, *The Search for Al Qaeda: Its Leadership, Ideology and Future*, Washington, DC: Brookings Institution, 2008.

Rohde, David, "Verses From bin Laden's War: Wielding the Pen as a Sword of the Jihad," *The New York Times*, 7 Apr. 2002.

Roy, Olivier, *The Failure of Political Islam*, Cambridge: Harvard University Press, 1994.

———, *Globalized Islam: The Search for a New Ummah*, New York: Columbia University Press, 2004.

"Sadiqi bin Ladin: Laysa Irhabiyyan," (Interview with ʿIsam Diraz, 19 Mar. 2002,) http://islamtoday.net/nawafeth/artshow-14–15817.htm, last accessed 14 May 2014.

Ryan, Michael W. S., *Decoding al-Qaeda's Strategy: The Deep Battle Against America*, New York: Columbia University Press, 2013.

Sageman, Marc, *Leaderless Jihad: Terror Networks in the Twenty-First Century*, Philadelphia: The University of Pennsylvania Press, 2008.

Saghi, Omar, "Osama bin Laden, the Iconic Orator," in *Al Qaeda in Its Own Words*, (eds) Gilles Kepel and Jean-Pierre Milelli, Pascale Ghazaleh, Cambridge: Belknap Press of Harvard University Press, 2008, pp. 11–40.

Saloman, Noah, "The Salafi Critique of Islamism: Doctrine, Difference and the Problem of Islamic Political Action in Contemporary Sudan," in *Global Salafism: Islam's New Religious Movement*, (ed.) Roel Meijer, London: C. Hurst & Co., 2009, pp. 143–68.

Sasson, Jean, Najwa bin Ladin and Omar bin Ladin, *Growing Up bin Laden: Osama's Wife and Son Take Us Inside Their Secret World*, New York: St. Martin's Press, 2010.

Scheuer, Michael (Anonymous), *Through Our Enemies' Eyes: Osama bin Laden, Radical Islam, and the Future of America*, Washington, D.C.: Brassey's, 2002.

———, *Osama bin Laden*, New York: Oxford University Press, 2011.

"Al-Shaikh ʿAbd al-Rahim Al-Tahhan bayn Al-Sunna wa-l-Sufiyya fa-ila Ayyahuma Aqrab?" (1995), http://www.d-sunnah.net/forum/printthread.php?t=43521, last accessed 13 July 2008.

Soufan, Ali H., *The Black Banners: The Inside Story of 9/11 and the War Against al-Qaeda*, New York: W.W. Norton, 2011.

Stampnitsky, Lisa, *Disciplining Terror: How Experts Invented Terrorism*, Cambridge: Cambridge University Press, 2013.

Steinberg, Guido, "The Wahhabi Ulama and the Saudi State: 1745 to the Present," in *Saudi Arabia in the Balance: Political, Economy, Society, Foreign Affairs*, (eds) Paul Aarts and Gerd Nonneman, London: Hurst and Co., 2005, pp. 11–34.

Stenersen, Anne, "Blood Brothers or a Marriage of Convenience? The Ideological Relationship between al-Qaida and the Taliban," Paper Presented at International Studies Association 50th Annual Convention, New York, Feb. 2009, http://www.allacademic.com/meta/p_mla_apa_research_citation/3/1/2/5/2/pages3 12525/p312525–6.php

———, "Arab and Non-Arab Jihadis," in *Self-Inflicted Wounds: Debates and Divisions within Al-Qaʿida and Its Periphery*, (eds) Assaf Moghadam and Brian Fishman, Westpoint: Combatting Terrorism Center, 2010, pp. 132–54.

Storer, Cynthia, "Working with al-Qaeda Documents: An Analyst's View before 9/11," in *Ten Years Later: Insights on al-Qaeda's Past and Future through Captured Records*, (eds) Lorry M. Fenner, Mark E. Stout and Jessica L. Goldings, National Defense University: The Johns Hopkins University Center for Advanced Governmental Studies, 2012, pp. 39–50.

Summers, Anthony and Robbyn Swan, *The Eleventh Day: The Full Story of 9/11 and Osama bin Laden*, New York: Ballantine Books, 2011.

Al-Suri, Abu Musʿab, *Daʿwah ila Al-Muqawamat Al-Islamiyyat Al-ʿAlamiyya*, 2006, http://www.megaupload.com/?d=D1Q8JDR1, last accessed 27 Aug. 2009.

Talbott, Strobe and Nayan Chanda, *The Age of Terror: America and the World After September 11*, New Haven: Basic Books, 2001.

Tammen, Ronald et. al., *Power Transitions: Strategies for the 21st Century*, New York: Chatham House, 2000.

Tawil, Camille, *Brothers in Arms: The Story of al-Qaʿida and the Arab Jihadists*, London: Saqi, 2010.

SOURCES CITED

"Two-page Letter from Usamah bin Ladin to Mullah 'Umar," n.d., http://www. ctc.usma.edu/wp-content/uploads/2010/08/AFGP-2002–600321-Trans.pdf

USA v. Enaam Arnaout (Government's Evidentiary Proffer Supporting the Admissibility of Coconspirator Statements), Chicago: File no. 02 CR 892, 2003.

USA v. Enaam Arnaout (Special April 2002 Grand Jury Charges), Chicago: File no. 02 CR 892, 2002.

"Usama bin Ladin: Islamic Extremist Financier," Central Intelligence Agency, 1996, http://www2.gwu.edu/~nsarchiv/NSAEBB/NSAEBB343/osama_bin_laden_file01 _transcription.pdf

Vertigans, Stephen, *Militant Islam: A Sociology of Characteristics, Causes and Consequences*, New York: Routledge, 2008.

Al-Wadi'i, Shaikh Hadi Muqbil, *Man Wara' Al-Tafjirat Fi Bilad Al-Haramayn?*, 1996.

Wagemakers, Joas, "Framing the 'Threat to Islam': Al-Wala' wa al-Bara' in Salafi Discourse," *Arab Studies Quarterly*, 30, 4 (2008), pp. 1–32.

———, "The Transformation of a Radical Concept: al-wala' wa-l-bara' in the Ideology of Abu Muhammad al-Maqdisi," in *Global Salafism: Islam's New Religious Movement*, (ed.) Roel Meijer, London: C. Hurst & Co., 2009, pp. 81–106.

Waugh, Billy and Tim Keown, *Hunting the Jackal: A Special Forces and CIA Soldier's Fifty Years on the Frontlines of the War Against Terrorism*, New York: Avon Books, 2004.

Whitlock, Craig, "After a Decade at War With West, Al-Qaeda Still Impervious to Spies," *The Washington Post*, 2008, http://articles.washingtonpost.com/ 2008–03–20/world/36926605_1_al-qaeda-qaeda-european-intelligence-officials

Worth, Robert F., "Ex-Jihadist Defies Yemen's Leader, and Easy Labels," *The New York Times*, 26 Feb. 2010.

Wright, Lawrence, *The Looming Tower: Al-Qaeda and the Road to 9/11*, New York: Alfred A. Knopf, 2006.

Yusufzai, Rahimullah, "In the Way of Allah," *The News* (Islamabad), 15 June 1998. *FBIS Report: Compilation of Usama Bin Laden Statements 1994—January 2004*, pp. 72–4, http://www.fas.org/irp/world/para/ubl-fbis.pdf, last accessed 15 May 2014.

Zaeef, Abdul Salam, *My Life with the Taliban*, New York: Columbia University Press, 2010.

Al-Zahrani, Faris (aka Abu Jandal Al-'Azdi), *Usama bin Ladin: Mujaddid Al-Zaman wa Qahir Al-Amrikan*, Minbar Al-Tawhid wa-l-Jihad website, n.d., http://www.tawhed.ws/dl?i=2v5pw774, last accessed 15 May 2014.

SOURCES CITED

Zaydan, Ahmad, *Bin Ladin bi-la Qinaʿ*, Beirut: Al-Sharikat Al-ʿAlamiyya li-l-Kitab, 2003.
Zernike, Kate and Michael T. Kaufman, "The Most Wanted Face of Terrorism," *The New York Times*, 2 May 2011.

INDEX

INDEX

Afghan War, 3, 36
The Age of Terror (Talbott and Chanda), 246
Al-Ahmar, ʿAli Muhsin, 171
Al-Ahram, 248
Aidid, Mohammad Farah, 277
ʿAlawites, 50, 54
Algeria, 20, 25, 84, 100, 118, 184, 187, 262, 310, 344, 414n75
ʿAli, ʿUmar ʿAbdalla, 421n7
al-Qaʿida: anti-American platform of, 9, 12–14, 17–19, 24, 28–29, 31–33, 41–45, 48, 77–78, 82, 85, 91–93, 112, 132–33, 141, 145–46, 150, 161, 167–68, 173, 175–76, 179–86, 197–204, 233–46, 248–73, 280, 292–305, 309–11, 324, 342–44, 359–60, 364–68, 375–76, 390n51, 392n8, 412n46, 420n14; asceticism and, 33, 36–37, 44–45, 62–71, 83–85, 89–93, 144–52, 166–67, 201–4, 262–63, 272, 281, 291–92; as "base," 5, 11, 14, 22, 27, 45–46, 80–93, 137–44, 263, 295–97, 300–305, 307, 370, 390n46; definitions of, 7, 371, 380n10; embassy bombings and, 14, 28, 44–45, 203, 275, 279–80, 291, 301–2, 304, 311, 352, 359, 414n76; founding of, 27, 227, 298–305, 393n11, 395n26; internecine strife in, 84–85; Islamic victims of, 4, 46, 251, 253, 255, 261, 287, 364–65, 408n4; media coverage of, 7–8, 113, 117–18, 275, 292–305, 358–61, 374, 400n35, 426n7; near enemy discourses and, 12, 27–28, 35, 37–38, 46, 57, 71, 88–89, 104–5, 123–35, 146–47, 153–60, 164–65, 167–68, 172–77, 193, 245–47, 256–70, 273, 302–5, 307–11, 331–44, 373–74, 387n7, 392n8, 401n44; as "rule," 5, 12, 14, 34, 307–23, 325–26, 329–44, 376; Soviet Union's resistance and, 67–71; Sudanese period of, 160–64, 176–77; Taliban's relationship with, 13, 108–9, 323–25, 383n20, 422n14; Western understandings of, 4–5, 7–8, 12, 35, 88–89, 137, 139–41, 174, 197–98, 249–50, 273–74, 283–86, 290–305, 312–13, 330, 374, 393n16, 394n22. *See also specific camps and leaders*
Al-ʿAnbari, Abu Hanifah, 316–17
Al-Andalusi, Suruqa, 112, 383n27
"And the Stories Circulate on the Ground" (Abu Salman), 349–50
Ansar Al-Sunna Al-Muhammadiyya, 164
Arab-Israeli War, 64, 76–77
Arafat, Yasser, 187–88
ARAMCO (Arabian American Oil Company), 372–73
Aramco (company), 50
Arnett, Peter, 263, 271–72, 303
Al-Asad, Hafez, 54
asceticism: American materialism and, 4, 33–34, 149–51, 233–44, 360, 363, 373, 391n14; Arab states' profligacy and, 31, 58–60, 193, 365–66; audiocassettes and, 109–10, 118–19; Bin Laden's reputation and, 29, 36–37, 44–45, 62–63, 67–71, 83–85, 89–93, 144–51, 166–67, 201–4, 262–63, 272, 281, 291–92, 321;

INDEX

Al-Ghazzali, Abu Hamad, 423n19
GIA (Groupe Islamique Armée), 344
Globalized Islam (Roy), 257
Golan Heights, 52
Gray, Matthew, 428n4
guesthouses, 87–88, 108–9,
    115–16, 142, 291, 300–301
Gulf War, 3, 19, 115, 160, 168,
    177, 188–93, 202, 247, 266–71,
    289, 293, 314, 351, 404n15
Gunaratna, Rohan, 143, 395n26

Hadhramis, 55
hadith analysis, 56–57, 59, 65, 75,
    128, 151, 158, 166, 201, 224,
    315, 327–28, 337–40, 361,
    423n20. *See also* Bin Laden,
    Osama; Islam
Al-Hamad, ʿAbdalla, 146, 377
Hamas, 86, 162, 375
Hamdan, Salim, 14, 283–89,
    293–95
Hamdi, Tarik, 14, 283–86, 293
Hamid, Mustafa, 6, 14, 46, 142,
    146, 171, 276, 307–12, 320–25,
    367–68, 377, 382n12, 386n61,
    419n1, 420n14
Hanafism, 67, 79, 192, 339,
    342–44, 372, 409n5
Al-Haqil, Riyad, 106
Al-Haqq, Muhammad Zia, 103–4
Haqqani, Jalaluddin, 87, 311
Haqqani House of Islamic Sciences,
    79
Al-Hawali, Safar, 19, 27, 67, 166,
    191–92, 194, 202, 324, 343, 377
Al-Hayat, 248
Al-Hazmi, Nawaf, 358
Hegghammer, Thomas, 170–71,
    382n19
Hekmetyar, Gulbuddin, 90, 278

Hezbollah, 162, 188, 399n30
High Council of Scholars, 195
Hindu Kush, 17–19, 27, 36,
    233–43, 247, 254, 320
Hizb-i Islami, 163
Hizb-ul Mujahideen, 163
human rights, 18
Hussein, Saddam, 3, 19, 26, 115,
    160, 190–91, 289, 293, 297, 371
hypocrisy, 62, 71, 104–5, 123–34,
    147–48, 153–60, 167, 176, 315,
    368, 372. *See also* Islam; Islamic
    Awakening; polytheism; United
    States

Ibn ʿAbbas, ʿAbdalla, 158–59
Ibn ʿAbd Al-Wahhab, Muhammad,
    11, 42, 47, 62, 66, 100, 112,
    189, 192, 372
Ibn ʿAbd al-Salam, Al-ʿIzz, 18
Ibn Abi Sufyan, Muʾawiyya, 409n14
Ibn Abi Talib, ʿAli, 68, 255, 409n14
Ibn Abi Talib, Jaʿfar, 254, 410n26
Ibn Abu ʿAsim, ʿUmar, 345–58,
    360, 362, 427n11
Ibn al-Hajjaj, 75, 158
Ibn al-Khattab, ʿUmar, 30–31
Ibn al-Qayyim Al-Jawziyya, 424n23
Ibn ʿAwf, ʿAbd al-Rahman, 234–35
Ibn Baz, ʿAbd al-ʿAziz, 6, 67, 106,
    115, 168–71, 188–96, 200, 264,
    314–19, 332–33, 377
Ibn Al-Fujaʾa, Qatari, 186, 201
Ibn Hajar Al-Asqalani, 193
Ibn Al-Hajjaj, 75, 158
Ibn Hanbal, Ahmad, 237
Ibn Haritha, Zayd, 410n26
Ibn Hind, ʿAmru, 236, 254–55,
    409n6
Ibn Jibrin, ʿAbdalla, 195
Ibn Hisham, ʿAmr, 408n1

449

INDEX

INDEX

Quraish tribe, 2, 201, 241, 256, 272, 317, 403n4
Qutb, Muhammad, 59–60, 64, 190, 390n46, 392n9
Qutb, Sayyid, 57, 59–60, 192, 336, 377, 385n33

Randal, Jonathan, 170
Raphel, Robin, 382n11
Al-Rashid, Harun, 238, 254, 409n15
Al-Rashidi, Ali, 83
Rassler, Don, 398n14
"The Rectitude of the Summons to God's Calling" ('Abd al-Rahman), 164
Red Crescent, 81, 138
"rejectionism" (*rafidiyya*), 124, 154, 165, 372, 392n10, 397n1. *See also* Islam; Shi'ism
Revolutionary Command Council for National Salvation, 162–64
"The Roots of Power in Islam" (Al-Dawsari), 169
Roy, Olivier, 257–58
Al-Rumi, Suhayb, 360
Rumsfeld, Donald, 369

Al-Sabt, 'Abdalla, 146
Sadat, Anwar, 70–71, 168, 363
Sahih Al-Jami (Al-Bukhari), 44
"Salafi Precepts in Matters of Summoning" (Al-Qarni), 313
Salafism, 112–13, 151, 163–64, 259, 264, 275, 303, 313–14, 333–44, 362, 371–72, 376, 422n14
Saleh, 'Ali 'Abdalla, 173, 175, 308–9
Salim, Mamdouh, 393n16
Salman Al-Farsi (camp), 80

Al-Sanoussi, Ibrahim, 191
Saudi Arabia: American ties with, 3, 19, 25–27, 31, 41–44, 46–47, 61, 68, 91, 115, 150, 153–62, 179–86, 188, 190–91, 194, 202–3, 240–41, 245–46, 258–64, 266–71, 321, 332, 372–73, 404n15; audiocassette culture in, 99–100; Bin Laden's relationship with, 3–4, 9–10, 19–20, 22, 29, 35–36, 45, 48–53, 90, 134, 147–48, 160–64, 166, 172, 176, 179–89, 191–92, 196, 200–201, 228–29, 245, 250–51, 256–57, 272–74, 277–78, 289–90, 302–5, 332, 373–74, 383n3, 404n15; Islamic Awakening and, 9, 12–13, 28, 46–48, 53, 55–56, 61, 64–66, 138, 153–60, 163, 167, 172, 193–95, 197–204, 247–48, 270–74, 314, 332, 373; memoranda in, 246–48, 250; militants from, 84, 113, 118, 254, 280, 295, 342–44; National Guard of, 123–34, 164, 187, 251, 289–90, 298, 304, 408n4, 413n65; religious authority in, 67–71, 188–91, 193–96, 240, 374–75, 397n47; Soviet Union's resistance and, 19–20, 22, 66–67, 80, 82, 86, 137, 236, 278, 301, 397n47, 403n9; Wahhabism and, 11, 42, 47, 55–67, 100, 118, 172, 189–95, 200, 274–75
Al-Sayigh, Tawfiq, 106
Sayyaf, 'Abd al-Rasul, 75
Scheuer, Michael, 137, 165, 297, 387n7, 399n29, 413n59, 413n65
secularism, 4, 24–25, 33–34, 150–51, 157, 162, 167–68, 243–44, 258–70, 332–44, 363

455